SIGNING EXACT ENGLISH

BY
GERILEE GUSTASON
ESTHER ZAWOLKOW

FOREWORD BY
BARBARA LUETKE-STAHLMAN

ILLUSTRATIONS BY
LILIAN LOPEZ

LAYOUT DESIGN BY
MARIA ANGEL

Published by
Modern Signs Press, Inc.
Los Alamitos, CA 90720

International Standard Book Number
Soft Bound 0-916708-23-3
Hard Bound 0-916708-22-5
Pocket Edition 0-916708-26-8

Library of Congress Catalog Number 93-86649

Publisher
Modern Signs Press, Incorporated
P.O. Box 1181
Los Alamitos, CA 90720
562/596-8548,562/493-4168 V/TDD
FAX 562/795-6614
modsigns@modernsignspress.com
www.modernsignspress.com

Cover Design by Raya Designs

The publisher welcomes your comments and suggestions

Twenty Third Printing, 2013

Printed in the United States of America

Some Comments from Individuals Throughout the United States Who Use and Teach Signing Exact English

Our decision to use Signing Exact English was really quite simple--we want our son to be literate in the language our society uses as its primary means of communication, English. While respecting and nurturing his deafness and the deaf community in which he is a part, we found SEE a perfect choice for us to facilitate Hob's language acquisition and education. This system works! It is "user friendly"-- allowing English speaking family and friends to naturally express their thoughts. Even as this book is being printed, our son has over fifty signs and frequently uses two and three word expressions. Compare that to other 17-month-olds!

—Sarah and Hobby Howell
Waco, Texas

Congratulations to the authors of the new SEE Sign Dictionary and your continued commitment, sensitivity and significant contribution to deaf education, especially during these controversial and challenging times. As a professional in the field of Deaf Education for more than 20 years, as an interpreter, college sign language instructor, classroom teacher, program consultant, parent-infant specialist, and administrator, I am convinced that SEE offers deaf children a complete literal approach to learning English naturally with all members of their family. This new dictionary is filled with new signs that will give hearing parents, educators and friends the invaluable tool of "language" in which to share information and experiences that are important and essential to deaf children of all ages and academic levels. The wait was worth it!

—Jill Ellis, Director, Center for Education of the Infant Deaf
Berkeley, California

There is no reason why you shouldn't be signing in exact, authentic English and there are thousands of reasons why you should. Those reasons have names like Jennifer and Kayla and Tony and Daniel, they go to your school, and they are deaf. Signing Exact English has made it possible for our parents and staff to be consistent in the way we communicate with the students.

—Claire Wells, Temple ISD
Temple, Texas

Our son, Christopher, born with a profound hearing loss, was not diagnosed until he was two years old. Immediately we all began learning SEE signs. Within six months he had a vocabulary to several hundred signs; within a year he was signing such long sentences so quickly that we had to slow him down to read his signs. Now Christopher is six, is reading at the seventh grade level and has been mainstreamed since preschool. We feel emphatically that SEE sign language, which we will always refer to as Christopher's first language, provided the basis for his amazing success with the English language.

—Dr. Michelle Weil, Clinical Psychologist, and Dr. Larry Rosen, Professor of Psychology
Orange, California

The Umatilla County Education Service District has used Signing Exact English since 1979. Many of our students who have been raised with SEE since infancy are performing at or above grade level. They are English users. In rural America, SEE provides deaf students with the English that is so necessary to interact with hearing people in their home community. We have found that it is relatively easy for hearing people to learn SEE, which expands the deaf child's communication network. Our deaf, English using students, find themselves capable in both the deaf and hearing worlds.

—Malina Lindell, Resource Specialist for Educational Interpreters
Pendleton, Oregon

As parents of a 15 year old daughter who is deaf, it is easy to forget where we were 15 years ago having the normal teenager that we do. Erica was diagnosed at 12 months as being profoundly deaf and our whole world was turned upside down. We were devastated and petrified from our own ignorance. The big yellow SEE book was the first sign language book to enter our home and it opened a world of communication for us with our beautiful, smart baby. Learning sign language erased our fears, like how will our child learn to read or how will she think?! Erica's first sign was "light" only three months after we started signing and she has been signing ever since with a great deal to say. She is a freshman now and reads at about grade level and we are very proud of her. We're so happy the new SEE book is out, knowing that it will be the door to many more success stories! Communication is freedom: our children deserve it!!!

—Maria & Chuck Smyrniotis
San Jose, California

If you will take the time to read the information and instructions in the front of this book, and then learn and practice the signs demonstrated, I believe you will find this book to be one of the best tools available for the academic education of our deaf children. I know I do !

—Jan Foreman
Fort Wayne, Indiana

Signing Exact English has helped me retain and develop my English language proficiency since I was deafened at the age of four. It has enabled me to succeed in school and is presently helping me in college (where I entered as a sophomore due to nearly 50 hours of exam credit I acquired before I arrived).

—Jonathan N. Winkler
Kansas State University, Manhattan, Kansas

We have used SEE in our family for 18 years. We are hearing parents with three daughters, two of whom are profoundly deaf. SEE has allowed us to have excellent communication with all our daughters, in our native language, English. We are able to share our values, customs, religious beliefs, and everything that is important to us with our children. Our girls have very strong academic skills and we know that this is due to early and complete communication in English. We believe that without the use of SEE our daughters would never have had the opportunity to reach their true potential.

—Jim and Joan Hipskind
San Jose, California

In the world of education, people are so often judged by their command of the English language. If we, as parents, can provide that skill for our deaf or hard of hearing children, we will give them a valuable tool for success. For our deaf child, born of hearing parents, S.E.E. provided a manual representation of perfect English easily and quickly acquired. Therefore, communication and language could occur early in childhood, when language acquisition is most efficient and so vital to the development of thought processes.

—Patrice and David Stephenson
Goddard, Kansas

As a teacher of the deaf who has worked with 18 month old to 18 year old deaf students in programs which supported SEE and others which did not, I can definitely say that the programs which utilize the SEE sign system made a dramatic difference in the student's acquisition of English.

—Sue Tellez
Vista, California

Signing Exact English is the only sign system that would allow us to share the richness of the English language, while not losing any of the beauty and expressiveness of American Sign Language. —In time Signing Exact English has proven itself—We now have a child who has wonderful reading and writing skills because of the extensive use of the English language, while his hands and face express the poetry-like motion of American Sign Language. To us, Signing Exact English is the best of both worlds. Thanks for making it possible.

—Dave and LuAnn Berens
Stratton, Colorado

I am very glad to say that SEE is one of the sign systems I rely on most to serve the needs of many students and parents. The system is consistent with spoken English and provides a complete language model. It also employs the visual features of sign language to complete the delivery of a model that is as beautifully pictorial as it is linguistic. I have seen <u>much</u> success come from the combination of the system, the users, and the commitment to provide complete communication.

—Dennis Davino, M.A., Teacher, Interpreter
Irvine, California

As parents of three children, two of which are deaf, we know the importance of sign language. We have been using Signing Exact English for eight years. We chose it because we believe that we are Americans and we speak English, our children should speak and sign English. SEE has fulfilled our wishes for our children's language.

—Scott and Kristeen Gough
Highland, Utah

Signing Exact English is the power tool our family uses. To date its 21 year service contract provides personal instruction, multi-level teaching materials, and sustaining friendships with people who understand and respond. The product is a total communication family free to explore life in our unique way with investments unlimited. A best buy !

—Tom and Billie McDavitt, Parents, Teacher, Interpreter
Wichita, Kansas

Words fall short of the gratitude we feel towards the founders of SEE signs for having the insight to see a need, the courage to implement a change and the ability to make a difference. It is through the use of SEE signs coupled with the spoken English language that has been the key factor in the freedom our child enjoys. Her growth has been amazing and her potential knows no bounds. We have enjoyed Alaina's ability to communicate her every desire, her funny sense of humor, and her above grade level of literacy. After raising our daughter with SEE and seeing such profound results, we strongly recommend its usage.

—Lew and Nita Talbot
San Juan Capistrano, California

In search for the most fitting language in our situation as hearing parents, we feel SEE sign is the answer. We feel a need for a balance provided in that system:

1) one that makes "English Sense", that is, a sign for every word spoken;

2) one that incorporates feeling through inflection and intensity of expression;

and finally,

3) a language that is ever changing and constantly improving to meet the ongoing needs of our child in his/her world.

—Kim and Bob Kropp
Omaha, Nebraska

Signing Exact English was a very important part of our philosophy in educating James, our deaf son. It was stressed to us from the very first stages of learning about deafness that everything we said should be conveyed visually as he has a severe/profound hearing loss. Throughout the years of parenting, we were always careful to sign everything we said to him. James recently graduated from Louisiana State University. It is my opinion that he would never have had the language necessary to compete academically if he had not acquired language through the exact English model.

—June Street
Baton Rouge, Louisiana

SEE II has given our child a complete visual code for English that maximizes his ability to use lip reading and his residual hearing. Reading and writing are facilitated because he brings the complete code to the task. In an inclusive setting, hearing children can much more easily bridge the communication gap by learning this same code for their language. The SEE II book is easy to use and works well for beginners and advanced signers alike.

—Pope and Kathy Moseley
Iowa City, Iowa

We started using Signing Exact English with Kurt when he was nine months old. We were always able to communicate! Kurt was born profoundly deaf, yet has developed good speech. Our family, some neighbors, and his school interpreter all used SEE consistently. Kurt's reading and language skills tested on the 99 percentile on his high school ACT college assessment exams. SEE provided the ability to communicate clearly and made a quality education possible.

—Jo Ann Stoskopf
Salina Kansas

We are grateful to the founders of SEE for providing the tools which allowed our son the opportunity to firmly grasp the English language. We feel Signing Exact English has contributed to our son Mick's ability to function at grade level along with his hearing peers. Many thanks to those individuals who dedicated so much of their time and energy in order that Mick and many children like him can obtain their education in "full view" using Signing Exact English.

—Chris and Barbara Martin
Irvine, California

I have used the S.E.E. book with autistic, aphasic, cerebral palsied, brain damaged and/or laryngectomized hearing children as well as deaf and hard of hearing children. In other words, non-verbal children. They have all improved in their communication skills with their English speaking parents. This has reduced both parents' and children's frustration levels. Most have begun using voice more often.

—Evelyn Lawyer
Reedsport, Oregon

In the course of our lives, some of us are fortunate enough to encounter a few individuals who truly represent the highest ideals by which humanity can be measured. Those of us involved with Signing Exact English have had the good fortune to have been touched by two such people.

Donna Pfetzing was one of the founders of the system. As the mother of a deaf daughter she knew the frustrations associated with establishing communication and determining education directions. She was a bright, vivacious, spirited part of the early efforts. Donna died in 1976 but her energetic and dynamic personality remain in the memories of the developers of this new volume.

Sadie DeFiore came on the scene a bit after the early efforts. She was one of the early students in Signing Exact English classes. Sadie exhibited immediate interest and capability, becoming one of the premier interpreters in the field. Her recognition of the needs of deaf children from preschool through high school and her willingness to lovingly address those in a forthright manner positively affected the lives of literally thousands. Although Sadie died in 1992, her ready smile, laughter, and strength of her convictions remain as bright and vivid guides to the future.

To these two wonderful people and all the other parents, teachers, interpreters, and children who have touched our lives through their use of Signing Exact English, this book is humbly dedicated.

ACKNOWLEDGEMENTS

Countless individuals and groups have contributed to the continuing development on which this volume is based. To everyone who has given us their input in ways great and small we offer our thanks, with special mention to:

--Carolyn Norris, for her creative drawings in the original book which set the tone for this one;

--everyone who sent lists of words needed and suggestions for signs for their interests and ideas;

--Claire Wells and the staff of Temple Regional School for the Deaf for sharing their local signs for our consideration;

--Maria Angel for her computer and graphic art skills used to develop the format of this book;

--Lilian Lopez for her flexibility and creativity in providing clear and interesting sign drawings in an atmosphere of continuous change;

--Betty Barrus for her patient attention to detail during the many, many hours of proof reading;

--the instructors of SEE sign classes, workshops, and seminars for their dedication and long hours spent upgrading participants signing skills;

--to the parents, teachers, and interpreters whose tireless efforts to provide clear communication for countless deaf and hard of hearing people of all ages;

--our families , friends, and colleagues for their patience and support which made this edition possible;

--and especially Dave Zawolkow for his "word sense", dry humor, constructive criticism, putting up with us and always being there.

TABLE OF CONTENTS

FOREWORD

A LOOK AT SEE IN THE 1990'S

Barbara Luetke-Stahlman, Ph.D.
Director, Teacher Preparation Program, Deaf and Hard of Hearing
University of Kansas Medical Center

BEING invited to write the introduction of this new edition of the Signing Exact English text is a bit like writing a brief history of my professional career. This must be true, too, for the many parents and teachers who have waited so patiently for this new, improved version! But the stories our tattered old "yellow" books could tell...

Any hearing teacher of the deaf who is my age or older "came of age" in our field of deaf education at a time when no one cared *how* we signed—only that we *could* sign. Rudimentary as the signing was then for those of us who were converting from oralism to "total communication", we all can recount stories of principals who thought our awkward beginning signs were fascinating, of our panic and embarrassment as we tried to communicate with the patient deaf adults who taught us, and of our sheer delight when the deaf children in our care began to progress: oralism augmented by an accessible signed message!

At that time, as I studied like many of you to become a teacher of the deaf, I was required to complete one student teaching practicum in a total communication (or T.C.) placement and one in an oral program. Within hours of signing on my first day in my assigned second grade, T.C. classroom, I came face-to-face with the gaps in my sign training: reading seemed to necessitate different signs for different words because the children were confused when sight words like "brook" and "lake" or "mom" and "mother" were signed the same way.

Later that afternoon, after the children had left, my cooperating teacher handed me a new sign book, Signing Exact English (1972). Like many teachers of the time, I studied that book without the assistance of an instructor and began to differentiate the way I communicated. I signed "conceptually" to deaf adults and in SEE 2 with the deaf students in my charge. For the next seven years, my colleagues and I never questioned the appropriateness of either.

A few years later, as a new professor of deaf education, I moved to Omaha, Nebraska. Public school programs there had both oral and SEE 2 "tracks" and the school for the deaf used PSE. As I visited my student teachers in these various sites, I began to design research projects to address the questions that my teachers-in-training were asking me. Some of these studies weren't presented or published until after I had left Omaha, but this initial research demonstrated that SEE students could understand stories told in American Sign Language as well as residential children (Luetke-Stahlman, 1990), that SEE 2 children could read better than PSE students (Luetke-Stahlman, 1988), that building a first language or system base was essential if age appropriate reading and writing abilities were a goal (1982 and 1986), and that hearing parents of young deaf children could improve their SEE 2 signing and retain that improvement over time (Luetke-Stahlman and Moeller, 1990). These studies marked the beginnings of a research agenda that has become my career and has afforded me the opportunity to meet many families and professionals who are committed to signing in accurate and consistent SEE 2. Their children are thriving because of that commitment.

Until 1988 I approached my research, teaching, and consulting as a professional. That year, with the adoption of a deaf toddler into my family, I was forced to put the theory behind my work to the test. Earlier that year, I had published a study demonstrating that deaf children exposed to SEE 2 outscored users of oral English only, Seeing Essential English, Signed/Manual English, and Pidgin Signed English on tests of reading and English language (Luetke-Stahlman, 1988). My school district was basically following my lead as to how we would all sign to Mary Pattie...that decision was facilitated by my research, but was actually decided by a conversation I had with my then five year old hearing daughter, Hannie. She had asked me around that time to sign the word "run" so she could comment to her new sister. I started to explain conceptual signing, how the sign used depended on the meaning or context. I gave Hannah several examples.

"Mama," she interrupted impatiently and looking at me innocently, "how do you sign run?" She was a little girl with a young mind; she didn't understand what I had explained at all. To her (and to the founders of SEE 2) a word like "run" should have one sign. I knew in that moment that our signing would need to be done in the language of our home: English. I immediately ordered two SEE 2 books, one for our home and one for the car. Little did I know then what we all have experienced since: that we would have to advocate assertively, and often unconvincingly, to have others accept the legitimacy of our deaf daughter's first language.

Even in the year that I write this introduction, it is almost impossible to get a SEE 2 interpreter for a high school choir concert or a community theater presentation, but ASL interpreters are a "given" at these same types of events in our community. This is America where the majority of the population uses English, and yet many parents must fight for their home language to be signed with their deaf children at school.

In 1989 Mary Pat Moeller completed a study based on communication assessments conducted with deaf children in Sedalia, Missouri. The parents and teachers in this small rural town had utilized SEE 2 since its beginnings. Moeller's research demonstrated that the majority of the children were reading at or above grade level. Analyzed language samples of the teachers in this same program had illustrated that these professionals, like their colleagues in Omaha, were able to almost perfectly sign what they said while teaching deaf students (Luetke-Stahlman (in press) and Luetke-Stahlman (1989a and 1989b). Propelled by a discussion of numerous studies compiled by Hyde and Power (1991), even the most ardent opponents of SEE 2 were agreeing publicly that some people could sign English with a high degree of accuracy. It was well-documented that if motivated to do so, both parents and professionals could sign English, a code as accurate as written English (Moores, 1992), to deaf children.

Work by Schick and Moeller (1989) was another important contribution to the growing SEE 2 literature that was accumulating. These researchers completed a detailed analysis of language samples from Sedalia and Omaha students who used SEE 2. They found that the students had acquired some of the most complex rules of syntactic structure in English and had internalized the rules of English. Further, they stated that SEE 2 had served as an input for the native language learning of English for these students. They concluded that the acquisition of ASL is not a "universal eventuality" (Schick and Moeller, 1989). At a time when most of the country had jumped blindly on the "ASL bandwagon," this research made an important contribution to the field.

The justification for the invention of SEE 2, and the history of how deaf adults, children of deaf parents, and parents met to design this new system, is a story that all users of this text will find interesting. They are referred to a chapter in Bornstein (1990) by Gerilee Gustason. A series of research articles has also been collected and is available through Modern Signs Press, Inc. (Gustason, 1988).

The long and difficult road that many of us travel in deciding which communication system to use with a deaf child, and then becoming especially proficient in the use of that method, is one made easier for me by information about reading. My investigation into the complexity of the reading process caused me to discover that figurative English is used in one in eight utterances of the "through the air" conversations (Nippold, 1985) and that it appears in 10 of every 1,000 words in 5th and 6th grade basal reading stories (Arter, 1976). Often the main idea of a story is expressed in a figurative expression (Lockhard, 1972). SEE 2 unlocks for deaf children what PSE can not: figurative English, authentic English, genuine English, exact English.

English has one combination of sounds for one word. Likewise, one word, one sign: that is Signing Exact English. Signing Exact English differentiates words like electric, electrical, electricity, non-electric, electrician. English itself is not "conceptually accurate;" it is riddled with non-literal expressions, and to learn what those groups of words mean, children must be exposed to them in routine ways. How do deaf children understand that a nose doesn't physically run? Just as hearing children do. The expression is directly explained to them or just used in context (for example, "cut that out, stop that, please cut that out"). Those of us who have hearing children know this is how children learn. In fact, just this week, my hearing nine year old asked if we could get a car "without a lid" (a convertible) and if she could get new glasses with a lighter "outline" (frame)! Parents and teachers simply attend to the child's message and respond with the correct grammar and vocabulary of English. It matters not whether the child is hearing or deaf. It matters not whether we are speaking or signing to the child.

Parents, administrators, teachers, and interpreters who are impressed by the available research to date regarding SEE 2 believe that there is a literacy payoff for signing the exact form (grammar and syntax) of what we say. They believe in authentic English... signing what you want to say, not just what you know how to sign. Transcription of our signed and spoken communication has told us that we need to remember to start our hands signing immediately as we utter the first words in our sentences, that always adding the -s marker can be a challenge, and that it takes practice to use the less common affix markers like the -ity on "electricity" or the -ous on "dangerous." Adults should know how to calculate their sign-to-voice ratio (see Luetke-Stahlman and Luckner, 1991), set goals to improve their signing, and receive specific feedback from knowledgeable others as to their progress.

Setting goals and obtaining feedback is also a relatively new advancement. Mayer and Lowenbraun (1990) were first to document the logical relationship between supervisors' expectations in terms of teacher signing and the sign proficiency of teachers. A growing number of administrators and supervisors are now expecting the teachers and interpreters in their programs to sign SEE 2 proficiently. Some progressive principals now state during job interviews that SEE 2 will be used at their school and regularly evaluate personnel progress. These programs should be congratulated, especially when they can be compared with the vast majority of school programs that have no consensus or policy on what teachers and interpreters will use or how well they will sign. After all, there is no magic formula to what is required for deaf children to acquire English as do their hearing peers: they must have access to mature users of the system, who sign it consistently and accurately.

The challenges are endless, as they always have been in the volatile field of deaf education. However, I sincerely believe that this text is a key. It is a reference for your home, your classroom, your car, your church, your neighbor. Reward yourself when you take time in your busy day to stop and consult it for a sign or sit down and page through it to see if there are some new ones you can learn. Rest assured that when used completely, consistently, and in genuine communication with deaf children, their age-appropriate literacy obtainment will be your reward.

REFERENCES

Arter, J. (1976) The effects of metaphor on reading comprehension. Unpublished doctoral dissertation, University of Illinois.

Bornstein, H. (1990) Manual Communication. Washington, D.C.: Gallaudet University Press.

Gustason, G. (1988) Signing English: Exact or Not? Los Alamitos, CA: Modern Signs Press, Inc.

Gustason, G., Pfetzing, D., & Zawolkow, E. (1972) Signing Exact English. Los Alamitos, CA: Modern Signs Press, Inc.

Hyde, M.B., & Power, D.J. (1991) Teachers' use of simultaneous communication: effects on the signed and spoken components. American Annals of the Deaf, 136(5), 381-387. Mayer, P. & Lowenbraun, S. (1990) T.C. use among elementary teachers of deaf children. American Annals of the Deaf, 135(3), 257-263.

Moeller, M.P. (1989) The expressive language of deaf students exposed to SEE 2. Paper presented at the American Speech and Hearing Conference (ASHA), St. Louis, MO, November.

Moores, D. (1992) Blueprints for the future: two programs. In M. Walworth, D. Moores, and R. O'Rouke (eds.) A Freehand. Silver Spring, MD: T.J. Publishers.

Nippold, M. (1985) Comprehension of figurative language in youth. Topics in Language Disorders, 5(3), 1-20.

Lockhart, M. (1972) A description of similes from children's fiction. Unpublished master's thesis, University of Alberta.

Luetke-Stahlman, B. (in press) Can teachers sign English form? Submitted to the American Annals of the Deaf.

Luetke-Stahlman, B. (1990) Can SEE 2 children understand ASL-using adults? American Annals of the Deaf, 135(1), 7-8.

Luetke-Stahlman, B. (1989a) Input and literacy. Paper presented at the Illinois Supervisors of the Deaf meeting. Lyle, IL, March.

Luetke-Stahlman, B. (1989b) Documenting syntactically and semantically incomplete bimodal input to deaf subjects. American Annals of the Deaf, 133(3), 230-234.

Luetke-Stahlman, B. (1988) The benefit of oral English-only input as compared with signed input to deaf students. Volta Review, 90(7), 349-361.

Luetke-Stahlman, B. (1986) Building a language base in deaf students. American Annals of the Deaf, 131 (3), 220-228.

Luetke-Stahlman, B. (1982) A philosophy for assessing the language proficiency of deaf students to effectively promote English literacy. American Annals of the Deaf, 127 (7), 844-851.

Schick, B. & Moeller, M.P. (1989) The expressive English language of deaf students exposed to SEE 2. Paper presented at ASHA, St. Louis, MO, November.

A LOOK AT SEE IN THE 1980'S

(Reprinted from the 1980 edition of Signing Exact English)

Hilde Schlesinger, M.D.
Co-author of
Sound and Sign: Children, Deafness and Mental Health

FOR those of you—parents, teachers and others—who have had introductions to prior editions of this impressive work—read no more. Undoubtedly, by now, you have gone through the many steps that lead to the exciting discovery that you can communicate with a deaf child or adult through an intricate system of movements of the body and face but more especially the hands as you continue to use spoken English. You have become an adept participant in dialogue in two modalities, through the hand and voice, through signs and words.

For those of you, however, who pick this book up for the first time—pause awhile, and consider the following. What are the steps that have led to your interest in this book? A recent encounter? A novel experience? A successful (or unsuccessful) communication? A frequent reason is that of a recent encounter with an individual, who due to an impairment in the sense of hearing, depends to a large extent on his or her eyes for the acquisition or understanding of language. To meet an individual who acquires and uses language in a way unfamiliar to you leads to a novel experience.

Novel experiences can be exciting and rewarding or sad and fear-provoking. Most novel experiences combine all of these feelings to some extent. When the novel experience is related to the powerful human need to communicate, the feelings can become intense. Communication—dialogue between human beings—can and does occur in a variety of ways that are essential to our well being: the eyes through sight, the body through touch can convey a variety of meanings. Most human communication, however, is accompanied by or initiated through a very complex human achievement—the language of the society wherein the child was born. A language can be seen as a system of symbols used with certain rules by which people have come to abide. The symbols and their rules of usage become the vehicle for dialogue between people. Yet there are other important features of dialogue-shared interests, shared focus, shared social rules, and shared functions of language are numerous and subject to considerable research and debate. There appears to be some general agreement that a number of thought processes and concepts can develop fully without language, that some are promoted by language, and that still others require language for full development.

Language provides freedom from the "here and now," ability to anticipate the future, to recall the past, to describe objects and events beyond the field of vision, to develop solutions to some problems, to share or maybe even to develop imagination and cultural products of imagination such as stories and songs. In addition, language enhances the ability to understand the complex relationships between people and the feelings of other people. Although almost all members of the human species develop competence in the language of a culture, they differ markedly in the way in which they use language. Some use it more freely to comment on or ask questions about the world, the relationships between objects, between people, between feelings and action, between cause and effect. Others are more taciturn and tend to use language (despite full competence in its usage) less frequently for the functions mentioned above. Yet other individuals use language at great length and with much fervor and skill primarily for special areas of human endeavors such as sports, mechanics, hobbies, etc.

The Deaf Child and Dialogue

Despite the fact that acquisition of language is a complex phenomenon, most children learn it easily and playfully and by age five have achieved a nearly adult level of linguistic competence. Children do not acquire language primarily through imitation of adults. First, they are the creators of a language that has childrenese words and childrenese rules. This exciting process of first creating a language and then somehow adopting the adult version of the language of society is also subject to much research and debate. It does appear, however, that human beings are preprogrammed to develop a viable means of communication and that a certain amount of exposure to a specific language is a prerequisite for competence. For many years there existed massive confusion between speech and language. Because most of our linguistic interchanges occur through speech, language and speech were seen as identical, and yet speech is only one of the ways that can be used by the participants in a dialogue.

Under previous conditions deaf children, although continuously "exposed" to language through speech, could benefit only minimally or perhaps not at all from this exposure. The language they saw on the lips of the people around them was extremely limited because only 40 percent of the English language can be seen on the lips. In earlier times, deaf children learned neither language nor speech playfully and easily from their parents, nor did most of them become proficient in the language or speech of their hearing parents. In earlier times, deaf children of hearing parents learned the language of the deaf community—American Sign Language—from their peers and from the few deaf adults permitted to be in contact with them. They learned English with great difficulty and with unimpressive results.

Even in those earlier times, deaf children of deaf parents learned the language of their parents easily, playfully, and with great proficiency. The language of the deaf parents was either American Sign Language, a language in its own right with a word order and syntax different from English, or manual English. The language of the deaf parents was expressed through symbols made by the hands with or without the use of voice. This early parent-child dialogue resulted in clear-cut psychological and academic advantages for the deaf child of deaf parents. Exciting changes have taken place in the recent past of deaf children and their hearing parents due in large part to the existence of this volume and its prior editions. Hearing parents observing the advantages that deaf children of deaf parents had throughout their lives wanted to share in the process that led to these advantages.

The process is similar and yet different in crucial ways. Deaf and hearing parents both can use the hands to express the symbols of language. Most deaf parents, however, have a language system readily available to them, with their deaf children. Although some deaf parents may choose to use American Sign Language with their children, others may choose to sign English and still others may want their children to know both and to alternate their usage.

Most hearing parents initially feel more comfortable in using an English version of sign language than in using ASL. This is because learning a new modality is easier than learning a completely new language, or perhaps they feel more comfortable because they want their children to know the language that they themselves know best, or perhaps they feel more comfortable because they can combine the sign and the spoken word.

Dialogue and the Deaf Infant

Our experience indicates that the most ideal situation for the deaf infant and its hearing parents include the following: early diagnosis, accurate audiological evaluation, appropriate consistent amplification, and appropriate emotional support during the time of the diagnostic crisis. None of the above can be obtained from this volume. You, who want to engage in a dialogue with a deaf infant most optimally, will need to seek out the most competent professionals in your area. But while taking those steps, you can become engrossed in this book. You can seek out the vocabulary items that you want to share with your infant, repeat them to your infant, and teach them to your parents and your friends to use with your infant.

The period before the exciting moment when the infant returns the first sign to you will seem interminable, but it will come. All infants—even hearing ones learning sign language—will reproduce signs before they can reproduce spoken words. The ease with which the deaf infant acquires language depends in a large part on the early introduction of signs, the comfort and competency of the parents learning the new modality, the attitudes and competencies of the infant's teacher. The ease with which the deaf infant will learn the use of speech depends to a large extent on the residual hearing, the efficacy of the hearing aids and a combined use of sign and word.

You who start with the deaf infant have a distinct advantage. You can keep ahead of your infant in your acquisition of S.E.E. signs. You will experience the excitement of early language acquisition and of early dialogues. You will be spared the frustration of delayed language onset. Nevertheless, you must experience some of the pain and frustration of having a deaf infant: learning a new modality of English, meeting numerous professionals, resolving conflicting advice. It won't always be easy, but it will be easier than it was ten years ago. The deaf children we know who started S.E.E. signs about ten years ago are doing well. They learned English as their first language from their parents. They are using it in dialogues with their parents, their peers and their teachers. They are conducting their dialogues in a combination of signs and speech and they are doing well in school.

Children and parents who come upon S.E.E. signs in the early childhood years can benefit almost as well as the infants, if they begin to use signs before they have experienced a massive feeling of failure in communication and before they have been labeled failures by teachers and other professionals.

This book is useful for deaf children of all ages, but older children will usually have had experiences of failure with language and dialogue. Some may have developed an aversion to human communication, some may have developed a very personal system of communication, still others may have acquired American Sign Language as their first language. The feelings and language style of these youngsters must be respected before we require their acceptance of another language we want them to learn.

It is my hope that all these groups of deaf children will acquire the skills that will enable them to communicate happily and competently with a wide variety of people, and that they do not come to believe that one means or mode of communication should be used to exclude the possibility of any other.

INTRODUCTION

To The 1993 Edition

Changes from previous editions...

THE present edition of Signing Exact English includes both some revisions of previously published signs and the addition of new sign vocabulary. The past decade has seen a great increase of interest in the use of signs, how children learn language, and how deaf children can best learn English. There has also been increased sensitivity to and respect for American Sign Language and the deaf community in the world at large. Research in all of these areas is still growing. This research information, plus comments and suggestions from users in the field, has been taken into account in the development of this new edition.

We are aware that revision, or change of any previously published sign book may lead to complications and confusion for the users of the book. However, we felt we would be remiss if we did not make every effort to adjust the signs published here according to two criteria: what has proved most feasible in use, and what is consistent with American Sign Language (ASL) features without sacrificing Signing Exact English principles. While ASL and English are two quite distinct languages, and the overlap can never be complete, we wish to stay as close as possible to signs and principles or features used in ASL, while at the same time representing English as clearly and completely as possible. By respecting and considering both ASL and English, we believe we can better facilitate the learning of a first and a second language by native users of both ASL and of English, and in so doing aid in bridging the gap between users of these two languages. It must be remembered, also, that these are two different languages, and that this is not a text of American Sign Language. Signs are presented in this book without any attempts at identifying which are also used in ASL. It should be pointed out, however, that in the original 1972 edition roughly three-quarters of the signs were either borrowed from ASL or based on an ASL sign with the addition of an initial. Such borrowed signs are used to represent only one English word in Signing Exact English; for instance, the sign for "girl" is the same in this book and in ASL, but while the sign for "run" in this book is borrowed from ASL, ASL has many other ways to sign "run" depending on the idea being conveyed, and there is no one-for-one correspondence between signs in this book and ASL.

Variations in signs exist around the country. For instance, there are several ways to sign "could". In some instances we decided to include such variations in this book, which means that users will need to choose which version they prefer. This choice should, of course, be dependent on what is used in the geographical area concerned. As with our past editions, the signs in this book are presented as suggestions. This means that if we have modified a sign in the present text, and users are comfortable with the previous sign, they should feel no compulsion to change. Finally, some pictures have been changed in an attempt to improve their clarity, as in placement or direction of arrows, without any actual change in the sign itself.

Vocabulary Development

We are aware that we have not included in this book all the words for which individuals may desire signs...for instance, names of characters from children's stories or advanced vocabulary items. All of us, however, are sometimes faced with the need to invent. Thus, included are some guidelines and suggestions for sign development based on principles drawn from research on American Sign Language. Our general recommendation is that other sign books, and skilled signers in the local community who are supportive of signing in English, be consulted before a new sign is developed. Fingerspelling should be considered a viable alternative in some circumstances. The problem here is, of course, to avoid irresponsible, uncoordinated creation of new signs by too many individuals in the child's environment. It is always necessary to guard against the danger of assuming that, because a child knows a sign, s/he can spell, read, or write the word s/he is signing. The transfer to spelling and print is no more automatic for manual or signed English than for spoken English.

Modifying Signs

There are some features of sign production, such as location or place where the sign is made, and size or intensity of the sign, which can and should reflect the concept or message being signed. For instance, the sign for "bow" as presented in this book should be signed in various places and various sizes depending on whether one is speaking of a bow tie, a bow in one's hair, a bow and arrow, and the like. This kind of creative signing does not come from a strict adherence to a single picture and description of a sign, but is important in effectively using this kind of communication. Accordingly, we have listed some ideas for creative signing and have identified with a star some of the signs which can thus be expanded. While this is most applicable to multiple meaning words, it may also be used in an adverbial or adjectival sense. One should not sign "very big" with quite small movements—unless one is being sarcastic—or talk about "walking fast" with very slow hand movements.

Sign Families

To aid in instruction and learning, printed word groups for "families" of signs that are related both in meaning and in formation have been provided at the end of the book. Within the book, members of a given sign family are identified by placing the "head of the family" in parentheses following each sign description. For instance, the description for the sign "group" is followed by the head of the family (CLASS), the description for the sign "author" is followed by its head (WRITE), and so on. In cases of two-sign families, these signs are cross-referenced. Family heads appear with a ♔ in the book.

Right or Left Hand?

The signers pictured in this book are all right handed. Therefore, if only one hand is used or moves in the production of a sign, this is always the right hand unless otherwise indicated. Left-handed persons should, of course, reverse these pictures and sign with the left hand.

Sign What You Say

To maximize the amount of visual language input and contribute to the child's feeling of self-worth, it is important to sign everything that is said in the child's presence, whether or not the communication is addressed to the child. On the one hand, this aids incidental learning. Also, it does not take advantage of the child's lack of hearing to discuss in his or her presence what would not be discussed in the presence of a hearing child. While we are aware that this is difficult for the beginning signer, the payoff in language development, self-concept, awareness of the world, and sophistication is well worth the cost.

Communication, vital though it is to the teaching-learning process, is not the only requisite. Obviously, good teaching and good parenting involve much more.

It is our hope that the updating and revisions discussed above will add to the clarity and helpfulness of the book, and we welcome responses from users. Language and communication are dynamic, and Signing Exact English is open to continuing development as more is learned about the use of sign language both alone and with speech.

Why Signing Exact English Was Developed

IN January, 1969, a group of deaf individuals, parents of deaf children, children of deaf parents, teachers of the deaf, interpreters, and program administrators met in southern California to discuss appropriate, effective ways to represent English in a gestural mode. From this group developed three published systems, originally similar but now quite different: Seeing Essential English (SEE 1), Linguistics of Visual English (LOVE), and Signing Exact English (SEE 2).

As was pointed out in the winter 1974-75 issue of Gallaudet Today: *The main concern of the original group was the consistent, logical, rational, and practical development of signs to represent as specifically as possible the basic essentials of the English language. This concern sprang from the experience of all present with the poor English skills of many deaf students, and the desire for an easier, more successful way of developing mastery of English in a far greater number of such students. (Gustason, 1975)*

Achievement Levels

The educational retardation of deaf students had been well documented over the years, and had caused deep and widespread concern. In 1965, the Secretary of Health, Education, and Welfare's Advisory Committee on Education of the Deaf stated in the Babbidge report that

...the American people have no reason to be satisfied with their limited success in educating deaf children and preparing them for full participation in our society...the average graduate of a public residential school for the deaf...has an eighth grade education. (Babbidge, 1965)

Many studies over the previous sixty years had reported the low English language skills of deaf students, with reading and English scores reported for older deaf students hovering around the level attained by fourth and fifth grade hearing children. In Wrightstone's 1963 survey, 88% of 1075 deaf students aged 15-1/2 and above scored below grade level 4.9 in reading. Boatner (1965) and McClure (1966) classified roughly one third of deaf students sixteen and older as functionally illiterate, or unable to read well enough to cope with ordinary circumstances in life. These findings were not new. In 1918, a fill-in-the-blanks English test given to 1098 deaf students showed the average for fourth grade hearing children to be higher than the average for any grade level of the deaf. (Pintner, 1918)

Yet research had shown that the intelligence range for deaf persons, with no other disability, was the same as in the hearing population. (Vernon, 1969). Given this level of intellectual ability among deaf students, their low test scores in reading and English structure took on a new dimension, and it is not surprising that little correlation had been found between intelligence and such test scores.

Normal Language Development

At the same time that such studies were pointing out the normal intelligence range of deaf students and their problems with English, other researchers were studying normal language development in hearing children. Children exposed to English, they reported, mastered much of the structure of that language, including basic sentence patterns and inflections, by about age three. Language structures are fairly stable by age six, and extremely difficult to modify after the age of puberty. Between two and three years of age, children make a great jump in the use of prepositions, demonstratives, auxiliaries, articles, conjunctions, possessive and personal pronouns, and the tense, plural, and possessive markings. (See, for instance, Braine, 1963; Brown & Bellugi, 1964; Cazden, 1968; Weir, 1962; Labov, 1965; Penfield, 1964; Moskowitz, 1978). What hearing children learn is the language of their environment, be it French, Chinese, Standard American English, the English of Great Britain, or whatever language they perceive. Many children in Europe learn two or more languages with little or no formal instruction. Adults who know only one language, on the other hand, often experience great difficulty trying to learn a different language.

English Problems of Deaf Students

Studies focusing on the English problems of deaf children identified specific areas of weakness. These weaknesses included omission of necessary words or incorrect use of words. Sentence structures were simple and rigid, with those of 17-year-old deaf students comparable to eight-year-old hearing children. Lexical, or dictionary, meanings were learned more easily than structural meanings, and deducing the meaning of words from context was not a common skill. While studies with hearing children indicated consistent sequences of structures mastered in English language development, no such sequences appeared in the English skills of deaf children; what was learned first was what was taught first in school, and this varied from school to school. Deaf students used fewer adverbs, auxiliaries and conjunctions than hearing children. (See Myklebust, 1964; Heider and Heider, 1940; Hart and Rosenstein, 1964; Cooper, 1965; Simmons, 1962, as examples.) Many of these problems, especially discomfort with the idiomatic nature of many American English word meanings, are experienced by native speakers of other languages attempting to learn English, and indicate the difficulty of learning this complex language when the optimal language-learning years of childhood are past.

Incomplete Input

These problems are not surprising when it is remembered that language input must precede output, that this input is most beneficial when it takes place during the critical language learning years before age six, and that the deaf child's perception of English is often very imperfect, depending on the communication mode.

Even a partial hearing loss cuts off some of the auditory input, and hard-of-hearing children have very real problems learning English. For the profoundly deaf child, the problem can be even more serious. Since 40%, to 60% of the sounds of English look like some other sound on the lips (as in the old examples of pan, ban, man), it is not surprising that even the best speechreaders with a ready command of English must use educated guesswork and knowledge of the topic and the language to fill the gaps. The problem of speechreading for infants is compounded when it is remembered that young children do not ordinarily differentiate the parts of what they perceive, especially if the stimuli are unfamiliar or have no meaning for them. They perceive largely in terms of context. (Mussen, 1963)

Although three-year-old hearing children, as noted above, are well on their way to mastery of tenses and function words,

...in lipreading...the child does not perceive every word in an utterance, but rather, catches the key words, or even only the root parts of words (e.g. BOY instead of BOYS, WALK instead of WALKED). The words that are ignored are words that are not understood, as well as the function words (e.g. TO, AT, THE, FOR) that tie the communication together. (Hart and Rosenstein, 1964)

Similarly, -ing and -ed are difficult to speechread. It is not surprising, then, that some older deaf students who have learned that -ed is used for the past and -ing for a present action believe that the movie was interest<u>ed</u> because they saw it yesterday, while they are interest<u>ing</u> in TV because they are watching it now. It should be noted, also, that while hard-of-hearing children may pick up more vocabulary, many of these structural affixes are as difficult to hear as they are to speechread, and such students often have difficulty with -s, -ed, and the like.

Obviously, dependence on speechreading as a means of providing clear and unambiguous English input is a very dangerous dependence. What was needed was some way to make use of an unimpaired input channel, a more visual mode of representing English.

Fingerspelling

Fingerspelling, or forming words by spelling the letters of the alphabet on the hand, is larger and easier to perceive than speechreading. However, there is still the perception problem for very young children, since the child's eyes do not fully mature until age eight (hence the use of large print in primary storybooks). Moreover, skilled adult fingerspellers normally spell at a 300-letter-per-minute rate (Bornstein, 1965), while the average speaking rate ranges from 120 to 270 words per minute (Calvert and Silverman, 1975). If the average word length is calculated at five letters, this would mean spelling 600 to 1350 letters per minute. Using fingerspelling and speech together would thus mean either the speech rhythm would be distorted or letters would be left out or distorted in the fingerspelling.

Speech

Speech alone is obviously the easiest mode for hearing persons to use with a deaf child, but it is too often unsatisfactory in terms of the amount of information the child is able to perceive. Fingerspelling, while relatively easy to learn (26 letters are, after all, not that many) is not easy to learn to use well, and still presents perception problems for a very young child as well as production problems if the parent or teacher wishes to speak simultaneously. (See Caccamise, Hatfield, and Brewer, 1978, for further discussion of research and problems with the use of fingerspelling alone and in combination with speech.)

Signs: American Sign Language

Signs present larger, more easily perceived and discriminated symbols in communication than either speech or fingerspelling for young deaf children. With early visual input of signs, it is not surprising that deaf children of signing deaf parents, able to communicate from infancy, had been shown to enter school with an advantage over deaf children of hearing parents, and had tended to maintain this advantage throughout school.

However, it must be remembered that American Sign Language (ASL), which is used by many deaf adults, is a language in its own right and not a visual representation of English. Children who learn ASL as their native language from their parents have been shown to develop better English skills than those who were not exposed to sign language; however, children of deaf parents who signed to them from infancy in English mastered English to an even greater degree. (See Brasel and Quigley, 1975, for a report of such research.)

Early Parent–Child Communication

This introduces another factor, since adults who know only one language often have some difficulty mastering a second. For parents, the problem of becoming fluent during the early language-learning years is a very real problem. Accordingly, it may be simpler for most hearing parents of deaf children to begin with a form of signing in English than to attempt to become fluent in a foreign language (ASL) during what is for many parents a psychologically trying period of adjustment to their child's deafness.

The important issue is that comfortable parent-child communication be established as early as possible in a language readily available to the parents and a mode clearly perceivable by the child. If the parents know and use ASL with their child, English is still needed at some point for maximal function in our society, and should be taught in a clearly perceivable mode.

Simultaneous Communication

Research has tended to focus on the receptive abilities of older deaf students rather than younger, but showed consistently that understanding is greater with the use of simultaneous communication (speech, spelling, and signs used in combination) than with the use of speech alone, signs alone, spelling alone, or spelling and speech without signs. (See Caccamise and Johnson, 1978, for a summary of such research). While there are, of course, individual differences, the rule seems to be that the larger the number of modes used, the greater the chances for reception and understanding. A summary of research on the effect of the use of signs on English and on oral/aural communication skills finds not only that signs can assist in the development of English, but that they may facilitate the development of speech, speechreading, and listening skills. If attention is not given these oral/aural skills, they may not develop, but if such attention is given, the use of signs is not a detriment. (See Caccamise, Hatfield, and Brewer, 1978; Weiss, McIntyre, Goodwin, and Moores, 1975 and 1978, for more discussion of this research.)

Some individuals expressed concern that the use of all modes and the inclusion of manual English signs for word-endings may overload the child. Research with deaf children of deaf parents acquiring ASL as their native language has shown that these children are quite similar to hearing children in terms of increasing length of utterance and in their progressive mastery of structures of language. In studies of language acquisition by deaf children whose parents use manual English signs, the appropriate use of signed markers for past tense, plurals, and -ing has been reported in children at age three (Schlesinger and Meadow, 1972). One study of preschoolers using manual communication reported that what the mother used at home had greater influence than what the teacher used at school, and that if the mother used markers, the child also developed skill in using them. (Crandall, 1978)

Results of Signing English

The ability to use signs does not automatically transfer to the ability to read and write, and there was some question whether indeed signing English would result in better reading and writing skills.

Babb (1979) studied deaf children of hearing parents who used SEE at home and found the students equal in English skills to those reported in earlier studies of deaf children of deaf parents who signed English. Some researchers reported that the key factor associated with higher English skills in the students was teacher consistency in SEE usage (Gilman, Davis, and Raffin 1980; Raffin, Davis, and Gilman 1978). Wodlinger-Cohen (1986) found that the children were able to learn the system, and that they adjusted their use of signs and speech based on the speech and sign language abilities or preferences of their communication partners—their mothers, their teachers, or other children. Gaustad (1986) reported on the long-term effects of such instruction on deaf students aged five to seven. She reported that the length of time students had been in an early intervention program using Manually Coded English had an influence on their spontaneous language production, and that the students with longer time in such a program were more like hearing children in overall English scores, types of errors, and grammaticalness of productions. She described the differences based on that criterion as "remarkable." Mayberry and Wodlinger-Cohen (1987) reported that reading skills of deaf students in their study were not related to speech skills, but to the students' ability to understand signing in either English or ASL. In 1989 a study by Moeller based on communication assessments conducted with deaf children in a SEE program found the majority of the children were reading at or above grade level. A detailed analysis of language samples from deaf students who used SEE 2 by Schick and Moeller (1989) found that these students had acquired some of the most complex rules of syntactic structure in English and had internalized the rules of English. Luetke-Stahlman stated that building a first language or system base was essential if age-appropriate reading and writing abilities were a goal (Luetke-Stahlman, 1982 and 1986). She conducted a series of studies and reported that SEE students could understand stories told in American Sign Language as well as could residential school children (Luetke-Stahlman, 1990) and that SEE children could read written English better than PSE students (Luetke-Stahlman, 1988).

SEE and ASL

The stress on the importance of exposing the child to English if we wish him or her to acquire the language easily must not be interpreted as a rejection of American Sign Language (Gustason, Pfetzing, and Zawolkow, 1974). There are many ways in which these two languages can and should go hand-in-hand for a fuller educational and developmental experience for deaf children. Ideally, we would like to see teachers and parents comfortable with both ASL and English, who could combine and otherwise utilize the two types of signing both in and out of the classroom in a variety of ways to enrich the communication experiences of students. Our goal is for deaf children to become truly bilingual, at ease in both ASL and English. How best to accomplish this is still an open question, and again we solicit constructive suggestions from users. We consider Signing Exact English a means of manual expression for those who are speaking English while they sign, and an introduction to the richness and variety of signs for parents of young deaf children. We also consider it a teaching tool for use with students who know ASL and are learning English as a second language. We would like to see the best of both languages in as many hands as possible. (See Caccamise and Gustason, 1979, Caccamise and Johnson, 1978, and Gustason and Rosen, 1975, for further discussion of the roles of both ASL and English in the education and general development of deaf children, and communication with the deaf adult.)

Signing Exact English, (SEE 2), is NOT a replacement for ASL and is meant for use by parents and by teachers of English. Persons working with deaf adults should understand that SEE 2 is not widely used currently among adults, although "new" signs crop up in common usage. The study of ASL is important not only for those desiring to work with adult deaf persons, but for parents and teachers. ASL is a rich and expressive language, worth studying for its own sake, and many of its principles should be put to good use in using Signing Exact English. While there is still a shortage of trained teachers of both ASL and SEE, those who wish to learn either are encouraged to learn as much as possible about the other. Incomplete understanding raises the possibility of misunderstanding and personal/psychological/ sociological problems—for parents, for teachers, and for the child.

Because we wish to see such problems minimized, we encourage a study of and acceptance of both ASL and manual English. In the following pages we list important principles of SEE, suggestions to follow in the development of additional signs, and some points to remember for clear, effective signing. In these, we have attempted to combine our knowledge of ASL and English into a sign system that can assist deaf and hard-of-hearing children in their development of English language skills. We present both theoretical principles and practical usage suggestions for the system. We recognize the dynamic nature of language and communication, and that any communication form must accommodate its users. Few language rules are strict, and exceptions to rules can be found in all languages. We are aware that some of the signs in this book may not seem consistent with the principles explained, but these exceptions are based on users, whose skills in language usage continue to go ahead of the knowledge of educators and linguists as to how languages may be used most effectively in various modalities (alone and in combination) for maximum communication and language development.

Important Principles of Signing Exact English

1 The most important principle in Signing Exact English is that ENGLISH SHOULD BE SIGNED IN A MANNER THAT IS AS CONSISTENT AS POSSIBLE WITH HOW IT IS SPOKEN OR WRITTEN IN ORDER TO CONSTITUTE A LANGUAGE INPUT FOR THE DEAF CHILD THAT WILL RESULT IN HIS MASTERY OF ENGLISH. This means, for instance, that idioms such as "dry up," "cut it out," "stop horsing around" would be signed as those exact words, rather than as "quiet" or "stop" or "finish." It also means that inflections or markers must be shown, such as talks, talked, talking, government.

2 A second important principle is that A SIGN SHOULD BE TRANSLATABLE TO ONLY ONE ENGLISH EQUIVALENT. Initialized signs contribute a great deal here, providing such synonyms as HURT, PAIN, ACHE, and so on. But this principle also means that only one sign should be used for such English words as RUN, which has a number of different meanings and a number of different translations in ASL.

These two principles have led to a number of problems and jokes. How does one sign "I saw you yesterday" or "he left home last week"? Is the sign for saw the same as in sawing wood, and the sign for left the same as the opposite of right? For that matter, what of right, rite, and write? In an attempt to come to terms with these problems, more principles were developed. Words are considered in three groups: 1) Basic, 2) Compound, and 3) Complex.

3 "BASIC WORDS" ARE WORDS THAT CAN HAVE NO MORE TAKEN AWAY AND STILL FORM A COMPLETE WORD (GIRL, TALK, THE, the noun SAW, etc.). For these basic words, the three-point criteria of sound, spelling, and meaning is utilized. If any two of these three factors are the same, the same sign is used. This covers multiple-meaning words such as RUN, which would have the same sign in:

The boys will *run*. The motor will *run*.
Your nose will *run*.

These are all signed differently in ASL. (See the following "points to remember for expressive signing" for suggestions on combining ASL principles with English words in such cases.)

To take a different example, a different sign would be used for W-I-N-D in:

The *wind* is blowing. I must *wind* my watch.

In this case only the spelling is the same; sound meaning both differ, and since two of the three factors are different a different sign is used. In the case of RUN, spelling and sound are the same, and meaning varies; since two of the three factors are the same, the same basic sign is used.

4 "COMPLEX WORDS" ARE DEFINED AS BASIC WORDS WITH THE ADDITION OF AN AFFIX OR INFLECTION: GIRLS, TALKED, the past tense verb SAW. Once such an addition has been made the combination is no longer considered a basic word. Accordingly, the past tense of SEE is added to produce the verb SAW, which is not the same as either the noun SAW or the verb to SAW (which would have past tense added to produce SAWED). An affix is added in signs if it is added in speech or writing, regardless of the part of speech. The suffix -s, for instance, is used both for regular plurals (GIRLS, SAWS) and the third person singular of verbs (RUNS, SEES, SAWS).

5 COMPOUND WORDS ARE TWO OR MORE BASIC WORDS PUT TOGETHER. IF THE MEANING OF THE WORDS SEPARATELY IS CONSISTENT WITH THE MEANING OF THE WORDS TOGETHER, THEN AND ONLY THEN ARE THEY SIGNED AS THE COMPONENT WORDS. Thus UNDERLINE would be signed UNDER + LINE but UNDERSTAND, having no relation to the meaning of the words UNDER and STAND, would have a separate sign and would not be signed UNDER + STAND.

6 WHEN A SIGN ALREADY EXISTS IN ASL THAT IS CLEAR, UNAMBIGUOUS, AND COMMONLY TRANSLATES TO ONE ENGLISH WORD, THIS SIGN IS RETAINED. As pointed out previously, the sign for GIRL is the same in ASL and in this book. This is clearest with single meaning words. With multiple meaning words, while the sign may fit one ASL way of signing the word, ASL may have other signs for different meanings. This is handled by Principle 3 above. Principle 6 explains why signs are presented in this book for compound or complex words such as CARELESS, MISUNDERSTAND, BASEBALL, CAN'T, that could, by following the principles above, be signed CARE-+ LESS, MIS + UNDERSTAND, BASE-+ BALL, CAN + N'T. A single sign is borrowed from ASL when ease and economy of movement are possible with no loss of clear, unambiguous English.

7 WHEN THE FIRST LETTER IS ADDED TO A BASIC SIGN TO CREATE SYNONYMS, THE BASIC SIGN IS RETAINED WHEREVER POSSIBLE AS THE MOST COMMONLY USED WORD. For instance, the basic sign for MAKE is retained for that word, while the sign is made with C-hands for CREATE, and P-hands for PRODUCE. In some cases, as with GUARD, PROTECT, DEFEND, users have experienced difficulty remembering which is the uninitialized sign since all three words are used relatively equally; hence all three are initialized.

8 WHEN MORE THAN ONE MARKER IS ADDED TO A WORD, MIDDLE MARKERS MAY BE DROPPED IF THERE IS NO SACRIFICE OF CLARITY. For instance, the past tense sign is added to BREAK to produce BROKE, but BROKEN may be signed as BREAK plus the past participle or -EN. Similarly, EXAM may be joined by -INE for EXAMINE, but EXAMINATION may be signed as EXAM plus -TION. Such dropping of the middle markers serves to keep the flow of the sign smooth and efficient, while retaining the identifying marker which shows what word is used. Dropping is not done if confusion might result; for instance, WILL plus N'T creates WON'T, WILL plus -D (or the past participle marker -en) plus N'T creates WOULDN'T. Dropping the middle marker in this case would confuse the two words.

9 WHILE FOLLOWING THE ABOVE PRINCIPLES, RESPECT NEEDS TO BE SHOWN FOR CHARACTERISTICS OF VISUAL–GESTURAL COMMUNICATION. While sign languages vary just as do spoken languages, and what is possible in one language may not appear in another, awkward or difficult movements should be avoided whenever possible. For instance, English does not use the trilled R present in other spoken languages, and some phonetic combinations are not normal in English (e.g. WUG is a possible nonsense word, but PKT is not). The same is true of ASL, where simple hand shapes (A, 5, 1) are used much more commonly than more complex hand shapes (R, P, etc.) Small differences in shape or motion should not occur far from the visual center of attention. These points are addressed further in the next section.

Suggestions for the Development of Additional Signs

BOTH common sense and experience tell us that when manual English is used, words are sure to crop up that have no sign in this book. When this happens, we have several recommendations.

1 **SEEK AN EXISTING SIGN.** Check other sign language texts. Ask skilled signers in your community, especially deaf native signers, who support signing in English.

2 **MODIFY AN EXISTING SIGN WITH A SIMILAR OR RELATED MEANING.** Generally, this means adding the first letter of the word to a basic sign.

3 **CONSIDER FINGERSPELLING.** This depends, of course, on the age and perceptual abilities of the child, and the length and frequency of use of the word in question.

4 **IF ALL ELSE FAILS, AND YOU MUST INVENT, TRY TO STAY AS CLOSE AS POSSIBLE TO ASL PRINCIPLES.** We realize that many individuals using manual English are not yet familiar with ASL. In an attempt to give some guidance in this area, pertinent guidelines are summarized below. These guidelines were developed for collection, evaluation, selection, and recording of signs used in educational and work settings under the direction of Dr. Frank Caccamise of the National Technical Institute for the Deaf. The persons involved in developing these guidelines were for the most part concerned with college age deaf students. Most of the guidelines are, however, equally applicable when considering younger children. Those that need special consideration are noted.

There are four major components of signs: A) position, B) handshape, C) movement, and D) orientation (the direction of the palm and fingers). The guidelines discussed below are based on how these four components are combined in ASL signs, and they may be used in considering or assessing the acceptability or unacceptability of newly developed signs.

1) **THE SIGNING SPACE.** Signs generally fall within an area between the top of the head and just above the waist, within a comfortable, but not fully extended, arms reach to the sides and ahead. The center of this space is the hollow of the neck. Signs do occur outside this area, as in theatrical signing and for emphasis.

2) **THE VISUAL CENTER OF THE SIGNING SPACE** is the nose-mouth area, and while many signs are made near here, they are seldom made within this center. Vision is sharpest near this center, and less sharp as you move away from the center. When reading signs people usually watch the face of the signer rather than the hands, and facial expression and lip movement are important. An effort should be made not to obstruct the mouth area when signing since this interferes with speechreading. In addition to speechreading, the mouth area should not be blocked because the face and mouth area are important for grammatical expression in ASL and can and should be effectively used in SEE to enhance communication.

3) **POSITION.** Signs made near the center of the signing space can use smaller movements and finer distinctions among signs than signs made further away from the visual center (see e.g. APPLE, FRUIT, VEGETABLE, etc.).

4) **SYMMETRY.** Signs made near the center of the signing space often use one hand, while signs made further away tend to use two hands in symmetry (e.g. HEAVEN, RUSSIA). Signs made in the neck and face area generally use one hand. Signs made below the neck generally use two hands. If both hands move, the handshapes should be the same.

5) **DOMINANCE.** For two-handed signs in which only one hand moves, the non-moving or passive hand should have one of the seven neutral handshapes (l-A-S-B-C-5-0) or the same handshape as the moving hand. Ordinarily one attends to the moving hand. (Note: This need not occur when the moving hand brings attention to the non-moving hand, as in GOAL, AIM, OBJECTIVE, TARGET, COMMENCE, INITIATE, etc.)

6) **NUMBER OF HANDSHAPES PER SIGN.** Most signs in ASL use only one handshape on each hand. Some signs require a slight handshape change, as in MILK or PRINT, but do not involve more than two handshapes. Accordingly, invented signs should use no more than two handshapes. (Note: Markers or inflections may be added to a sign already having two handshapes.)

7) **SIGNS INVOLVING CONTACT.** Four major areas of contact in signs are the head, trunk, arm, and

hand. ASL signs are systematic in that signs made with double contacts are made within the same major area (e.g. INDIAN has both contacts on the head, WE has both contacts on the trunk, etc.). Exceptions to this are signs derived from compounds, as DAUGHTER from GIRL-+ BABY, etc.

8) SEMANTICALLY RELATED SIGNS. Signs which are related in meaning are often related in formation. For instance, the basic concept of a group is initialized to represent CLASS, GROUP, TEAM, and the like. (As stated previously, such related signs are grouped as "families" in this book.) This type of structural relationship should be considered in the development of new signs.

9) MOVEMENT AND WORD-TYPE: NOUN-VERB PAIRS. In ASL, some signs may have the same handshape, position, and orientation, but differ in movement, with nouns having short repeated movement and verbs having hold or continuous movement (e.g. AIRPLANE and GO-BY-AIRPLANE). (Note: This guideline may be applicable in terms of effective signing, as listed in the next section. Signing Exact English does not rely on this principle to distinguish between or among English words. See, for example, CHAIR and SIT.)

10) COMPOUNDING SIGNS. There are two kinds of compounding, lexical and grammatical. Lexical compounding refers to signs made up of several reduced signs; e.g. FRUIT in ASL may be signed APPLE-ORANGE-BANANA, etc., with shorter and assimilated movements. Grammatical compounding connects several signs to form a new one; e.g. LETTER-NUMBER for ZIPCODE, or HEART-STUDY for CARDIOLOGY. *(note: This type of compounding is clear to ASL users, and some signs derived from compounds–e.g. daughter–are used in manual English, but this guideline is at variance with the first principle of Signing Exact English, that we attempt to sign exactly the words we say. Relying on a slight difference in movement, as in Guideline 9 above, or on a compound sign, may not provide a clear, unambiguous representation of the English word as spoken/written. This is a criticism of neither ASL nor English, but a recognition of the difference between the two.)*

11) ITERATIONS. This refers to the number of times a sign is repeated. Some signs in ASL are limited to one repetition (e.g. the singular form of a noun such as GIRL). Signs needing at least two repetitions do not distinguish between two or more repetitions.

Points to Remember for Clear, Expressive Signing

AS stated previously, we believe ASL principles should be incorporated into English signs for more effective simultaneous communication. While the suggestions and guidelines listed before relate to the development of new signs, such guidelines can also be considered as an aid in production. Following are examples of this integration of principles or characteristics with SEE, and other points to remember in sign production.

1) Always speak when you sign, and let facial expression and body English aid communication.

2) Affixes, and word-endings for tense, person, and the like, should not be made as signs separate from the sign for the basic word itself, but should flow from the base sign for the word. Similarly, signs for word endings should not be made with an emphasis equal to that for the sign of the basic word. Be guided by the practice of spoken English. You do not say "swing ing" or "swingING" but "SWINGing". This may be compared to syllables in spoken words: they are not pronounced as separate words, but flow into each other. Similarly, combined words (compound words) should flow together. INTO should be signed INTO, not IN TO.

3) The past tense sign does not actually need to be made over the shoulder. A backward flip of the hand at the conclusion of the sign for the verb suffices to indicate the past tense (or the addition of -d, if preferred, for regular past tenses such as WALKED).

4) When adding a suffix to a two-handed sign, keep the left hand in the position of the sign (do not drop hand) while the right hand signs the suffix. This helps indicate that the suffix is part of the word and not a separate word.

5) Raising the eyebrows and freezing the hands in the air, or holding the end position of a sign instead of letting the hands drop, are ASL techniques for indicating a question that can be answered yes or no. A slight frown is often used with "WH" questions (What, Who, Where, When, Why, How). These expressions can and should be used in conjunction with manual English signs. A question-mark sign is only for emphasis.

6) When making a negative statement, as in "I don't think so," "She isn't here," and the like, shaking the head from side to side aids in clarifying the negative.

7) With many signs, clarity can be added by making the sign in the appropriate place. This is true not only of multiple meaning signs such as BOW tie (signed at the neck), BOW and arrow (signed in the position of a bow), and hair BOW (signed at the hair); but of signs such as PAIN (in the neck, in the side) and BUTTERFLY or BUTTERFLIES (in the stomach). Of course in the latter examples the entire phrase should be signed, and the sign executed in the appropriate location. In showing fear of something to your right, do not make the sign on your left.

8) When signing pronouns, if the person referred to is present, sign HE, SHE, HIM, or HER in the person's direction, or sign and point. If the person is not present, it helps to set him or her up in a specific location and orient your signs to that location when talking about him or her. When talking about more than one person, setting them up in different locations aids immeasurably in clarifying to whom you are referring. Try putting one of them on your right, the other on your left.

9) Body, eye, and hand orientation help! When signing LOOK, the motion should move toward where you want the person to look: at the sky, the floor, out the window, etc. If you are signing a dialogue between two characters, turning slightly to the left when one is speaking, and slightly to the right when the other responds, helps to indicate who is speaking. Looking up or down can indicate relative height.

10) Some verbs should show the direction of the action—towards the direct object. GIVE, for example, may be signed from the giver to the receiver, as can TEACH, SHOW, TEASE, and other such verbs. When you are the receiver, these signs can begin in front of you and move towards you, in a sort of mirror image of the sign.

11) Some signs can be made more than once when you are talking about plural nouns; e.g. make the sign for GIRL more than once before adding -s or for BOOK two or more times before adding -s. Repeating the sign also shows an action that is on going, as in I AM PAINT-PAINT-PAINTING A PICTURE or one that is very difficult as in I AM STUDY-STUDY-STUDYING VERY HARD.

12) Some signs can vary in size, a big dog is not as large as a big dinosaur, and BIG can be signed accordingly.

13) Signs can also vary in intensity, or be modified in their execution. A slow, thoughtful WALK should differ from from a business-like WALK; SYMPATHY can be more or less intense as shown by the motion; I LOVE YOU can be sincere or sarcastic depending on motion and facial expression.

14) Ham it up! Use facial expression and mime to help get the message across. You will find ASL a treasure trove of graphic and expressive signs, and you will find most children are natural hams.

15) ENJOY YOUR COMMUNICATION, AND ENJOY YOUR CHILDREN.

SELECTED REFERENCES

Babb, R. (1979) A study of the academic achievement and language acquisition levels of deaf children of hearing parents in an educational environment using Signing Exact English as the primary mode of manual communication. Doctoral dissertation, University of Illinois, Urbana.

Babbidge, H. D. (1965) *Education of the deaf: A report to the secretary of Health, Education, and Welfare by his Advisory Committee on the Education of the Deaf.* Washington, DC: U.S. Dept. of Health, Education, and Welfare.

Boatner, E.B. (1965) The need of a realistic approach to the education of the deaf. Paper presented to a joint convention of the California Association of Parents of Deaf and Hard-of-Hearing Children, California Association of Teachers of the Deaf and Hard-of-Hearing, and the California Association of the Deaf.

Bornstein, H. (1990) Manual Communication. Washington, DC: Gallaudet University Press.

Bornstein, H., and Saulnier, K. (1981) Signed English: A brief follow-up to the first evaluation. *American Annals of the Deaf 126*:69-72.

Bornstein, H., Saulnier, K., and Hamilton, L. (1980) Signed English: A first evaluation. *American Annals of the Deaf 125*:467-481.

Braine, M. D. S. (1963) The ontogeny of English phrase structure: The first phase. *Language* 39:1-13.

Brasel, K., and Quigley, S. (1977) The influence of certain language and communication environments in early childhood on the development of language in deaf individuals. *Journal* of *Speech and Hearing Research* 20:95-107.

Brown, R., and Bellugi, U. (1964) Three processes in the child's acquisition of syntax. *Harvard Educational Review* 39 :133-152.

Caccamise, F., Hatfield, N. and Brewer, L. (1978) Manual/Simultaneous Communication Research: Results and Implications. *American Annals of the Deaf* 123:7, 8.

Cazden, C. B. (1968) The acquisition of noun and verb inflections. *Child Development* 39:433-448.

Center for Assessment and Demographic Studies, Annual Report 1982-83. Gallaudet University, Washington, DC.

Cooper, R. L. (1965) The ability of deaf and hearing children to apply morphological rules. Doctoral dissertation, Columbia University, New York.

Crandall, K. (1978) Inflectional morphemes in the manual English of young hearing impaired children and their mothers. *Journal of Speech and Hearing Research* 21:372-386.

Fischer, S. D., Metz, D., Brown, P., and Caccamise, F. (1990) The effects of bimodal communication on the intelligibility of sign and speech. In *Theoretical Issues in Sign Language Research, Vol. 1: Linguistics,* ed. S. Fischer and P. Siple. Chicago: University of Chicago Press.

Gaustad, M. G. (1986) Longitudinal effects of manual English instruction on deaf children's morphological skills. *Applied Psycholinquistics* 7:101-128.

Gilman, L., Davis, J., and Raffin, M. (1980) Use of common morphemes by hearing impaired children exposed to a system of Manual English. *Journal of Auditory Research* 20:57-69.

Gustason, G. (1981) Does Signing Exact English work? *Teaching English to the deaf* (Winter).

Gustason, G. (1974) Signing Exact English, *Gallaudet Today* 5:2,11-12.

Gustason, G. (1973) The languages of communication. *Deafness Annual III.* Silver Spring, MD.: Professional Rehabilitation Workers with the Adult Deaf, 83-95.

Gustason, G., Pfetzing, D. and Zawolkow, E. (1974) The Rationale of Signing Exact English, *The Deaf American,* September, 5-6.

Gustason, G. & Rosen, R. (1975) Effective Sign Communication for Instructional Purposes: Manual English and American Sign Language. *Proceedings of the Convenion of American Instructors of the Deaf.*

Gustason, G., ed. (1988) *Signing English: Exact or Not?* Los Alamitos, CA: Modern Signs Press, Inc.

Hart, B. O., and Rosenstein, J. (1964) Examining the language behavior of deaf children.*Volta Review* 66:679-682.

Heider, F., and Heider, G. (1940) Comparison of sentence structure of deaf and hearing children. *Psychological Monographs* 52:42-103.

Jordan, I. K., Gustason. G., and Rosen, R. (1976) Current communication trends at programs tor the deaf. *American Annals of the Deaf* 121:327-532.

Jordan, I. K., Gustason, G., and Rosen, R. (1979) An update on communication trends at programs for the deaf. *American Annals of the Deaf* 124:4, 350-357.

Luetke-Stahlman, B. (1990) Can SEE 2 children understand ASL-using adults? *American Annals of the Deaf*, 135:1, 7-8.

——(1989a) Input and literacy. Paper presented at the Illinois Supervisors of the Deaf meeting. Lyle, Il., March.

——(1989b) Documenting syntactically and semantically incomplete bimodal input to deaf subjects. *American Annals of the Deaf*, 133:3, 230-234.

——(1988a)The benefit of oral English-only as compared with signed input to hearing-impaired students. *The Volta Review* 90:349-361.

——(1988b) A description of the form and content of four sign systems as used in classrooms of hearing impaired students in the United States. Paper submitted to *American Annals of the Deaf*.

——(1988c) SEE II in the classroom: how well is English grammar represented? In *Signing English: Exact or Not?* ed. G. Gustason. Los Alamitos, CA: Modern Signs Press, Inc.

——(1988d) A series of studies investigating SEE II use. In *Signing English: Exact or Not?* ed. G. Gustason. Los Alamitos, CA: Modern Signs Press, Inc.

——(1986) Building a language base in deaf students. *American Annals of the Deaf*, 131:3, 220-228.

——(1982) A philosophy for assessing the language proficiency of deaf students to effectively promote English literacy. *American Annals of the Deaf*, 127:7, 844-851.

Mayberry, R., and Wodlinger-Cohen, R. (1987) After the revolution: Educational practice and the deaf child's communication skills. In *They grow in silence*, 2nd ed., ed. E. Mindel and M. Vernon. San Diego, CA: College Hill Press.

Mayer, P. & Lowenbraun, S. (1990) T.C. use among elementary teachers of deaf children. *American Annals of the Deaf*, 135:3, 257-263.

McClure, W.J. (1966) Current problems and trends in the education of the deaf. *The Deaf American*, 18: 8- 14.

Moeller, M. P., et al. (1988) A long-term study of a SEE II program. Paper presented at the convention of the American Speech Language Hearing Association, Boston.

Moeller, M. P. and Luetke-Stahlman, B. (1988) Parents' use of SEE II: A descriptive analysis. *Journal of Speech and Hearing Research*.

Moskowitz, B. A. (1978) The acquisition of language. *Scientific American* (December):92-108.

Parkins, S., and Whitesell, K. (1985) Evaluating the manual communication skills of prospective teachers and currently employed teachers in two hundred and fifty-four schools/programs for hearing impaired children in the United States. Unpublished survey conducted for the North Carolina Council for the Hearing Impaired.

Penfield, W. (1964) The uncommitted cortex: The child's changing brain. *The Atlantic Monthly* (July):77-81.

Raffin, M., Davis, J., and Gilman, L. (1978) Comprehension of inflectional morphemes by deaf children exposed to a visual English sign system. *Journal* of *Speech and Hearing Research, 21*:387-400.

Reay, E. E. (1946) A comparison between deaf and hearing children in regard to the use of verbs and nouns in compositions describing a short motion picture story. *American Annals of the Deaf*, 91:331-349.

Schick, B., & Moeller, M.P. (1989) The expressive English language of deaf students exposed to SEE 2. Paper presented at ASHA, St. Louis, MO. November.

Schlesinger, H. S. (1978a) The acquisition of bimodal language. In *Sign language of the Deaf*. New York: Academic Press.

Schlesinger, H. S. (1978b) The acquisition of signed and spoken language. In *Deaf Children: Developmental Perspectives*. New York: Academic Press.

Simmons, A. A. (1962) A comparison of the type-token ratio of spoken and written language of deaf and hearing children. *Volta Review*, 64:417-421.

Swisher, M. W. (1985) Characteristics of hearing mothers' manually coded English. In *SLR '83: Proceedings of the III International Symposium on Sign Language Research*, eds. W. Stokoe and V. Volterra. Silver Spring, MD: Linstok Press.

Swisher, M. V., and Thompson, M. (1985) Mothers learning smultaneous communication: The dimensions of the task. *American Annals of the Deaf*, 130: 212-217.

Vernon, M. (1968) Fifty years of research on the intelligence of the deaf and hard of hearing: A survey of the literature and discussion of implications. *Journal of Rehabilitation of the Deaf*, 1:1-11.

——(1969) Sociological and psychological factors associated with hearing loss. *Journal of Speech and Hearing Research*, 12:511-563.

Wodlinger-Cohen, R. (1986) The manual representation of speech by deaf children, their mothers, and their teachers. Paper presented at the Conference on Theoretical Issues in Sign Language Research. Rochester, NY.

Suggestions For Signing Creatively

SEE has followed a one-word, one-sign criterion in sign-selection for most words, despite their multiple meanings in English. However, the varieties of meanings have not been ignored.

When a basic sign represents various–sometimes unrelated–meanings, then, by incorporating the principles of American Sign Language, the basic sign can be altered slightly to express each separate meaning more clearly.

Pictures of three examples of creative signing are given on the facing page.

1) The sense of lasting a long time comes from continuing the moving hand for the word "last" forward after striking the other hand at the fingertips. A past time is indicated by swinging the moving hand upward and backward for a short distance.

2) The sign for "duck," can be made with the body-movement for ducking an approaching object.

3) A clawing motion represents the animal, "bear." A carrying motion, swinging slightly to the side, means to "bear" an object. To indicate endurance, close the claws into fists and minimize the swinging motion.

Further examples to illustrate possibilities for creative signing:

BARK For a dog's bark, the sign is produced near the mouth area, with the fingers pointing outwards. For bark on a tree, the sign is produced in front of the body.

BOW The basic sign for "bow" (long o), is made in different places to show what kind of bow is meant. At the neck for a bow-tie, in midair for a rainbow, vertically to outline a bow used with arrows. In the hair means a hair-ribbon bow, and on an invisible box represents gift-wrapping.

POUND The meaning of a pound of weight is distinguished from the meaning of beating upon something, by signing "pound" with a pounding motion for the second meaning.

SOME OF THE SIGNS THAT CAN BE MADE CREATIVELY TO HELP INDICATE THE DIFFERENT MEANINGS OF THE ENGLISH WORD DESIRED ARE MARKED IN THE BOOK BY ✶

(Note: Fingerspelling the word is a viable alternative in cases in which the signer feels very uncomfortable with the connection between sign and sense.)

LAST IN LINE

LOLLIPOPS CAN LAST ALL DAY

REMEMBER LAST WEEK

A DUCK LOVES WATER

DUCK THAT BALL

THE BEAR IS BIG

BEAR YOUR LOAD

BEAR YOUR PAIN

EXPLANATION OF THE TEXT

Form of hands, position, and movement, if any, are shown in various ways:

1. Arrows show direction and line of movement.
2. Dotted hands represent original positions.
3. Pairs of pictures (1 and 2) show movement too complex for the use of dotted original positions only.

Hands are usually in the form of a letter of the alphabet or a number. Modifications are shown, such as "flat", "bent", "claw hand" and "bent hand." See Hand-Shapes on facing page.

Note whether movement is to be repeated. Pay special attention to whether there is touching, brushing, striking, or merely an approaching motion. For a right-handed person, use the right hand as the active hand. "Right" in the description refers to the right of the person signing—-you. Left-handed persons should reverse hands. Do not make a habit of switching from one hand to the other.

Pictures of the words represented are used, when possible, to aid in understanding why the sign is made as it is (see hippopotamus, child, caterpillar) and we feel pictures aid the preschool child.

A star symbol ★ follows a word that has two or more different meanings that should be indicated by the way the word is signed. For further explanation, see the Creative Signing pages.

A crown symbol ♔ follows a word that is the head of its sign family. See the family listings at the end of the book.

Alternative signs have been included for some signs which have several accepted versions. Use the sign most commonly used in your school or local area, or the sign most comfortable for you. These pairs of signs are indicated by "Alt.1" and "Alt. 2." See, for example, grip.

Some words are "Compound" or "Complex"; that is, made with the signs for two smaller words or a word plus an affix.

Example:	COMPOUND (Two words put together that do not change the meaning of the words)		
	Chalkboard—	signed:	Chalk + Board
	Overcook—	signed:	Over + Cook
	COMPLEX (A word preceded or followed by an affix)		
	Girls—	signed:	Girl + -s
	Unhappy—	signed:	Un- + happy
	Application—	signed:	Apply + -tion

We have included some of these words in the text when we felt the combination needed clarification.

After some word descriptions the initials (*p.t.* or *p.p.*) in italics will be used to show tenses:

p.t. which stands for Past Tense of verbs

Example:	Saw—	signed:	See + *p.t.* (-ed, alt.1)
	Spoke—	signed:	Speak + *p.t.* (-ed, alt.1)
	Drank—	signed:	Drink + *p.t.* (-ed, alt. 1)
	Talked—	signed:	Talk + *p.t.* (-ed, alt.1 or alt.2)

p.p. which stands for Past Participle of verbs

Example:	Seen—	signed:	See + *p.p.* (-en, alt.1 or alt. 2)
	Swum—	signed:	Swim + *p.p.* (-en, alt.1)
	Drunk—	signed:	Drink + *p.p.* (-ed, alt.1)

HAND-SHAPES

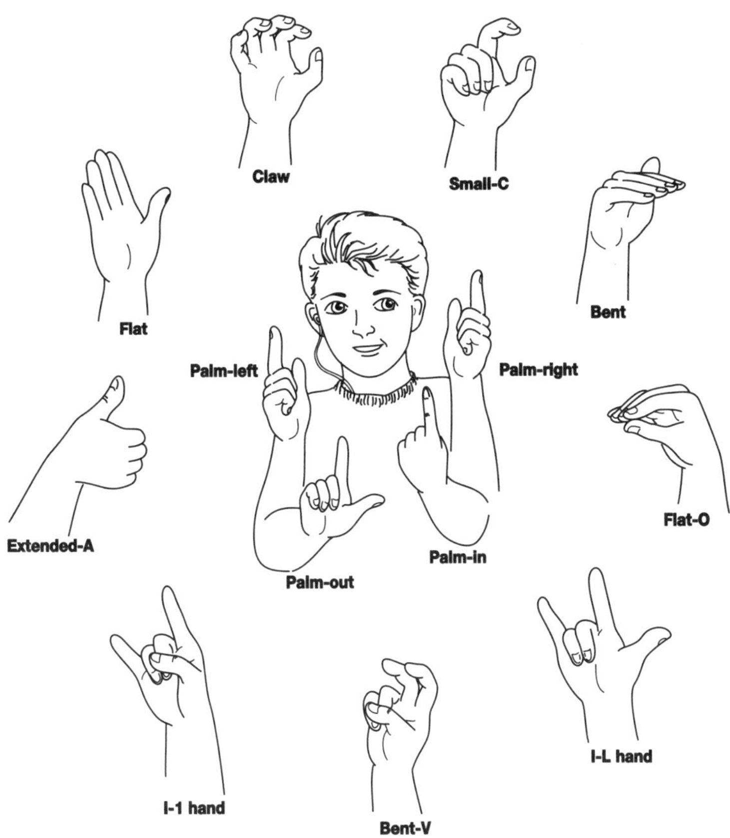
Claw
Small-C
Flat
Bent
Palm-left
Palm-right
Extended-A
Flat-O
Palm-in
Palm-out
I-1 hand
I-L hand
Bent-V

XXIV

THE PLEDGE OF ALLEGIANCE

I
pledge
allegiance
to
the
flag
of
the
United States
of
America
and
to
the
Republic

for
which
it
stands
one
nation
under
God
in-
divis-
-ible
with
liberty
and
justice
for
all

THE ALPHABET

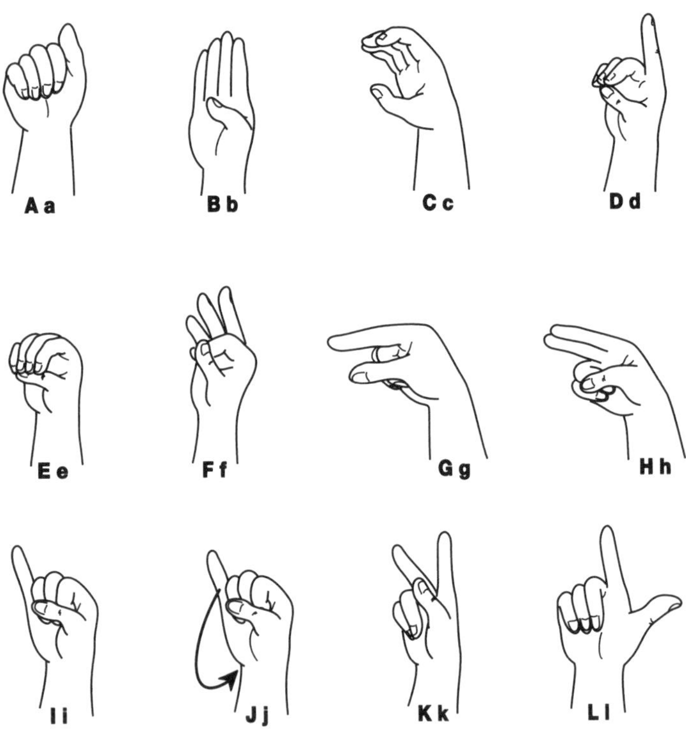

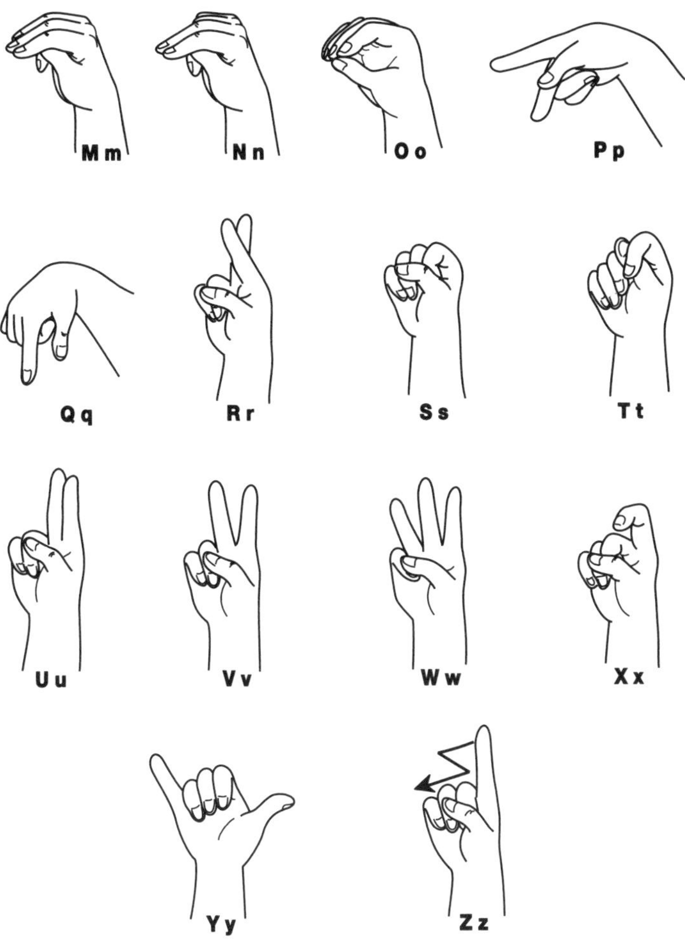
Mm
Nn
Oo
Pp
Qq
Rr
Ss
Tt
Uu
Vv
Ww
Xx
Yy
Zz

NUMBERS

One (1)
(can be done palm-in)

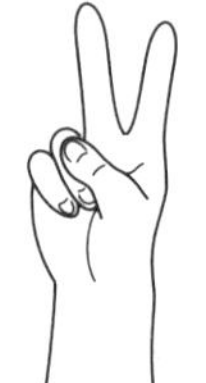

Two (2)
(can be done palm-in)

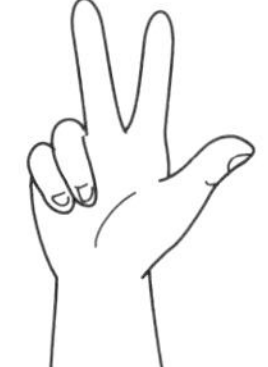

Three (3)
(can be done palm-in)

Four (4)
(can be done palm-in)

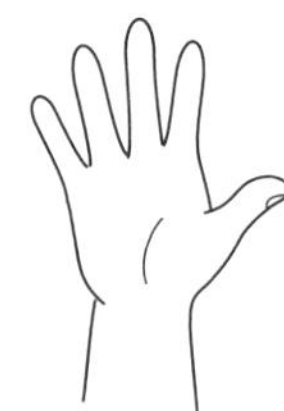

Five (5)
(can be done palm-in)

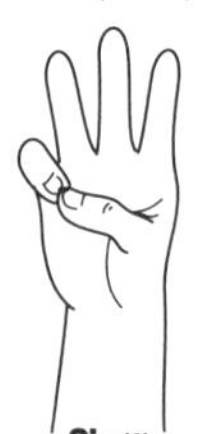

Six (6)

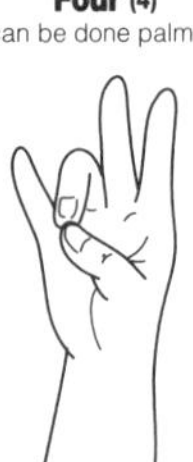

Seven (7)

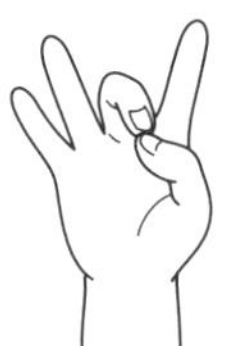

Eight (8)

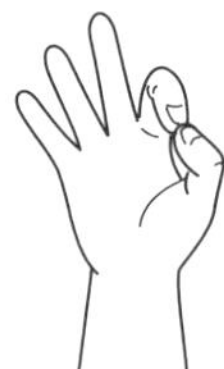

Nine (9)

Ten (10)

Eleven (11)
Index flips up

Twelve (12)
First two fingers flip up

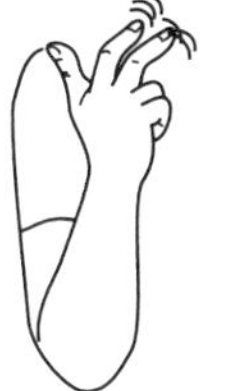

Thirteen (13)
(Alt. 1)
First two fingers of "3" wiggle together

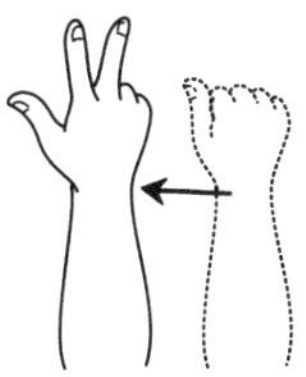

Thirteen (13)
(Alt. 2)
Palm-in A-hands open to 3-hand *(10 + 3)*

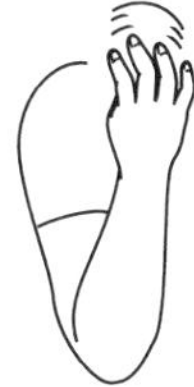

Fourteen (14)
(Alt. 1)
"4" fingers wiggle all together

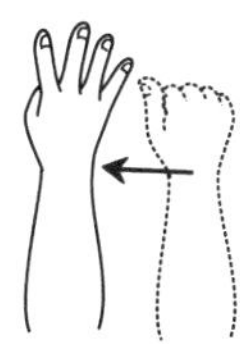

Fourteen (14)
(Alt. 2)
Palm-in A-hand opens to 4-hand *(10 + 4)*

Fifteen (15)
(Alt. 1)
Four fingers wiggle all together, thumb out

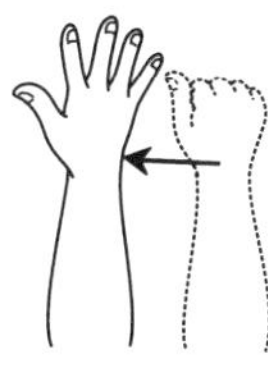

Fifteen (15)
(Alt. 2)
Palm-in A-hand opens to 5-hand *(10 + 5)*

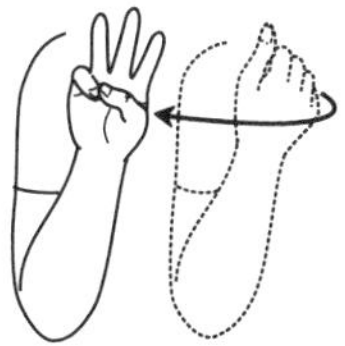

Sixteen (16)
Palm-in A pivots and opens to palm-out 6 *(10 + 6)*

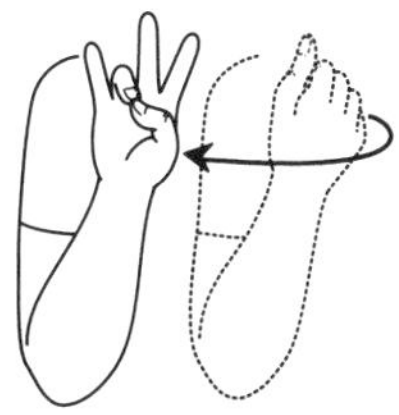

Seventeen (17)
Palm-in A pivots and opens to palm-out 7 *(10 + 7)*

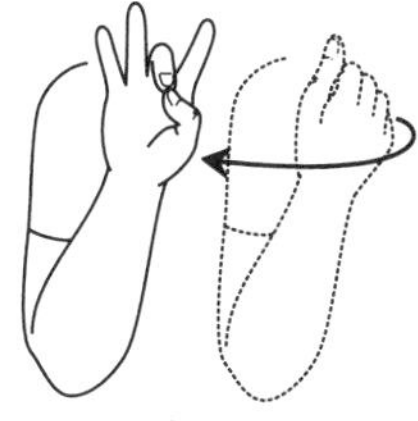

Eighteen (18)
Palm-in A pivots and opens to palm-out 8 *(10 + 8)*

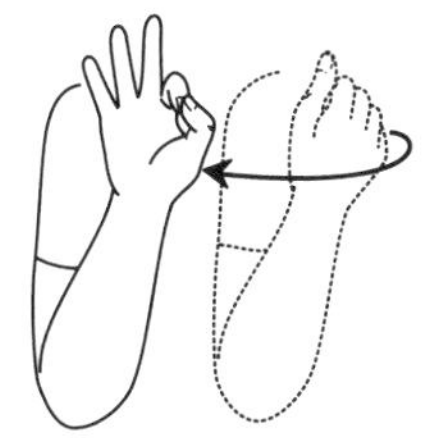

Nineteen (19)
Palm-in A pivots and opens to palm-out 9 *(10 + 9)*

Twenty (20)
Index of G closes several times on thumb

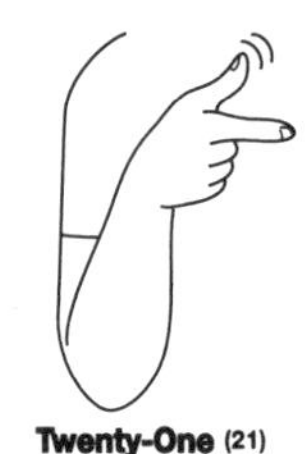

Twenty-One (21)
Thumb of L wiggles, index aiming forward

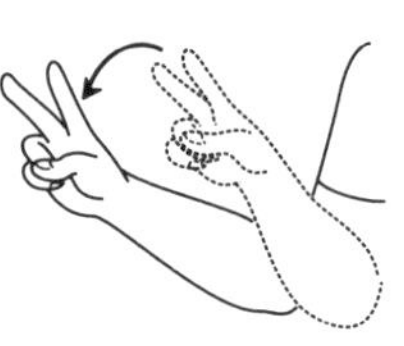

Twenty-Two (22)
V-hand makes two 2's

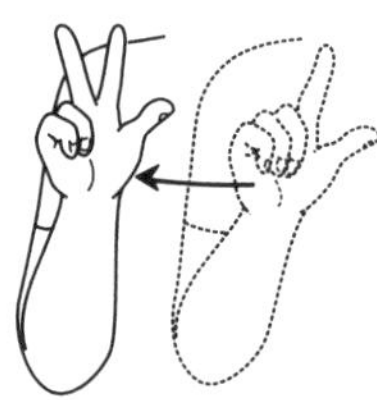

Twenty-Three (23)
"L" + 3

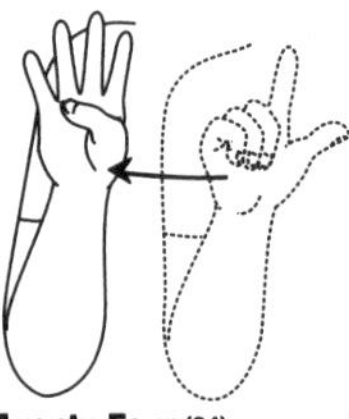

Twenty-Four (24)
"L" + 4

Twenty-Five (25)
(Alt. 1)
Last three fingers wiggle together

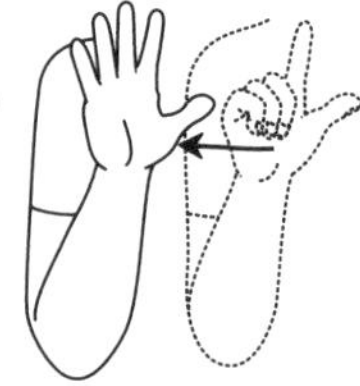

Twenty-Five (25)
(Alt. 2)
"L" + 5

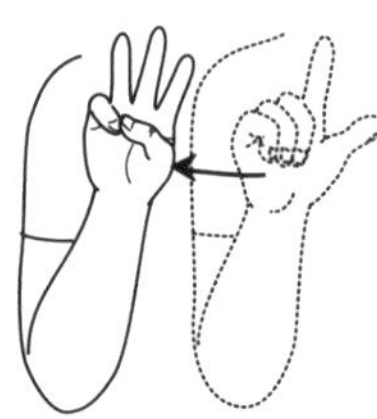

Twenty-Six (26)
"L" + 6

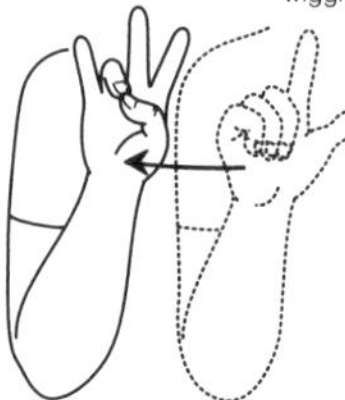

Twenty-Seven (27)
"L" + 7

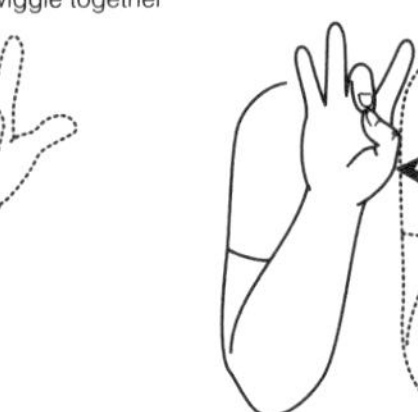

Twenty-Eight (28)
"L" + 58

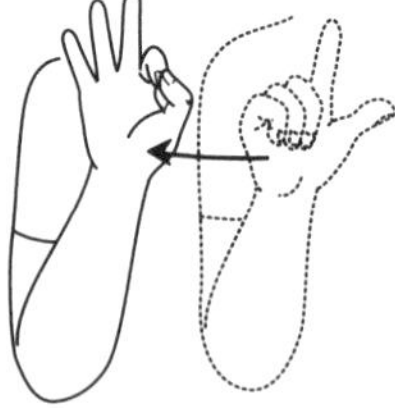

Twenty-Nine (29)
"L" + 9

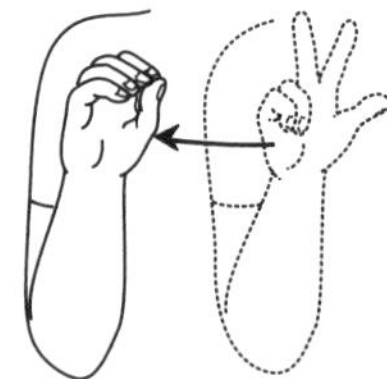

Thirty (30)
"3" + "0"

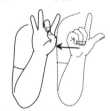

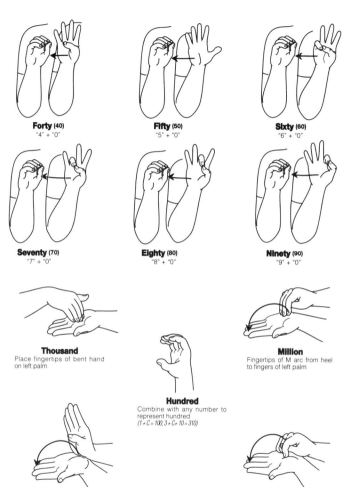

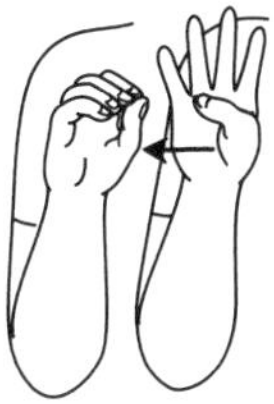

Forty (40)
"4" + "0"

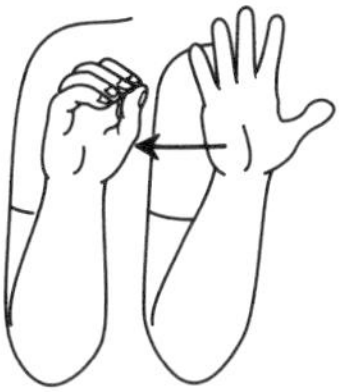

Fifty (50)
"5" + "0"

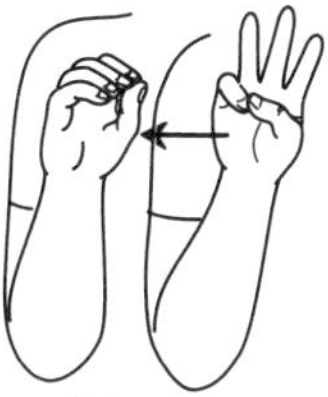

Sixty (60)
"6" + "0"

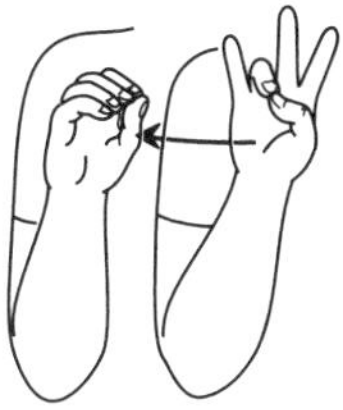

Seventy (70)
"7" + "0"

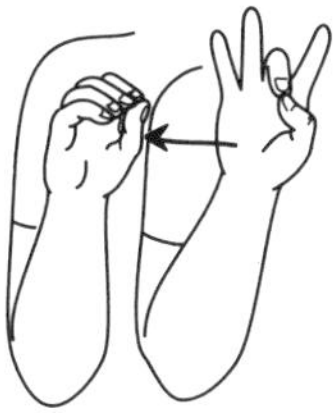

Eighty (80)
"8" + "0"

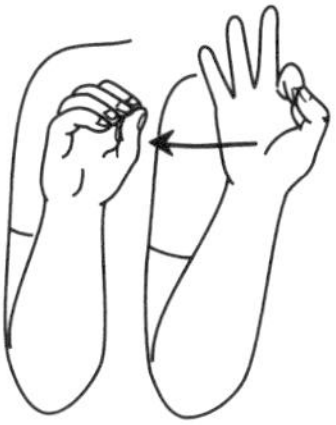

Ninety (90)
"9" + "0"

Thousand
Place fingertips of bent hand on left palm

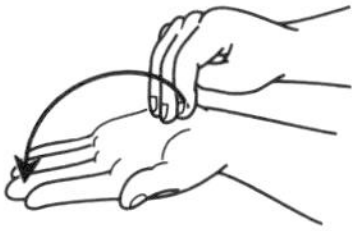

Million
Fingertips of M arc from heel to fingers of left palm

Hundred
Combine with any number to represent hundred
(1 + C = 100; 3 + C + 10 = 310)

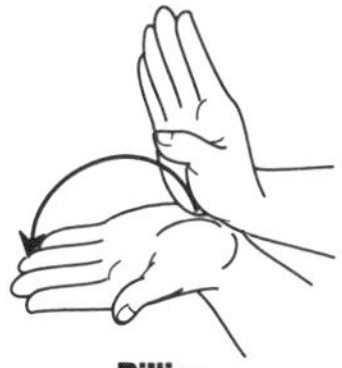

Billion
Heel of right B-hand arcs from heel to fingers of left hand

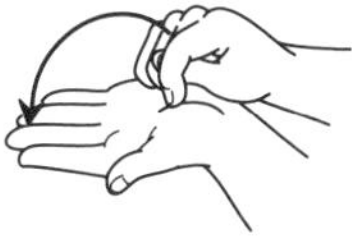

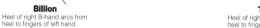

Trillion
Heel of right T-hand arcs from heel to fingers of left hand

CONTRACTIONS

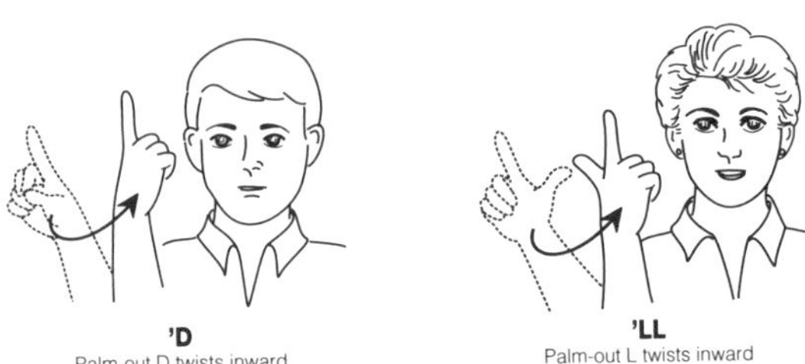

'D
Palm-out D twists inward

'LL
Palm-out L twists inward

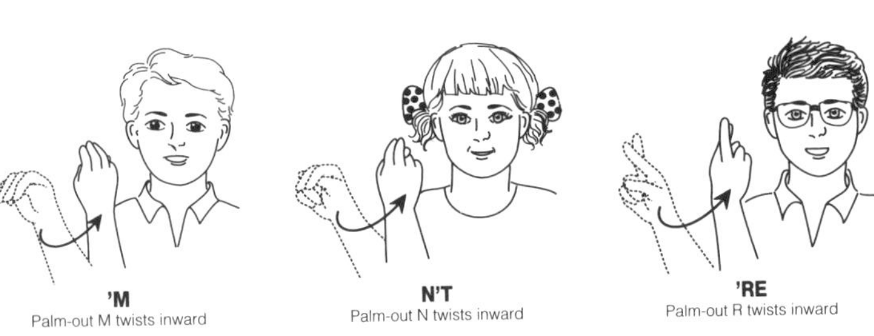

'M
Palm-out M twists inward

N'T
Palm-out N twists inward

'RE
Palm-out R twists inward

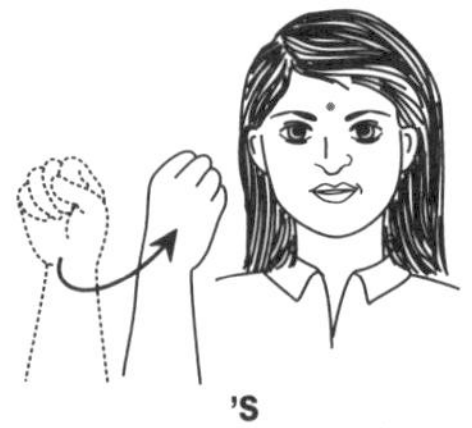

'S
Palm-out S twists inward

'VE
Palm-out V twists inward

AFFIXES

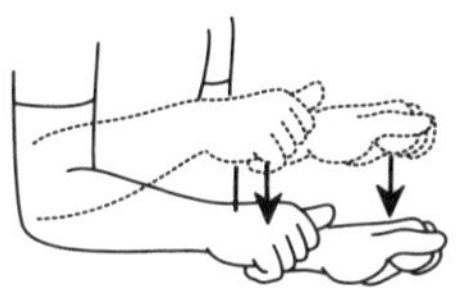

–ABLE, –IBLE
Palm-down A's drop slightly

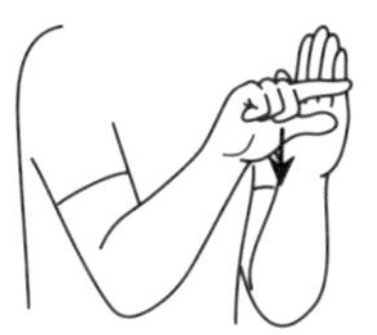

–AGE
Side of G slides down left fingers and palm

–AL
Palm-out L at end of preceding sign

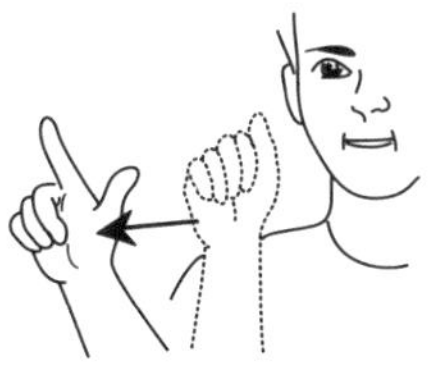

–AL, ALL–
Palm-out A slides right, changing to L

–AN, AN–
Palm-up A twists to palm down

–ANCE, –ENCE
Side of C slides down left fingers and palm

–ANT, –ENT
Side of T slides down left fingers and palm

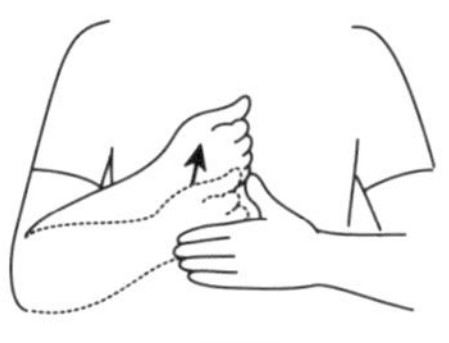

–ANTE
Palm-in A-hand moves toward body from left palm

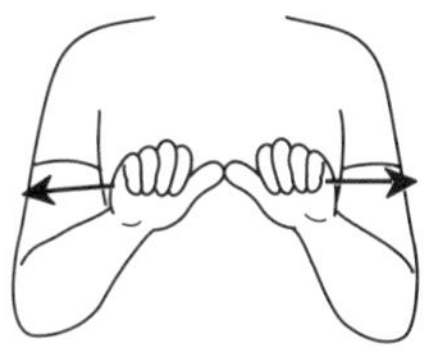

ANTI–
Thumbs of A's, touch; separate hands

–AR, –ER, –OR
Palm-out R

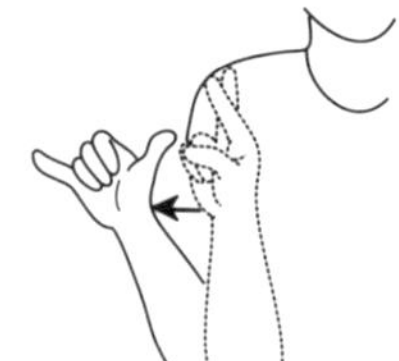

–ARY, –ERY, –ORY
Palm-out R and Y

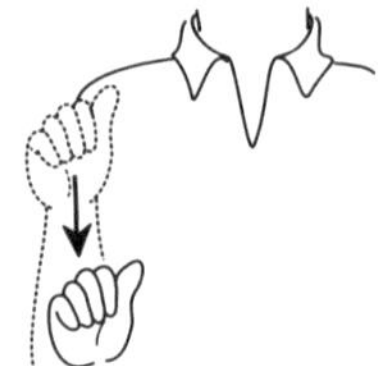

–ATE
Drop palm-out A down slightly

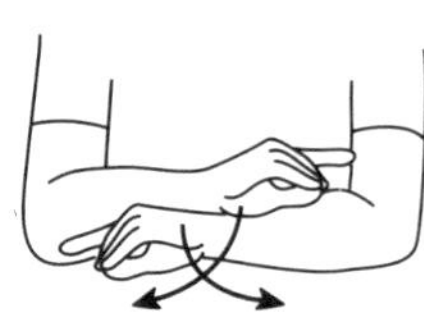

DIS–
Palm-down D's crossed at wrists separate sideways as in "not"
(see NOT)

–DOM
D on back of hand circles out, left and back along left arm
(see GROUND)

–E
Palm-out E at end of word

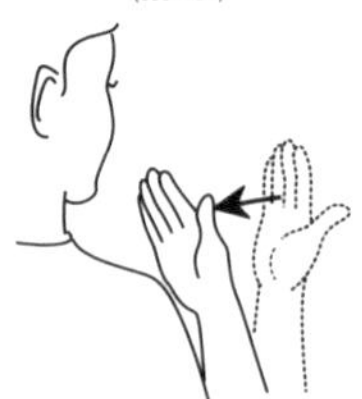

–ED (Alt. 1)
Palm of hand flips back toward shoulder (past tense)

–ED (Alt. 2)
For regular past tense (-ed), make a palm-out D at the end of the sign
(note: it is suggested that this alternate not be used with very young children)

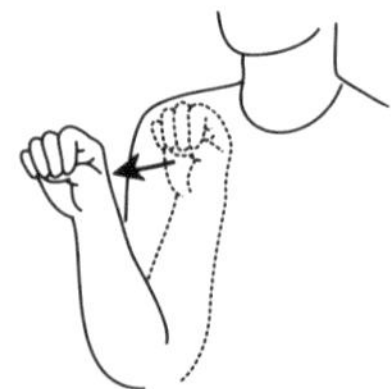

–EE
Move E slightly to the right

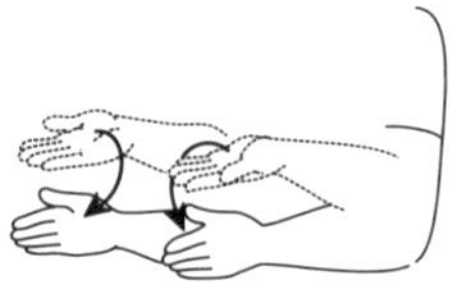

–EN (Alt. 1)
Flat hands twist from 5 palms-up to palms-facing *(past participle)*

–EN (Alt. 2)
For regular past participle (-en) add N at completion of sign
(note: it is suggested that this alternate not be used with very young children)

–ENCE, –ANCE
Side of C-hand slides down left fingers and palm

–ENT, –ANT
Side of T slides down left fingers and palm

–ER, –AR, –OR
Palm-out R

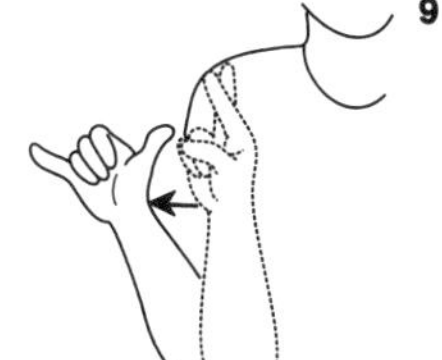

–ERY, –ARY, –ORY
Palm-out R and Y

–ESE
E moves down in a wavy motion

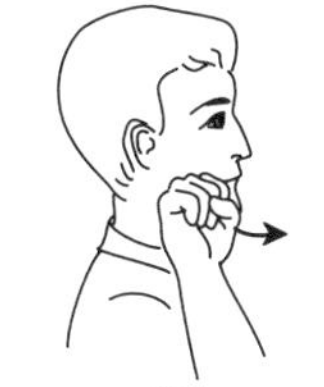

–ESS
Side of S slides along jaw forward

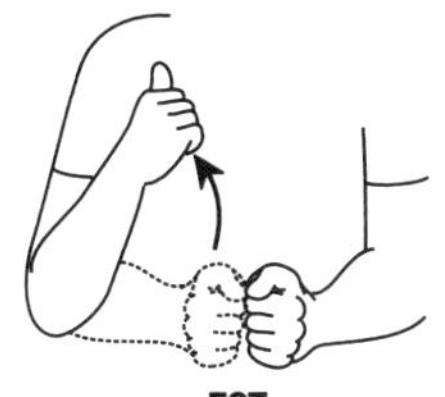

–EST
A-hands together; right A moves up

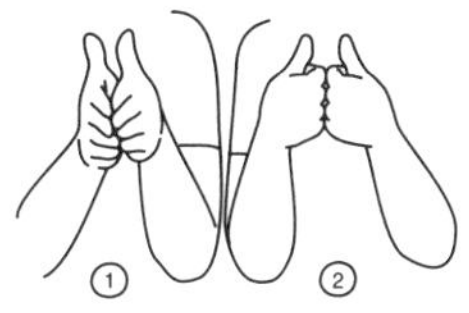

–FOLD
Palm-to-palm, keep fingertips together and bend hands back-to-back

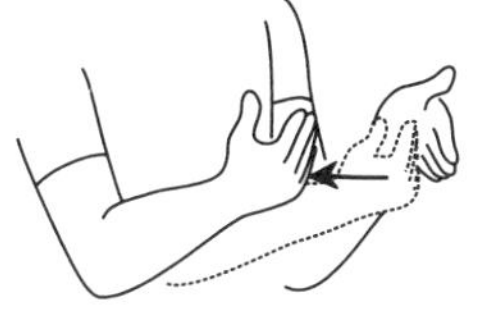

FORE–, –FORE
Bent right hand behind bent left; right moves back

–FUL, FUL–
Palm-down hand brushes inward across top of left horizontal S

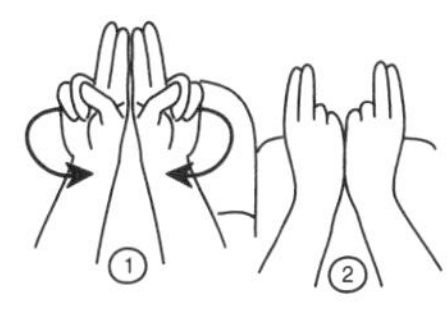

–HERD
Palm-out vertical H-hands circle horizontal to palm-in

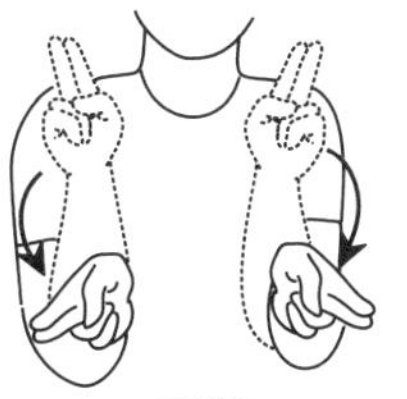

–HOOD
Vertical H to H-hands forward, as wrists cock

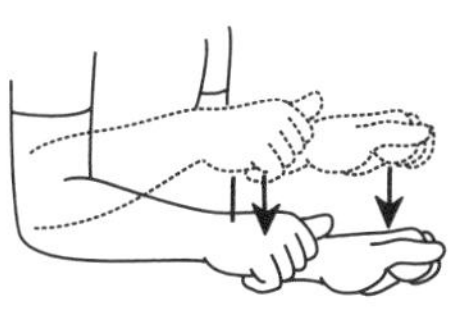

–IBLE, –ABLE
Palm-down A's drop slightly

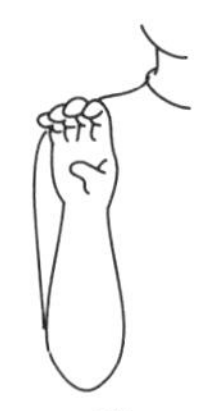

–IC
Palm-out C

–ICE
Palm-out C moves slightly down

–ICITY, –ITY
Thumbtip of Y slides down left fingers and palm

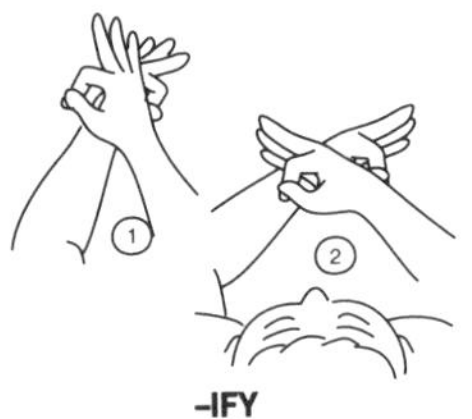

–IFY
F's, right on left, then pivot as in "make" and touch again

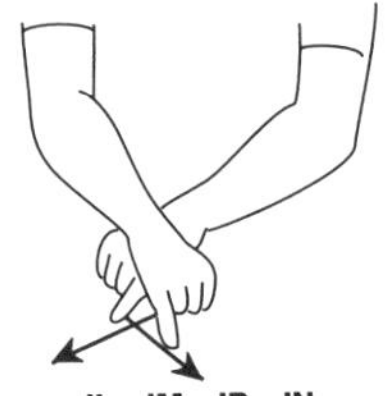

IL–, IM–, IR–, IN–
Palm-down I-hands, crossed at wrists, separate sideways
(see NOT)

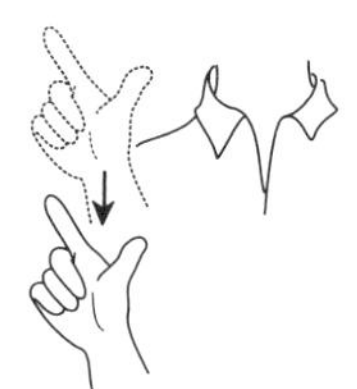

–ILE
L drops straight down

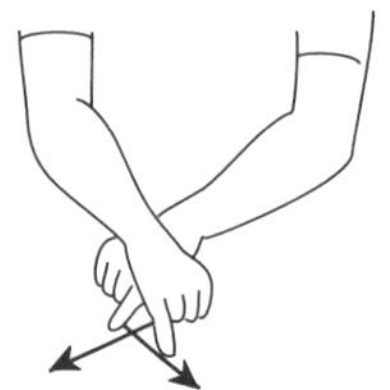

IM–, IR–, IN–, IL–
Palm-down I-hands, crossed at wrists, separate sideways
(see NOT)

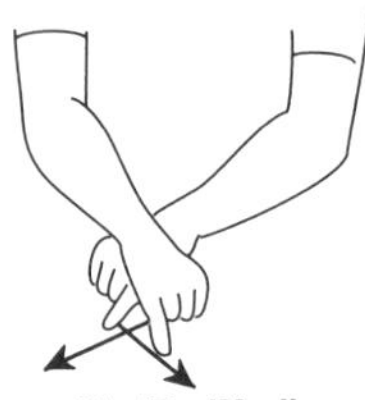

IN–, IR–, IM–, IL–
Palm-down I-hands, crossed at wrists, separate sideways
(see NOT)

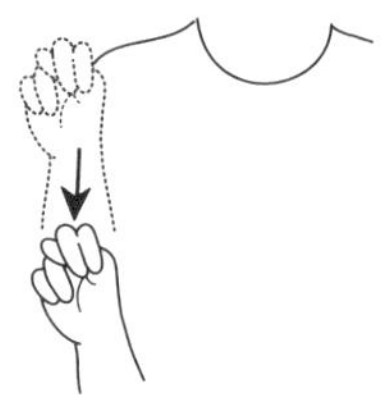

–INE
Palm-out N drops down slightly

–ING
Palm-in, I-hand twists in slight downward arc to right, ending palm-out

INTER–
Little finger of I weaves among fingers of left hand

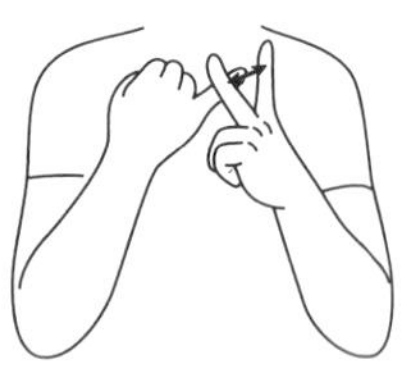

INTRA–
Little finger of I bounces between fingers of left hand

-ION, -TION, -SION
Side of S slides down fingers and palm

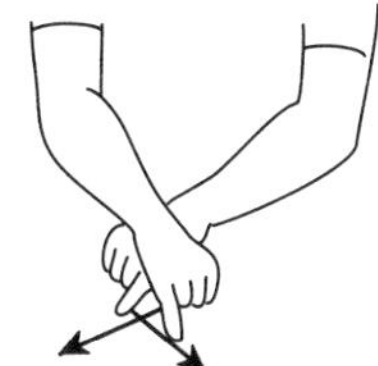

IR-, IM-, IN-, IL-
Palm-down I-hands, crossed at wrists, separate sideways
(see NOT)

-ISH
I points forward and draws a wavy downward line

-ISM
Hook little fingers, one hand palm-up, the other palm-down, reverse
(see FRIEND)

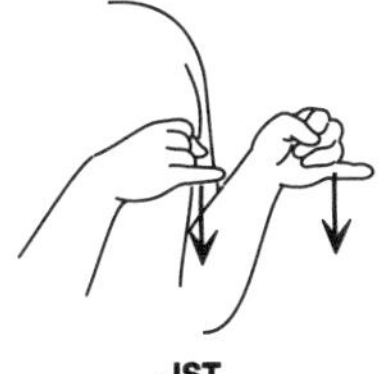

-IST
Drop palms-facing horizontal I's straight down near body
(see PERSON)

-ITE
Palm-out T moves slightly down

-ITY, -ICITY
Thumbtip of Y slides down left fingers and palm

-IVE
Palm-out V moves downward in a wavy line

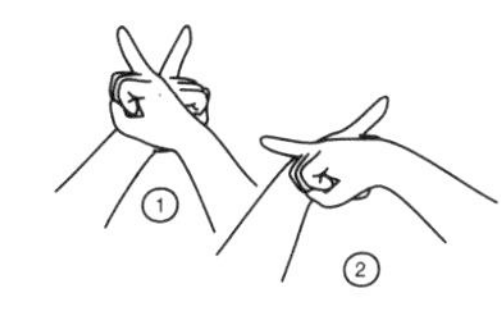

-IZE
I's, right on left, then pivot as in "make" and touch again

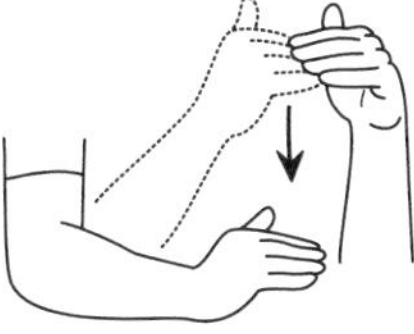

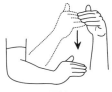

-LESS
Right bent hand under left bent hand; drop right hand downward

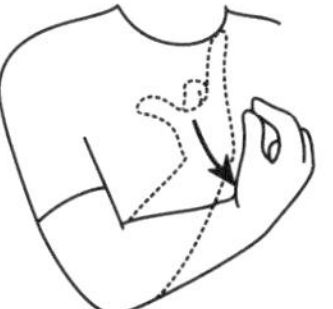

-LIKE
Palm-in L on chest moves forward, closing thumb and finger

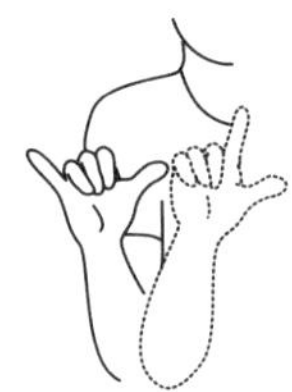

–LY(Alt. 1)
Form L and then Y

–LY(Alt. 2)
Palm-out I-L hand moves downward in a wavy line

–MENT
Side of right M slides down left fingers and palm

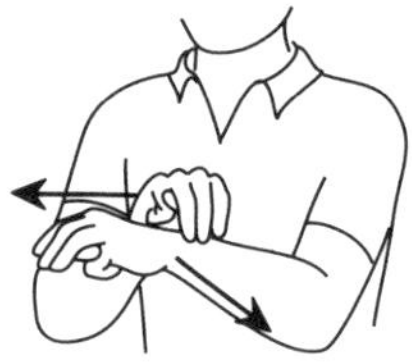

MIS–
Palm-down M's, crossed at wrists, separate
(see NOT)

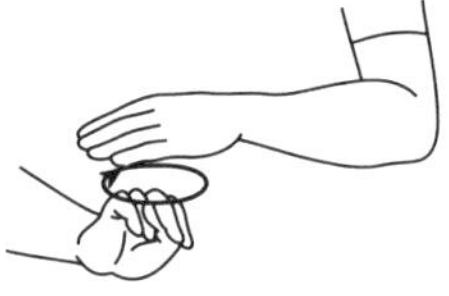

–NEATH
N circles below left palm

–NESS
Side of right N slides down left fingers and palm

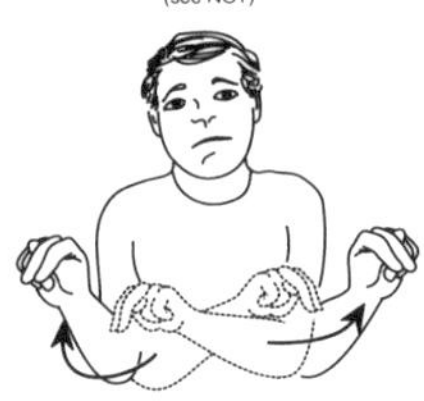

NON–
N-hands, crossed at wrists, separate hands to sides
(see NOT)

–OR, –ER, –AR
Palm-out R

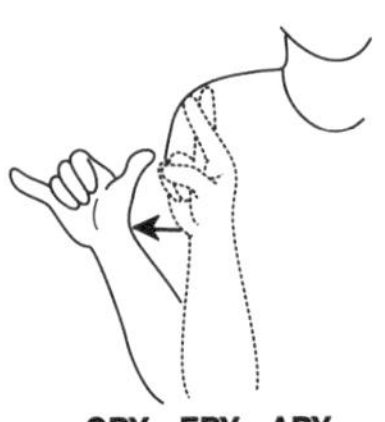

–ORY, –ERY, –ARY
Palm-out R and Y

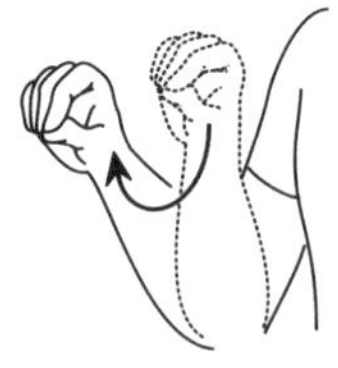

–OUS
Palm-out O draws a "U"

OVER–
Palm-down right hand circles over back of left hand

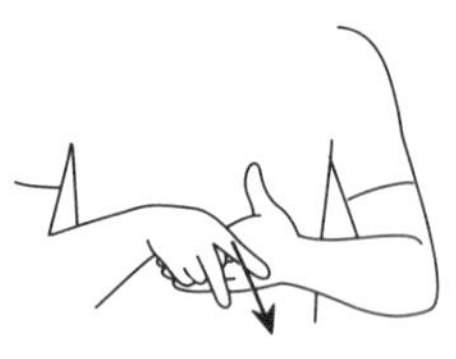

POST–
P moves from back of left hand straight forward

PRE–
P moves inward from behind left palm
(see FORE)

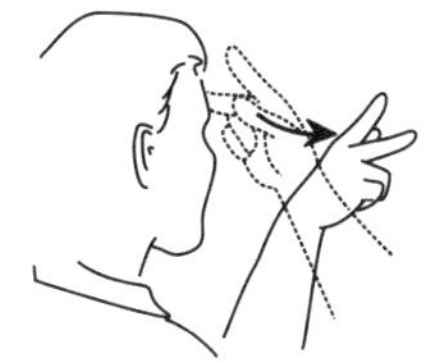

PRO–
Middle fingertip of P on forehead twists to palm-out
(see FOR)

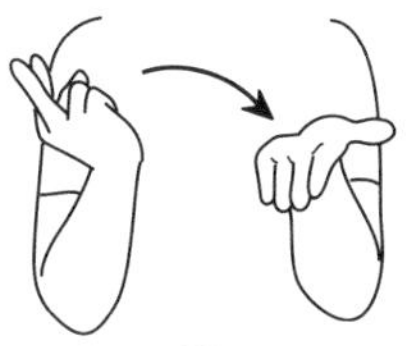

RE–
R fingertips hit left palm

–S
Palm-out S

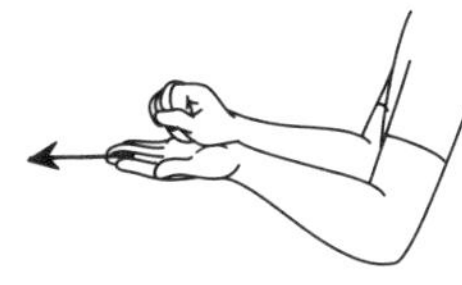

–SHIP
Palm-out S on left palm; both move forward together

–SION, –ION, –TION
Side of right S slides down fingers and palm of left hand

–SOME, SOME–
Side of right hand draws small arc across left palm

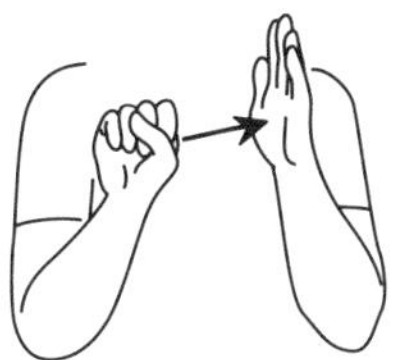

STEAD–, –STEAD
Side of S hits heel of left hand

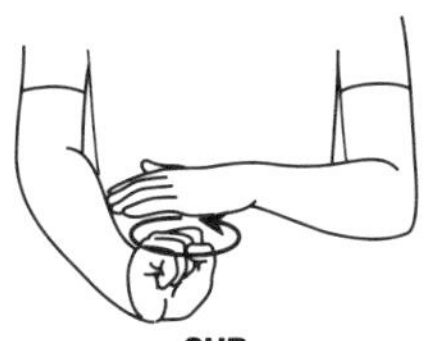

SUB–
S circles under palm
(see BASE)

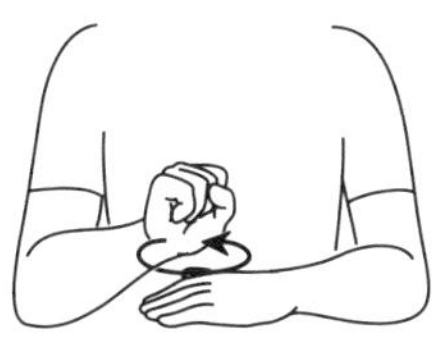

SUPER–
S circles over palm-down left hand

–T
Palm-out T

–TH
Make an H when you finish the sign for the word

-THING
Palm-up, arc hand slightly up and down to the right

-TION, -ION, -SION
Side of right S slides down fingers and palm of left hand

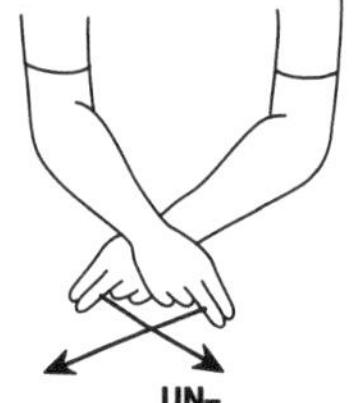

UN-
U hands, palm-down, cross at wrists; separate sideways

(see NOT)

-URE
Side of right U slides down left fingers and palm

VICE-
Touch temple with index of V

-WARD
Palm-out W moves forward

-Y
Palm-out Y

A
(article)
Palm-out A moves slightly right

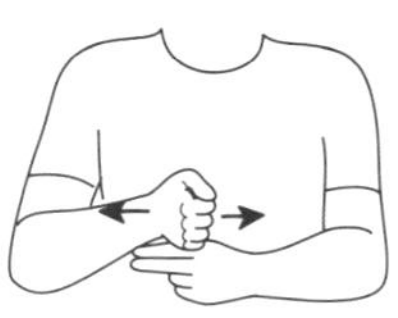

ABBREVIATE

Side of A-hand on side of left H, slide A back and forth

(see SHORT)

ABDOMEN

A-hand, palm-in, pats abdomen

ABLE
Palm-down A's drop slightly
(see VISIBLE)

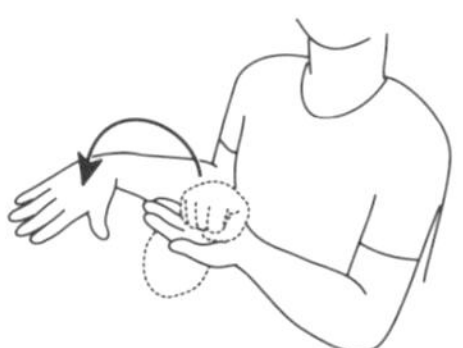

ABORT
Palm-down S on palm lifts up and throws down to open 5
(see DISPOSE)

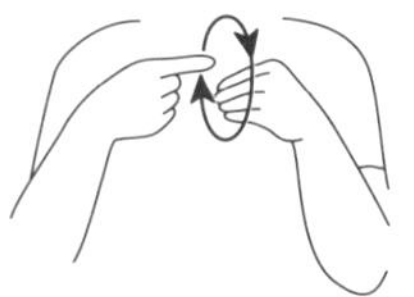

ABOUT
Index finger circles the tip of horizontal left palm-in flat-O hand

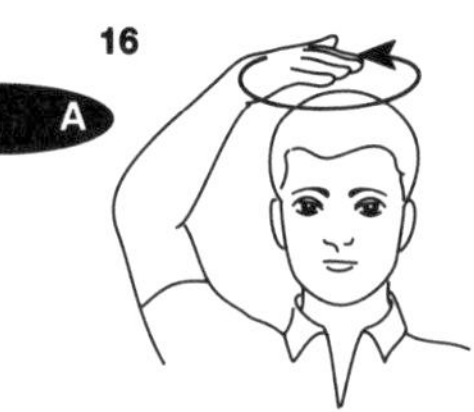

ABOVE
Palm circles once over head

ABSENT
Right index clips bent middle finger of palm-down left hand, right to left

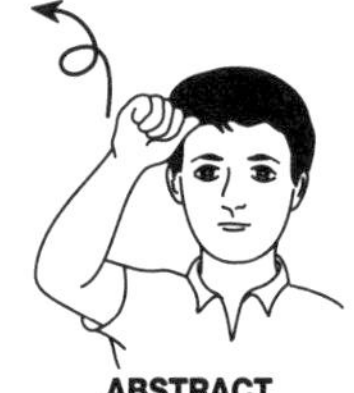

ABSTRACT
Right A-hand circles up and forward sideways from forehead
(see IDEA)

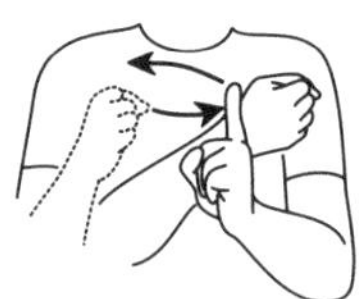

ABUSE
Right horizontal S beats left index back and forth

ACADEMIC
Right palm-down A claps on left palm
(see SCHOOL)

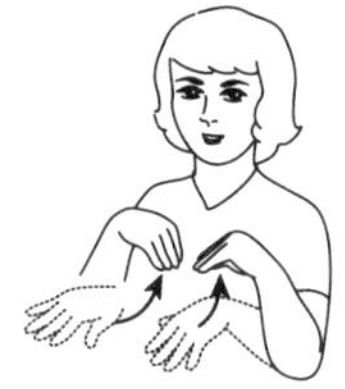

ACCEPT
Palm-down flat hands rise to flat-O's on chest
(see APPROVE)

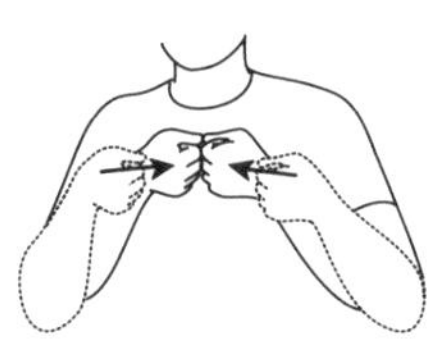

ACCIDENT
Palm-in horizontal S's at sides; hit knuckles together once

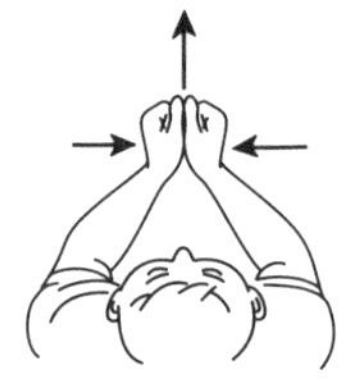

ACCOMPANY
A-hands come together, palm-to-palm, and move forward
(see WITH)

ACCOMPLISH
C-hands facing temples, twist out and up twice to palm-out C's
(see SUCCESS)

ACCOUNT
Index and thumbtip of right 9 brush up left palm; repeat
(see COUNT)

ACCUSE
A drops to hit top side of left index, both hands move slightly downward

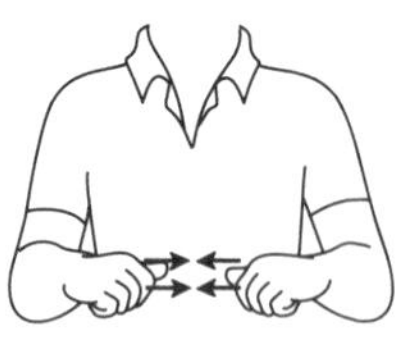

ACHE
A's jerk toward each other several times near area of ache (can be done with twisting motion)
(see HURT)

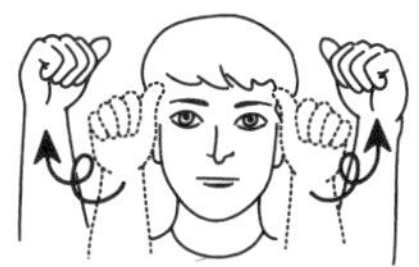

ACHIEVE
Palm-out, A's twist from temples out and up twice
(see SUCCESS)

ACQUAINT
Rest extended A-thumbs first right on left, then left on right
(see FRIEND)

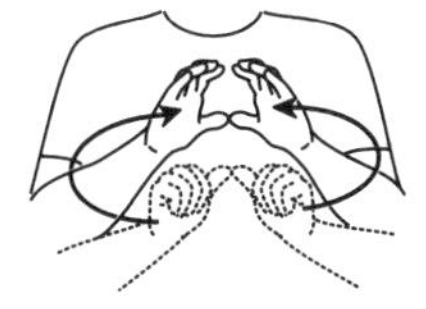

ACRE
Thumbtips of A's circle back towards body changing to C's touching again
(see PLACE)

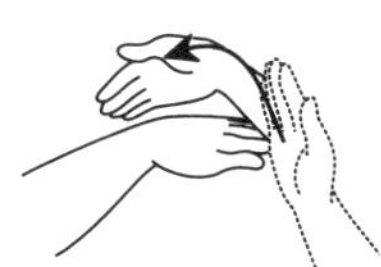

ACROSS
Right palm-left hand arcs across back of left palm-down hand

ACT ♔
Thumbs of A-hands facing each other brush alternately down chest,

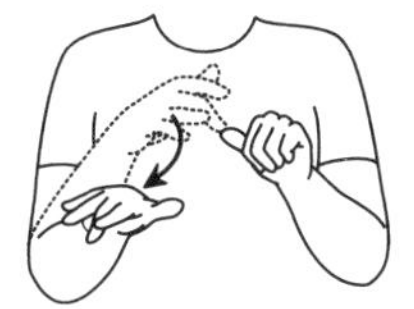

ACUTE
Bent middle finger of open right hand touches thumb of left A, flicks off
(see SHARP)

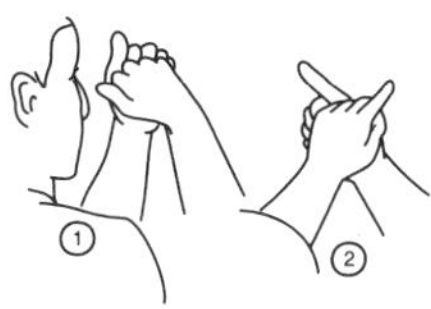

ADAPT
A-palms together, reverse position, changing to D's
(see CHANGE)

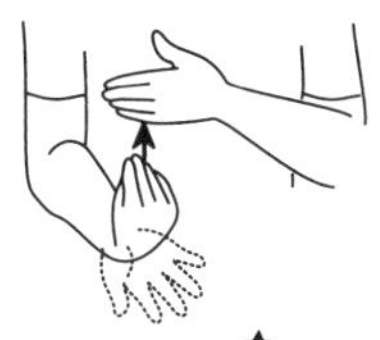

ADD ♔
Palm-up 5 to flat-O rises to touch little-finger side of palm-in left hand

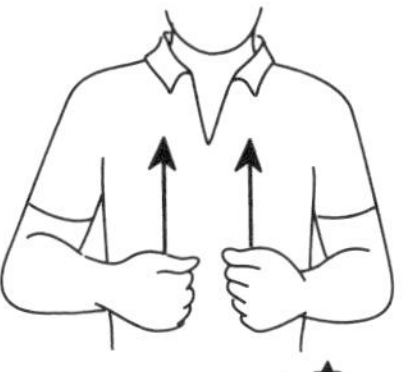

ADDRESS ♔
Palm-in A-hands move up body once

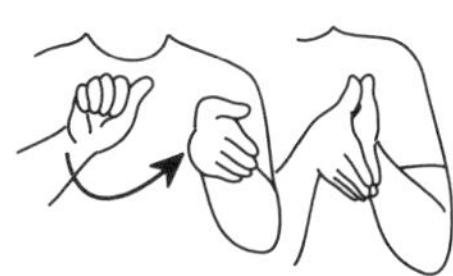

ADHESIVE
Horizontal left hand, palm-right, palm-out right A flattens against left palm
(see COHESIVE)

ADJECTIVE
Fingerspell A + D + J

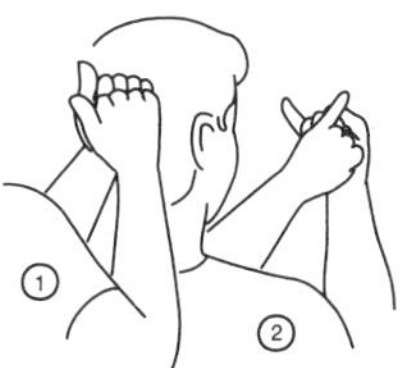

ADJUST
A-palms together, reverse position, changing to I's
(see CHANGE)

ADMIRE

From above, palm-left A arcs in toward forehead, down and outward

(see GOD)

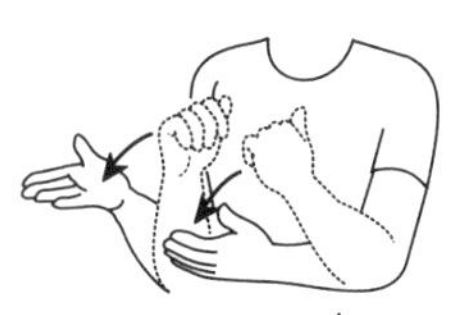

ADMIT

A-hands on chest turn over and out to palm-up open hands

(see CONFESS)

ADOLESCENT

Thumbtips of A's brush up on chest near shoulders

(see YOUNG)

ADOPT

Palm-down 5's rise to D's

(see ASSUME)

ADULT

A-thumb on temple then to side of jaw

(see PARENT)

ADVANCE

Bent hands, palms-facing, arc towards body and up twice

(see PROMOTE)

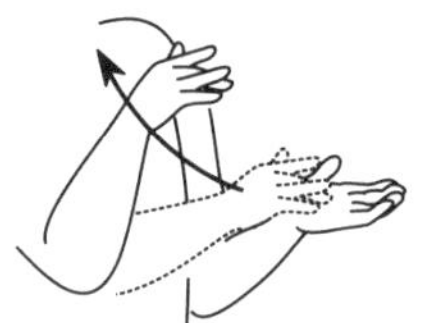

ADVANTAGE

Left palm-up; bent middle finger of right hand on palm flicks back on heel

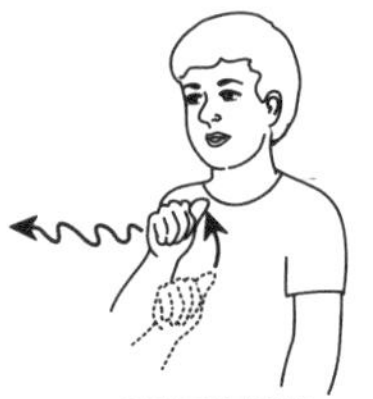

ADVENTURE

Thumbside of right palm-left A brushes up on chest and moves forward in wavy side to side motion

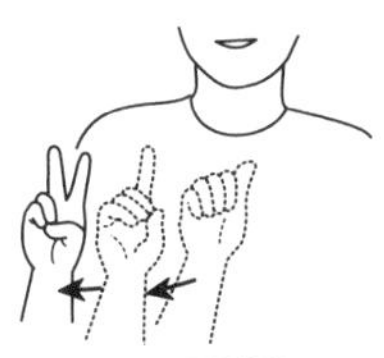

ADVERB

Fingerspell A + D + V

ADVERTISE

Right S in front of left S, right moves out (slightly right) and back twice

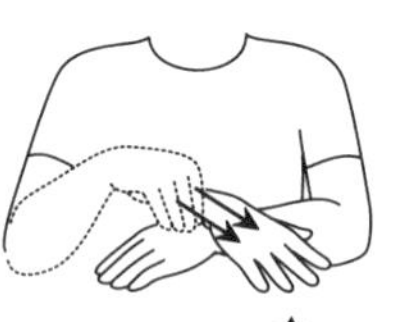

ADVICE

Right flat-O set on back of left hand moves forward to palm-down 5; repeat

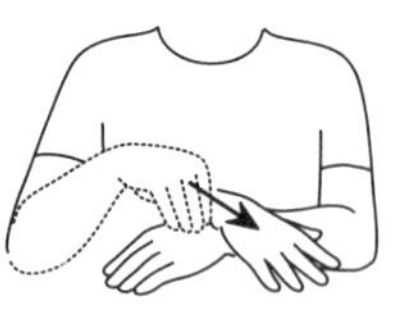

ADVISE

Right flat-O set on back of left hand moves forward to palm-down 5

(see ADVICE)

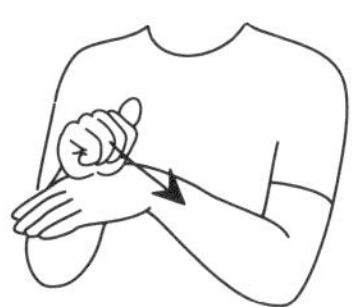

AFFECT
A moves forward off back of stationary palm-down left hand
(see ADVICE)

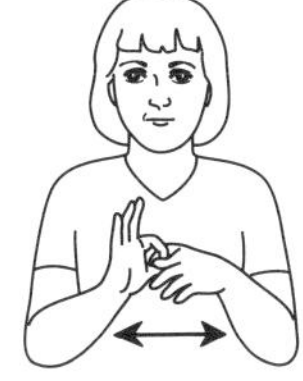

AFFILIATE
Link 9 hands; move from side-to-side
(see CONNECT)

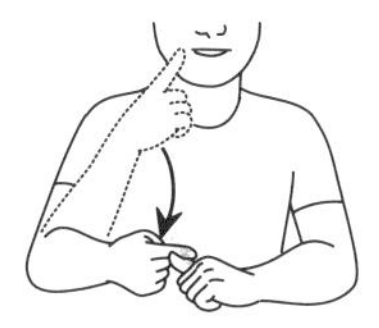

AFFIRM
Index at mouth moves down to make a cross with thumb of palm-down left A
(see POSITIVE)

AFFIX
Left index points right; palm-out right A arcs to touch tip of index

AFRAID
Slightly to left, palm-out A's move downward in shaking motion

AFRICA
(Alt. 1)
Palm-left A hand circles face

AFRICA
(Alt. 2)
Palm-out C moves slightly right, twists and moves downward ending with fingers closed (continent shape)

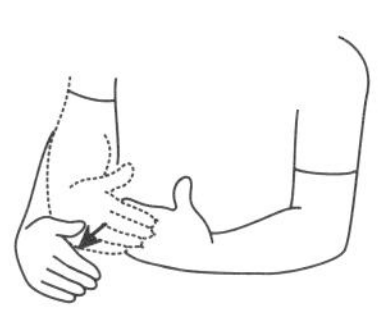

AFTER
Right palm on back of palm-in left hand; right moves out
(see POST)

AFTERNOON
Flat hand, arm resting on back of left hand, drops forward

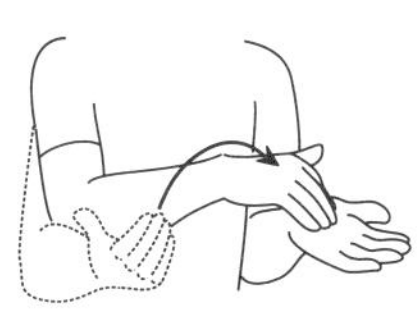

AGAIN
Fingertips of palm-up bent right hand arc over and strike heel of left hand
(see REPEAT)

AGAINST
Fingertips of flat hand hit left palm at right angles

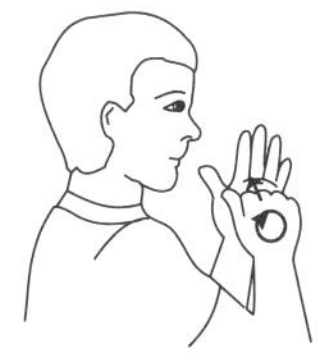

AGE
Palm-left A makes small circle, then touches left palm
(see HOUR)

AGENDA
Palm of right A on fingers of left palm, then move to heel
(see LESSON)

AGGRESS
Left hand palm-out, right A behind left; both move sharply forward
(see PUSH)

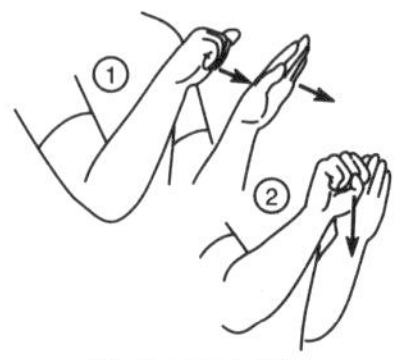

AGGRESSION
Left palm-out, right A behind left; both move forward sharply; right S slides down left vertical hand *(aggress + -ion)*

AGO
Palm-in right A twists out and back over shoulder, opening to G

AGREE
Index finger touches forehead, then drops to touch index fingers together

AGRICULTURE
Thumb of A on left side of chin, draw arc below mouth to right side on chin
(see FARM)

AHEAD
A-hands, palms facing together; right arcs forward horizontally

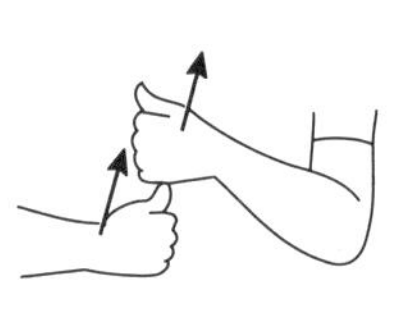

AID
Thumb of right A pushes left A upward, both palm-in
(see HELP)

AIL
Right A thumb on forehead; left A thumb on stomach
(see SICK)

AIM
Indexes point up, right behind and slightly lower than left; right jerks to point at left fingertip

AIR
A-hands sweep from side to side twisting at wrists
(see WIND)

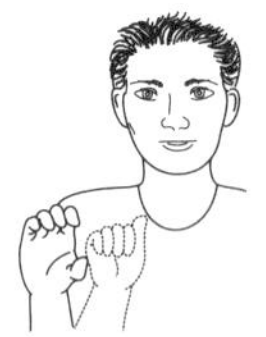

AIR CONDITION
Fingerspell A + C

AIRPLANE
Right I-L hand, palm-down, jerks forward; repeat

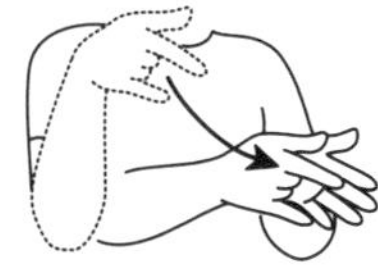

AIRPORT
Right palm-down I-L hand lands on palm-up left hand

ALARM
Side of right index hits vertical left palm repeatedly

ALASKA
Palm-down A-hand arcs around parka hood to an open flat hand

ALBUM
Palm-to-palm A-hands separate like a book opening
(see BOOK)

ALCOHOL
Circle tip of thumb of extended-A above palm
(see MEDICINE)

ALERT
Palm-out A's at corners of eyes move sharply forward to palm-out L's

ALFALFA
Palm-out A brushes up through left horizontal C twice
(see GRAIN)

ALGAE ♔
Extended A-thumb makes small circle on little finger of palm-up left I-hand

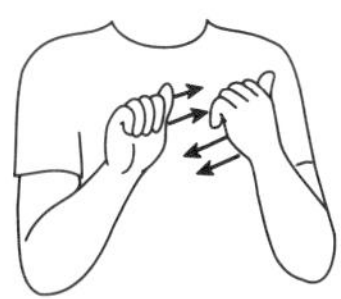

ALGEBRA
Left palm-in A and right palm-out A, brush each other sideways twice
(see ARITHMETIC)

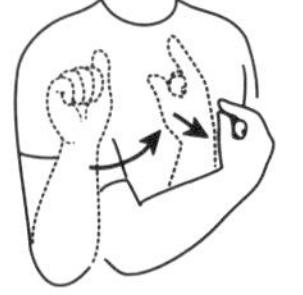

ALIKE
Make A, change to palm-in L on chest, close thumb and finger while moving forward

ALL
Palm-out A slides right, changing to L

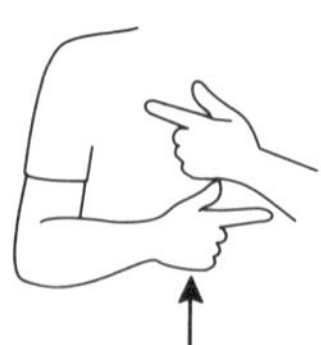

ALLEGIANCE
Thumb of right palm-in L pushes side of left L up
(see SUPPORT)

ALLERGY ★
Right index points at left A and both draw sharply apart
(see OPPOSE)

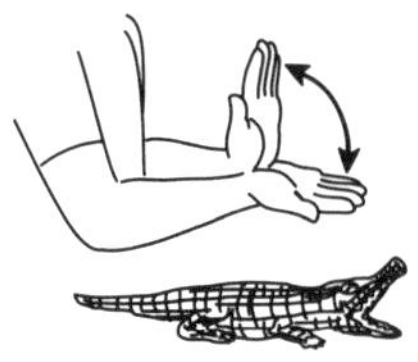

ALLIGATOR
Heels of flat hands touching, snap top "jaw" open and closed

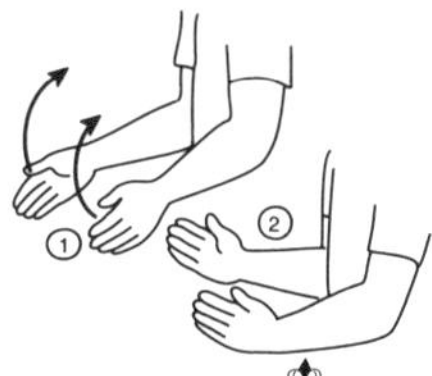

ALLOW ♕
Parallel palm-to-palm flat hands point downward, swing upwards

ALL RIGHT
Side of right hand slides forward across left palm, arcing slightly up
(see LEGAL)

ALLSPICE
Right V above palm-down left-A, fingers of V tap back of A alternately
(see SALT)

ALMOST
Right fingertips stroke upwards off back of left fingers once

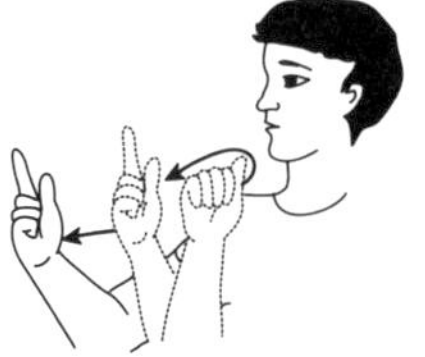

ALONE
Palm-out A moves slightly right, changes to L, twists to palm-in, and moves forward
(see WIDOW)

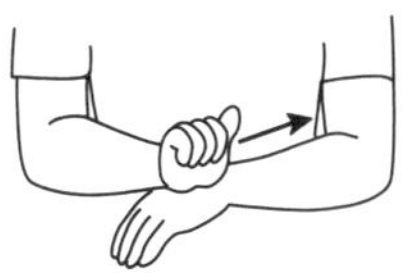

ALONG
Heel of right A slides up left arm towards elbow
(see LONG)

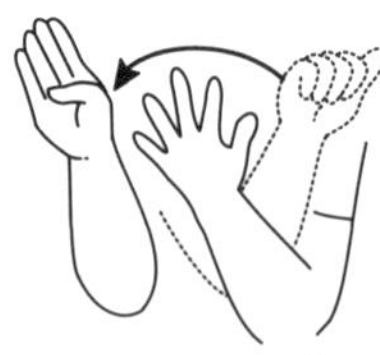

ALPHABET ♕
A-hand moves across left 5-fingers, changing to B-hand

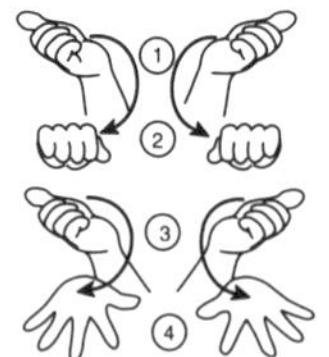

ALREADY
A-hands, palms-up, swing inward and down; repeat, ending in palm-down 5's

ALSO
Fingerspell A + L; change to S's, move right hand sharply down striking side of left S in passing *(al- + so)*

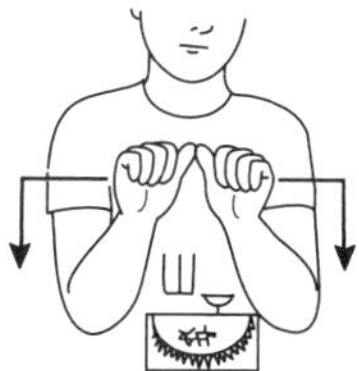

ALTAR

Palm-out A-hands separate to sides and move down

ALTER

A-palms together, reverse position, changing to L's

(see CHANGE)

ALTERNATE

A-hand brushes sidewards to left from off thumb, then brushes off tip of index

(see THEN)

ALTHOUGH

Fingerspell A + L; then alternately slap fingertips of hands forward and back against each other *(al- + though)*

ALUMINUM

Heel of A-hand hits down in an arc on index of left B-hand

(see METAL)

ALWAYS

Palm-up index, pointing forward, circles clockwise

AM

Thumbtip of palm-left A just below lips; move forward

AMAZE

Palm-out A-hands circle near eyes and flick index and thumb out

(see SURPRISE)

AMBITION

Thumbsides of A's brush alternately up chest *(reverse of "act")*

AMBULANCE

Thumb of A draws a cross on left upper arm

(see HOSPITAL)

AMEN

One hand folded atop the other, drop hands slightly and bow head)

AMEND
(Alt. 1)
A-palms together, reverse position, changing to M's
(see CHANGE)

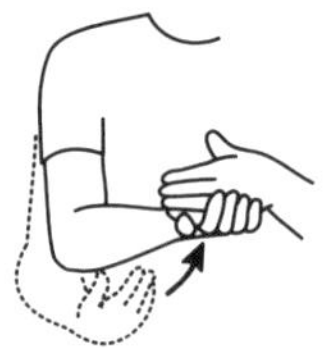

AMEND
(Alt. 2)
Arc right hand up from beneath to grasp side of palm-in left hand *(attaching amendment)*
(see ADD)

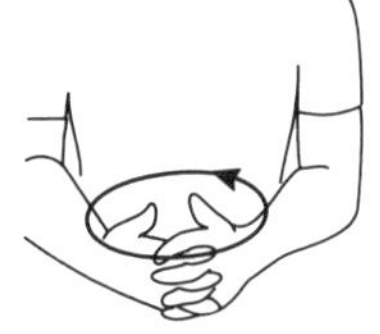

AMERICA
Mesh palm-in fingers, circle horizontally in front of body

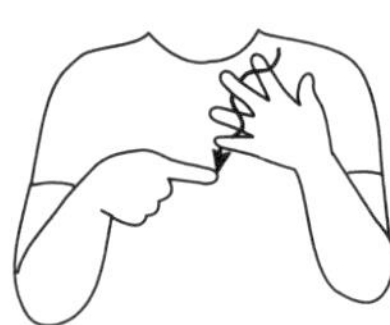

AMONG
Right index finger weaves through fingers of left 5-hand

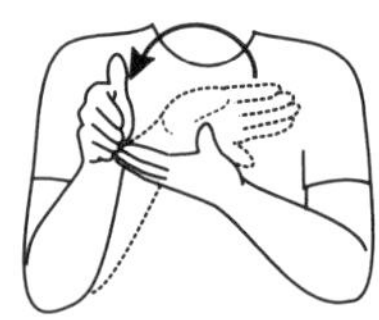

AMOUNT
Index side of flat hand on heel of left hand, outline amount to little-finger side of hand on left fingertips

AMUSE
Sides of A's rub in small opposing circles on chest and stomach
(see ENJOY)

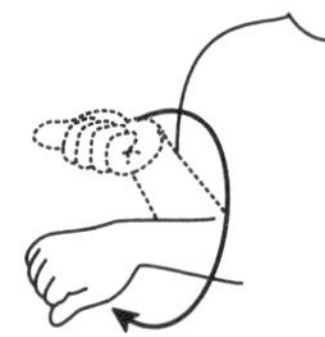

AN
Palm-up A twists to palm-down

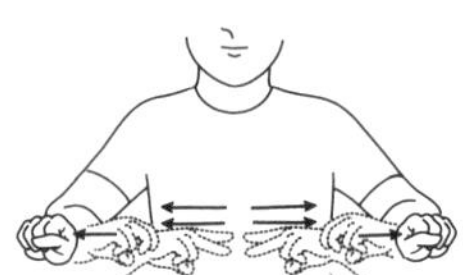

ANALYSIS
Palm-down V's point at each other, separate while bending fingers; repeat, ending with palm-out S's
(see DIAGNOSES)

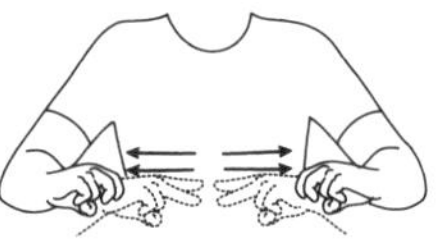

ANALYZE
Palm-down V's point at each other, separate while bending fingers; repeat slightly forward
(see DIAGNOSE)

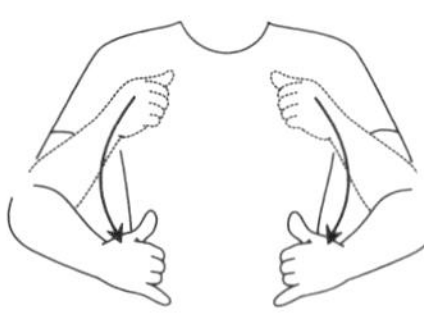

ANATOMY
A's on chest arc down trunk, changing to palm-in Y's
(see BODY)

ANCESTOR
Palm-in flat hands circle each other back to right shoulder

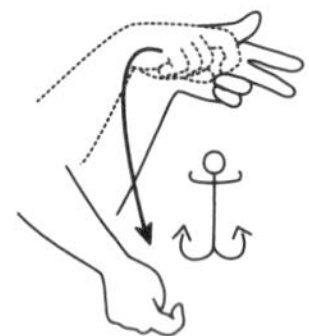

ANCHOR
X-hand drops anchor in sideways arc from palm-right horizontal 3-hand

ANCIENT
Left A-thumb supporting right A, move down together in wavy motion from near chin
(see OLD)

AND
Palm-in horizontal 5-hand pulls to right, closing to a flat-O

ANGEL
Fingertips of flat hands on shoulders, swing out

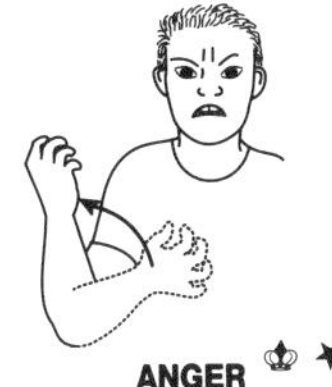

ANGER
Claw hand arcs up near chest to right *(can be done with two hands)*

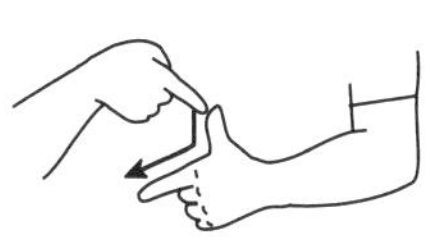

ANGLE
Right index finger traces angle of left horizontal L-hand

ANIMAL
Keep fingertips on chest; swing wrists toward center of body twice
(see MAMMAL)

ANKLE
Palm-out A touches behind left of wrist

ANNIVERSARY
Palm-in A's circle
(see CELEBRATE)

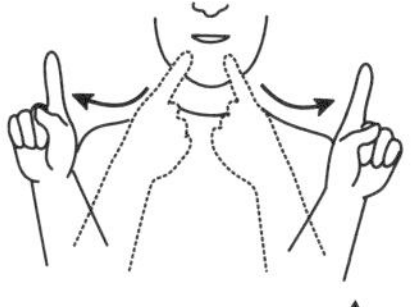

ANNOUNCE
Palm-in index fingers at side of mouth twist out and sideways to palm-out

ANNOY
Little finger side of A chops into thumb joint of palm-in left hand
(see BOTHER)

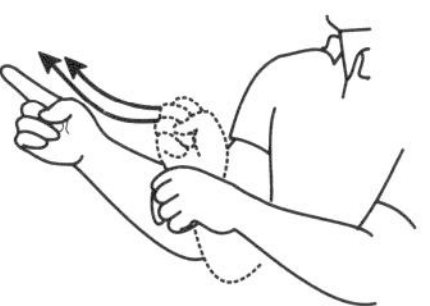

ANNUAL
Right S-hand brushes forward off side of left S-hand while index flicks forward; repeat several times

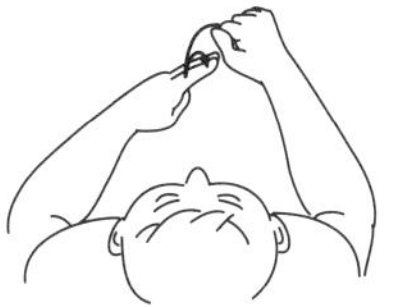

ANONYMOUS
Right A taps side of left H, first near base of fingers then further forward
(see NAME)

ANOTHER
Palm-up A twists to palm-down, then arcs right to palm-up

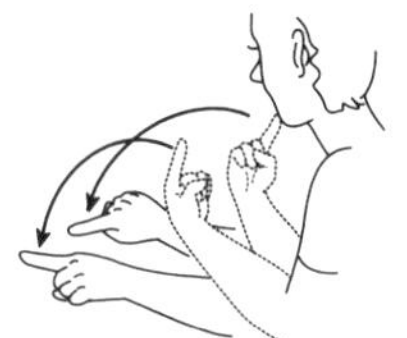

ANSWER
Right index finger on chin, left palm-in index slightly ahead; both hands turn palm-down
(see REPLY)

ANT ♔
Palm-out A rides forward on back of wiggling fingers of left hand

ANTELOPE
A-hands, thumbs extended, curve up and back from temples
(see DEER)

ANTLER
A's on temples move slightly out and up to 5's
(see DEER)

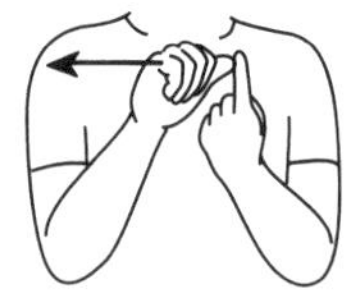

ANTONYM
Left index pointing up; thumb of right A touches tip and moves away to right
(see HOMONYM)

ANXIOUS
A's slightly at side shake
(see AFRAID)

ANY
Palm-up A twists to palm-down A, changes to Y *(an + -y)*

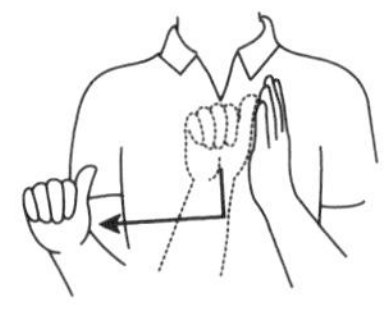

APART
Thumb-side of A-hand moves down left palm and away to side

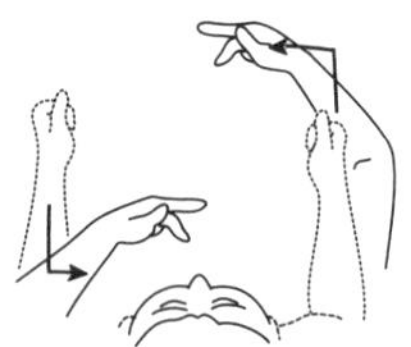

APARTMENT
Horizontal A-hands face each other, change to palm-in P hands one ahead of other
(see BOX)

APATHY
Flat-O, palm-in at nose, twists out to open and fling down
(see IGNORE)

APE
A-hand thumbs scratch sides upward
(see MONKEY)

APHASIC

Thumbs of right A at forehead, horizontal palm-in left A; right hand drops and hands twist

(see CONFUSE)

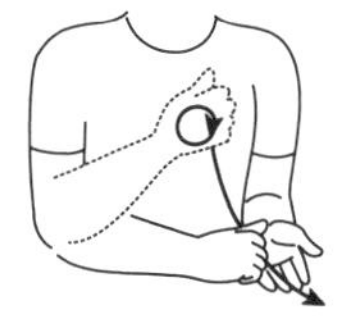

APOLOGIZE ✶

Palm-in A-hand circles on chest; moves down to left open palm and slides forward

(see EXCUSE)

APOSTROPHE

X-finger twists inward and down to make an apostrophe in the air

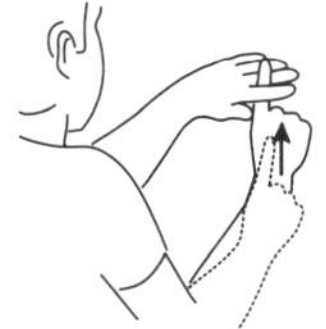

APPEAR

Right index rises to appear between index and middle fingers of palm-down left hand

APPETITE

A-hand palm-in, moves down on chest once

(see HUNGER)

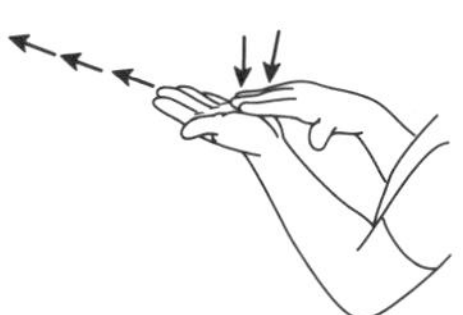

APPLAUD

Clap several times quickly while hands move forward

(see APPLAUSE)

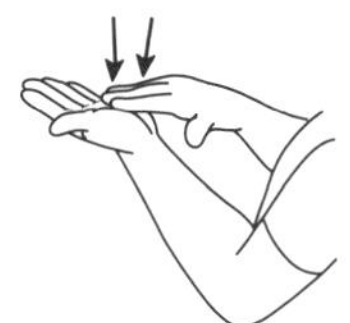

APPLAUSE

Clap several times quickly

(see APPLAUD)

APPLE ♔

X twists against corner of mouth

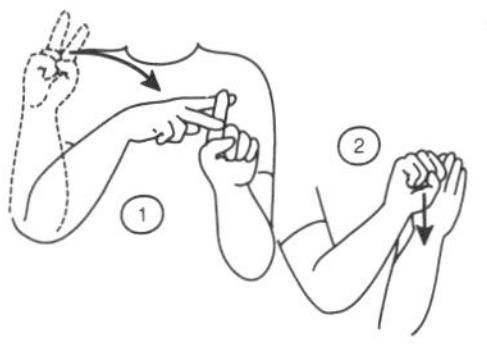

APPLICATION

Right V falls over left index; side of right S slides down left palm *(apply + -tion)*

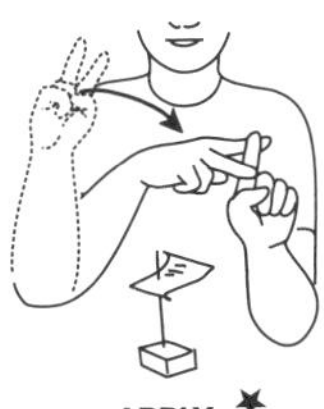

APPLY ✶

Right V falls over left vertical index

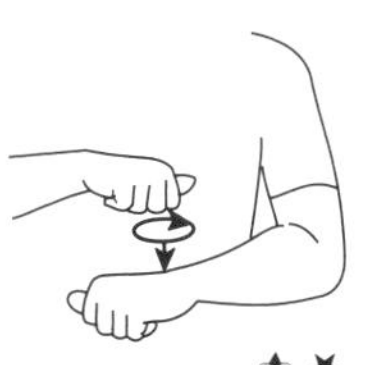

APPOINT ♔ ✶

Right A-hand circles over left, then drops to wrist

APPRECIATE

Side of A circles once on chest while changing to P

(see PLEASE)

APPROACH

Bent right hand moves in stages toward left palm; does not touch it

APPROPRIATE

Right index above left, both pointing forward; right makes clockwise vertical circle and drops onto left

APPROVE
(Alt. 1)

A-hands, palm-down, draw back to P's on chest

(see ACCEPT)

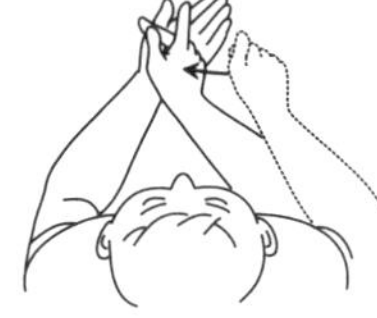

APPROVE
(Alt. 2)

Right palm-left A drops to hit as P on left palm

(see STAMP)

APPROXIMATE

Palm-out 5 moves in small circles

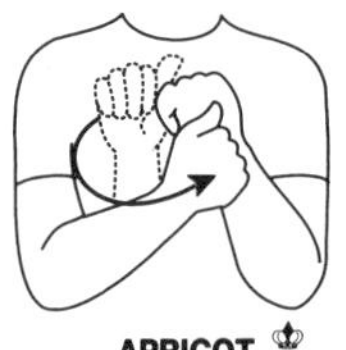

APRICOT ♔

Right A circles left palm-in S, touching

APRIL
(Alt. 1)

A-hand turns calendar page outward over left flat hand

(see CALENDAR)

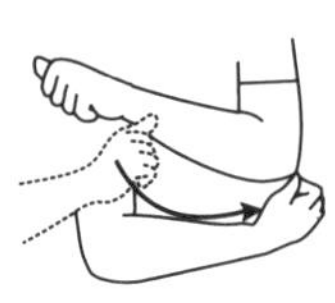

APRIL
(Alt. 2)

Right A-hand at wrist arcs down and up to touch near elbow

(see BASKET)

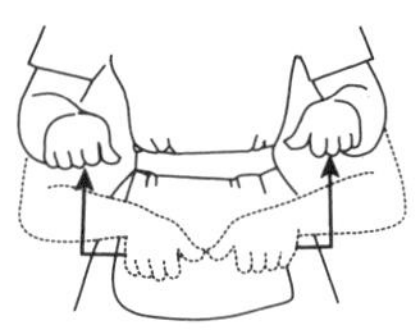

APRON

A-hands outline small apron at waist

ARCHITECT

Right A draws down vertical palm in wavy motion

(see ART)

ARE

R just below lips, moves forward

(see AM)

AREA

Palm-down A-thumbs touch, circle in toward chest, touch again

(see PLACE)

ARGUE
Palm-in index fingers move rapidly up and down from wrists
(see HASSLE)

ARISE
Palm-up right V rises and inverts to stand on left palm

ARITHMETIC ♔
Palm-in V's brush past each other sideways twice

ARIZONA
Touch left side of chin with A-thumb, then touch on right side

ARM ★
Pat upper arm with palm-in A

ARMADILLO
Right hand clasps back of left, left index extended; both move left, index flapping up and down

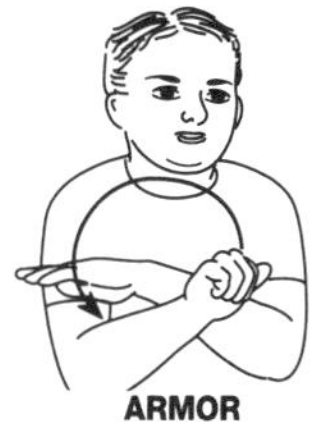

ARMOR
Palm-out right A circles vertically in front of horizontal left arm
(see SHIELD)

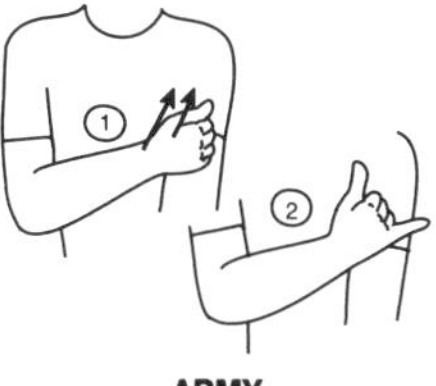

ARMY
Pat upper arm with right A, changing to Y-hand *(arm +-y)*

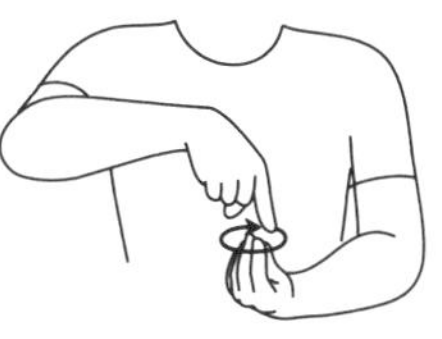

AROUND
(Alt. 1)
Right index points downward and circles fingertips of palm-up left flat-O

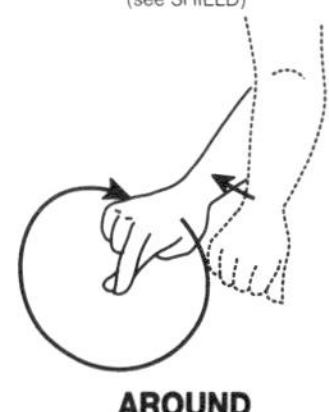

AROUND
(Alt. 2)
Palm-down A moves slightly right, changes to palm-down R and circles once horizontally

ARRANGE
Horizontal parallel palms move right in small vertical arcs

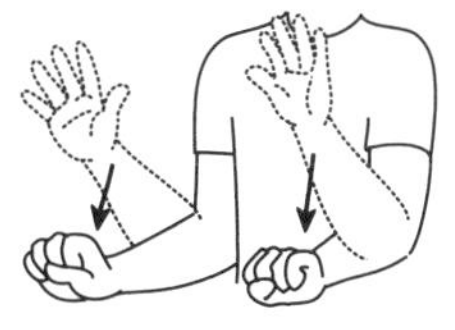

ARREST
5-hands drop downwards, closing sharply to S-hands

ARRIVE
Back of right hand arcs forward and touches left palm
(see REACH)

ARROGANT
Right index pointing up, brushes up by front of nose; repeat
(see SNOB)

ARROW
Pull bowstring back to right V from left S-hand
(see CUPID)

ART
I-fingertip draws wavy line on palm

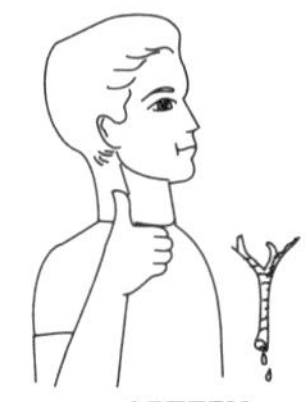

ARTERY
Extended-A thumb presses the side of neck near artery

ARTICHOKE
Hold left A-thumb and peel backward

ARTICLE
Curved index and thumb move down across horizontal left palm

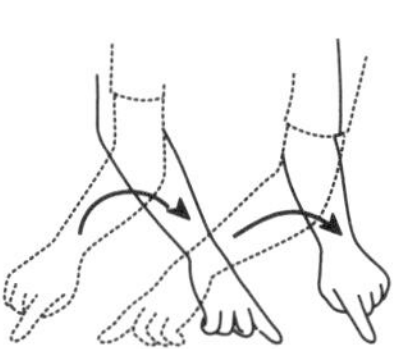

AS
Parallel palm-down indexes at right arc up and then drop to the left

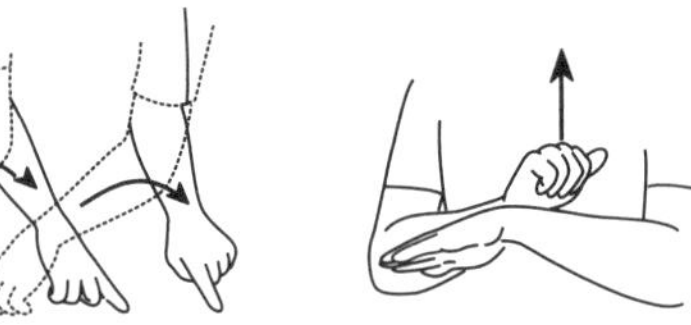

ASCEND
Right A on back of left arm rises

ASHAMED
Little finger side of A-hand on cheek opens, fingers brush up cheek; flat hand moves forward and slightly down
(see SHAME)

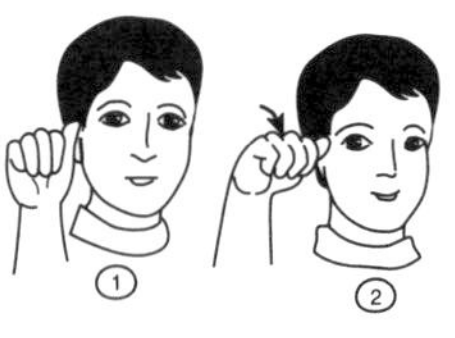

ASIA
Thumbtip of A at corner of eye; hand twists forward slightly
(see CHINA)

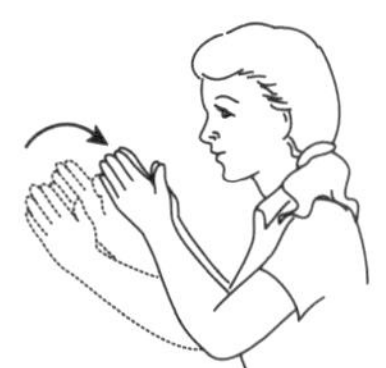

ASK
Palms of open hands come together and arc toward body
(see REQUEST)

ASLEEP

Palm-out A, changes to palm-in 5-hand before face, then drops to flat-O

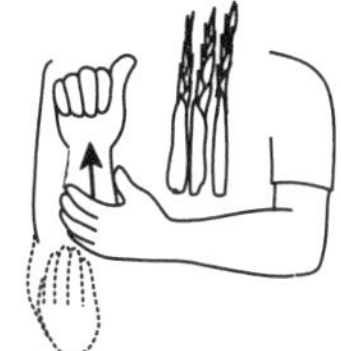

ASPARAGUS

(Alt. 1)

Flat-O twists up through left C to palm-out A-hand

(see GROW)

ASPARAGUS

(Alt. 2)

Left A; right G slides upwards off A thumb and closes

ASPIRIN

Left flat hand, palm-up; right extended A-thumb circles on edge of left palm

(see MEDICINE)

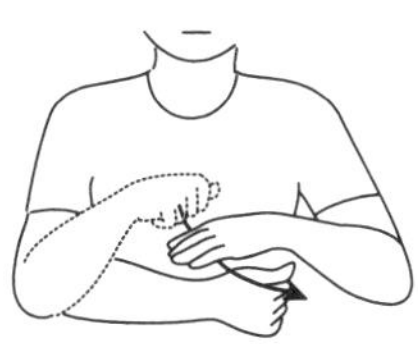

ASSASSIN

Thumb side of A twists diagonally under left palm

(See KILL)

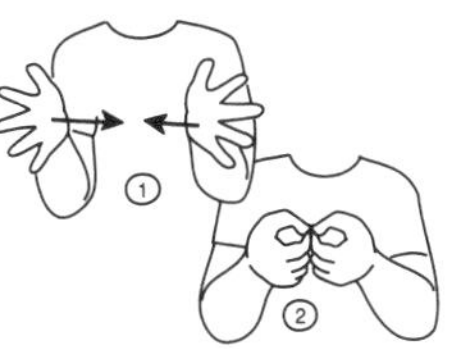

ASSEMBLE

Horizontal palm-out 5's approach, close to flat O's; touch

(see CONVENE)

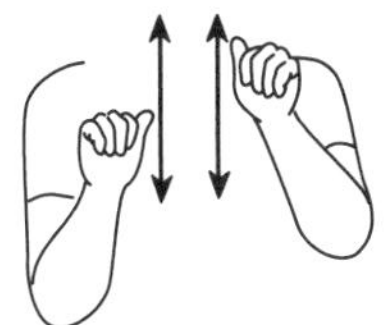

ASSESS

Palm-out A-hands move alternately up and down

(see BALANCE)

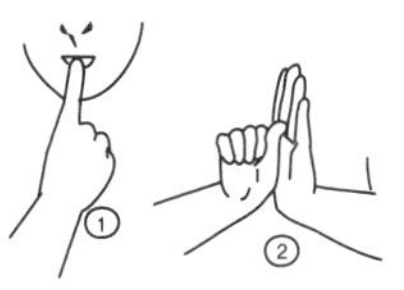

ASSIGN

Right index finger at mouth moves to palm-out A on vertical left palm

ASSIST

Thumbtip of left L pushes vertical right A upward

(See HELP)

ASSOCIATE

Thumbs of extended-A's circle each other, left hand pointing up, right pointing down

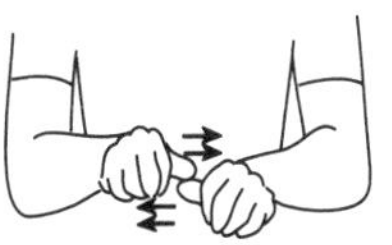

ASSORTED

Palm-down A's, right thumb brushes off left thumbnail as hands separate sideways; repeat

(see DIFFER)

ASSUME

Palm-down 5's draw up to S's

(See ADOPT)

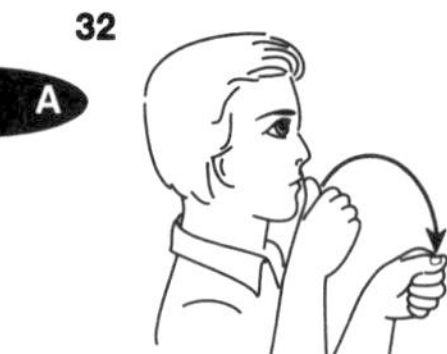

ASSURE
Thumb side of right A at lips, arc up and out; touches thumb of left A
(See POSITIVE)

ASTONISH
Palm-out A's at temples move to sides and open sharply to 5's
(See SURPRISE)

ASTRONAUT ♔
Right A slides up palm of vertical flat hand and takes off

AT
Right fingertips approach and touch back of vertical left fingers

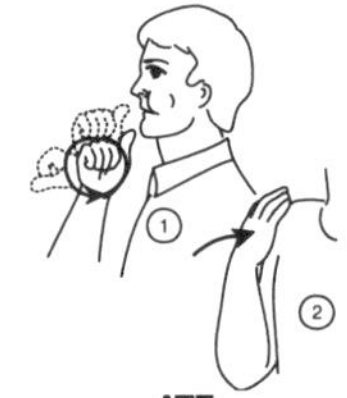

ATE
A-hands, thumb extended circles in and up near mouth; palm of open hand flips toward shoulder *(eat + p.t.)*

ATHLETE
A's lift weights (bar-bell); repeat

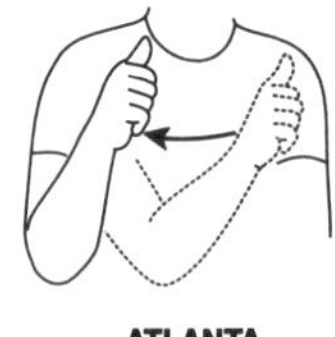

ATLANTA
Thumb of A-hand touches left and then right shoulder

ATLANTIC
Palm-out A's move wave-like up and down forward, opening to 5's
(see OCEAN)

ATMOSPHERE ♔
Right A-hand makes a half circle around left index

ATOM ♔
Left extended-A, palm-down; right A thumb circles near left thumb

ATTACH
Pinch left A-hand thumb between right index and thumb and draw back to left shoulder

ATTACK
Right claw hand approaches and hits palm-out left index

ATTEMPT

A-hands, facing each other, move forward away from body in a slight arc

ATTEND

Vertical palms drop to point forward

(see CONCENTRATE)

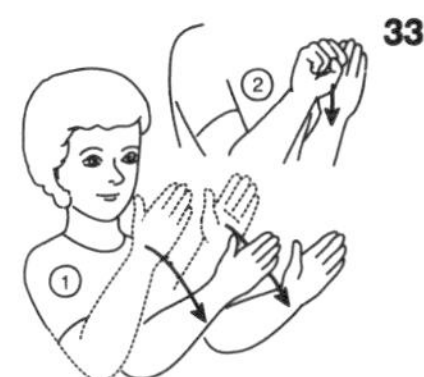

ATTENTION

Vertical palms drop to point forward; side of S slides down fingers and palm *(attend + -tion)*

ATTIC

Little finger side of A on back of left hand arcs up and makes small circle

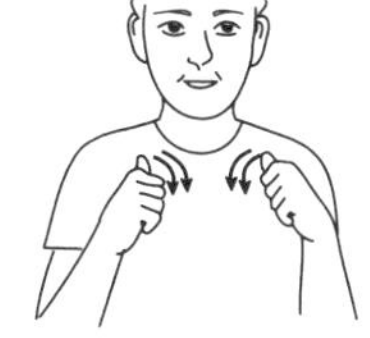

ATTIRE

A-hands brush downward off shoulders; repeat

(see DRESS)

ATTITUDE

Right A-hand circles the heart and touches chest

(see CHARACTER)

ATTRACT

(Alt. 1)

Thumb of right A on palm; both move toward body

(see BELONG)

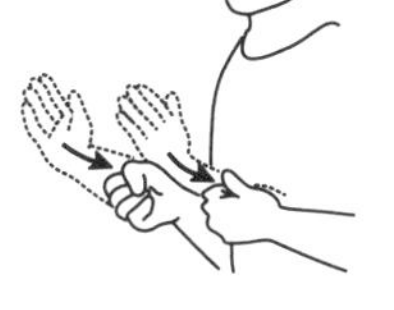

ATTRACT

(Alt. 2)

Palm-up open hands, left behind right, draw toward body and close to palm-up S's

AUCTION

Palm-in right A points toward palm-up left hand, wrist of A jerks up to palm-down; repeat

(see SELL)

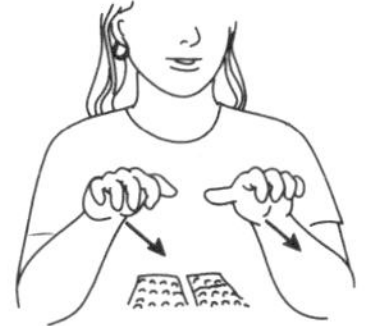

AUDIENCE

Palm-down claw hands move forward

AUDIO

Thumb of A touches ear, palm-out

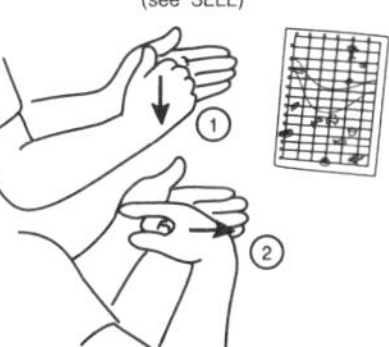

AUDIOGRAM

Right A slides down horizontal left palm, then G slides across

AUDIOLOGY

A faces right ear and circles

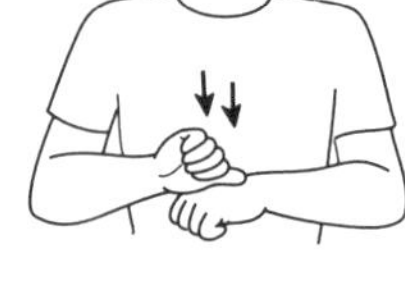

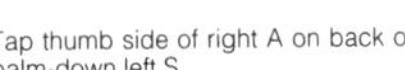

AUDITORIUM

Tap thumb side of right A on back of palm-down left S

(see CHURCH)

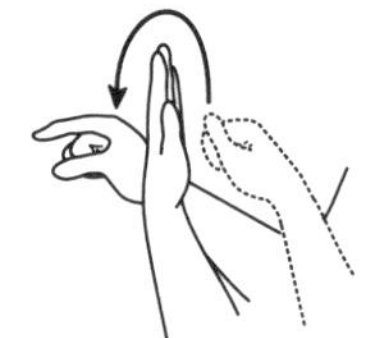

AUGUST

(Alt. 1)

Arc right A to G over vertical palm-in flat left hand

(see CALENDAR)

AUGUST

(Alt. 2)

Thumb of palm-left A-hand circles inward twice, touching chest

AUNT

A-hand shakes near jaw

AUSTRALIA

(Alt. 1)

Fingertip of right B at temple twists to palm-out touching side of head

AUSTRALIA

(Alt. 2)

Thumb of A-hand at temple twists to palm-out to touch side of head

AUTHOR

Palm-down A writes across left palm

(see WRITE)

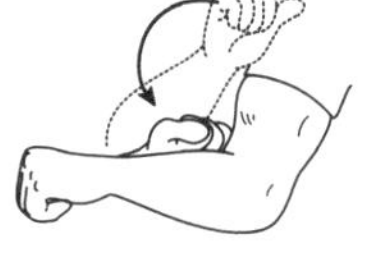

AUTHORITY

A-hand draws a muscle on left arm

(see STRONG)

AUTISM

Thumbside of palm-out A touches palm of left 5; A moves away to right

(see DISTINGUISH)

AUTO

Right A behind left A, right moves back toward shoulder

(see CAR)

AUTOMATIC

Back of fingers of right horizontal A tap vertical left index

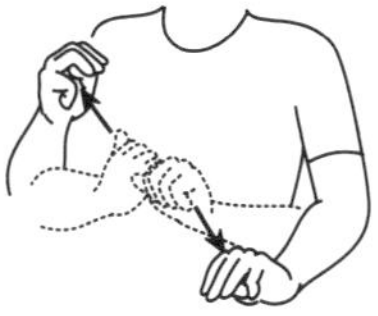

AUTOMOBILE
Right A behind left A, separate, changing to M-hands
(see CAR)

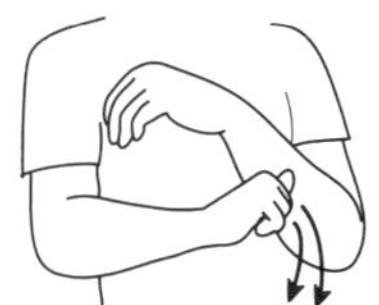

AUTUMN
Right A brushes down left elbow
(see SEPTEMBER)

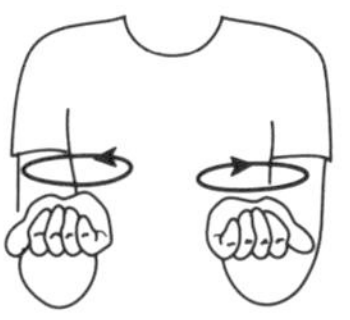

AVAIL
Palm-up A's circle slightly
(see HERE)

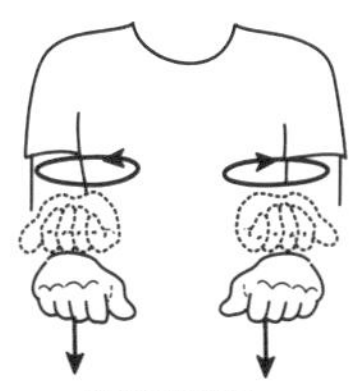

AVAILABLE
Palm-up A's circle, change to palm-down and drop slightly *(avail + -able)*

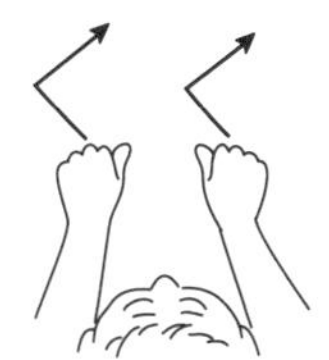

AVENUE
Palm-down A-hands move forward, zig-zagging
(see BOULEVARD)

AVERAGE
Side of right flat hand crossways on side of left hand, rock top one slightly side-to-side
(see MEDIUM)

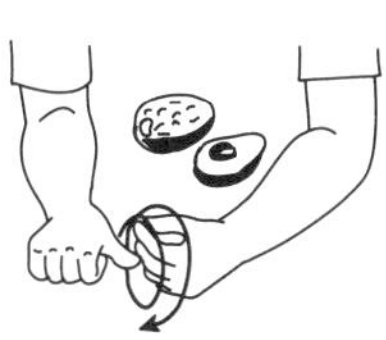

AVOCADO
Extended thumb of palm-down A circles around palm-in flat-O, peeling

AVOID ♔
Right A behind left A, right draws back toward body in wavy motion

AWAKE
A at corner of eye opens to L
(see AWARE)

AWARD
A's, palms-facing, right behind left, arc diagonally forward to left
(see GIFT)

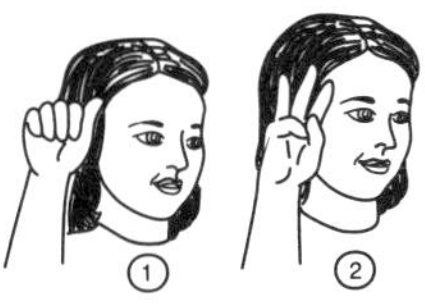

AWARE
Touch temple with palm-out A-hand then with W
(see AWAKE)

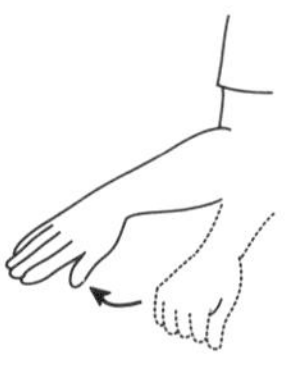

AWAY
Palm-in A-hand opens and flips forward to palm-down

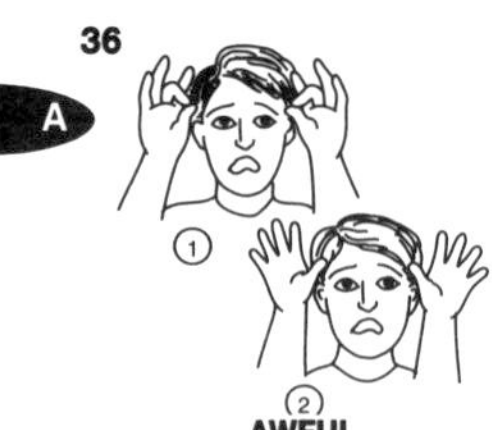

AWFUL

8-hands at temples flick open to 5's

AWKWARD

3-hands, palm-down, alternately move up and down

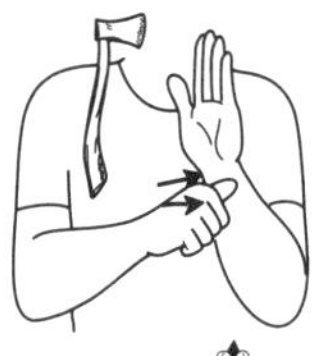

AXE ♔

Side of palm-down A chops at wrist of vertical left hand

BABBLE
Both flat-O's pointing forward near mouth, move forward opening and closing rapidly

BABY
Hold and rock baby

(see INFANT)

BACHELOR
Palm-left B-hand arcs from left side of mouth to right side

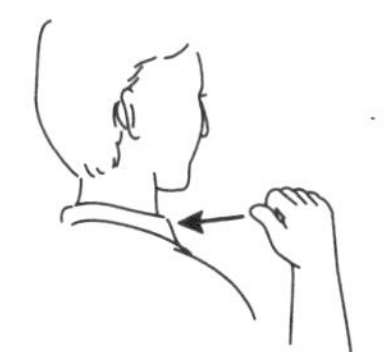

BACK
Extended-A thumb jerks back towards shoulder

BACKGROUND
Right palm-out B, on left vertical palm, drops slightly and changes to G

BACON
Palm-down H-fingertips touch and separate, waving

(see SPAGHETTI)

BACTERIA
Heel of B circles on little finger of palm-up left I
(see ALGAE)

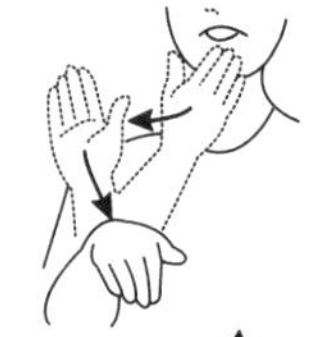

BAD ♔
Palm-in flat hand at mouth; twist to palm-out and throw down

BADGE
Side of small C's on chest near shoulder *(form a badge)*

BADMINTON
Hit bird twice sharply upward to right

BAG ♔
Right B draws bag under left S

BAKE ♔ ★
Right B slides under palm-down left flat hand

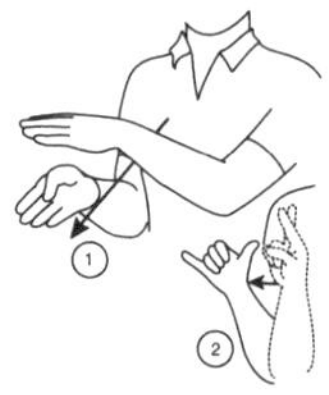

BAKERY
Right B slides under palm-down left hand; change to palm-out R then Y *(bake + -er + -y)*

BALANCE ♔
Palm-down hands rise and fall alternately

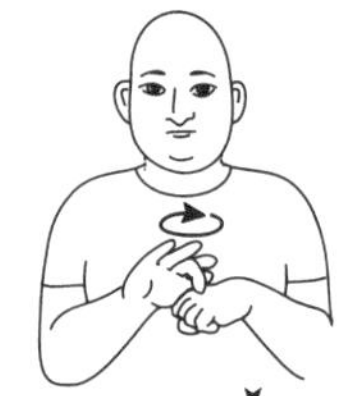

BALD ★
Bent middle finger of right hand circles on the back of left S-hand

BALL
Claw hands form ball shape

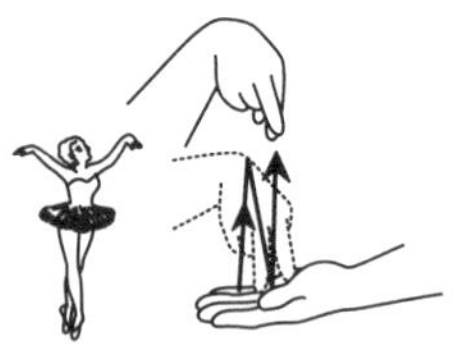

BALLET
Right V stands on left palm, jumps up to cross fingers into R; repeat
(see JUMP)

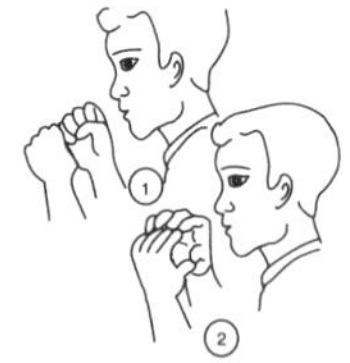

BALLOON
S-hands right behind left, near mouth open and form ball

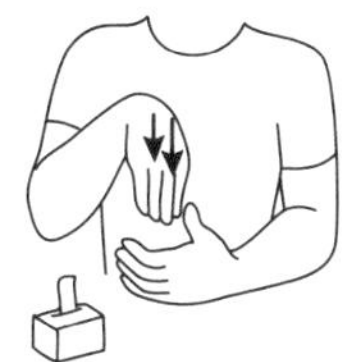

BALLOT
Fingertips of B-hand stick into left horizotnal C; repeat

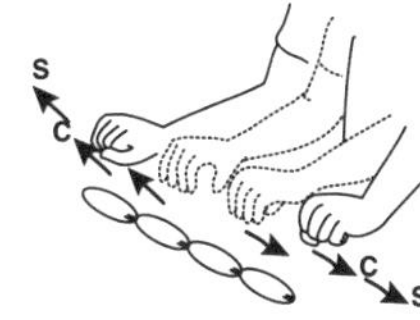

BALONEY
C-hands change to S-hands, twice, while separating

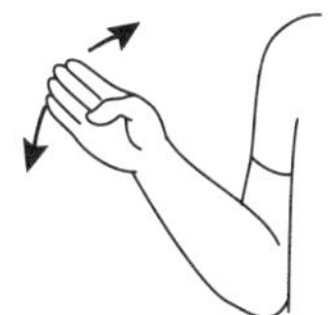

BALTIMORE
Shake palm-left B-tip up and down

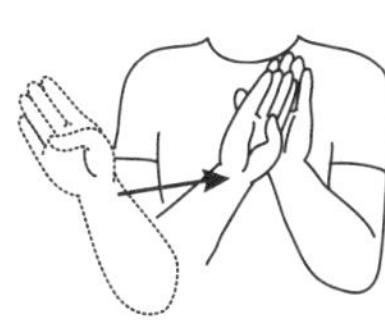

BAN
Side of right B strikes vertical left palm
(see FORBID)

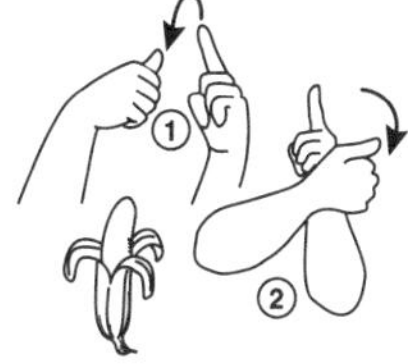

BANANA
Right A-hand peels left index finger twice

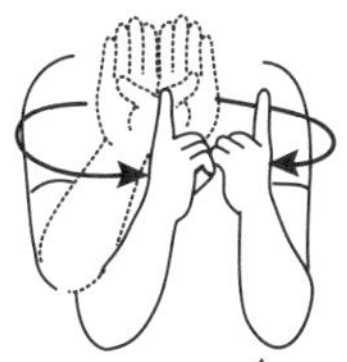

BAND
Palm-out B's together, circle outward to palm-in D's together

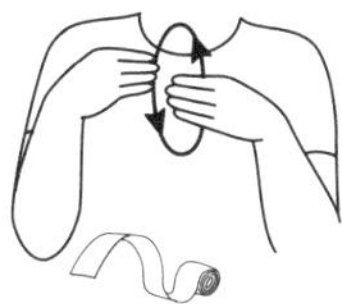

BANDAGE
Right B circles left B

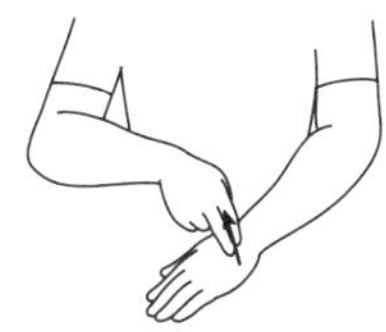

BANDAID
Right palm-down U slides inward across back of left hand

BANDANA
Flat hands brush down by sides of neck and cross under chin
(see BONNET)

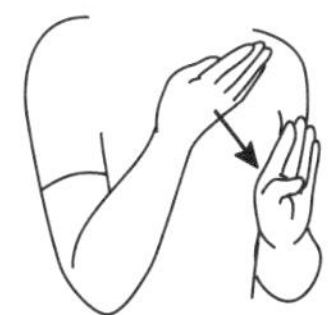

BANG
Hit back of B-hand with the back of the right B-hand
(see BUMP)

BANJO
Right hand strums banjo held by the left hand

BANK *
Palm-up horizontal B jerks slightly toward and away from side of left C; repeat
(see STORE)

B

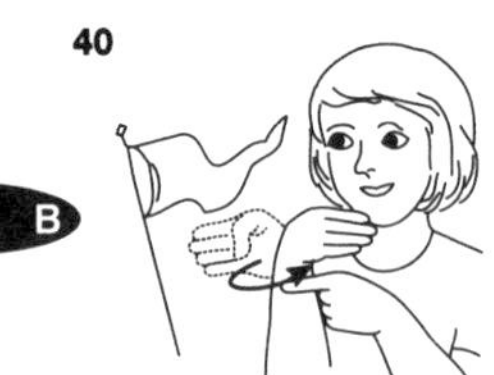

BANNER
Right B-hand waves in breeze with left index at wrist
(see FLAG)

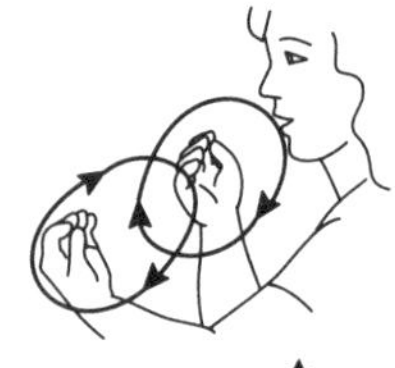

BANQUET
Flat O-hands, palm-in circle alternately up to chin

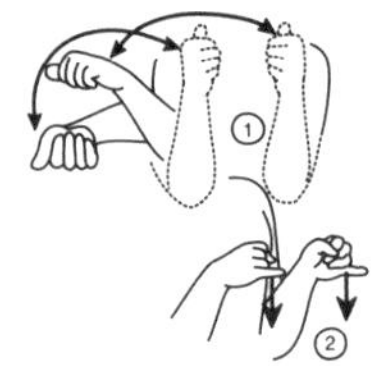

BAPTIST
A-hands move to the right, palm-up right and palm-down left, return to original position, then I's drop down body *(baptize + -ist)*

BAPTIZE
A-hands move to the right, palm-up right and palm-down left, *(dipping person)*, return to original position

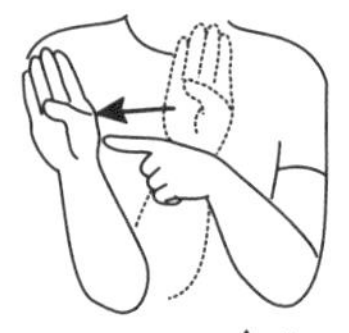

BAR
B moves right, palm-out, off left horizontal index

BAR/BAT MITZVAH
Right A-hand winds twice around left palm-down horizontal forearm

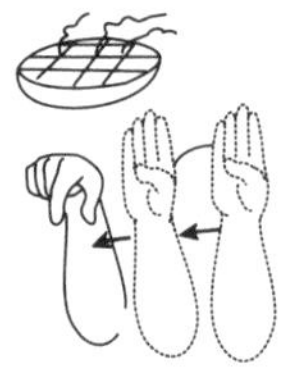

BARBECUE
Fingerspell B + B +Q

BARBER
Finger of V-hand clips hair

BARE
Right middle finger brushes forward along back of horizontal left hand

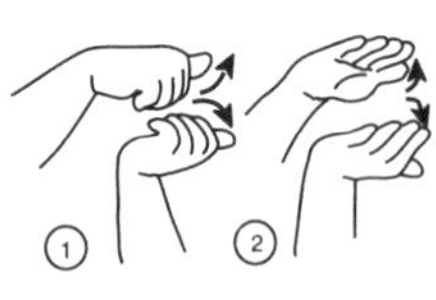

BARK
Bent hands, one above the other, palms-facing, open; repeat

BARLEY
Palm-out B brushes up through left hoaizontal C twice
(see GRAIN)

BARN
Palm-out B's outline barn
(see HOUSE)

BAROMETER
Side of right B slides up and down left vertical index
(see THERMOMETER)

BARREL ★
Open hands outline barrel upward

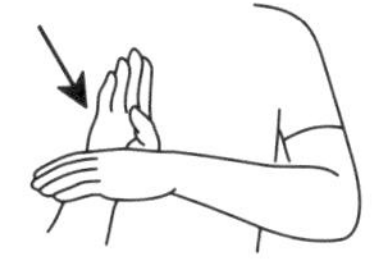

BARRIER
Palm-out right B pushes outward until it hits side of palm-down left hand
(see GUARD)

BASE ♔
Horizontal B circles under left palm

BASEBALL
Swing bat a short way; repeat

BASEMENT
Horizontal B circles under left palm; then side of M slides down left fingers and palm

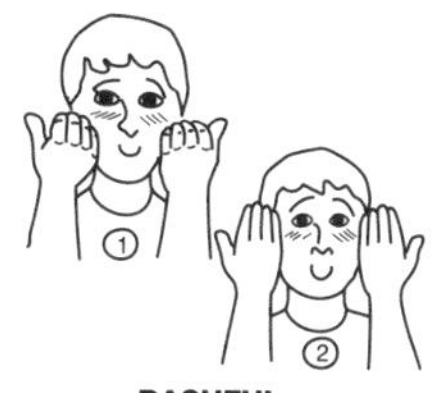

BASHFUL
Palm-in bent hands on cheeks change to palm-in open hands on cheeks
(see SHAME)

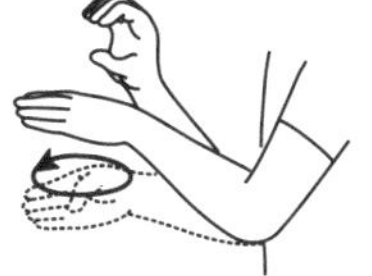

BASIC
Horizontal B circles under left palm, changes to palm-out C

BASIL
Right V-fingers tap alternately on back of palm-down left B
(see SALT)

BASKET ♔
Flat hand draws basket under left arm

BASKETBALL
Claw hands flip ball upward

BAT
Palm-out B bats to palm-in

BATCH
Heel of palm-out B hops from palm to fingers of flat left hand
(see AMOUNT)

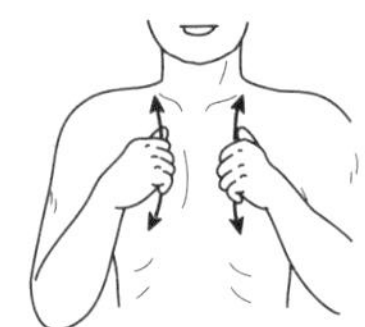

BATH
Rub knuckles up and down on chest

BATTER ★
Right B fingers pointing down, circle above left horizontal C

BATTERY
Right horizontal X-finger bumps side of B; repeat
(see ELECTRIC)

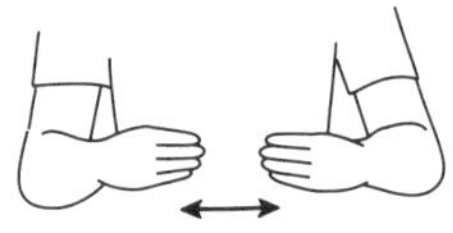

BATTLE
Palm-in B's point at each other; move together from side-to-side
(see WAR)

BAWL ★
S's by cheeks drop and open, palms-down (*tears*), *(note: for vocals, hands open and move outward from cheeks)*

BAY ♔ ★
Palm-out B-hand outlines curve of palm-down left hand, index to thumb ending palm-in

BE
Palm-left B below lips; move forward
(see AM)

BEACH
Palm-down B's ripple forward to the left

BEAD ★
Tap side of F across palm, *like beads*
(see SEQUIN)

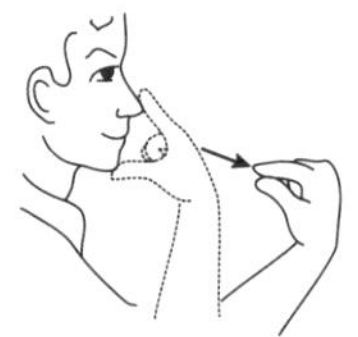

BEAK
G-hand on nose and chin moves forward to close
(see WOLF)

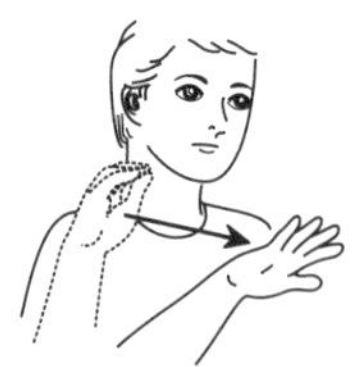

BEAM
Palm-out flat-O projects forward, opening to 5, slightly palm-down

BEAN
(Alt. 1)
Slide thumb of A along thumbside of palm-in horizontal B-hand; repeat

BEAN
(Alt. 2)
Right X taps down left horizontal index
(see PEA)

BEAR ✶
Swing crossed wrists of palm-in claw hands to the right, still crossed

BEARD
Thumb and fingers on chin drop and close to flat-O

BEAST
Thumb sides of B-hands alternately beat on chest

BEAT ♔ ✶
Back of right B hits left index finger

BEAUTY
Circle face with 5-hand closing to palm-in flat-O
(see FACE)

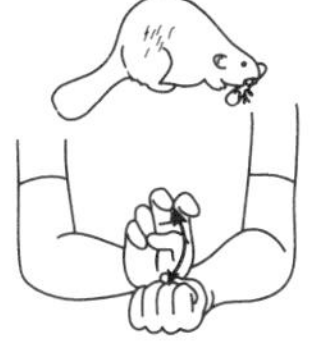

BEAVER
Tap right bent-V on palm-up left S, heels together

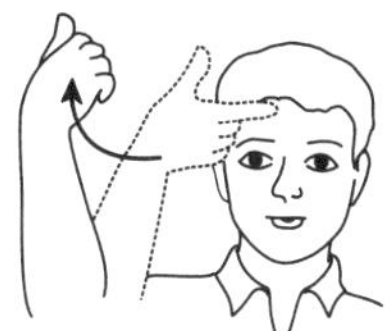

BECAUSE
Index of L on forehead, moves up and right, closing to extended-A

BECOME
Palm-to-palm flat hands twist to their reverse position

BED ♔
Rest cheek on back of palms-together hands

BEE
9 on cheek, then brush off bee
(see WASP)

BEEF
Right thumb and forefinger grasp side of left horizontal palm-in B and shake
(see MEAT)

BEEN
B at chin moves outward; then flat palm-up hands turn to palms-facing
(can be done with a N ending)

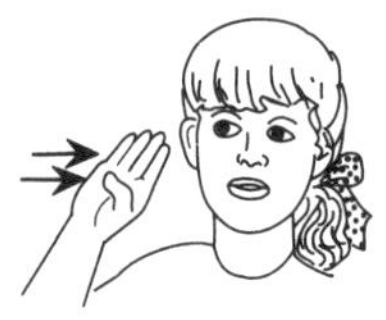

BEEP
Palm-out B taps ear

BEER
Vertical B circles on right cheek
(see WINE)

BEET
Right index finger slices side of left palm-out B; repeat
(see TOMATO)

BEETLE
B rides forward on back of wiggling fingers on left hand
(see ANT)

BEFORE
Make palm-out B, then right palm-in hand behind left palm-in hand, right hand moves inward

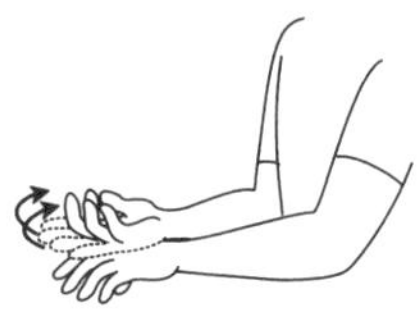

BEG
Palm-up right hand on back of left; flex fingers
(see COAX)

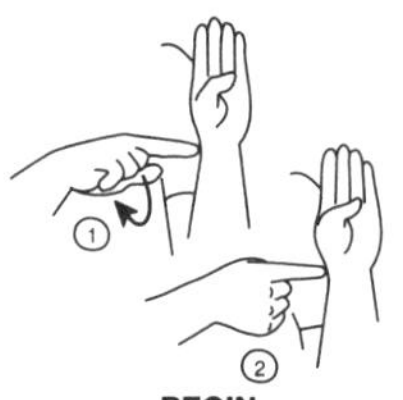

BEGIN
Index twists on wrist of left B-hand
(see START)

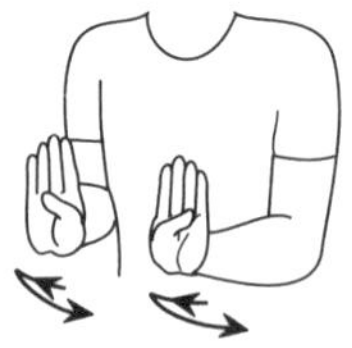

BEHAVE
Palm-out B's move from side-to-side
(see DO)

BEHIND
Palm-out B behind horizontal A-hand changes to A and arcs back to rest against left A-wrist
(see HIND)

BEIGE
B at side of mouth drops slightly to G
(see BROWN)

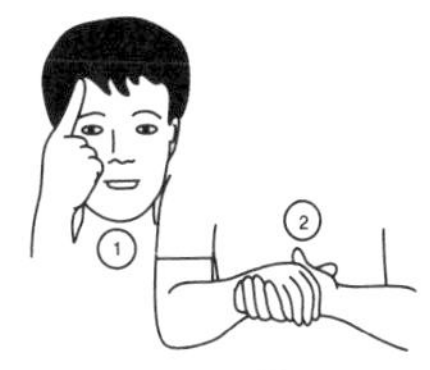

BELIEVE
Right index finger on forehead; drops to clasp hands

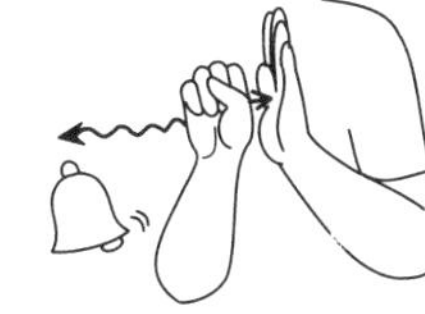

BELL ♔
Right S hits vertical left palm, then shakes to the right

BELLY
Open hands outline big belly

BELONG
Right thumb and finger hold thumb of left B while moving to left shoulder
(see ATTRACT)

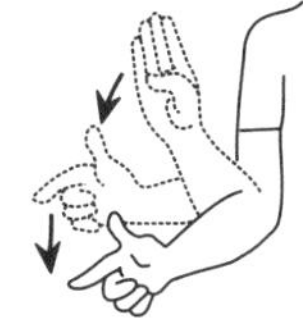

BELOW
Palm-out B drops to L, which falls slightly

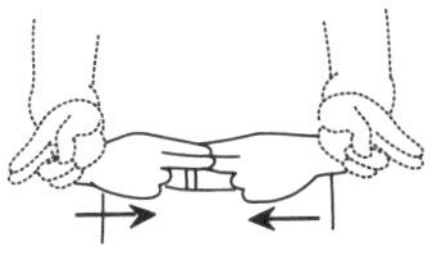

BELT ✶
H-hands overlap fingertips across belt-line, snapping at wrists
(see BUCKLE)

BENCH
Two fingers sit on side of left palm-in horizontal B-hand
(see SIT)

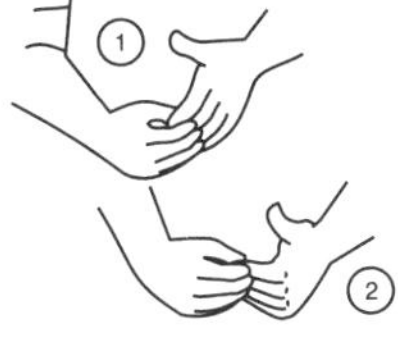

BEND
Grasp left hand fingertips and bend them inward

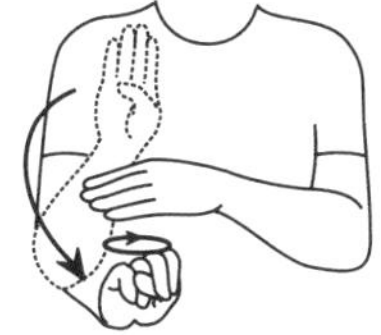

BENEATH
Palm-out B drops; changes to N, circles below left palm

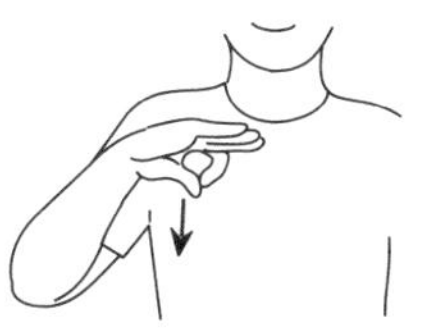

BENEFIT
Move thumb and finger of 9-hand down chest near shoulder

BERRY
Twist C around I-fingertip; *(shake first letter of name of berry by little finger before signing "berry" e.g., "Raspberry" = shake R, sign "berry")*

BESIDE
Palm-out B drops to palm-in flat hand that brushes past outside of left palm-down flat-hand

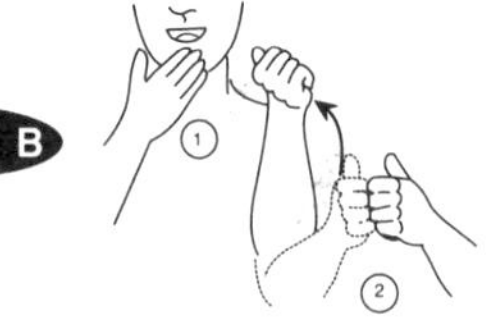

BEST
Hand on chin; A-hand brushing up from left-A

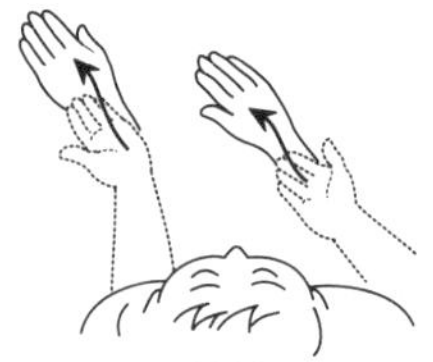

BET
Palm-up hands, right to the rear of left, move slightly forward to the left and turn palm-down
(see COMPROMISE)

BETHLEHEM
Palm-out B circles and then taps fingertips of left B

BETRAY
Index finger flicks around vertical left B, near mouth
(see TRAITOR)

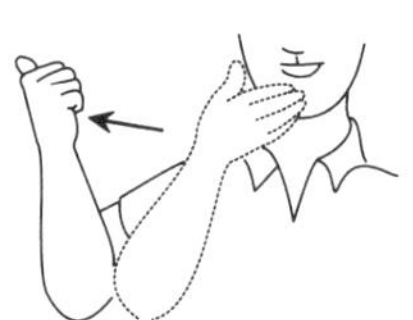

BETTER
Flat palm-in hand slides off chin into palm-in A

BETWEEN
Right flat hand bounces between 1st and 2nd fingers of left hand

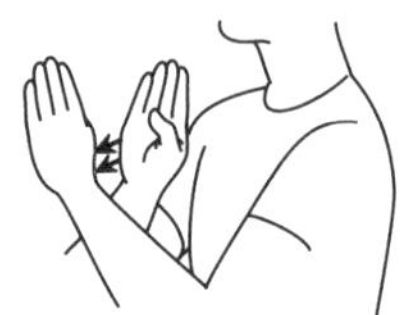

BEWARE
Little finger side of right B taps thumb side of left B at right angle
(see KEEP)

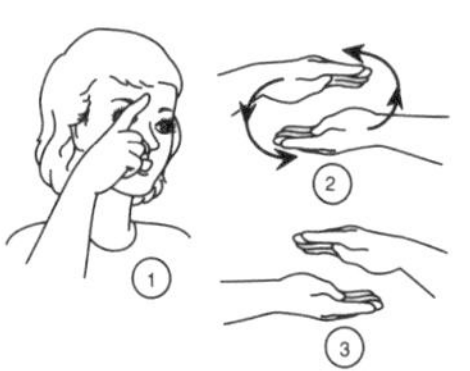

BEWILDER
Index touches forehead, palm-down right B above palm-up left B, reverse
(see CONFUSE)

BEYOND
Right B changes to palm-left Y and passes palm-right left Y

BIB
Both index fingers outline bib

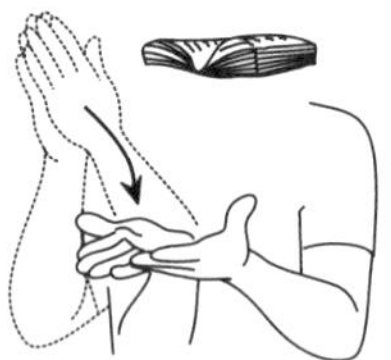

BIBLE
Praying hands drop open like book

BIBLIOGRAPHY
Palms-together "book" moves down, opening repeatedly
(see BOOK)

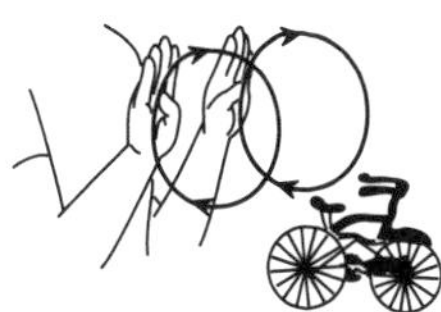

BICYCLE

Palm-out B-hands pedal

BID

Flat right hand, palm-up, moves up and out to bid

(see NOMINATE)

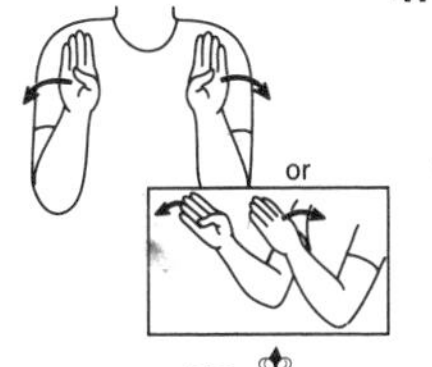

BIG

Palm-out B's separate and arc sideways *(can be done palms-facing)*

BIKE

Palm-down S-hands pedal

(see BICYCLE)

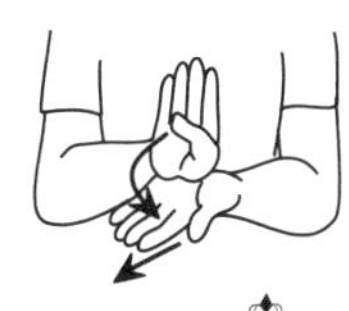

BILLION

Heel of right B on heel of left hand; arc B to fingertips as both hands move forward

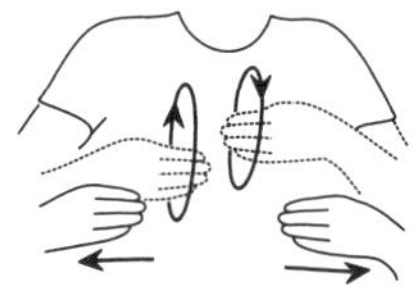

BIND

B's point toward each other, circle each other, and separate

(see TIE)

BINOCULARS

O-hands twist around eyes, in place

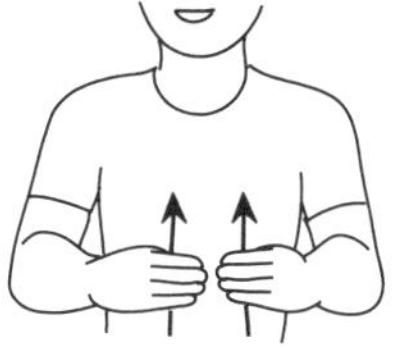

BIOGRAPHY

Palm-in B's move up trunk

(see ADDRESS)

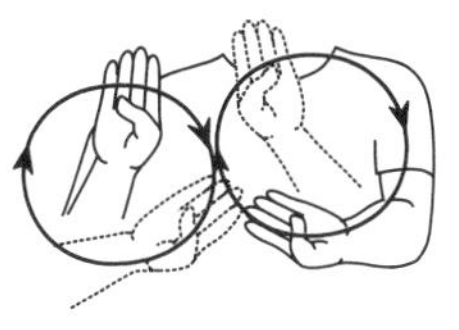

BIOLOGY

Palm-out B's circle towards each other alternately

(see SCIENCE)

BIRD

Close index finger on thumb twice, hand at chin

BIRTH

Palm-up hands move from sides forward and slightly down to rest right hand on left

BIRTHDAY

Palm-up hands move from sides forward; slightly down to rest, right on left; right 1-hand drops down on left arm

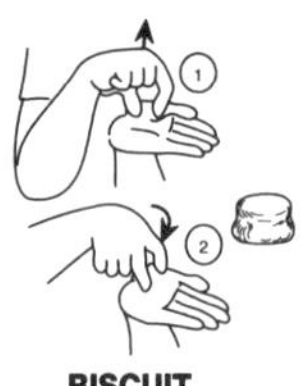

BISCUIT

Thumb and curved index on left palm lift slightly, rotate and touch again

(see COOKIE)

BISHOP

Kiss ring on right fist

BIT
(Alt. 1)

Little finger flips forward from unde the thumb

BIT
(Alt. 2)

Palm-up fist; thumb flips up from under index

(see SLIGHT)

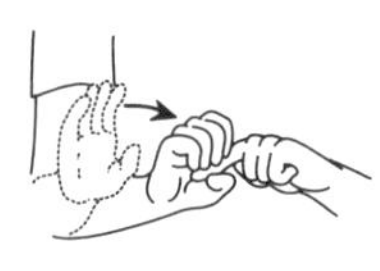

BITE

Right hand bites left index finger

BITTER

Index finger of B on chin, palm-left, twist to palm-in

(see SOUR)

BLACK

Index finger moves across forehead to right

BLADE

Shake heel of B upward from left index fingertip

(see SHARP)

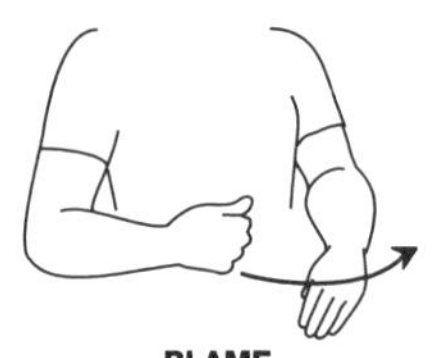

BLAME

Little finger side of A arcs forward, hitting back of left hand

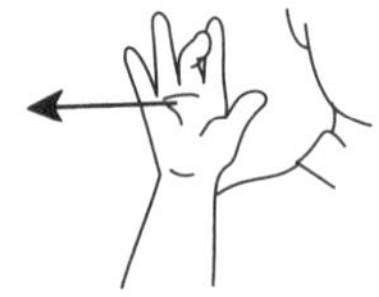

BLANK

Bent middle finger of 5-hand draws a line in the air

(see DASH)

BLANKET

From in front, right arm sweeps across left arm to shoulder near neck *(drawing up blanket)*

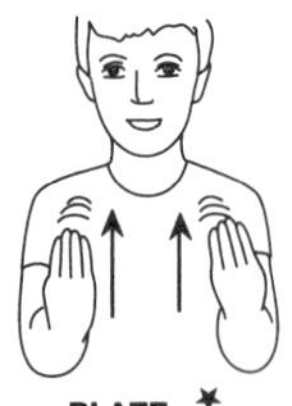

BLAZE

Palm-in B's flutter upwards

(see FIRE)

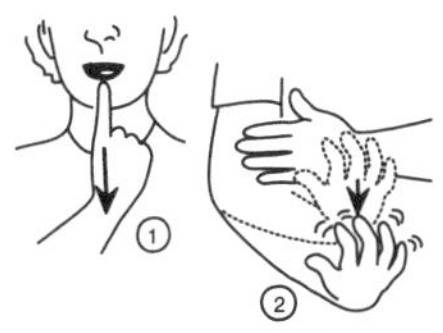

BLEED
Index at chin drops, changing to palm-in 5 on back of left hand, moving downwards with fluttering fingers

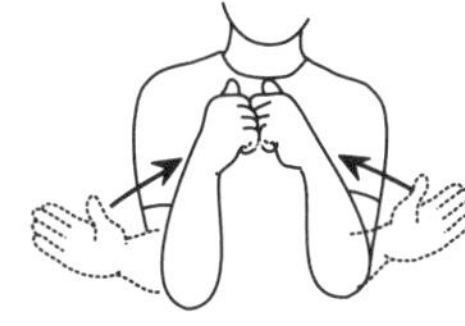

BLEND
Flat hands draw up to A's with knuckles together

BLESS
Thumbs of A's on chin; move down, opening slowly to palm-down 5's

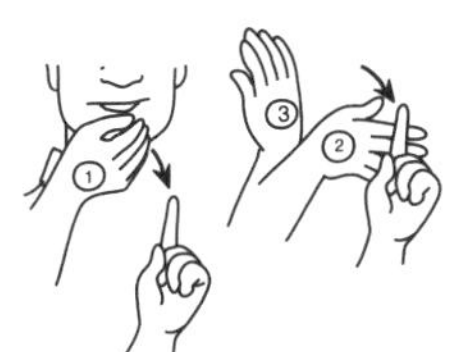

BLEW
Palm-in flat-O at mouth moves out and opens to palm-in 5; hits side of vertical index finger, then hand flips back *(blow + p.t.)*

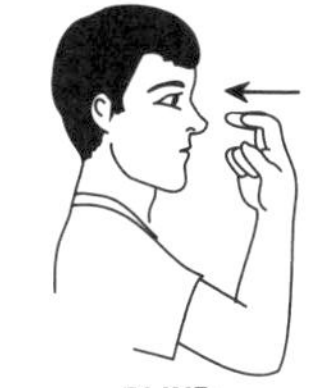

BLIND
Bent-V, palm-in, jerks toward eyes

BLINK
Thumbs and index fingers of L's, near eyes open and shut again

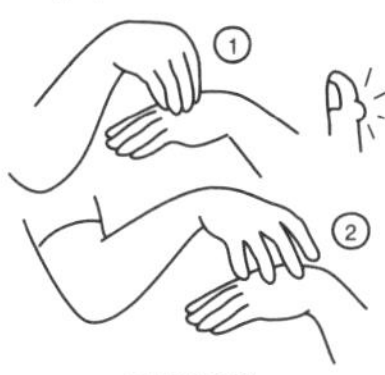

BLISTER
Tips of right flat-O on topside of palm-down left hand pops to claw

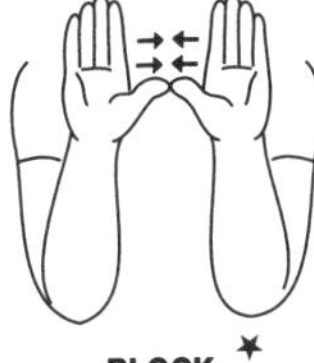

BLOCK *
Thumb-tips, palms out, tap

BLOND
B makes a wavy motion down the side of hair

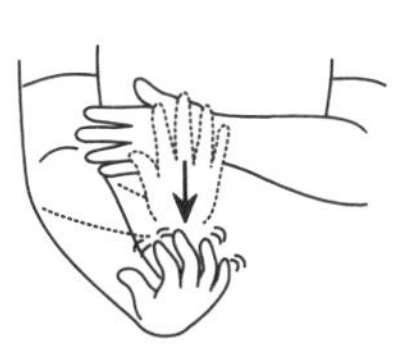

BLOOD
Palm-in 5 touches back of hand, then drops down with fluttering fingers *(blood dripping)*

(see BLEED)

BLOOM
Flat-O's touch tips, slowly change to bent 5's

BLOSSOM
Flat-O's touch tips, change to bent 5's, move slightly to right and repeat

(see BLOOM)

BLOUSE
Palm-out B's on chest, then on waist
(see COAT)

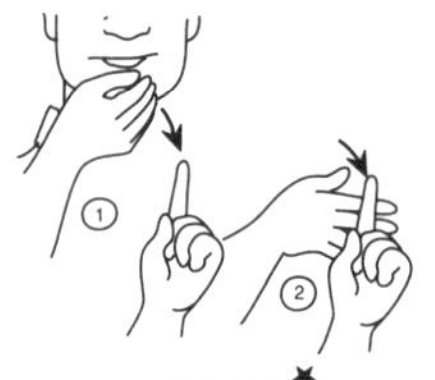

BLOW ★
Palm-in flat-O at mouth moves out and opens to palm-in 5; hits side of vertical index finger

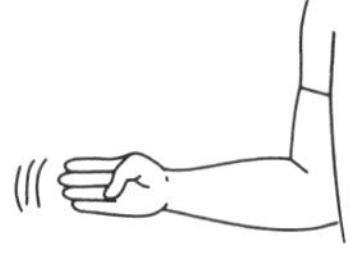

BLUE
Palm-left B shakes from wrist

BLUSH
Flat-O at cheek rises and opens to a 5-hand

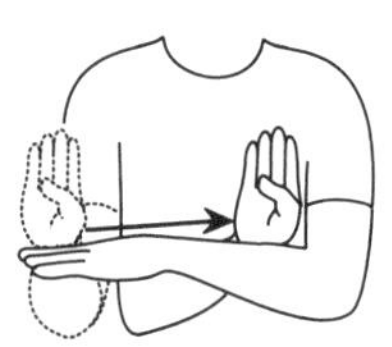

BOARD
Palm-out right B on back of left hand moves left along arm to elbow

BOAST
Palm-down extended-A thumbs strike waist alternately

BOAT
Flat hands joined at little finger side, move forward in wavy up-and-down motion

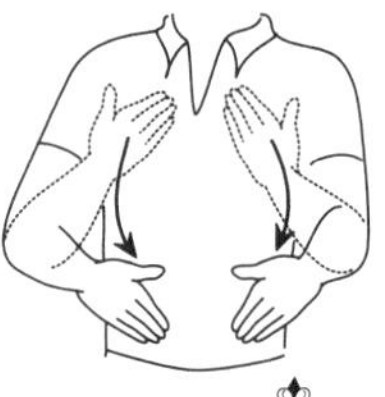

BODY
Touch the chest and then ribs with flat hands

BOIL
Palm-in hands "juggle" alternately while fluttering fingers

BOLD
Little finger side of fist strikes right chest circularly

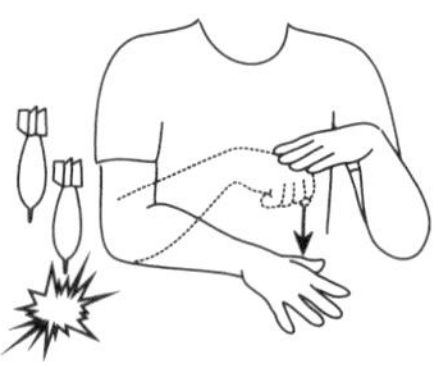

BOMB
Drop bomb from under left hand, right hand opening from S to 5

BONE
Bent-V's palms-in, wrists tap against each other

BONFIRE
Palm-in 5's flutter fingers as they separate and rise
(see FIRE)

BONNET ♔
With A-hands start at top of head outline and tie on bonnet

BOOK ♔
Palm-to-palm hands open to palms-up

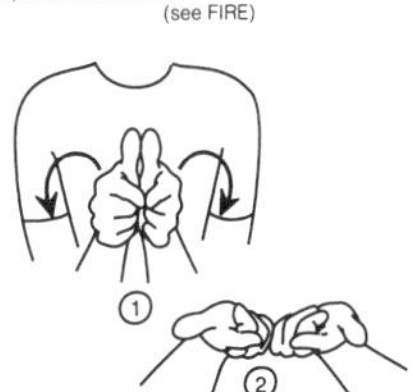

BOOKLET
L's palm-to-palm, open booklet
(see BOOK)

BOOST
Right palm-in S boosts heel of left B
(see SUPPORT)

BOOT *
Tap sides of plam-out B-hands together twice
(see SHOE)

BORDER
Left hand palm-down, right B brushes around edge of hand ending palm-in
(see EDGE)

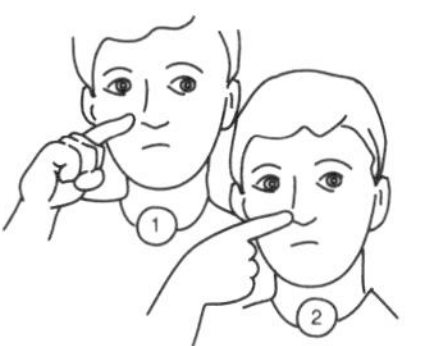

BORE
Tip of index finger on side of nose; twist in place

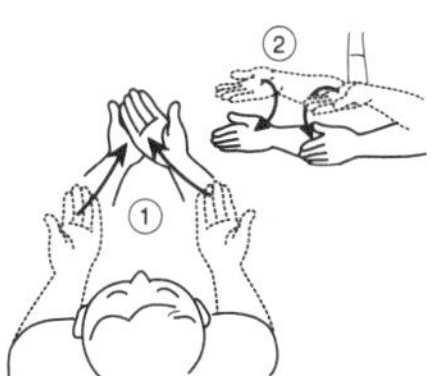

BORN
Palm-up hands move from sides forward, slightly down to rest on left, then flat hands twist to palms-facing *(birth + p.p.)*

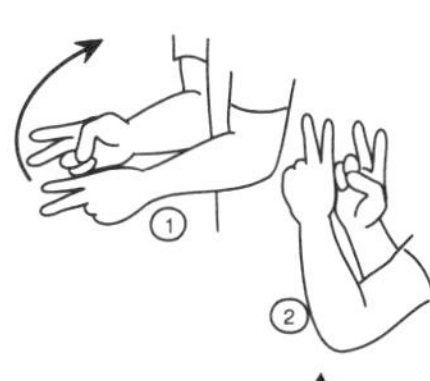

BORROW ♔
Horizontal right V on top of left V, both arc up together toward body

BOSS
Tap side of right B on right shoulder
(see OFFICE)

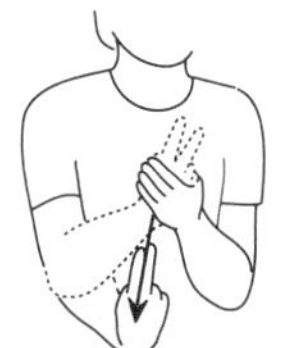

BOTH
Palm-in V slides through left C, left hand closes V to a U-hand

B

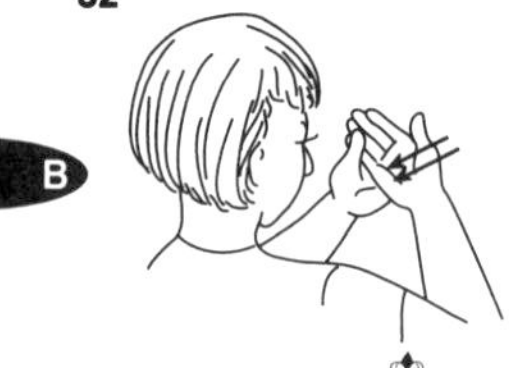

BOTHER ♔
Side of right hand chops into thumb-base of left hand; repeat

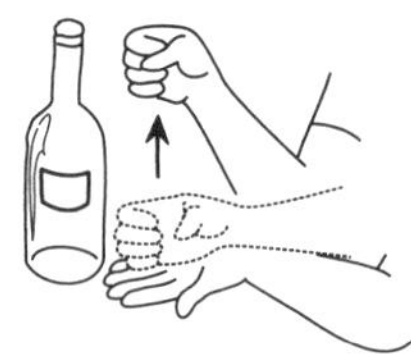

BOTTLE
Side of right C on left palm rises and closes into S, outlining a bottle

BOTTOM
Right fingertips tap heel of palm-out left B-hand

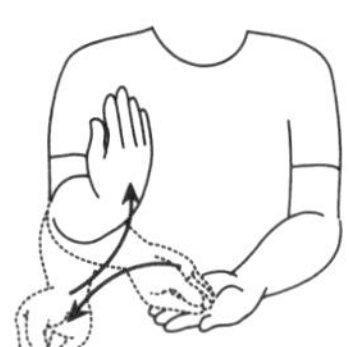

BOUGHT
Back of palm-up flat-O on left palm, lift off, arc forward, right hand flips back *(buy + p.t.)*

BOULEVARD
B's, palm-out and parallel, zig-zag away from body

(see AVENUE)

BOUNCE
5-hand bounces

BOUND
Left index points right; palm-out right B jumps over it

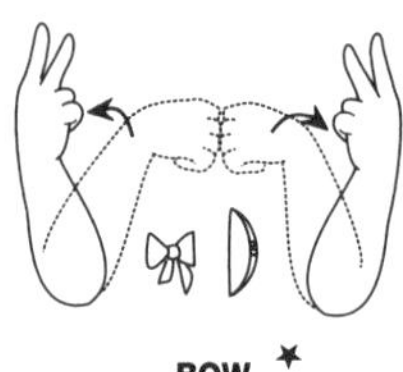

BOW ★
(noun)
Palm-in S-hands touch knuckles, arc away from each other changing to V's

BOW
(verb)
Arm at waist, bow forward slightly

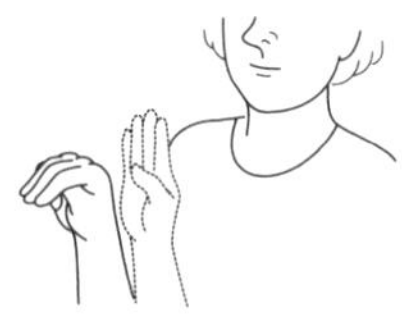

BOWEL MOVEMENT
Fingerspell B + M

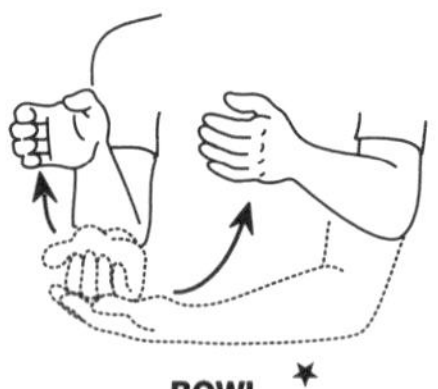

BOWL ★
Palm-up cupped hands, right on left, rise to sides

(see JAR)

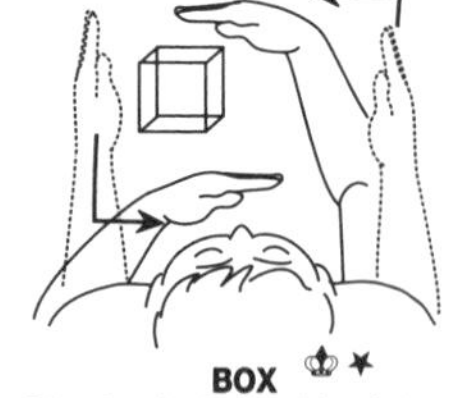

BOX ♔ ★
B-hands make the four sides of a box

BOY

4-fingers touch thumb several times near temple, grasping cap brim

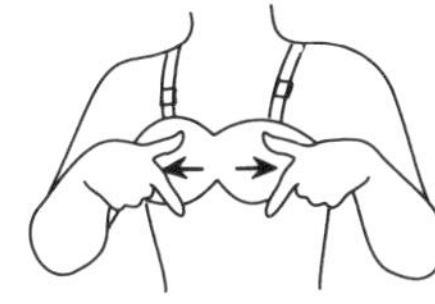

BRA

L-hands, pointing down, move from mid chest to sides

BRACELET

Middle finger and thumb circle left wrist and twist "bracelet" slightly

BRAG

Extended-A thumb strikes waist several times

(see BOAST)

BRAID ★

Both palm-down R-hands, arc over each other alternately while moving downwards as if braiding *(may be made wherever the braid is)*

BRAILLE

Flutter fingers slightly across "page" palm of palm-up hand

BRAIN

Thumb of horizontal C taps on forehead

BRAKE

A-hand palm-down, presses down abruptly, as if braking

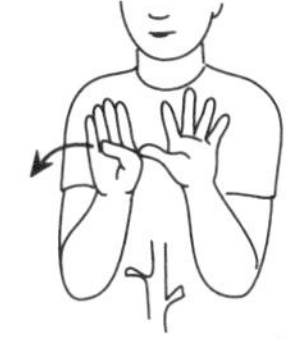

BRANCH ♔ ★

Right palm-out B, at thumb of left palm-out 5, arcs sideways

(see LIMB)

BRAND ★

Draw fingers of palm-in horizontal B across vertical palm-out palm

(see LABEL)

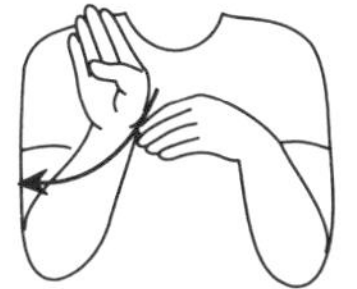

BRASS

Heel of the right B arcs down and to side hitting side of horizontal palm-in left B-hand

(see METAL)

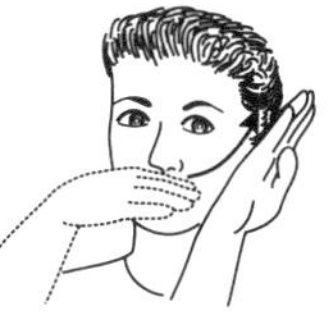

BRAT

Palm-down B under nose, brush sharply up to left

(see KID)

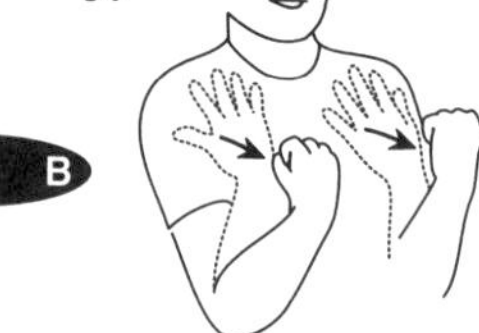

BRAVE

5's on chest; pull out to S-hands

(see HERO)

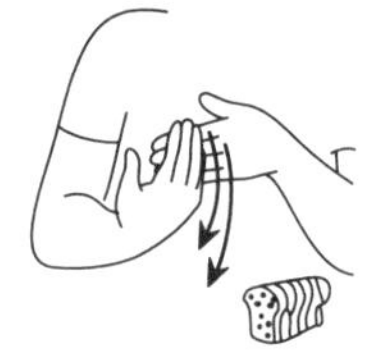

BREAD

Little finger side of right hand slices down back of left hand several times

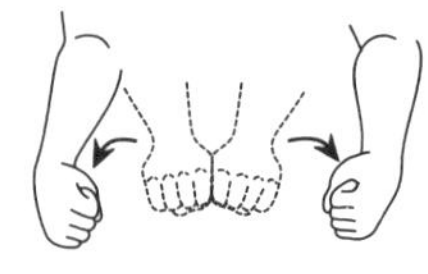

BREAK

Sides of S-hands touch, then separate sharply, twisting to face each other

BREAKFAST

B-hand rotates at wrist up to mouth, spooning food in

(see EAT)

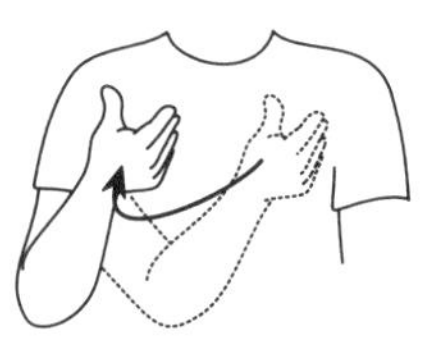

BREAST

Fingertips of bent hand touch on each side of chest

BREATH ★

Flat hands move together from and to chest *(breathing motion)*

(see SIGH)

BREED

Palms-in B on B; then circle each other vertically

(see KIND)

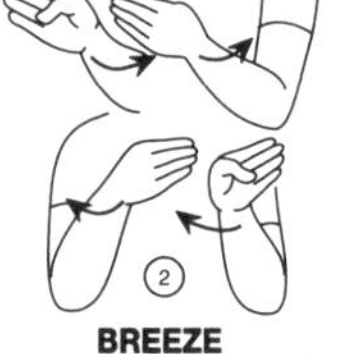

BREEZE

B-hands swing side-to-side twisting at wrists *(as breeze "blows")*

(see WIND)

BRIBE

Palm-up flat-O passes under left-palm toward left

(see UNDER)

BRICK

Back of B taps on back of left palm-down S

(see STONE)

BRIDE

Extended-A thumb strokes down cheek, opens, and goes into clasp of other hand, palms-in

BRIDEGROOM

Extended-A touch near temple, then hand swings down to enter clasp of other hand

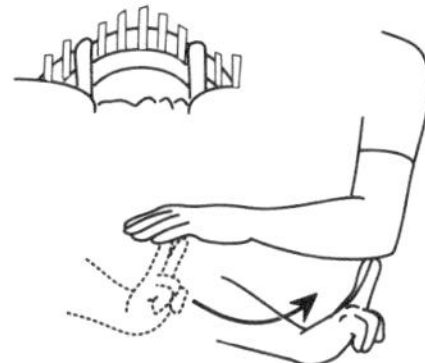

BRIDGE
Fingertips of V touch palm of palm-down left, arc to touch arm near elbow

BRIEF
Little finger side of right B slides back and forth on the side of the left H-index finger
(see SHORT)

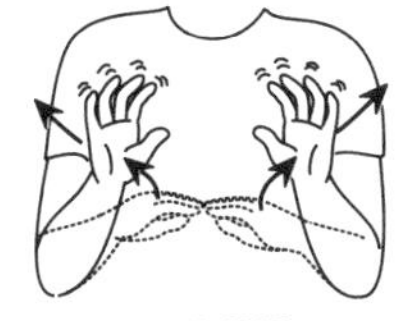

BRIGHT
Tips of flat-O's together open and separate upwards with fluttering fingers
(see CLEAR)

BRILLIANT
Bent middle finger shakes slightly upward from forehead
(see SMART)

BRING ♔
Palm-up hands at left; move back toward body

BRITAIN
Thumb and bent index grasp chin, wiggle chin slightly side-to-side

BRITISH
Thumb and bent index wiggles chin, slightly, right I-hand draws a wavy downward line *(Britain + -ish)*

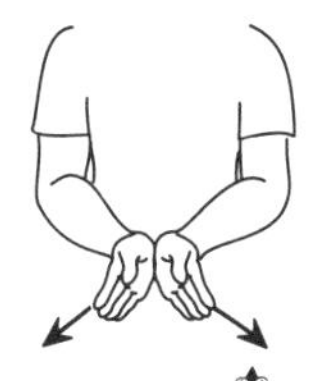

BROAD ♔
Heels of B-hands together, then separate forward

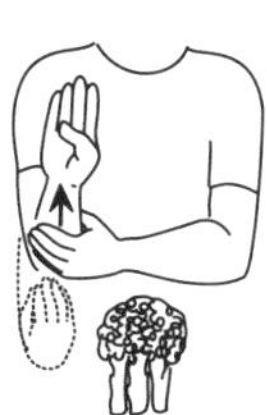

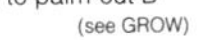

BROCCOLI
Flat-O grows up through C-hand, twisting to palm-out B
(see GROW)

BROCHURE
Right palm-up B fingertips brush along little finger side of horizontal left B; can repeat
(see MAGAZINE)

BROIL
Flutter fingers while circling palm-up hand under left palm
(see OVEN)

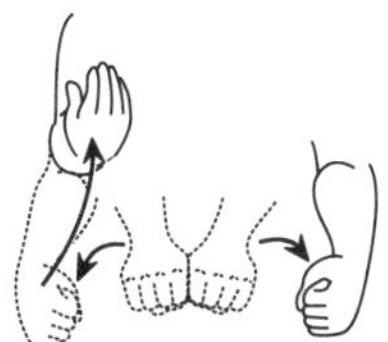

BROKE
Sides of S-hands touch, then separate sharply, twisting to face each other; right hand flips back *(break + p.t.)*

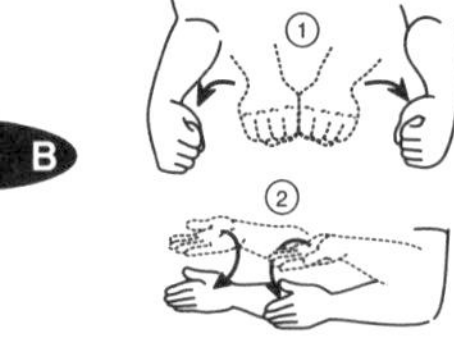

BROKEN
(Alt. 1)
Sides of S-hands touch, then separate sharply, twisting to face each other, then flat hands twist from palms-up to facing each other *(break + p.p.)*

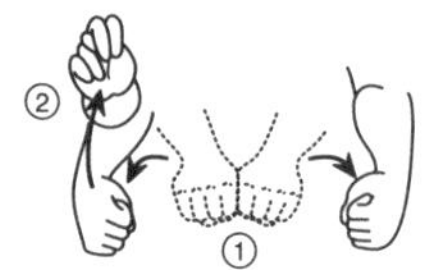

BROKEN
(Alt. 2)
Sides of S-hands touch then separate sharply, twisting to face each other, add N with right hand *(break + p.p.)*

BRONTOSAURUS
B moves downward in wavy motion, left to right, outlining back of dinosaur

BRONZE
Palm-in horizontal left B; right B brushes off side of left and draws a Z

BROOCH
Index finger draws a small circle near left shoulder

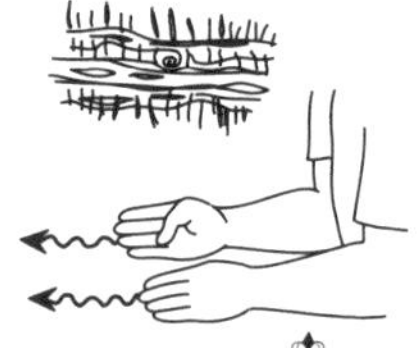

BROOK
Parallel B-hands shake forward slightly to the side *(like brook-water)*

BROOM
Right S on left S, sweep to left; repeat

BROTH
Ladle palm-up B-hand up to mouth twice from palm-up left hand
(see SOUP)

BROTHER
Palm-out A-hand at temple drops, then index fingers touch sides
(see SISTER)

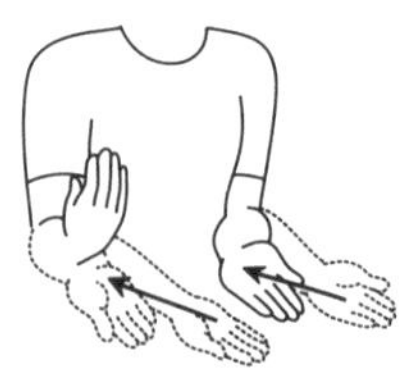

BROUGHT
Palm-up hands at left; move back toward body, right flat hand flips back *(bring + p.t.)*

BROW
Fingertips of palm-out B brush across forehead

BROWN
Palm-left B moves down cheek at side of mouth
(see TAN)

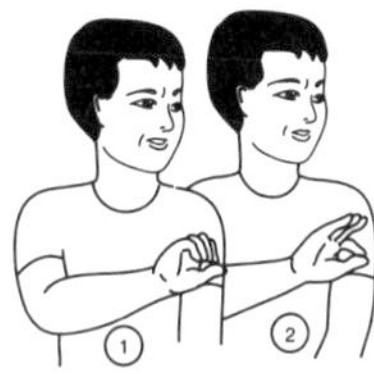

BRUISE
Thumb-side of O on upper arm, open to F *(note: make on body where bruise is)*

BRUSH ✶
Brush top of left hand with back of right fingers several times

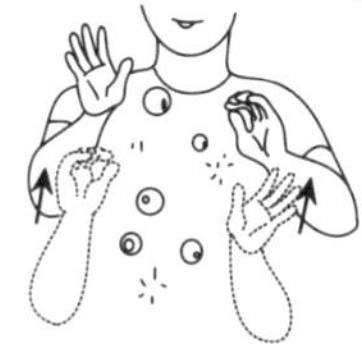

BUBBLE
O-hands rise, alternately opening several times with a flicking motion

BUCKET
B-hand points down at side, rises, still pointing down
(see PAIL)

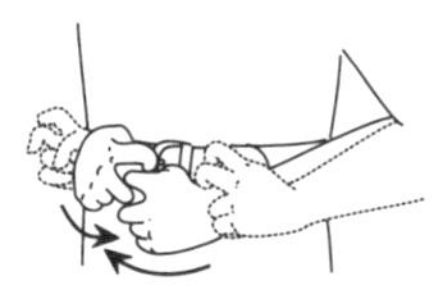

BUCKLE ✶
Bent-V's curve toward each other at waist and mesh
(see BELT)

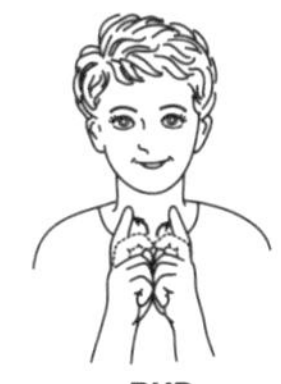

BUD
Palm-to-palm X-hands, index tips touch thumbtips, indexes open like a bud
(see BLOOM)

BUFFALO
Place sides of I-hands at temples

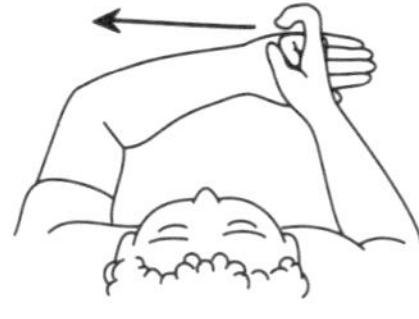

BUFFET
Horizontal palm-left X moves from back of left hand along arm
(see CAFETERIA)

BUG
Thumb of 3-hand on nose, wiggle the two fingers

BUGGY
Palm-out B-hands move straight forward to Y-hands
(see PUSH)

BUILD
Palm-down hands build alternately on top of each other

BULB ♔ ✶
Vertical B-hands, heels together, circle down and together again

BULL
Palm-out Y on center of forehead

BULLDOZER
Right index in the palm of left palm-in hand, push hand forward with index

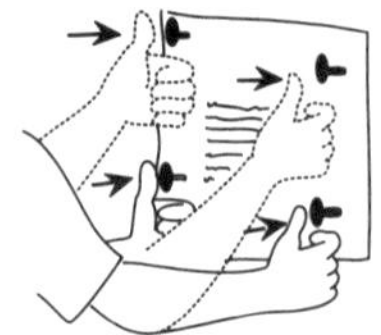

BULLETIN
Extended-A hands tack up bulletin, top and bottom

BUMP ♔★
S-hand hits left palm from behind and bounces back

BUN
Right flat C envelopes left flat-O

BUNCH
Palm-out B's circle out to touch again, palm-in

(see CLASS)

BUNDLE
Right hand pointing down quickly rotates around left hand pointing up

BUNNY
B's at temples, fingers of both hands flop forward and back

(see RABBIT)

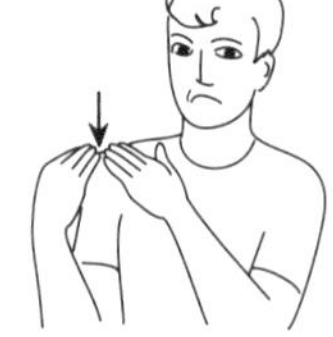

BURDEN
Slightly bent hands push right shoulder down

(see RESPONSIBLE)

BURN ★
Right fingers flutter under palm-in horizontal B

(see HEAT)

BURP
Index points at and touches chest, arcs up slightly

BURY ♔
(Alt. 1)
Palm-down flat hands arc back toward body

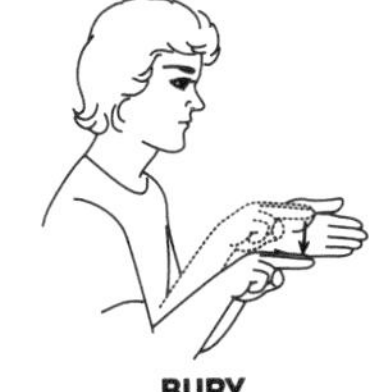

BURY
(Alt. 2)
Flat left hand points forward; right palm-down U against left slides downward

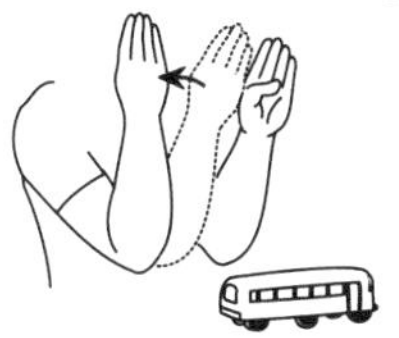

BUS
Left B, palm-right, in front of right B, palm-left; right moves back towards right shoulder

(see CAR)

BUSH ★
Wrist of palm-out B against side of palm-down hand; shake top of B slightly

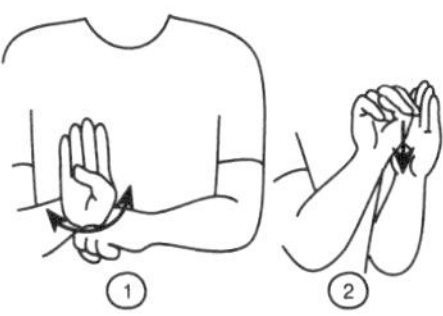

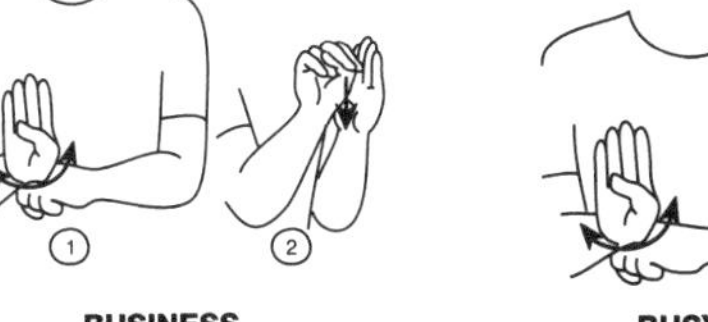

BUSINESS
Palm-out B arcs from side-to-side, hitting back of S-hand; then side of N slides down left fingers and palm *(busy + -ness).*

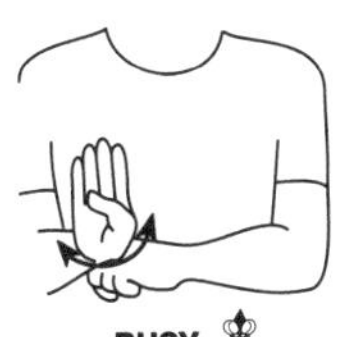

BUSY ♔
Palm-out B arcs from side-to-side, hitting back of palm-down S-hand

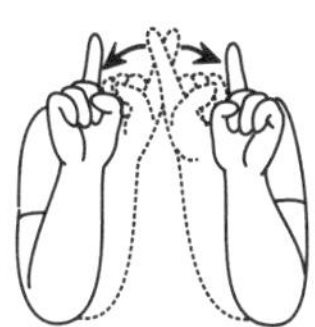

BUT
Palm-out crossed index fingers separate *(wrist action)*

BUTCHER
Thumb of extended-A slices side of neck backwards

BUTTER ♔
U-fingers flick backwards off heel of left hand; repeat

BUTTERFLY
Hook thumbs of palms-in hands and flutter fingers

BUTTON
Side of 9-hand placed on chest arcs down to touch again *(wherever button is)*

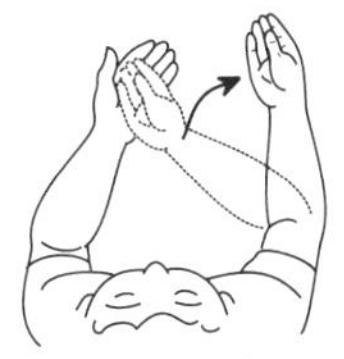

BUY ♔
Back of palm-up flat-O on left palm, lift off, arc forward

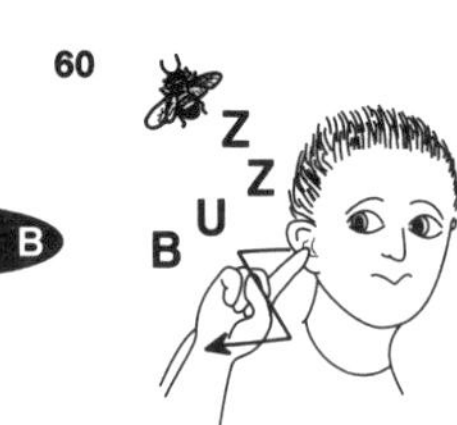

BUZZ
Starting with index finger on ear, draw a letter Z

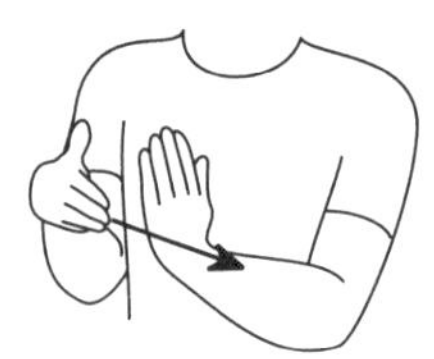

BY
Palm-in right hand points left, brushes by side of left vertical palm-right hand

BYE-BYE
Wave goodbye

CABBAGE
Heel of C-hand taps side of head

CABIN
Palm-out C's draw roof and sides of cabin

(see HOUSE)

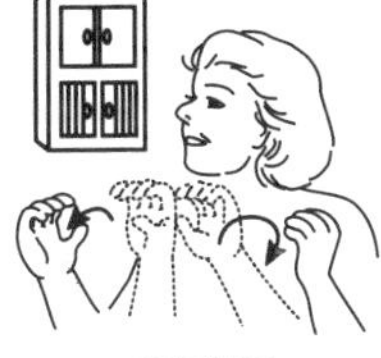

CABINET
Palm-out C's open doors

(see CUPBOARD)

CABLE
Right C moves away from thumb of left C in wavy motion

(see CORD)

CABOOSE
Right C-thumb rubs back and forth on left palm-down U

(see TRAIN)

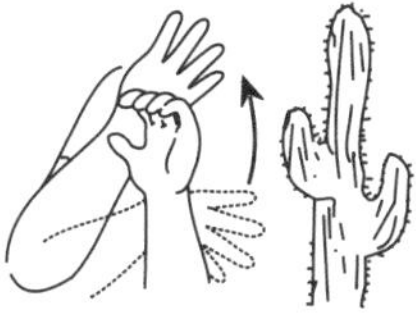

CACTUS
Palm-in right 4 behind left C, raise 4 from pointing left to vertical

CAFE

C fingers tap at corner of mouth

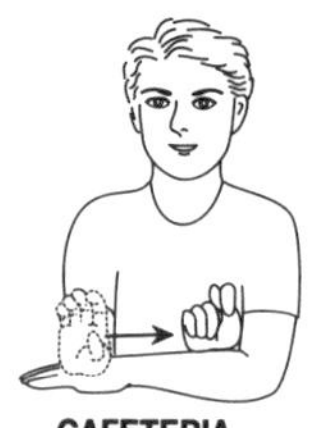

CAFETERIA

(Alt. 1)

Palm-out C on back of hand slides up left arm into T

(see BUFFET)

CAFETERIA

(Alt. 2)

C touches at one side of mouth, then at the other

(see RESTAURANT)

CAGE

Palm-in right 4 hits side of left C

(see JAIL)

CAKE

Fingertips of right claw hand bounce on back of left hand

CALCULATE

Right palm-in V and left C brush past each other sideways; repeat

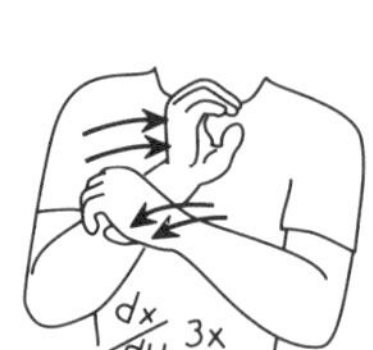

CALCULUS

C's brush past each other sideways; repeat several times

(see ARITHMETIC)

CALENDAR

Side of right C slides up palm-in left hand, over, and down back

CALF

Palm-in extended-A's at corners of head (for calf of leg, just point)

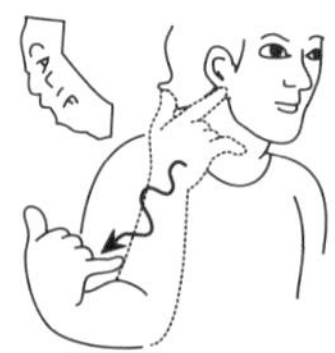

CALIFORNIA

Index at earlobe changes to Y, shaking down and slightly out

CALL

Thumb of right palm-left C touches corner of mouth; hand moves short distance forward

CALM

C-hands slightly crossed near chin, separate downwards

(see QUIET)

CALORIE
Small C moves up left palm
(see COUNT)

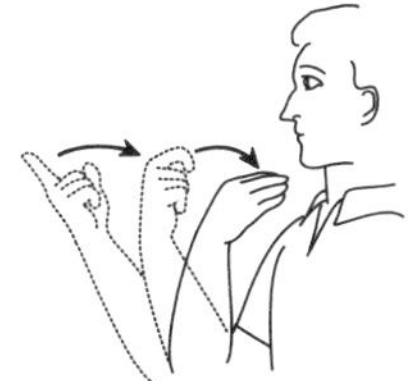

CAME
Palm-up index, points out, beckons once; flat hand flicks back

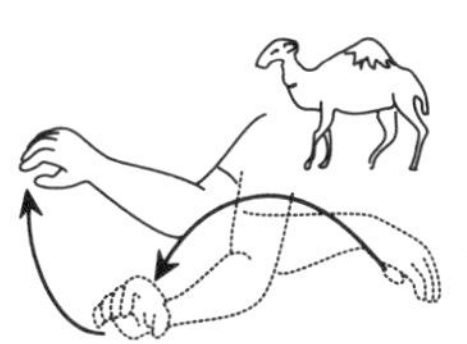

CAMEL
C-hand draws a camel's back

CAMERA
Hold camera near eyes; index finger "clicks the shutter"

CAMP
Tap little and index fingers twice

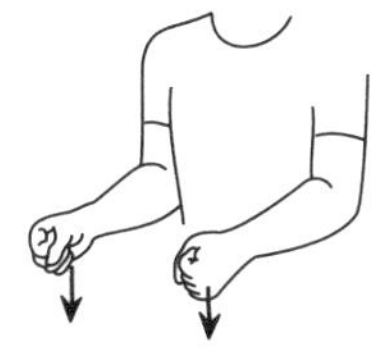

CAN
(Alt. 1)
Horizontal S-hands face each other, drop sharply downwards a short way
(see COULD)

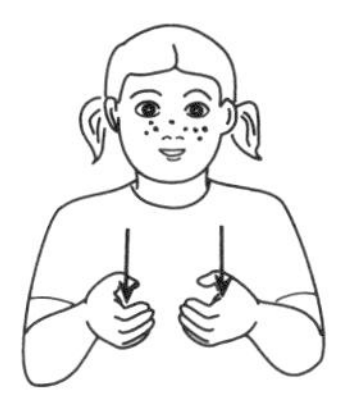

CAN
(Alt. 2)
Horizontal C's face each other and drop a short way
(see COULD)

CANADA
A grasps clothes on right side and taps chest

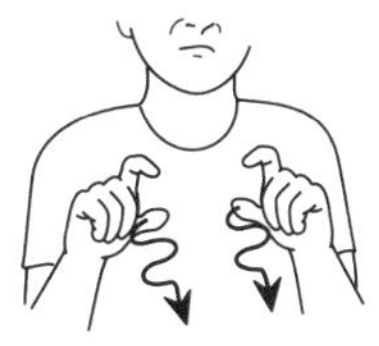

CANAL
Palm-out small C's move forward in wavy motion
(see WAY)

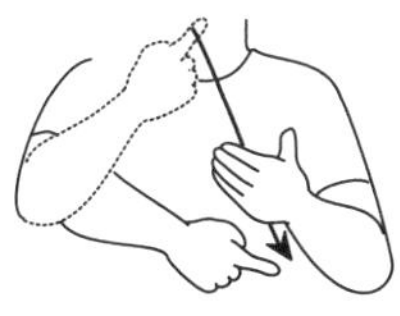

CANCEL
Right index finger slashes diagonally across palm of left hand

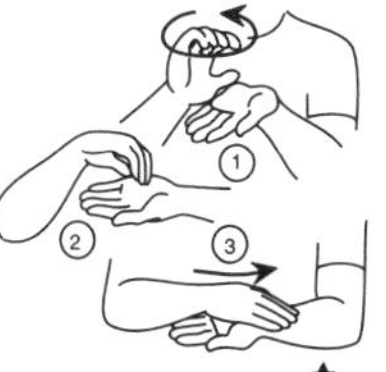

CANCER ♔
C circles on palm, changes to flat-O, opens and spreads up arm

CANDLE
Palm of right 5 on tip of left index finger; flutter fingers

CANDY
Index finger on cheek, twist hand

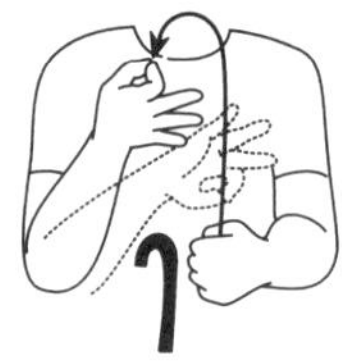

CANE
Lift right 9-hand from left S-hand up into shape of cane

CANNON
Indexes pointing forward, right on left; right shoots forward and recoils

CANOE
Paddle canoe to left and right

CAN'T
Right index strikes down hitting tip of left index *(may also be signed Can + -n't)*

CANTALOUPE
Middle finger thumps top of left C-hand
(see MELON)

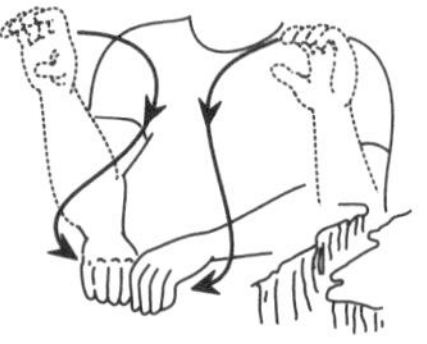

CANYON
C-hands outline canyon
(see VALLEY)

CAP ♔ ★
Flat right hand pats top of left C

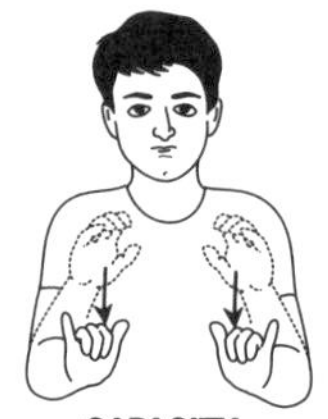

CAPACITY
Palm-out C's drop slightly to Y's

CAPITAL
Thumb of C taps shoulder
(see OFFICE)

CAPITOL
C circles near temple pivoting at wrist, then thumb touches temple
(see GOVERN)

CAPTAIN
Claw hand taps right shoulder twice
(see OFFICE)

CAPTION
Right palm-down 9 draws right from stationary left 9

CAPTURE
Claw hand "attacks" left index; closes, and pulls it back to shoulder

CAR ♔
Right C-hand behind left C; right moves backwards

CARAMEL
Right C on back of flat left hand circles and changes to L-hand

(see CHOCOLATE)

CARD
Right C grasps left palm-in flat hand, then slides off

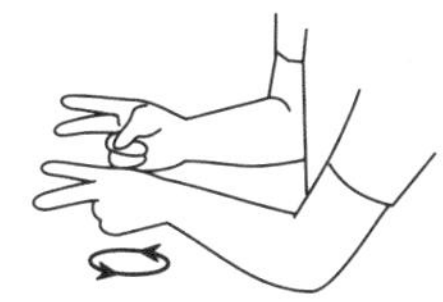

CARE ♔
Right V-hand on left V-hand, both circle horizontally

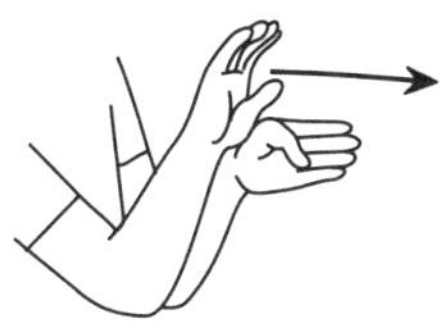

CAREER
Thumb of C slides forward along side of left B-hand

(see STRAIGHT)

CARELESS
Palm-left V fans back and forth at forehead several times

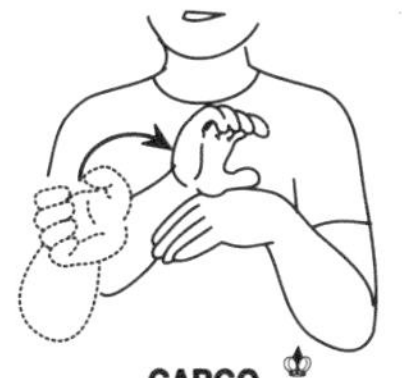

CARGO ♔
Palm-up C arcs over to palm-out on top of palm-down hand

CARNIVAL ♔
Palm-out C arcs down to palm-out L, and moves right

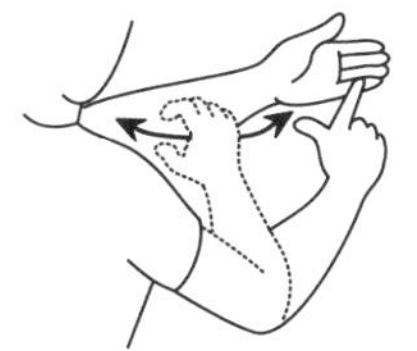

CAROL
Right C swings left, then right to L behind left arm

(see MUSIC)

CARPENTER
Side of S on open left palm moves forward several times like planing

CARPET
Palm-left C-hand drags to the right across back of left hand

CARROT
Scrape top of left C with thumb of extended-A
(see BEAN)

CARRY
Palms-up, move to side in small vertical arcs
(see VESSEL)

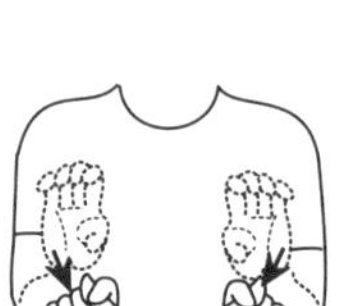

CART
Palm-out C-hands move straight forward to T-hands
(see PUSH)

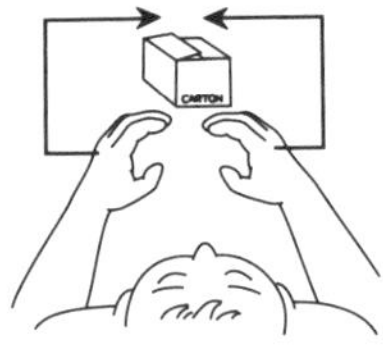

CARTON
Horizontal C's face each other, outline box

CARTOON
Index of C brushes downward twice off nose
(see DOLL)

CARVE
Flat right hand carves side of left C-hand; repeat
(see SLICE)

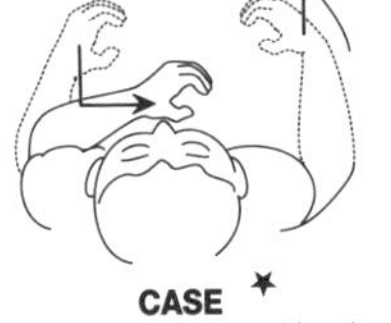

CASE ★
C's outline box, first at sides then front and back
(see BOX)

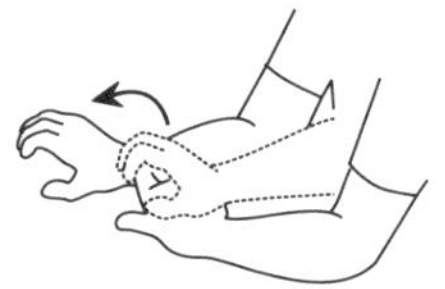

CASH
Palm-out right C on left palm, arcs slightly, moving forward
(see BUY)

CASSEROLE
Slide C under flat left hand as if sliding casserole into oven
(see BAKE)

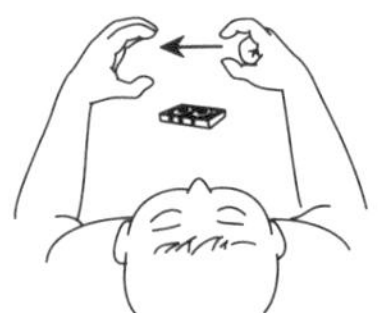

CASSETTE
Horizontal right small C inserts into horizontal left C

CASTLE
Bent-V's build a castle shape

CAT ♔
9-hand draws out whiskers; repeat

CATALOGUE
Right palm-up C grasps side of left hand, slides forward and off
(see MAGAZINE)

CATCH
Palm-out right claw above side of left claw; right drops onto left; both close to S's

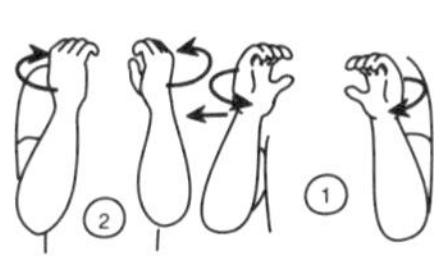

CATEGORY
C's quickly twist from palm-out to palm-in, move sideways and repeat

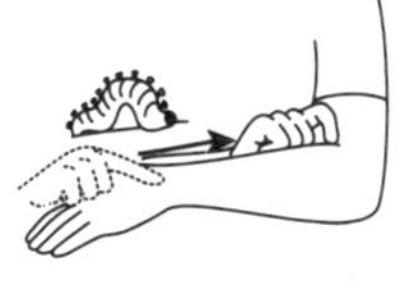

CATERPILLAR ♔
Index alternating with X-finger several times, pulls right hand along left arm

CATHOLIC
Palm-in U-fingers make a cross near forehead, vertical, then horizontal

CATSUP/KETCHUP
Side of K shakes downward like a bottle

CATTLE
Y-hands, thumb of palm-out at temples, twist slightly
(see COW)

CAULIFLOWER
Heel of 9 taps on side of head
(see CABBAGE)

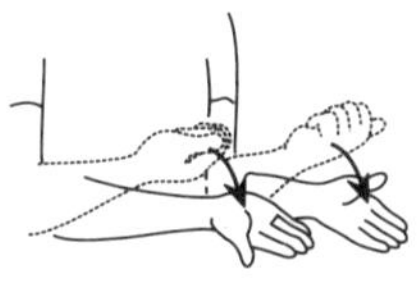

CAUSE
Palm-up A's, left more ahead than right, drop and open

CAUTION
Right palm-out C taps back of palm-down left hand
(see WARN)

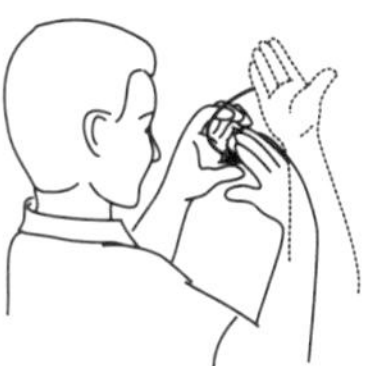

CAVE
Little finger side of right hand hollows out left C
(see HOLLOW)

CEASE
Palm-out right C falls onto left palm
(see STOP)

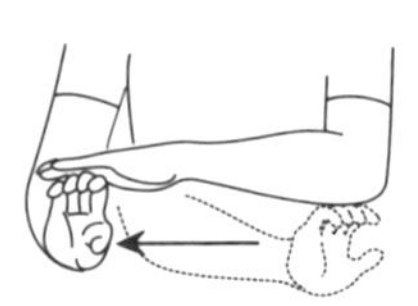

CEILING
Palm-out C-hand slides along underside of left arm from elbow to hand

CELEBRATE
A-hands spiral upward toward head

CELERY
Flat-O grows up through C, twisting to palm-out C
(see GROW)

CELL
Right thumb of small C circles on little finger of left hand
(see ALGAE)

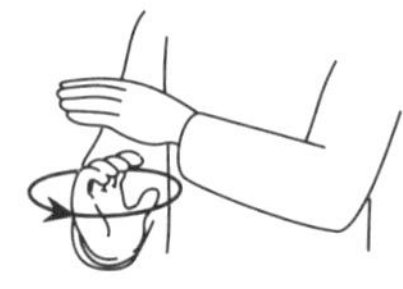

CELLAR
C circles under flat left hand
(see BASE)

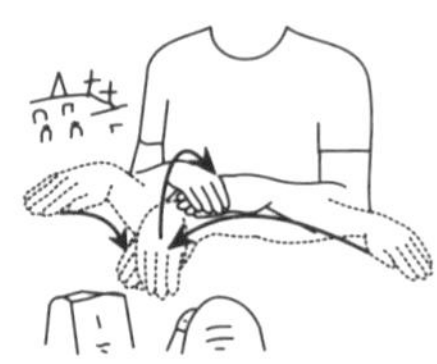

CEMETERY
Palm-down hands arc horizontally toward each other, right rests on left, both arc back toward body

CENT
Touch index finger to forehead, then move hand out with small jerk

CENTER
C circles over, drops on left palm
(see MIDDLE)

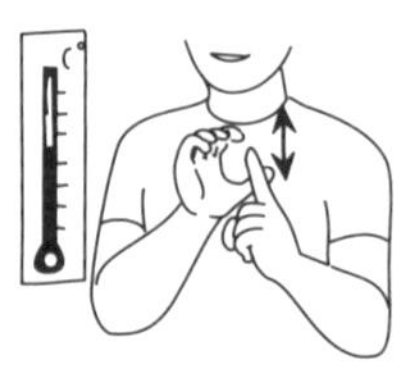

CENTIGRADE
Right C moves up and down behind left index finger
(see THERMOMETER)

CENTIGRAM
Fingerspell C + G
(see CENTIMETER)

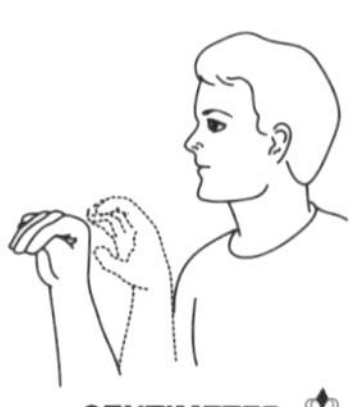

CENTIMETER
Fingerspell C + M

CENTURY

Side of C touches left palm, circles once vertically, then touches again

(see HOUR)

CEREAL

(Alt. 1)

C-hand ladles up to mouth from left hand

(see SOUP)

CEREAL

(Alt. 2)

Index changes to X; repeat, moving sideways under lips

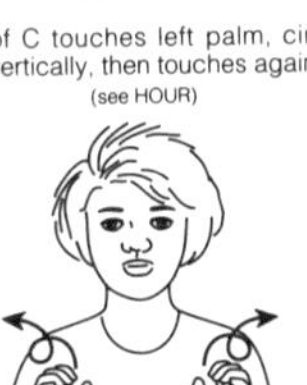

CEREMONY

Palm-out C's circle out and upward

(see CELEBRATE)

CERTAIN ♔

Right C jerks from chin forward and slightly down

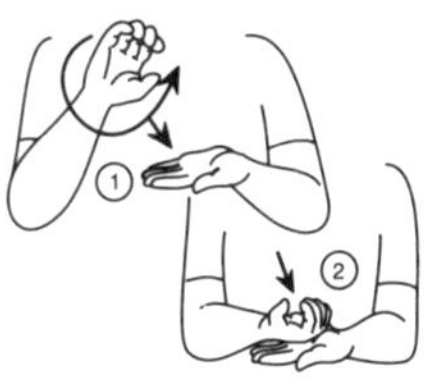

CERTIFY

Right palm-out C-hand inverts and back hits flat left palm

(see WHOLE)

CHAIN

Link 9-hands, release, reverse, and link again, moving slightly right with each reversal

CHAIR

2 fingers "sit" on thumb of left C

(see SIT)

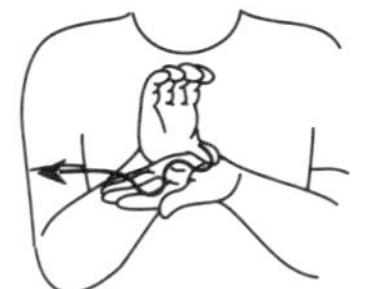

CHALK

Thumb of C writes on left palm

(see WRITE)

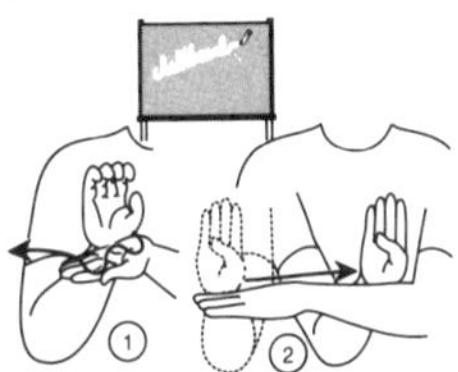

CHALKBOARD

Thumb of C writes on left palm; palm-out right B on back of left arm, moves left along arm to elbow (chalk + board)

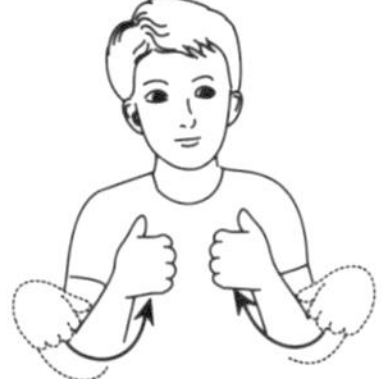

CHALLENGE

Extended-A's point downward then arc toward each other, then upward, but do not meet

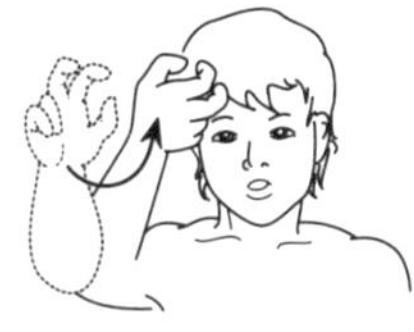

CHAMP

Palm-out bent-3 hand twists inward to top of forehead

C

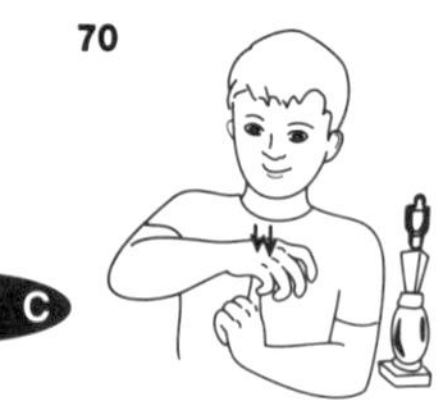

CHAMPION
Palm of claw taps left index

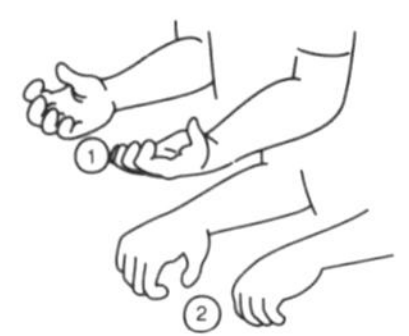

CHANCE
Palm-up C's twist to palm-down C's
(see HAPPEN)

CHANGE
X's touch heels, stay together, twist to reverse hands

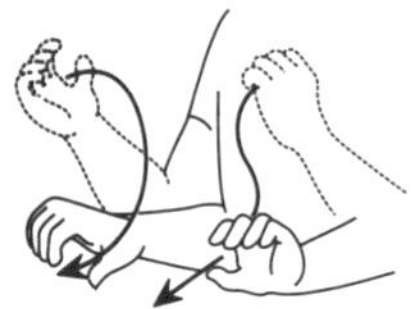

CHANNEL
Palm-in C's twist to palm-out, moving forward and down slightly

CHANT
Small C at mouth arcs forward twice
(see SING)

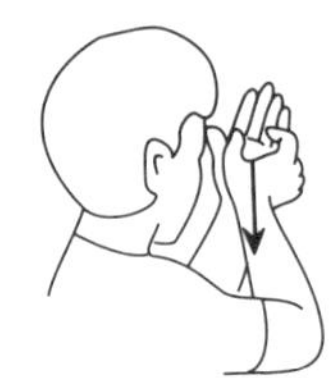

CHAPTER
Thumb and fingertips of C slide down vertical left palm

CHARACTER
C circles clockwise, then touches on left chest

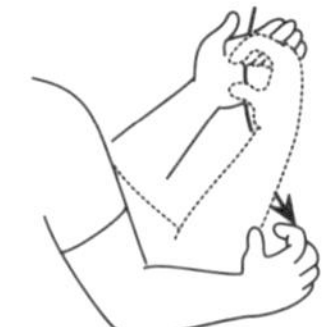

CHARGE
Back of fingers of palm-in C strike downward across left palm
(see COST)

CHARITY
Flat-O at heart moves to palm-up on left palm, both move forward
(see GRACE)

CHARM
Thumb of right C slides down outside of left wrist, wiggling fingers

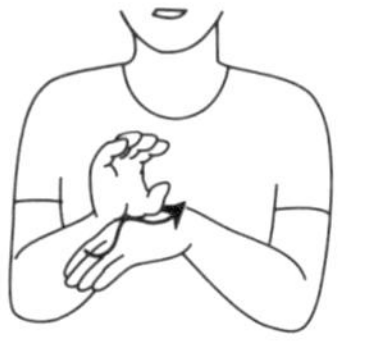

CHART
Thumb of right C draws wavy line backwards on back of left hand
(see MAP)

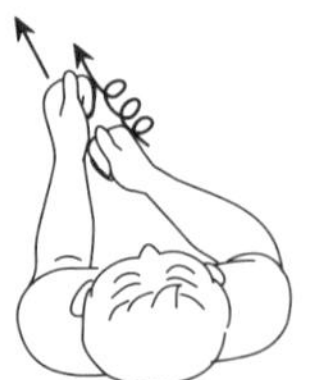

CHASE
Right extended-A behind left extended A; both move forward and left, right hand circling slightly
(see PURSUE)

CHAT

Hands face each other, one near mouth, open and close simultaneously and repeatedly

CHATTER

Heels together, right claw fingertips rise and fall quickly on left several times

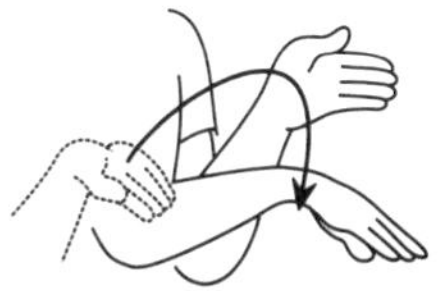

CHEAP

Palm-up right hand turns and slaps down off horizontal palm-right left hand

CHEAT

(Alt. 1)

Horizontal V-hand chops side of palm-down left hand; repeat

CHEAT

(Alt. 2)

Right horizontal I-1 hand, moves right from left wrist to elbow *(putting card in sleeve)*

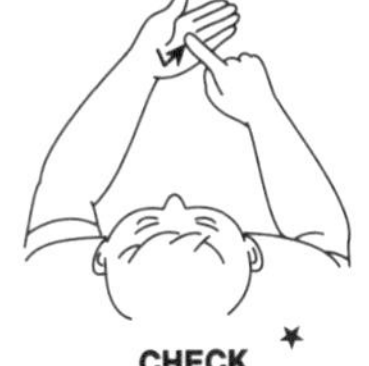

CHECK *

Index finger makes check mark near left palm

(see EDIT)

CHEEK

Thumb and finger grasp skin of cheek

CHEER

Thumb side of C brushes up side of chest; repeat

(see HAPPY)

CHEESE

Hands pointing in opposite directions right heel on left heel mashes and twists slightly

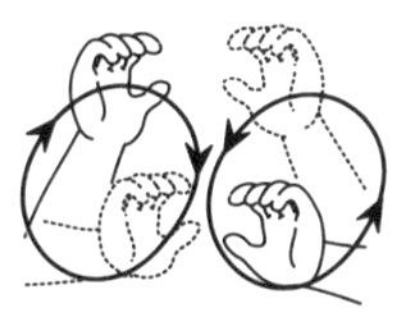

CHEMISTRY

Palm-out C's circle (pour) alternately

(see SCIENCE)

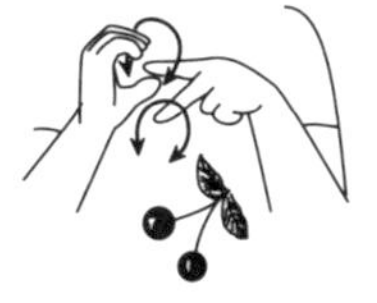

CHERRY

Twist right C first around left hand's upper V-finger, then around lower finger

CHESS

Small C moves chess pieces

C

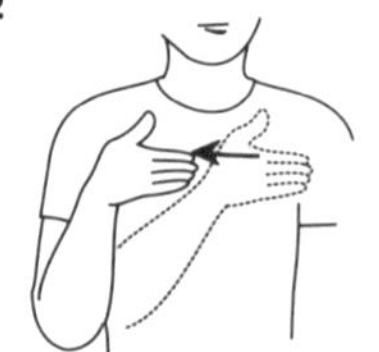

CHEST
Draw hand palm-in across chest

CHEW
Right A circles knuckles on palm-up knuckles of left A
(see DIGEST)

CHICAGO
Palm-out C-hand arcs sharply down to right

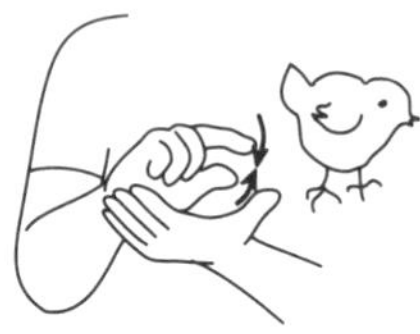

CHICK
G-hand rests on cupped palm-up hand, opens and closes
(see DUCKLING)

CHICKEN
Right G drops from mouth to close on left palm
(see BIRD)

CHIEF
Right C-hand taps top of left index twice

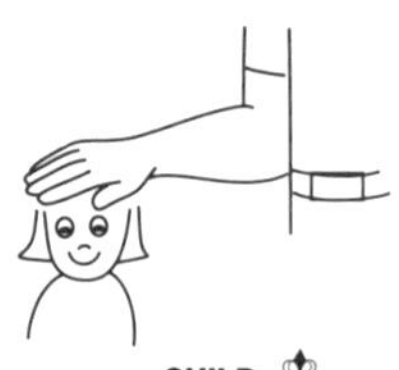

CHILD
Waist high palm-down flat hand indicates child's height

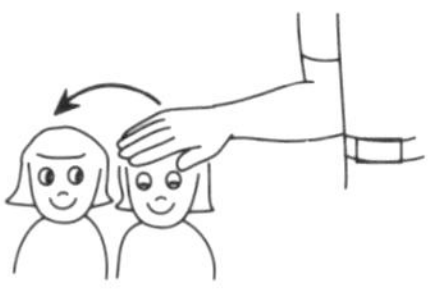

CHILDREN
Palm-down hand bounces to side, waist high

CHILI
Right palm-in claw hand near mouth, twists to palm-out I

CHILL
C-hands face each other, hands shiver slightly
(see COLD)

CHIME
Side of right C against vertical left palm, shakes away to right
(see BELL)

CHIMNEY
Outline chimney upward with C's
(see TOWER)

CHIN
Index finger circles slightly on chin

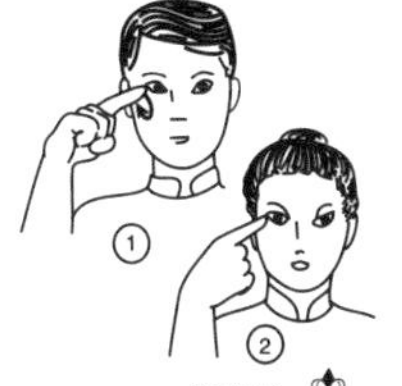

CHINA
Index finger at corner of eye twists slightly inward

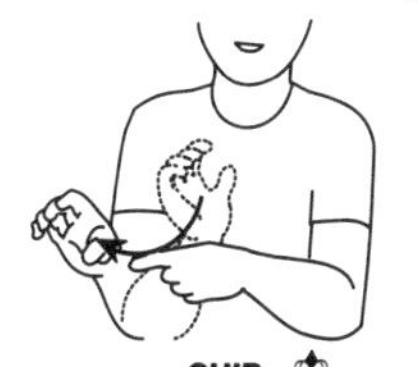

CHIP
Right C arcs down and up, hitting side of left index with thumb

CHIPMUNK
Finger of bent hands under chin flap up and down

CHIROPRACTOR
Thumb of C taps palm-up left wrist
(see DOCTOR)

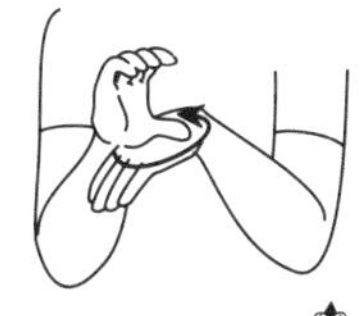

CHOCOLATE
C-thumb circles on back of left hand

CHOICE
Right palm-out C touches index of palm-in V, moves back
(see CHOOSE)

CHOIR
Palm-in C's circle horizontally back to palm-out at shoulders

CHOKE
Right hand chokes self

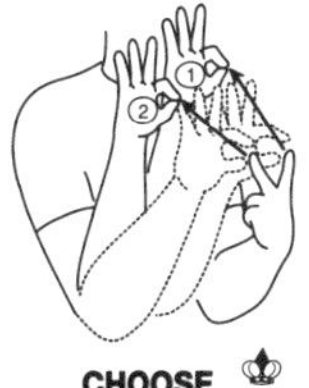

CHOOSE
Thumb and finger of 9 pick index and then middle finger of left palm-in V

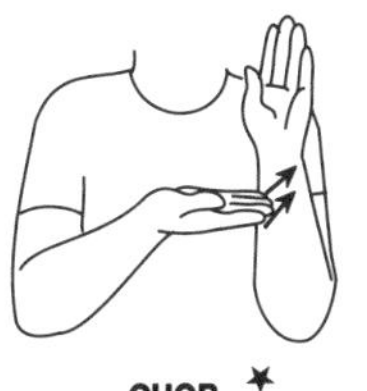

CHOP
Side of palm-up hand chops at wrist of vertical left hand
(see AXE)

CHORD
Right palm-out C touches fingertips of left palm-in horizontal 4; then shakes to right
(see BELL)

CHORE

Palm-down left S, palm-out right small C bounces side-to-side on back of palm-down left S

(see BUSY)

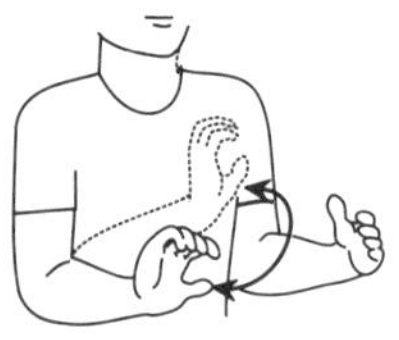

CHORUS

Right C swings back and forth inside left flat hand and left arm

(see MUSIC)

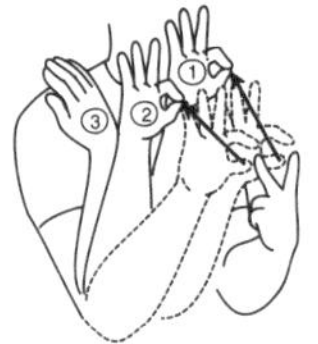

CHOSE

Thumb and finger of 9 pick index then middle finger of left palm-in V; right flat hand flicks back *(choose + p. t.)*

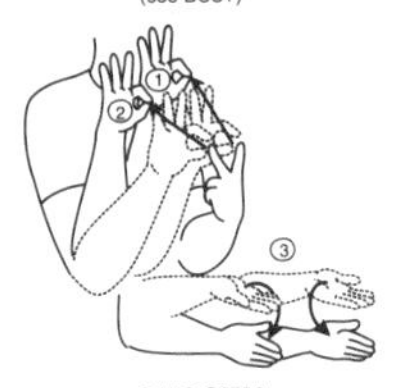

CHOSEN

(Alt. 1)

Thumb and finger of 9 pick index then middle finger of left V; flat hands twist to palms-facing *(choose + p. p.)*

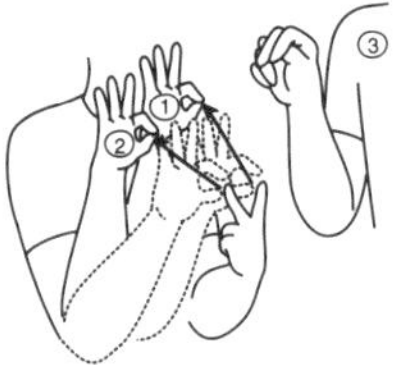

CHOSEN

(Alt. 2)

Thumb and finger of 9 pick index then middle finger of left V; ending in right N *(choose + p. p.)*

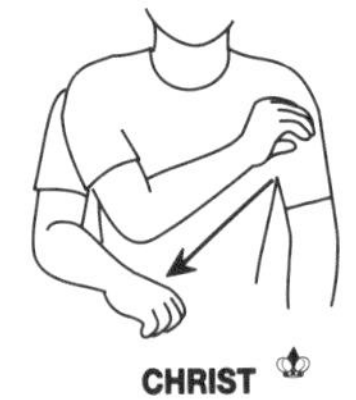

CHRIST

Right C at left shoulder moves to right side of waist

CHRISTMAS

(Alt. 1)

Twist palm-out C inward

(see DECEMBER)

CHRISTMAS

(Alt. 2)

Palm-out C arcs to right

CHUBBY

Claw hands tap on cheeks

(see FAT)

CHUCKLE

Thumbtips of L's at side of mouth, hands stationary, thumbs brush to sides; repeat

(see LAUGH)

CHURCH

Palm-out C thumb taps back of left palm-down S twice

CIDER

Right C-thumb cuts down back of left palm-in S

(see JUICE)

CIGAR
Back of right R-hand resting against chin, fingers wiggle

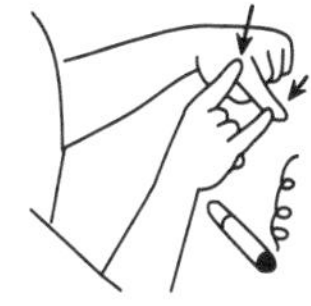

CIGARETTE
Index and little fingers tap on left index finger

CINNAMON
First 2 fingers tap alternately on top of left C-hand
(see SALT)

CIRCLE
Palm-out index finger draws circle

CIRCUIT
Left C; right index touches fingertip, arcs to thumbtip

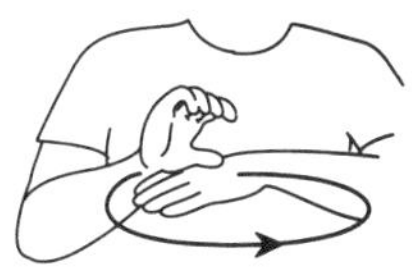

CIRCUMSTANCE
C on back of left hand, both move in horizontal circle
(see STANDARD)

CIRCUS
V-fingertips touch, separate in two sideways arcs

CITE
Right palm-out C drops on palm-in left H-hand
(see NAME)

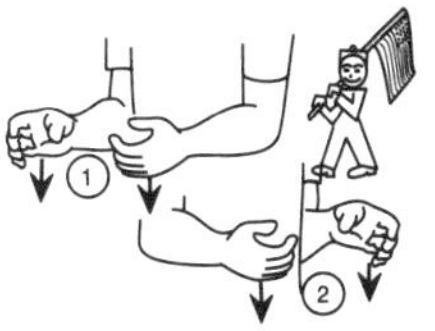

CITIZEN
Both C's, palms-facing, drop downward first at left then at right
(see INDIVIDUAL)

CITY
Tip of palm-out right C taps fingertips of flat left hand while both circle
(see TOWN)

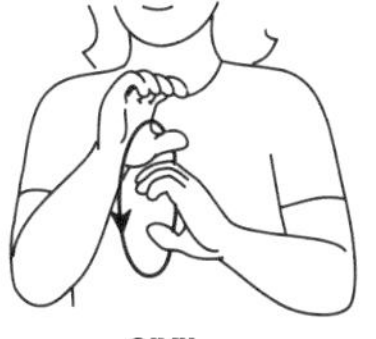

CIVIL
Top C circles left C vertically
(see WORLD)

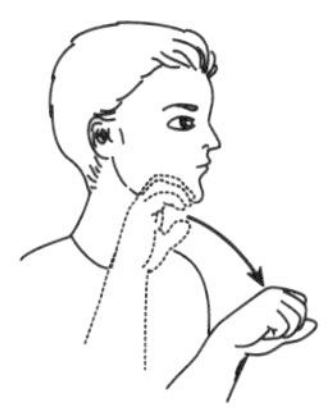

CLAIM
Palm-out C-hand near mouth drops, closing to S-hand
(see ORDER)

CLAM
Palms-together, slightly cupped, right flat hand opens and closes at little finger side

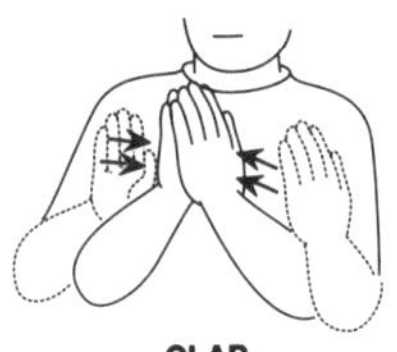

CLAP
Vertical hands clap; repeat

CLASH
A-hands face each other; arc toward each other, opening and meeting sharply

CLASS ♔
Palm-out C-hands circle horizontally out to palm-in

CLAUSE
Palm-out C's separate to L's

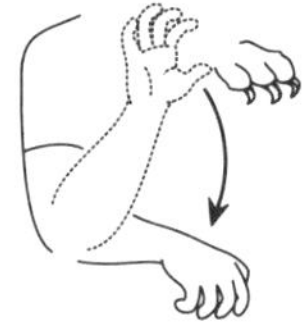

CLAW
Right hand claws forward

CLAY
Cupped hands squeeze clay

CLEAN
Right palm wipes once off left palm
(see NEAT)

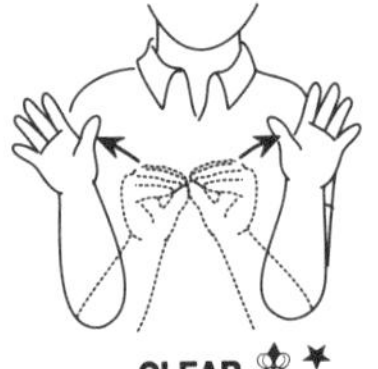

CLEAR ♔ ★
Flat-O's touching tips; open to 5-hands

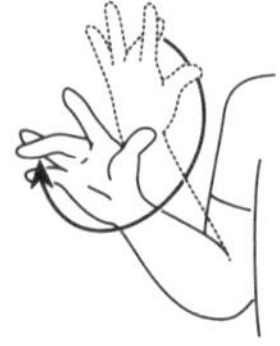

CLEVER
Middle finger bent, palm-in hand flicks to palm-out

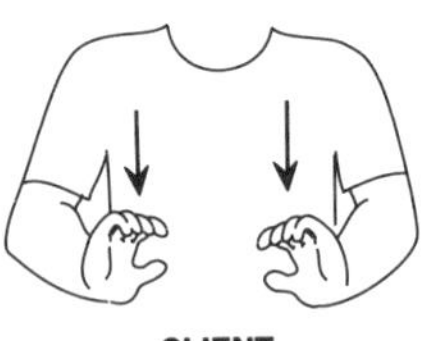

CLIENT
C's move down each side of chest

CLIMATE
Palm-out C hand moves downward in curvy motion
(see WEATHER)

CLIMAX
Flat hands move upward, tips touch to form a peak
(see PEAK)

CLIMB
Palm-out bent-V's climb, alternately

CLINIC
C draws cross on upper arm
(see HOSPITAL)

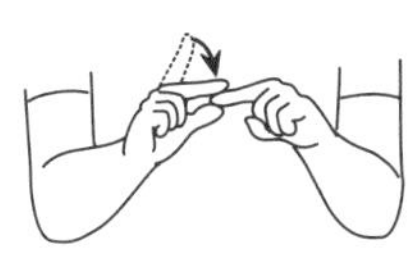

CLIP
Right L clips left index

CLOCK
Index circles clockwise in left C

CLOSE
(adjective)
Side of C approaches back of bent left hand but does not touch it
(see NEAR)

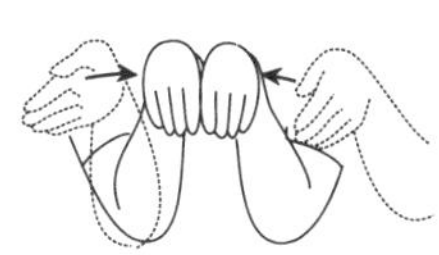

CLOSE
(verb)
Flat hands palms-facing, close to palms-down sides meeting

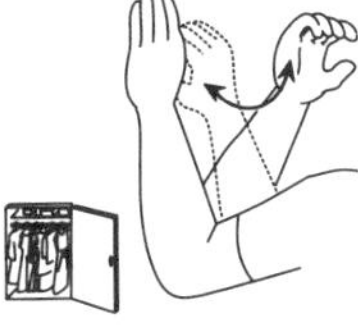

CLOSET
Palm-out C-hand beside palm-out left B opens toward you, then returns
(see DOOR)

CLOTH ♔
Right fingertips rub side of chest

CLOUD
C-hands face each other above eyes; move right in small arcs

CLOVER
Indexes together, right one outlines 3-leaf clover and returns to left fingertip

CLOWN
Palm-in claw hand shakes slightly in front of nose

CLUB ★

C's palms-facing, circle forward and touch as palm-in B's

(see BAND)

CLUE

Palm-out C at eye drops to touch thumb on left palm and traces curvy line forward on palm

(see INSPECT)

CLUMSY

Palm-down 5-hands, fingers slightly curved, move alternately up and down

(see BALANCE)

CLUSTER

Palm-out C's circle outward, changing to palm-in R's

CLUTCH

Grasp thumb of left C

(see HOLD)

COACH ★

Palm-out right C-hand on left index finger brushes back and forth

(see PRACTICE)

COAL

Slide thumb of C across forehead

(see BLACK)

COARSE

Left palm-out C; right claw scrapes forward across fingers of left hand

(see ROUGH)

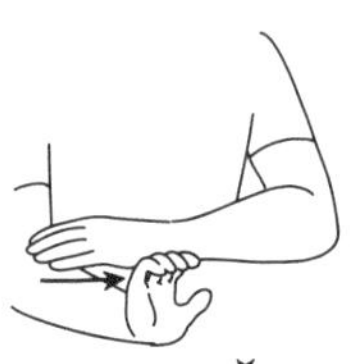

COAST ★

Back of palm-out C moves left along outside of left hand

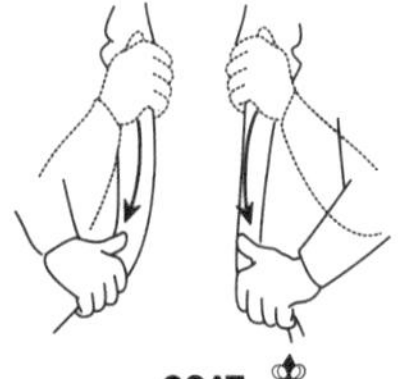

COAT ♔

Extended thumbs of A-hands slide down lapels

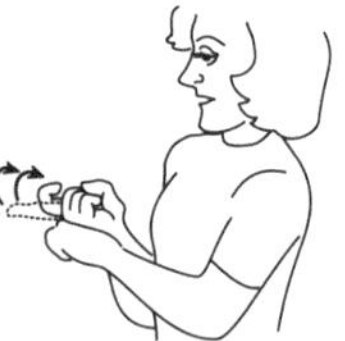

COAX

Right index on back of palm-down S-hand beckons

(see BEG)

COCOA

Thumb of small C traces circle on back of hand twice

(see CHOCOLATE)

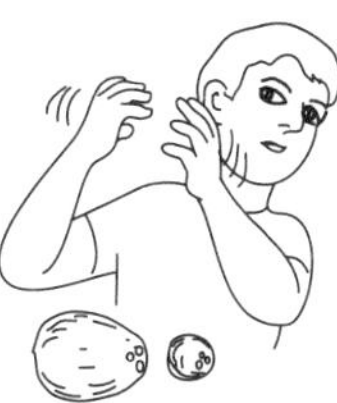

COCONUT
Shake coconut beside ear

COCOON
Palms-in, hook thumbs together, close hands on chest

CODE
Side of palm-out right C against fingers of left vertical palm; both move slightly forward
(see SHOW)

COFFEE
Right-S on left S, right circles in a grinding motion
(see GRIND)

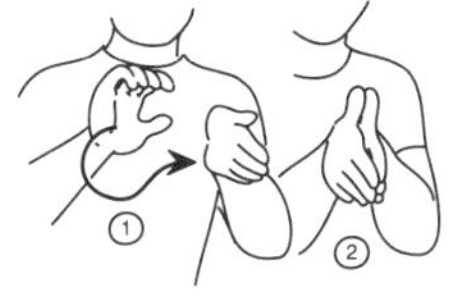

COHESIVE
Palm-out right C flattens against left flat hand

(see ADHESIVE)

COIN
Thumb and index of right 9 lie flat on palm of left hand

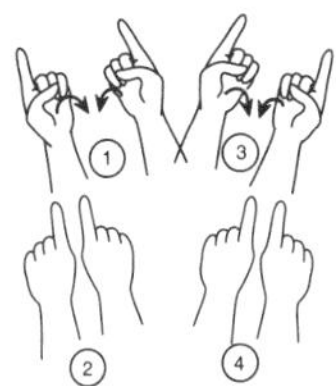

COINCIDE
Indexes extended, hands turn over from palm-up to palm-down, first toward left, and then toward right

COKE
Index of L-hand sticks left arm

COLD
S-hands shake as if shivering

COLE SLAW
Palm-up C-hands toss salad
(see SALAD)

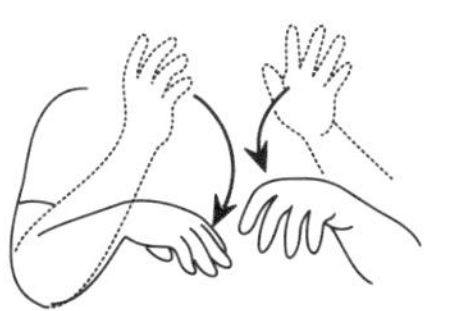

COLLAPSE
5-hands fall toward each other, briefly meshing palm-down, en route
(see CRUMBLE)

COLLAR
Fingers of G draw across neck to front

C

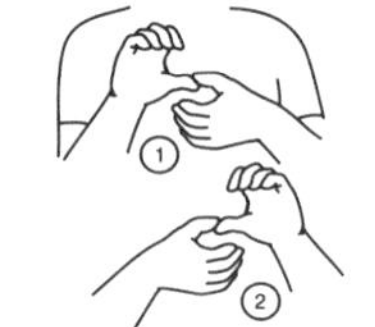

COLLEAGUE
Cross thumb of right C on thumb of palm-up left C; reverse hands
(see FRIEND)

COLLECT
Right hand, fingers together and flapping, circles left palm, gathering in

COLLEGE ♔
Right hand on left, palm-to-palm; right rises, circling

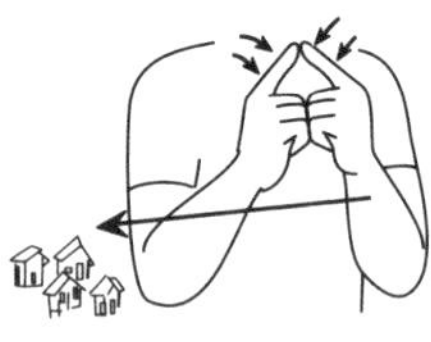

COLONY
With knuckles together, indexes tap moving right
(see TOWN)

COLOR
Fingers flutter in front of chin

COLORADO
Right C-hand above left arm outlines big and small mountains

COLT
C at temple nods twice from wrist
(see HORSE)

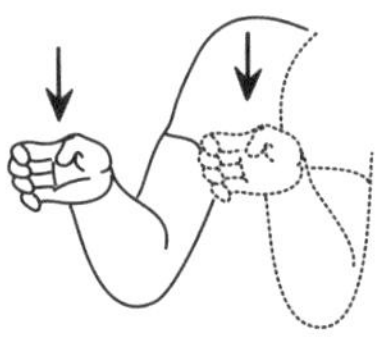

COLUMN
Horizontal palm-out C moves downward, shifts to right, and repeats

COMB ✶
Palm-left claw near side of hair makes a combing motion

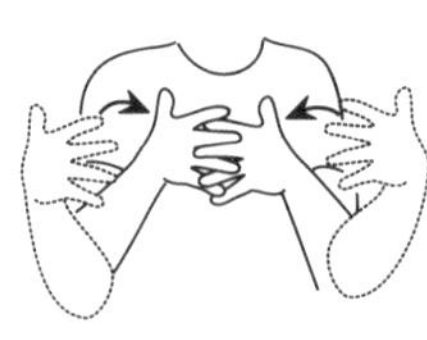

COMBINE
Horizontal 5-hands, palms-in, move together, meshing fingers

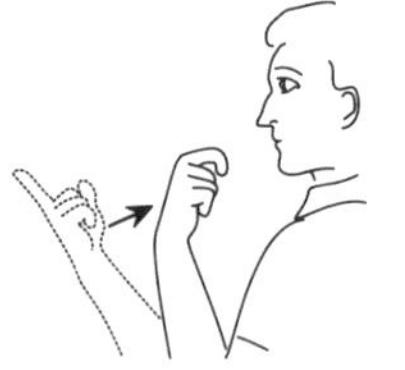

COME
Palm-up index points out; beckons once

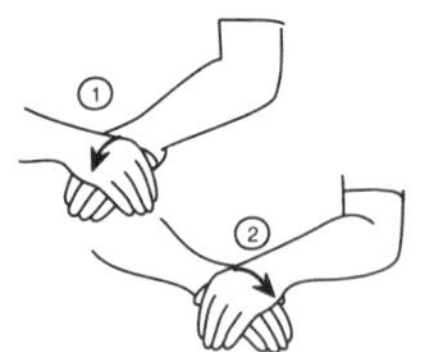

COMFORT
Stroke back of left hand down fingers, then stroke back of right hand
(see COZY)

COMIC
C-hands near face pull up smile
(see SMILE)

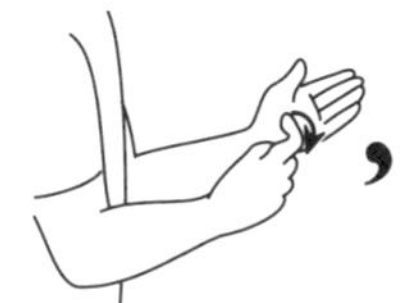

COMMA
Right hand with bent index finger twists to make comma near left palm

COMMAND
Index at chin twists to palm-out C, and moves sharply down
(see ORDER)

COMMANDMENT
Index at chin twists to palm-out C, and moves sharply down; right M slides down left flat hand from fingers to heel *(command + -ment)*

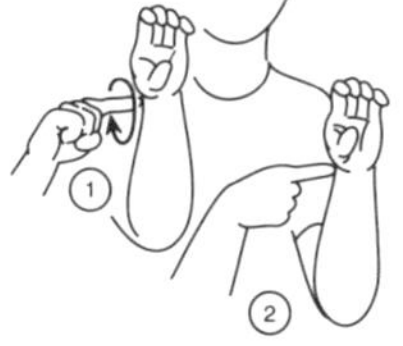

COMMENCE
Index fingertip on wrist of palm-out left C twists to palm-in
(see START)

COMMERCE
C on left S bounces back and forth
(see BUSY)

COMMERCIAL
Right C in front of palm-right left C, moves out and back several times
(see ADVERTISE)

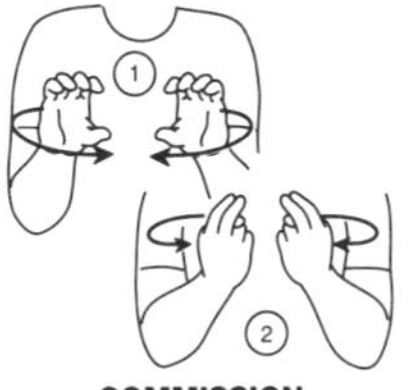

COMMISSION
Palm-out C's circle outwards to palm- in N-hands
(see BAND)

COMMIT
C-hand touches chest, moves forward to open palm-up
(see ADMIT)

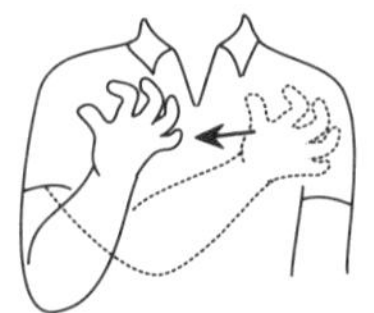

COMMITTEE
Palm-in claw hand on left shoulder, then right shoulder
(see MEMBER)

COMMON
Both palm-out C's move in a horizontal circle
(see STANDARD)

COMMUNICATE
Palms-facing C-hands move alternately to and from chin
(see TALK)

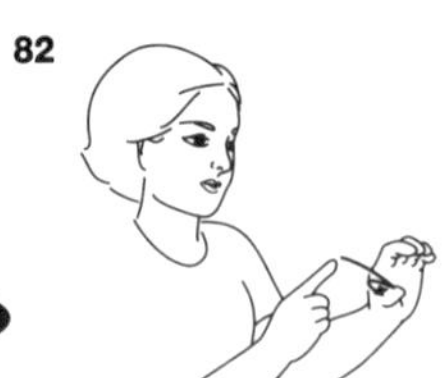

COMMUNIST
Side of right index approaches and hits thumb of left C

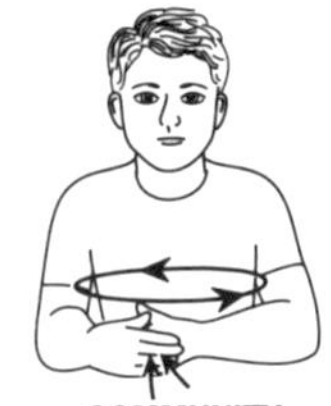

COMMUNITY
Palm of right taps back of left hand repeatedly while circling

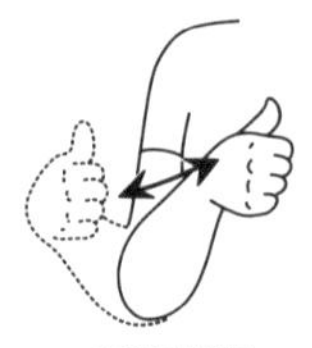

COMMUTE
Palm-in extended-A moves forward right and back; repeat

COMPACT *
Horizontal C's jerk slightly toward each other; repeat
(see SMALL)

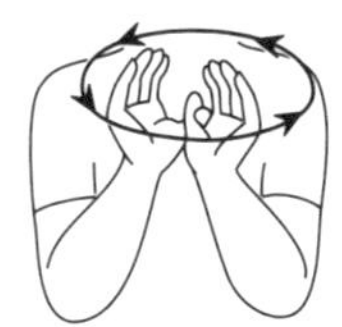

COMPANY
Thumbs of C-hands interlock and circle horizontally
(see STANDARD)

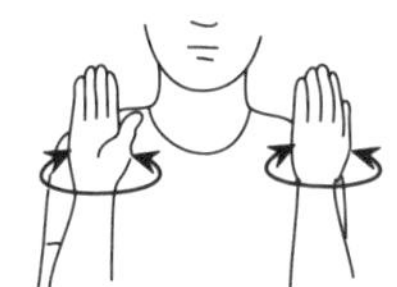

COMPARE
Slightly bent hands alternately pivot in and out several times

COMPASS
Right index finger moves like needle behind left small C

COMPASSION
C at heart, then 5-hands, right behind left, stroke forward with middle fingers
(see SYMPATHY)

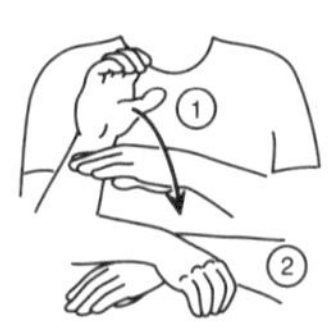

COMPEL
Right C, behind palm-down left, drop forcefully over left hand to palm-down
(see ENFORCE)

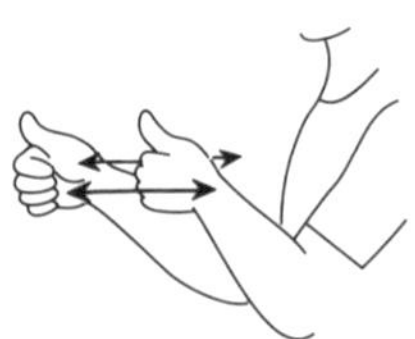

COMPETE
Extended-A's palms-facing, move alternately back and forth, not touching
(see RACE)

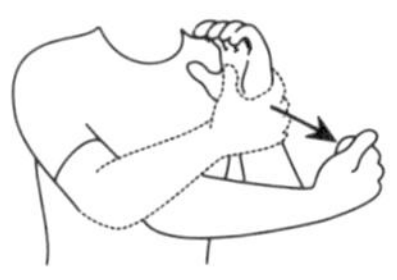

COMPETENT
Right hand grasps side of left C and slides off to A-hand
(see EXPERT)

COMPLAIN
Tips of claw hand tap on chest

COMPLETE
Palm-out C slides along side of left B-hand and down at fingertips
(see FINISH)

COMPLEX
Hands rise alternating X and I-hand, and cross in front of chest
(see COMPLICATE)

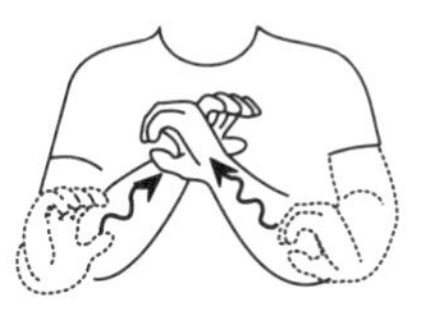

COMPLICATE
C's shaking slightly, rise from sides, to cross in front of chest
(see COMPLEX)

COMPLIMENT
Index at chin drops to flat hand which claps left hand
(see PRAISE)

COMPONENT
Palm-up C-hand arcs slightly up and down to right
(see THING)

COMPOSE
Palms-facing C's at sides; shake C's together to link, right above left

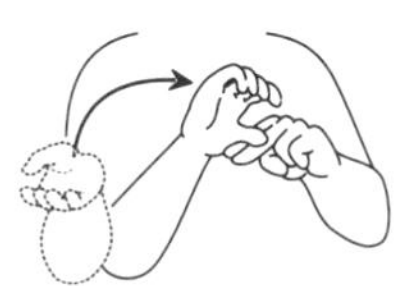

COMPOUND
Palm-up C arcs over to rest on top of left palm-down U-fingers

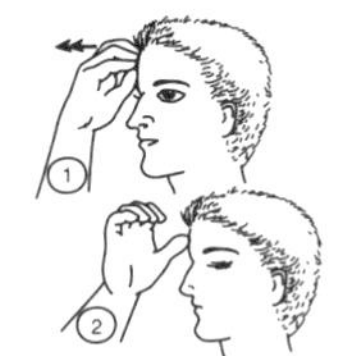

COMPREHEND
Fingertips of flat-O at temple open to C; may repeat
(see UNDERSTAND)

COMPROMISE
Index on forehead, then palm-up C's turn to palm-down, left ahead of right
(see BET)

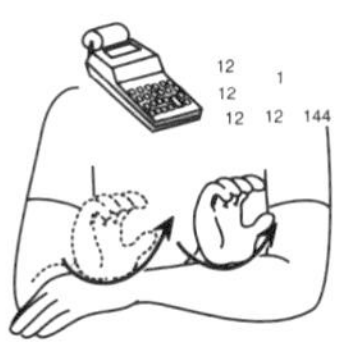

COMPUTE
Right C bounces up left arm

COMPUTER
Thumbtip of right C taps forehead
(can be compute + -er)

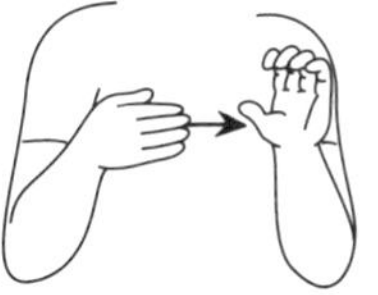

CON
Flat right hand approaches side of left C till fingertips hit side
(see AGAINST)

CONCEAL
Right C moves from chin to under left palm-down flat hand
(see HIDE)

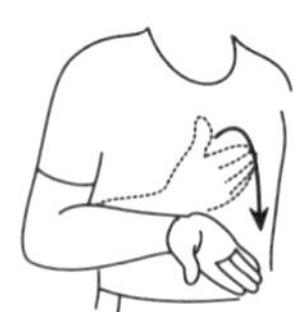

CONCEDE
Flat hand on chest swings to palm-up

CONCEIT
Thumb and bent indexes near head jerk out and slightly forward

CONCENTRATE
C-hands at temples move forward a short distance
(see ATTEND)

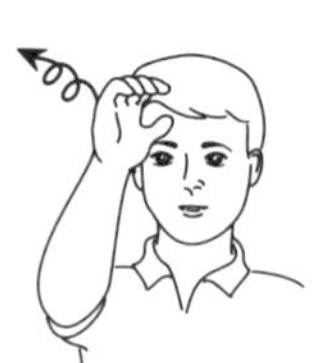

CONCEPT
Thumb of C-hand on forehead; spiral up and out
(see IDEA)

CONCERN
Middle fingers alternately touch chest

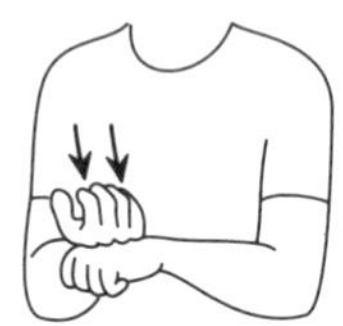

CONCRETE
Back of C strikes back of left palm-down S-hand
(see STONE)

CONDENSE
Right above left, open hands come together as palm-together S's

CONDITION
Right C-thumb in left palm, pull left hand toward body
(see REQUIRE)

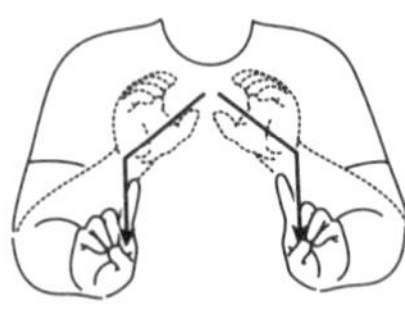

CONDOMINIUM
(Alt.1)
Palm-out C's draw roof, change to D's and drop downwards
(see HOUSE)

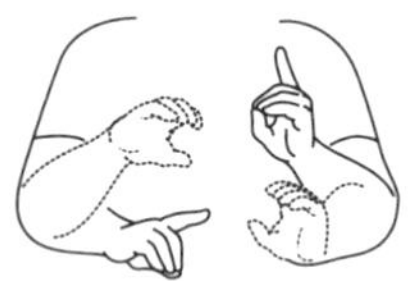

CONDOMINIUM
(Alt. 2)
Parallel palm-out C's change to palm-in D's, left behind right
(see BOX)

CONDUCT ♔ ★
Palm-out C's swing apart and together

CONE
Open palm-out G drops downward narrowing in cone shape

CONFEDERATE
Right C-hand makes confederate flag on chest

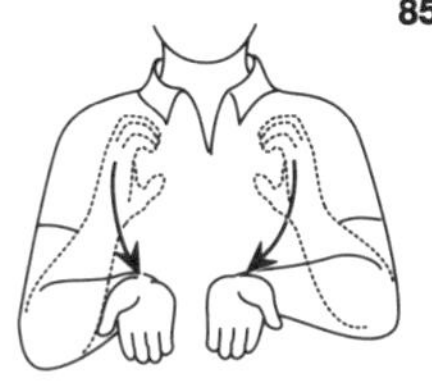

CONFESS
C-hands on chest turn over and out to palm-up open hands
(see ADMIT)

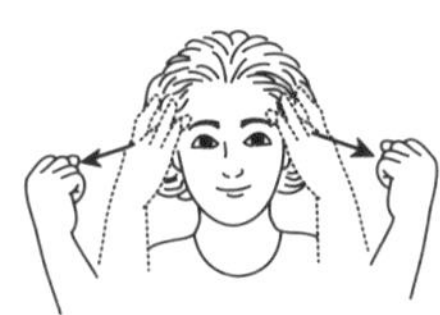

CONFIDENT
Middle fingertips of 5's touch sides of forehead, move forward and close to S-hands

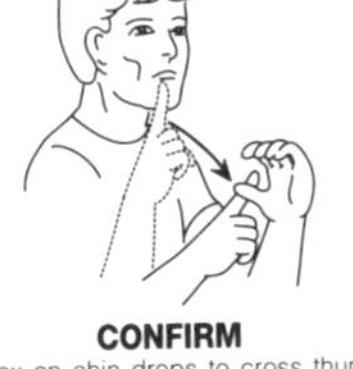

CONFIRM
Index on chin drops to cross thumb of left C
(see POSITIVE)

CONFLICT
Index fingers move forward to cross
(see PARADOX)

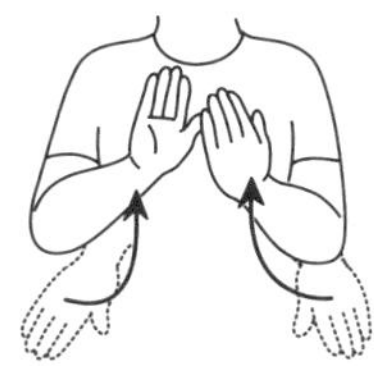

CONFRONT
Palm-down flat hands swing up to face each other, not touching
(see PRESENCE)

CONFUSE
Right index on temple, then both claw hands, right above left, reverse

CONGRATULATE
Clasped hands shake near head

CONGRESS
Side of right C touches left side of chest, then right side
(see MEMBER)

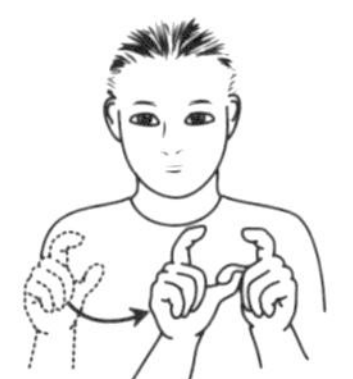

CONJUNCTION
Small C's, right moves towards left and hooks onto left thumb
(see LINK)

CONNECT
G's face each other, come together and link, move linked hands slightly side-to-side
(see AFFILIATE)

CONQUER
Wrist of palm-out right S on wrist of palm-down left S, snap to palm-down, wrist-on-wrist
(see DEFEAT)

CONSCIENCE
Side of index finger taps heart twice
(see GUILT)

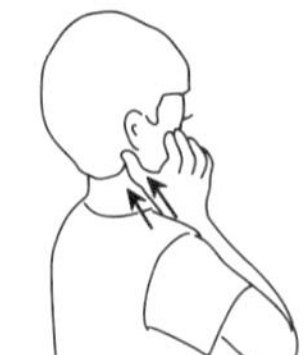

CONSCIOUS
Tip of thumb of C taps head behind ear
(see SENSE)

CONSERVE
Right palm-in V-hand taps side of left palm-right C
(see SAVE)

CONSIDER
Palm-in index fingers circle alternately in front of forehead

CONSISTENT
Thumb of right extended-A on thumb of left extended-A, both move forward in three short movements
(see CONTINUE)

CONSONANT
Palm-out C moves over fingers of palm-in left 5
(see ALPHABET)

CONSOLE
Left hand palm-in near chest, right hand strokes back of left

CONSTANT
C-hands, thumbs touching move forward
(see CONTINUE)

CONSTELLATION
Side of right C strikes upwards off index of 1-hand, then index off C, while moving upwards
(see STAR)

CONSTIPATE
Extended-A thumb moves up into small finger side of left A

CONSTITUTE
Side of right C touches on left fingertips, then on heel
(see LAW)

CONSTRUCT
Palms-facing C's alternately build on top of each other
(see BUILD)

CONSUME
Bent hand arcs past cheek

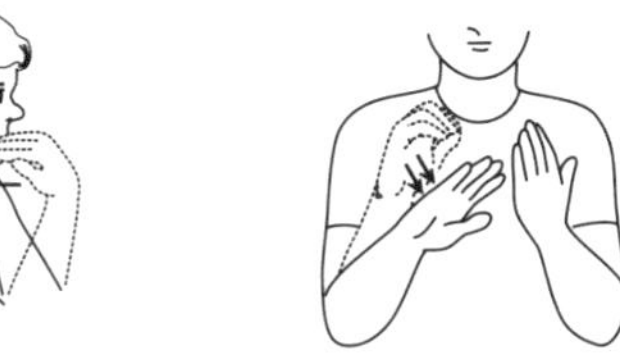

CONSULT
Right flat-O faces left palm, "throws" to open 5 towards palm; repeat

CONTACT
Bent middle fingers, left palm-in and right palm-out, make contact

CONTAIN
Vertical right C-hand drops into horizontal left C

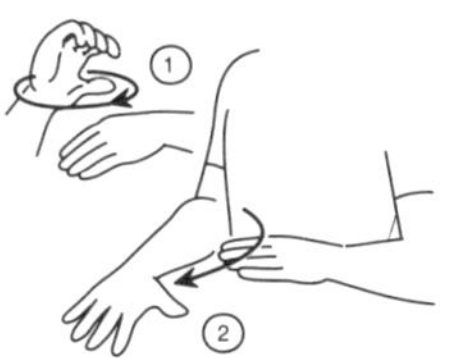

CONTAGIOUS
C circles slightly over left palm-down hand and opens to spread outward
(see INFLUENCE)

CONTENT
(*adjective*)
Sides of C's on chest, one above the other, move down slightly
(see SATISFY)

CONTEST
Small C's face each other, move alternately up and down
(see TOURNAMENT)

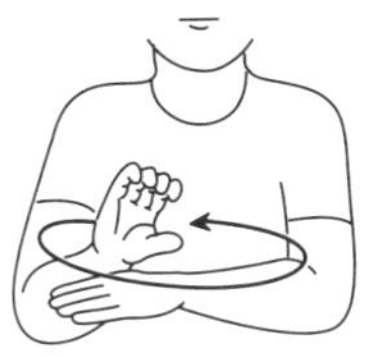

CONTINENT
Palm-out C on back of left hand circles out and back along arm
(see GROUND)

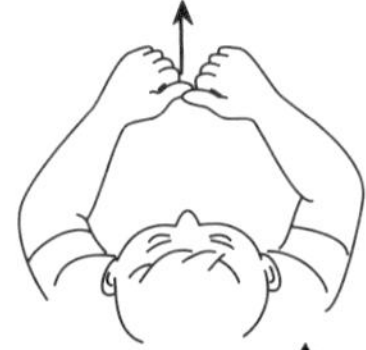

CONTINUE
Thumb of right extended-A on thumb of left A, both move forward
(see MOMENTUM)

CONTOUR
Palm-out C's outline form
(see SHAPE)

CONTRACT
Right palm-down U-fingers tap palm of left hand twice

CONTRAST
Right index points at left palm-out C; jerk hands apart
(see OPPOSE)

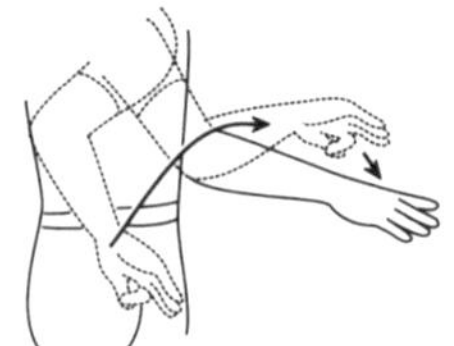

CONTRIBUTE
9 pulls "out of pocket," moves forward and opens to palm-down 5
(see PROVIDE)

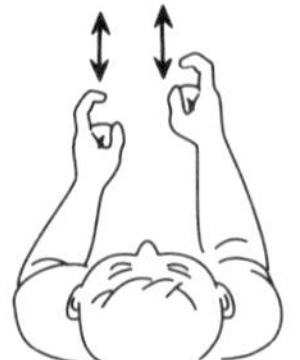

CONTROL
Palms-facing X-hands alternately move forward and back
(see MANAGE)

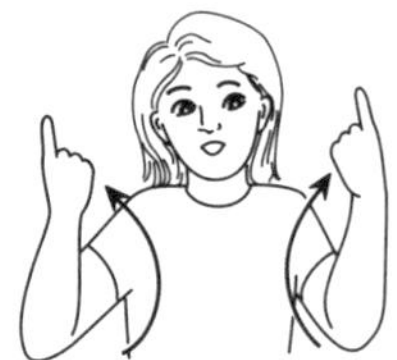

CONTROVERSY
Indexes point at each other; swing sharply up and out

CONVENE
Vertical 5's face each other, come together to meet fingertips in flat-O's
(see ASSEMBLE)

CONVENIENT
Thumb of C brushes up back of bent fingers; repeat
(see EASE)

CONVENTION
Relaxed 5's come togther to meet in flat-O hands; right S slides down left palm-right, vertical hand *(convene + -tion)*

CONVERSE
Bent 4-hands face each other near face, move back and forth from wrists
(see TALK)

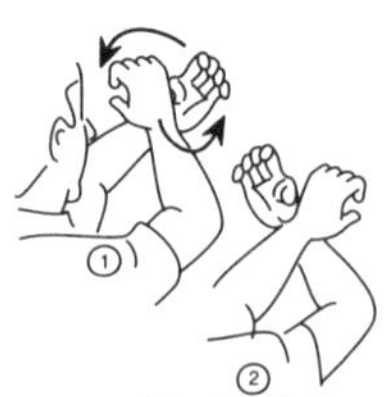

CONVERT
Heels of C's together; reverse position
(see CHANGE)

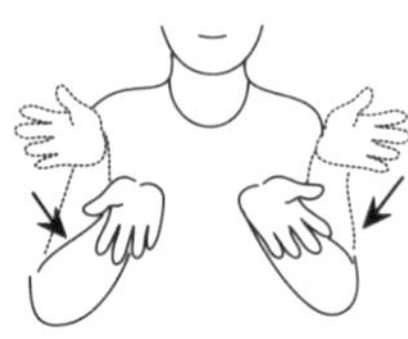

CONVINCE
Palm-up hands jerk sharply toward each other and slightly down

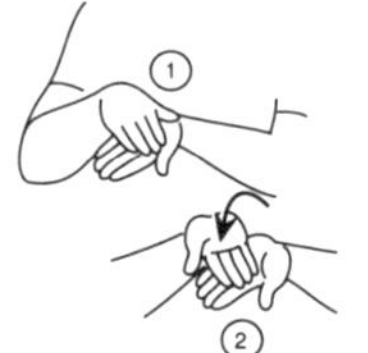

COOK
Fingers of right hand palm-down on left palm, turn over to palm-up
(see FRY)

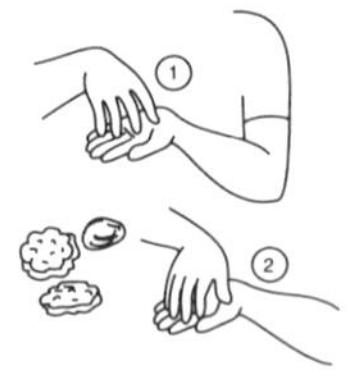

COOKIE
Right fingertips touch left palm, twist and touch again *(cookie cutter)*
(see BISCUIT)

COOL

Palms-in flat hands by sides of head; fingers together flap

COOPERATE

9's interlock; circle horizontally

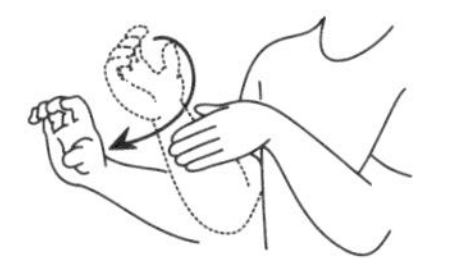

COPPER

Thumb of C arcs right, twisting, hitting side of left index of horizontal palm-in B

(see METAL)

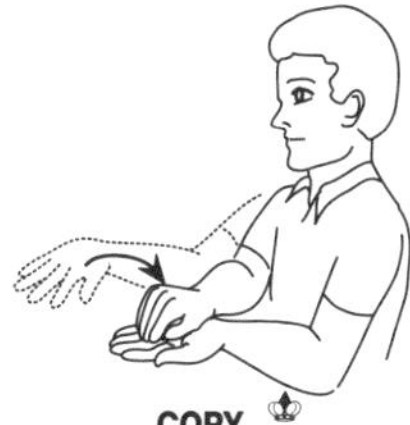

COPY ♔

Palm-down 5 arcs back to make a flat-O on left palm

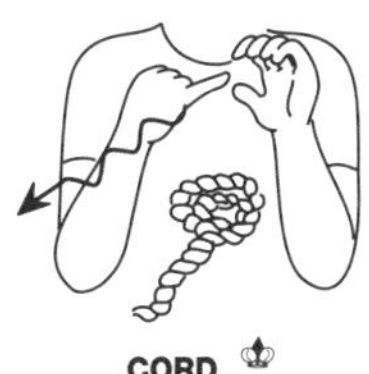

CORD ♔

Right palm-in I-hand wiggles down and to side from C

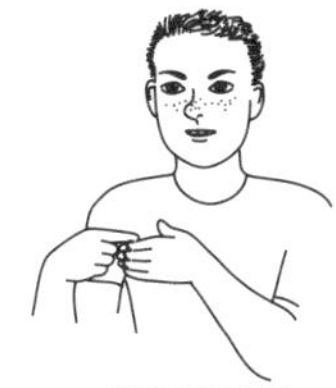

CORDUROY

Left flat palm-in near shoulder, right index points left between fingers, arcing down over each finger in turn

CORE

Right index points towards left small C and circles towards it in coring motion

CORK

Right extended-A thumb pushes cork into side of left horizontal S

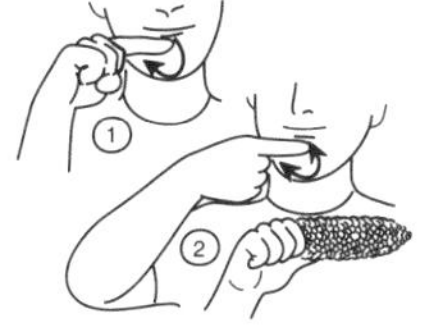

CORN

Palm-down 1-hand twists inward and out near chin

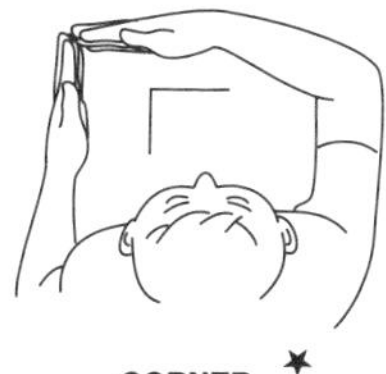

CORNER ★

Fingertips of flat hands tap creating a corner shape

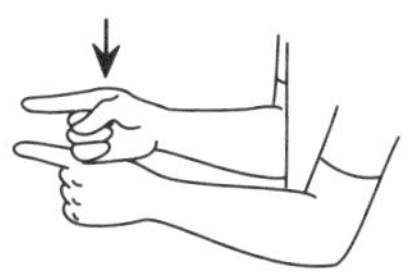

CORRECT

Right 1-hand drops on top of left 1; index fingers at slight angles

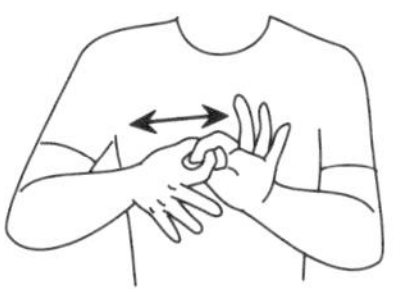

CORRELATE

Interlocked 9's move side-to-side

C

CORRESPOND

Right S-hand slightly behind left S, index fingers flick from S to G-hands toward each other several times *(note: can alternate flicking hands)*

COSMETIC

Flat-O's decorate cheeks

COST

Right palm-in X; knuckle strikes downward on horizontal left palm

COSTUME

Thumbs of C's brush down chest near shoulders; repeat

(see DRESS)

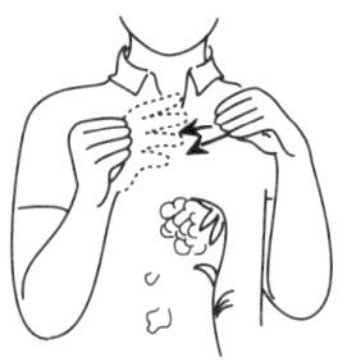

COTTON

Right hand "pulls cotton" off left flat-O to the right; repeat

COUCH

Two fingers sit on thumb of left C; slide off to right

(see SIT)

COUGH

Fingertips of claw remain stationary on chest; hand swings up and down

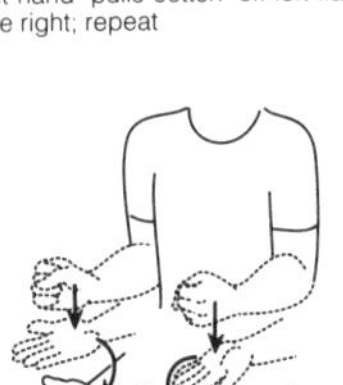

COULD

(Alt. 1)

S-hands palms-facing, drop slightly; then flat hands, palms-up, drop to palms-facing *(can + p. p.)*

COULD

(Alt. 2)

Palm-out right C, near head, arcs forward to D

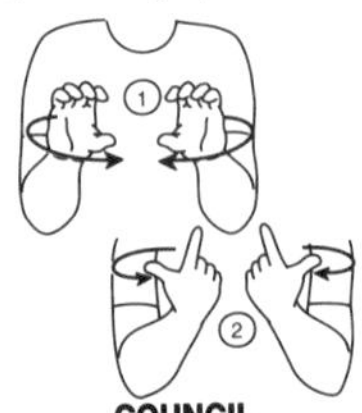

COUNCIL

Palm-out C's circle out to palm-in L's

(see BAND)

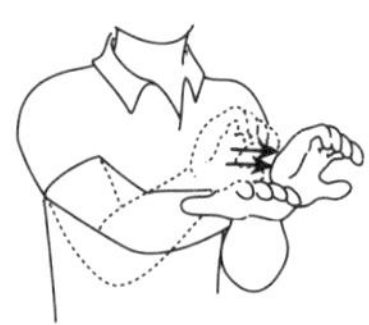

COUNSEL

Palm-out C on back of left hand brushes forward; repeat

(see ADVICE)

COUNT

Thumb and index finger of 9 slide up vertical left palm

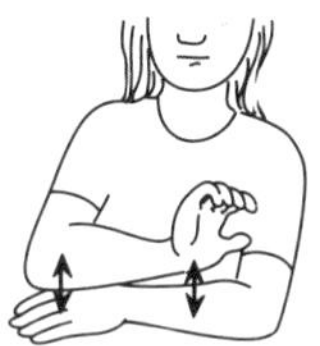

COUNTER
Right C above left elbow, C and elbow bounce on left arm
(see TABLE)

COUNTRY
Palm-in Y rubs arm in circle near elbow

COUNTY
C circles on left elbow
(see COUNTRY)

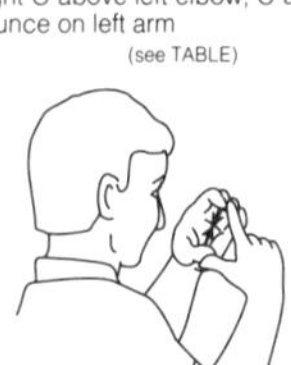

COUPLE
Thumb and finger of right hand close fingers of C to left thumb
(see PAIR)

COUPON
G's, tips touching, separate and close, outlining coupon

COURAGE
Bent middle finger on heart, then hand moves out to palm-in S

COURSE
Side of C touches left flat fingertips, then heel of left hand
(see LESSON)

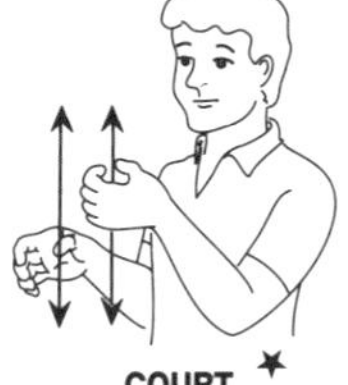

COURT
Horizontal C-hands, palms-facing, move alternately up and down
(see BALANCE)

COURTESY
Side of C-hand taps upward twice in middle of chest
(see FINE)

COUSIN
Shake C near ear
(see AUNT)

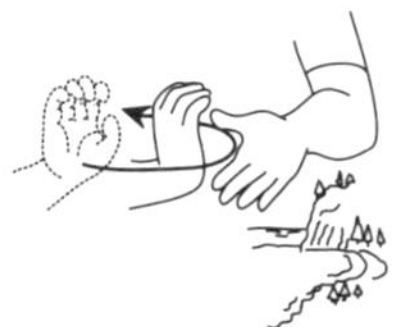

COVE
Right C outlines curve of palm-down left thumb and index
(see BAY)

COVER 
Curved hand, palm-up, turns to cover left S-hand

COW
Thumb of Y on side of forehead, twist slightly down
(see CATTLE)

COWARD
Palm-out C's, right slightly behind left, shake downwards
(see AFRAID)

COZY
Small C's, stroke thumb side down back of opposite hand, alternating hands
(see COMFORT)

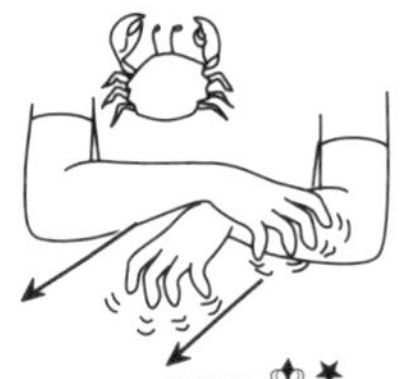

CRAB ♔ ★
Crossed hands move forward to right, wiggling fingers

CRACK ★
Palm-left flat hand outlines crack in wall

CRACKER ♔
Palm-in A taps arm near elbow

CRACKERJACK
Make C and J at left elbow
(see CRACKER)

CRADLE
Right U in left C, both hands palms-up, rock both

CRAFT
Thumb of palm-out small C draws wavy line on left palm
(see ART)

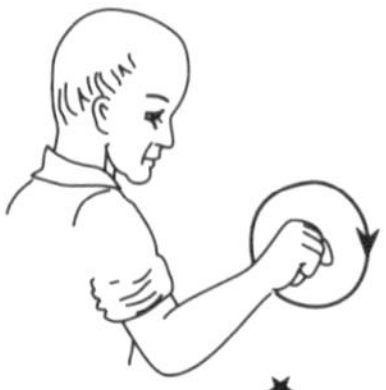

CRANK ★
Right fist cranks

CRASH
Right palm-in S hits side of left C
(see BUMP)

CRAWL
Inverted bent-V's twist from "knee to knee" across left palm

CRAYON
Fingertip of index circles on left palm

CRAZE
Index rotates near temple

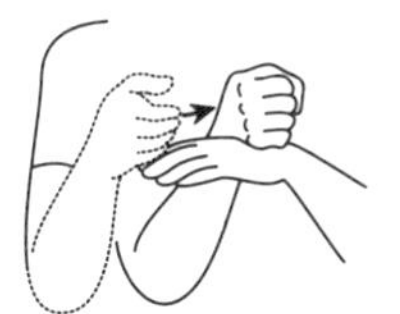

CREAM ★
Horizontal right C changing to S-hand moves across back of left hand

CREATE
Horizontal C's, right on left, both twist to palm-in
(see MAKE)

CREDENTIAL
Tips of C-thumbs tap
(see LICENSE)

CREDIT
Horizontal C's, right on left, both arc up toward body
(see BORROW)

CREEK
Palm-out C's ripple up and down while moving forward
(see BROOK)

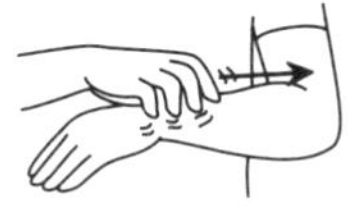

CREEP
Fingers creep up left arm
(see CATERPILLAR)

CREW
Palm-out C's circle out to touch as palm-in W's
(see BAND)

CRIB
Mesh fingers downward

CRICKET
Palm-out C rides forward on wiggling fingers of left hand
(see ANT)

C

CRIED
(Alt. 1)
Drag index fingers alternately down cheeks; flip right hand toward shoulder *(cry + p. t.)*

CRIED
(Alt. 2)
Drag index fingers alternately down cheeks; add D-hand. *(cry + p. t.)*

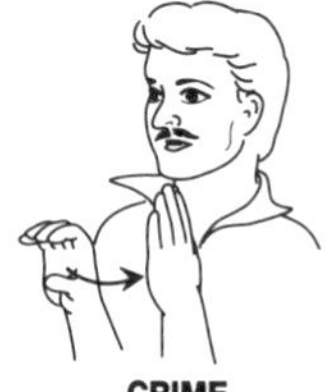

CRIME
Side of right C hits forcefully against vertical left flat hand
(see FORBID)

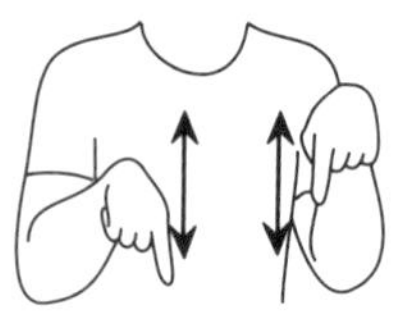

CRIPPLE
1-hands point down; alternately move up and down

CRISIS
Palm-down bent-V's grip each other and pull apart

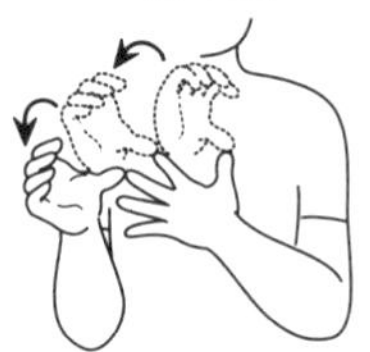

CRITERIA
Palm-in left 5, pointing right; thumb of palm-out right C touches left thumb, index and middle fingers
(see PRIORITY)

CRITIC
Index makes large X on left palm
(see DISCRIMINATE)

CROCHET
Cross horizontal index fingers; right slides off end of left into X; repeat several times

CROCODILE
Top "jaw" of C snaps open and closes, C-heels touching

CROISSANT
Palm-out G's touch, separate and close, drawing croissant shape

CROOKED
(Adjective)
B's pointing forward, right on left; right moves forward in zigzag motion

CROP
C brushes up through left C twice
(see GRAIN)

CROQUET
Bend over with mallet and strike ball to left

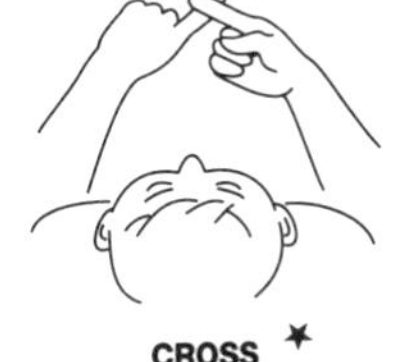

CROSS ★
Palm-in right index on palm-down left index
(see HYBRID)

CROW ★
Flat-O at chin opens and closes beak
(see BIRD)

CROWD
Horizontal S's approach each other, then press outward, lifting shoulders *(elbowing through a crowd)*

CROWN ★
C's hold crown above head, put it on

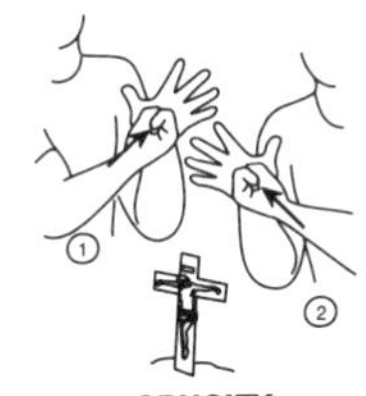

CRUCIFY
Side of S strikes left palm at side; reverse hands, strike palm on the other side

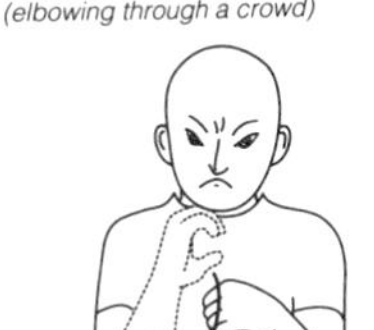

CRUEL
Thumb of C strikes across back of left S

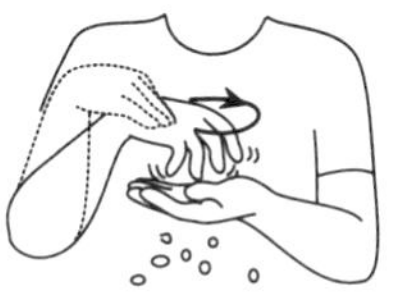

CRUMB ★
Right flat-O above left palm opens to scatter crumbs in circling motion, fingers fluttering

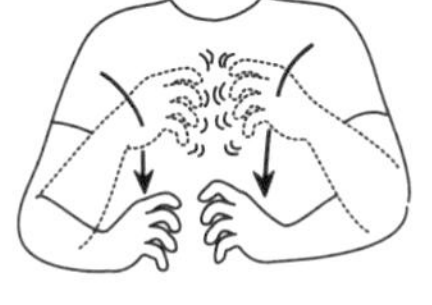

CRUMBLE
Palm-down 5's point at each other, converge downward, fingers fluttering
(see COLLAPSE)

CRUNCH
Right palm-down A on left palm-up A; twist forcefully
(see CRUSH)

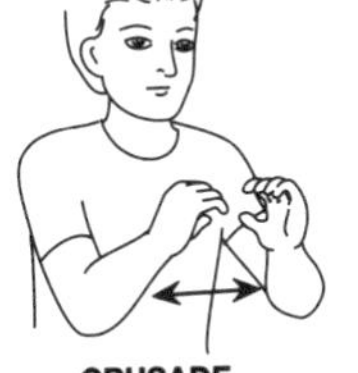

CRUSADE
C's face each other and move from side-to-side
(see WAR)

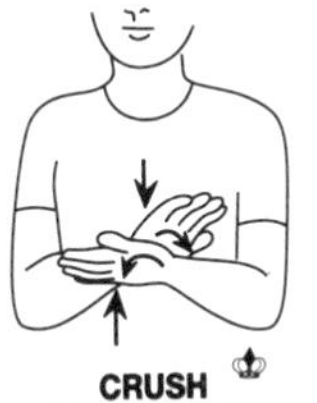

CRUSH
Heels of 5-hands twist forcefully on each other

CRUST
C moves around edge of left hand
(see EDGE)

CRUTCH
Right C approaches and pushes up little finger side of palm-in fist
(see SUPPORT)

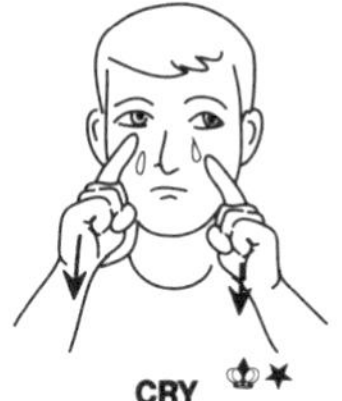

CRY ♔ ★
Drag index fingers alternately down cheeks, marking tear-tracks

CRYSTAL
Thumb of small C taps teeth

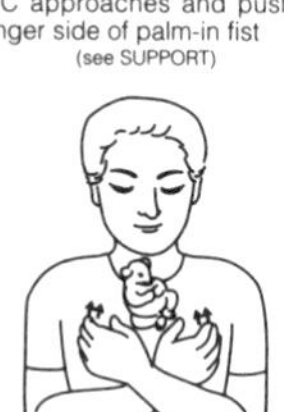

CUB
Cross wrists of palm-in C-hands, fingertips tap chest

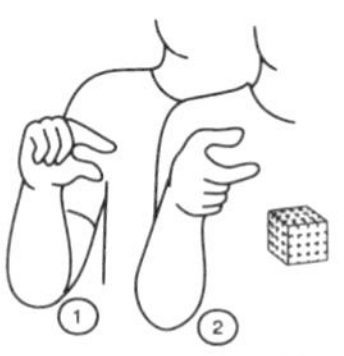

CUBE ★
Thumb and index of G-hand outline 2 sides of cube

CUCUMBER
Right index slices past thumb side of C several times
(see TOMATO)

CUFF ★
Thumb and index finger outline cuff on left wrist

CULTURE
Right C curves around vertical left index finger
(see ATMOSPHERE)

CUP ★
Right X-hand is set on left palm *(as if holding a cup handle)*

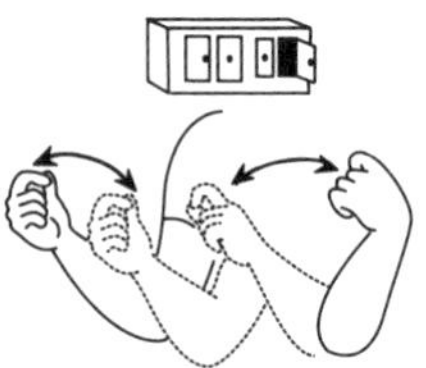

CUPBOARD
Indexes and thumbs open and close cupboard doors
(see CABINET)

CUPID
Right fist pulls back to a horizontal V from left C-hand
(see ARROW)

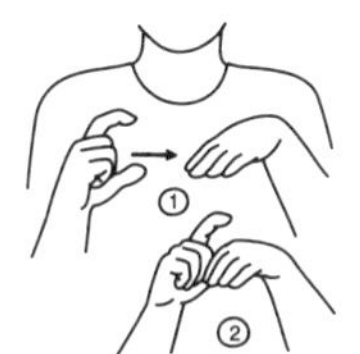

CURB

Left B palm-down; right small C approaches until stopped by left hand

(see GRIP)

CURE

Palm-out C's turn over and slide closed to palm-up A's

(see MELT)

CURIOUS

Right 9 on throat twists

CURL ✶

Index outlines curl from ear down

CURRENT ✶

Palm-down flat hand flows through left C-hand

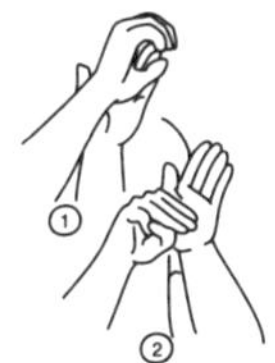

CURRICULUM

Side of C on fingers of vertical left palm, then side of M on heel

(see LAW)

CURSE

(Alt. 1)

Palm-in right C from front of mouth strikes side of vertical left index

(see BEAT)

CURSE

(Alt. 2)

Palm-down Y above left horizontal index shakes along index and off

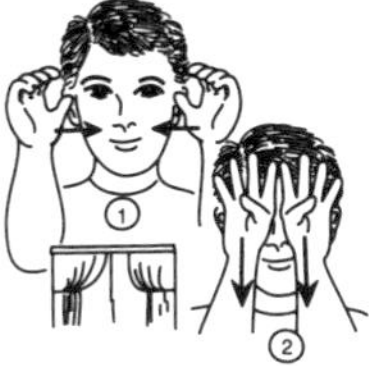

CURTAIN

C-hands meet in front of face, change to 4's and slide down

(see DRAPE)

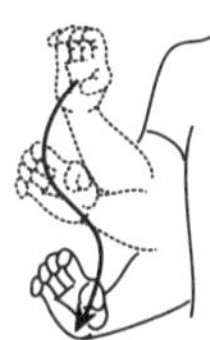

CURVE

Palm-out C curves downward

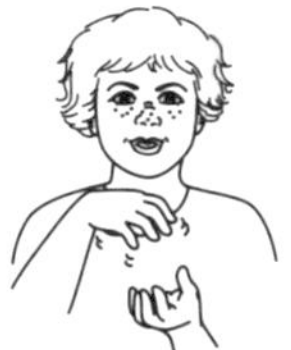

CUSTARD

Claw hands, palms-facing, right above left, right hand shakes slightly

(see JELL)

CUSTODY

Left horizontal V, right C on top, both circle horizontally

(see CARE)

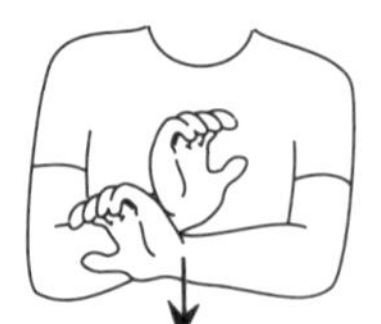

CUSTOM
Wrist of right C on wrist of left C, both drop slightly

(see HABIT)

CUT
V-fingers snip off end of middle fingertip of flat left hand

CUTE
Palm-in U-fingers brush chin down to N; repeat

(see SUGAR)

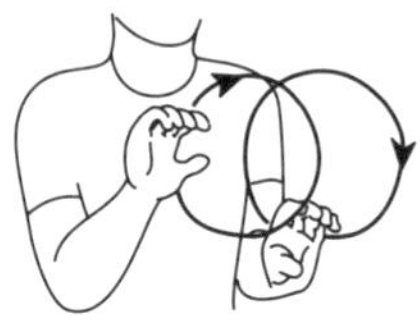

CYCLE
Palm-out C's alternately pedal forward

(see BICYCLE)

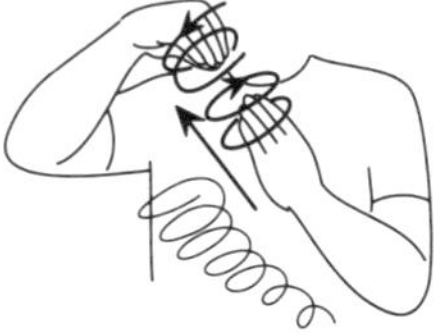

CYCLONE
Flat-O's, right above left, rotate around each other, rising to the right

(see STORM)

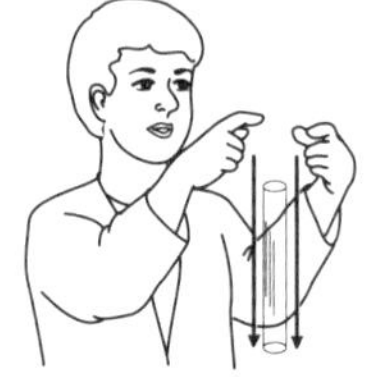

CYLINDER
Slightly to one side, small horizontal C's face each other and drop, outlining cylinder

CYMBAL
Holding cymbals with A's strike cymbals together

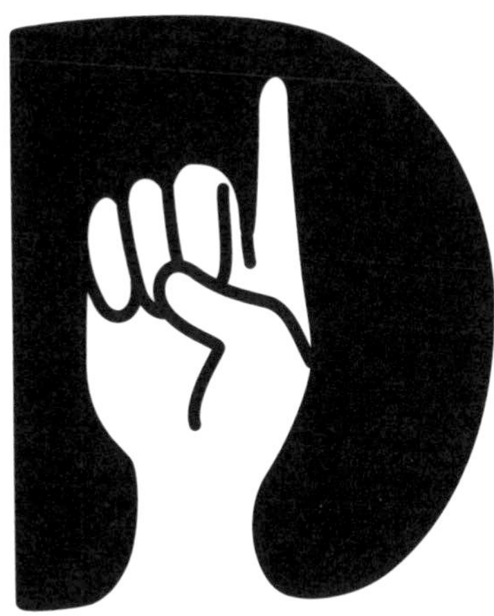

DAD
D touches temple
(see FATHER)

DAFFODIL
Palm-left D on side of nose, twists to touch other side
(see FLOWER)

DAILY
A on cheek, brush forward; repeat
(note; may be made as day + -ly)

DAISY
G-hand plucks petals from left index

DAM
Palm-down left hand points right; palm-out right D approaches and is stopped by side of left hand
(see IMPAIR)

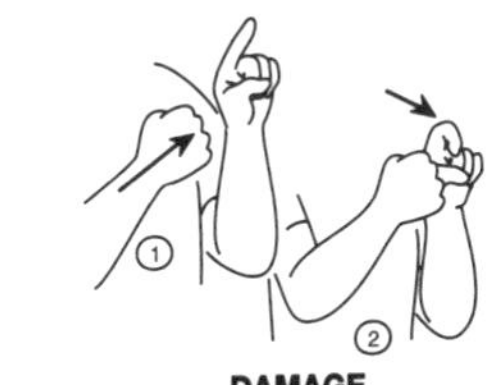

DAMAGE
Right S strikes side of left I-hand; left index bends to X
(see BUMP)

DAMN
D moves sharply to the right

(see HELL)

DAMP
Left hand palm-up, right 5 palm-in at chin; right drops to palm-up flat O on left palm, opens slightly and closes

(see WET)

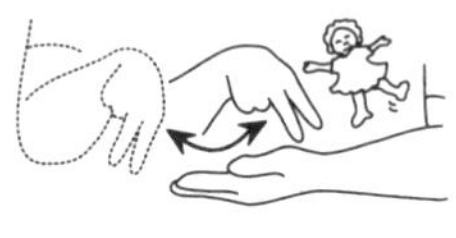

DANCE
Palm-in inverted V-fingertips arc from side-to-side, brushing left palm

DANDELION
Flat-O on left index-tip, pull fluff off to side, fingers fluttering

DANDY
Palm-out D's near shoulders, jerk out slightly; repeat

DANGER
Thumb-side of A arcs up, hitting back of left horizontal S; repeat

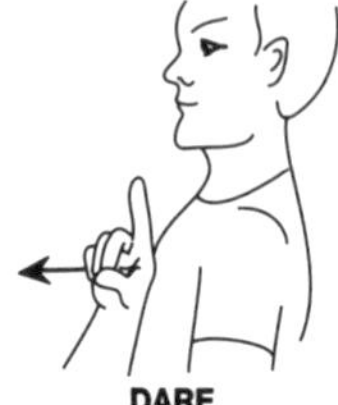

DARE
Palm-left D on heart moves sharply forward slightly

DARK
Palm-in hands cross in front of body

DARLING
Right D-hand circles on back of left hand over heart

DART
Index and thumb hold dart and throw

(see THROW)

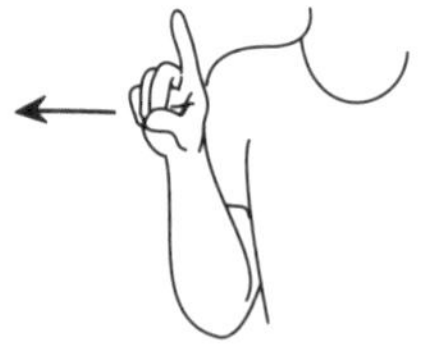

DASH
D moves right a short distance

(see BLANK)

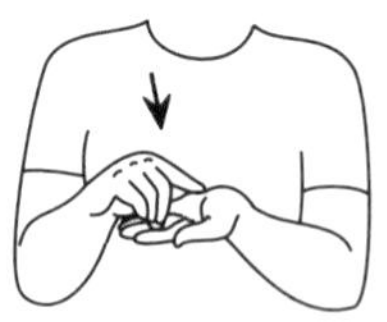

DATE
Right D touches left palm

DAUGHTER
Extended A-hand drops from chin to open palm-up hand on left arm

DAWN
Right D rises past outside of palm-down left hand

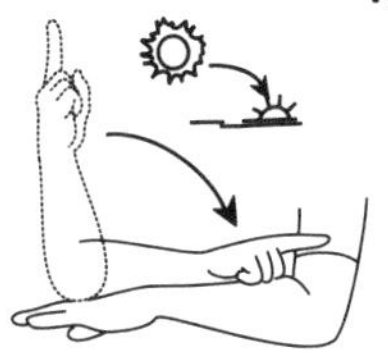

DAY
Elbow on back of hand, right 1-hand drops down on left arm

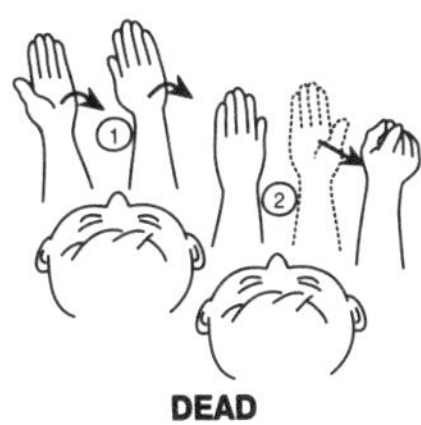

DEAD
Right hand palm-down, left hand palm-up, turn hands over to the right; add D-hand *(die + p.t.)*

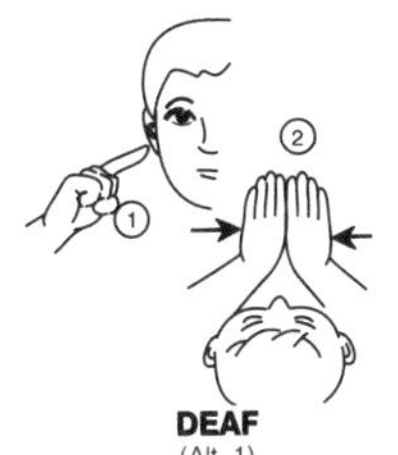

DEAF
(Alt. 1)
Right index touches ear, then sides of palm-down B's touch

DEAF
(Alt. 2)
Right index touches ear, then mouth

DEAL
Deal several cards

DEAR
D-hands cross on heart
(see LOVE)

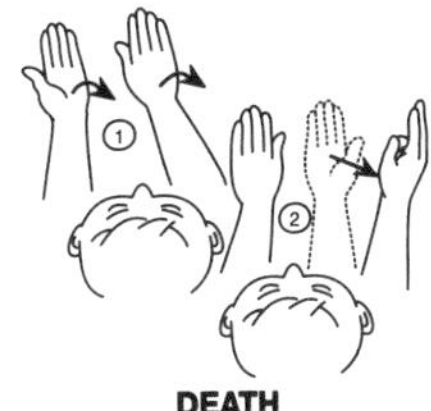

DEATH
Right hand palm-down, left palm-up, turn hands over to right; add H-hand *(die + -th)*

DEBATE
1-hands pointing at each other, right slightly in front of left, move together back and forth

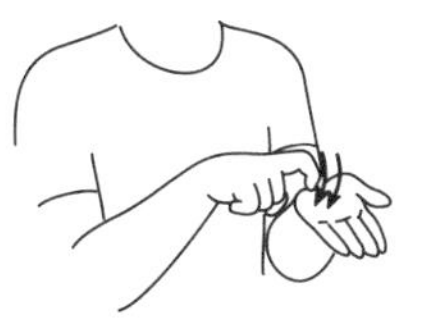

DEBT
Right bent index finger taps heel of palm-up left hand
(see OWE)

DECADE
Side of D on left palm, circle once then touches palm again
(see HOUR)

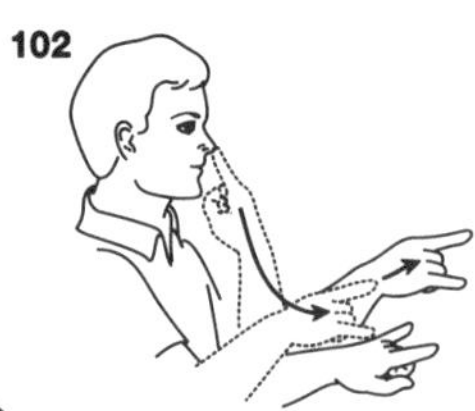

D

DECEIVE

Right palm-in index of I-1 hand on nose drops to palm-down, brushes outward across back of palm-down left I-1 hand

DECEMBER

(Alt. 1)

Right D arcs over top of vertical flat left hand

(see CALENDAR)

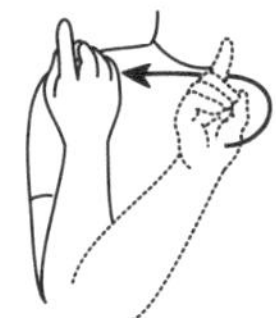

DECEMBER

(Alt. 2)

Palm-out D twists inward

(see CHRISTMAS)

DECENT

Palm-in left B points right; palm-out right D slides along index and off

(see NICE)

DECIDE

Palm-in right index on forehead; then both 9-hands jerk slightly down

DECIMAL

Left D, palm-right; right index makes dot next to D

(see MARK)

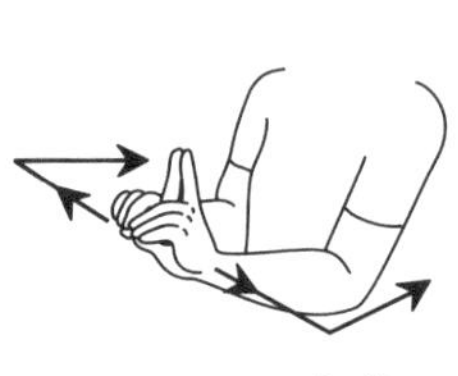

DECK ♔ ★

Palm-out D's touching; separate to sides then moves toward body

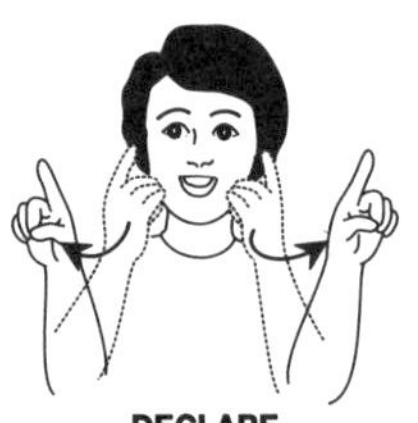

DECLARE

Palm-in D's touch corners of mouth, swing out and twist to palm-out

(see ANNOUNCE)

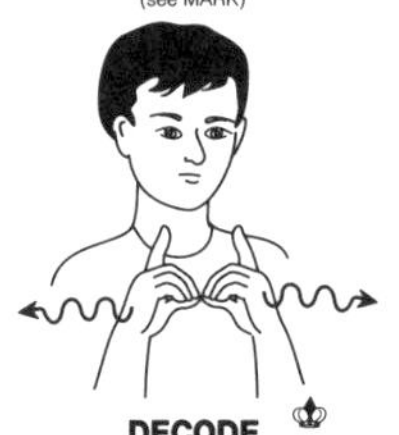

DECODE ♔

Thumbtips of palm-facing D's touch; right D shakes to right; may repeat

DECODER

Thumbtips of palm-facing D's touch; right D shakes to right and changes to palm-out R

DECORATE

Palm-out flat-O's alternately twist while putting up decorations

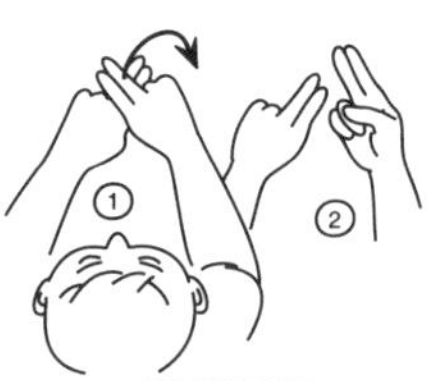

DECREASE

Right palm-down H on left palm-down H, right H twists off to palm-up

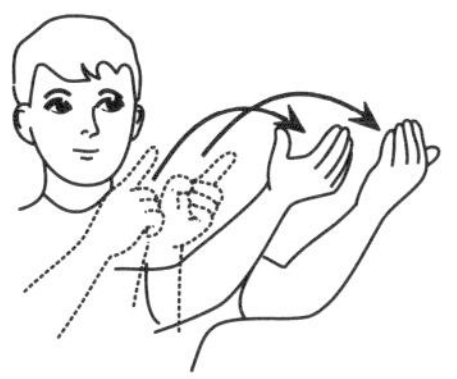

DEDICATE
D's, palms-facing, arc forward to left and upward to open palms-up
(see GIFT)

DEDUCE
D's brush past each other sideways, right behind left; repeat
(see ARITHMETIC)

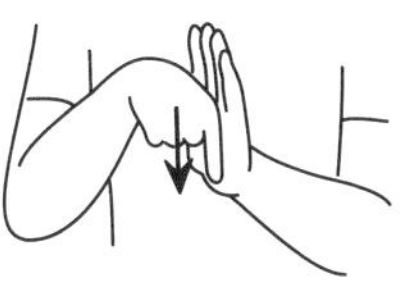

DEEP
Side of index pointing down, slides down vertical left palm

DEER
Both 5-hands move up from temples to sides

DEFEAT
Right D over and behind palm-down left S jerks down at wrist to palm-down, wrist on wrist
(see CONQUER)

DEFEND
One D behind the other D; both move forward slightly
(see GUARD)

DEFENSE
Right palm-down fist, elbow out, hand moves sharply forward

DEFICIT
Right index slides down between index and middle fingers of left palm-down hand

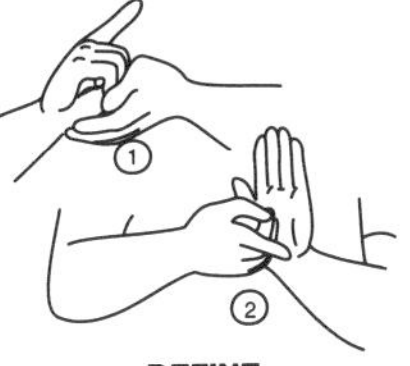

DEFINE
Right palm-down D touches left palm, then hands twist and touch again
(see MEAN)

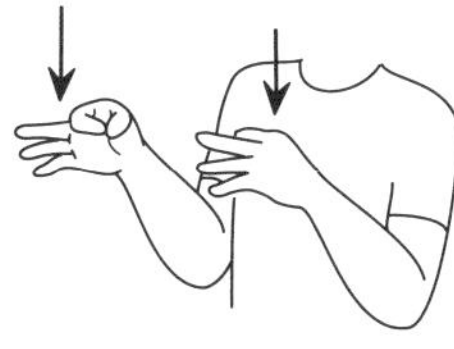

DEFINITE
Horizontal 9's, palms-facing, jerk down
(see DETERMINE)

DEFLATE
Flat C-thumb, on palm-up left finger-tips; close C-fingers to thumb

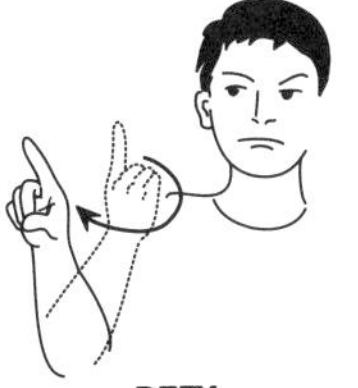

DEFY
Palm-in D near shoulder swings sharply to palm-out
(see REBEL)

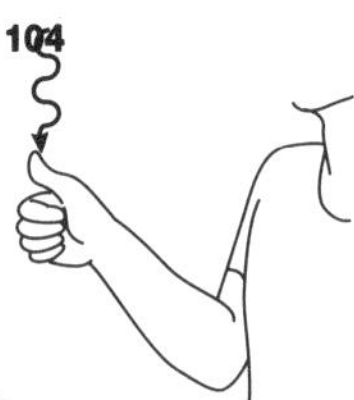

DEGENERATE

Palm-left extended A-hand, wriggles downward in front of body *(can be done with two hands)*

DEGREE

Thumb and finger of right D move up and down index finger of palm-out D

(see THERMOMETER)

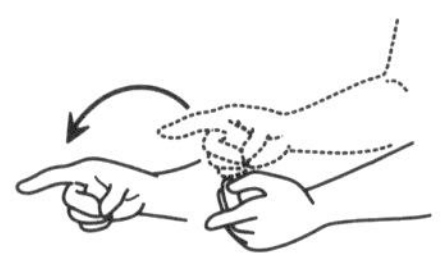

DELAY

Horizontal D's, palms-facing, touch; right D arcs forward

(see POSTPONE)

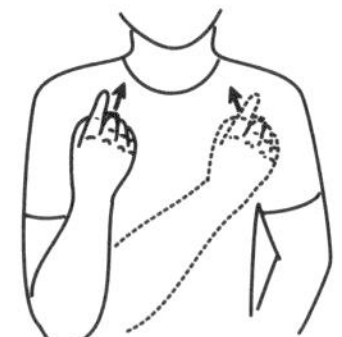

DELEGATE

(Alt. 1)

Palm-in D-fingers touch one shoulder, then the other

(see MEMBER)

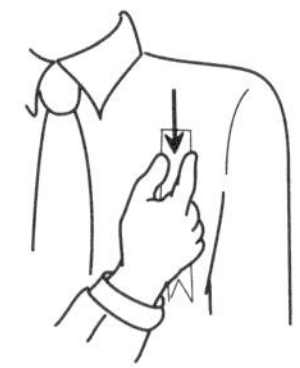

DELEGATE

(Alt. 2)

Right palm-in G touch below left shoulder, move slightly downward

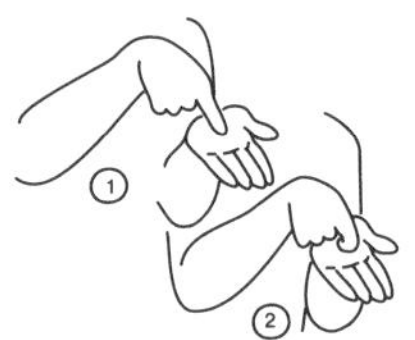

DELICATE

Right inverted index finger does push-ups on left palm

(see WEAK)

DELICIOUS

Bent middle finger on mouth, as hand moves out, thumb rubs middle finger *(can be done with two hands)*

DELIGHT

Fingertips of both palm-in D's brush up shoulders

(see GAY)

DELINQUENT

Left palm-down D; right index clips past fingertips inwards

(see ABSENT)

DELIVER

Fingers of right palm-down D on back of left hand flip forward to palm-out

(see SEND)

DEMAND

Thumb and fingers of D on left horizontal palm; both hands arc toward body

(see REQUIRE)

DEMOCRAT

Palm-out D-hand wiggles

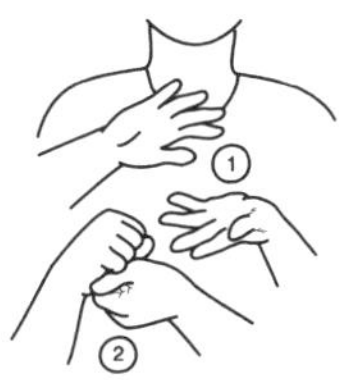

DEMOLISH
Right 5 palm-down above left palm-up 5, approach and change to fists as hands touch

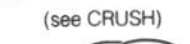
(see CRUSH)

DEMON
Fingertips of D at temple, crook index sharply to X
(see DEVIL)

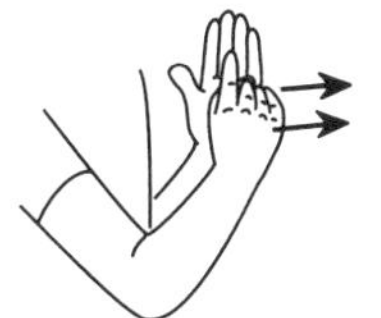

DEMONSTRATE
Fingertips of D on left vertical palm; both move forward
(see SHOW)

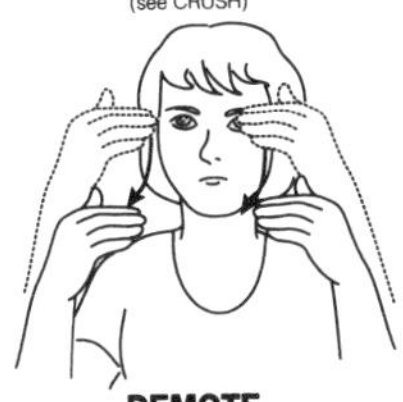

DEMOTE
Bent hands, palms-facing at eye level arc inward and down

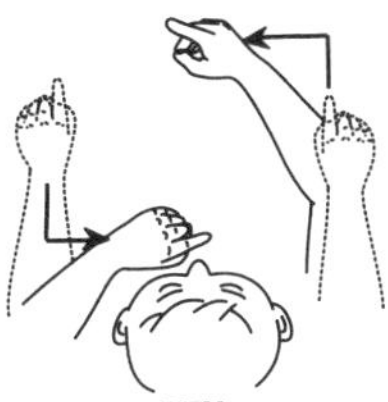

DEN
Palm-down D-hands shape box
(see BOX)

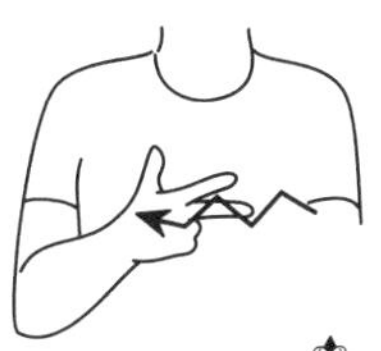

DENMARK ♔
Palm-in 3 moves in wavy motion across chest to right

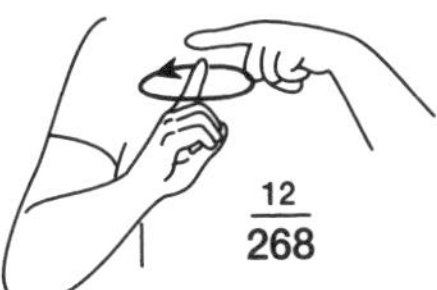

DENOMINATOR
D circles below left palm-down index
(see FRACTION)

DENTIST
Right palm-in D taps at corner of mouth twice

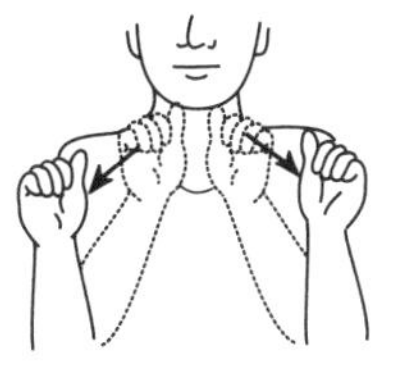

DENY
Thumbs of both A-hands under chin, brush forward to palm-out

DEODORANT
Spray deodorant can under palm of left hand

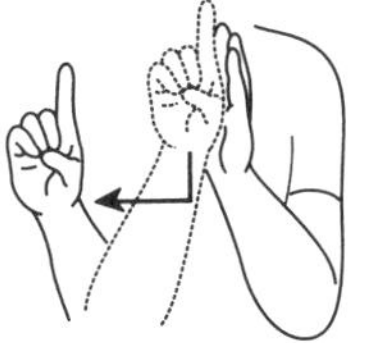

DEPART
Side of right D moves down vertical left palm, then away to the side
(see APART)

DEPARTMENT
D-hands, palm-out, circle horizontally out to palm-in
(see CLASS)

DEPEND
Right X hangs on horizontal left index, both drop slightly
(see PARASITE)

DEPLETE
Left flat palm-up; right palm-in 5 on top moves outward to close into S

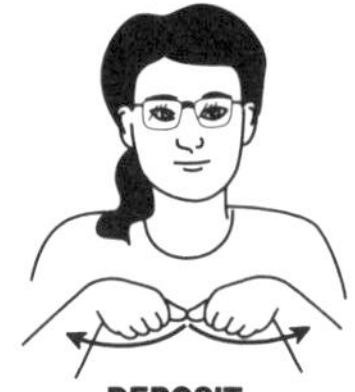

DEPOSIT
Thumbs of palm-down A's touch; separate to sides as if taping something down with thumbs

DEPRECIATE
Left flat-hand palm-up; right bent hand above shakes downwards towards left palm
(see DIMINISH)

DEPRESS
Middle finger of right hand slides down middle of chest
(see HUNGER)

DESCRIBE
D-hands, palms-facing, indexes pointing forward, move hands alternately forward and back
(see EXPLAIN)

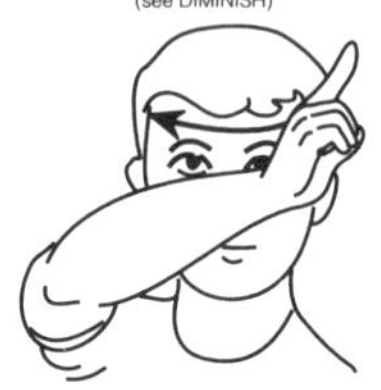

DESERT
Side of palm-left D brushes across forehead to right
(see SUMMER)

DESERVE
Side of D on flat left palm moves toward body, closing
(see EARN)

DESIGN
Palm-down D draws "S" on back of left palm-down S

DESIGNATE
Left vertical index; palm-out right D arcs towards index

DESIRE
Palm-in D moves down chest
(see HUNGER)

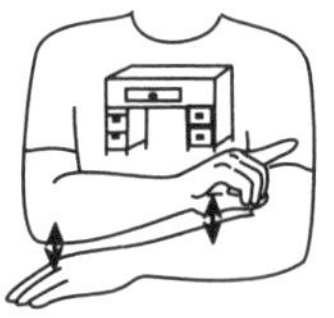

DESK
Right palm-down D and elbow bounce on left arm
(see TABLE)

DESPERATE

Palm-up D's pull back toward body as index fingers crook

(see WANT)

DESSERT

(Alt. 1)

Right palm-up D-hand ladles up to mouth twice from left palm

(see SOUP)

DESSERT

(Alt. 2)

Horizontal D's, palms-facing, tap fingertips together

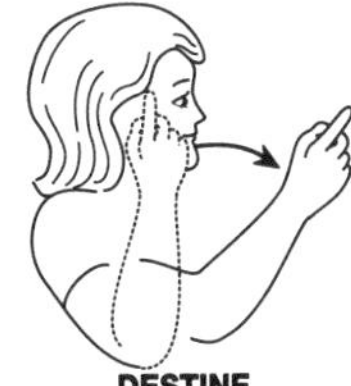

DESTINE

Palm-left D near head arcs forward

(see WILL)

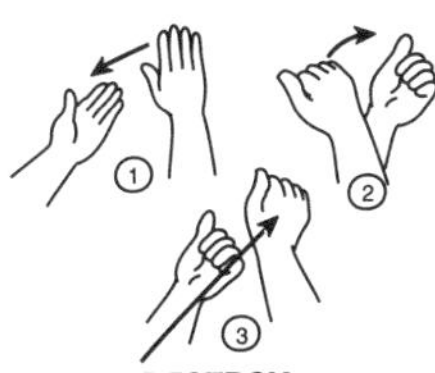

DESTROY

Palm-down right hand sweeps back over palm-up left, closing left; right closes, then brushes forward, striking left in passing

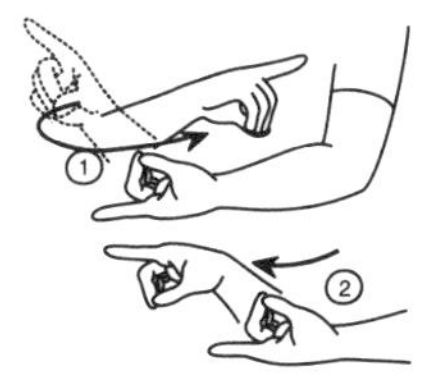

DESTRUCT

Right palm-down D sweeps back, brushing palm-up D; then forward again, brushing palm-up D fingertips

(see DESTROY)

DETAIL

Palm-down D taps down left palm

(see LIST)

DETAIN

Right X pulls index of left D backwards

DETECT

D near eye drops to flat left palm

(see NOTE)

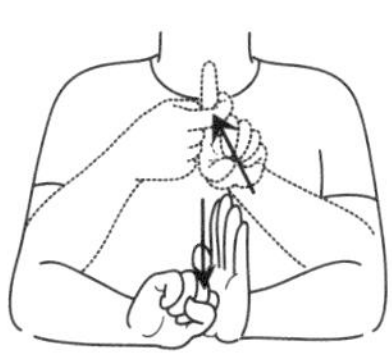

DETENTION

Right X pulls index of left D backwards; side of S slides down vertical palm *(detain + -tion)*

DETERIORATE

Side of right hand on back of left arm, hops down arm

(see REGRESS)

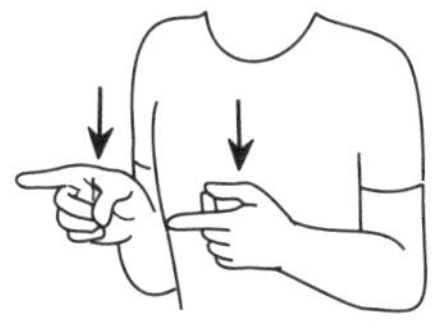

DETERMINE

Horizontal D's, facing each other, jerk downward

(see DEFINITE)

DETROIT
With D-hand, arc sharply down to right, palm-out
(see CHICAGO)

DEVELOP
Thumb and finger of right D slide up left vertical palm
(see TALL)

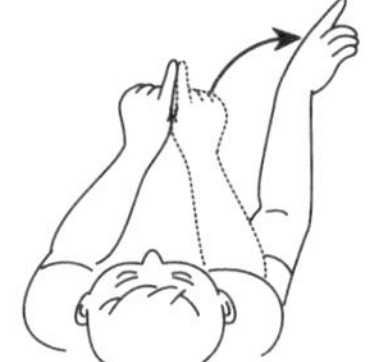

DEVIATE
Palm-down indexes touch; one curves off to side
(see STRAY)

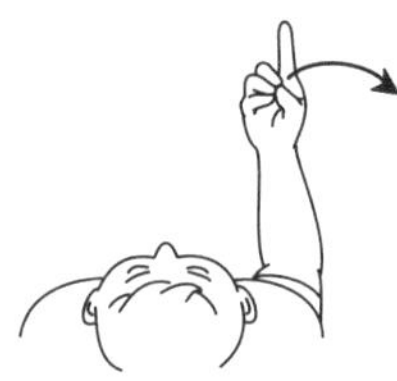

DEVICE
Palm-up D arcs once towards the side
(see THING)

DEVIL
Thumb of 3 on temple, bend 2 fingers at the same time; repeat

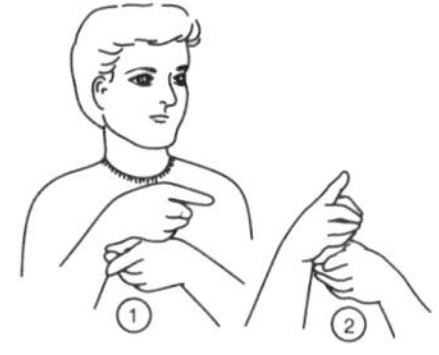

DEVISE
Both palm-in D's, right on left, twist to indexes pointing forward
(see MAKE)

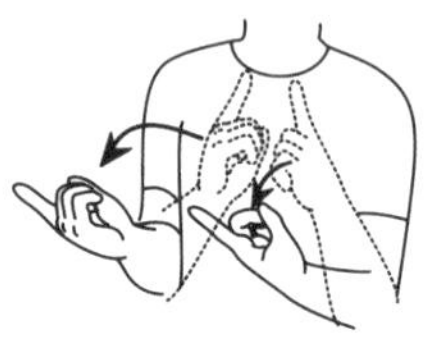

DEVOTE
Palm-in D's touch heart, then arc outward to palm-up

DEW
Left claw palm-up; right 5 palm-in at chin drops to close to flat-O against back of left fingers
(see WET)

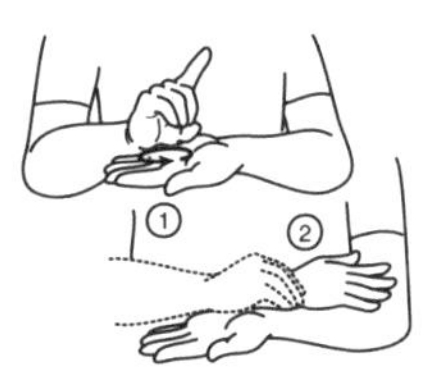

DIABETES
Right D makes small circle above left palm, changes to flat-O which opens and spreads up arm
(see CANCER)

DIAGNOSE
D's, fingertips almost touching, indexes separate while bending, repeat while moving downwards.
(see ANALYZE)

DIAGNOSES
D's fingertips almost touching, indexes separate while bending, repeat while moving downwards ending with right S
(see ANALYSIS)

DIAGNOSIS
D's fingertips almost touching, indexes separate while bending, repeat while moving downwards ending with S's

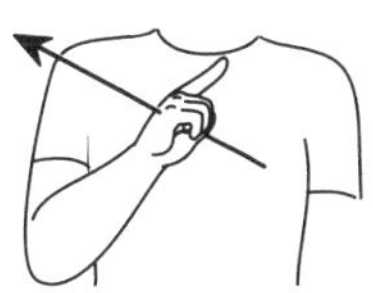

DIAGONAL

Right D moves up to right diagonally

DIAGRAM

Left palm-in 5 points left; right palm-out D moves down in wavy line inside left hand

(see ART)

DIALECT

(Alt. 1)

Palm-in D shakes from lips outward

DIALECT

(Alt. 2)

Horizontal D's fingertips touching, separate to sides, shaking slightly

DIALOGUE

D's move alternately from near corners of mouth forward and back

(see TALK)

DIAMETER

Left C, palm-right; right palm-out D draws diameter

(see RADIUS)

DIAMOND ♔

D rises shaking from left ring-finger

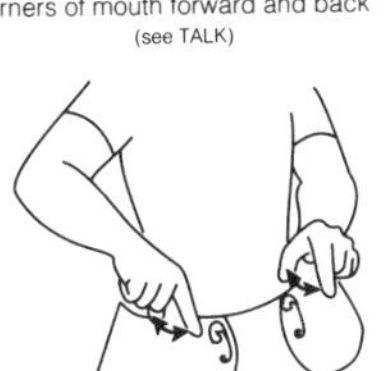

DIAPER

Both G-hands open and close at hips *(like 2 pins)*

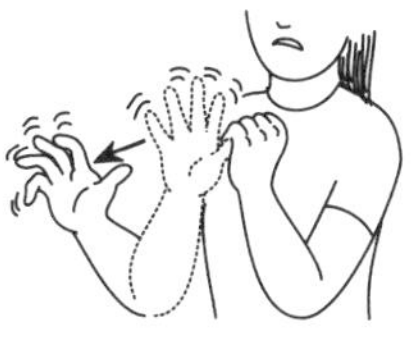

DIARRHEA

Left hand grasps right 5-thumb, which pulls out, fingers fluttering

DICE ★

D-hand shakes dice, then throws to left, opening hand

DICTIONARY

Palm-down D arcs down and left brushing left palm; repeat

(see ENCYCLOPEDIA)

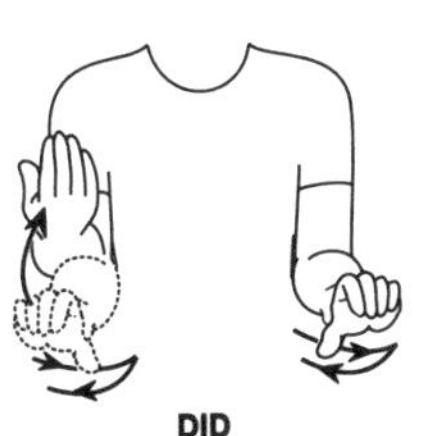

DID

Palm-down C-hands move left to right; right hand flips toward shoulder *(do + p.t.)*

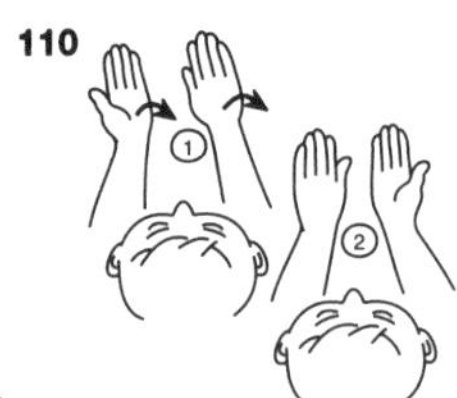

DIE
Right hand palm-down, left palm-up, turn hands over to the right

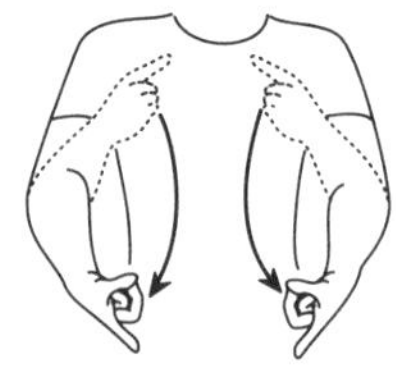

DIET
Palm-in D's twist inward and arc down body

(see SLIM)

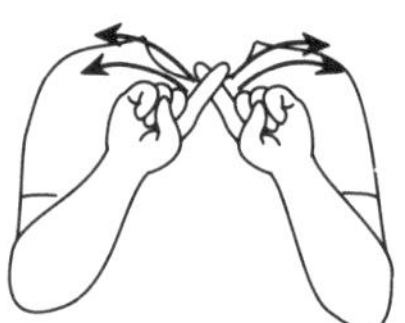

DIFFER
Palm-out crossed index fingers separate; repeat

(see ASSORTED)

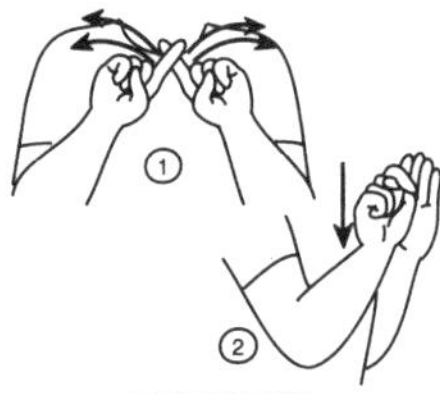

DIFFERENT
Palm-out crossed index fingers separate; side of right T slides down left fingers and palm *(differ + -ent)*

DIFFICULT
Fingers of palm-in bent V's brush up and down

(see HARD)

DIG ★
S's one palm-up and one palm-down, *(like holding handle of a shovel)* make digging motion

DIGEST ★
Palm-down D on palm-up left D grind on each other alternately

(see CHEW)

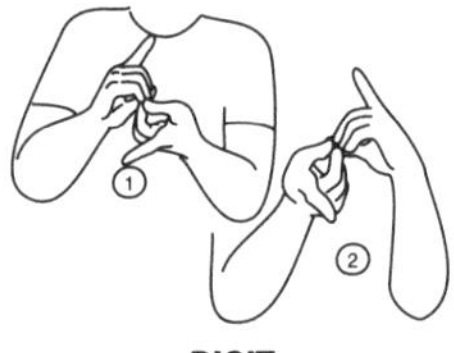

DIGIT
Fingers and thumbs of D's touch, one palm-up, one palm-down; reverse position and touch again

(see NUMBER)

DIM
Palm-out D's cross in front of face, moving down

(see DARK)

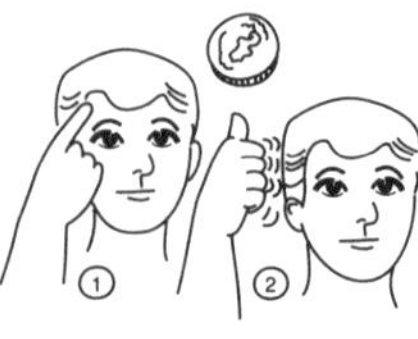

DIME
Index finger touches temple; moves out to extended-A hand; shake

(see CENT)

DIMINISH
Left index, palm-up; right index palm down above shakes downward towards left index

(see DEPRECIATE)

DIMPLE
Index pokes dimple in cheek

DINE
Palm-in D's circle alternately up toward mouth
(see BANQUET)

DINNER
Right D circles in and up near mouth, with wrist motion
(see EAT)

DINOSAUR
Elbow of flat-O arm moves along behind left horizontal arm

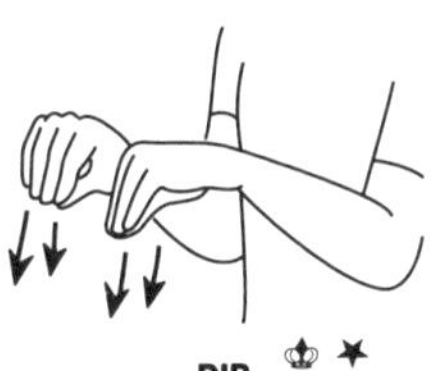

DIP ♔ ★
Palm-down flat-O's dip down twice

DIPLODOCUS
Palm-out D's touch; right moves down right in wavy motion

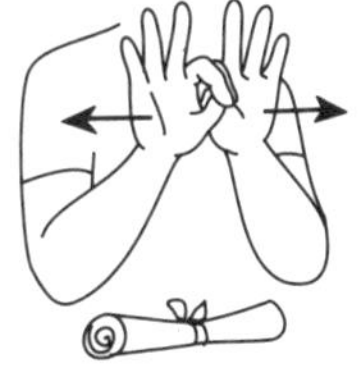

DIPLOMA
Palm-out F's touching, separate
(see FLOOR)

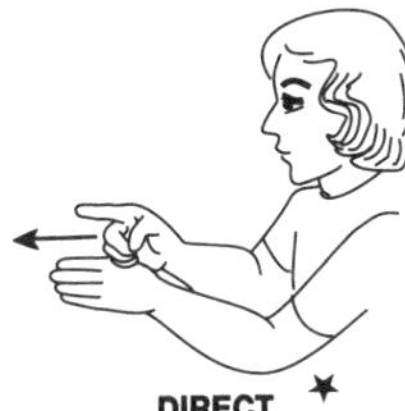

DIRECT ★
Right D on index side of flat left hand, D slides forward
(see STRAIGHT)

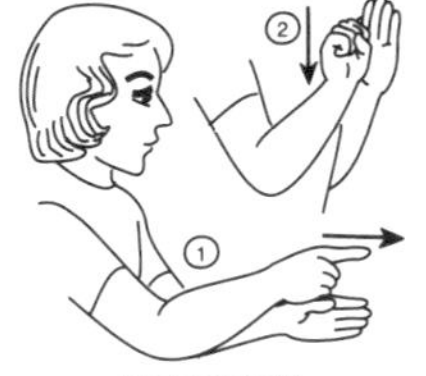

DIRECTION
Right D on left index, D slides forward; side of S slides down vertical hand *(direct + -tion)*

DIRT ♔
Fingers of palm-down hand wiggle under chin

DISAGREE
Index at side of forehead moves to touch end of left index tip to tip, then hands pull sharply apart
(see OPPOSE)

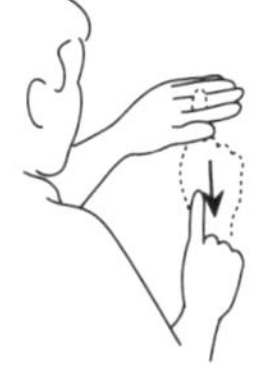

DISAPPEAR
Index between fingers of palm-down left hand, then drops down
(see DROWN)

DISAPPOINT
Index finger hits chin sharply

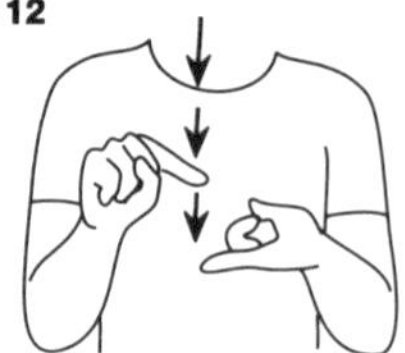

DISCOUNT
Right palm-down index finger lowers in stages toward palm-up left index, not touching

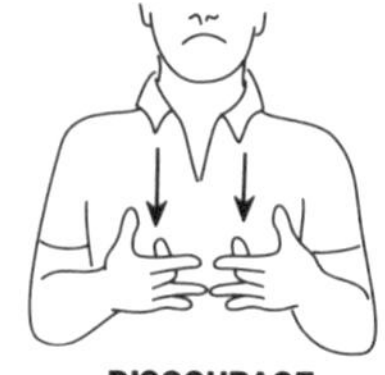

DISCOURAGE
Both middle fingers slide down chest

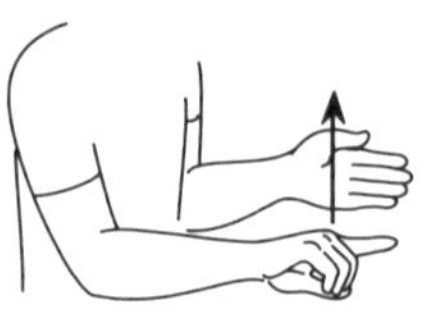

DISCOVER
Palm-down D moves up across palm
(see FIND)

DISCRIMINATE
Thumb and fingertips of right D make large X on left palm
(see CRITIC)

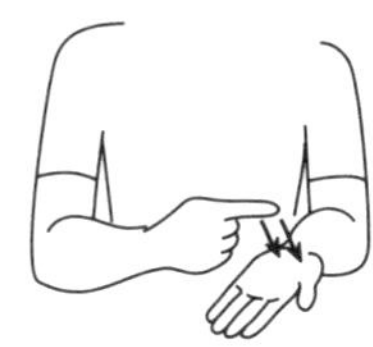

DISCUSS
Palm-in index taps palm of palm-up left hand

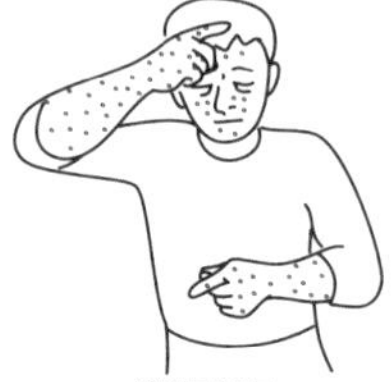

DISEASE
Palm-in D's right on forehead and left on stomach
(see SICK)

DISGUISE
D-hand, palm-in, passes across face

DISGUST
Palm-in claw hand circles on chest
(see NAUSEA)

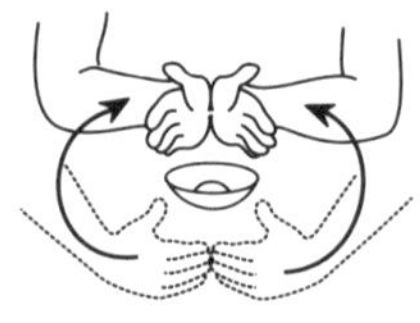

DISH ★
With palms outline dish
(see PLATE)

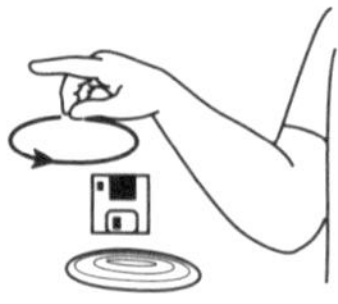

DISK
Palm-down D circles

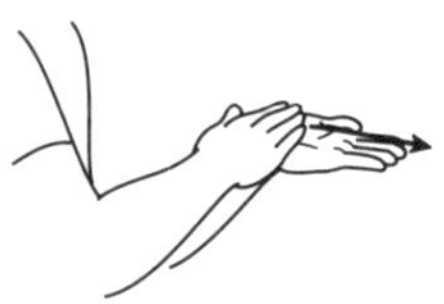

DISMISS
Right palm-down flat hand wipes once forward off palm-up left hand
(see EXCUSE)

DISPLAY ♔
Thumb and fingers of D on palm-left hand; circle both hands horizontally

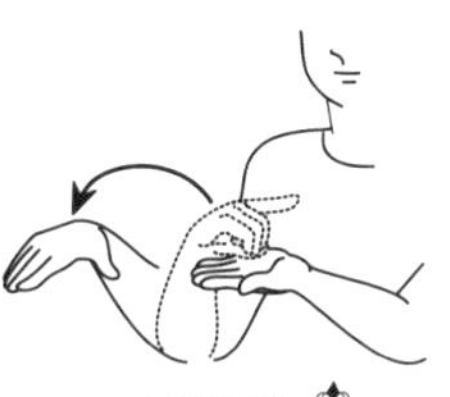

DISPOSE ♔
Right palm-left D on left palm slides out and off to palm-down 5-hand

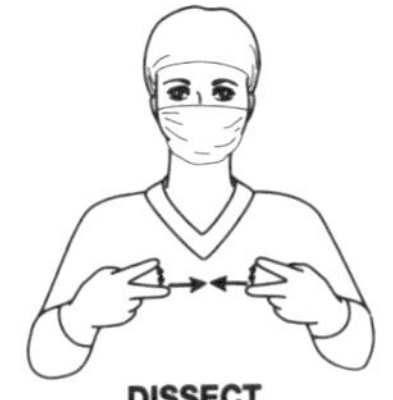

DISSECT
Palm-in V's point towards each other, both "cut"

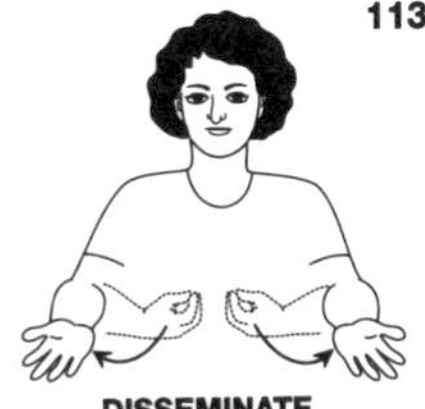

DISSEMINATE
Palm-up flat-O's point towards each other, move forward and outward, opening to flat hands

DISSOLVE
Palm-up D's separate, closing to A's
(see MELT)

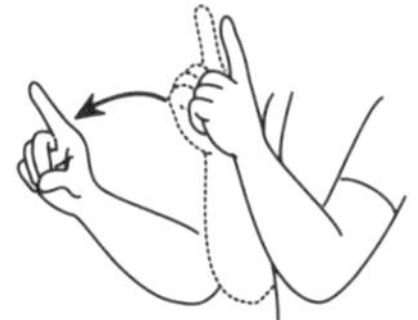

DISTANT
Thumbs and fingers of D's touch, right D arcs forward
(see FAR)

DISTINGUISH
Left 5, palm-right, pointing up; right D touches left palm, then hands separate, arcing slightly
(see AUTISM)

DISTORT
Heels of D's touch, crossing, stay together as hands reverse
(see CHANGE)

DISTRACT
Right D touches palm; D moves forward and slightly to the side

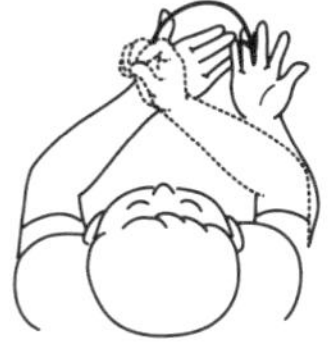

DISTRIBUTE
Palm-up flat-O opens to 5 while moving across fingers of left flat hand

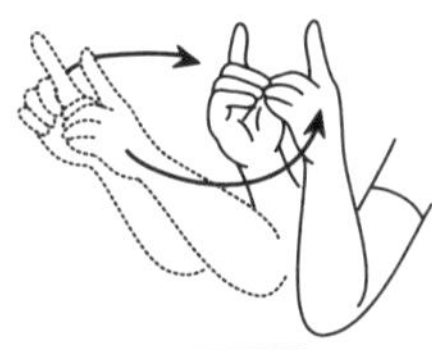

DISTRICT
Palm-out D's circle back towards body
(see PLACE)

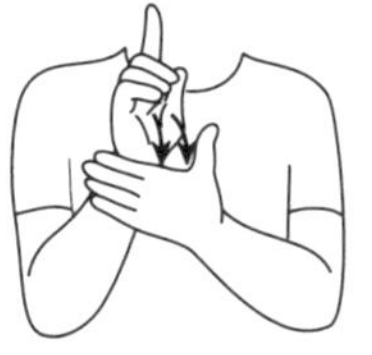

DISTURB
Thumb-side of D chops into thumb-base of open hand several times
(see BOTHER)

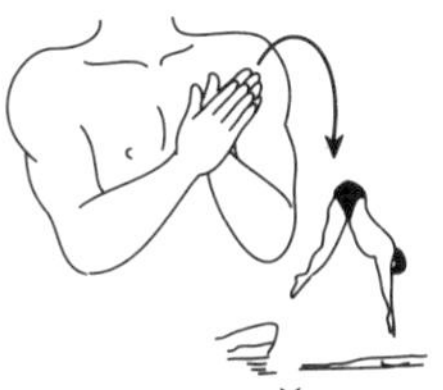

DIVE ★
Hands together dive

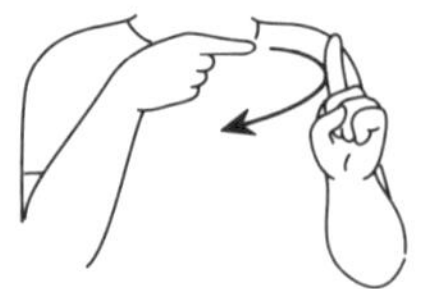

DIVERGE
Right index points at vertical left index and veers off to side

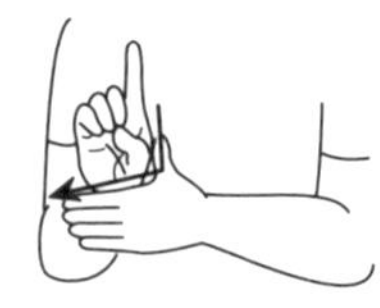

DIVIDE
Palm-out D moves down thumb and out finger of palm-in flat hand

DIVINE
D circles above palm, then open hand slides straight off end of palm
(see HOLY)

DIVORCE
D-hands, thumbs and fingers touching, then twist to sides

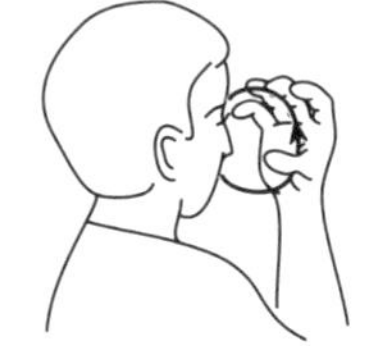

DIZZY
Palm-in right claw hand circles in front of eyes

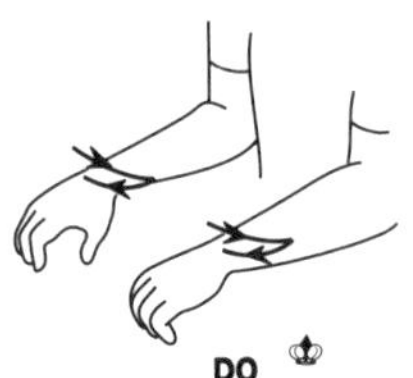

DO
Palm-down C-hands move side-to-side left to right

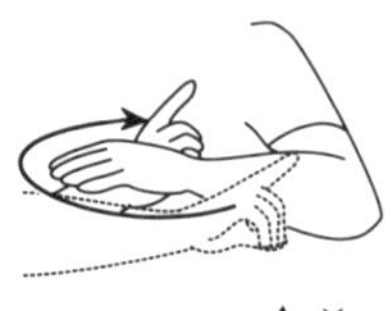

DOCK
D outlines left palm-down arm, starting on outside

DOCTOR
Thumb and finger of D tap pulse of left wrist

DOCTRINE
Index side of D touches fingers and then heel of left vertical hand
(see LAW)

DODGE
Right D wiggles back toward body from palm-right A
(see AVOID)

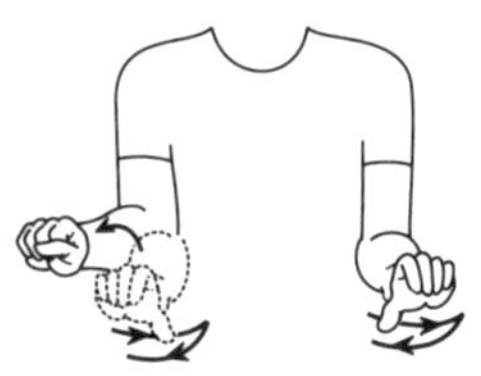

DOES
Palm-down C-hands move left to right; add S-hand *(do + -s)*

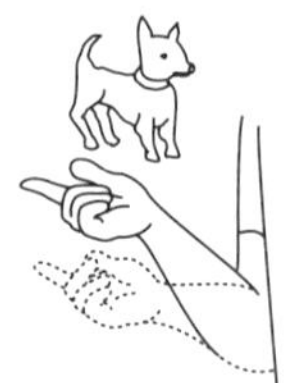

DOG
Palm-up fingers of D-hand snap several times *(to call a dog)*
(see PUPPY)

DOLL
Right X-finger brushes off tip of nose

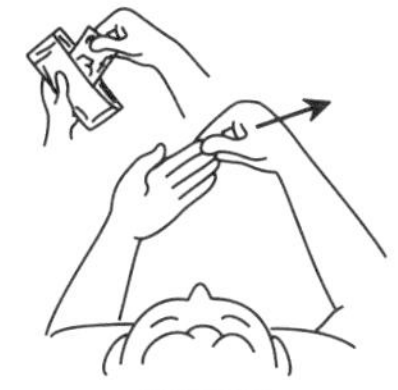

DOLLAR
Flat-O grasps end of palm-up flat hand, then slips off

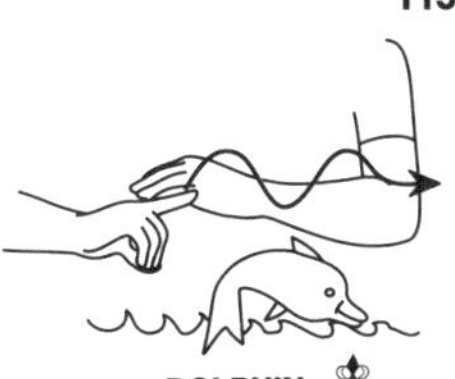

DOLPHIN
Palm-left D makes 2 curves to the left outside of arm

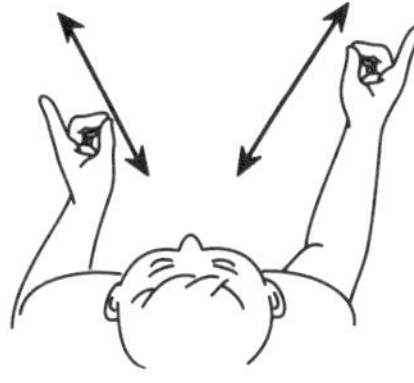

DOMINATE

D's point forward at each side of body, move forward and back alternately in large motions tending slightly outward
(see MANAGE)

DOMINO

Fingertips of two G-hands make the shape of a domino

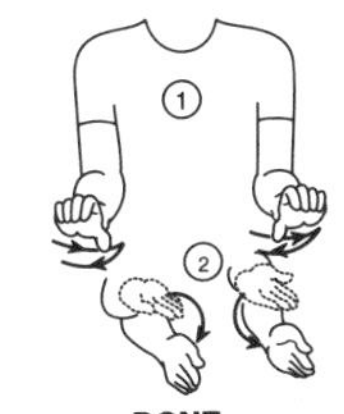

DONE
(Alt. 1)
Palm-down C-hands move left to right, flat palms-up twist to palms-facing
(do + p.p.)

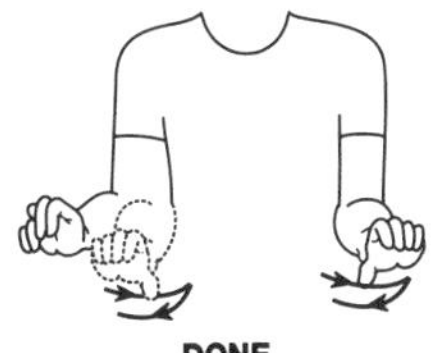

DONE
(Alt. 2)
Palm-down C-hands move left to right, add N-hand *(do + p.p.)*

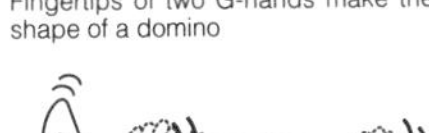

DONKEY

Thumbs of flat hands on temples, fingers flap forward
(see STUBBORN)

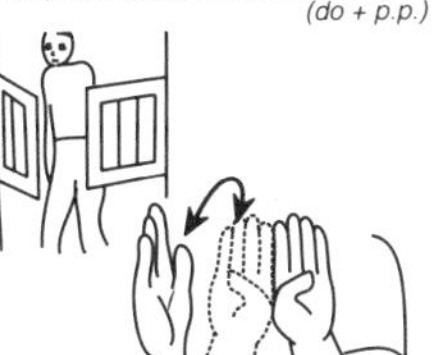

DOOR

Palm-out B's together, swing right hand open to palm-in and return

DOOR KNOB
Palm-out B's together, swing right hand to palm-in and return; C-hand twists

DORM
D on chin, then on cheek
(see HOME)

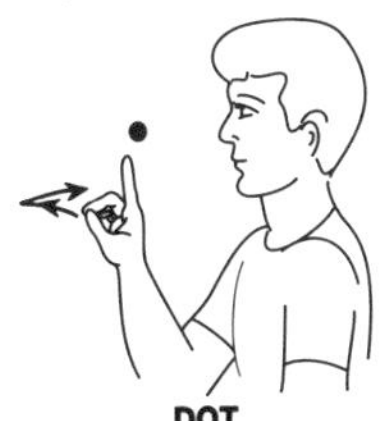

DOT
D moves forward to make dot

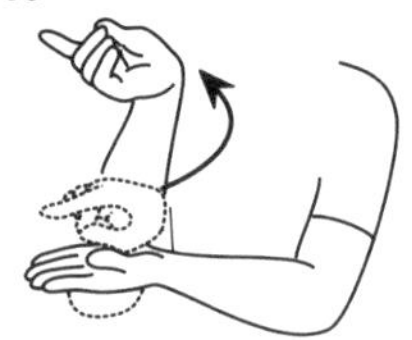

DOUBLE
D on left palm arcs up to palm-up
(see ONCE)

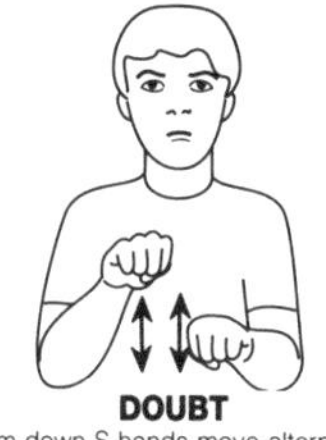

DOUBT
Palm-down S-hands move alternately up and down
(see BALANCE)

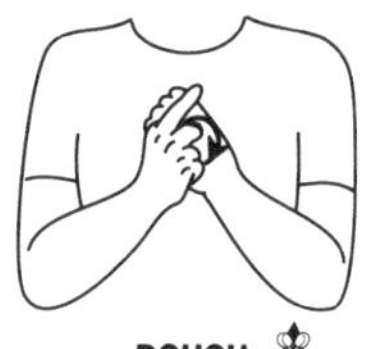

DOUGH ♔
Circle palm-in D on back of palm-in S

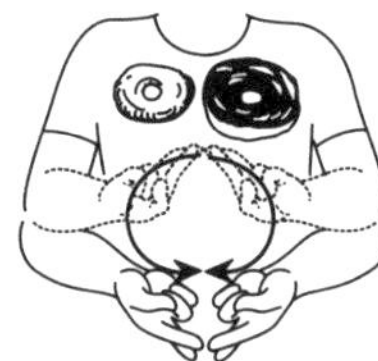

DOUGHNUT
R's touching, circle downward to palm-up and touching

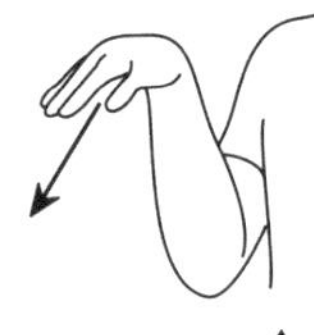

DOWN ♔ ★
Palm-in flat hand moves down

DOZEN
Palm-out D draws Z

DRAG
S's near shoulder, left in front of right, both move forward

DRAGON
Palm-out S's at chin move forward to palm-down 5's; fingers fluttering while moving forward

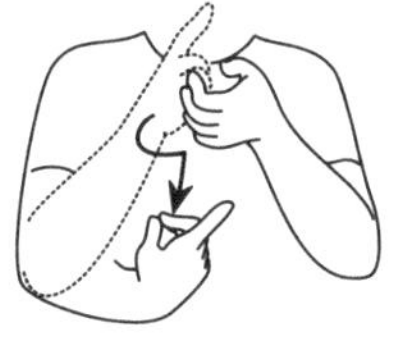

DRAIN
D rotates as it falls through left C-hand
(see EXTINGUISH)

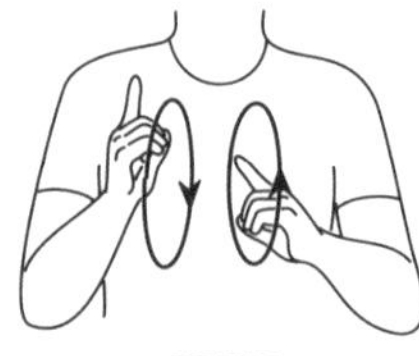

DRAMA
Thumbs and fingers of D's brush down chest alternately
(see ACT)

DRAPE
Palm-out D-hands meet, change to 4's, and slide down
(see CURTAIN)

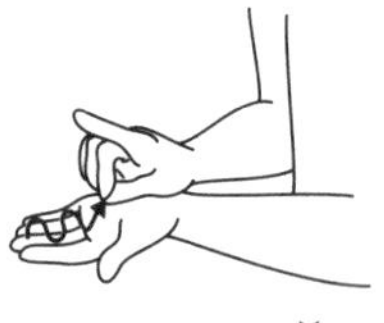

DRAW ★
With D-hand draw backwards on palm in wavy line
(see ART)

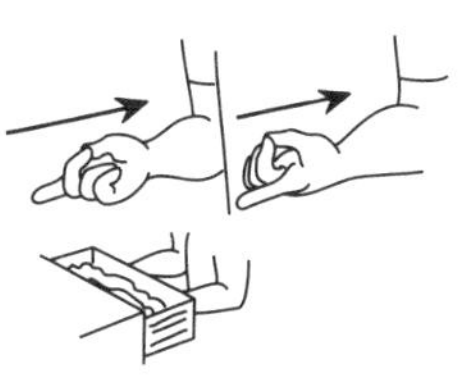

DRAWER
Palm-up D-hands draw toward body

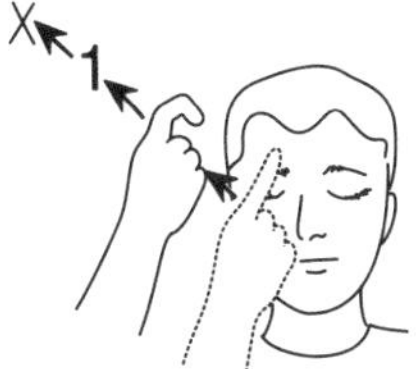

DREAM
Palm-in 1 on forehead move up to right, alternating X and 1
(see SCHEME)

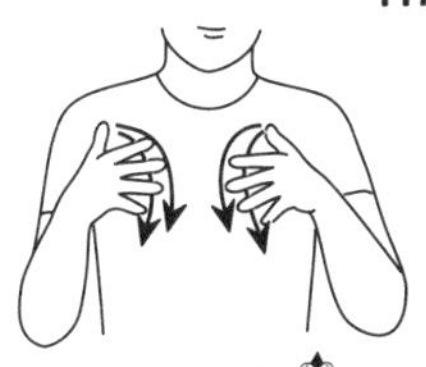

DRESS ♔
Thumbs of palm-in 5-hands brush down chest; repeat

DRIFT ♔
Right palm-down D on back of left hand, both drift forward

DRILL ★
D bounces back and forth on side of left index
(see PRACTICE)

DRINK
Thumb of C-hand on chin, drink from C
(see SIP)

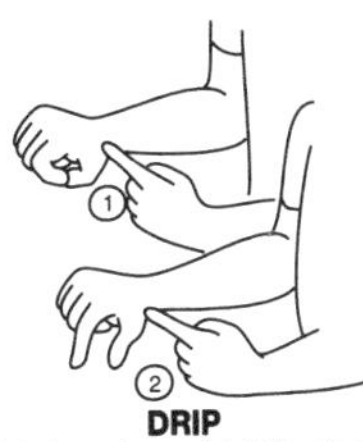

DRIP
Left index on base of right thumb of S-hand; right index "drips" by flicking off thumb repeatedly

DRIVE ★
Palm-in S-hands grasp invisible wheel, and steer
(see TRACTOR)

DRIZZLE
Palm-down relaxed 5 fingers fluttering, circles over back of flat left hand
(see SPRINKLE)

DROOL
Index of 4 at corner of mouth, pointing left; hand moves downward with fluttering fingers

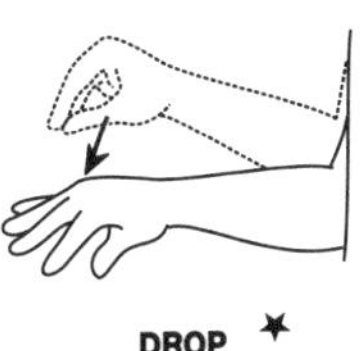

DROP ★
Flat-O drops and opens *(can be done with 2 hands)*

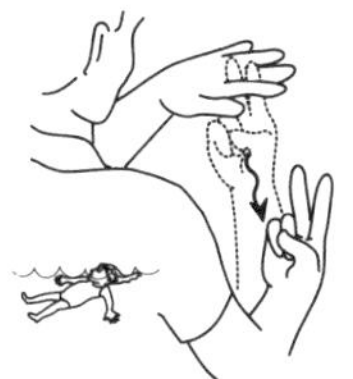

DROWN
Palm-in right V-fingers between left palm-down fingers, right hand drops, twisting slightly
(see DISAPPEAR)

DRUG

D circles on palm

(see MEDICINE)

DRUM

Both A-hands drum alternately

DRUNK

(noun, adj.)

Palm-out extended-A hand swings past mouth

DRUNK

(verb)

Thumb of C-hand on chin, drink from C; both palm-up flat hands twist to palms-facing *(drink + p.p.)*

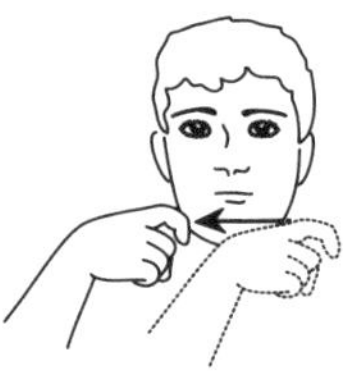

DRY

Palm-down X drags across chin as if wiping it

(see PRUNE)

DUCK

At chin, index and middle fingers close on thumb twice

(see BIRD)

DUCKLING

Right hand resting in left palm, two fingers open and close on thumb

(see CHICK)

DUKE

Right D-hand at left shoulder arcs down to right waist

(see CHRIST)

DULL

Side of X pulls back across fingertips of left D

(see STALE)

DUMB

Knuckles of palm-in A hit forehead

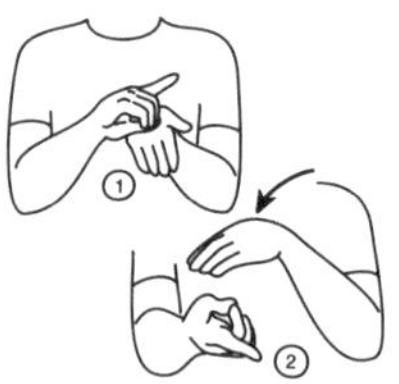

DUMP

Right palm-down D on left palm-up hand; turn hands over, dumping D-hand off palm

DUPLICATE

Palm-out D closes down to flat-O on left palm

(see COPY)

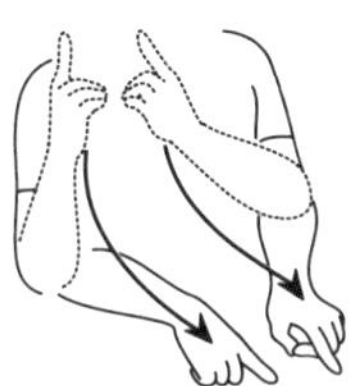

DURING
Indexes of D-hand near right shoulder, arc down and out
(see WHILE)

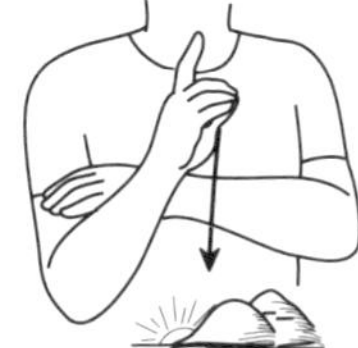

DUSK
Left arm horizontal; right D in front drops below arm level
(see SUNSET)

DUST
Back of palm-up D circles on back of palm-down left S
(see WAX)

DUTCH
Both hands touch temples with fingertips and thumb, arc to sides and slightly up closing to flat-O's

DUTY
Right D taps back of left hand
(see WORK)

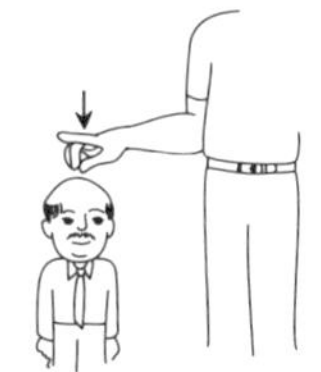

DWARF
Palm-down D shows height of dwarf
(see CHILD)

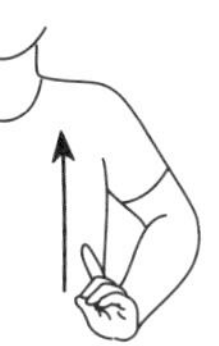

DWELL
Sides of D's, indexes pointing up, brush up trunk of body
(see ADDRESS)

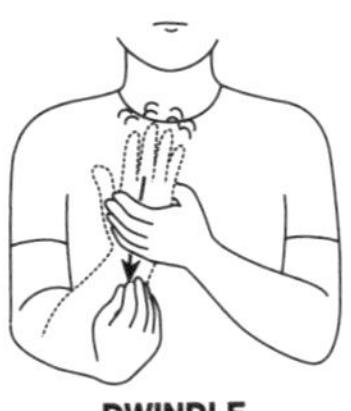

DWINDLE
Left C around wrist of right palm-in relaxed 5, 5 fingers fluttering slowly drops through C, closing into flat-O

DYE
Parallel palm-down 9-hands move down and up several times
(see DIP)

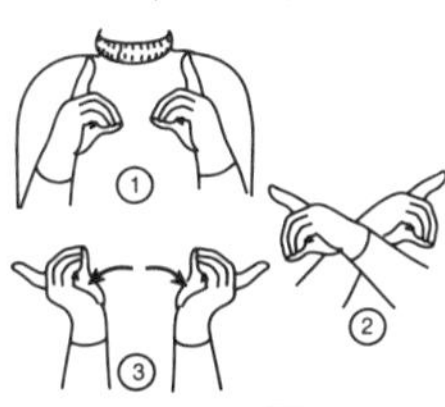
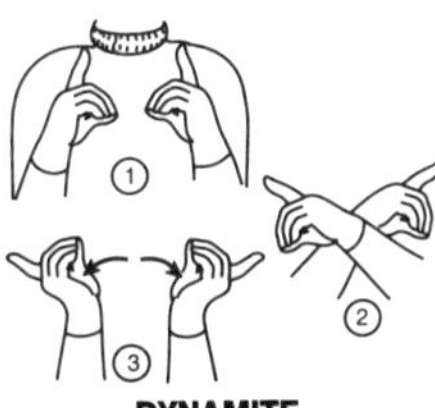

DYNAMITE
D's face each other, move to cross wrists, jerk sharply apart
(see EXPLODE)

NOTES

EACH

Thumb of right A brushes once down side of left thumb

(see PER)

EAGER

Palm-to-palm E-hands pointing forward, knuckles rub back and forth on each other

(see ENTHUSE)

EAGLE

X pointing forward on nose

EAR

Right Index points to ear

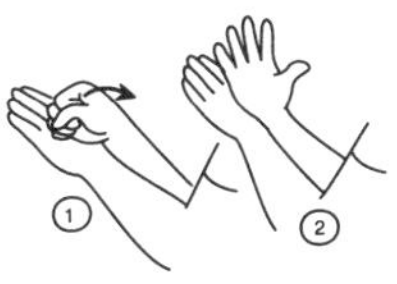

EARLY

(Alt. 1)

Horizontal S on back of left hand slides inward, opening to 5

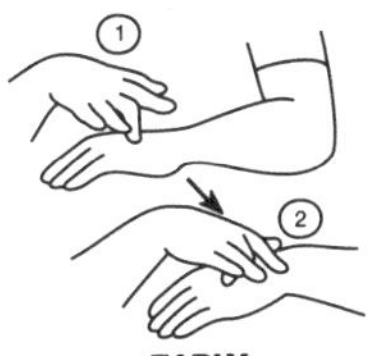

EARLY

(Alt. 2)

Right middle finger on back of left flat hand stays put as right hand moves forward

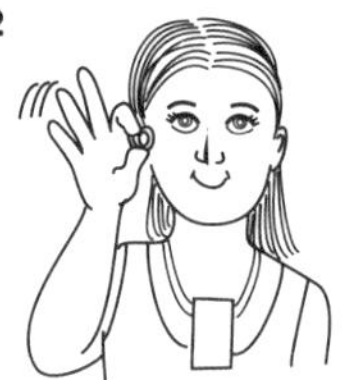

EARMOLD
Index and thumb of right 9-hand put mold in ear

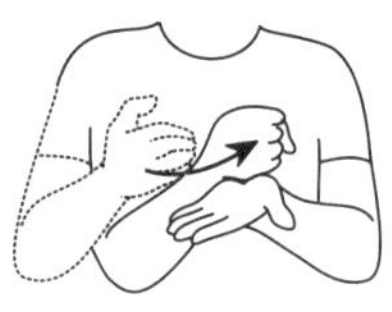

EARN
Side of horizontal C on flat left palm, C moves inward closing to S-hand
(see DESERVE)

EARNEST
Side of right E on horizontal left palm, E brushes forward on palm
(see HONEST)

EARPHONES
Claw hands tap over ears

EARRING
With thumb and index of right 9-hand clip earring on ear

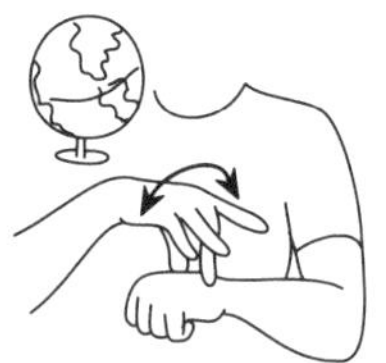

EARTH
Thumb and middle finger hold sides of left palm-down S; right hand rocks back and forth as on axis

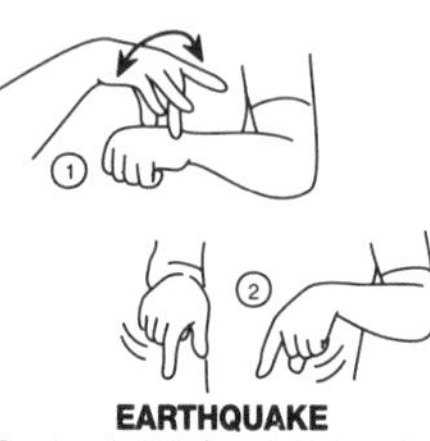

EARTHQUAKE
Thumb and middle finger hold sides of left S; right hand rocks back and forth; change to Q-hands and shake *(earth + quake)*

EASE ♔
Right fingertips stroke upwards on back of bent left fingers, circling up and out; repeat

EASEL
Right palm-left V-hand angles down from vertical flat left palm *(like an easel's legs)*

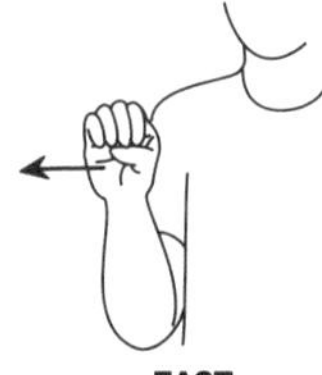

EAST
Palm-out E moves right

EASTER
Palm-to-palm horizontal E-hands separate, shaking

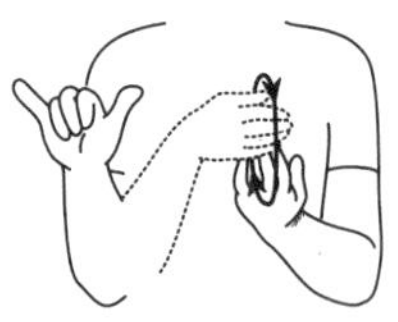

EASY 
Right fingertips stroke upwards on back of bent left fingers, circling up and out; repeat, ending in Y-hand *(ease + -y)*

EAT

Thumb of extended-A circles in and up near mouth spooning food in

ECHO

Side of E hits left vertical palm, shakes to right, "bouncing off"

(see BELL)

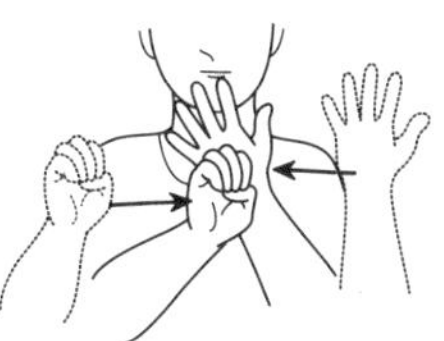

ECLIPSE

Palm-in left 5, palm-out right E cross in front of chin

(see DARK)

ECOLOGY

Palm-up E on back of left hand circles slightly out and back

(see GROUND)

ECONOMY

Palm-up E taps left palm; repeat

(see MONEY)

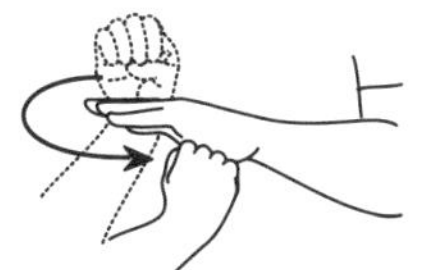

EDGE

E moves around fingertips of palm-down left hand

EDIT

Palm-out E makes check mark over left palm

(see CHECK)

EDUCATE

E's near temples move forward slightly; repeat

(see TEACH)

EFFECT

E moves across back of left hand

(see ADVICE)

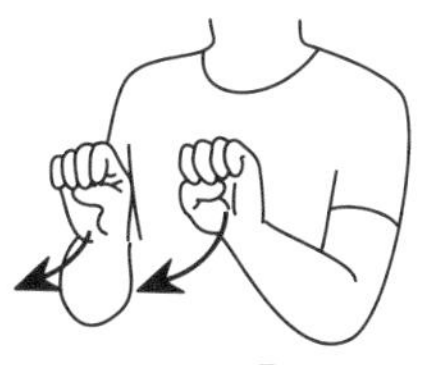

EFFORT

Palm-out E's move down and forward with slight arc

(see ATTEMPT)

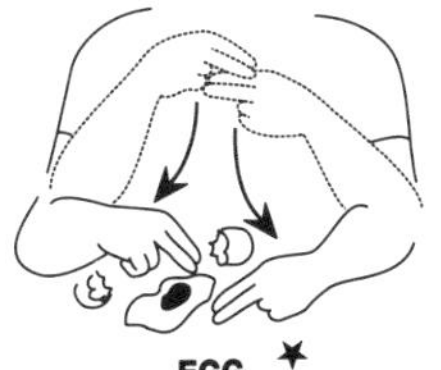

EGG

Right H breaks on the left H and both hands pivot down

(see OMELET)

EGYPT

Palm-out X on forehead

E

EITHER

Palm-out E brushes from tip of left thumb, then off fingertip of index

(see THEN)

EJECT

Palm-out E rockets up side of vertical palm and away

(see ASTRONAUT)

ELABORATE

Palm-out claws in front of body circle vertically in opposite directions

(see FABULOUS)

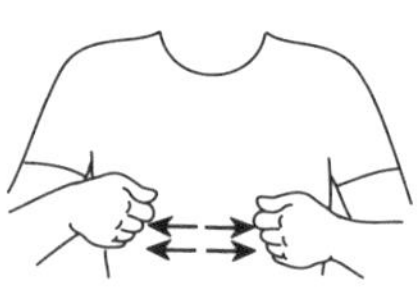

ELASTIC

Palm-in horizontal A's mime pulling elastic twice

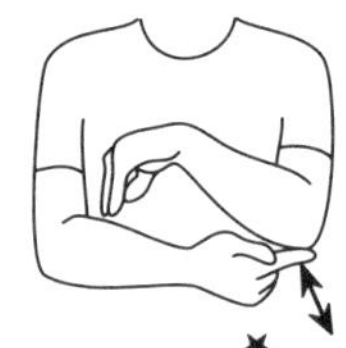

ELBOW ★

Index finger taps left elbow

ELDER

E waves downward from chin

(see OLD)

ELECT

Right 9-hand moves to touch left index, then moves back

(see CHOOSE)

ELECTRIC ♔

Knuckles of palm-in horizontal X-fingers bump twice

ELECTRON

Left extended-A, palm-down; right E circles near left thumb

(see ATOM)

ELEGANT

5's facing, alternately circle upward, thumbs brushing chest

(see FANCY)

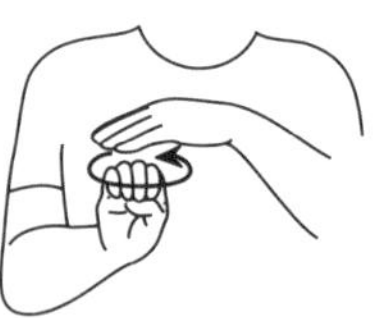

ELEMENT

E circles under palm

(see BASE)

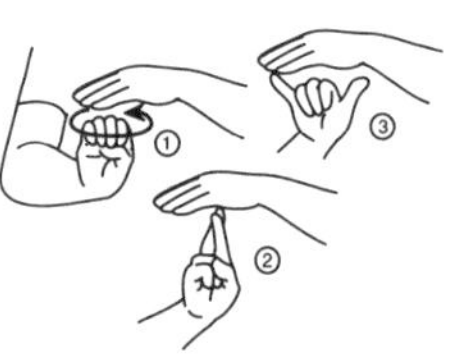

ELEMENTARY

Right E circles under left palm, changes to palm-out R, then to Y-hand *(element + -ar + -y)*

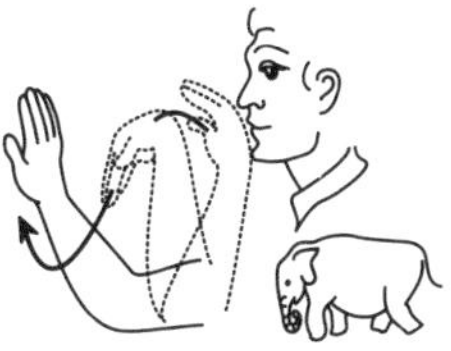

ELEPHANT
From nose, trace elephant's trunk with open hand

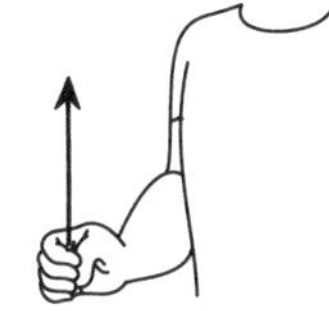

ELEVATE
Palm-left E pointing forward, rises
(see UP)

ELF
E-hands inward on shoulders turn outwards and to sides
(see ANGEL)

ELIMINATE
From index of left 5-hand flick right thumb out and away

ELK
Both palm-out E's move up and out from temples
(see DEER)

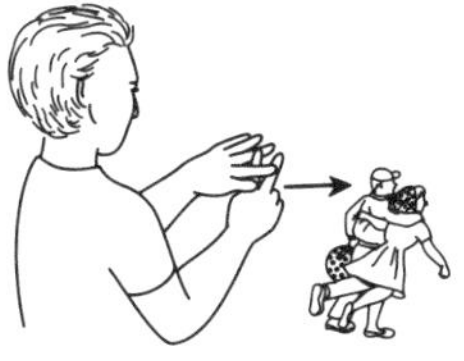

ELOPE
Palm-out 2-hand, between index and middle finger of palm-down left hand; 2 slips out to side
(see ESCAPE)

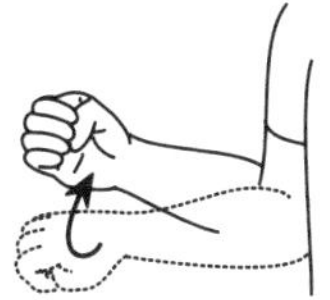

ELSE
Palm-down E twists over to palm-up and slightly to right

EMBARRASS
Palm-in 5-hands alternately circle in front of face while fingers flutter

EMBLEM
Index side of E touches left upper arm

EMBROIDER
9 sews up and down between fingers of palm-down left hand

EMBRYO
Left hand covers right E-hand

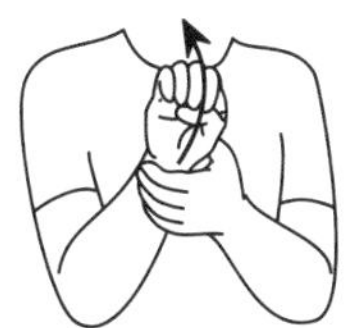

EMERGE
Palm-out E grows up through left horizontal C
(see GROW)

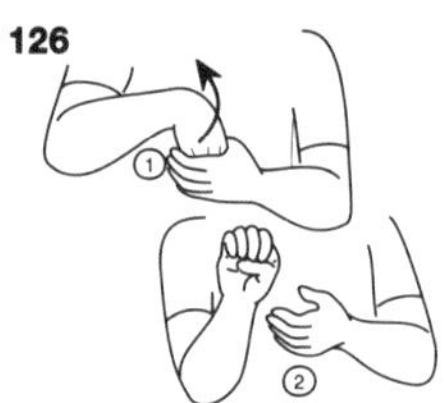

EMIT
Upside-down E pulls out of left horizontal C to palm-out
(see OUT)

EMOTION
Palm-in E-hands alternately circle up and outward from chest; right S slides down left vertical palm
(see FEEL)

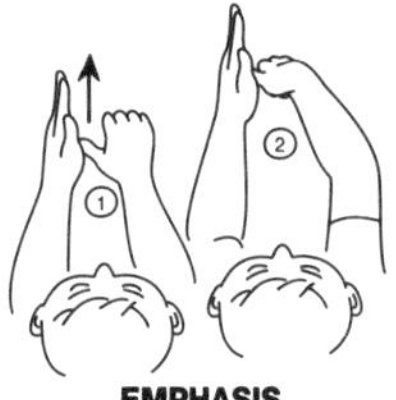

EMPHASIS
Tip of extended-A thumb on left palm twists to palm-in
(see STRESS)

EMPEROR
Side of right E touches left chest near shoulder, then right side of waist
(see CHRIST)

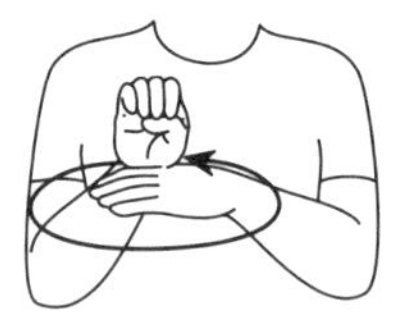

EMPIRE
Palm-out E on back of left hand circles out, around, and along arm
(see GROUND)

EMPLOY
Palm-out E arcs side-to-side, hitting back of left palm-down S
(see BUSY)

EMPRESS
Side of right E touches left chest near shoulder, right chest near shoulder, then right side of waist

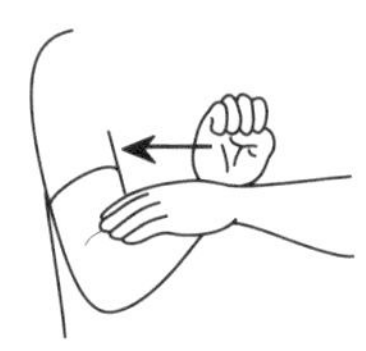

EMPTY
Right E brushes along back of left hand and off
(see BARE)

ENCHILADA
E-hands, palm-up; right "folds" over, then the left "folds" on top
(see TORTILLA)

ENCOURAGE
Flat hands gently push (someone) forward in short movements
(see MOTIVE)

ENCYCLOPEDIA
Palm-down E arcs down and toward self, brushing left palm; repeat
(see DICTIONARY)

END
Palm-out E slides along top of palm-in left hand and down fingertips
(see FINISH)

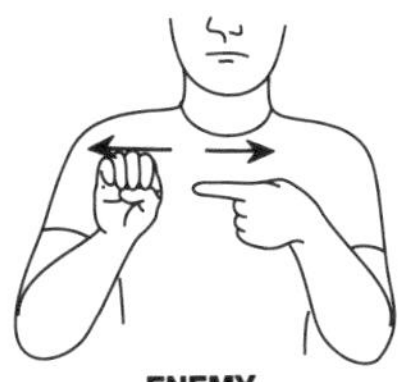

ENEMY

Palm-out E and left horizontal index pull away from each other

(see OPPOSE)

ENERGY

Right E-hand draws muscle on left upper arm

(see STRONG)

ENFORCE

Palm-out E behind palm-down left hand, drop forward forcefully to palm-down E-hand

(see COMPEL)

ENGAGE

Palm-out E circles once horizontally over left S and drops on back of S

(see APPOINT)

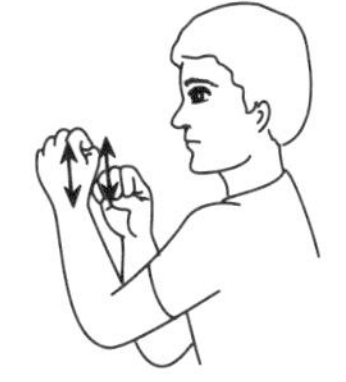

ENGINE

E's, palms-facing, right behind left, hands move piston-like alternately up and down

(see MOTOR)

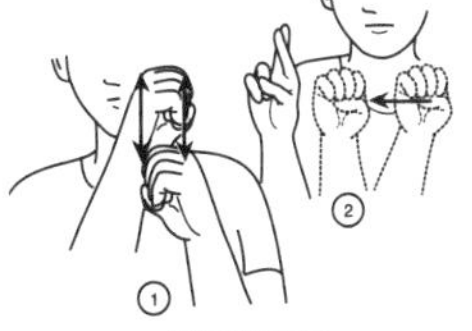

ENGINEER

E's right behind left, move up and down alternately; right E slides to right, changes to R *(engine + -ee + -er)*

ENGLAND

Palms-down, right hand pulls left hand toward body

ENGLISH

Palms-down, right pulls left hand toward body; right I draws a wavy downward line *(England + -ish)*

ENGROSS

Bent L's, palms-in, left in front of chest and right in front of mouth, both hands move forward

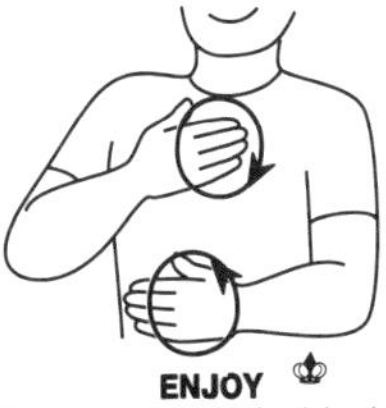

ENJOY ♔

Palm-in hands, on body, right above left, circle in opposite directions

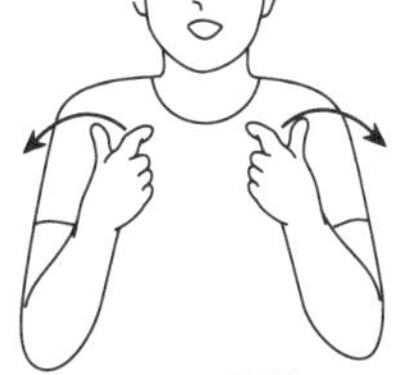

ENORMOUS

Bent L's, face each other slightly palm-in; arc towards sides, raising shoulders slightly

(see BIG)

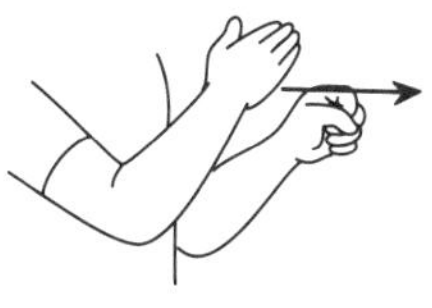

ENOUGH

Flat palm brushes forward across top of left S; may repeat

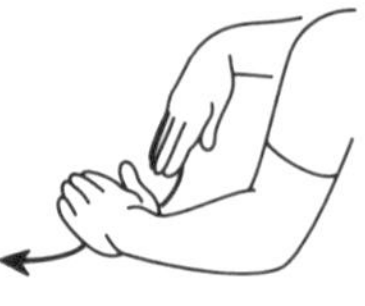

ENTER ♔
Right palm-down flat hand arcs down under horizontal left palm

ENTERTAIN
Circle side of E's on chest in opposite directions
(see ENJOY)

ENTHUSE
Palms rub together
(see EAGER)

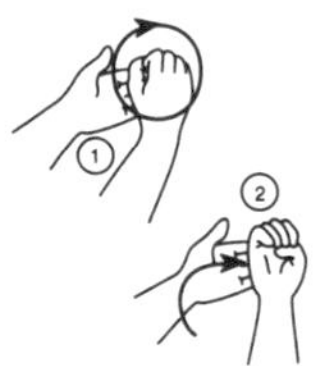

ENTIRE
Palm-down E on left palm, circles horizontally and returns palm-up
(see WHOLE)

ENTRANCE
Right palm-down arcs down under horizontal left palm; C slides down left hand *(enter + -ance)*

ENVELOPE
Flat hand passes under lip *(as if licking the flap)* and inserts in left hand

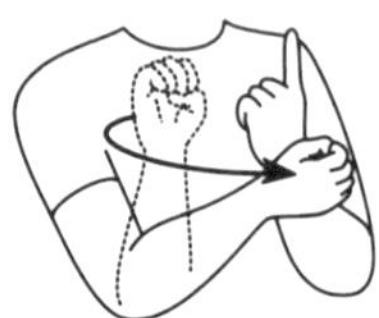

ENVIRONMENT
Right E curves around vertical palm-in left index
(see ATMOSPHERE)

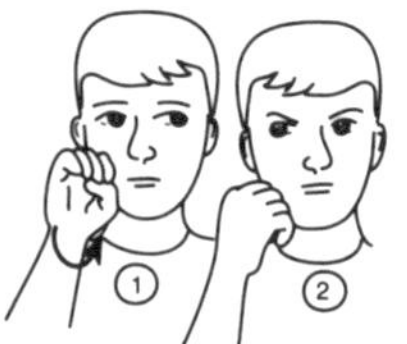

ENVY
Side of palm-out E at corner of mouth twists to palm-in
(see JEALOUS)

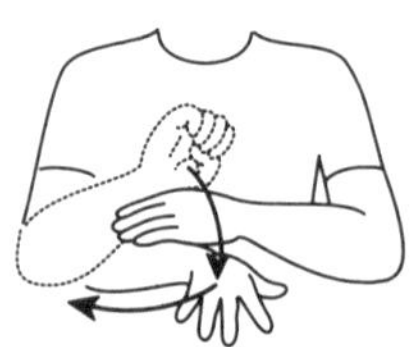

EPIDEMIC
E on back of hand moves forward to palm-down 5 over left hand and spreads outward

EPISCOPAL
With right index, outline full sleeve under left horizontal arm

EQUAL ♔
Fingertips of bent hands tap

EQUATE
E's, palm-out, tap sides together
(see EQUAL)

EQUATOR

Right E circles left palm-in S, from palm-out to palm-in position

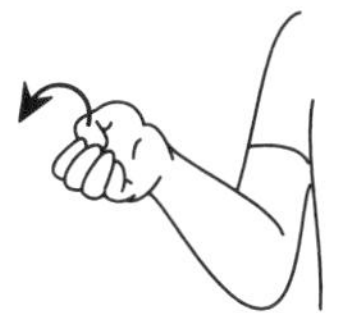

EQUIP

Palm-up E arcs to the right

(see THING)

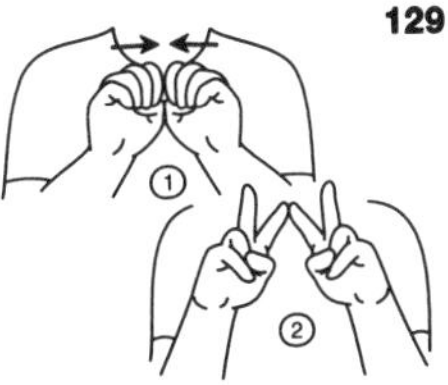

EQUIVALENT

E's, palm-out, tap; then change to palm-out V's with indexes touching

(see EQUAL)

ERA

E on vertical left palm, circles forward once, then touches palm again

(see HOUR)

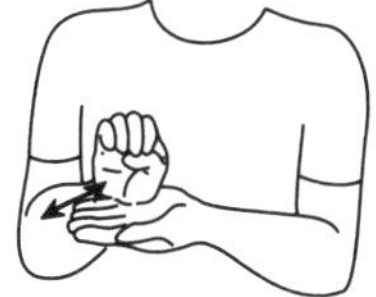

ERASE

Bottom of right E rubs back and forth on left palm

ERECT

Palm-out E slides up vertical left palm

(see TALL)

ERROR

With side of E, hit chin lightly; repeat

(see MISTAKE)

ESCALATE

E on side of horizontal left index; both move forward and up together

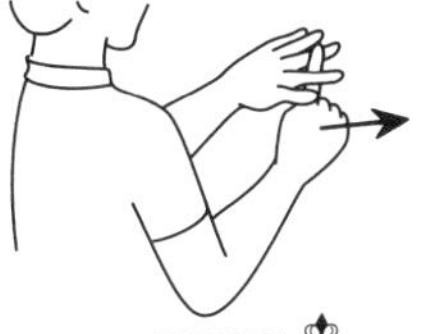

ESCAPE

Index finger between fingers of left hand; "escapes" sharply to side

ESCORT

Vertical 1-hands come together and move forward

(see WITH)

ESKIMO

E-hands outline parka hood

ESPECIALLY

Palm-out E on tip of middle finger of palm-in left 5, both move up

(see EXCEPT)

ESSAY
E moves down left palm in wavy motion
(see READ)

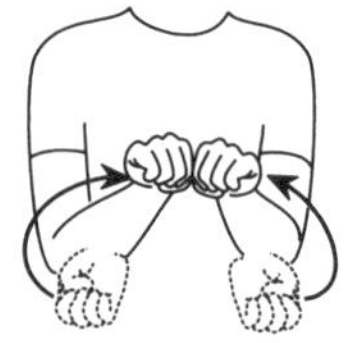

ESSENCE
E-hands palms-up to palms-down in vertical circle
(see IMPORTANT)

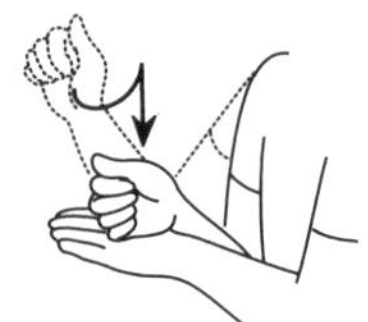

ESTABLISH
Palm-out A-hand twists to palm-left and comes down on back of left hand
(see FOUND)

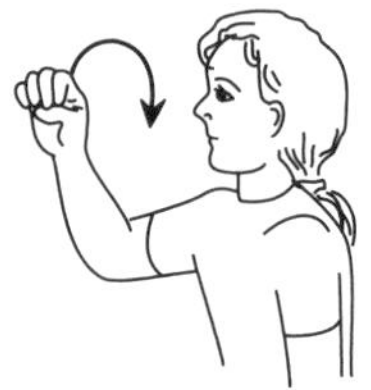

ESTEEM
Palm-left E arcs down in front of face
(see GOD)

ESTIMATE
Right palm-left E arcs sideways in front of forehead
(see GUESS)

ETCH
With palm-down E "draw" on palm
(see ART)

ETERNAL
E circles and then moves forward

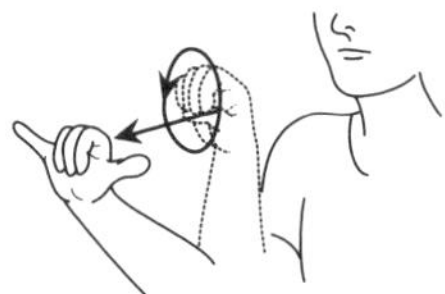

ETERNITY
E circles, moves forward while changing to Y-hand *(eternal + -y)*

EUROPE
E faces temple, circles vertically

EVACUATE
E-hand from between fingers of palm-down left hand moves sharply away
(see ESCAPE)

EVADE
Right E wiggles back from left palm-right A-hand
(see AVOID)

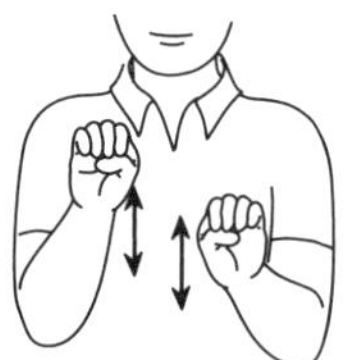

EVALUATE
E's move alternately up and down
(see BALANCE)

EVAPORATE
E shakes up out of left horizontal C

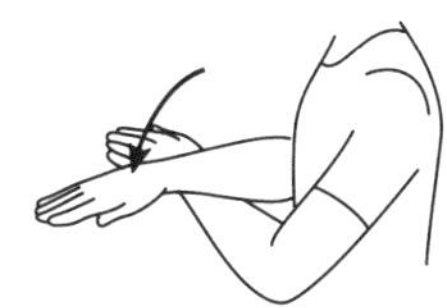

EVE
Flat right hand "sets" over left to a level position

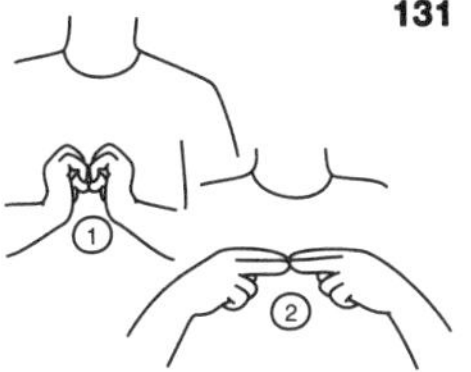

EVEN
E-fingertips touch, then N-fingertips
(see EQUAL)

EVENT
Palm-up E's twist to palm-down
(see HAPPEN)

EVER
Palm-out E circles
(see CIRCLE)

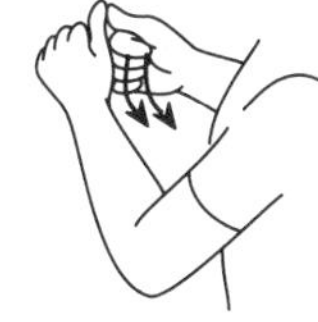

EVERY
Thumbtip of right A slides twice down thumb of left A
(see EACH)

EVIDENT
Palm-up E falls on left palm
(see PROVE)

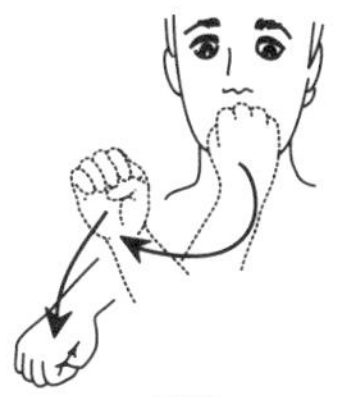

EVIL
Palm-in E at mouth, moves sharply to palm-down
(see BAD)

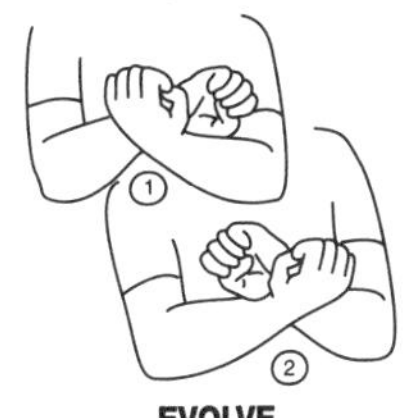

EVOLVE
Heels of E's touch, crossing, and stay together as hands reverse
(see CHANGE)

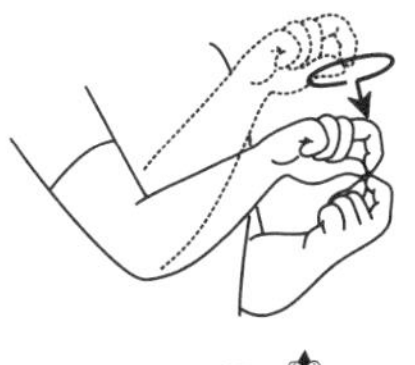

EXACT
Right hand with closed thumb and fingertip circles and drops on palm-up closed thumb and fingertip

EXAGGERATE
Right S in front of left; right S moves forward in short up and down arcs
(see PROPAGANDA)

EXAM
Right index faces left palm, moves downward, alternating index and X

EXAMPLE
Palm-out E on left vertical palm; both move forward
(see SHOW)

EXCAVATE
Palm-up E digs down and upward from left palm

EXCEED
Bent right on bent left hand; right arcs upward to new level
(see EXCESS)

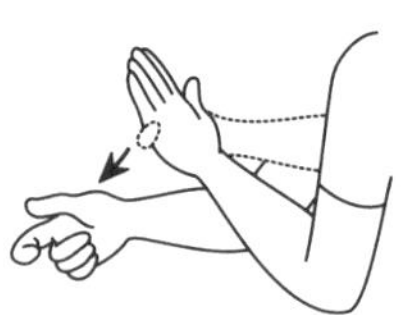

EXCEL
Right X holds side of left hand, jerks away forward
(see EXPERT)

EXCEPT
9 grasps finger of palm-in left index finger and pulls hand up

EXCESS
Bent hands, right atop left; right arcs inward and up twice
(see EXCEED)

EXCESSIVE
Bent hands, right atop left; right arcs inward and up, changes to V and shakes downward

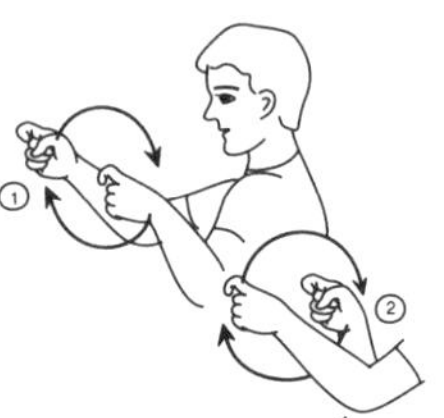

EXCHANGE
Horizontal X-hands, right in front of left, circle each other once

EXCITE
Bent middle fingers alternately brush upward on chest

EXCLAIM
Palm-left E-hand near side of mouth, twists to palm-out, moves slightly out and downward
(see ORDER)

EXCLUDE
Index finger side of open right hand brushes forward off left palm

EXCLUSIVE
Index finger side of open right hand brushes forward off left palm, changes to V and shakes downward

EXCUSE

Right fingertips brush off left fingertips several times

EXERCISE

Palm-down S's move up and down above shoulders

EXHAUST

Back of right V on palm-up left hand drags inward across palm

(see LIE)

EXHIBIT

Palm-out E against left palm; both circle horizontaly

(see DISPLAY)

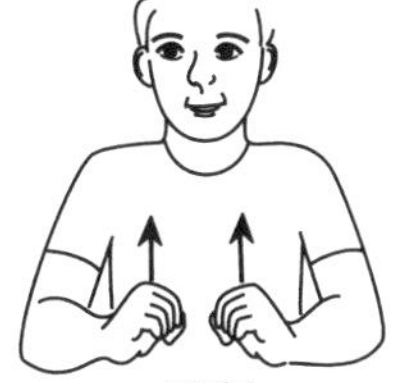

EXIST

E-hands, palms-facing, move upwards on body

(see ADDRESS)

EXIT

Right E rises toward body from under left flat palm

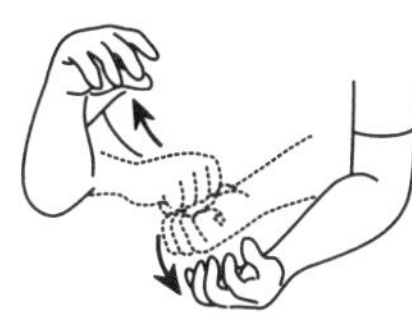

EXPAND

Palm-down right S on palm-up left S, separate vertically, opening

EXPECT

Index at temple, then slightly to side, hands face each other, right behind left, and bend quickly

EXPENSE

Back of right palm-up flat-O on left palm, rises, throws (money) down to palm-down 5

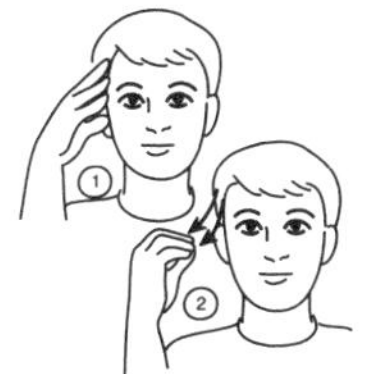

EXPERIENCE

Palm facing head, relaxed 5 on temple closes into flat-O; repeat

(see VETERAN)

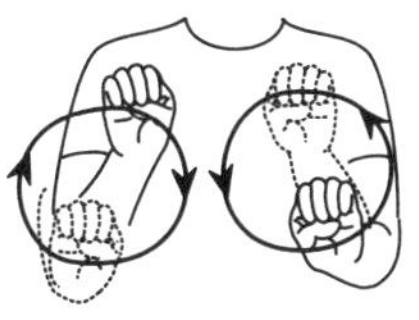

EXPERIMENT

Palm-out E's circle alternately

(see SCIENCE)

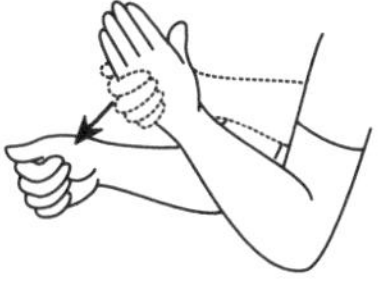

EXPERT

Grasp side of left hand, slide off forward into A

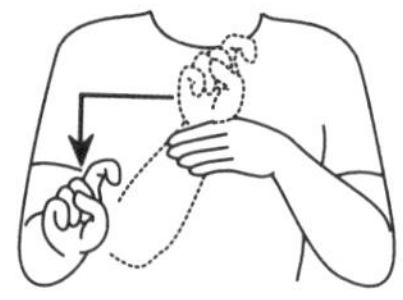

EXPIRE
Palm-out X slides along index of palm-in left hand and down fingers
(see FINISH)

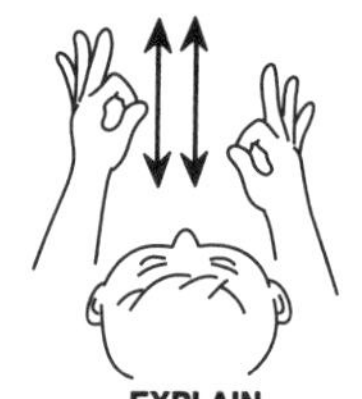

EXPLAIN
Horizontal 9-hands, palms-facing, alternately move forward and back
(see DESCRIBE)

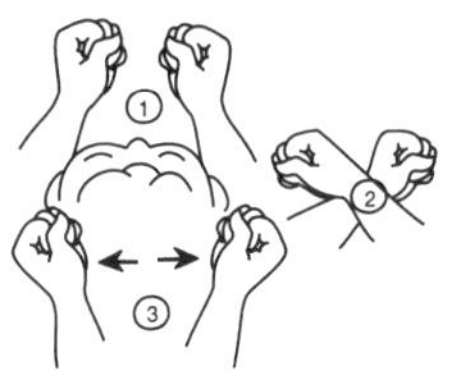

EXPLODE
Horizontal S's face each other, cross at wrists, jerk apart sharply
(see DYNAMITE)

EXPLORE
Palm-out E at eye moves down and out across left palm
(see INSPECT)

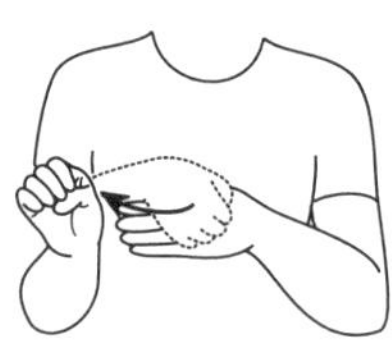

EXPORT
Inverted palm-in E on back of palm-in hand, flips forward to palm-out
(see SEND)

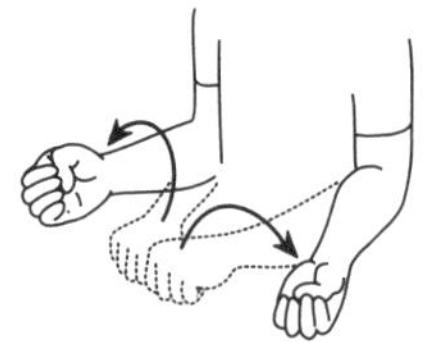

EXPOSE
E's, palms-down and touching, twist apart sideways to palms-up
(see OPEN)

EXPRESS
E-hands facing each other near chin, left ahead of right, move forward in slight arc

EXPRESSIVE
E's, palms-facing near chin, left ahead of right, move forward in slight arc; right V shakes downward *(express + -ive)*

EXTEND
Horizontal 9's touch, palms-facing; one arcs forward
(see POSTPONE)

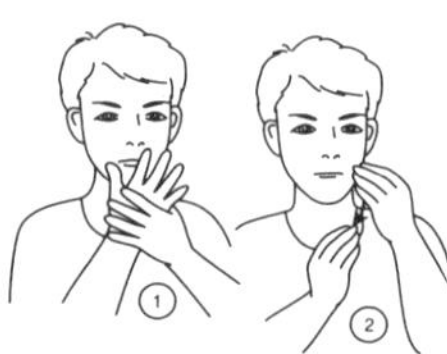

EXTINCT
Palm-in 5-hand, draws down through left C-hand while both hands close

EXTINGUISH
Wrist of palm-out X in left C, X turns inward dropping through C-hand
(see DRAIN)

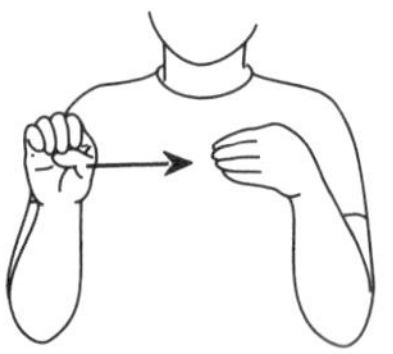

EXTRA
Palm-out right E moves toward and touches fingertips of left flat-O
(see MORE)

EXTRACT
Inverted E pulls sharply upward through palm-in C, tilting forward
(see OUT)

EXTREME
Palms-facing E's touch; right E arcs up and forward
(see FAR)

EYE
Right index points to eye

EYEBROW
Outline eyebrow with index

EYELASH
Relaxed palm-down 4 at eye moves forward to palm-out

NOTES

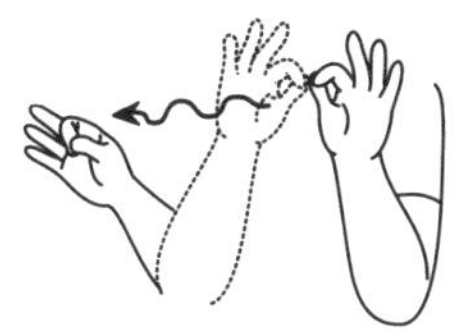

FABLE
Palm-out, right F-hand shakes away from stationary left F
(see DECODE)

FABRIC
Fingers of palm-in F rub shoulder
(see CLOTH)

FABULOUS ♔
Palm-out F's near temples make small outward circle, then palm-out, flat hands push forward

FACE ♔
Index finger circles face

FACILITATE
Fingers of right palm-up F tap little finger side of horizontal left S, pushing it upwards
(see HELP)

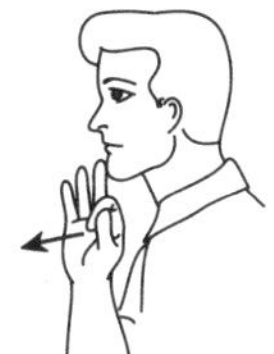

FACT
Fingers of F at chin; move forward
(see CERTAIN)

FACTOR
Side of F arcs inward across left palm
(see SOME)

FACTORY
Palm-out F-hands touch, and outline roof and sides
(see HOUSE)

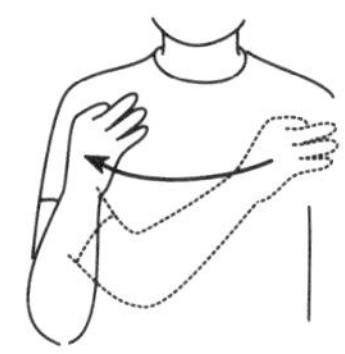

FACULTY
F-hand at left, then right shoulder
(see MEMBER)

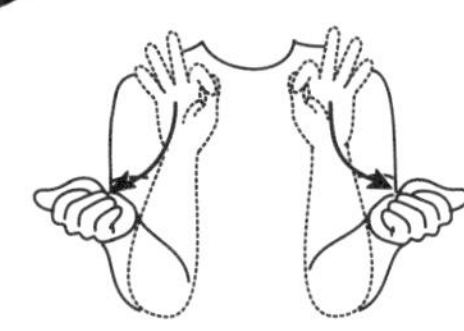

FADE
Palm-out F's fall; gradually closing to palm-up A's
(see MELT)

FAHRENHEIT
Thumb and fingertip of F move up and down left index
(see THERMOMETER)

FAIL
Back of right V slides outward across left palm

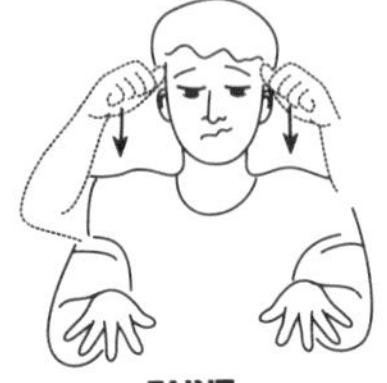

FAINT
Palm-down A's, drop from near temples to 5's

FAIR
Middle finger of palm-left F taps chin

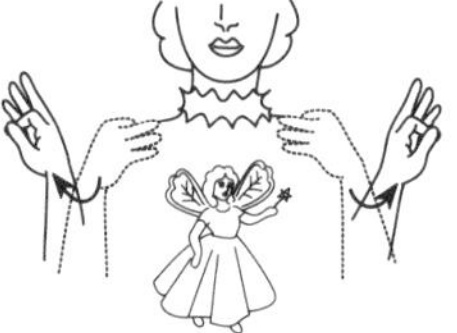

FAIRY
Fingers of F's on shoulders, twist to point out *(wings)*
(see ANGEL)

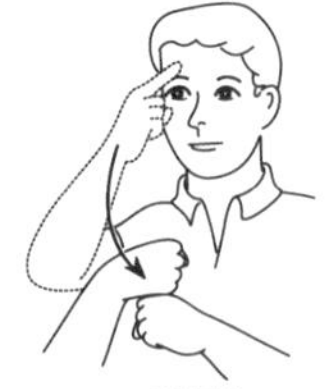

FAITH
Touch forehead with index; drop to S on S at shoulder level

FAKE
Fingers of F brush past mouth
(see FALSE)

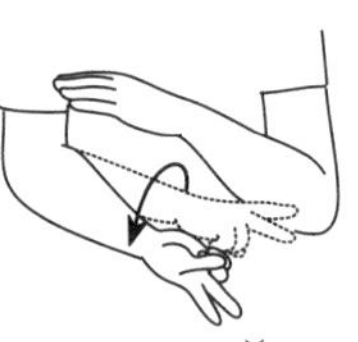

FALL ★
Palm-down V on elbow twists over and out to palm-up

FALSE ♔

Palm-left index brushes past mouth

FAME

Palm-in index fingers at corners of mouth spiral up and out

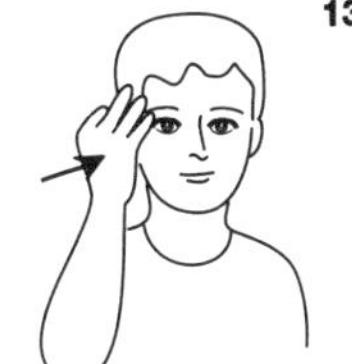

FAMILIAR

Fingertips of right palm-in F tap side of forehead

(see THINK)

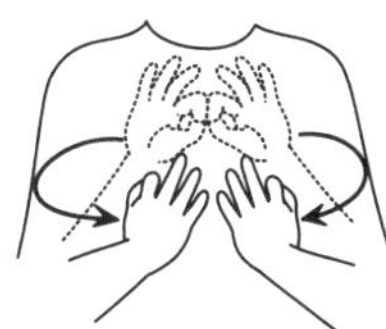

FAMILY

F-hands first touch indexes, and then circle to touch little fingers

(see CLASS)

FAMOUS

Index fingers at corners of mouth spiral up and out; right palm-out O arcs slightly to right *(fame + -ous)*

FAN

Palm-in 4-hand fans face

FANCY ♔ ★

Thumb of palm-left 5 brushes upward on chest several times

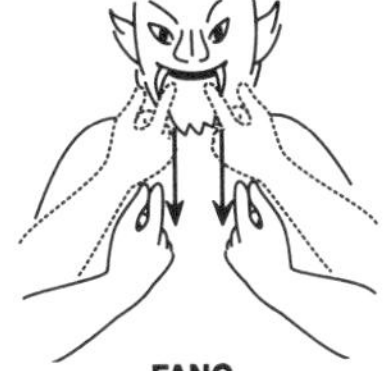

FANG

Fingers of G-hands close, pulling fangs downward from mouth

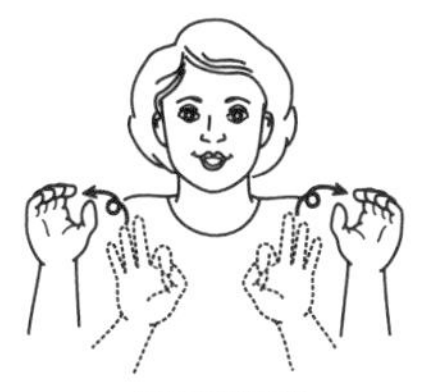

FANTASTIC

F's make small outward circles, then palm-out C's push forward

(see FABULOUS)

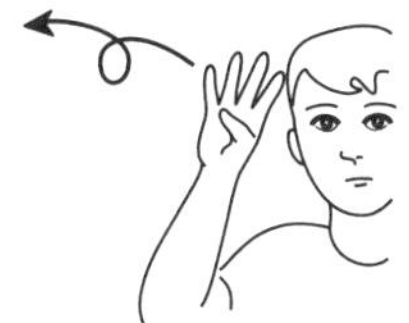

FANTASY

Palm-out 4 off temple loops forward

(see IDEA)

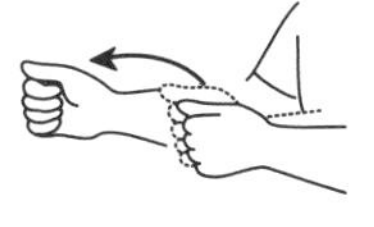

FAR ♔

A-hands palms-facing together, right hand arcs forward

(see YONDER)

FAREWELL

Palm-out 5 waves from side-to-side

F

FARM ♔
Right thumb of open hand is drawn across the chin left to right

FASCINATE
C-hands, right behind left in front of face, draw forward, closing to S's

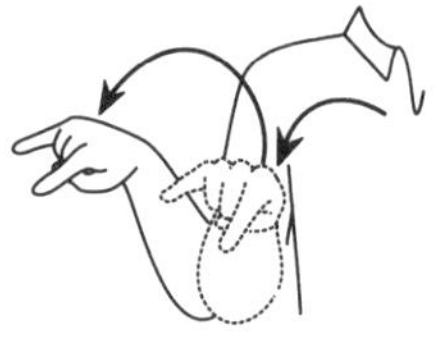

FASHION
Index and little finger out, hand nods down, arcs, and nods to right

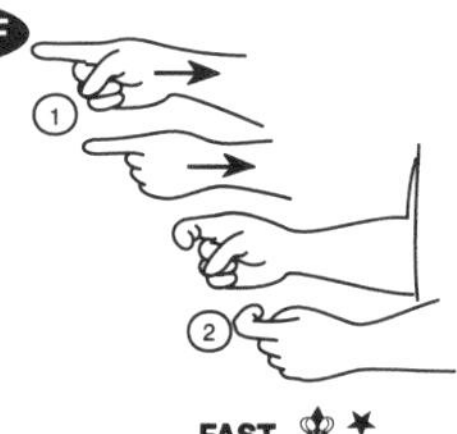

FAST ♔ ★
Indexes point forward, one ahead of the other, jerk back to X's

FASTEN
Right palm-up X drops to hook into hole of horizontal F

FAT
Both claw hands face the neck, move out to sides
(see CHUBBY)

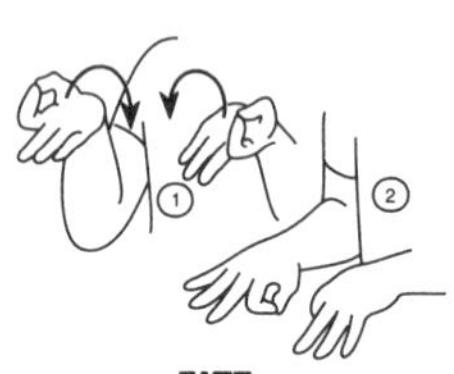

FATE
(Alt. 1)
Palm-up F's flip over to palm-down

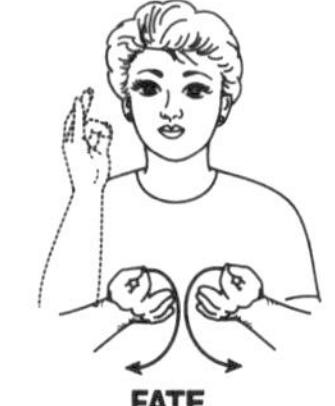

FATE
(Alt. 2)
Right F near side of head arcs forward; both F's twist to palm-down
(see HAPPEN)

FATHER
Thumb of right 5 on forehead
(see DAD)

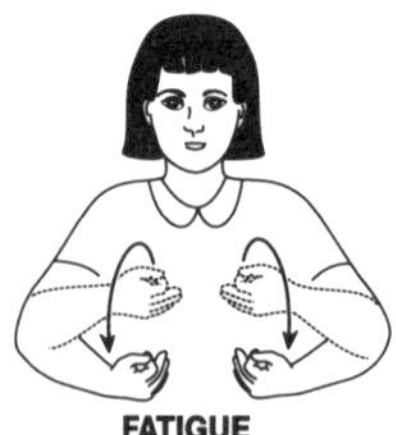

FATIGUE
Fingertips of F's on chest; hands arc down to palm-up
(see TIRE)

FAUCET
Bent 3-hand twists twice to the right as if turning on faucet

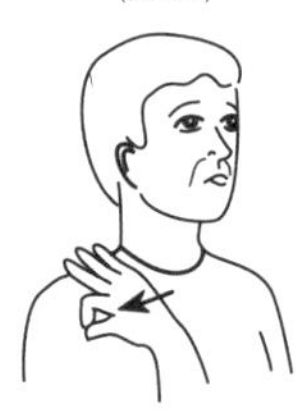

FAULT
Palm-in fingertips of F push down on right shoulder

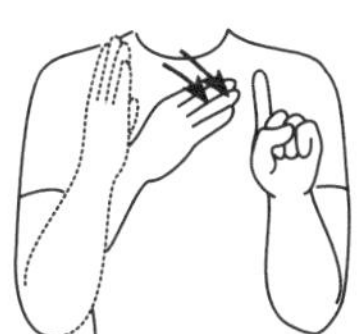

FAVOR
Fingertips of right palm-in B-hand nod up and down toward left index finger several times

FAVORITE
Tap middle finger on chin; repeat. *(may be signed favor + -ite)*

FEAR
Slightly at left, palm-out F's shake downward toward body
(see AFRAID)

FEAST
Palm-in F's circle alternately to mouth
(see BANQUET)

FEATHER
F-hand arcs up from back of head

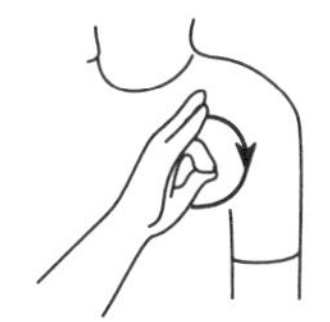

FEATURE
Side of F-hand circles heart clockwise once on chest
(See CHARACTER)

FEBRUARY
(Alt. 1)
F arcs over at side of palm-in vertical left hand
(see CALENDAR)

FEBRUARY
(Alt. 2)
Draw heart over own heart with F-hands
(see HEART)

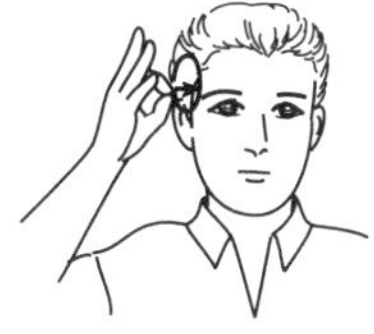

FEDERAL
Palm-left F circles once near temple, then touches temple
(see GOVERN)

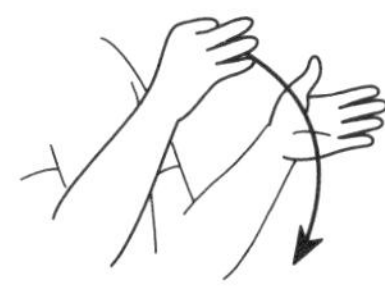

FEE
Middle fingertip of F brushes down across horizontal left palm
(see COST)

FEED *
Flat-O's, left hand ahead of right, hand food from near mouth in 2 small jerks

FEEDBACK
Palm-out F moves back toward body, changing to B

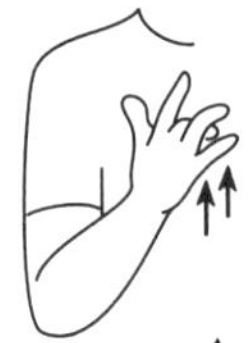

FEEL

Bent middle finger brushes middle of chest upwards

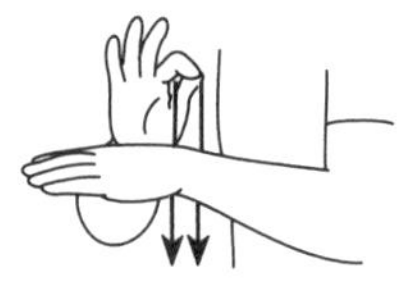

FEET

Palm-out F moves down behind flat left wrist twice

(see FOOT)

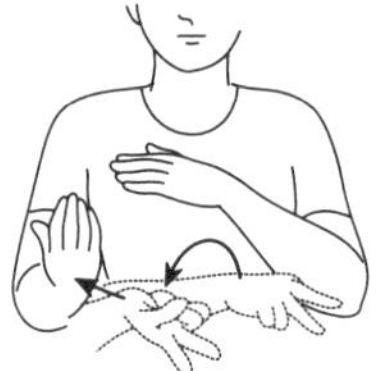

FELL

Right palm-down V on left elbow twists over and out to palm-up; flat hand flips towards shoulder *(fall + p. t.)*

FELLOW

Side of right F-hand moves forward from temple

(see HE)

FEMALE

Tips of thumb and index of palm-out F brushes down jawline

(see GIRL)

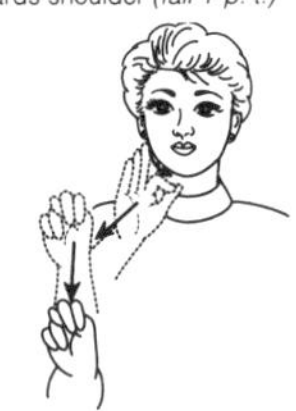

FEMININE

Tips of thumb and index of palm-out F brushes down jaw line; N-hand drops down *(female + -ine)*

FENCE

Fingers of both palm-in hands mesh; separate sideways

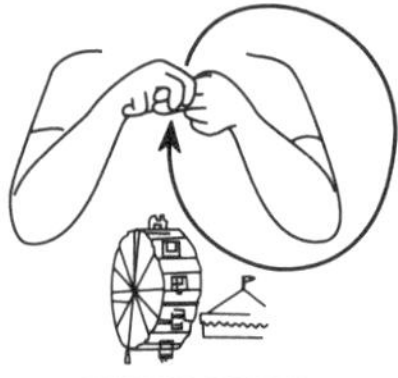

FERRIS WHEEL

Two fingers sit on side of left H; make large circle forward with both hands

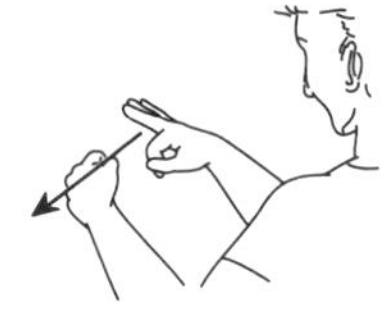

FERTILE

Fingers of right F brush backwards across thumb side of horizontal left S

(see FULL)

FESTIVAL

Palm-out F curves right and down, changes to L and continues right

(see CARNIVAL)

FEVER

Back of flat hand on forehead

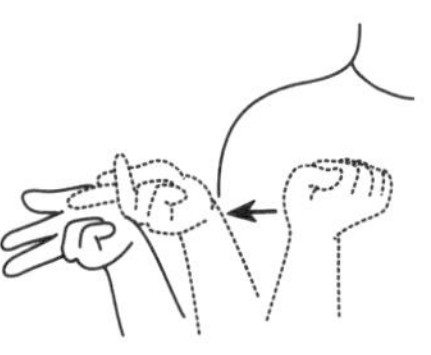

FEW

Palm-up A, while moving to right opens slowly to 3-hand

FIB
Palm-down index passes to left under lip; may repeat
(see LIE)

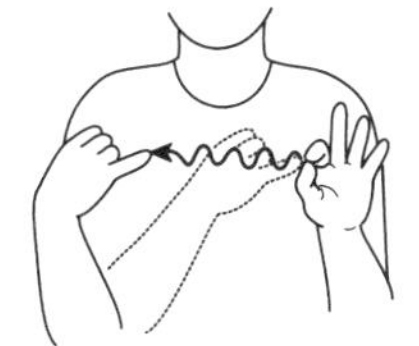

FIBER
Left palm-out F, little fingertip of palm-in right I touches left thumb and shakes off to right
(see CORD)

FICTION
Middle finger of F on temple circles up to right
(see IDEA)

FIELD ★
Palm-down F on back of hand, circle out, back to elbow, along arm to hand
(see GROUND)

FIERCE
Claw in front of face arcs to side, fingers closing slightly
(see ANGER)

FIG
Finger and thumb of F on palm-in left S, goes around S
(see APRICOT)

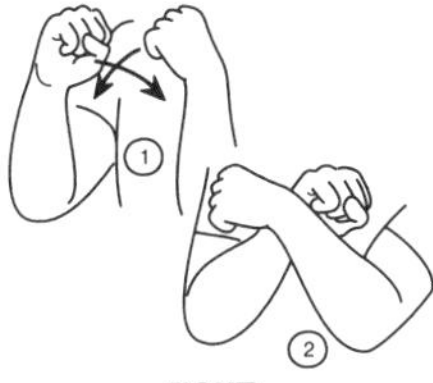

FIGHT
S-hands face each other, jerk to cross at wrists; repeat

FIGURE ★
Left palm-in F, right palm-out F, palms brush sideways twice
(see ARITHMETIC)

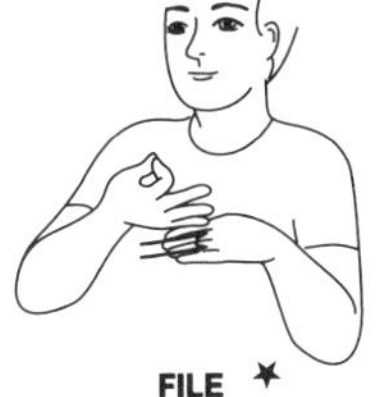

FILE ★
Side of F-hand pushes toward left wrist along each finger

FILL
Right palm-down flat hand rises inside horizontal left C

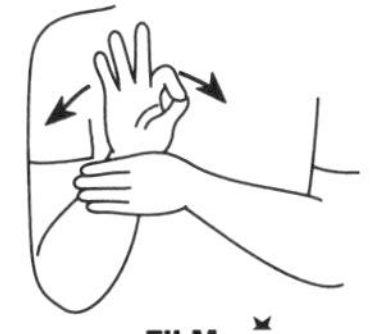

FILM ★
Heel of F-hand stays on side of left, fingers of F move side-to-side slightly
(see MOVIE)

FILTH
Right hand opens sharply under chin from S to 5

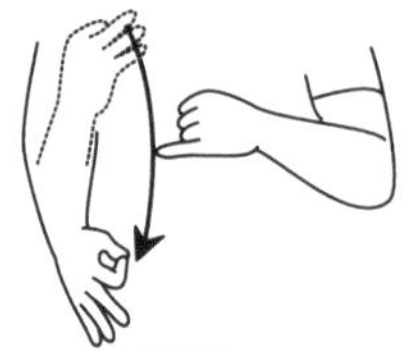

FINAL

Right F-hand moves down past the little finger of the left I-hand

(see LAST)

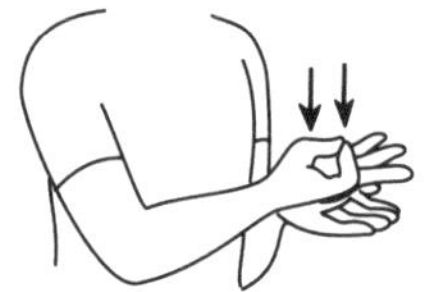

FINANCE

Palm-up right F taps left palm twice

(see MONEY)

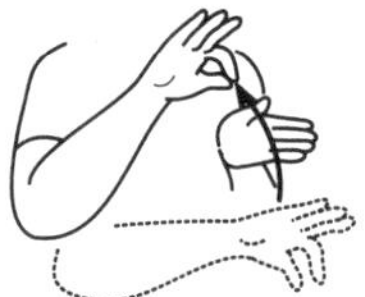

FIND

F-hand pulls up past palm of left hand

FINE

Thumb of palm-left 5-hand on chest, move hand forward *(may be done sharply with F-hand)*

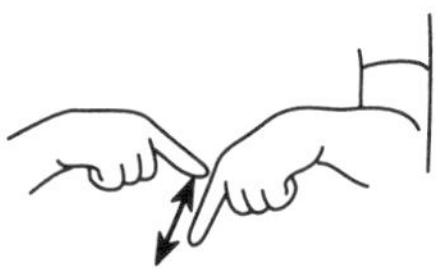

FINGER

Fingertip rubs back of index finger

FINISH

Side of right hand on side of left moves to end and drops down

FINLAND

(U.S. Sign)

Side of F-hand circles near forehead

(see DENMARK)

FINLAND

(Finnish Sign)

Bent index taps teeth

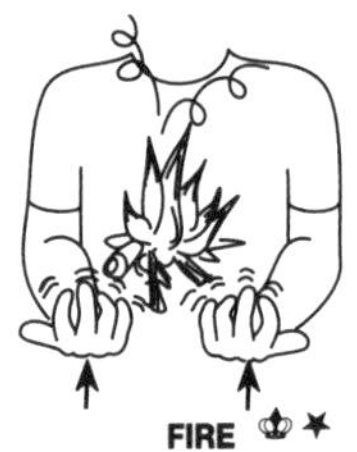

FIRE

Palm-up bent 5's move upward fluttering fingers

FIRM

Left S, palm-down; side of right F hits back of hand

(see HARD)

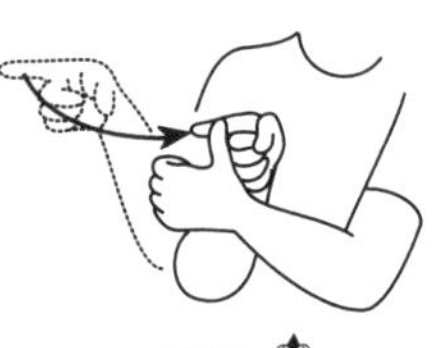

FIRST

Right index finger hits tip of left extended-A thumb

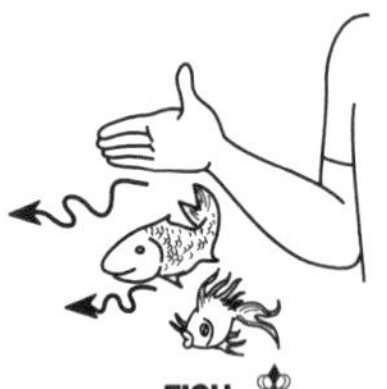

FISH

Palm-left flat hand flutters forward like fish swimming

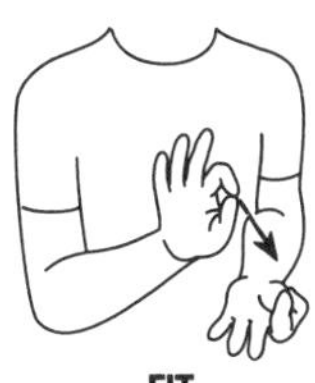

FIT

Right palm-out F moves down to touch thumbtips of palm-up left F

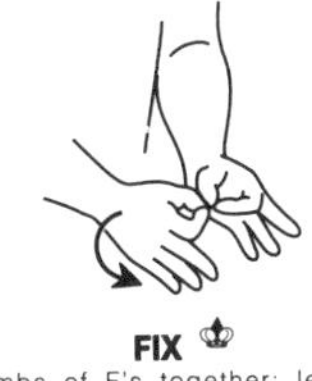

FIX ♔

Thumbs of F's together; left is stationary, right twists down from wrist; repeat

FLABBERGAST

Bent-V's near chin, right palm-in, left palm-out; right falls to palm-up *(dropping jaw)*

FLAG ♔

Right flat hand waves in breeze, left index on arm

FLAKE

Palm-up F arcs downward, striking side of left index in passing

(see CHIP)

FLAME

Palm-in F moves up, fluttering fingers

FLANNEL

(Alt. 1)

Thumb and index of right palm-down F circle on palm-up left hand

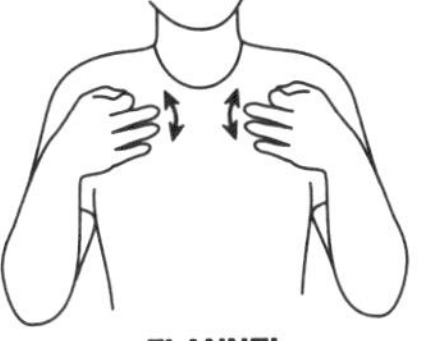

FLANNEL

(Alt. 2)

Fingers of F's rub chest near shoulders

(see CLOTH)

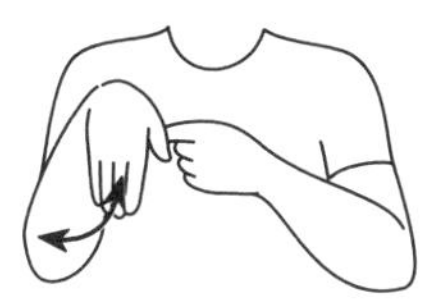

FLAP

Right hand hangs over left index and flaps up and down

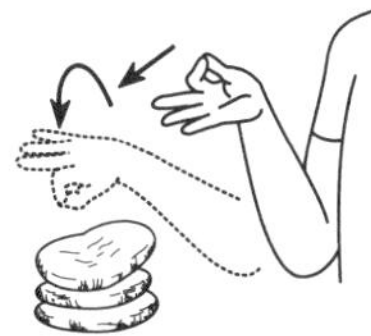

FLAPJACK

Palm-up F slides forward and flips

(see PANCAKE)

FLARE

Wrist of right O on horizontal left index finger; opens to 5 and rises, fingers fluttering

(see TORCH)

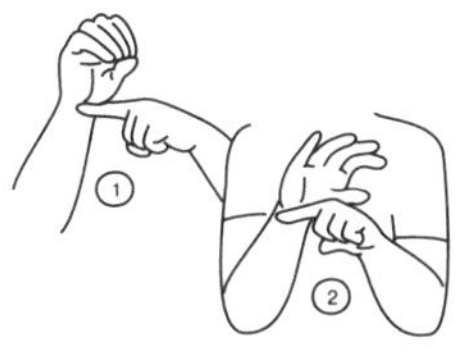

FLASH

Flat-O and 5-hand open and close supported on left index; can repeat

(see SIGNAL)

FLASHLIGHT
Left index on wrist of right palm-down 5, move around like flashlight

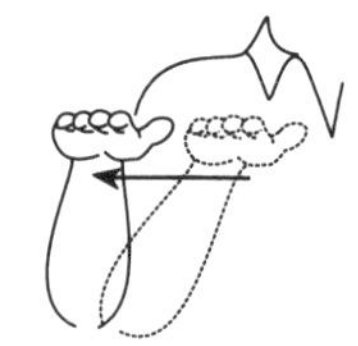

FLAT ♔
Open hand swings right, on a level

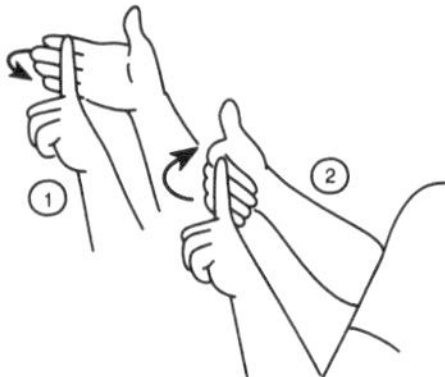

FLATTER
Right hand "paints" left index finger

FLAVOR
Palm-in, middle finger of F taps chin
(see TASTE)

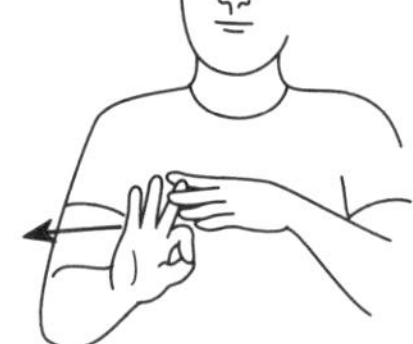

FLEE
Palm-out F between fingers of palm-down left hand moves sharply away
(see ESCAPE)

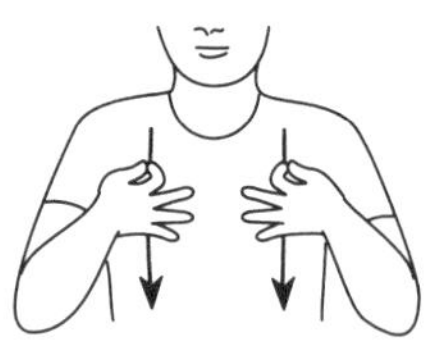

FLESH
Palm-in horizontal F-hands move down body from chest
(see BODY)

FLEW
Bent hands at shoulders flap fingers like wings; right flat hand flips toward shoulder *(fly + p.t.)*

FLEX
Right hand holds left index finger and flexes forward and back
(see PLASTIC)

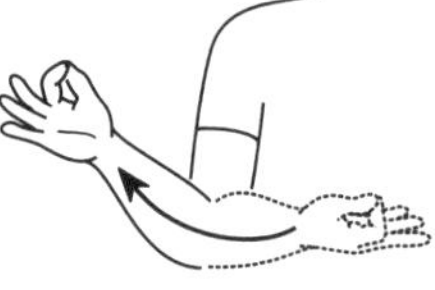

FLING
Palm-up F throws forward
(see THROW)

FLIRT
Palm-down 5-hands, thumbtips together, wiggle fingers *(like eyelashes)*

FLOAT
Right F, palm-up on back of left flat hand; float forward together
(see DRIFT)

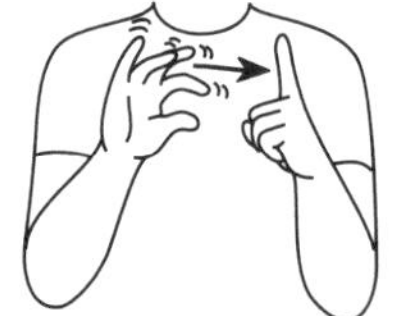

FLOCK ✶
Palm-out 5 moves toward vertical left index while fluttering fingers

FLOOD
Palm-down 5-hands point to each other; rise, fluttering fingers

FLOOR ♔
Palm-down B-hands separate

FLOUR
Palm-in F circles on back of palm-in S
(see DOUGH)

FLOW
Palm-down hands right behind left; fingers flutter while hands flow forward to the left

FLOWER ♔
Flat-O at right of nose, then at left

FLU
Palm-in F-hands, right on forehead, left on stomach
(see SICK)

FLUID
Right F moves downward from lips with wavy motion

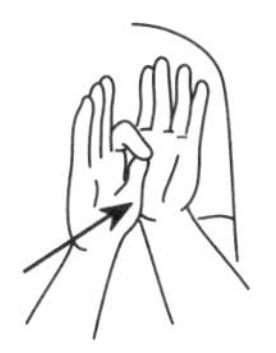

FLUNK
Side of F-hand hits left palm sharply
(see FORBID)

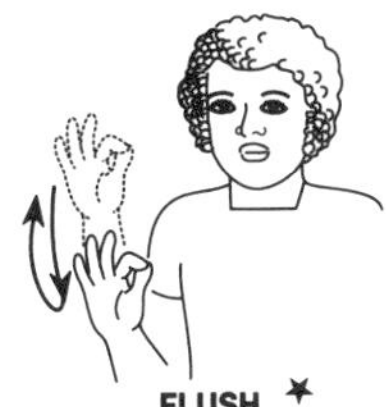

FLUSH ✶
Palm-out F, move down and back up again *(can be done near cheek)*

FLUTE
Palm-in F's play flute, fluttering fingers

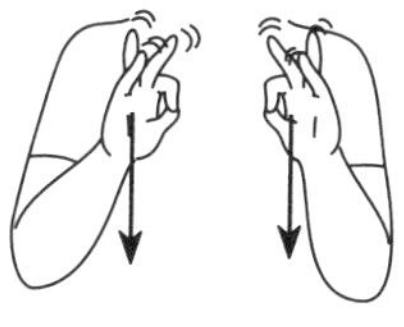

FLUTTER
Fingers of F-hands flutter downward

FLY ✶
Bent hands at shoulders flap fingers like wings

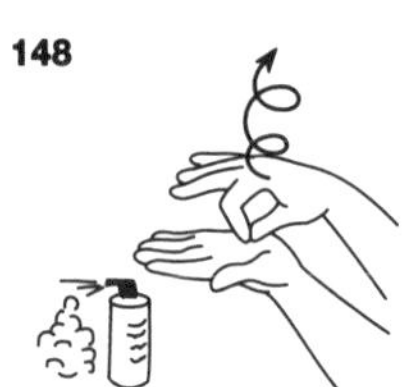

FOAM
F-hand spirals up from left palm

FOCUS
F's at side of eyes drop and come together to a focus

FOE
F-hand and horizontal left index move sharply apart
(see OPPOSE)

FOG
From sides, arc up and cross palm-in F's at wrists, near face
(see DARK)

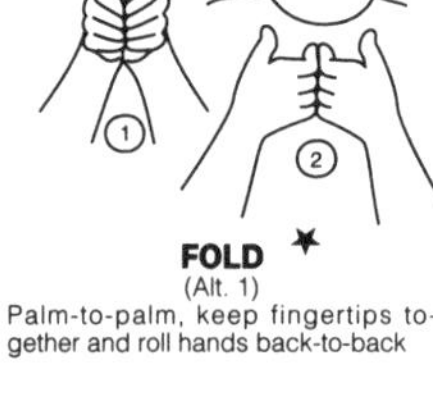

FOLD ✱
(Alt. 1)
Palm-to-palm, keep fingertips together and roll hands back-to-back

FOLD
(Alt. 2)
Both hands palm-up, right folds over to palm-down on top of left

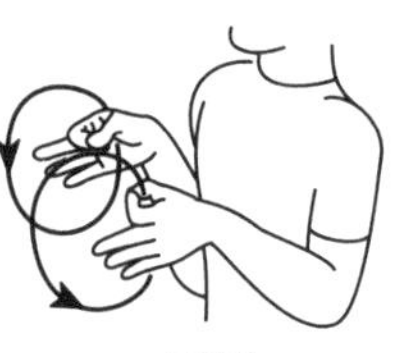

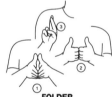

FOLDER
Palm-to-palm; keep fingers together and roll hands back-to-back; then add R-hand *(fold + -er)*

FOLK
Horizontal F's, palms-facing each other; circle alternately up and down forwards
(see PEOPLE)

FOLLOW
Right A follows left A; both move forward left

FOND
Palm-in F's cross over heart
(see LOVE)

FOOD
Palm-in flat-O nods toward mouth *(putting food in)*

FOOL
Palm-left F arcs in front of eyes
(see STRANGE)

FOOT
Right F-hand moves down behind flat left wrist
(see PAW)

FOOTBALL
Mesh fingers of almost horizontal 5-hands several times

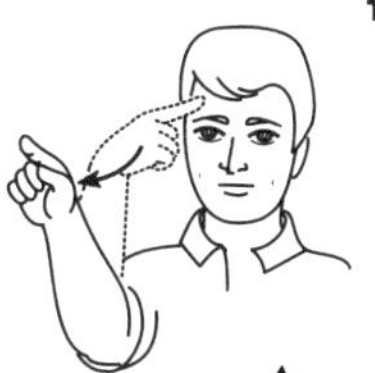

FOR ♔
Palm-in right index on forehead twists to palm-out

FORBID ♔
Side of right vertical 1-hand strikes vertical left palm

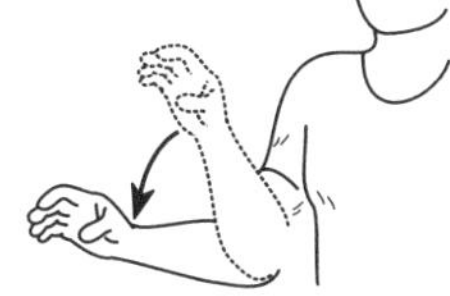

FORCE
Thumb of palm-out C at shoulder level; move sharply forward

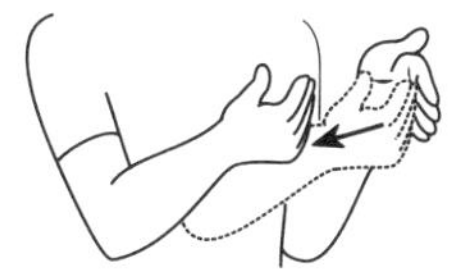

FORE
Bent right hand behind bent left; right moves back
(see PRE)

FOREIGN
Fingers of palm-in F rub left arm in circles near elbow
(see COUNTRY)

FOREST
Elbow of F on back of left hand, shake F slightly to right
(see TREE)

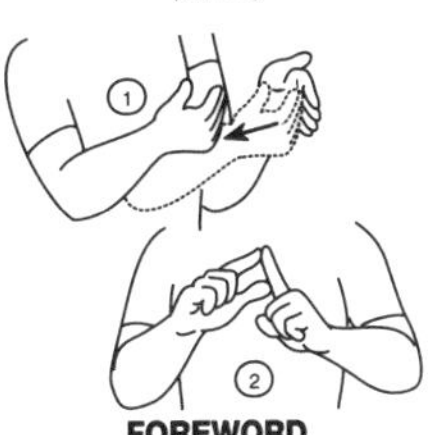

FOREWORD
Bent right hand behind bent left, right moves back; right G-fingers rest against left index *(fore + word)*

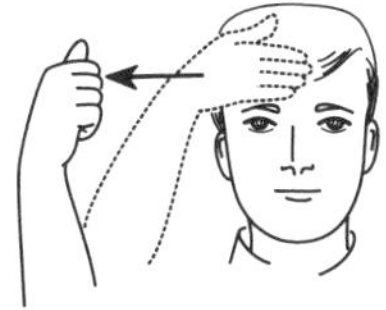

FORGET
Palm-in hand on forehead; wipe off to right, to palm-in A

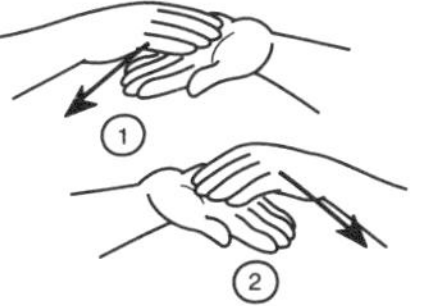

FORGIVE
Fingertips brush off palms, right off left; turn over, then left off right

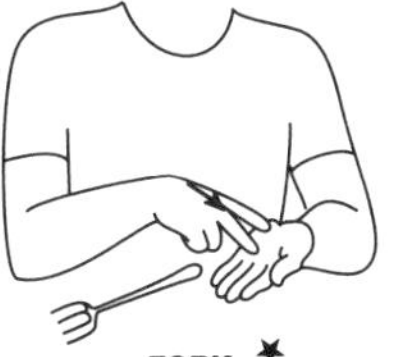

FORK ★
"Tines" of V stab palm

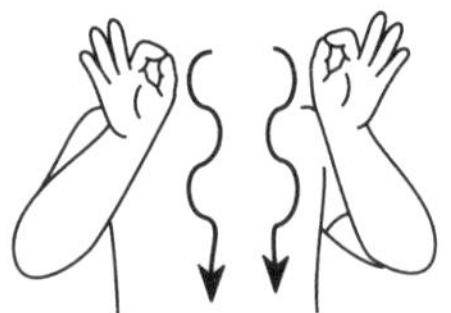

FORM

Thumb and index of F's outline form

(see SHAPE)

FORMER

Thumb of open hand brushes backward on front shoulder several times

FORMULA

Side of right F on fingers of left vertical hand, then on heel

(see LAW)

FORT

Left arm horizontal in front of body; palm-out right 4 moves right in front of left hand

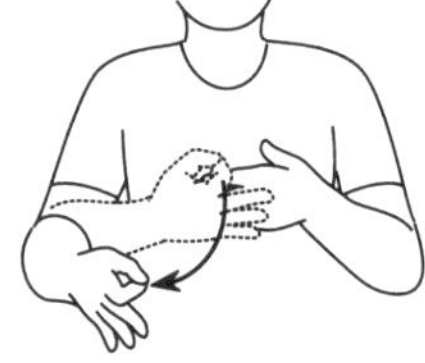

FORTH

Left hand palm-in pointing right, right F palm-in against back of fingers; right moves forward

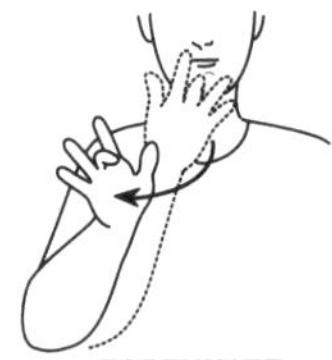

FORTUNATE

Palm-in 5, bent middle finger touches chin and flicks forward to palm-out

FORTUNE

Palm-up F on left palm, swing up over palm, inverting

(see RICH)

FORWARD

Bent right hand behind bent left; right moves back, changes to W, moves forward *(for + ward)*

FOSSIL

(Alt. 1)

Fingertips and thumb of right F make elongated circle in palm-up left hand

FOSSIL

(Alt. 2)

Back of palm-up right F taps back of palm-down left S

(see STONE)

FOSTER

Finger and thumb of F touch temple, then side of jaw

(see PARENT)

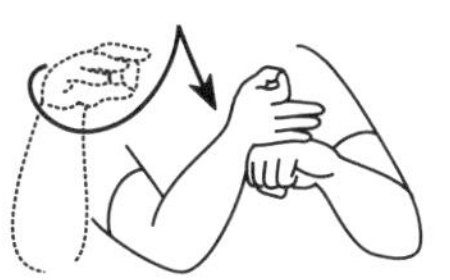

FOUND
(verb)
Palm-down F twists, and side of F falls on back of left S
(see ESTABLISH)

FOUND
(past tense)
F-hand pulls up past palm of left hand; right hand flips towards shoulder *(find + p. t.)*

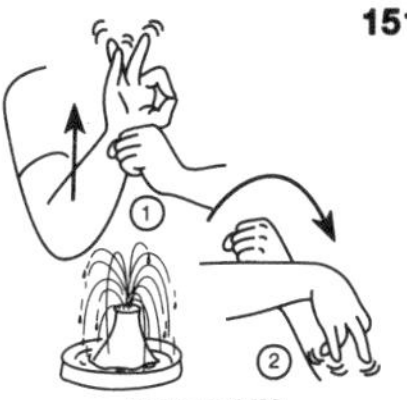

FOUNTAIN
F rises behind left S, fingers fluttering, and "flows" down other side

FOX
Nose in center of F, twist F around nose, wrist stationary

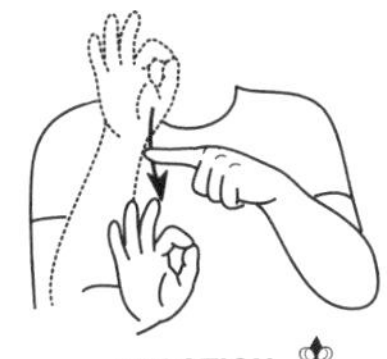

FRACTION ♔
Place F above and then below horizontal left index

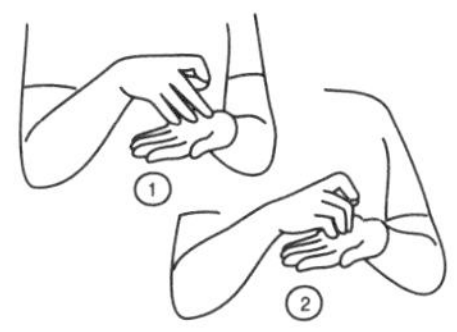

FRAGILE
Three fingertips of F do push-ups on left palm
(see WEAK)

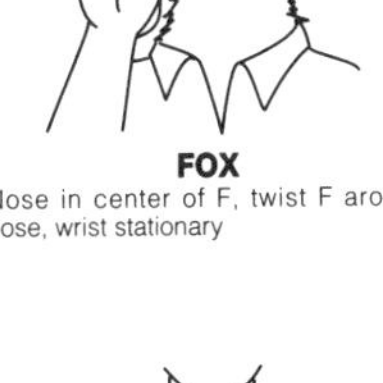

FRAGMENT
Left I-hand points slightly right; right F arcs down across end of little finger
(see CHIP)

FRAGRANT
Palm-in F circles vertically near nose
(see SMELL)

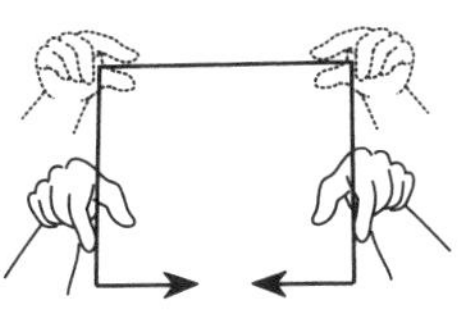

FRAME ★
Palm-out G's outline frame

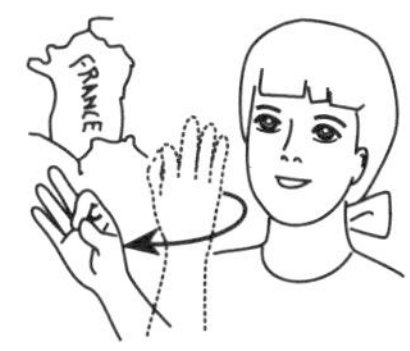

FRANCE
(U.S. Sign)
Palm-in F-hand twists to palm-out

FRANCE
(French Sign)
F twists outward from heart

FRANK
Side of right F on left palm; slide F straight forward
(see HONEST)

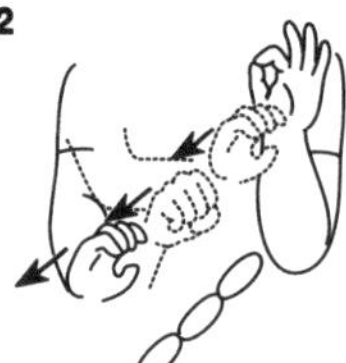

FRANKFURTER
C to S hand pulls alternately out of left F-hand
(see BALONEY)

FREAK
F-fingers flutter past forehead
(see STRANGE)

FRECKLE
Spot face with thumb and fingertip of F
(see MEASLES)

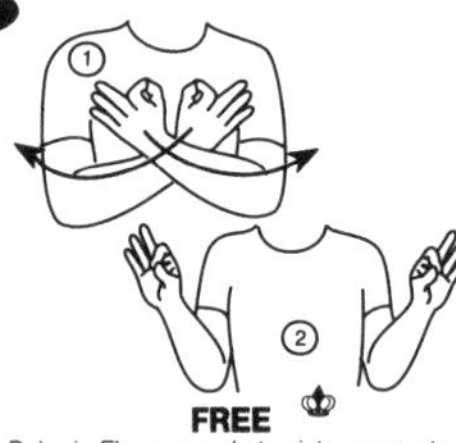

FREE ♔
Palm-in F's, crossed at wrists, separate and twist to palm-out

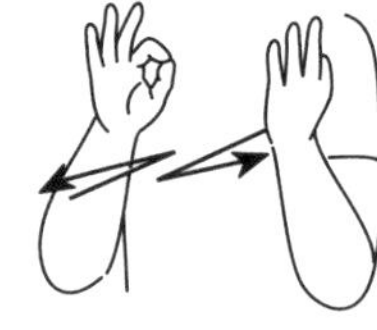

FREEWAY
Palms-facing F's brush past each other, moving rapidly back and forth *(can be free + way)*
(see TRAFFIC)

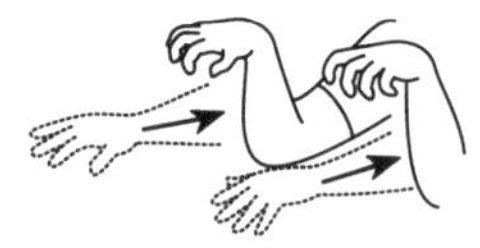

FREEZE
Palm-down 5's draw back to claws

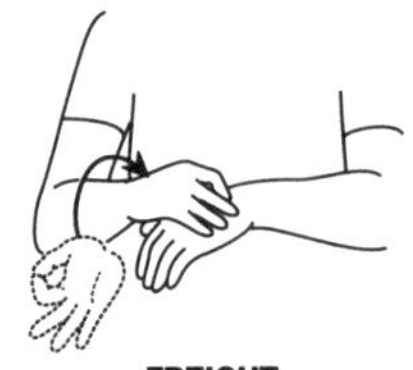

FREIGHT
Palm-up F arcs over to palm-down on top of left palm-down hand
(see CARGO)

FRENCH FRY
Palm-down F arcs once to right
(see THING)

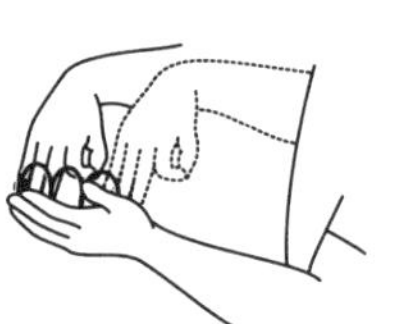

FREQUENT
Fingertips of palm-in F tap forward on left palm-up hand
(see OFTEN)

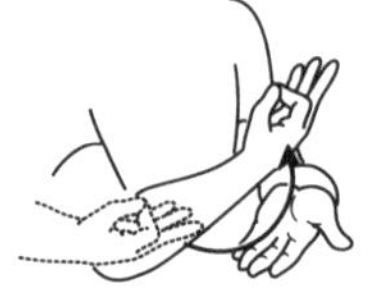

FRESH
Back of F-hand slides left across left fingers and palm, arcing up
(see NEW)

FRESHMAN ♔
Right index taps tip of palm-in left 5's ring finger

FRIDAY
Palm-out F-hand circles slightly
(see MONDAY)

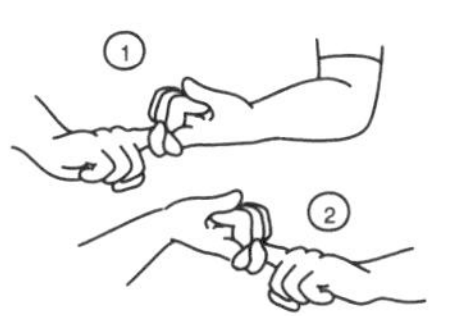

FRIEND
Index fingers hook, first right over left, then left over right

FRIGHT
Palm-in F's jerk toward each other and cross

(see SCARE)

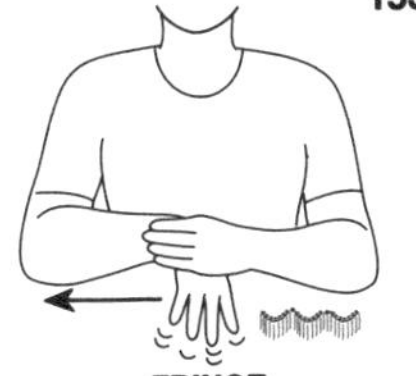

FRINGE
Palm-in left B, palm-in right 4 inside with fingers dangling down moves slightly right with fingers wiggling

FRISBEE
Right A, palm-in, throws frisbee, opening hand

FRISK
Both F-hands, palms-facing, pointing forward, twist slightly while arcing upwards twice

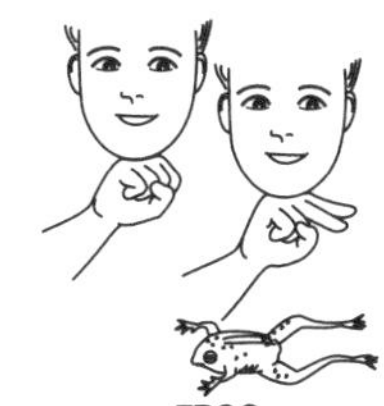

FROG
Back of right S under chin; two fingers flick out; repeat

FROM
Knuckle of palm-in right X touches palm-out left index, and then moves toward body

FRONT
Palm-in flat hand moves downward in front of face

FROST
3-fingers of F smooth up and over back of S-hand

(see COVER)

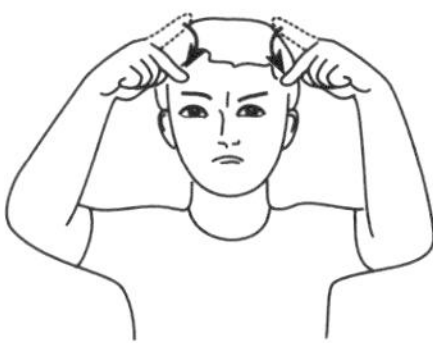

FROWN
Indexes above eyes drop to point downwards over eyes

FRUIT
Finger and thumbtip of F on cheek; twist wrist

(see APPLE)

FRUSTRATE
Flat hand flips up in front of mouth

FRY
Right palm-down F on left palm flips over to palm-up
(see COOK)

FUDGE
F circles on back of left hand
(see CHOCOLATE)

FUDGSICLE
Fingers of palm-in F-hand near chin move down and out; repeat
(see ICE CREAM)

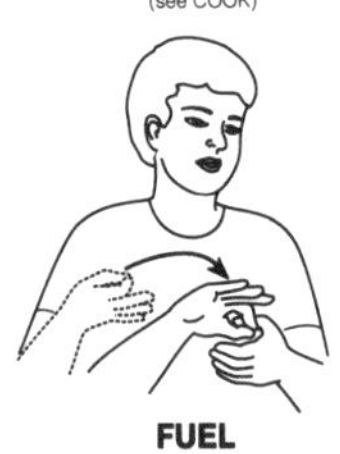

FUEL
Side of right F pours into left O
(see GASOLINE)

FULL
Palm-down flat hand brushes inward across top side of left S
(see MATURE)

FUN
(Alt. 1)
Right palm-in U-fingertips on nose drop to palm-down U; fingertips of both U's brush each other alternately up and down

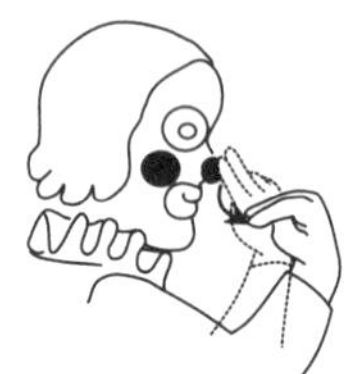

FUN
(Alt. 2)
Palm-in U on nose strokes downward to palm-in N
(see DOLL)

FUNCTION
Palm-out F arcs, side-to-side, hitting back of left S
(see BUSY)

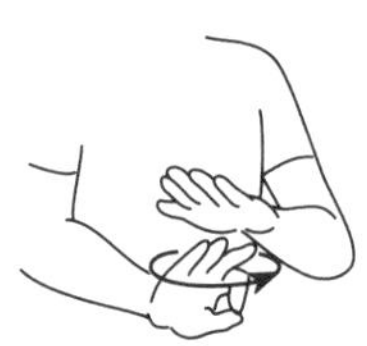

FUNDAMENTAL
Circle right palm-out F below left palm
(see BASE)

FUNERAL
Right V behind left V; move forward both hands slightly in down and up motion twice
(see TROOP)

FUNGUS
Heel of F-thumb circles on little fingertip of left palm-up I-hand
(see ALGAE)

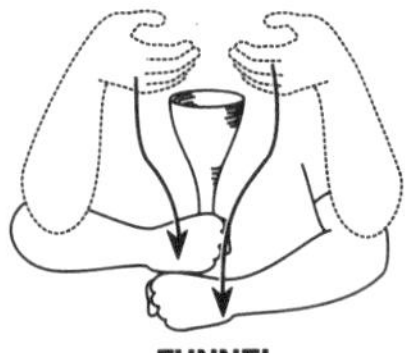

FUNNEL
Horizontal C's approach each other and close to S's, moving down to one on the other

FUNNY
Palm-in U on nose strokes downward to palm-in N's; add Y-hand *(fun + y)*

FUR
Right F-hand slides up left arm and over shoulder

FURNACE
Fingers of relaxed 5 flutter upward through left horizontal C

(see GROW)

FURNISH
F-hand, palm-up, arcs to the right

(see THING)

FURNITURE
F-hand palm-up, arcs to the right; right U-hand slides down left vertical palm (*furnish + -ure)*

FURY
Right palm-in F jerks up chest

(see ANGER)

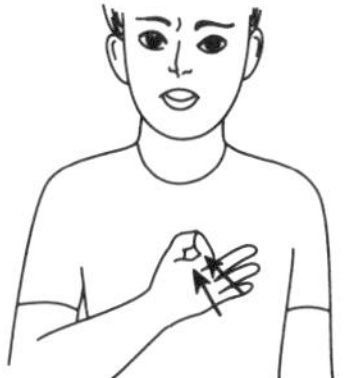

FUSS
Palm-in F taps on chest sharply

(see COMPLAIN)

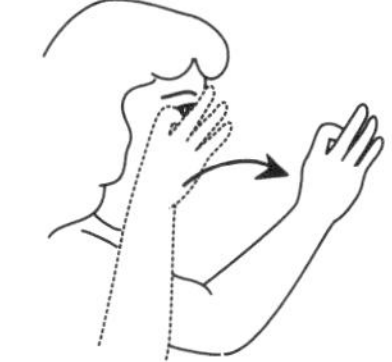

FUTURE
Palm-left F-hand near side of head arcs forward

(see WILL)

NOTES

GAIN
Right palm-up H swings over to hit top of left G; may be repeated
(see INCREASE)

GALAXY
Thumb sides of G's brush each other alternately, moving upwards
(see STAR)

GALLAUDET
G closes and moves backwards from side of eye

GALLERY
Parallel G's, pointing forward, move forward together
(see HALL)

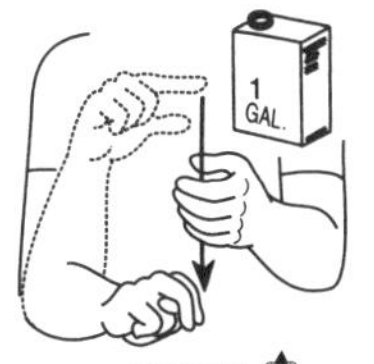

GALLON ♔
Right G passes down to N through left horizontal C

GALLOP
Right behind left, bent-V's leap forward to open V's; repeat

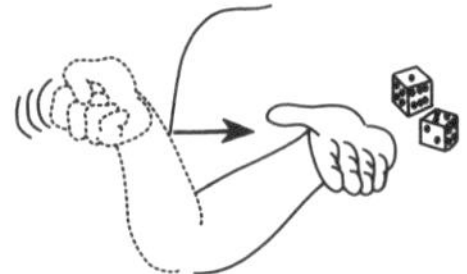

GAMBLE

Mime shaking dice and throwing them

(see LOTTERY)

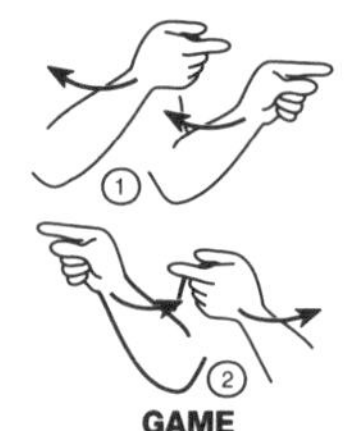

GAME

(Alt. 1)

G-hands, one palm-out, one palm-in, swing back & forth, pivoting at wrists

(see PLAY)

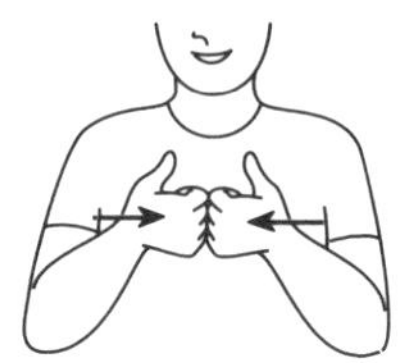

GAME

(Alt. 2)

Palm-in A's, thumbs up, bump knuckles

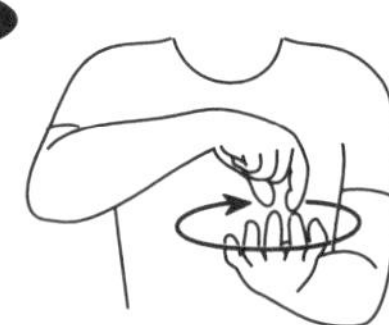

GANG

Left relaxed 5 palm-up; right palm-down G circles above

GARAGE

Thumbs and fingertips of G's touch, outline garage

(see HOUSE)

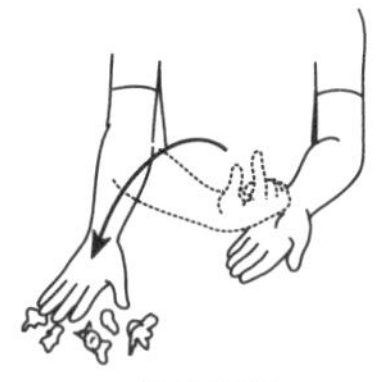

GARBAGE

Back of G on palm, slide forward and off, throwing down as palm-down 5

(see DISPOSE)

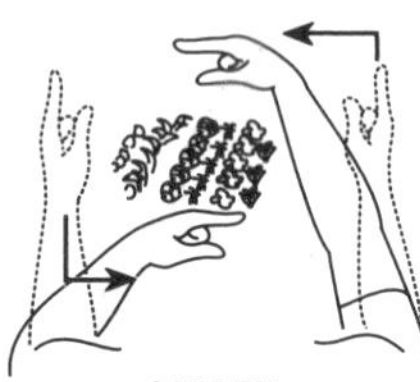

GARDEN

Box in a garden with G-hands

(see BOX)

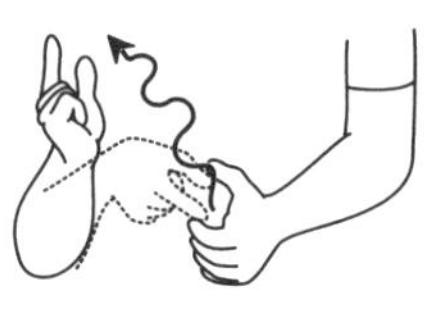

GAS

Right G rises up in wavy motion from top of left horizontal C

(see EVAPORATE)

GASOLINE

Extended thumb of right A pours into left horizontal O

(see FUEL)

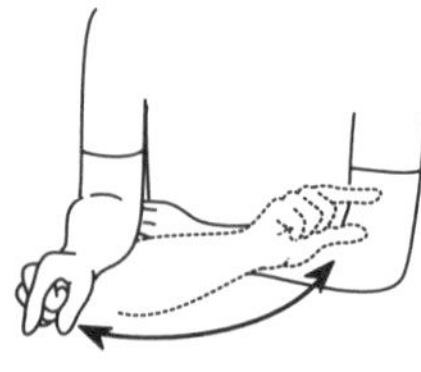

GATE

(Alt. 1)

G swings out from elbow and back

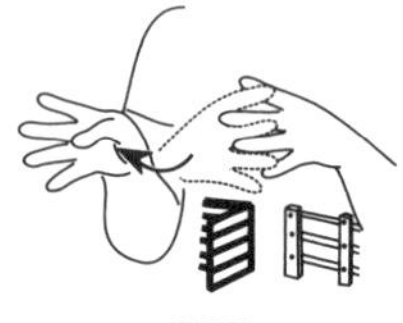

GATE

(Alt. 2)

Fingers of palm-in horizontal 4 hands mesh; right opens outward and closes again

GATHER 

Starting at sides, horizontal flat hands flap slightly forward toward each other several times to meet, palm-in

(see COLLECT)

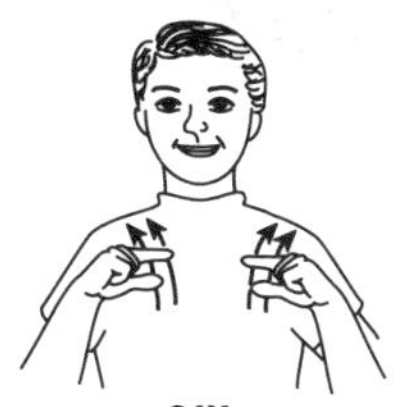

GAY
Sides of G-hands brush upwards on sides of chest; repeat
(see DELIGHT)

GAZE
V at side pf right eye points forward; move forward with steady movement
(see STARE)

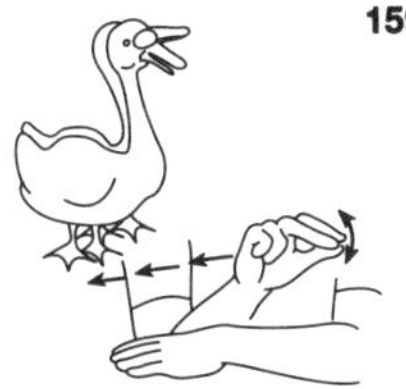

GEESE
First two fingers and thumb open and close, arm against left arm; move to left wrist, opening and closing

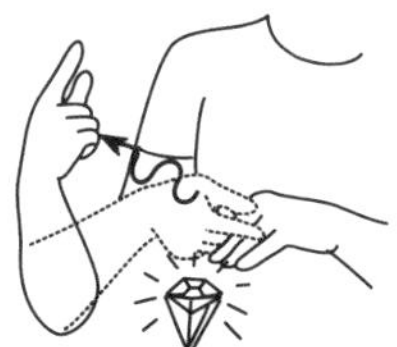

GEM
G shakes away from left ring finger
(see DIAMOND)

GENDER
G at temple, then at jaw
(see PARENT)

GENE
Left I-hand palm-up, heel of right G circles on end of little finger
(see ALGAE)

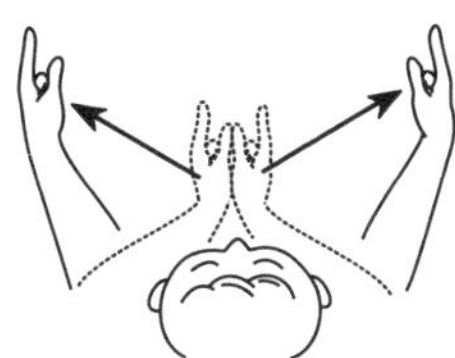

GENERAL
Palms of G-hands touch; then separate forward
(see BROAD)

GENERATE
G's, palms-facing, circle each other forward from right shoulder

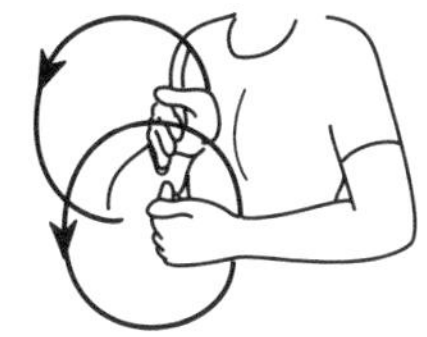

GENEROUS
Bent hands circle each other vertically near heart
(see KIND)

GENIUS
Thumb of horizontal left C on forehead; thumb of right C in front of fingers of first one

GENTLE
G-hands, one behind the other at chin; separate downward
(see QUIET)

GENTLEMAN
A-thumb on forehead drops to 5-hand, thumb touching chest

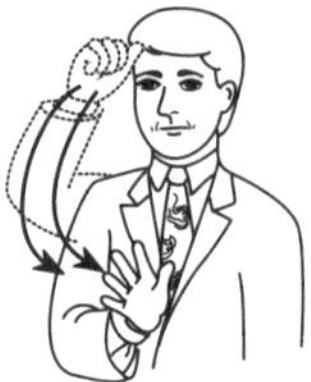

GENTLEMEN
Make the sign for "Gentleman" twice

GENUINE
Side of right G-hand on palm, slide off forward
(see HONEST)

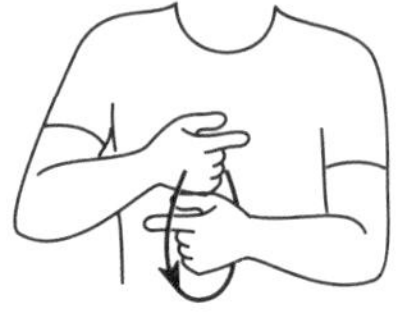

GEOGRAPHY
Right G on left; then circle each other vertically once and touch again
(see WORLD)

GEOMETRY
Little finger side of G hits thumb and finger of left G; repeat
(see ARITHMETIC)

GERBIL
G brushes off tip of nose; repeat
(see MOUSE)

GERM
Side of G circles on left palm, changes to flat-O over palm and spreads up arm using 5-hand
(see CANCER)

GERMAN
(U.S. Sign—Alt. 1)
S-hands cross at wrists, open to 5's

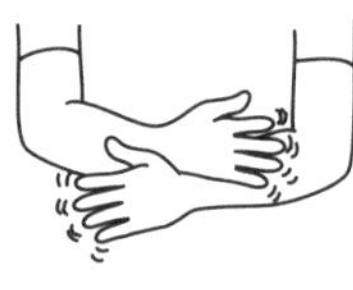

GERMAN
(U.S. Sign—Alt. 2)
Open hands crossed at wrists, wiggle fingers

GERMANY
(German Sign)
Back of hand with vertical index touches forehead

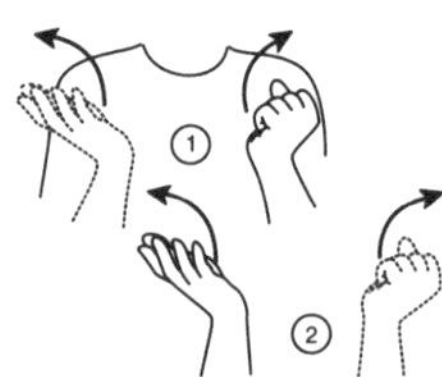

GESTURE
Begin with both hands in loose palms-up S's; hands alternate in brushing fingers out, becoming palm-in loose 5's while moving slightly up and out

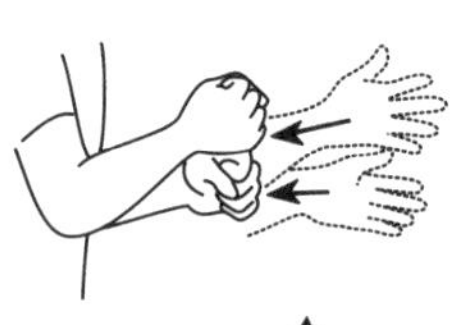

GET
Right open hand above left, draw toward body, closing to S-hands

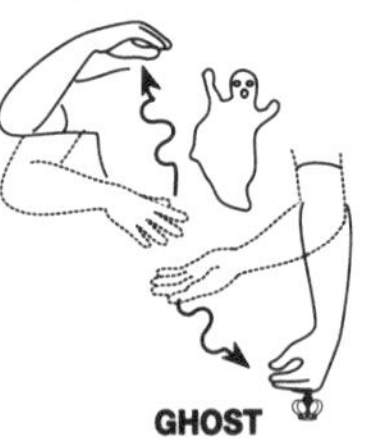

GHOST
Palms-facing, right above left, right rises and left drops in wavy motion, closing to flat-O's

GIANT
Both G-hands move in big arc to sides from shoulders
(see GIGANTIC)

GIFT
G's point up, left ahead of right, drop to left to level position

GIGANTIC
G's at shoulders move in large arcs to sides, change to palm-out C's
(see GIANT)

GIGGLE
Wiggle indexes of palm-in L's at corners of mouth

GILL
Tips of G-hand draw curved gill on side of neck

GINGER
Right G above left, tap twice

GIRAFFE
Palm-in C-hand traces up neck

GIRL
Thumb of extended-A hand moves down jawline

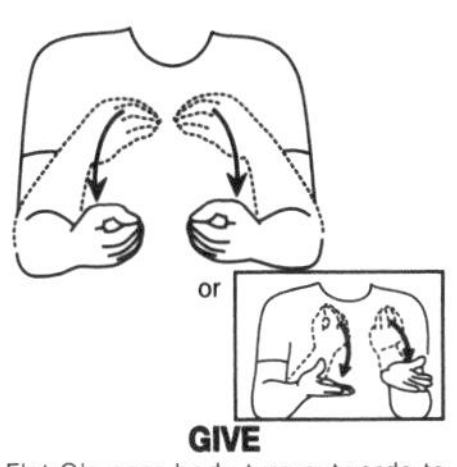

GIVE
Flat-O's near body turn outwards to palm-up *(or can end with flat palm-up)*
(see ISSUE)

GLACIER
Both parallel G-hands move forward in a zigzag motion
(see WAY)

GLAD
Side of G-hand brushes chest upward; repeat
(see HAPPY)

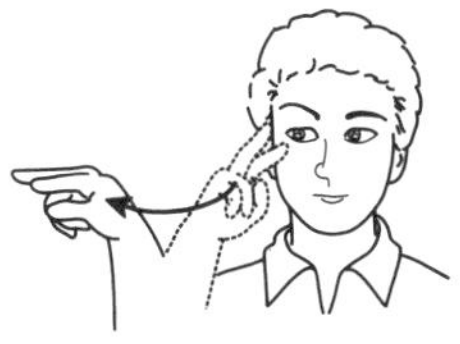

GLANCE
V at side of right eye flicks off to point towards side

GLASS
Drop G from temple to palm

GLAZE
Fingers of palm-down G arcs to cover back of palm-in left S
(see COVER)

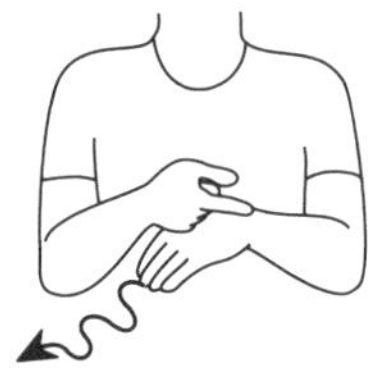

GLIDE
G rests on back of left hand, both glide forward
(see DRIFT)

GLIMPSE
Horizontal palm-in right hand shields right eye; open and close index to peek through

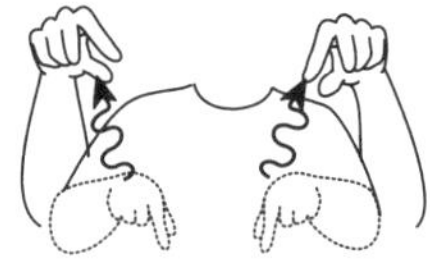

GLISTEN
Both G-hands move up and out with wavy motion
(see CLEAR)

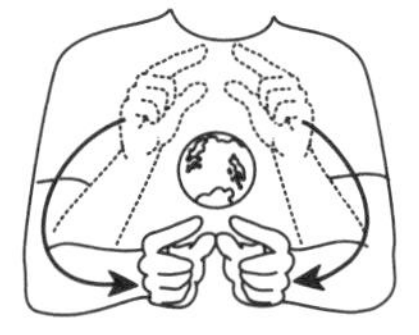

GLOBE
2 G's separate, outline globe and touch again
(see BULB)

GLORY
Palm of 5 on palm, right lifts off, fingers fluttering

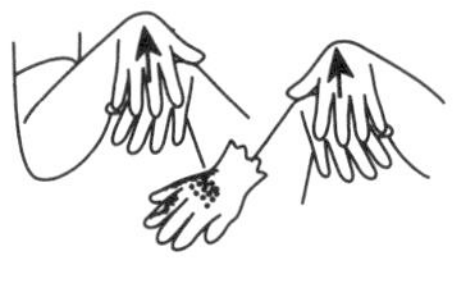

GLOVE
Draw on invisible gloves

GLOW
G's palm-facing, change to 5's moving upwards and out fingers wiggling

GLUE
G-hand twists to palm-down; sweeps across left palm
(See PASTE)

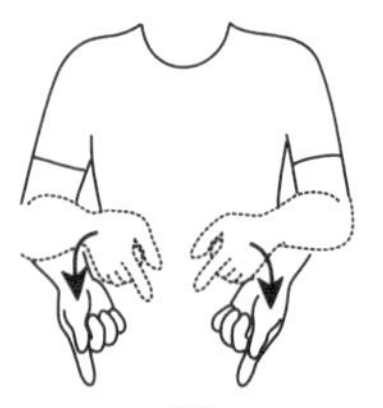

GO
G-hands face each other, roll out to point forward

GOAL
Left G at head height, slightly to left; right index, behind left G, jerks down to point at G
(see AIM)

GOAT
Palm-in fist on chin, two fingers flick out; fist moves to forehead, two fingers flick out again

GOBBLE
Palm-in G circles up and in near mouth; repeat
(see EAT)

GOBLET
Side of right G on palm-up left hand, right rises and opens to C

GOBLIN
G's pull away from each other vertically with wavy motion
(see GHOST)

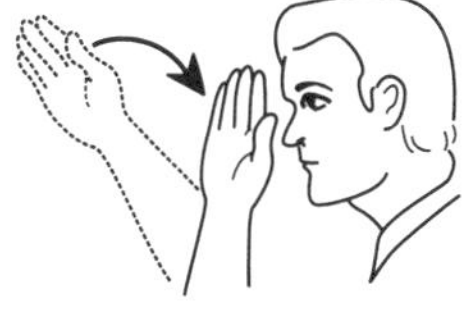

GOD
Palm-left hand arcs down from above to near forehead

GOLD
G at ear shakes downward to right
(see CALIFORNIA)

GOLF
Hold and swing invisible golf club

GOOD
Palm-in fingers on chin, fingers together, drop to palm of left hand
(see INDEED)

GOOF
Back of right G hits forehead
(see DUMB)

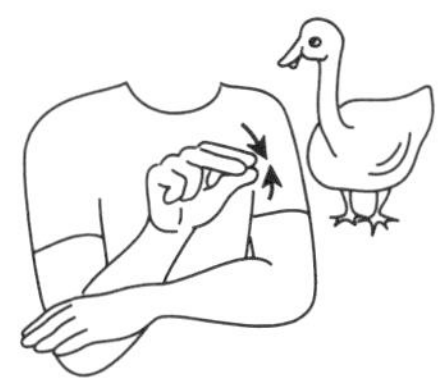

GOOSE
Arm on back of left wrist, first two fingers open and close on thumb; repeat several times

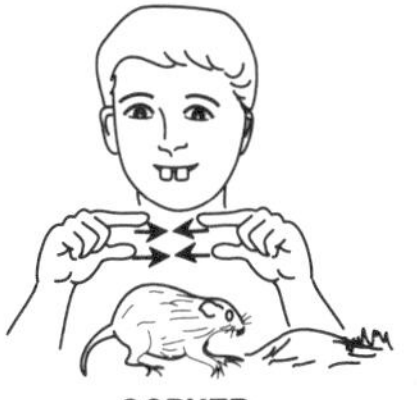

GOPHER
Tips of G's tap under chin

GORGEOUS
G circles face
(see FACE)

GORILLA
G-hands scratch sides
(see MONKEY)

GOSPEL
Little finger side of G-hand brushes up left palm; repeat
(see NEW)

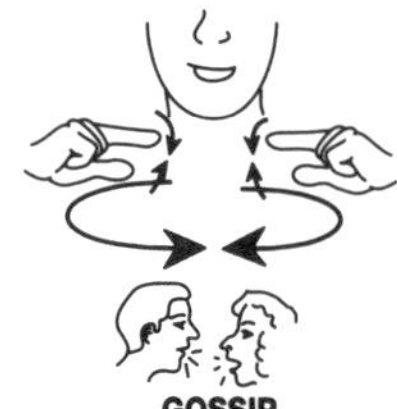

GOSSIP
G-hands facing near chin, circle outwards, horizontally, with indexes and thumbs opening and closing
(see RUMOR)

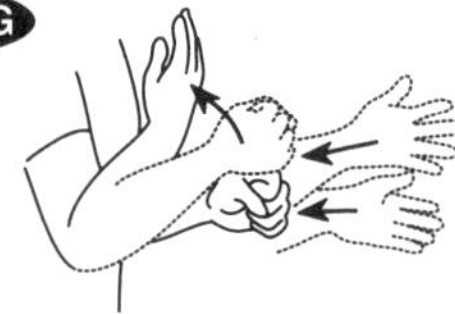

GOT
Right open hand above left, draw toward body, closing to S-hands; right hand flips toward shoulder

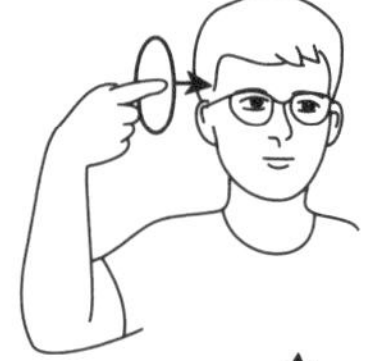

GOVERN
Index finger circles near temple, then touches temple

GOVERNOR
Index circles near temple, then touches temple; add R-hand *(govern + -or)*

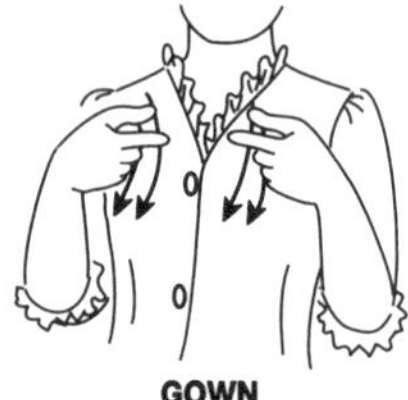

GOWN
Thumbtips of G-hands brush down off chest twice
(see DRESS)

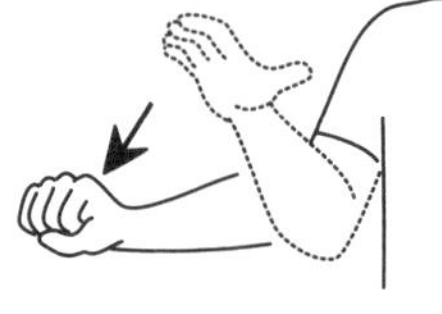

GRAB
Palm-down hand closes sharply to S, grabbing something
(see ARREST)

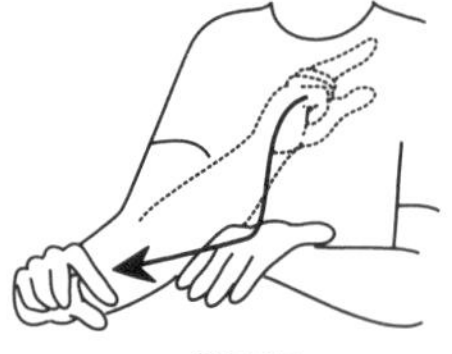

GRACE
Right G from heart glides off left palm and forward
(see CHARITY)

GRADE
G circles over and drops on left palm

GRADUAL
Left hand palm-down, right G palm-down above brushes backwards along left hand
(see SLOW)

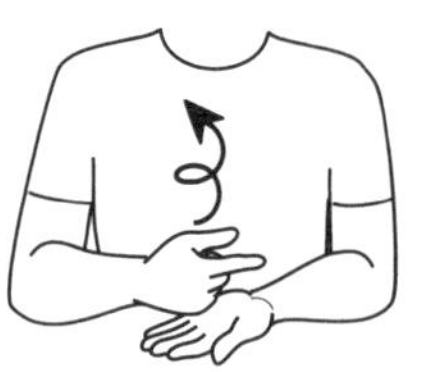

GRADUATE
G circles up from left palm
(see COLLEGE)

GRAHAM

G circles on back of palm-in left S-hand

(see DOUGH)

GRAIN ♔

Right G brushes up twice through left horizontal C-hand

GRAM

Right G makes small circle once

GRAMMAR

G-hands, palms facing each other, touch, then separate, shaking slightly

(see SENTENCE)

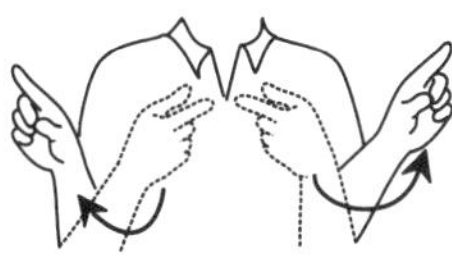

GRAND

G-hands face each other, twist apart to palm-out D's

GRANDDAUGHTER

G from chin falls to inside of left elbow *(holding baby)*

(see DAUGHTER)

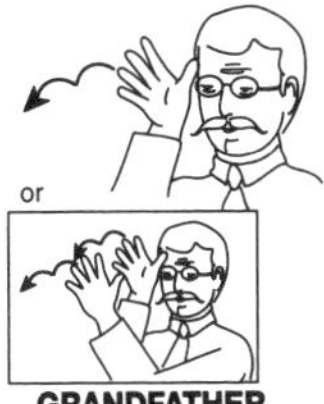

GRANDFATHER

Thumb of palm-left 5 at temple, makes two arcs diagonally to the right *(sometimes done with two hands)*

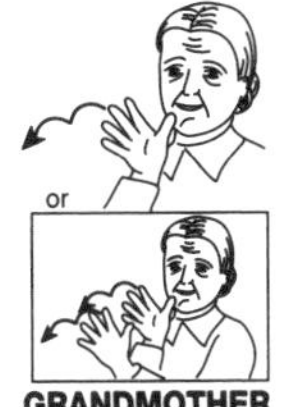

GRANDMOTHER

Thumb of palm-left 5 at chin, makes two arcs diagonally to the right *(sometimes done with two hands)*

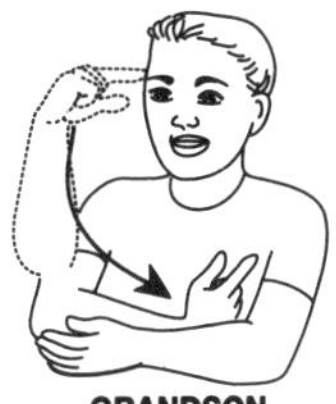

GRANDSON

G at temple falls to inside of left elbow *(holding baby)*

(see SON)

GRANOLA

Back of right G on palm-up left hand; right circles inward and up to mouth several times

(see SOUP)

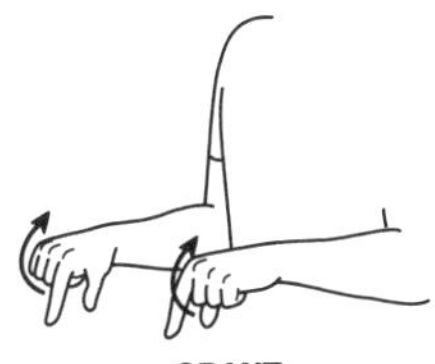

GRANT

(Alt. 1)

Both G-hands point downward, then swing upward

(see ALLOW)

GRANT

(Alt. 2)

Tips of thumb and bent index touching, arc forward and down

GRAPE
Fingers of claw hand hop down back of left hand
(See RAISIN)

GRAPEFRUIT
G fingertips twist on cheek
(see APPLE)

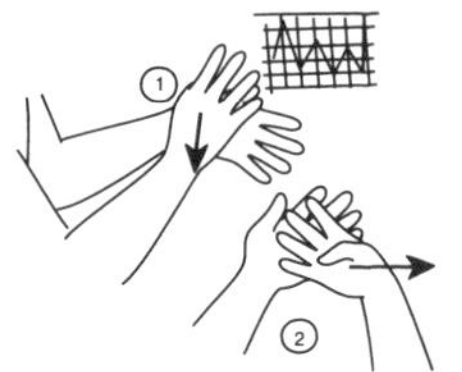

GRAPH
4-hand draws a cross on left palm

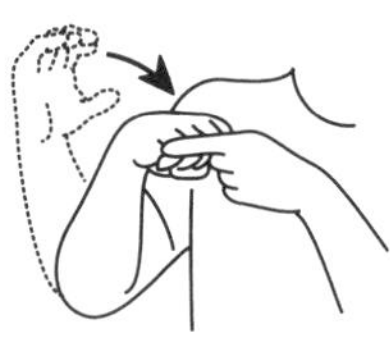

GRASP
Right hand grabs thumb of left G

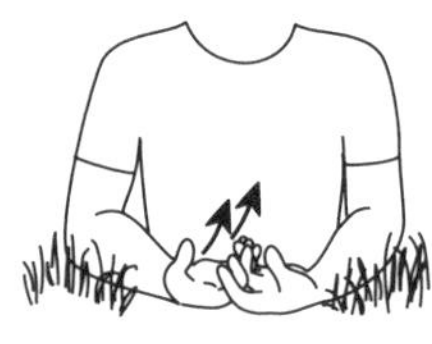

GRASS
(Alt. 1)
Fingers of right palm-up claw move up through fingers of palm-up left claw several times

GRASS
(Alt. 2)
Heel of palm-up claw hand brushes forward under chin several times

GRASSHOPPER
Right G rides forward on hopping left bent-V hand
(see LOCUST)

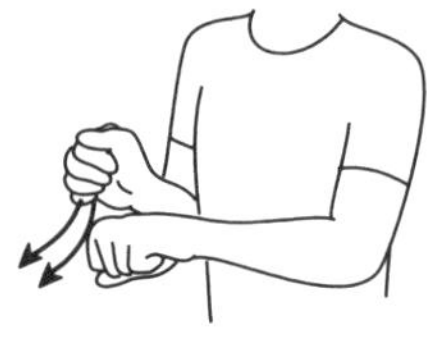

GRATE
Mime holding grater with left S; grate downwards with right A

GRATEFUL
Fingertips of hands touch chin, move slightly forward; right palm-down hand brushes inwards across side of horizontal S *(gratitude + -ful)*

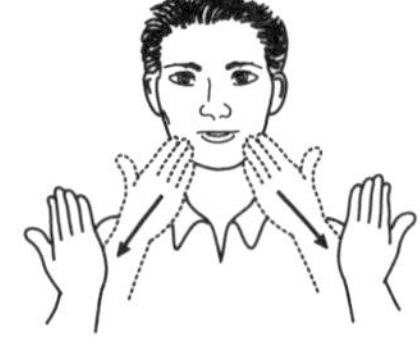

GRATITUDE
Fingertips of both hands touch chin, move slightly forward
(see THANK)

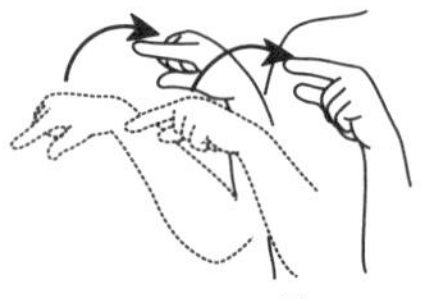

GRAVE ★
Palm-down G-hands arc back toward body, ending palm-out
(see BURY)

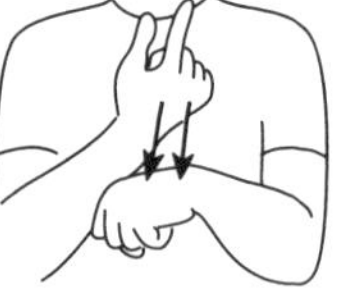

GRAVEL
Back of G taps on back of left S
(see STONE)

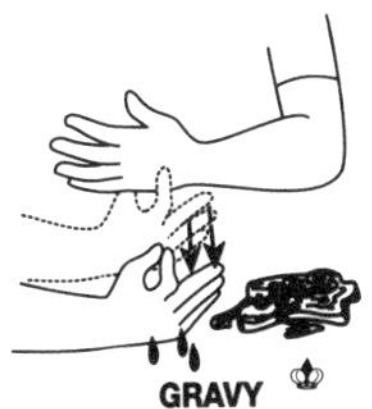

GRAVY

Right 9-hand grasps lower edge of left hand, slides off and closes; repeat

GRAY/GREY
(Alt. 1)

Side of G moves right across forehead
(see BLACK)

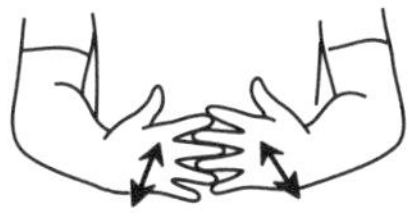

GRAY/GREY
(Alt. 2)

Fingers of open horizontal hands move alternately back and forth between fingers
(see THOUGH)

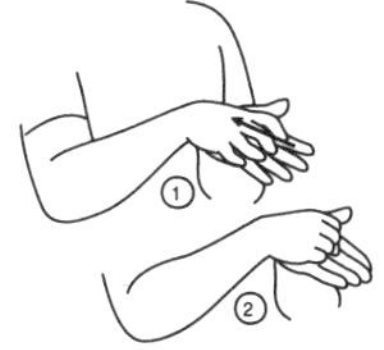

GRAZE

Right claw on left palm; repeatedly closes into S, moving slightly backwards
(see GREED)

GREASE

Thumb and index grasp thumb-base of left vertical G and pull off downward, closing
(see GRAVY)

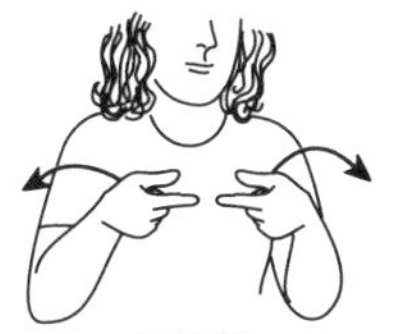

GREAT

G-hands face each other, arc apart
(see MUCH)

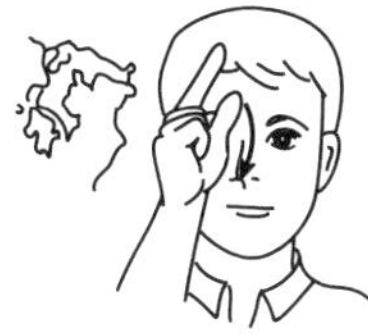

GREECE

G arcs down inward near nose

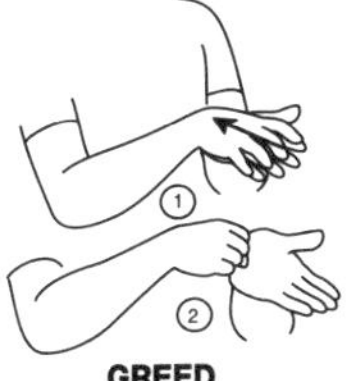

GREED

Left flat hand, palm-up; fingertips of right palm-down claw hand scratch closed on left heel
(see GRAZE)

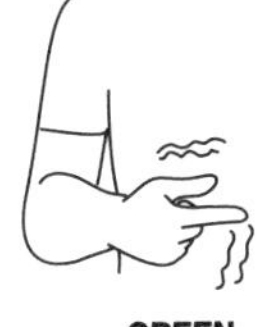

GREEN

Palm-left G shakes
(see BLUE)

GREMLIN

Fingertips of G's on shoulders swing off to palms-out
(see ANGEL)

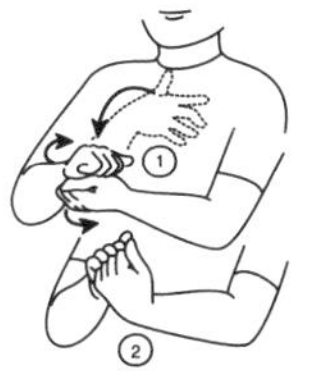

GRIEF

Bent middle right finger touches heart; press together A-hands knuckles and twist slightly
(see GRIEVE)

GRIEVE

Right bent middle finger touches heart; A-hands together twist slightly while moving forward
(see GRIEF)

GRILL ★
Palm-up G circles under left palm
(See OVEN)

GRIM
G-hands at sides of mouth curve slightly downward

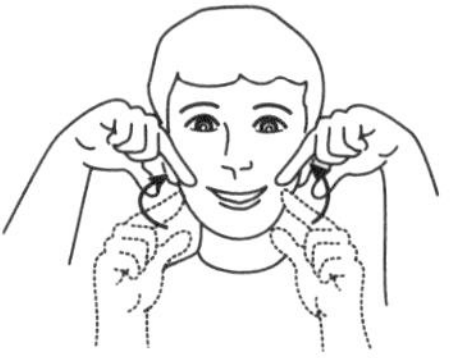

GRIN
G-hands twist upwards near corners of mouth
(see SMILE)

GRIND
G circles on G in grinding motion

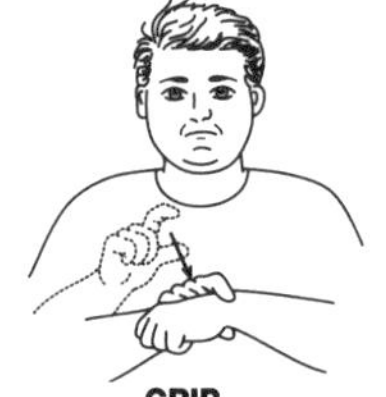

GRIP
(Alt. 1)
Palm-down left S; right small C grips left wrist
(see CURB)

GRIP
(Alt. 2)
G grips vertical left index finger
(see HOLD)

GRIPE
Fingertips of palm-in G hit chest sharply; repeat
(see COMPLAIN)

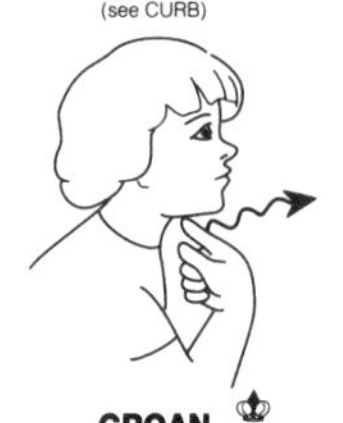

GROAN ♔
Fingertips of G-hand at throat shakes up and out under chin

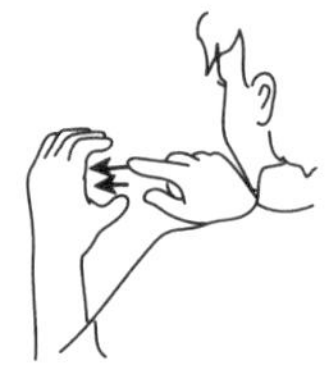

GROCER
Right G nods toward side of left C
(see STORE)

GROSS
Right G on fingertips of left flat hand circles slightly outward, back to heel, then back to fingertips

GROUCH
G outlines half of sour mouth

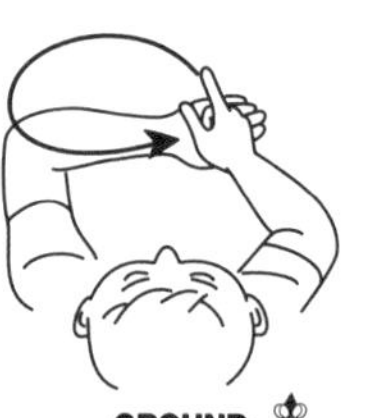

GROUND ♔
(noun)
Right G on back of left hand circles out and back

GROUND

(verb)

Side of right G circles on left G in grinding motion; right hand flips toward shoulder *(grind + p.t.)*

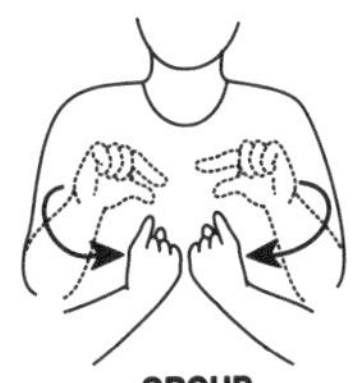

GROUP

G-hands circle outward horizontally from palm-out to palm-in

(see CLASS)

GROVE

Right elbow on back of left hand, shake right G slightly to right

(see TREE)

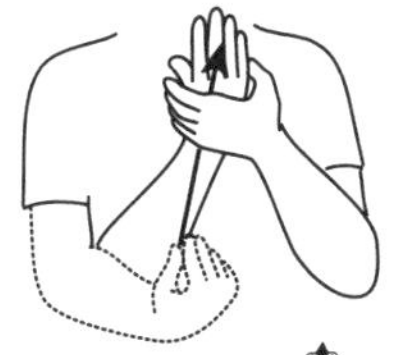

GROW ♔

Palm-up flat-O "grows" through left C, to a palm-in 5

GROWL

Palm-in claw hand at throat shakes

(see GROAN)

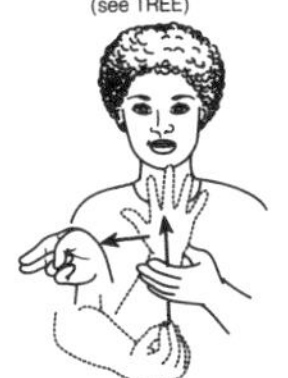

GROWTH

Palm-up flat-O "grows" through left S to palm-in 5; then changes to an H *(grow + -th)*

GRUMBLE

Claw hand on chest circles, fingers fluttering and tapping

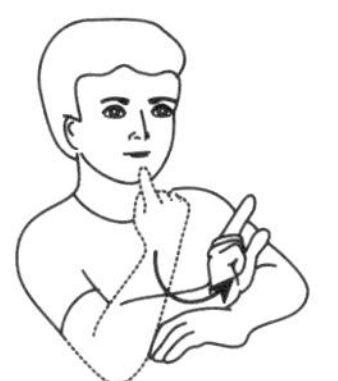

GUARANTEE

Index from chin moves to rest as a palm-out G against top of left hand

(see PROMISE)

GUARD ♔

G-hands one behind the other, both jerk forward

GUESS

Palm-left C-hand arcs past eyes, closing to S

(see ESTIMATE)

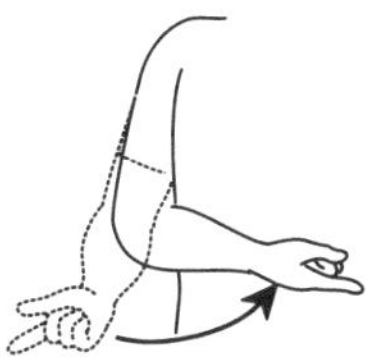

GUEST

Palm-up G-hand arcs downward toward body

(see INVITE)

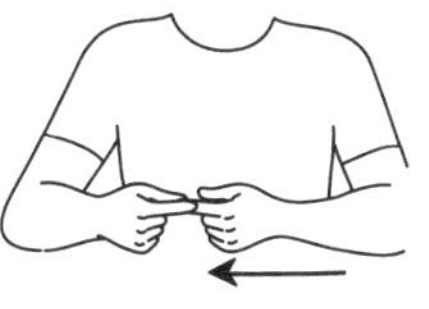

GUIDE

Right G grasps left G index and pulls hand toward right

(see LEAD)

GUILT
G taps on left chest
(see CONSCIENCE)

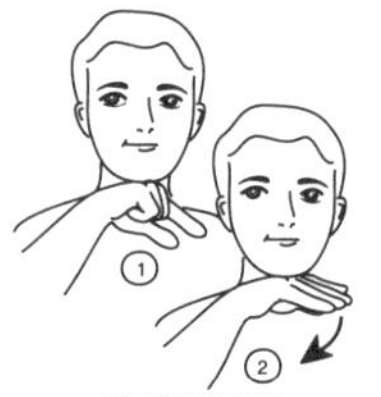

GUINEA PIG
G under chin, then flat hand fingers flap together for "pig"

GUITAR
Hold and strum on invisible guitar

GULF
Palm-out to palm-in G outlines curves of left hand from index to thumb
(see BAY)

GULL
Nod right G-hand while resting elbow on back of left hand
(see OSTRICH)

GULP
Thumb and index of 9 at throat move forward and back to throat

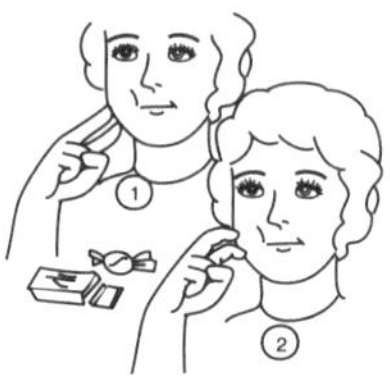

GUM
Fingertips of V-hand touch cheek; bend and straighten fingers
(see TOBACCO)

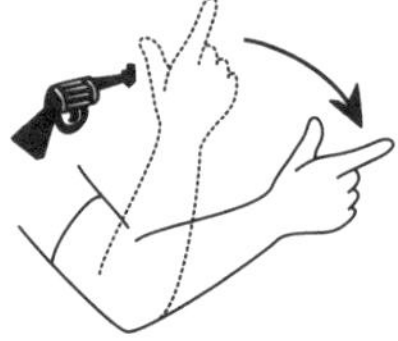

GUN
L-hand drops down and forward

GUY
Side of G at temple moves forward slightly right
(see HE)

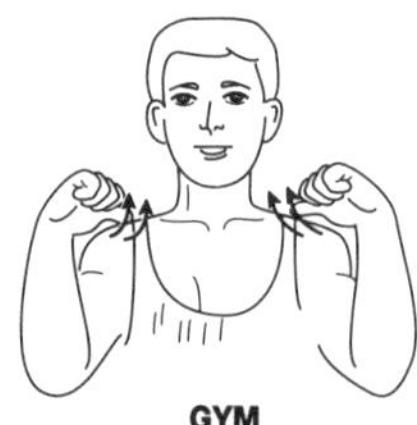

GYM
Thumbs of A's hit upward and inward on shoulders; repeat

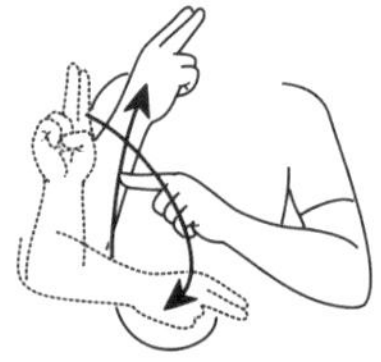

GYMNASTIC
Palm-out U-hand twists around left index finger and moves upward

GYPSY
Index and thumb of L open and close on earlobe

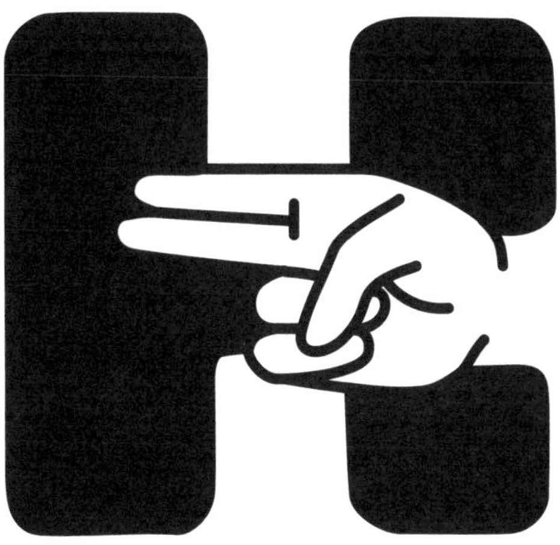

HABILITATE

Right H on flat left palm, both rise

HABIT ♔

Wrist of right S on wrist of left S, both hands drop slightly

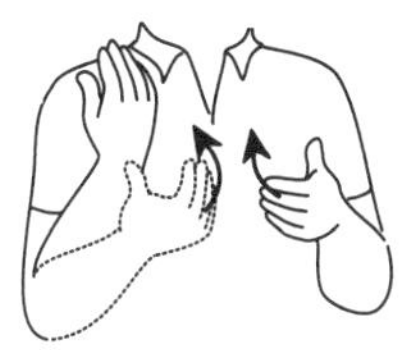

HAD
(Alt. 1)

Fingertips of slightly bent hands touch chest, right hand flicks back slightly (have + p.t.)

HAD
(Alt. 2)

Palm-in D's touch sides of chest
(see HAVE)

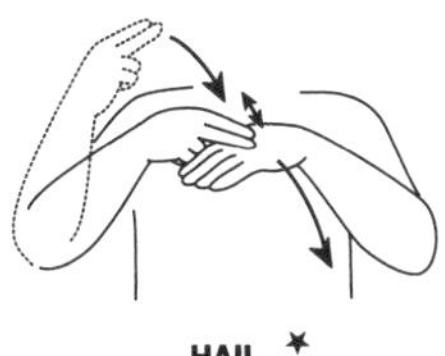

HAIL ★

H beats on back of left hand as both move diagonally left and down

HAIR

Hold hair with 9-hand

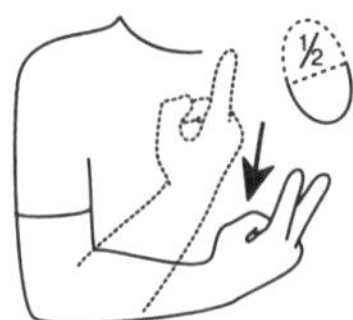

HALF
Palm-in 1 drops to palm-in 2

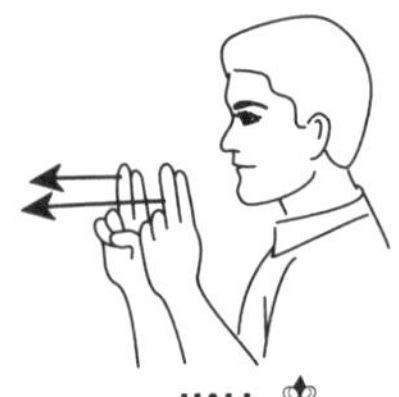

HALL ♕
Parallel vertical H-hands move forward, not touching

HALLOWEEN
Palm-in vertical H's at eyes move around to sides
(see MASK)

HALLUCINATE
Palm-in H's circle upwards alternately at sides of head
(see IMAGINE)

HALO
Index fingers and thumbs outline halo above head

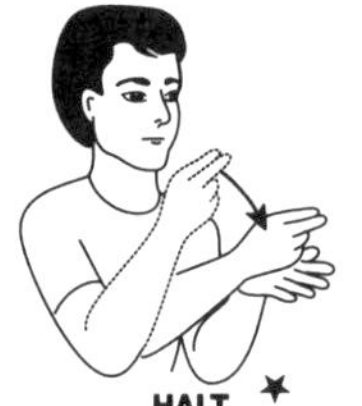

HALT ★
Side of right H falls on left palm
(see STOP)

HAM
Thumb and finger of 9 pinch side of H-hand and shake hand slightly
(see MEAT)

HAMBURGER
Clasp hands, right on left, separate, then left on right *(make a patty)*

HAMMER
A-hand pounds with invisible hammer

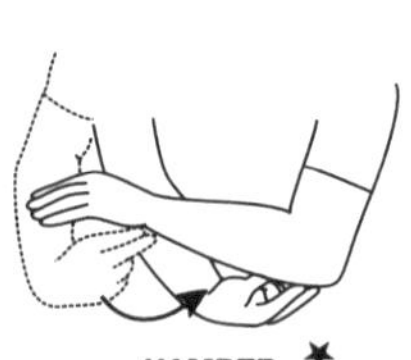

HAMPER ★
H outlines hamper from wrist to elbow of left arm
(see BASKET)

HAMSTER
Horizontal H-hand brushes off tip of nose; repeat
(see MOUSE)

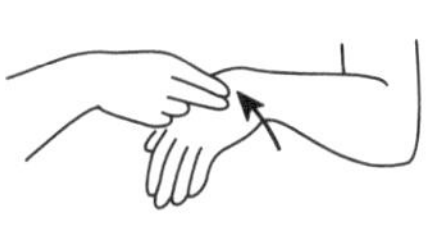

HAND
Right H-fingers draw across back of left hand

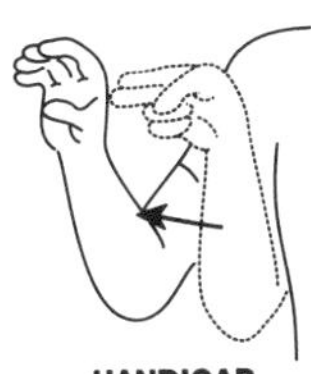

HANDICAP
Finger spell H + C

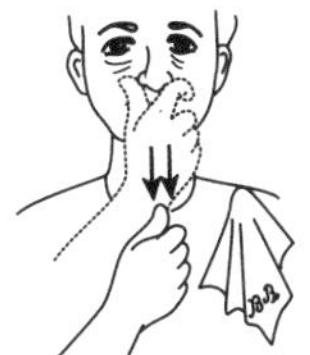

HANDKERCHIEF
Bent index finger and thumb at nose pull down and close; repeat

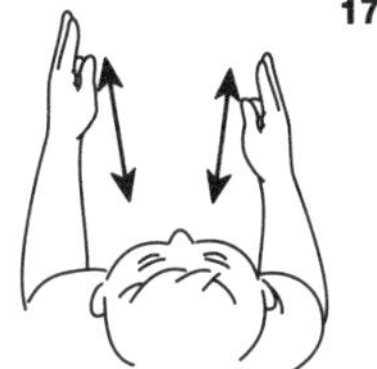

HANDLE
Palms-facing H's move alternately in and out *(like reins)*
(see MANAGE)

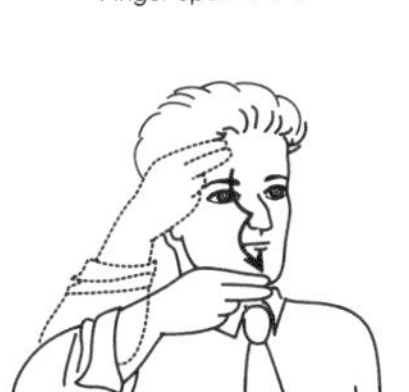

HANDSOME
H moves down at side of face in two arcs *(outlining profile)*
(see PROFILE)

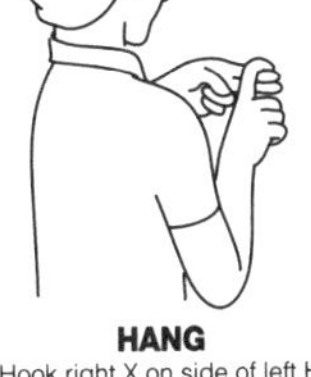

HANG
Hook right X on side of left H

HANGAR
Right L-Y hand slides beneath palm *(as in sheltering a plane)*

HANGER
Hook right X on side of left H, change to palm-out R hand *(hang + -er)*

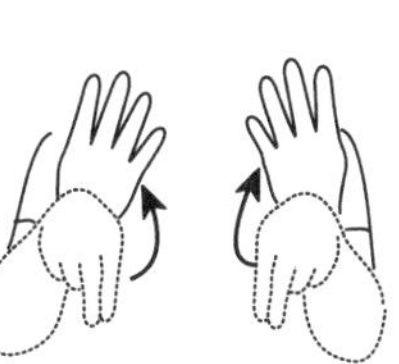

HANUKKAH
H's point down, palms-in, swing up to palms-in 4's
(see MENORAH)

HAPPEN
Both palms-up index fingers twist to palms-down

HAPPY
Open hand brushes middle of chest upward; repeat

HARBOR
Palm-out vertical H outlines curves of palm-down left hand's index and thumb, ending palm-in
(see BAY)

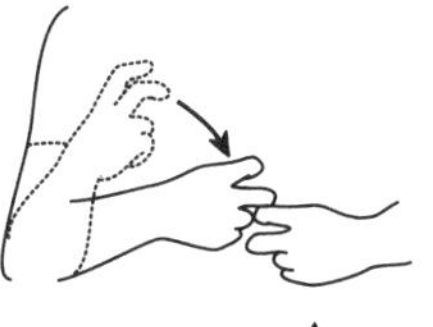

HARD
Palms-in, right bent-V hits topside of left bent-V

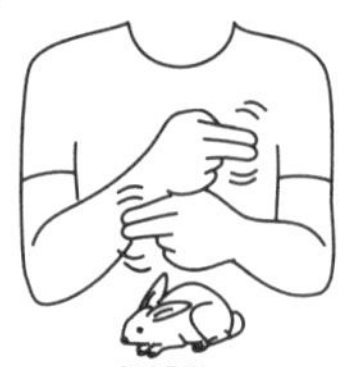

HARE
H-hands one on the other, wiggle fingers together in and out

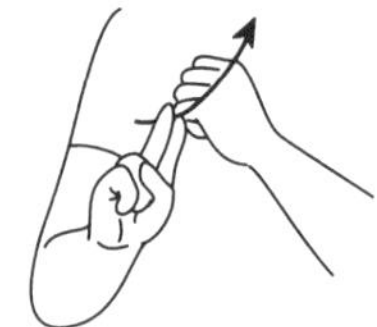

HARM
Vertical H arcs up, striking back of left S several times
(see DANGER)

HARMONICA
Palm-in flat-O's move harmonica back and forth in front of mouth

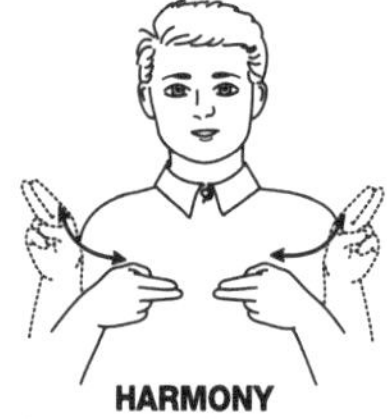

HARMONY
Conduct orchestra with two H-hands
(see CONDUCT)

HARP
Fluttering fingers, draw 5-hand toward body past flat left hand

HARSH
Left fist; right H hits forward off thumbside of left hand
(see HARD)

HARVEST
Curved right index slices toward and across side of horizontal left S

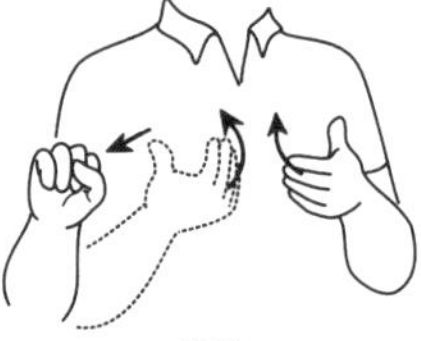

HAS
(Alt. 1)
Fingertips of slightly bent hands touch chest, right hand changes to S
(see HAVE)

HAS
(Alt. 2)
Palm- in S's touch sides of chest
(see HAVE)

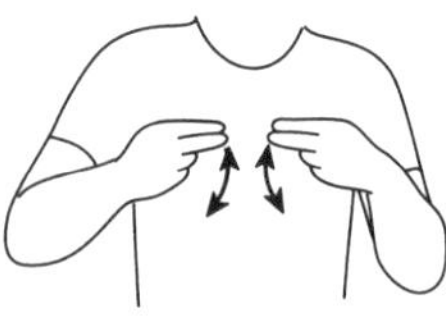

HASSLE
Palm-in H's point at each other; move rapidly up and down from wrist; repeat
(see ARGUE)

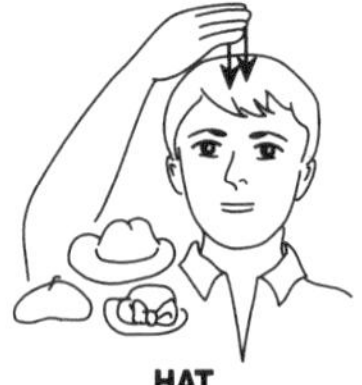

HAT
Right hand pats top of head

HATCH ★
Palm-down H's together, turn over and out to palm-up
(see OPEN)

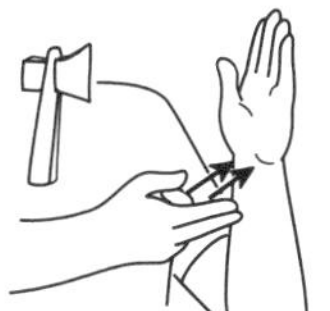

HATCHET
Side of palm-up H chops at wrist of vertical left hand
(see AXE)

HATE
Parallel 8's snap open to 5's

HAUL
Palm-up H's pull toward body
(see PULL)

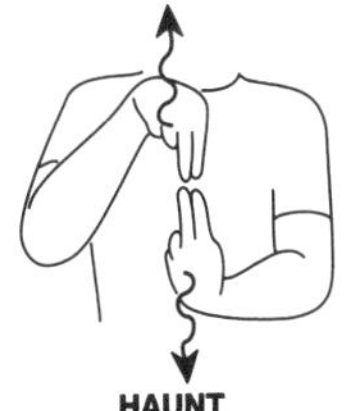

HAUNT
Palm-in H's pull away from each other vertically in wavy motion
(see GHOST)

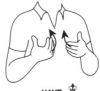

HAVE
(Alt. 1)
Fingertips of both slightly bent hands touch chest

HAVE
(Alt. 2)
Palm-in V's touch sides of chest

HAWAII
Palm-in H-hand circles face
(see FACE)

HAY
Horizontal palm-out H brushes up through left C-hand
(see GRAIN)

HAZE
Palm-in H's arc from sides to cross in front of face
(see DARK)

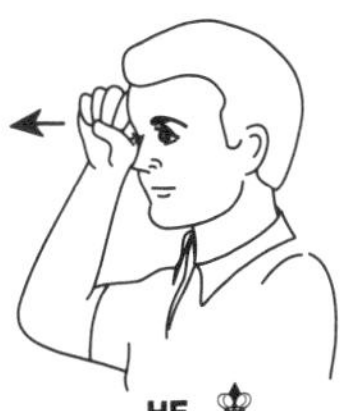

HE
E at temple moves forward

HEAD
Fingertips of right bent hand touch temple, then jaw

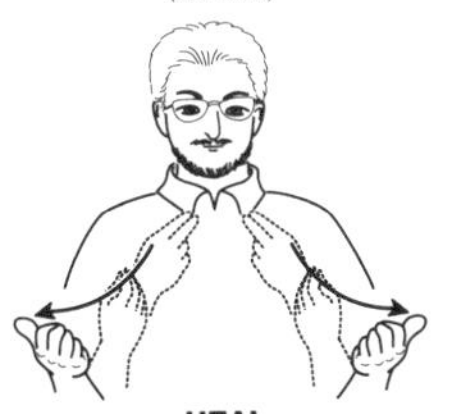

HEAL
Palm-in H's near shoulders move outwards, closing to palm-up A's
(see MELT)

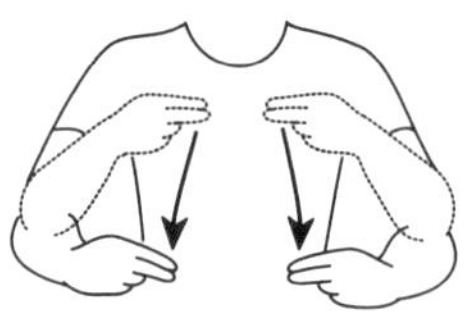

HEALTH
Palm-in H's touch chest, then ribs
(see BODY)

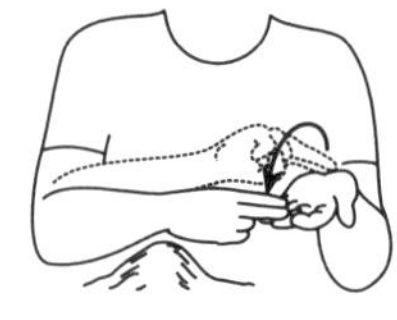

HEAP
Index side of H touches left hand heel, arcs to fingertips, palm-in
(see AMOUNT)

HEAR
H-hand rises to ear
(see SOUND)

HEARING AID
Right X crooks over and behind ear

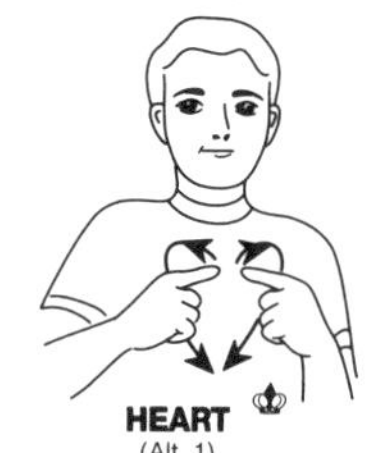

HEART ♔
(Alt. 1)
Index or bent middle fingers draw heart over heart

HEART ♔
(Alt. 2)
Middle finger taps over heart

HEAT
Right palm-in 5-hand flutters under left palm-in H
(see BURN)

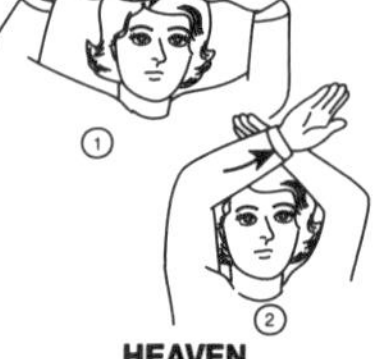

HEAVEN
Above head right flat hand passes under left hand and continues up *(entering heaven)*
(see PARADISE)

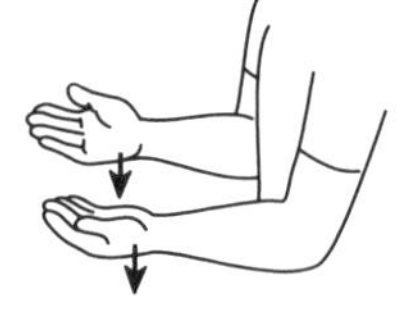

HEAVY
Slightly bent palms-up drop slightly

HEBREW
Palm-in hands on chin drop touching thumbs to fingers; repeat

HEEL ★
Right L-thumb touches heel of palm-down left hand *(can tap)*

HEIGHT
H-hand moves upward; add T *(high + -t)*

HELICOPTER
Palm of claw hand on tip of vertical left index fingertip; right hand shakes

HELL
H moves sharply to the side
(see DAMN)

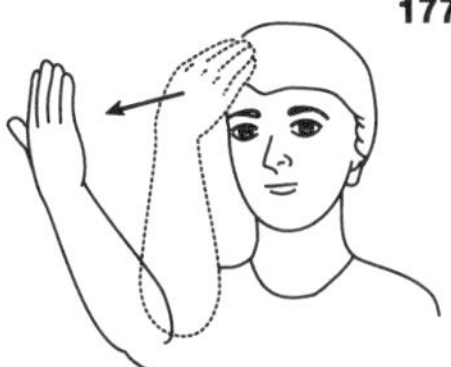

HELLO
Flat hand, fingertips at forehead, moves forward slightly right

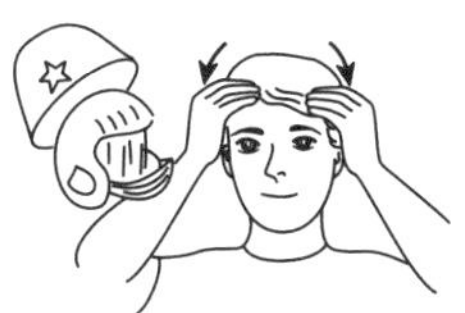

HELMET
Claw hands put on helmet

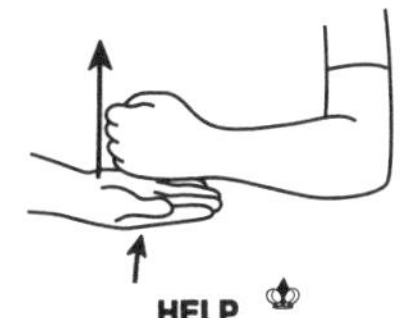

HELP
Palm lifts bottom of left S and pushes it slightly up

HEM
Palms-down relaxed 5's grasp edge of cloth and turn inwards and upwards, ending in flat-O's

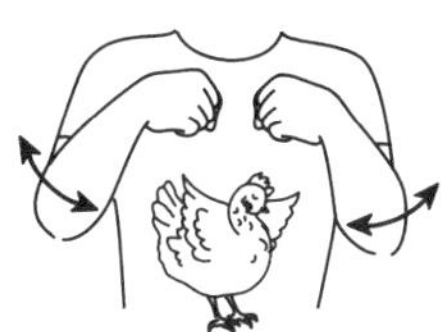

HEN
(Alt. 1)
S's on chest, flap elbows twice

HEN
(Alt. 2)
Thumb of 3 taps on chin

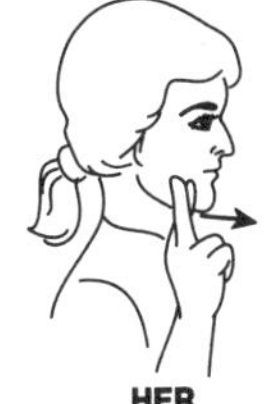

HER
Fingertips of R-hand slide down jawline forward
(see GIRL)

HERB
Right U grows through horizontal left C into palm-out H
(see GROW)

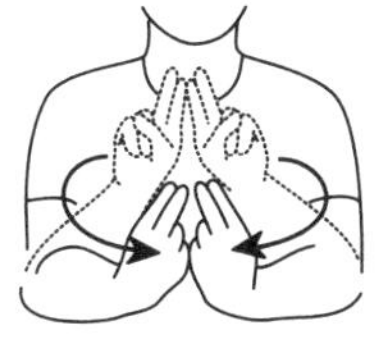

HERD
Touching palm-out vertical H-hands circle horizontally to palm-in
(see CLASS)

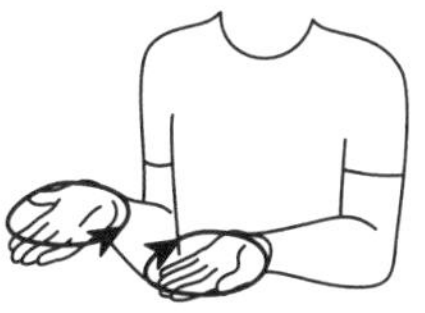

HERE
Palm-up hands circle horizontally in opposite directions
(see AVAIL)

HEREDITY
Palms-in, H's circle each other forward from right shoulder
(See GENERATE)

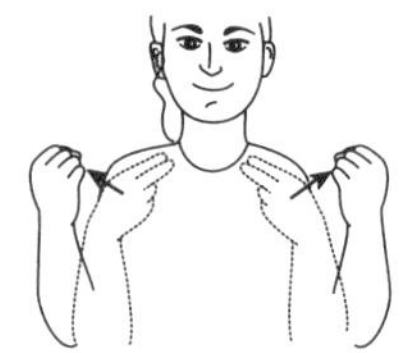

HERO
H's on upper chest move out to S's
(see BRAVE)

HESITATE
Right H points to palm-up left hand that flutters fingers
(see WAIT)

HICCUP
Side of index finger jumps up and down chest

HIDE ♔ ★
A at chin moves down under bent hand, top of thumb against left palm

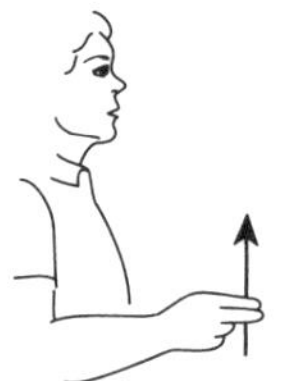

HIGH
H-hand moves upward
(see UP)

HIGH SCHOOL

Fingerspell H + S

HIGHWAY
(Alt. 1)
Palms-down H's point towards each other, approach and separate; repeat

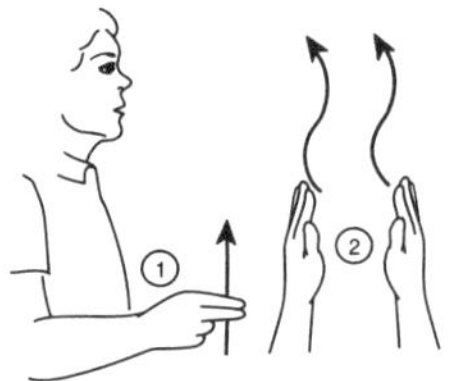

HIGHWAY
(Alt. 2)
H-hand moves upward; parallel flat hands move forward, weaving slightly side-to-side *(high + -way)*

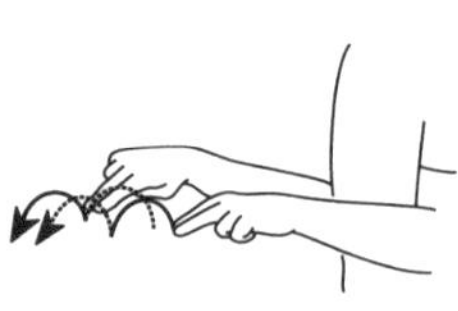

HIKE
Both palms-down, H-hands walk alternately forward
(see WALK)

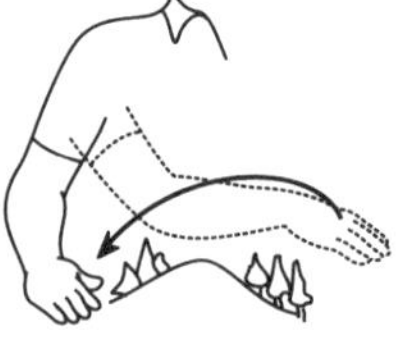

HILL
Palm-down hand draws hill

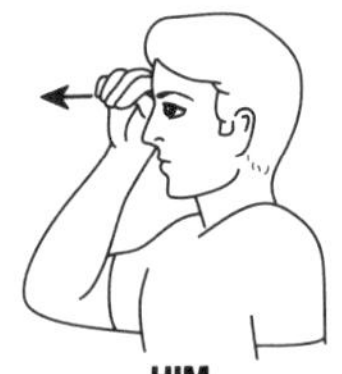

HIM
M-hand at temple moves forward and slightly right
(see HE)

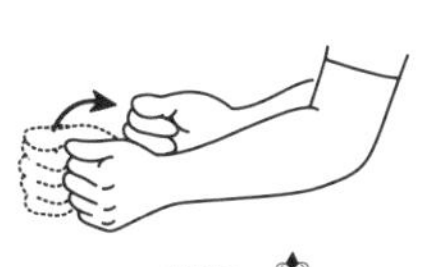

HIND

A-hands together; right arcs sideways to behind left

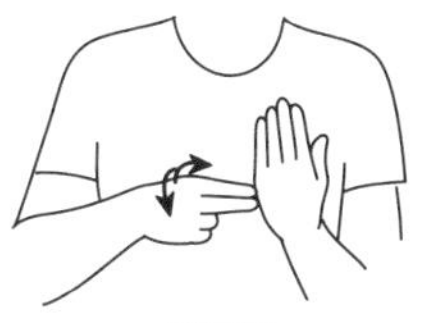

HINGE
(Alt. 1)

Palm-in right H tips touch side of left palm-in vertical hand; right H-hand rocks forward and back on hinge

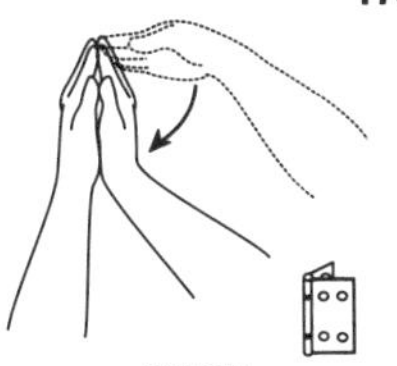

HINGE
(Alt. 2)

Flat hands joined at fingertips, fingers pointing forward, right hand opens and closes

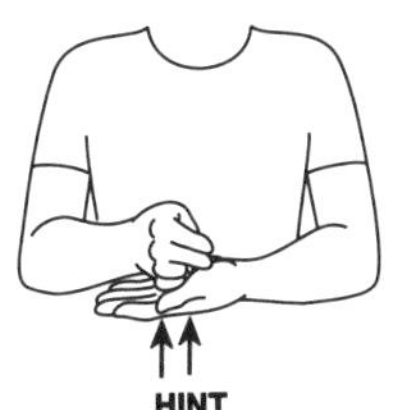

HINT

Fingers of palm-up right flat hand tap little finger side of left H

(see HELP)

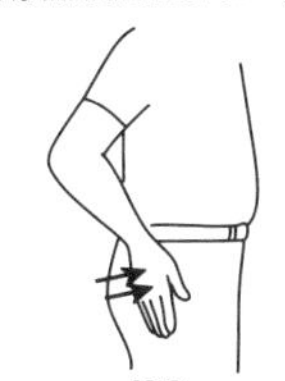

HIP

Right hand pats hip

HIPPOPOTAMUS

Y's, palms-together, right over left; open and close at wrists

HIRE

Palm-up H moves in toward body

(see INVITE)

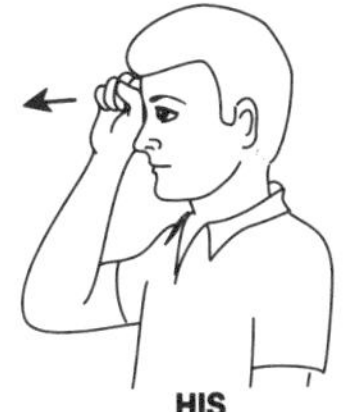

HIS

S at forehead moves forward and slightly right

(see HE)

HISPANIC

Palm-in H's at shoulders move out and forward to touch fingertips

(see SPAIN)

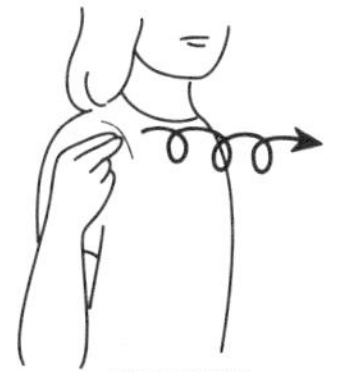

HISTORY
(Alt. 1)

H circles forward from right shoulder

HISTORY
(Alt. 2)

Right H-hand shakes

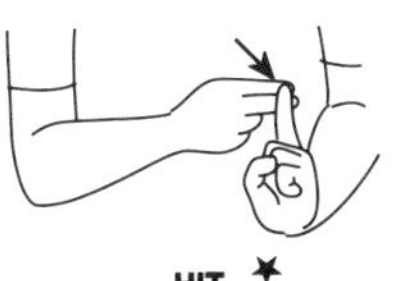

HIT

Back of H hits left vertical index

(see BEAT)

HITCH
Left H pointing right, right X hooks onto top of H and both move backwards

HOARSE
Palm-in right claw points left near throat, moves across throat to left

HOCKEY
Back of right X scrapes across left palm; repeat

HOE
(Alt. 1)
Bent hand hoes on left palm; repeat

HOE
(Alt. 2)
Hold handle of hoe with A's and chop towards body; repeat

HOG
H under chin; H-fingers flutter
(see PIG)

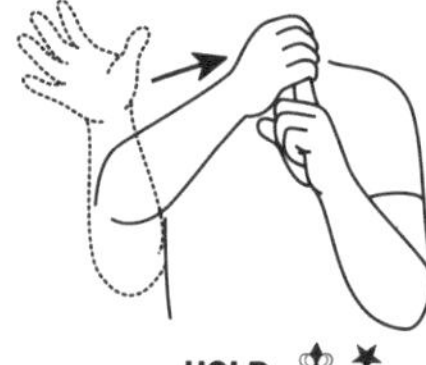

HOLD ♔ ★
Right hand seizes left index finger

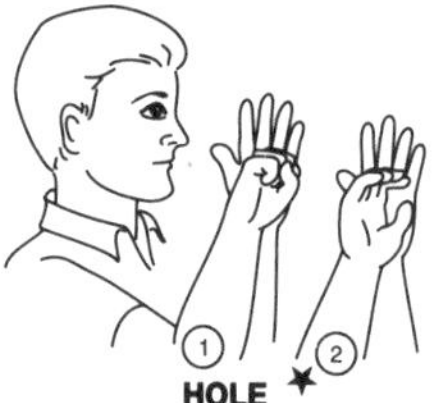

HOLE ★
Thumb side of right S on left palm opens to C-hand

HOLIDAY
Extended thumbs of palm-in H's tap on sides of chest
(see LEISURE)

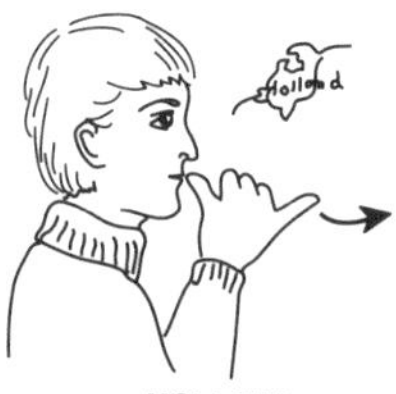

HOLLAND
Thumb of Y at mouth, arcs out

HOLLER
H from mouth shakes upward
(see SCREAM)

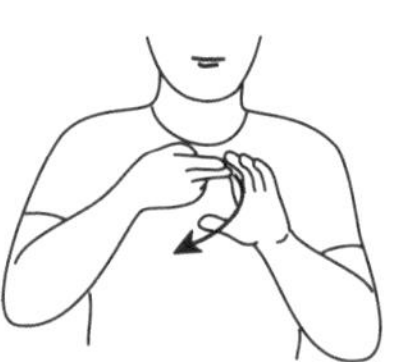

HOLLOW
Fingers of palm-up H carve out left C, ending palm-down
(see CAVE)

HOLLY

Starting on left index tip, outline holly leaf with thumb and finger

HOLSTER

L index sticks into C on hip

(see SWORD)

HOLY

Right H circles horizontally above left palm, then flat hand wipes off palm

HOME

Flat-O fingertips on chin then flat palm on cheek *(can be flat-O on cheek)*

(see DORMITORY)

HOMONYM

Left index points up; right palm-in H taps first joint of index

(see ANTONYM)

HONEST

Middle fingertip of H-hand slides forward on left palm

HONEY

Palm-in H rubs chin in circle

(see SWEET)

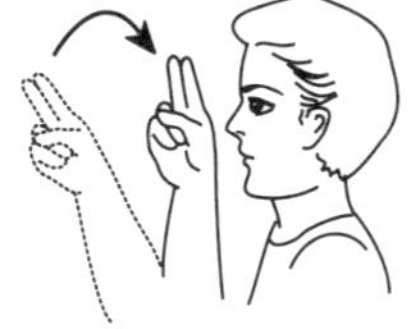

HONOR

Right H-hand arcs down and back to near forehead

(see GOD)

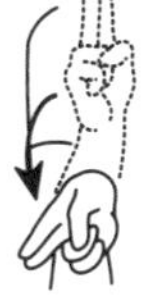

HOOD ★

Vertical H's, palms-facing, cock forward at wrists

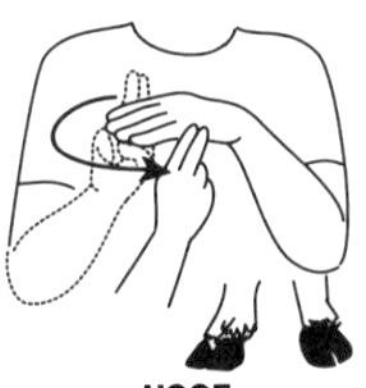

HOOF

Fingers of vertical H move around fingertips of palm-down left hand

(see EDGE)

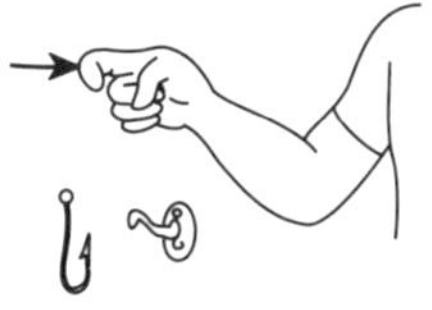

HOOK

Palm-left horizontal X-hand hooks toward body

HOOP

Right H draws circle in midair

(see CIRCLE)

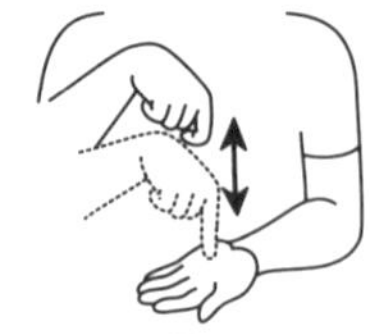

HOP
Inverted index fingertip on left palm hops up to X several times
(see JUMP)

HOPE
At head level palms-facing, left hand in front of right, fingers crossed

HOPSCOTCH
Right P hops to H on palm of left hand

HORIZON
Palm-in H moves along flat arm to right

HORN ★
Palm-in, right H on left H near lips; right moves forward and then returns *(sign can be made where horn is, e.g. on head)*

HORROR
H-hands shake down toward body
(see AFRAID)

HORSE ♕
Thumb on temple, flap H-fingers

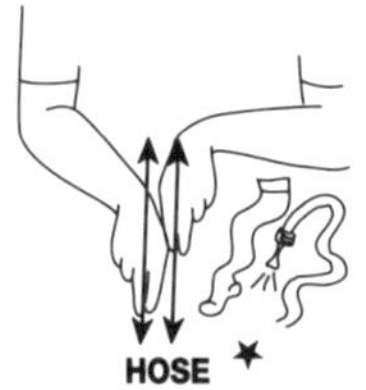

HOSE ★
Pointing down, H-hands slide up and down against each other alternately
(see STOCKING)

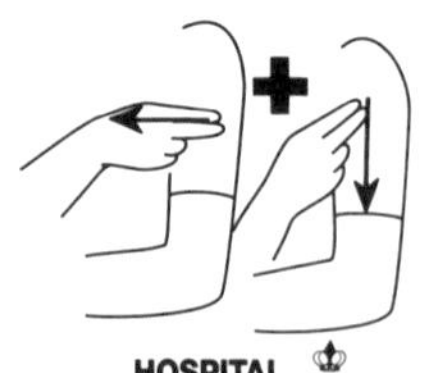

HOSPITAL ♕
H draws cross on upper left arm

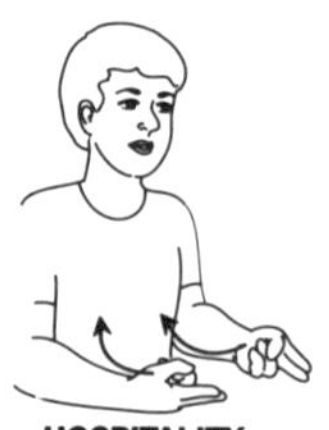

HOSPITALITY
Palm-up H's circle back towards body

HOSTAGE
Left vertical H palm-out, right S behind left, both hands pull back towards body

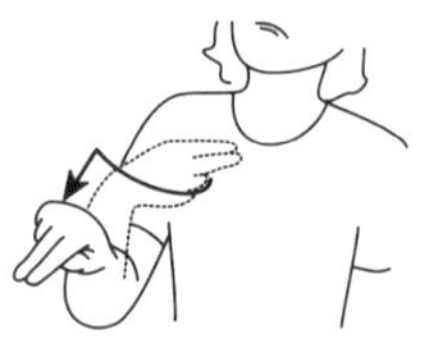

HOSTILE
H twists sharply down from chest to palm-down
(see RESENT)

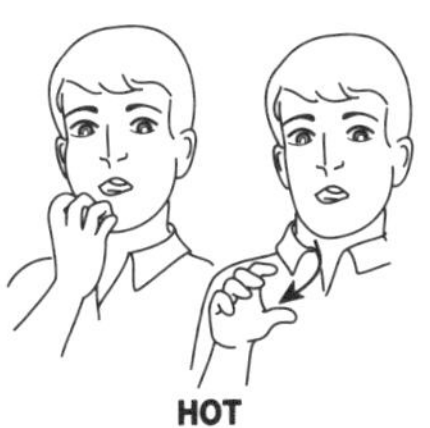

HOT

Palm-in claw at mouth; twist downward and to side

HOTEL
(Alt. 1)

Cheek rests on back of left hand; H under palm

(see BED)

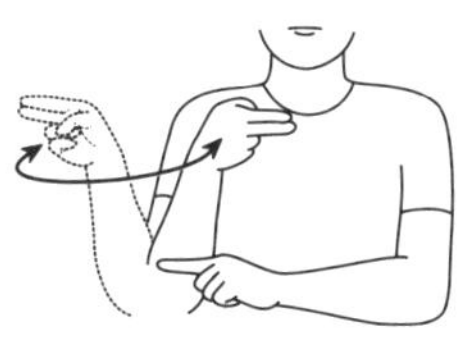

HOTEL
(Alt. 2)

H-hand waves in breeze, left horizontal index on arm

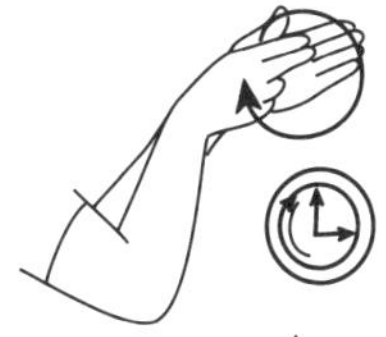

HOUR

Palm-left H touches left palm, circles forward once, touches again

HOUSE

Flat palms outline roof and sides

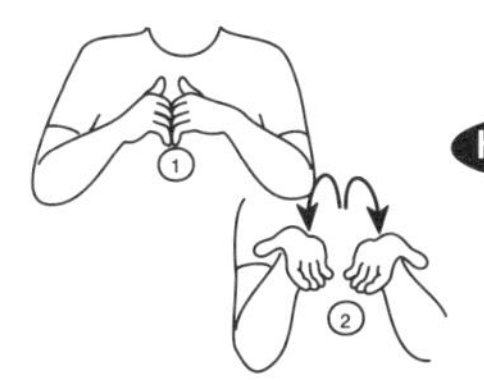

HOW

Knuckles of palm-down bent hands touching, roll hands from inward to outward ending palm-up

HOWL

Right palm-in H at throat vibrates slightly outward

(see GROAN)

HUG

Hug self with H's

(see LOVE)

HUGE

Parallel H-hands, palms-facing; then arc sideways

(see MUCH)

HULA

Do hula on each side

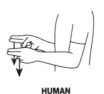

HUMAN

Parallel H-hands, palms-facing; move down

(see PERSON)

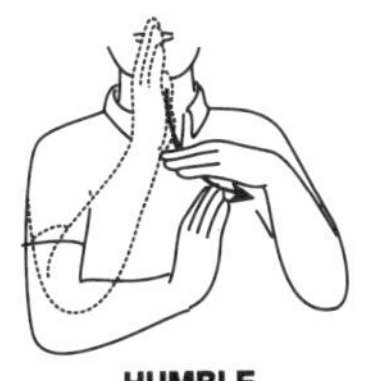

HUMBLE

Right B, palm-left near lips, moves down under left palm-down hand

(see SUBTLE)

HUMID
H-hand moves right across forehead
(see SUMMER)

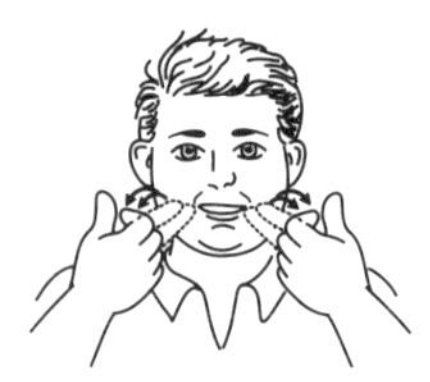

HUMOR
H's at side of mouth, thumbs out; fingertips brush to sides; repeat
(see SMILE)

HUNDRED
Fingers pull inward to palm-out C

HUNG
Hook right X on side of left H; right hand flips toward shoulder *(hang + p.p.)*

HUNGER ♔
Palm-in C moves once down chest

HUNGRY
Palm-in C moves once down chest ending in Y *(hunger + -y)*

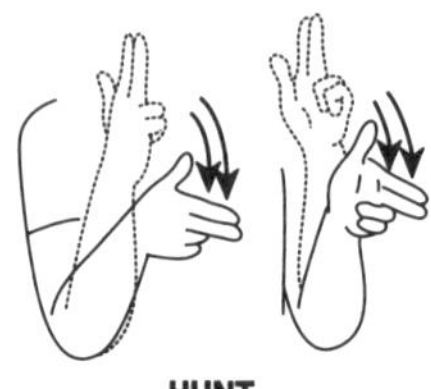

HUNT
Vertical H-hands with extended thumbs, left a bit ahead of right, drop to point forward; repeat

HURRICANE
Vertical H's rotate around each other, rising to right
(see STORM)

HURRY
Parallel H-hands, palms-facing, shake while moving forward
(see RUSH)

HURT ♔
Palm-in index fingers jerk toward each other; repeat

HUSBAND
Thumb of A-hand at temple drops to clasped C-hands
(see WIFE)

HUSH
H fingers palm-left tap closed mouth

H

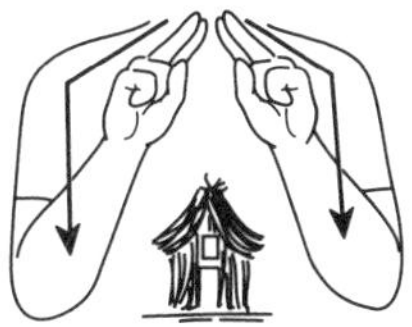

HUT
H-hands draw hut
(see HOUSE)

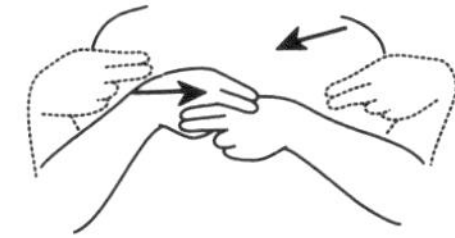

HYBRID
Palm-in H's move toward each other and cross
(see CROSS)

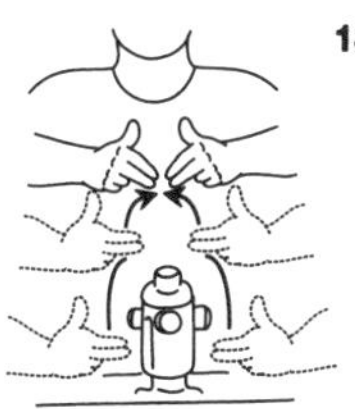

HYDRANT
Starting at bottom, outline hydrant with H's and extended thumbs

HYMN
Right palm-left H swings from side-to-side behind palm-in left hand
(see MUSIC)

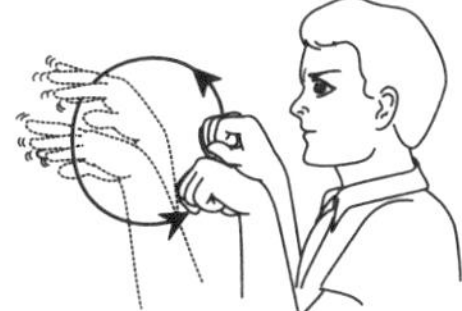

HYPNOSIS
Palms-down, 5's in front of eyes, right slightly behind left; flutter fingers while moving in small outward circle, ending in both hands palm-down S's

HYPNOTIZE
Palms-down, 5's in front of eyes, right slightly behind left; flutter fingers while moving in small outward circle

HYPOCRITE
Palm-down flat hands, right on left; top hand pushes bottom fingers down

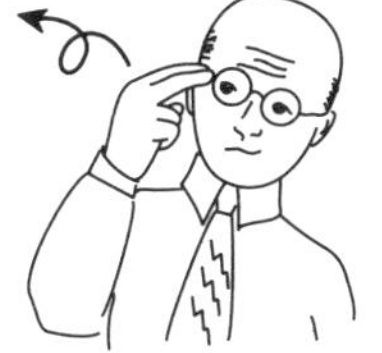

HYPOTHESIS
H circles from forehead up to right
(see IDEA)

HYSTERIC
Fingers of H's point at sides of head and circle alternately

NOTES

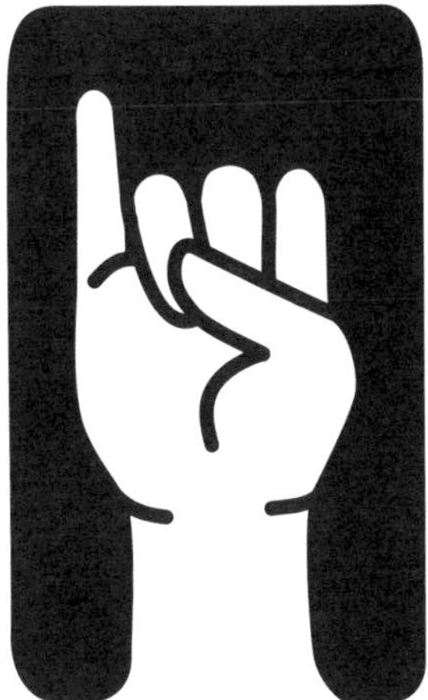
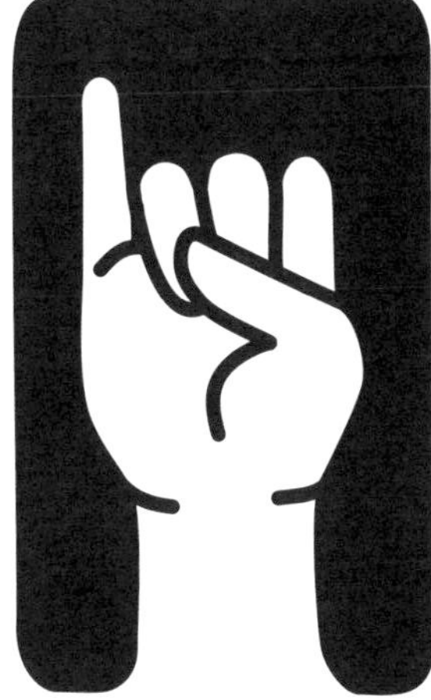

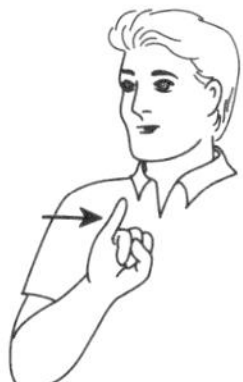

I
Palm-left I-hand on chest

ICE
W on chin moves forward, fingers bending *(contracting)*

ICE CREAM
Right S circles inward at mouth

ICICLE
Tips of I's touch; right wiggles downward from left

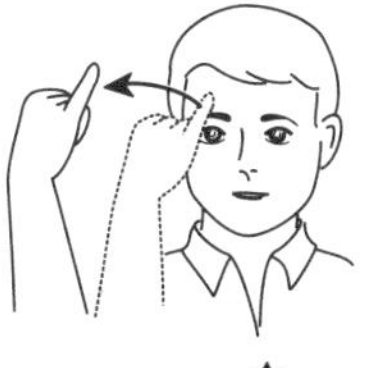

IDEA
From side of forehead; palm-in I arcs up and out

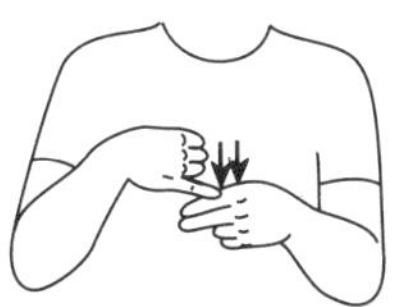

IDENTIFY
Side of little finger taps index of left H
(see NAME)

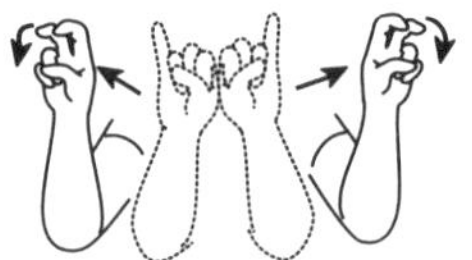

IDIOM
Palm-out I's together, separate to bent-V's that twist slightly down (as if making quotation marks)
(see QUOTE)

IDIOT
Back of I-hand strikes forehead
(see DUMB)

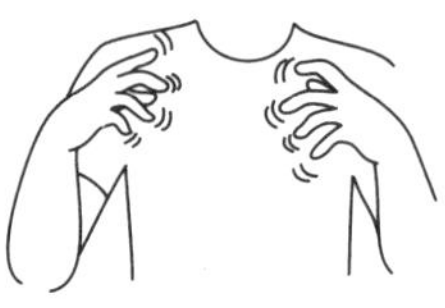

IDLE
Five hands with thumbs resting on side of chest, wiggle fingers
(see LEISURE)

IF
I-hand; two middle fingers move up into a F-hand; may repeat

IGLOO
Palm-out I's outline igloo

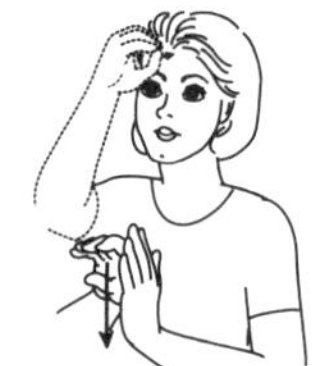

IGNORANCE
Side of O-hand hits forehead; right C-hand slides down left vertical hand *(ignorant + -ance)*

IGNORANT
Side of O-hand hits forehead

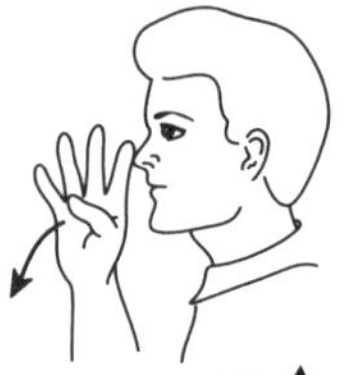

IGNORE
Index of 4 on nose, flip hand down and to left

ILL
Fingertips of palm-in I's touch forehead and stomach
(see SICK)

ILLUSION
Right palm-in I at forehead arcs up and out twice
(see IDEA)

ILLUSTRATE
Side of palm-out I-hand moves from cheek to left palm
(see PICTURE)

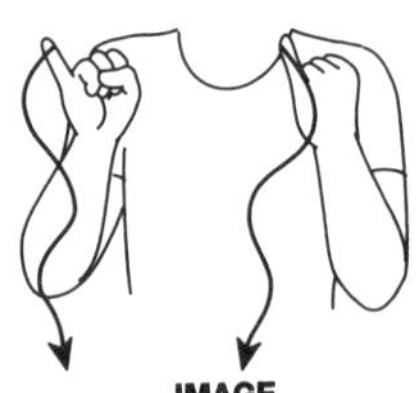

IMAGE
Palms-facing each other, I's outline shape downward
(see SHAPE)

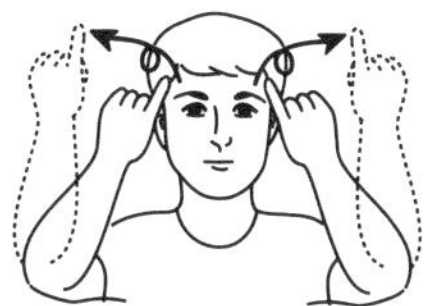

IMAGINE
Palm-in I's on forehead, alternately circle up and out
(see HALLUCINATE)

IMITATE
Palm-out I-hand closes to flat-O on horizontal left palm
(see COPY)

IMMACULATE
Heel of right palm-out I slides along left palm
(see CLEAN)

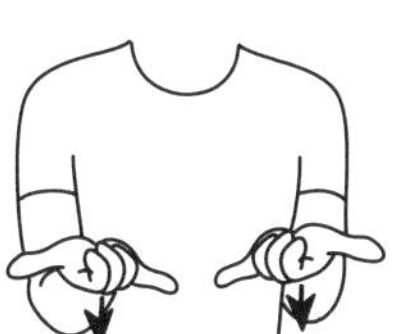

IMMEDIATE
Palm-up Y's slightly drop
(see NOW)

IMMENSE
I's facing each other arc to each side
(see MUCH)

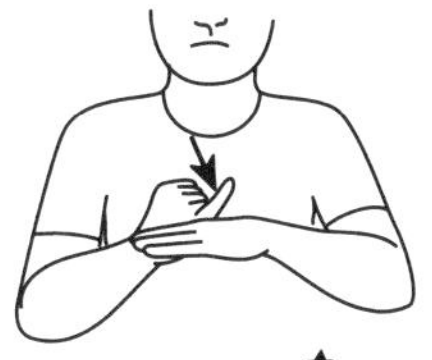

IMPAIR ♔
Little finger side of I strikes side of palm-down left hand
(see OBSTACLE)

IMPLY
Palm-in I-hand circles out at mouth
(see SAY)

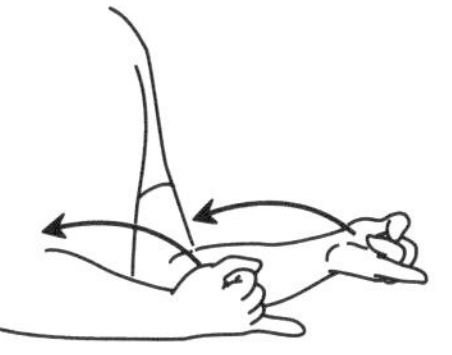

IMPORT
Palm-up I's, left slightly ahead, both arc towards body
(see BRING)

IMPORTANT ♔
Palm-up 9's circle up to touch ending palm-down

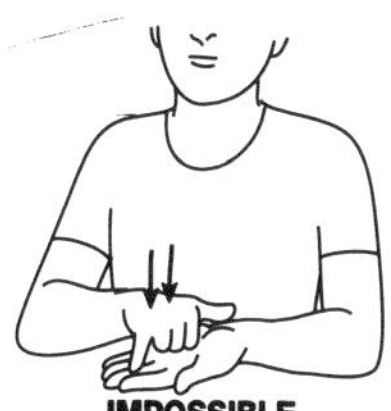

IMPOSSIBLE
Right palm-down Y-hand drops several times on palm-up left hand
(can be im + possible)

IMPRESS
Thumb of extended-A on left palm, move both back toward body
(see REQUIRE)

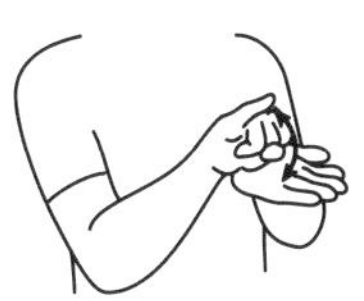

IMPRINT
Heel of I on left heel; little finger taps left palm
(see PRINT)

IMPROVE
Side of right hand on back of palm-down left hops up arm

IN
Fingertips of right flat-O enter left horizontal O

INCH
Right I moves down on first joint of left index finger

INCIDENT
Palm-up I's twist to palm-down
(see HAPPEN)

INCLUDE
Palm-out I circles to palm-in, back of hand lands in palm of left hand
(see WHOLE)

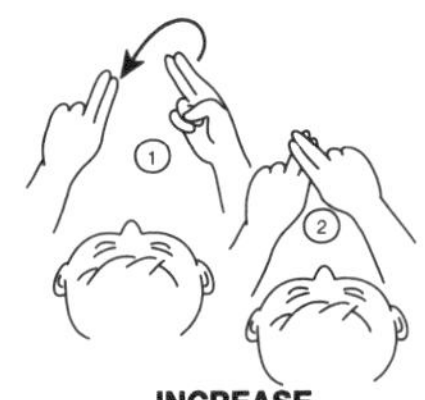

INCREASE
Right palm-up H twists up and over onto palm-down H *(may be repeated)*
(see GAIN)

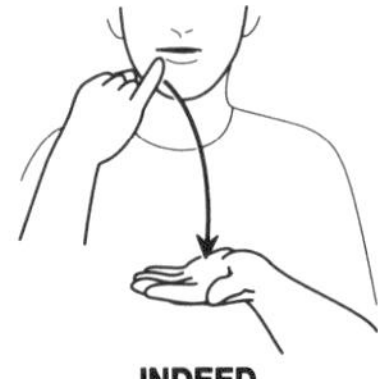

INDEED
Palm-in I at corner of mouth drops to palm of left hand
(see GOOD)

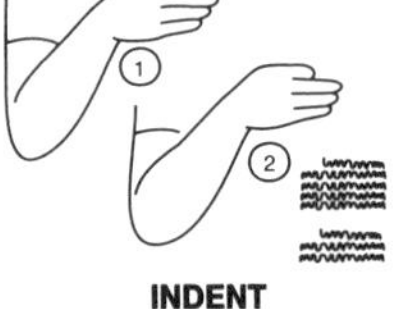

INDENT
Palm-in flat hand bends index

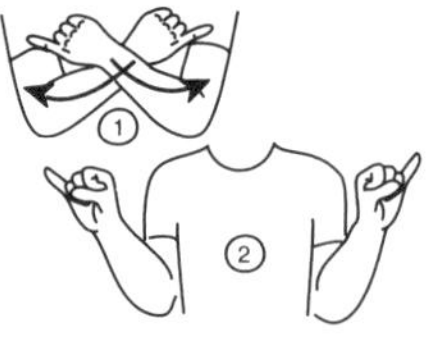

INDEPENDENT
Crossed wrists of palm-in I's turn outward and separate
(see FREE)

INDIA
Thumb of extended-A marks dot in middle of forehead

INDIAN
9 at corner of mouth, then on cheek in front of ear

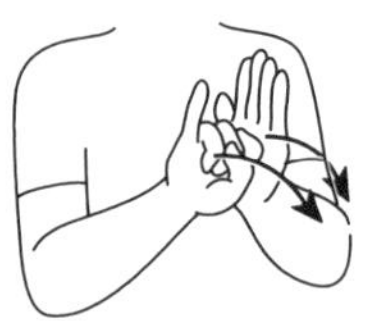

INDICATE
Palm-out I against left palm, both arc forward together
(see SHOW)

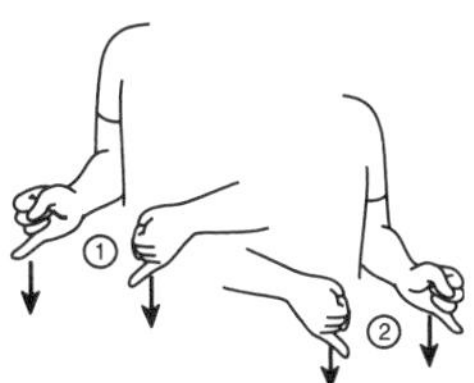

INDIVIDUAL

I-hands pointing forward, face each other, move downwards; first at right then at left

(see CITIZEN)

INDUSTRY

Palm-out I arcs side-to-side, hitting back of left S

(see BUSY)

INFANT

Wrists crossed and hands bent up, rock tiny infant

(see BABY)

INFATUATE

Palm-up flat-O opens and closes slowly at heart, moving slightly up and down *(heart beat)*

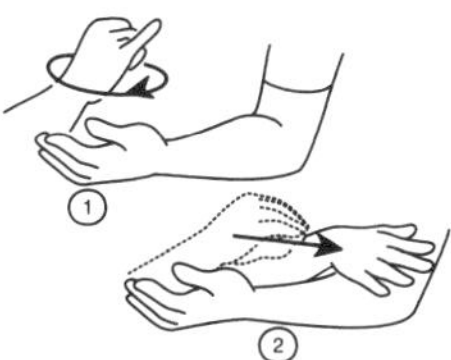

INFECT

I-hand circles on left palm, changes to flat-O, opens and spreads up arm

(see CANCER)

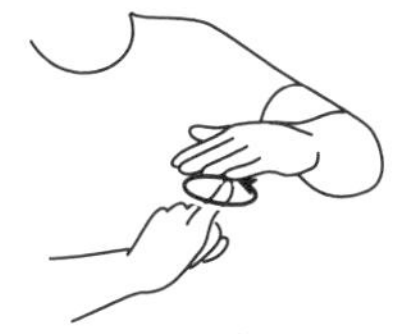

INFERIOR

Right I-hand circles under left palm

(see BASE)

INFEST

Palm-out I on back of left hand moves forward to palm-down 5 and circles

(see INFLUENCE)

INFILTRATE

Left hand curved palm-down in front of chest, right palm-down fingers creep beneath and out

INFINITE

I circles slightly then moves forward

(see ETERNAL)

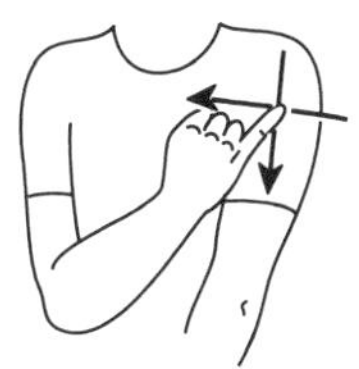

INFIRMARY

I-finger draws cross on shoulder

(see HOSPITAL)

INFLATE

Flat-O on left palm opens *(inflates)* to C

INFLECT

Index finger pointing left, moves to right while nodding up and down

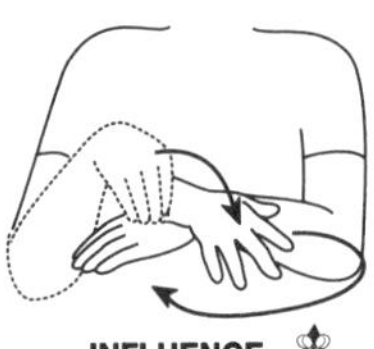

INFLUENCE

Inverted flat-O on back of left hand opens to 5 and then circles to the right *(spreading influence)*

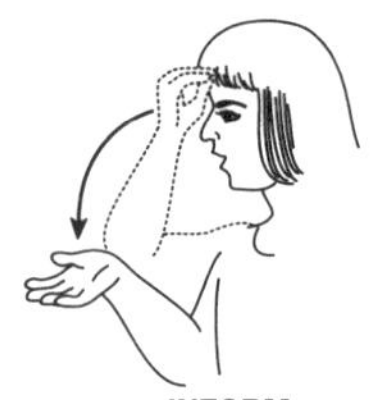

INFORM
(Alt. 1)

Flat-O at forehead moves forward and down, opening to palm-up

INFORM
(Alt. 2)

Both flat-O hands at forehead move downward and out, opening to palms-up

INGREDIENT

Side of I taps down left palm

(see LIST)

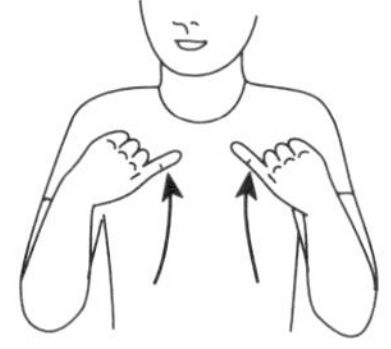

INHABIT

Palm-in I's move up chest

(see ADDRESS)

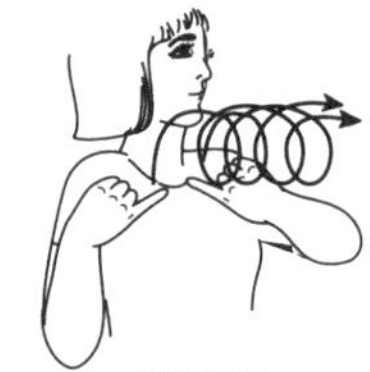

INHERIT

Palm-in I's roll forward from right shoulder, little fingers circling each other

(see GENERATE)

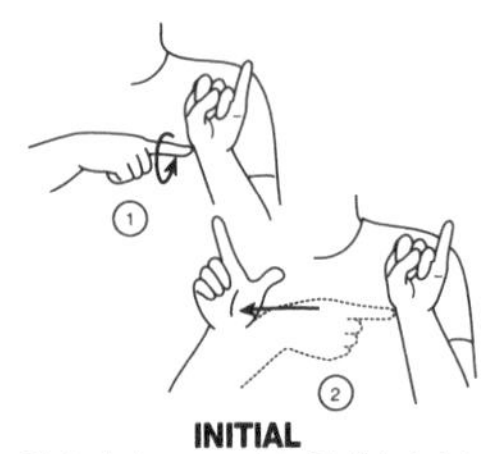

INITIAL

Right index on wrist of left I; twist index, change to L-hand *(initiate + -al)*

(see START)

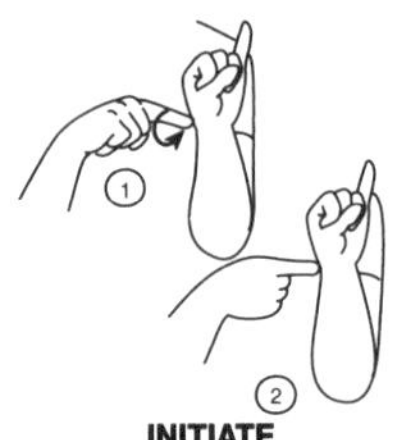

INITIATE

Right index on wrist of palm-out left I; twist index

(see START)

INJURE

Palm-in I-hands fingers pointing, jerk toward each other twisting slightly

(see HURT)

INNOCENT

Palm-in I-fingers, near mouth, swing out, twisting to palm-out

(see NAIVE)

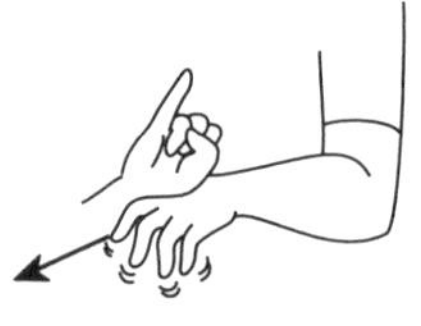

INSECT

I rides forward on back of wiggling left fingers

(see ANT)

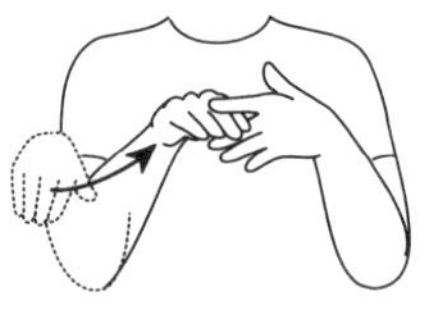

INSERT

Flat palm-down right hand slides in between index and middle finger of palm-in left hand

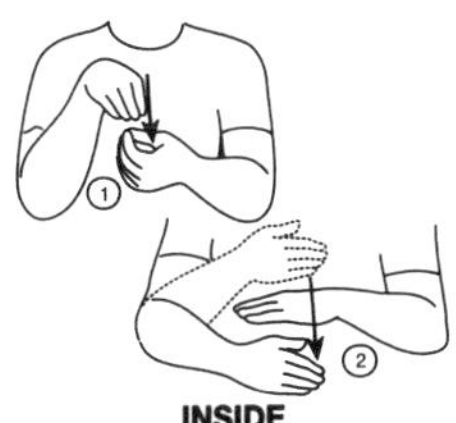

INSIDE

Fingertips of right flat-O enter left O; right palm-in flat hand brushes down past side of left hand *(in + side)*

INSIST

Tip of right I on left palm, both arc toward body

(see REQUIRE)

INSPECT

Index at eye, then brushes forward off left palm two or more times

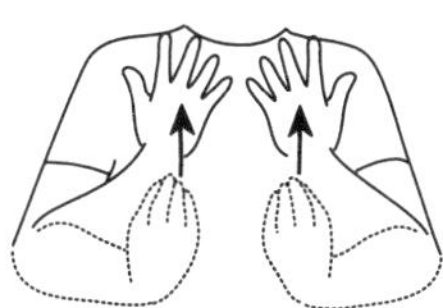

INSPIRE

Palm-in flat-O's on chest slide up opening to 5's

INSTALL

Right flat-O slightly behind left C, wrist of right twists forward toward C

(see PUT)

INSTANT

Palm-out I-hand rests against other palm; twist forward to palm-down

(see MINUTE)

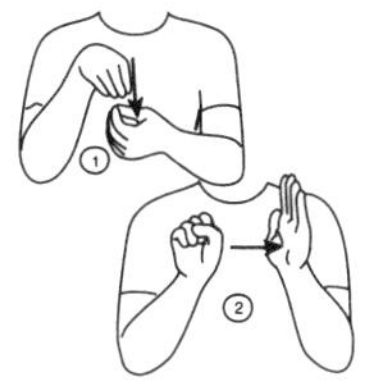

INSTEAD

(Alt. 1)

Fingertips of flat-O enter left O; side of S hits heel of left hand *(in + -stead)*

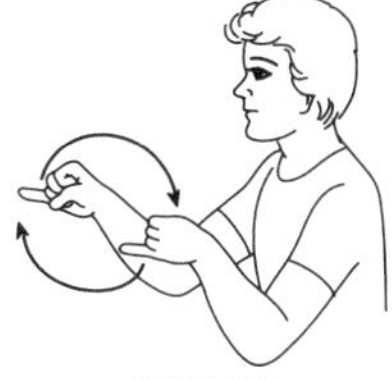

INSTEAD

(Alt. 2)

Both I-hands point forward, right ahead of left; reverse

(see EXCHANGE)

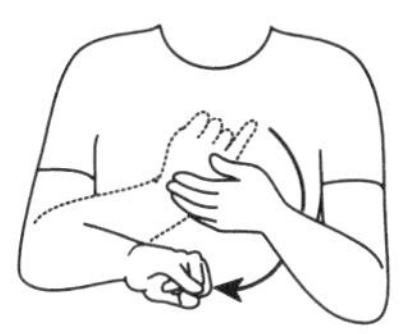

INSTINCT

Back of I-hand on left palm; I twists down and under to palm-down

(see NATURE)

INSTITUTE

Little finger side of right I taps on index side of left I-hand

INSTRUCT

I-hands at forehead jerk slightly forward; repeat

(see TEACH)

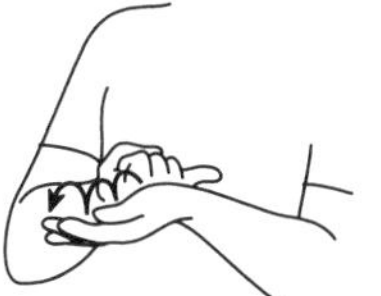

INSTRUMENT

Back of I on heel of left palm, bounce across palm to fingertips

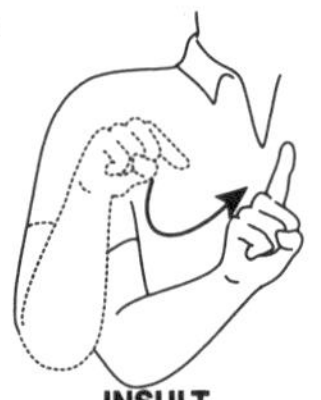

INSULT

Index finger, pointing forward, moves sharply out and up *(jab)*

INSURE

Palm-out I shakes

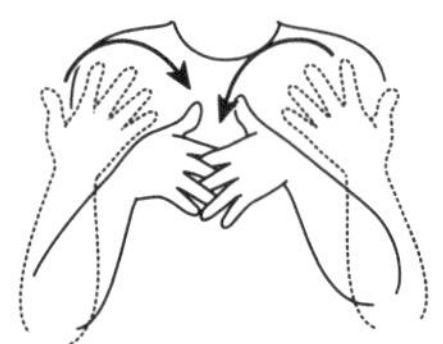

INTEGRATE

Palm-in 5-hands arc toward each other, meshing fingers

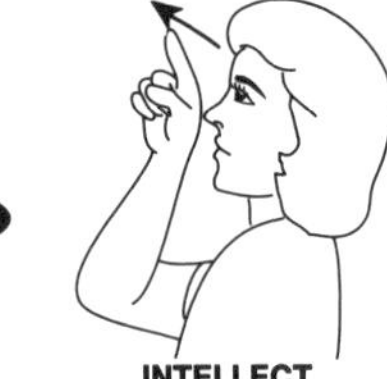

INTELLECT

Side of index on forehead, slide up and forward

(see INVENT)

INTELLIGENT

Side of index on forehead, slide up and forward; right T-hand slides down left vertical hand *(intellect + -ent)*

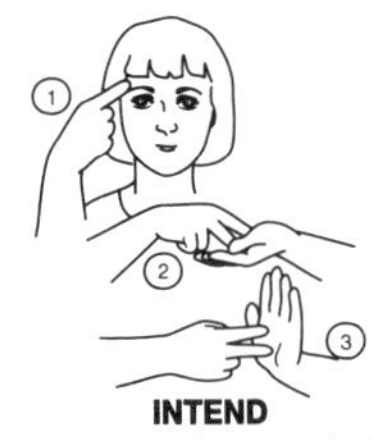

INTEND

Index on temple drops to palm-down V on left palm; hands separate; twist and touch again

(see MEAN)

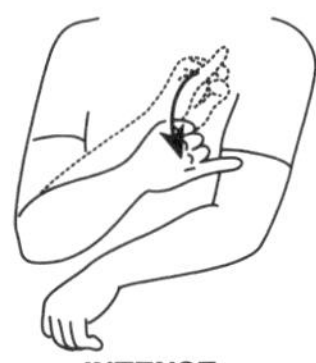

INTENSE

Little finger of right I outlines muscle on upper left arm

(see STRONG)

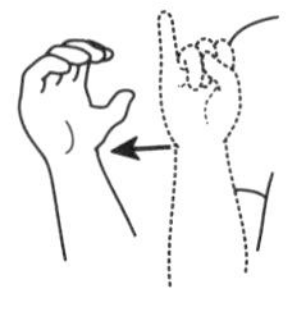

INTERCOURSE

Fingerspell I + C

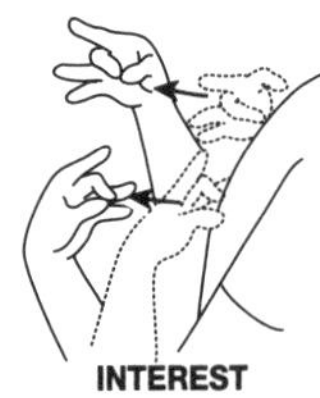

INTEREST

Palm-in 5's, thumbs and middle fingers on chest, one hand above other, pull out closing to palm-in 8's

INTERFERE

Side of I-hand chops into thumb-joint of left hand

(see BOTHER)

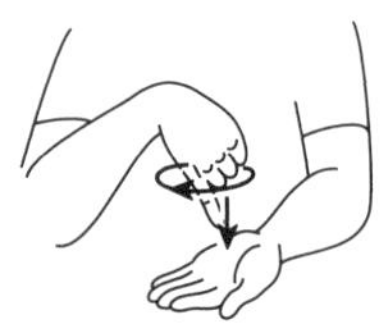

INTERMEDIATE

Circle inverted I over left palm, then touch tip to mid-palm

(see MIDDLE)

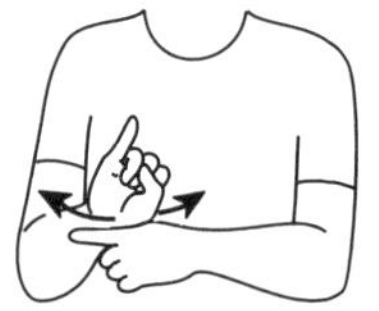

INTERN

Heel of I-hand brushes back and forth on horizontal left index

(see PRACTICE)

INTERNATIONAL

I-hands, one on top of other; circle each other vertically and touch again

(see WORLD)

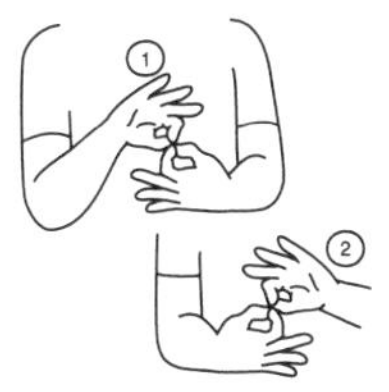

INTERPRET

9's, thumb-on-thumb, one palm-up and one palm-down; reverse; repeat

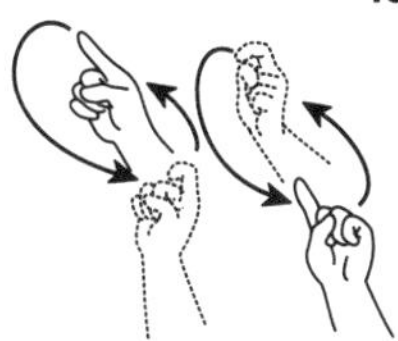

INTERROGATE

Hands move alternately in small in-and-out circles while changing from 1 to X

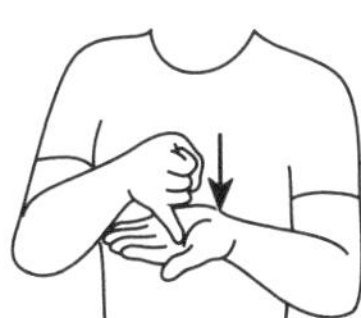

INTERRUPT

Little finger side of I hits left palm

(see STOP)

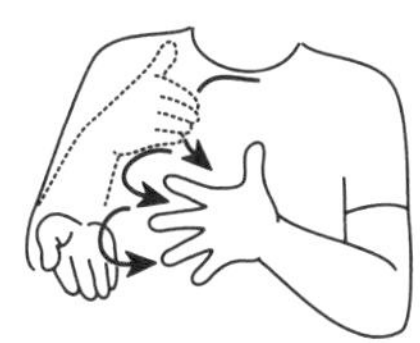

INTERVAL

Right flat hand arcs over left thumb and between finger gaps

INTERVIEW

Palm-facing I's move alternately towards and away from face

(see TALK)

INTIMATE

(adjective)

I moves near back of palm-in left hand

(see NEAR)

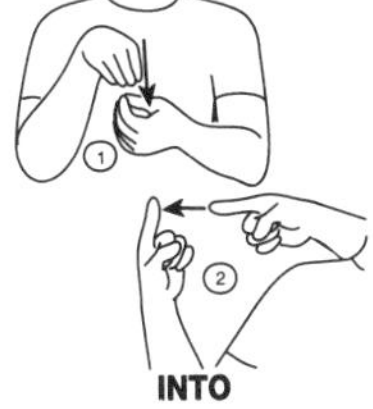

INTO

Fingertips of right flat-O enter left O; horizontal index finger approaches and touches left index finger *(in + to)*

INTRIGUE

I moves from chin to under left hand

(see HIDE)

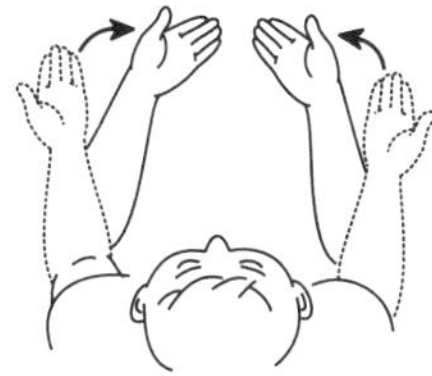

INTRODUCE

Palm-up flat hands swing to point at each other

(see PROLOGUE)

INTRUDE

Right flat hand swings down between index and middle finger of palm-in left hand

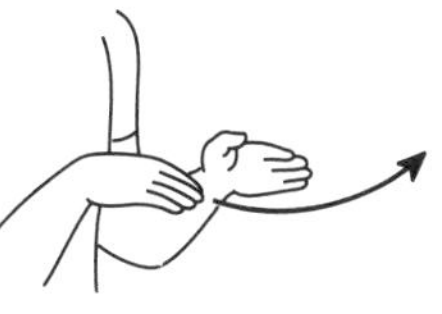

INVADE

Palm-down right hand arcs sharply out under palm-down left hand

(see ENTER)

I

INVENT
Index of 4 on forehead; arc up and out
(see INTELLECT)

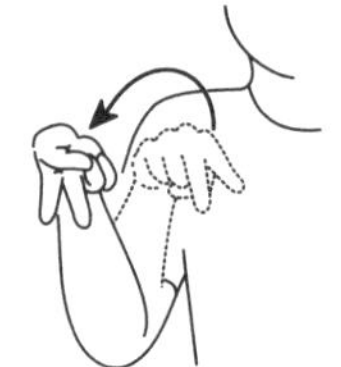

INVERT
Palm-down V swings over to palm-up

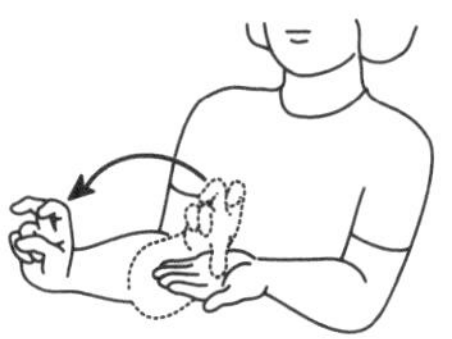

INVEST
Extended thumb of palm-out bent-V on left palm arcs forward
(see BUY)

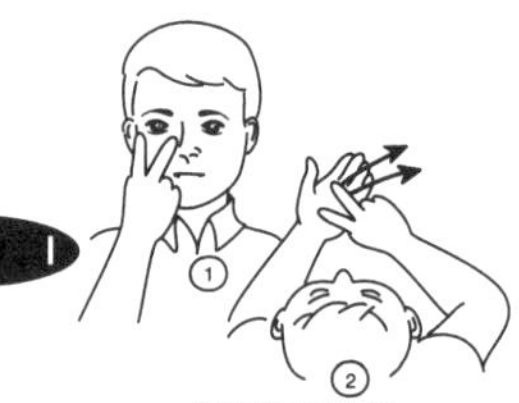

INVESTIGATE
Palm-in V at eye; then palm-down V brushes forward on palm twice
(see INSPECT)

INVISIBLE
Palm-down I-hands cross at wrists and separate; palm-out V's at sides of eyes drop to palm-down A's *(in + visible)*

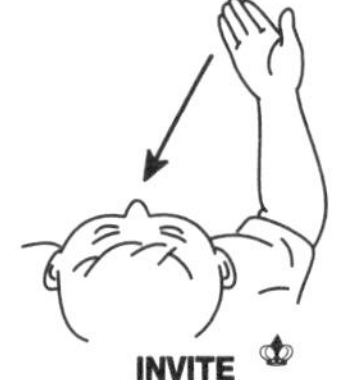

INVITE ♔
Palm-up flat hand moves in toward body

INVOLVE
Palm-down right 5-hand circles horizontally, goes into grasp of horizontal left C

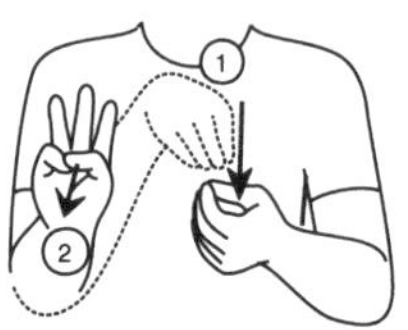

INWARD
Fingertips of right flat-O enter horizontal left O; right W moves forward *(in + ward)*

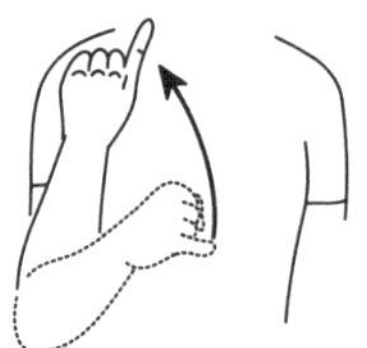

IRATE
Palm-in I jerks up body
(see ANGER)

IRELAND
Palm-down bent-V circles over, then drops on back of left fist

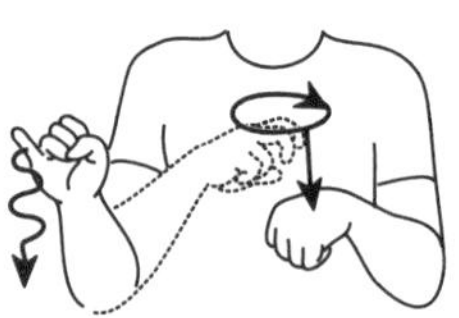

IRISH
Palm-down bent-V circles over, drops on back of left fist; right I draws a wavy downward line *(Ireland + -ish)*

IRON ★
Palm-in I arcs right, hitting side of left horizontal hand and ending palm-out
(see METAL)

IRONY
Fingertip of right I touches side of mouth, then arcs down past outside of palm-down left I, then twists inward
(see TRICK)

IRRESPONSIBLE
Palm-down I-hands, crossed at wrists, separate sideways; R-hands tap right shoulder *(ir + responsible)*

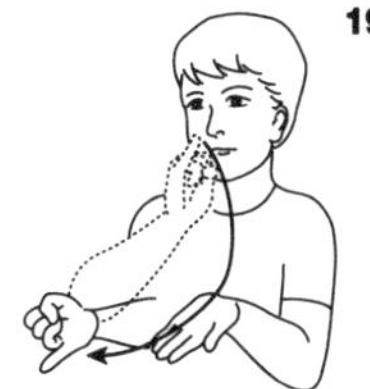

IRRIGATE
I at mouth, side of I then slides across left palm and to right, ending palm-up

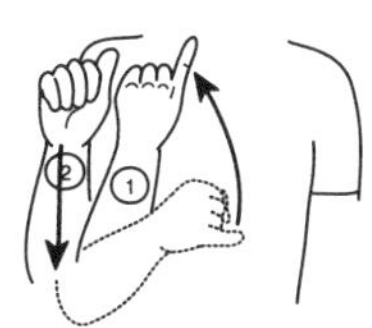

IRRITATE
Palm-in I jerks up body, changes to palm-out A and moves downward

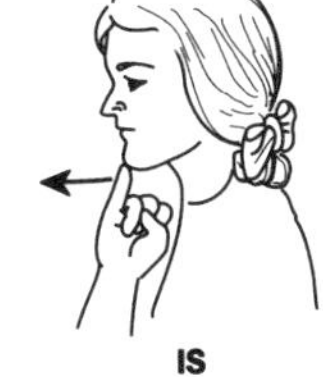

IS
I on chin moves straight forward
(see AM)

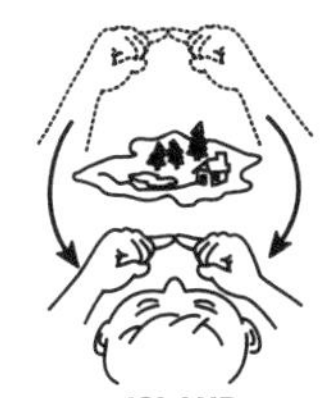

ISLAND
(Alt. 1)
Horizontal I's face each other, circle horizontally toward body and touch
(see PLACE)

ISLAND
(Alt. 2)
Side of I-hand circles on back of palm-down left S-hand

ISOLATE
I-hands touch and separate sideways
(see SEPARATE)

ISRAEL
Palm-in I strokes downward on each side of chin

ISSUE
Both palm-down I-hands, arc outwards to palm-up
(see GIVE)

IT
Tip of I touches palm of left hand

ITALY
Little finger makes cross near forehead

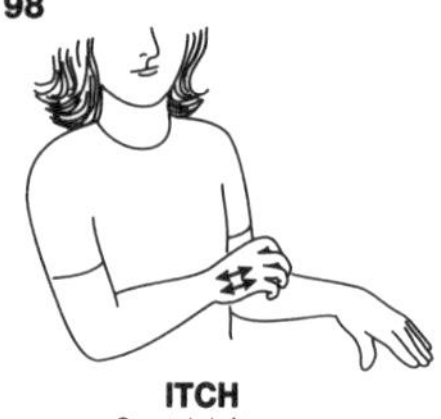

ITCH
Scratch left arm

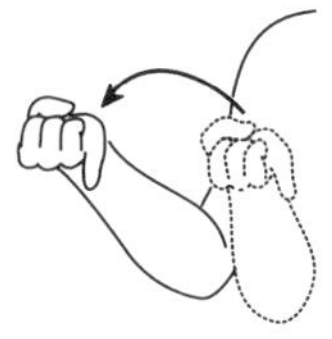

ITEM
Palm-up I-hand arcs to the right
(see THING)

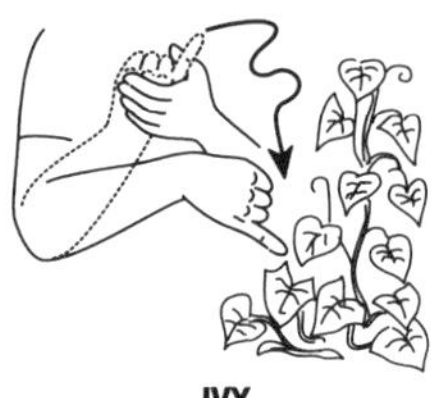

IVY
I grows up and out of horizontal left C and spirals downward
(see GROW)

JACK-IN-THE-BOX
Left hand clasped over right fist; left unbends and right fist pops up

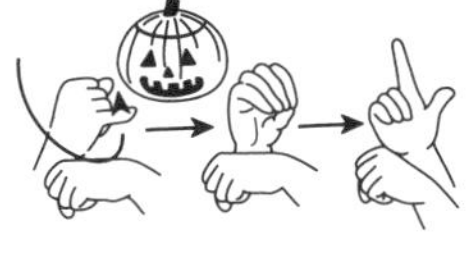

JACK O'LANTERN
Make J + O + L above back of left S, hitting left hand slightly each time
(see MELON)

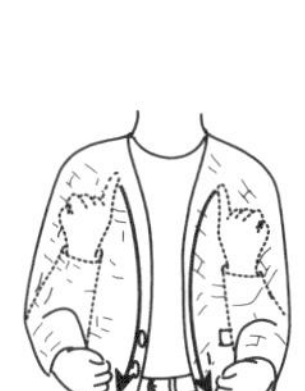
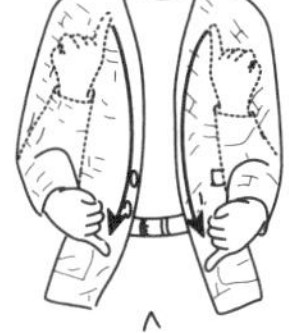

JACKET
Palm-in I-fingertips draw lapels down chest to waist
(see COAT)

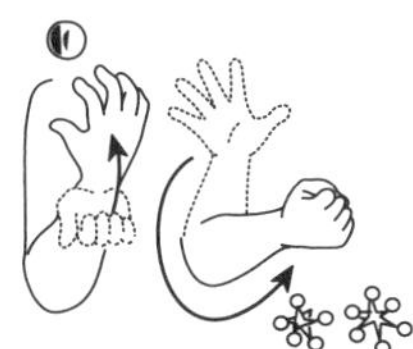

JACKS
Toss up ball and snatch up jacks

JAIL ♔
Palm-in V-hands, right behind left crosswise; right hits left

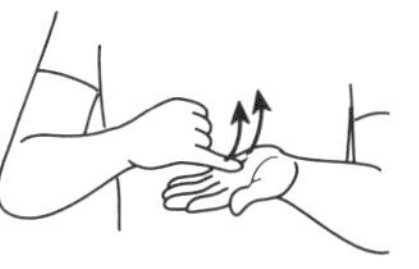

JAM ★
Tip of I flicks inward off left palm-up hand twice
(see BUTTER)

JANITOR

Right S on top of left, push broom in front; repeat

JANUARY
(Alt. 1)
J arcs over at side of vertical hand
(see CALENDAR)

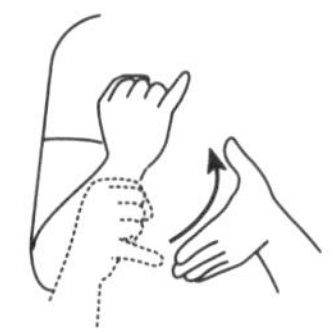

JANUARY
(Alt. 2)
Little finger of I-hand brushes off thumb of left hand
(see FIRST)

JAPAN
(U.S. Sign)
Little fingertip at corner of eye, hand twists slightly to palm-in
(see CHINA)

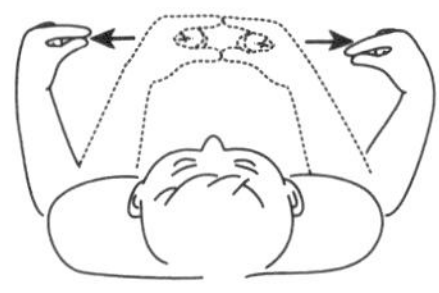

JAPAN
(Japanese Sign)
Index and thumb of horizontal G's touch, separate and close

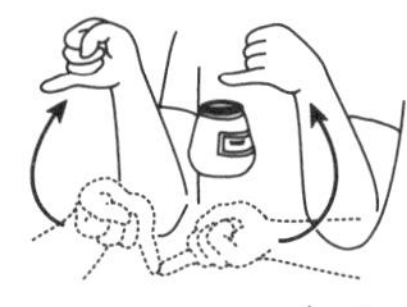

JAR ♔ ★

Palm-up I-fingers outline jar-bottom to palms-facing

JAY
G on head moves back on top of head and closes

JEALOUS
Draw a J near corner of mouth
(see ENVY)

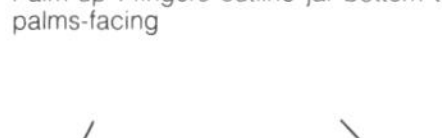

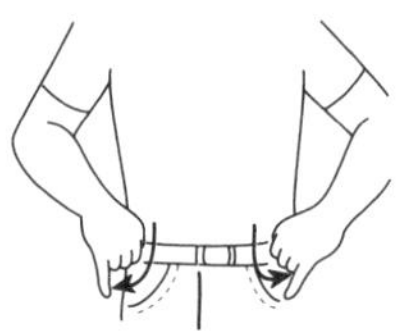

JEANS
Little finger of I-hands, palms-in, make J's at waist

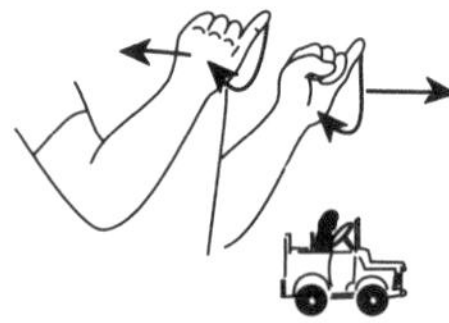

JEEP
Make J's, one in front of the other, and then move apart
(see CAR)

JELL
Right claw jiggles over left palm
(see CUSTARD)

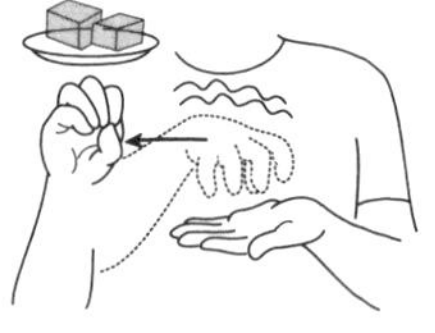

JELLO
Claw jiggles over palm; right hand changes to O *(jell + -o)*

JELLY
Claw jiggles over palm; right hand changes to Y *(jell + -y)*

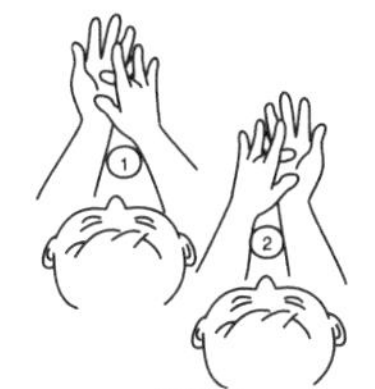

JESUS
Bent right middle finger touches left palm; reverse *(nails in Jesus' hands)*

JET
Palm-down I near shoulder darts forward, makes J

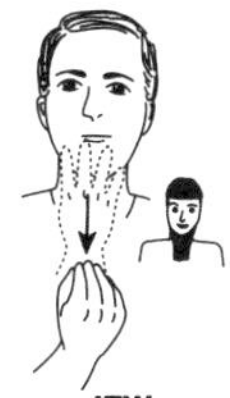

JEW
Palm-in, four fingers and thumb grasp chin, drop slightly to flat-O; repeat
(see ISRAEL)

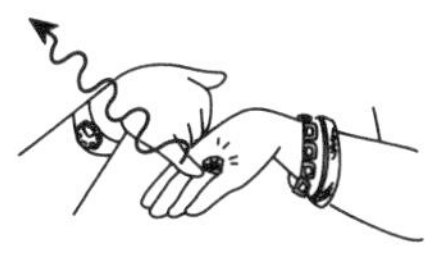

JEWEL
I-finger shakes off left ring-finger
(see DIAMOND)

JINGLE
Palm-down 9 strikes left vertical palm and shakes to side
(see BELL)

JOB
I-hand arcs once from right to left, hitting back of left S and ending palm-in
(see TASK)

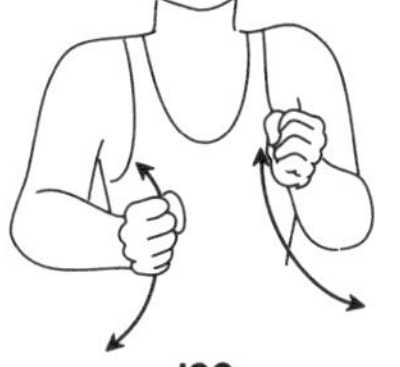

JOG
S's face each other, swing alternately back and forth with arm movement

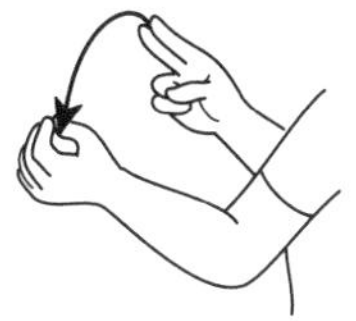

JOIN
Right H-fingertips arc into side of horizontal left O
(See PARTICIPATE)

JOINT
Both I-hands, palms-out, twist to palms-in and cross little fingers

JOKE
Palm-in H-hands arc slightly to cross before face; repeat

JOURNAL
Little finger of I brushes off edge of flat hand twice
(see MAGAZINE)

JOURNEY

Right I-hands points down and wanders forward

(see WANDER)

JOY

Fingertip of palm-in I brushes up chest; repeat

(see HAPPY)

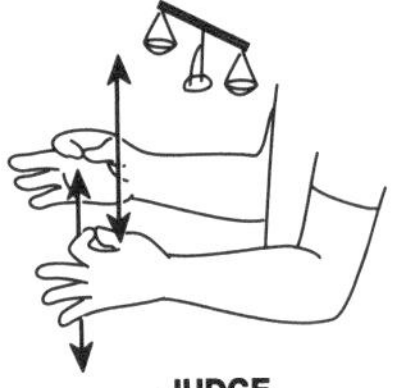

JUDGE

Palms-facing, parallel 9-hands move alternately up and down

(see BALANCE)

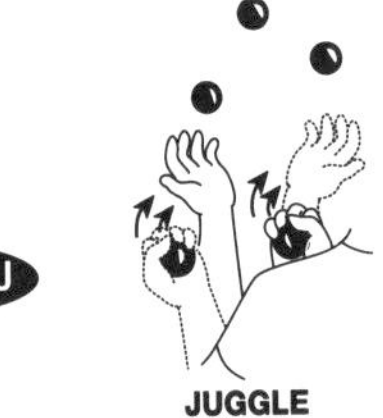

JUGGLE

Palm-up S's throw balls alternately up to 5-hands; repeat

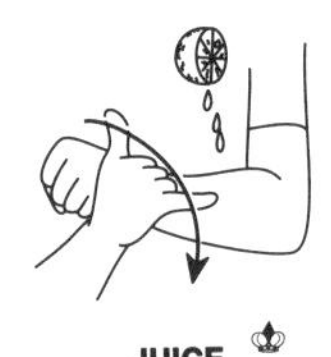

JUICE

Thumb side of Y cuts down back of S

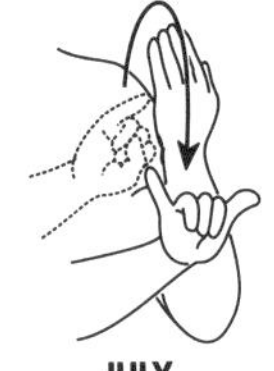

JULY
(Alt. 1)

Right J arcs over vertical left hand changing to Y

(see CALENDAR)

JULY
(Alt. 2)

Palm-in little finger brushes straight across forehead

(see SUMMER)

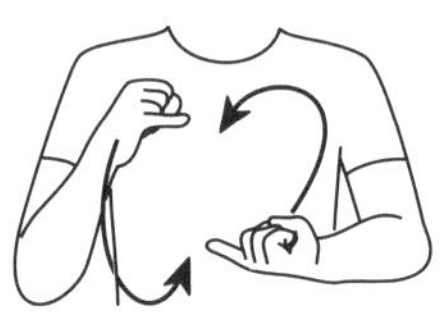

JUMBLE

Left I palm-up, right I palm-down above left; reverse positions

(see MESS)

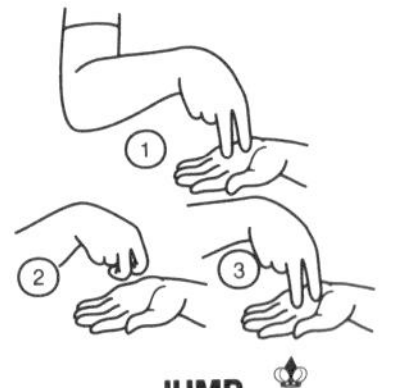

JUMP

V-fingertips stand on left palm, jump up to bent fingers and down again

(see HOP)

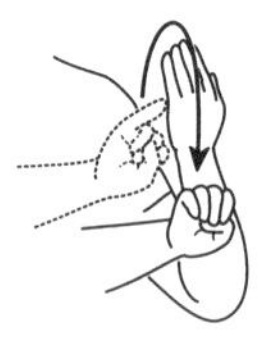

JUNE
(Alt. 1)

J arcs over vertical left hand, changing to E

(see CALENDAR)

JUNE
(Alt. 2)

Right I traces J around left fingertips

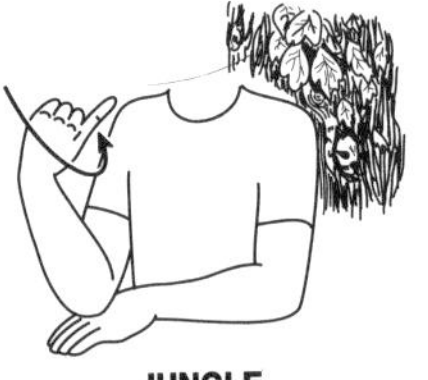

JUNGLE

Right elbow resting on back of left hand, make J; repeat slightly to right

(see TREE)

JUNIOR

Right index taps left index of palm-in 5

(see FRESHMAN)

JUNK

Back of palm-up I brushes off left palm, twists to palm-out, then throws *(junk)* down to 5

(see DISPOSE)

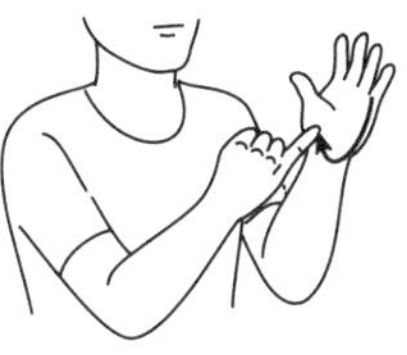

JUST

I-fingertip draws "J" on left palm

JUSTICE

I-fingertip draws "J" on left palm; palm-out C moves down slightly *(just + -ice)*

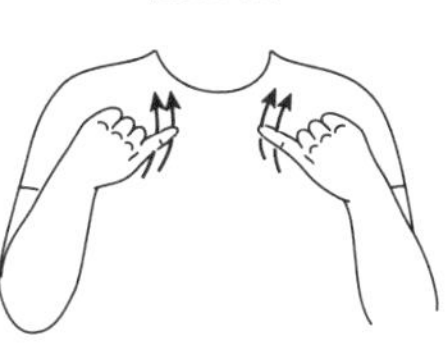

JUVENILE

Palm-in I fingertips brush upward twice off chest; repeat

(see YOUNG)

NOTES

KANGAROO
Body stationary, bent hands hop forward together

KARATE
Both palms-down, horizontally bent arms, one behind the other; mime several karate chops

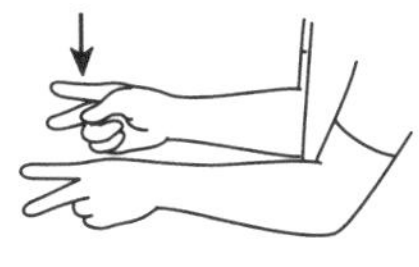

KEEP
Horizontal right K drops on left K

KERCHIEF
K's outline and tie kerchief on
(see BONNET)

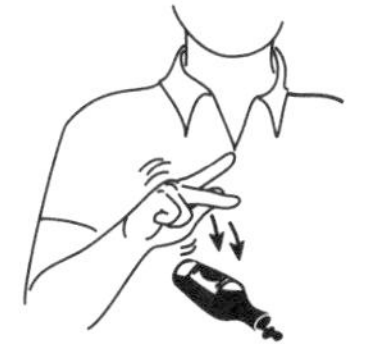

KETCHUP/CATSUP
Side of right K shakes downward, like a bottle

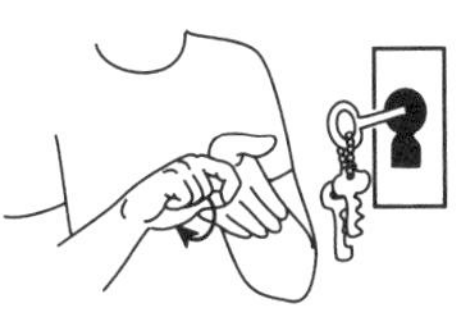

KEY
Hold imaginary key with thumb and index and twist on left palm

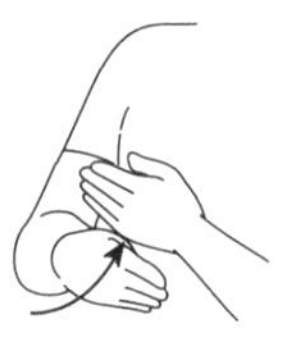

KICK

Side of right B-hand arcs from below to strike side of left hand sharply

(see SOCCER)

KID
(Alt. 1)
K-hand shakes in front of nose

KID
(Alt. 2)
I-1 hand shakes in front of nose

KIDNAP

Right K pulls back sharply to A-hand near shoulder

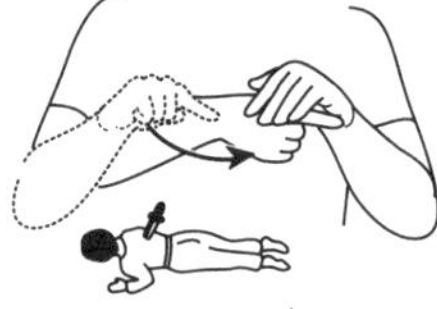

KILL ♔

Side of right index twists under palm-down left hand

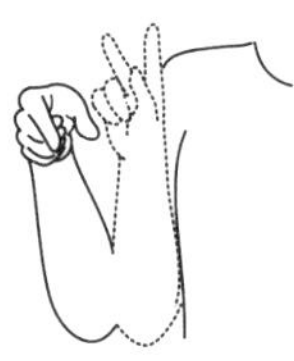

KILOGRAM
(Kg)
Fingerspell K + G

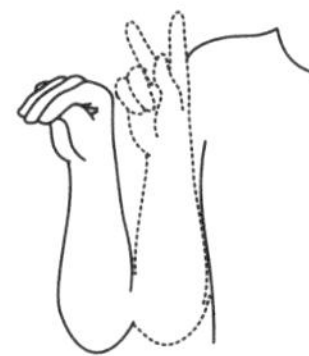

KILOMETER
(Km)
Fingerspell K + M

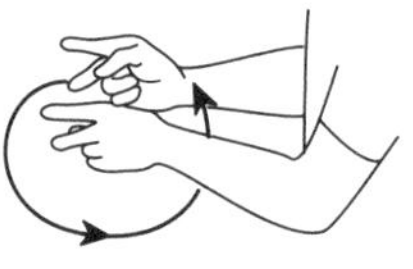

KIND ♔ ★

K-hands fingers pointing forward, circle vertically around each other, stopping one on top of the other

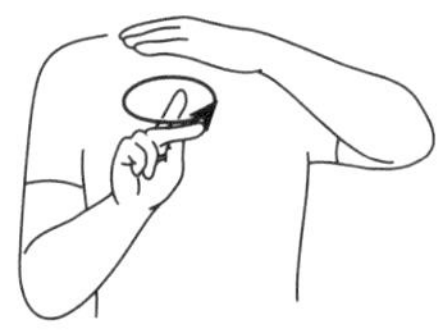

KINDERGARTEN

K circles under left palm

(see BASE)

KING

Right K on left shoulder, then moves to right hip

(see CHRIST)

KISS

Fingertips of palm-in hand touch below lips and on cheek

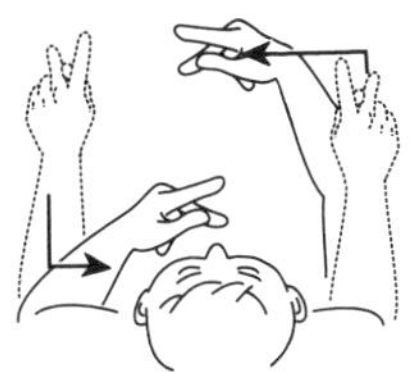

KITCHEN
(Alt. 1)
Palm-down K's point forward, form box-shape, changing to palms-in
(see BOX)

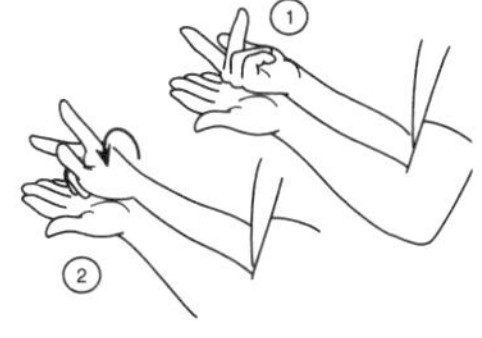

KITCHEN
(Alt. 2)
Flip right palm-up K to palm-down on left palm

KITE
K moves upward in wavy motion

KITTEN
Middle finger of right K brushes side of mouth; repeat
(see CAT)

KLEENEX
Heel of right K strikes across left heel several times
(see PAPER)

KNEE
Tap knee twice

KNEEL
Bent-V fingers kneel on left palm

KNIFE
Side of right H-hand flicks off side of left H twice

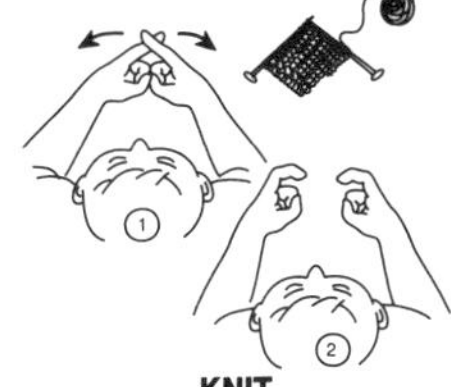

KNIT
Horizontal index fingers cross; separate to X's; repeat several times

KNOB
C-hand twists knob

KNOCK ★
Right A-hand knocks several times on left palm

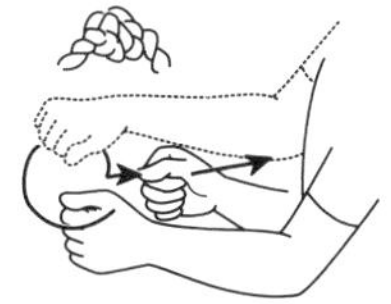

KNOT
Right A circles thumb of left A and jerks back to tie knot

KNOW
Fingers of palm-in hand hit forehead lightly; may repeat
(see THINK)

KOOL AID
Right K moves back to A at mouth
(see LEMONADE)

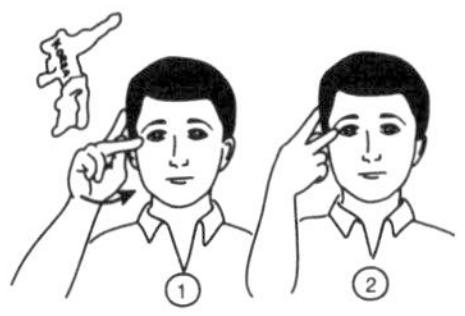

KOREA
Middle fingertip of K at corner of eye; hand twists slightly inward
(see CHINA)

KOSHER
(Alt. 1)
Side of right palm-left flat hand moves from mouth to slide along top of left palm-right hand

KOSHER
(Alt. 2)
Heel of K-hand rests on left palm-up wrist; then moves across hand

LABEL

H-fingers slide across heel of vertical left palm

(see BRAND)

LABOR

Palm-out L brushes side-to-side hitting back of left S

(see BUSY)

LACE

Palm-in I-hands with little fingers crossed; fingers reverse repeatedly, moving upwards

LACK

Left L points downward; index of horizontal right L moves inward and clips tip of left index

(see ABSENT)

LADDER

Two fingers walk up inverted V

LADY

A-hand, thumb on chin, moves to 5-hand, thumb on chest

LAKE
Palm-down L-thumbs touch; circle outward, shaking, and touch again
(see POND)

LAMB
Palm-up L moves twice up left arm
(see SHEEP)

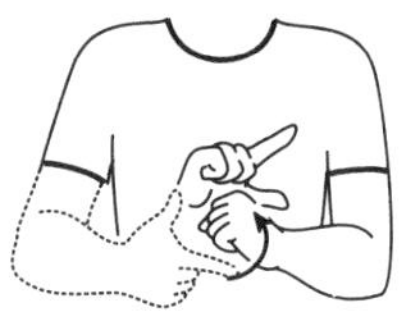

LAMINATE
Horizontal L-hand sweeps over back of palm-down left S
(see COVER)

LAMP
Place thumb on chin and flick middle finger out from thumb several times

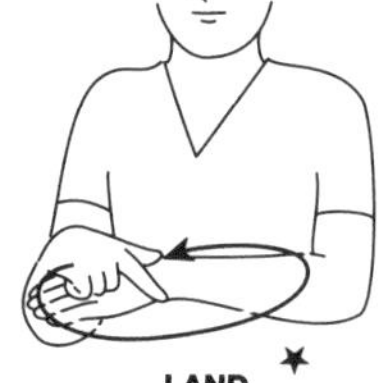

LAND ★
Palm-down L on back of left hand circles out, back to elbow and along arm to hand
(see GROUND)

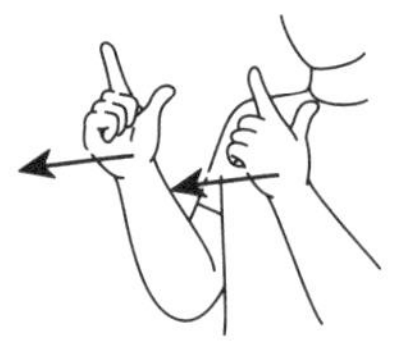

LANE
Parallel and vertical palms-facing; L's move forward
(see HALL)

LANGUAGE
Thumbtips of palm-down L's touch, then separate, shaking slightly
(see SENTENCE)

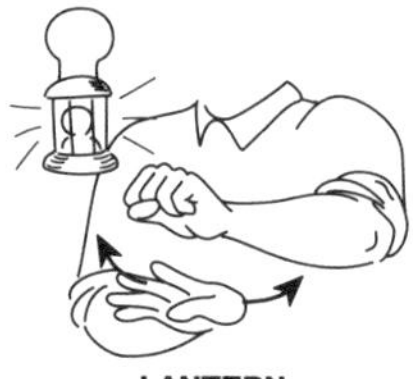

LANTERN
Palm-down left S *(as though holding lantern handle)*; palm-down 5 swings side-to-side under left S

LAP ★
Inverted L arcs forward twice, knuckles hitting left palm; repeat
(see SLIP)

LARD
H-fingers brush toward body off heel of palm-up left L
(see BUTTER)

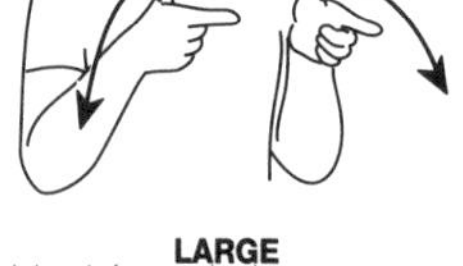

LARGE
L-hands face each other, arc apart
(see MUCH)

LASH ★
Index of palm-in right L moves out to strike vertical left index
(see BEAT)

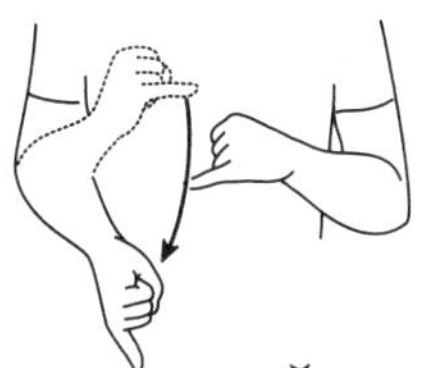

LAST ✶

Right little finger chops past end of horizontal left little finger

(see FINAL)

LATE

Thumbtip of palm-out L on left palm, twist to palm-down

(see MINUTE)

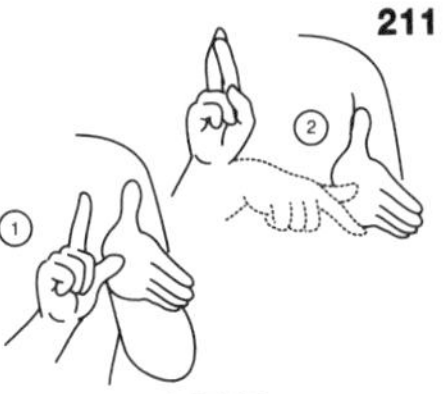

LATER

Thumbtip of palm-out L on left palm, twists to palm-down; add R-hand *(late +-er)*

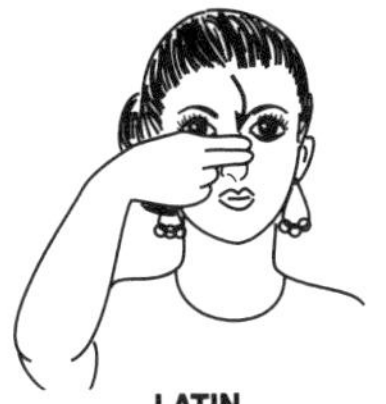

LATIN

Palm-in U-hand fingertips touch forehead, then nose

(see ROME)

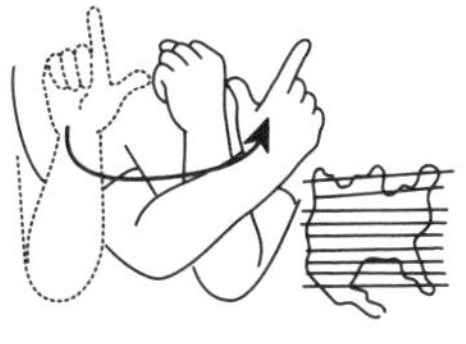

LATITUDE

Thumb of right L slides around palm-in left S-hand

(see EQUATOR)

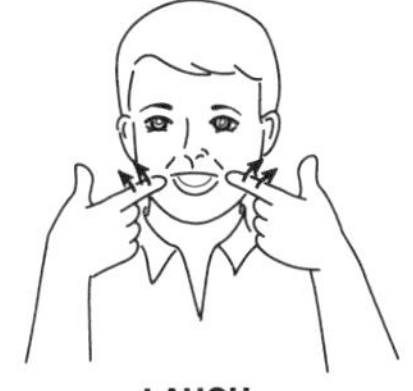

LAUGH

Index fingers of L's brush outward at corners of mouth several times

(see SMILE)

LAUNCH ✶

Palm-left right L pointing forward on flat left palm, arc L forward and off

LAUNDER

Knuckles of L-hand circle on left palm

(see WASH)

LAW ♔

Right L on left fingertips, then on heel

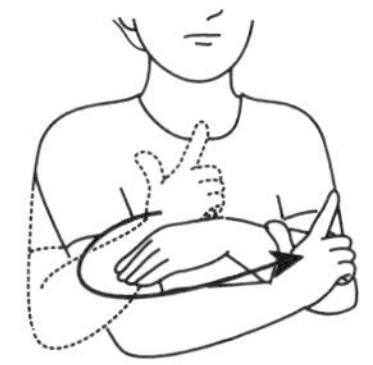

LAWN

Right L moves from inside left palm-down hand around to the outside

(see EDGE)

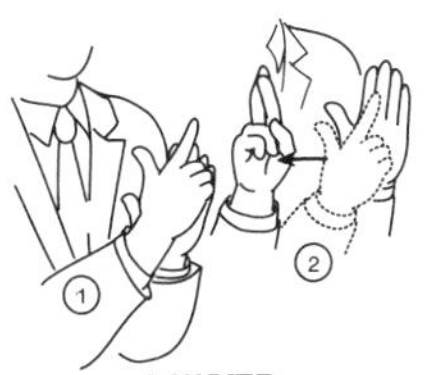

LAWYER

Right L on left fingertips, then on heel; add R-hand *(law + -er)*

LAY ✶

Set back of right palm-up V on back of left hand

(see SET)

LAYER ★

Palm-down G's separate, move down one layer and repeat; move down and repeat again

LAZY

Right L taps below left shoulder

LEAD

(verb)

Grasp tip of left hand and pull forward at an angle *(leading hand)*

(see GUIDE)

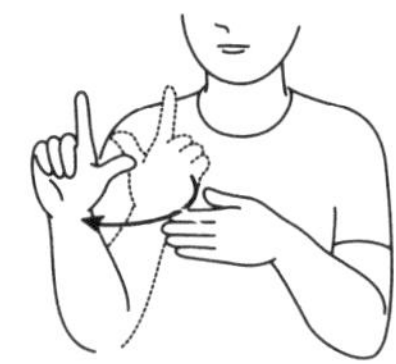

LEAD

(metal)

Heel of L strikes off index side of left hand, from palm-in to palm-out

(see METAL)

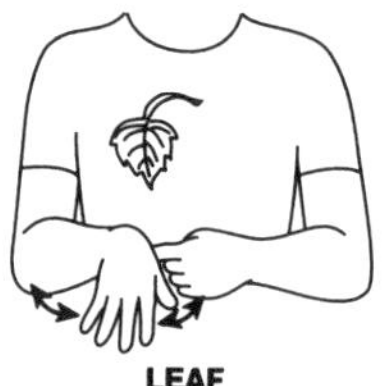

LEAF

Right wrist of 5-hand on left index; wave 5 side-to-side

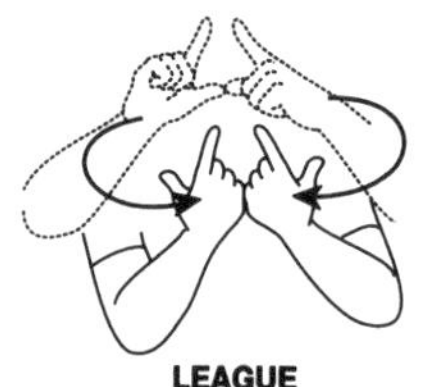

LEAGUE

Thumbtips of L's together circle out and touch little finger side of hands

(see CLASS)

LEAK

Right 4-hand "leaks" down from left horizontal left S; repeat

LEAN

Thumb of right L on vertical left palm; right index leans towards left palm and touches

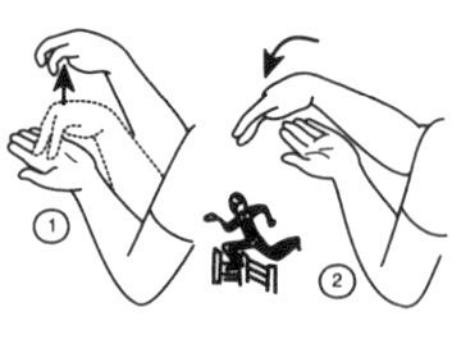

LEAP

Inverted V on left palm jumps up and bends, then leaps forward while straightening back to V-hand

LEARN

Right open palm-down fingers on palm-up left hand rise, closing to flat-O at forehead

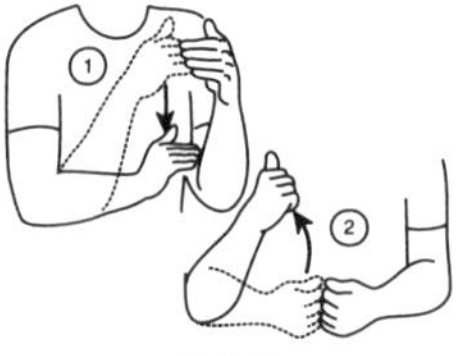

LEAST

Bent hands, right under left, drop downward; knuckles of A-hands together, right A jerks up *(less + -est)*

LEATHER

Palm-in L brushes down back of palm-in left hand

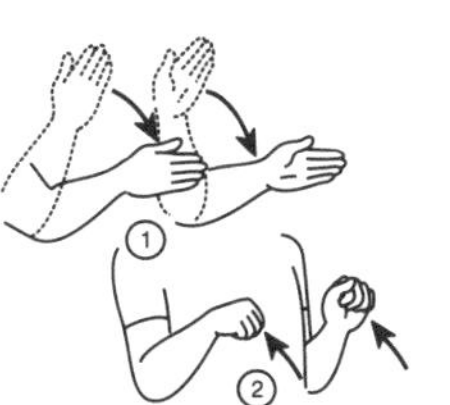

LEAVE
Flat palms-facing at side, pointing slightly up; drop down to pointing forward, withdraw back and up, closing to A's

LECTURE ♔
Right palm facing side of head, move hand slightly and quickly forward and back from wrist

LEDGE
Palm-down right L at fingertips of left palm-in hand, right moves right, down, and right again

LEDGER

Thumb of right L brushes off bottom edge of palm-in left flat hand
(see MAGAZINE)

LEFT

Palm-out right L moves left

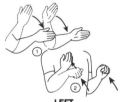

LEFT
(verb)
Flat palms-facing, at side, pointing slightly up; drops pointing forward, withdraw back and up, closing to A's; right hand flips back *(leave + p.t.)*

LEG
Right L-hand pats thigh

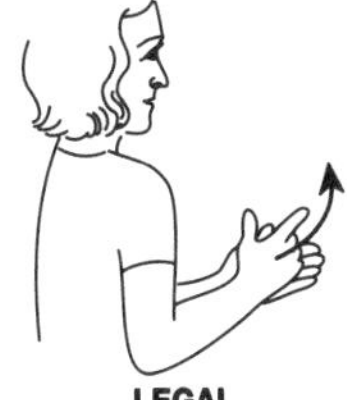

LEGAL
Right L pointing outward, side of hand slides out across left palm to point slightly upward
(see ALL RIGHT)

LEGEND
Palm-in horizontal L's circle each other forward from right shoulder
(see GENERATE)

LEGISLATE
Thumb of L touches left, then right side of chest
(see MEMBER)

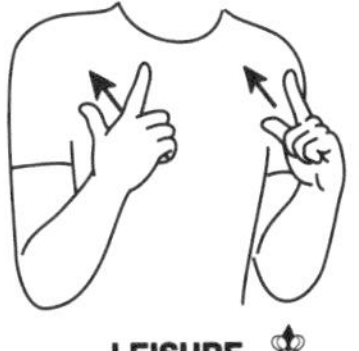

LEISURE ♔
L-thumbs tap into sides of chest

LEMON
Thumb of L taps chin

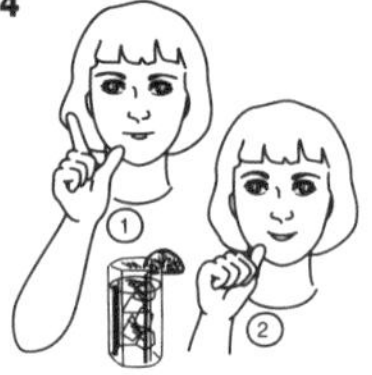

LEMONADE
Thumb of L on chin closes to A
(see KOOL AID)

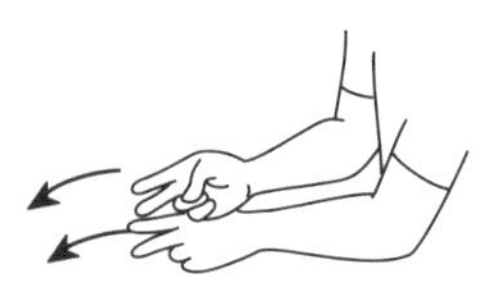

LEND
Horizontal V's, right on left, both hands arc forward
(see LOAN)

LENGTH
Index finger of right hand slides up left arm; then add H-hand *(long + -th)*

LENS
Thumb of right L circles in front of eye

LEOPARD
Thumbs of L's on cheeks move to sides; repeat
(see CAT)

LEPRECHAUN
Indexes of L's at shoulders swing out to palms-out
(see ANGEL)

LESS
Right bent hand under left bent hand; drop right downward

LESSON
Side of right bent hand on palm-up left fingertips, then on heel

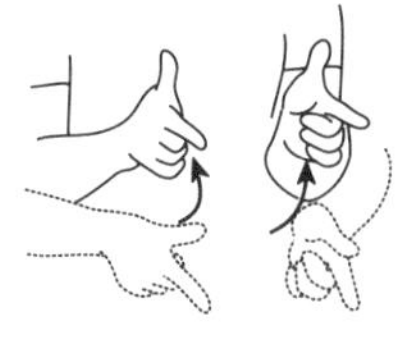

LET
L-hands face each other, pointing down; swing to point forward
(see ALLOW)

LETTER
Extended-A thumb at mouth moves down to touch palm-up left fingers

LETTUCE
Heel of L taps upwards on side of head; repeat
(see CABBAGE)

LEVEL ★
Palm-down L-hand moves to right
(see FLAT)

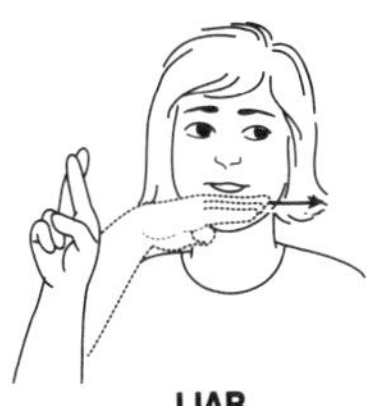

LIAR

Side of palm-down B moves left below mouth; add R-hand *(lie + -ar)*

LIBERTY

Palm-in L's, crossed at wrists, separate and twist to palm-out *(breaking bonds)*

(see FREE)

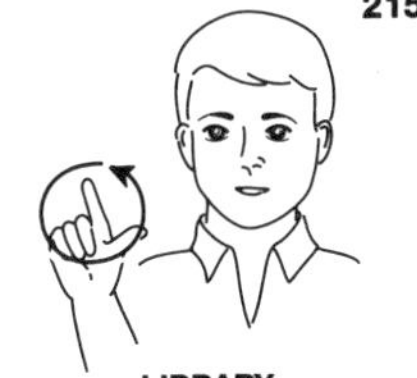

LIBRARY

Palm-out L makes a small vertical circle twice

LICENSE

Palms-out L-thumbs tap

(see CREDENTIAL)

LICK ✶

Fingertips of right hand brush upward against left palm; repeat

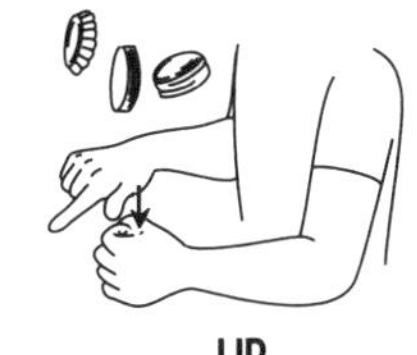

LID

Palm-down L drops on side of left S

(see CAP)

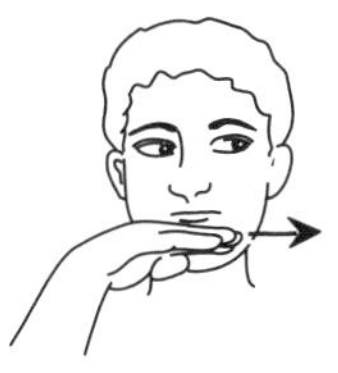

LIE

(To tell a ...)

Side of palm-down B moves left across chin *(below mouth)*

(see FIB)

LIE ♔

(Recline)

Back of right V on left palm; slide toward body

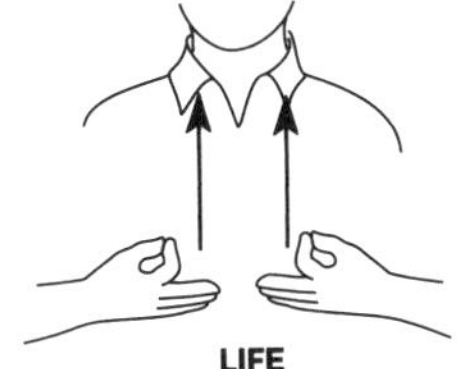

LIFE

Palm-in 9-hands move up body

(see ADDRESS)

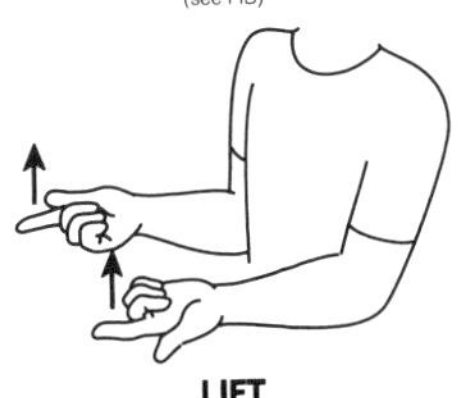

LIFT

Palms-up, L's lift

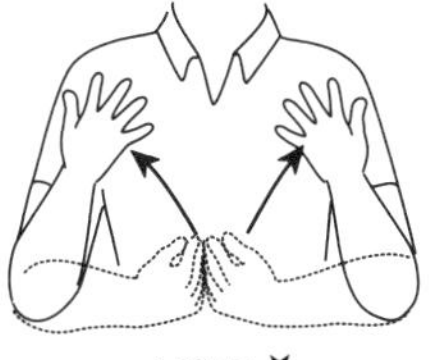

LIGHT ✶

Palm-in O-hands touch tips and open to palm-in 5-hands while moving up and outward

LIGHTNING

Index finger draws a large Z rapidly

LIKE
Palm-in L on chest moves forward, closing thumb and finger

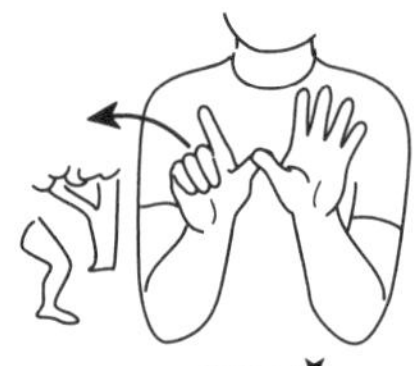

LIMB ★
Palm-out L at thumb of left palm-out 5, L arcs sideways
(see BRANCH)

LIME
Thumb-edge of L cuts down back of left palm-in S
(see JUICE)

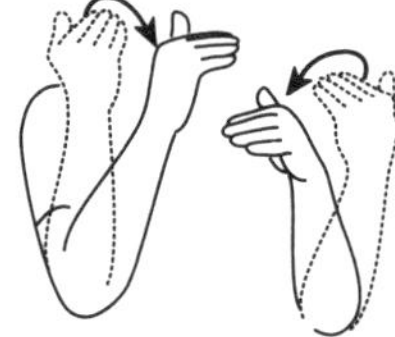

LIMIT
Palm-in bent hands, right higher than left, pivot to face each other, right above left
(see MAXIMUM)

LINCOLN
Right L-thumb taps temple

LINE ★
Palm-out L slides along and off side of horizontal left index
(see BAR)

LINGUISTIC
Thumbtips of L's touch, separate with slight shaking motion, change to palm-out C's *(language + -ic)*
(see SENTENCE)

LINK ★
Thumb and index of right hand grasp thumb of left L
(see CONJUNCTION)

LINOLEUM
Bottom of L-hand drags across back of left flat hand
(see CARPET)

LION
Claw hand combs backward once with a shaking motion over mane

LIP
Index draws across chin to the right under lower lip

LIPSTICK
Closed thumb and finger apply lipstick

LIQUEUR
Side of right L-hand taps index side of left I-1 hand
(see WHISKEY)

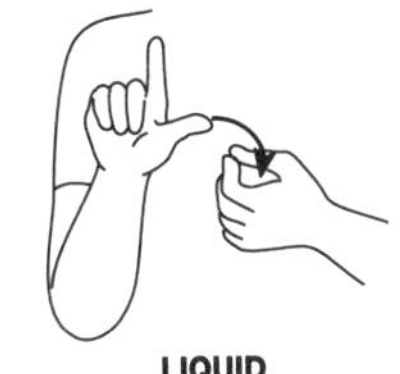

LIQUID
Thumbtip of L pours into left horizontal O

LIQUOR
Side of right I-1 hand taps index side of left I-1 hand
(see WHISKEY)

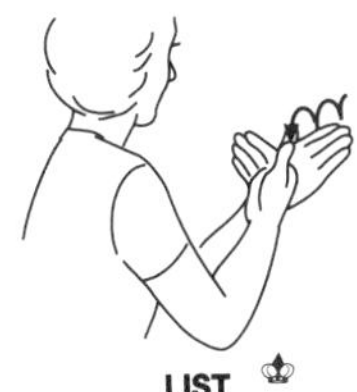

LIST ♔
Bent right hand makes short hops down left palm

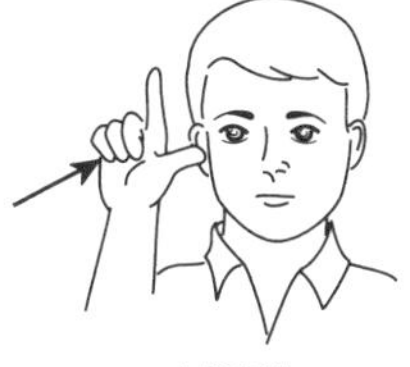

LISTEN
Thumb of palm-out L moves to ear
(see SOUND)

LITER
Left horizontal C; right L drops into C
(see GALLON)

LITERATE
Index of inverted right L writes across left palm-up hand
(see WRITE)

LITERATURE
Index of right L writes across left palm-up hand; U-hand slides down vertical left palm *(literate + -ure)*

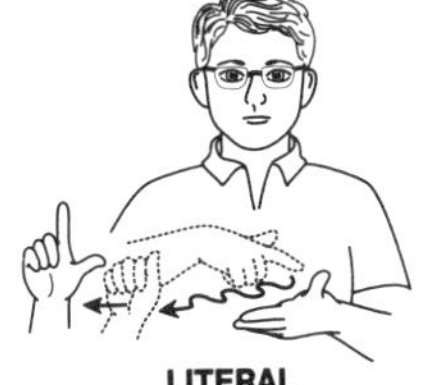

LITERAL
Index of inverted right L writes across left palm-up hand; add A + L *(literate + -al)*

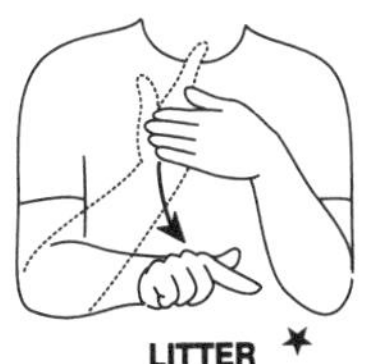

LITTER ★
Palm-in L behind left palm swings under and out to palm-down
(see NATURE)

LITTLE
L-hands face each other, jerk slightly toward each other; repeat
(see SMALL)

LIVE
Palm-in L-hands move up body
(see ADDRESS)

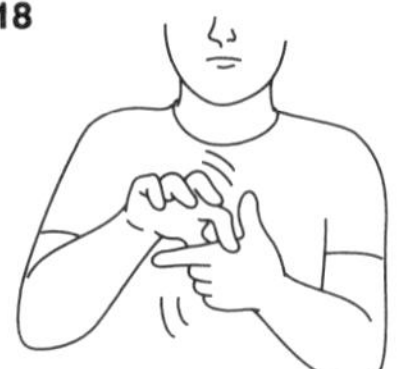

LIVER

Thumb and index grasp base of left palm-in L index; shake

(see MEAT)

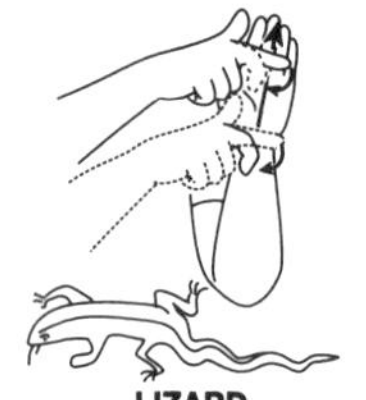

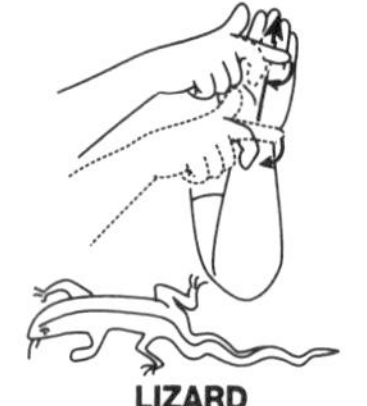

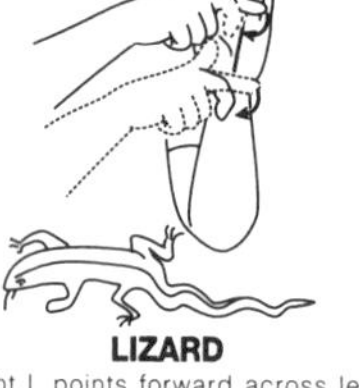

LIZARD

Right L points forward across left vertical palm and moves upward, bending index several times

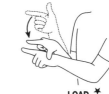

LOAD ★

Palm-up L flips to palm-down on left palm-down L

(see CARGO)

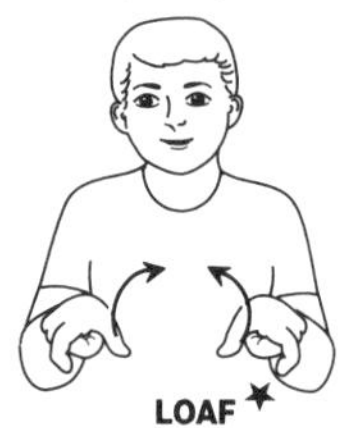

LOAF ★

Small C-hands, palms-down and turned slightly outwards, arc back towards body

LOAN

Horizontal 1-hands, right on left, both arc forward

(see LEND)

LOBSTER

Palm-down V-hands, crossed at wrists, move forward and to right while V's scissor

(see CRAB)

LOCAL

Right L behind vertical left index circles around index to palm-in

(see ATMOSPHERE)

LOCATE

Left hand palm-right points forward, right palm-down L rises past left hand

(see FIND)

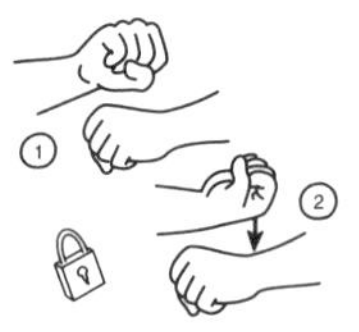

LOCK ★

Palm-down S's, right over left; right twists to palm-up, drops wrist-on-wrist

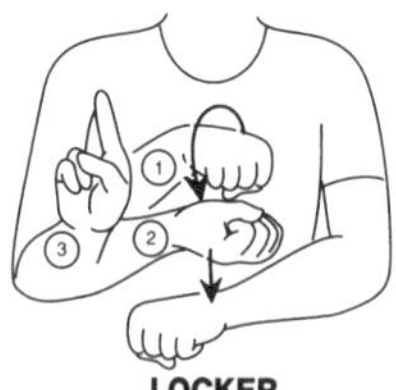

LOCKER

Palm-down S's right over left; right twists to palm-up, drops wrist-on-wrist; add R-hand *(lock + -er)*

LOCKET

Index and thumb of 9-hand form circle at base of throat

LOCUST

Palm-out L rides forward on hopping bent-V left hand

(see GRASSHOPPER)

LOW
Palm-left L drops slightly
(see DOWN)

LUCK
Palm-up L's turn to palm-down
(see HAPPEN)

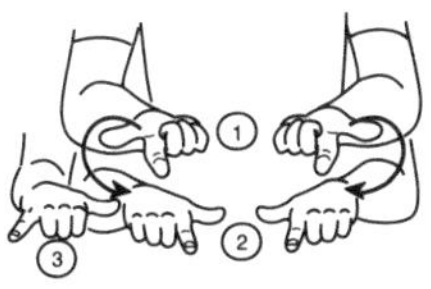

LUCKY
Palm-up L's turn to palm-down; add Y
(luck + -y)

LUGGAGE
Mime carrying suitcase

LUMBER
Right L-hand shakes while resting elbow on back of left hand
(see TREE)

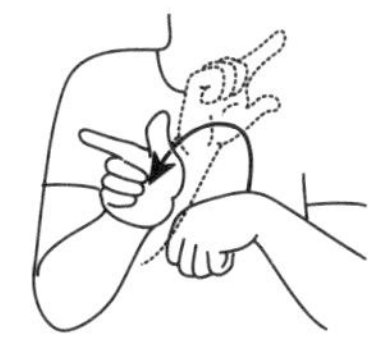

LUMP
Thumb of right L on back of left S arcs to heel of L

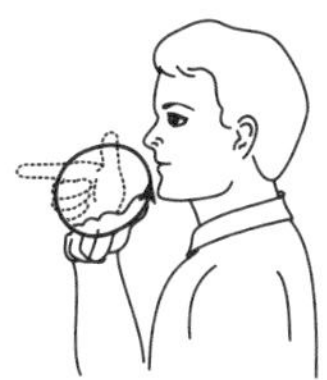

LUNCH
Thumb of L circles in and up near mouth several times
(see EAT)

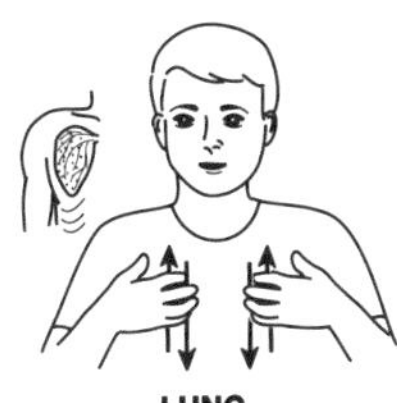

LUNG
Fingertips of palm-in relaxed 5's move up and down slightly on chest

LUST
Palm-in L on chest slides down slowly
(see HUNGER)

LUTHERAN ♔
Right L-thumb taps twice on palm-right left palm

LUXURY
Thumb of L brushes up middle of chest; repeat
(see FANCY)

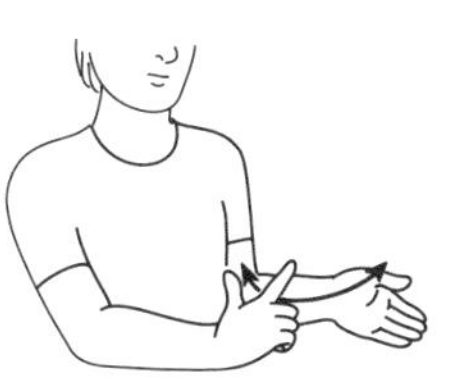

LYRIC
Right palm-left L swings back and forth behind bent left arm
(see MUSIC)

NOTES

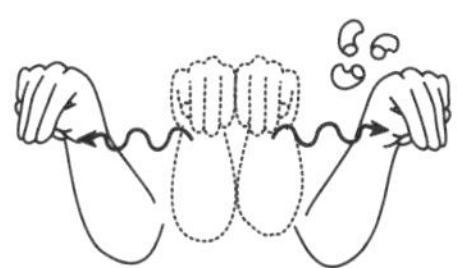

MACARONI
Shaking M's separate to sides
(see SPAGHETTI)

MACHINE
Bent fingers mesh like gear teeth and shake up and down

MAD
Palm-in 5-hand in front of face contracts to claw hand

MAGAZINE ♔
Thumb and finger of palm-up hand grasp little finger side of flat left hand and slide forward; may repeat

MAGIC
Palm-down flat-O's circle sideways and forward opening to palm-down 5-hands

MAGNET
Palm-down M's meet at index tips

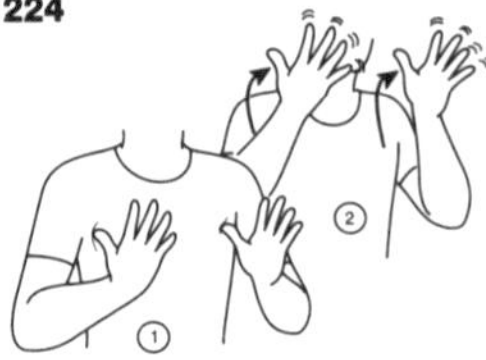

MAGNIFICENT
Thumbs of palms-facing 5's at sides of chest, arc up with wiggling fingers

MAGNIFY
Side of small C on horizontal left palm; C rises to eye

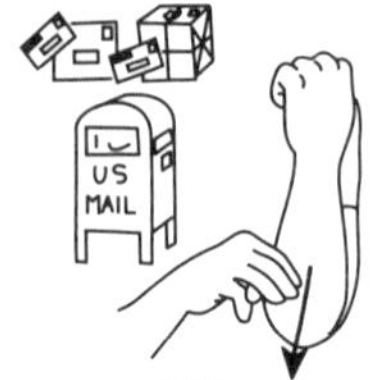

MAIL
Palm-down M brushes down left elbow

MAIN
M-hands, palm-up, arc up and touch sides, palm-down
(see IMPORTANT)

MAINSTREAM
Palm-down 5's at sides curve together forward, one on top of the other; move forward

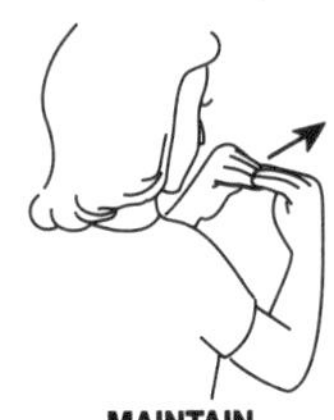

MAINTAIN
Tips of M's touch; move both hands forward together
(see CONTINUE)

MAJESTY
Right M touches left shoulder and then opposite hip
(see CHRIST)

MAJOR
Fingertips of right M on side of left B; right moves forward
(see STRAIGHT)

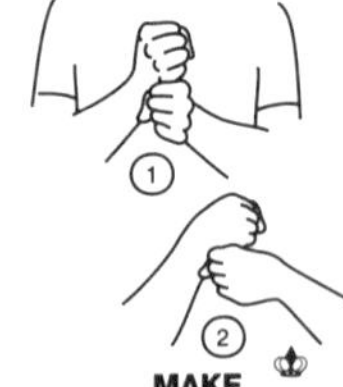

MAKE
Side of S touches on side of S; lift off, both twist to palm-in and touch again

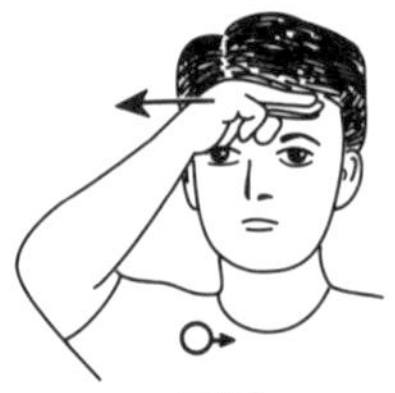

MALE
Palm-down flat M hand slides right across forehead

MALL
Palm-down M's face each other, move forward
(see HALL)

MAMMAL
Fingertips of M's on sides of chest remain stationary as hands swing slightly in and out
(see ANIMAL)

MAN
A on temple, then measure height with bent hand
(see MEN)

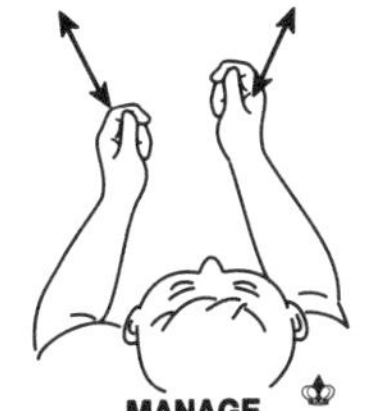

MANAGE
Palms-facing A-hands move alternately forward and back, diagonally

MANE
Fingertips of M-hand passes over head, front to back

MANNER
Palm-down M's move side-to-side
(see DO)

MANICURE
A-hand moves back and forth along edge of left fingernails

MANSION
M's face each other at sides of body, rise, approach, rise and meet
(see CASTLE)

M

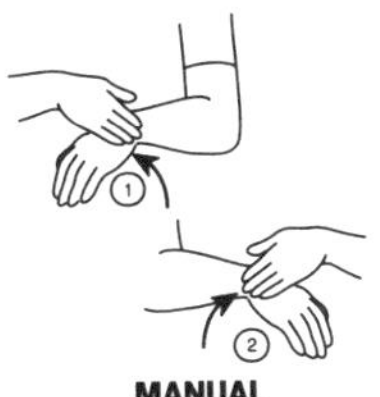

MANUAL
Sides of open hands slide inward alternately across each other's wrists *(cut off hands)*
(see HAND)

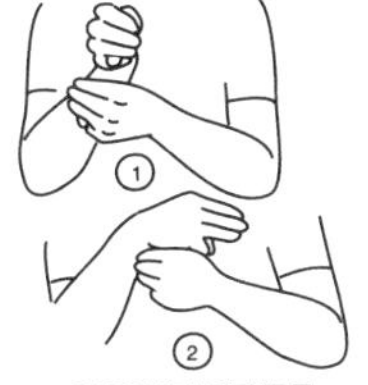

MANUFACTURE
Side of M on side of M; lift one slightly, twist both to palm-in and touch again and back again
(see MAKE)

MANUSCRIPT
M writes forward on palm-up left hand
(see WRITE)

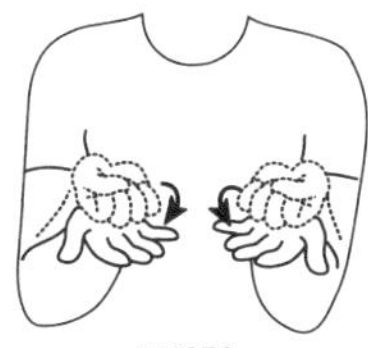

MANY
Palm-up S-hands spring open into 5-hands; repeat

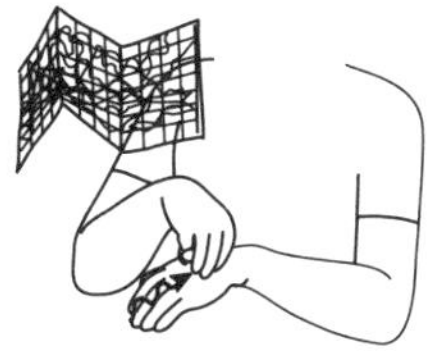

MAP
Right M-hand draws wavy line on back of left hand
(see CHART)

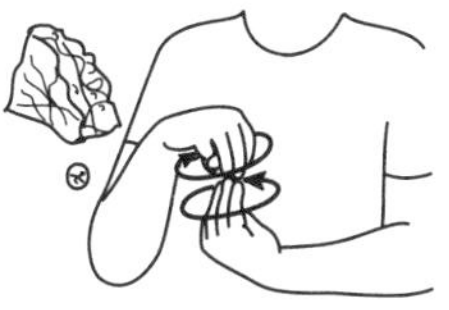

MARBLE
Palms-facing M's, one above the other, rotate in small circles
(see MIX)

MARCH
(Alt. 1)
M arcs over side of vertical left hand
(see CALENDAR)

MARCH
(Alt. 2)
With one 5-hand behind the other, swing hands sharply out and repeat
(see PARADE)

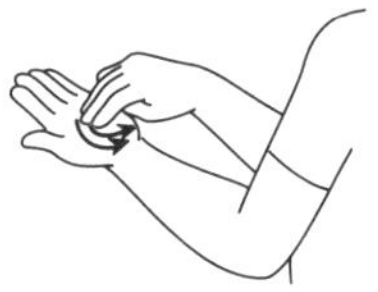

MARGARINE
Fingertips of right M flick off heel of open palm-up left hand twice
(see BUTTER)

MARGIN
G-thumb slides down outside of palm-in left hand *(showing size of margin)*

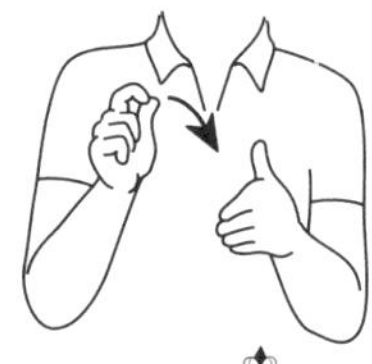

MARK
Closed thumb and fingertip jerk toward left palm

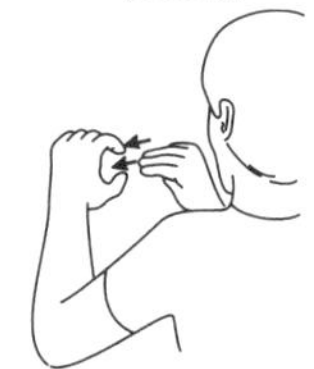

MARKET
Fingertips of flat M nod towards side of left C-hand
(see STORE)

MAROON
M circles on cheek

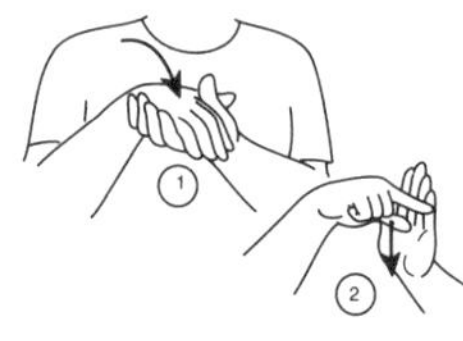

MARRIAGE
Clasp hands right on left; then side of right G slides down vertical left palm *(marry + -age)*

MARRY
Clasp hands, right on left

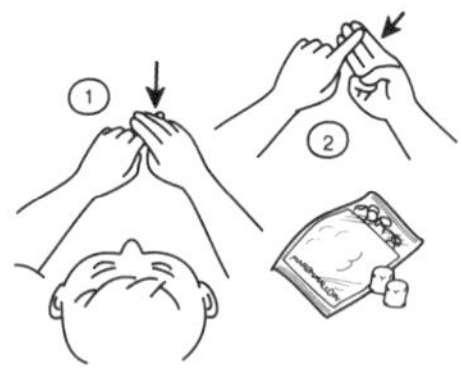

MARSHMALLOW
M-hand touches top of horizontal left index, then bottom

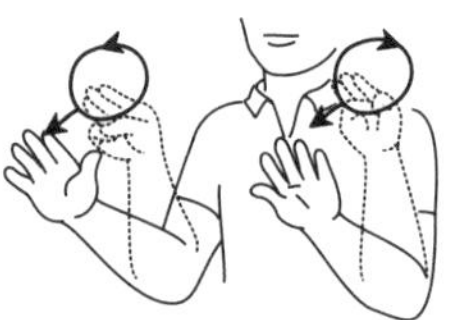

MARVEL
Palm-out M's make small circle; jerk slightly forward to 5's
(see FABULOUS)

MASH
Side of S drops in left palm and twists

MASK
Palm-in open M's before eyes move around to sides

MASSAGE
Palm-down hands open and close in massaging motion

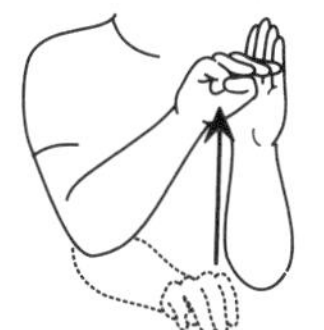

MAST
Side of palm-down M, slides up vertical left arm

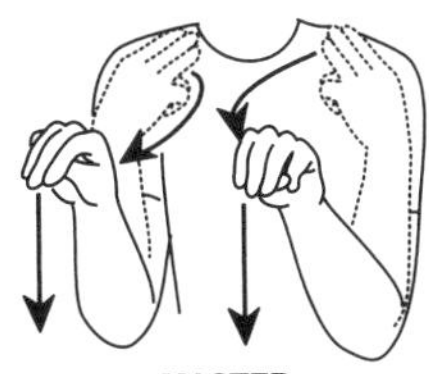

MASTER
M-fingertips on shoulders pivot to palm-out and drop

MAT
M drags across back of left hand
(see CARPET)

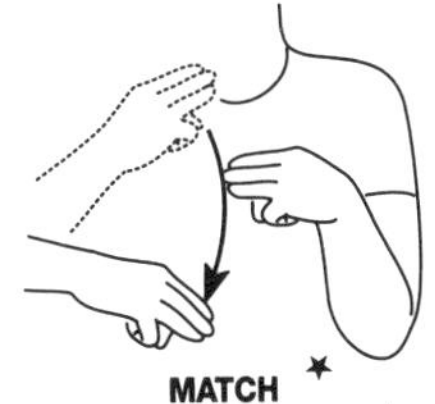

MATCH ★
Palm-in M's; tip of right arcs down, striking tip of left

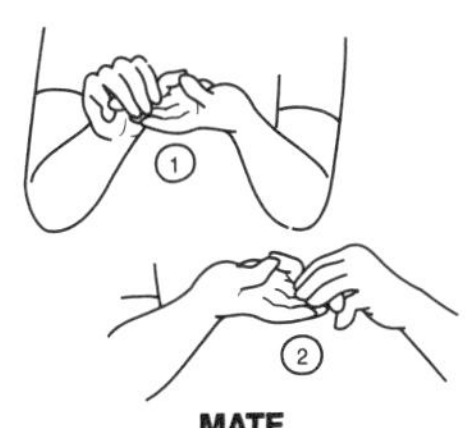

MATE
Both hands of M-fingers touch, palms-facing; right on left, then left on right
(see FRIEND)

MATERIAL
Palm-up M arcs once to the right
(see THING)

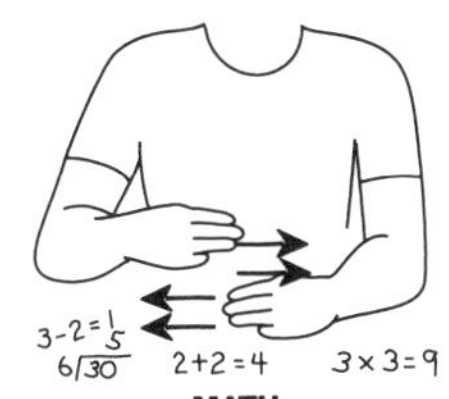

MATH
Little finger side of palm-in right M brushes on index finger of palm-in left M twice
(see ARITHMETIC)

MATTER
Fingertips of M's alternately slap back and forth
(see THOUGH)

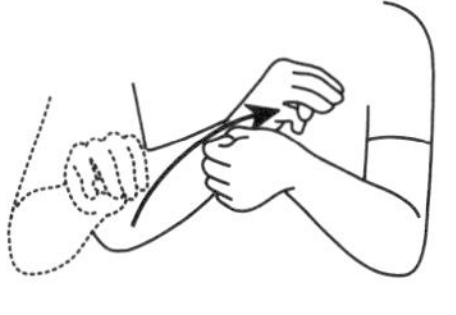

MATURE
Right M brushes inward across top of palm-in S
(see FULL)

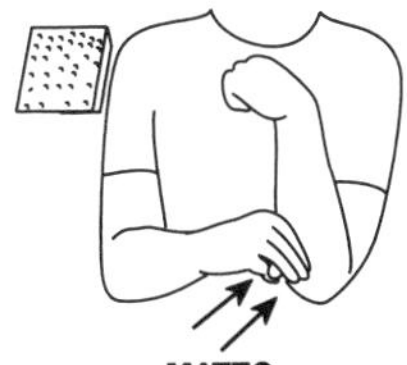

MATZO
Tap left elbow with side of M
(see CRACKER)

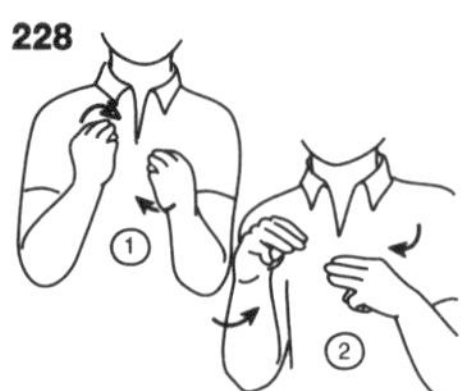

MAXIMUM

M-hands, palms-in, twist to face each other, right above left

(see LIMIT)

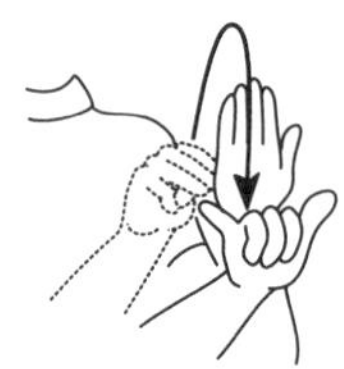

MAY

(Alt. 1 *for month*)

M arcs to Y over side of vertical palm-in left hand

(see CALENDAR)

MAY

(*verb* or Alt. 2 *for month*)

Palm-up flat hands move alternately up and down *(for the month or verb)*

(see BALANCE)

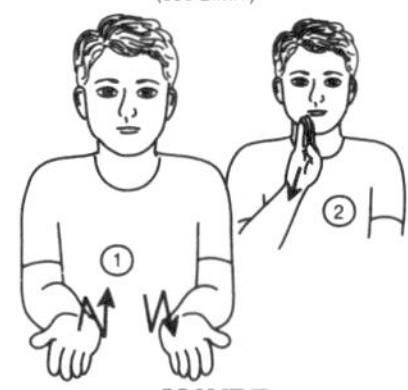

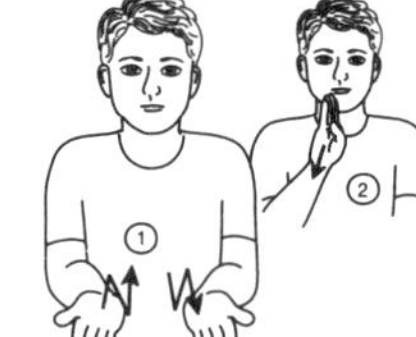

MAYBE

Palms-up flat hands move alternately up and down; B-hand moves forward below lips *(may + be)*

MAYOR

Fingertip of M circles by forehead and then touches temple

(see GOVERN)

MAYONNAISE

Fingers of palm-down right M brush heel of left palm toward body; repeat

(see BUTTER)

McDONALDS

M makes the arches

ME

Index points to and touches chest

MEADOW

M on back of left hand circles out and back along left forearm

(see GROUND)

MEAL

M circles in and up near mouth

(see EAT)

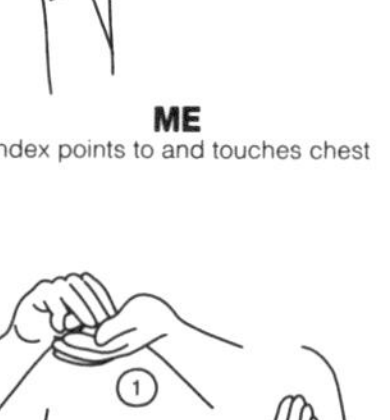

MEAN ♔ ★

Palm-down M touches left flat palm-up; twists and touches again

MEASLES ♔

Claw fingertips spot face several times

MEASURE
Palm-down, thumbtips of Y's tap; repeat

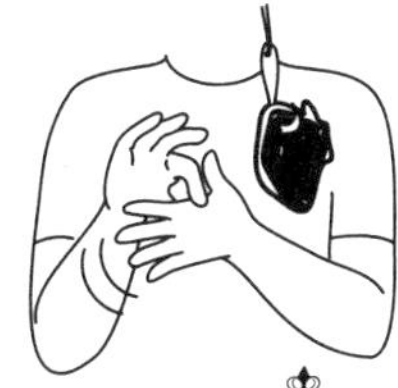

MEAT ♔
Thumb and finger of 9 pinch side of left 5-hand; shake both hands

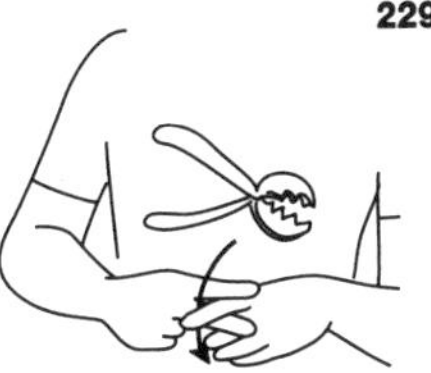

MECHANIC
With V-fingers, "tighten" left index; repeat *(like using wrench)*
(see WRENCH)

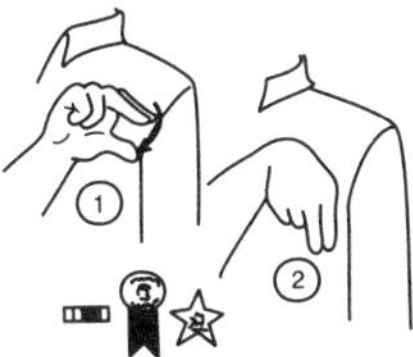

MEDAL
On left chest, fingers of U close on extended thumb *(pinning on medal)*

MEDIC
M fingertips tap left wrist on pulse
(see DOCTOR)

MEDICINE ♔
Tip of bent middle finger rubs circle on left palm

M

MEDITATE
Fingertips of M circles at temple
(see REASON)

MEDIUM
Right M rocks back and forth on side of palm-in left B
(see AVERAGE)

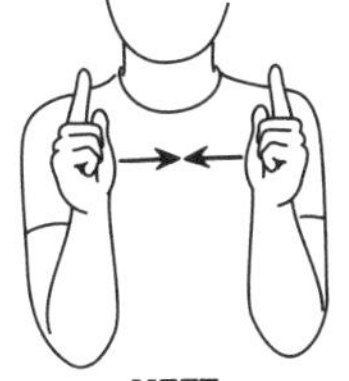

MEET
1-hands, palms-facing, meet

MELODY
Right M behind horizontal palm-in left arm, right arcs side-to-side
(see MUSIC)

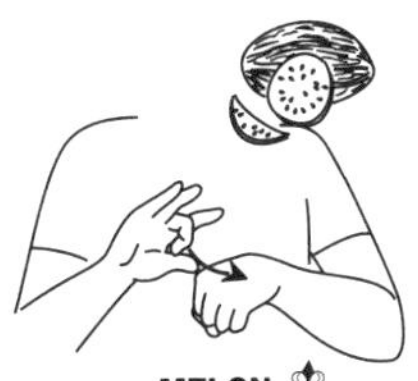

MELON ♔
Middle finger snaps on back of left S *(as if testing ripeness)*

MELT ♔
Palm-up flat-O's, thumbs rub across fingertips, changing to palm-up A's

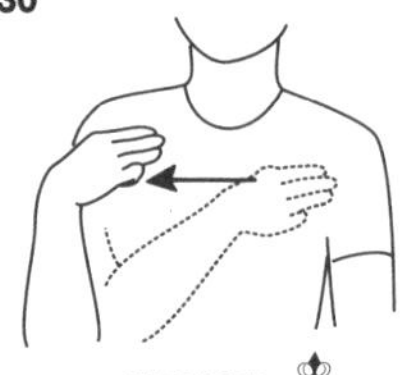

MEMBER
Right M-fingers touch left shoulder, then right

MEMO
Right M moves from below eye to touch palm-up left hand
(see NOTE)

MEMORIZE
Palm-in 5, middle finger on forehead; move forward and down, closing to S

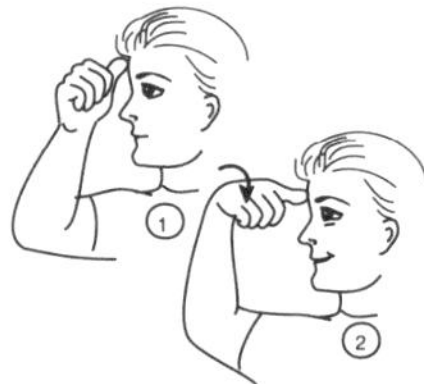

MEMORY
Extended-A thumb on forehead, twist at wrist

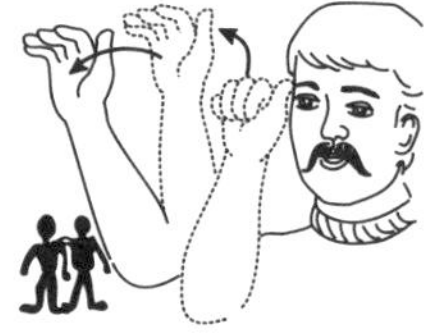

MEN
A on temple then measure two heights with bent hand
(see MAN)

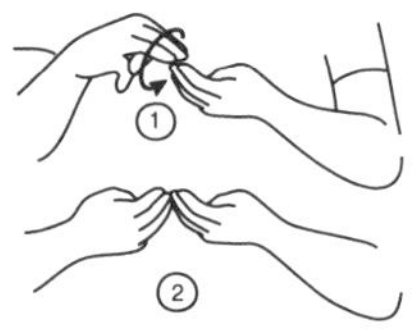

MEND
Fingertips of M-hands touch, then right hand twists
(see FIX)

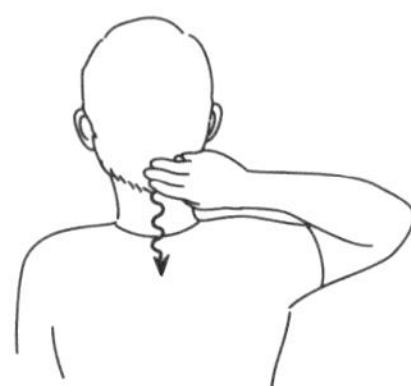

MENINGITIS
M at back of head shakes down neck
(see SPINE)

MENORAH
Little fingers of palm-in 4's touch; separate, rising to sides
(see HANUKKAH)

MENSTRUATE
Tap knuckles of A against cheek twice

MENTAL
Tip of M touches temple; then right hand changes to L

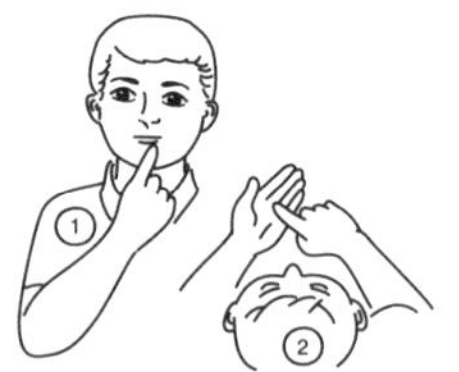

MENTION
Index below mouth drops to touch palm-up left hand
(see REPORT)

MENU
M-fingertips move down left palm; repeat *(as if scanning menu)*

MERCY
Right M touches heart, then both palm-down M's stroke outwards, right slightly behind left
(see SYMPATHY)

MERMAID
Fingertips of M stroke down jaw; palm-left M shimmies forward
(see FISH)

MERRY
Side of M brushes up chest; repeat
(see HAPPY)

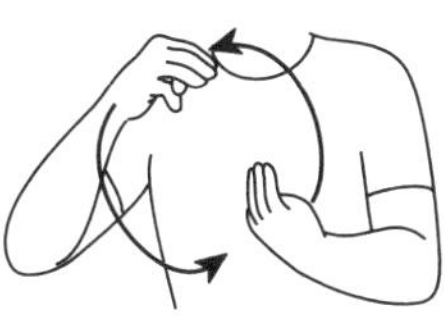

MESS
M's, right above left; reverse

MESSAGE
Fingertips of palm-in M-hand at mouth drop to touch left palm-up index finger
(see LETTER)

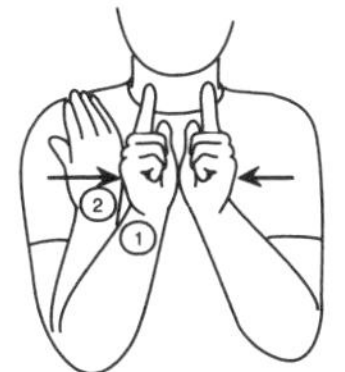

MET
1-hands, palms-facing, meet; right hand flips back *(meet + p.t.)*

METER
Fingertips of right M slide up and down left index finger
(see THERMOMETER)

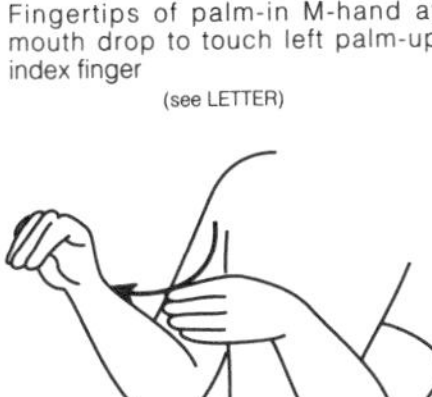

METAL
Palm-in M arcs right, to palm-out, after hitting side of left index

METHOD
Palm-down M's move forward weaving slightly side-to-side
(see WAY)

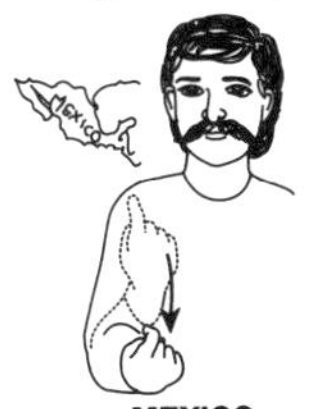

MEXICO
Index on shoulder drops to palm-up X
(see SPAIN)

MICE
Both index fingers brush past nosetip twice, alternately
(see MOUSE)

MICROPHONE
Palm-right S-hand by chin as if holding a microphone

MICROSCOPE
Horizontal palms-in S's, right on left, focus microscope

MICROWAVE
Flat-O's face each other, throw open to 5's; repeat

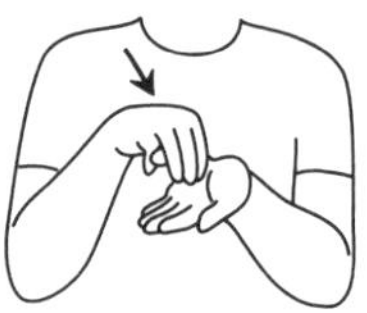

MID
Fingertips of M fall on left palm

MIDDLE
Fingertips of right M circle once over left palm, then touch mid-palm

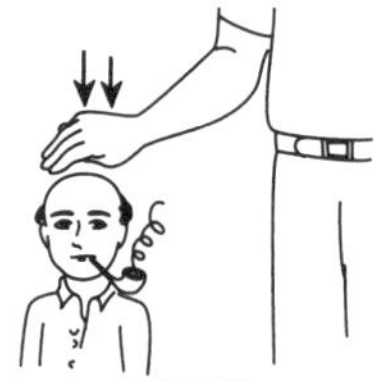

MIDGET
Palm-down M pats head of midget
(see CHILD)

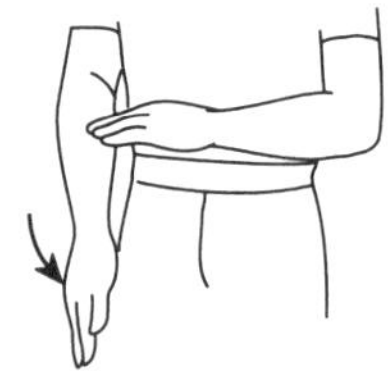

MIDNIGHT
Flat right hand swings downward, as you touch inside of right elbow

M

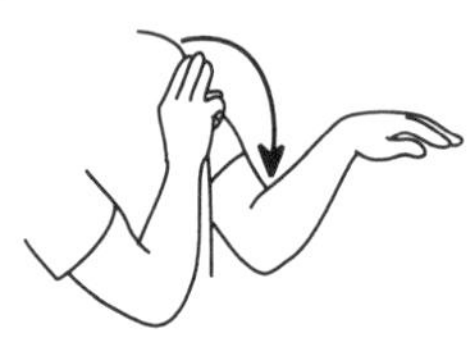

MIGHT
(Power)
M-fingertips draw muscle on left arm
(see STRONG)

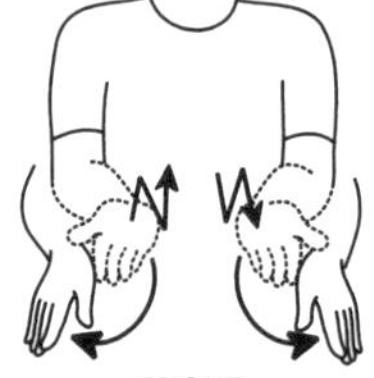

MIGHT
(Alt. 1)
Palm-up flat hands move alternately up and down; twist to palm-down *(may + p.p.)*

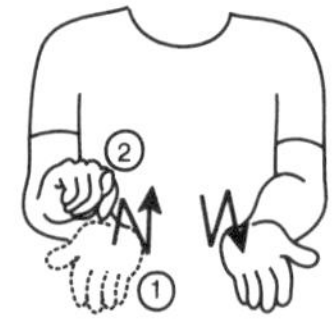

MIGHT
(Alt. 2)
Palm-up flat hands move alternately up and down; right changes to T-hand *(may + p.p.)*

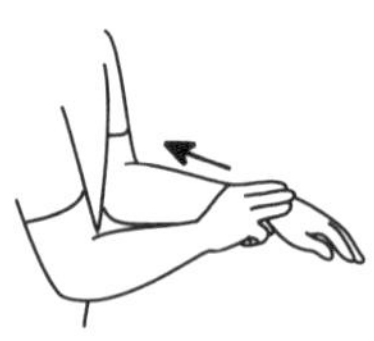

MILE
M Brushes up left arm
(see YARD)

MILITARY
Palms-in M's, right hand at left shoulder; left hand at left waist
(see SOLDIER)

MILK
Horizontal C to horizontal S squeezes in a milking motion; repeat *(can do with 2 hands)*

MILL
Side of right M on side of left M, grind

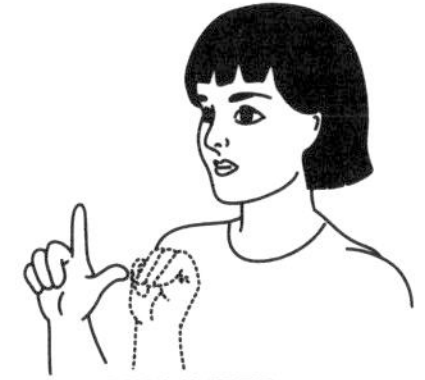

MILLILITER (ml)
Fingerspell M + L

MILLIMETER (mm)
Fingerspel M + M

MILLION
Fingertips of M hit heel, then fingers, of left hand
(see BILLION)

MILWAUKEE
Index finger moves back and forth under lip

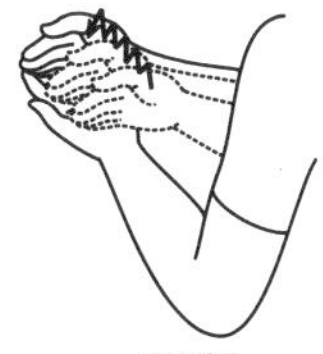

MINCE
Side of flat hand mimes mincing action on flat left palm

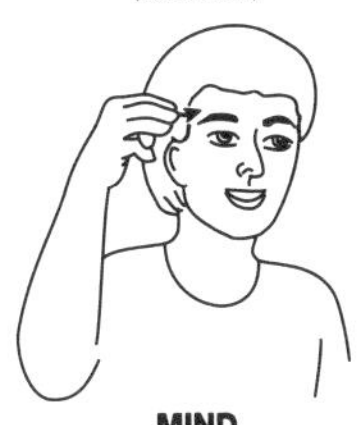

MIND
Tips of M touch temple
(see THINK)

MINE
(noun or verb)
Index finger picks at left horizontal palm several times

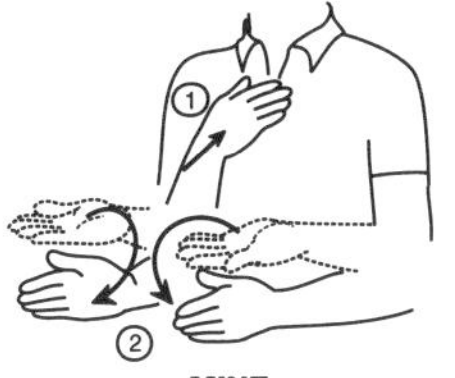

MINE
(Alt. 1)
Flat hand palm on chest; both flat hands, palm-up twist to palms-facing *(my + p.p.)*

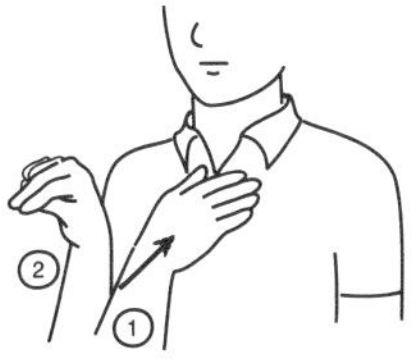

MINE
(Alt. 2)
Flat hand palm on chest; changes to an N-hand *(my + p.p.)*

MINERAL
Back of right M taps back of left S
(see STONE)

MINIATURE
Palms-facing I's, right above left, right drops slightly several times
(see TINY)

MINIMUM

Right M over left M, right hand moves down toward left hand

MINISTER

Palm-out M near head jerks slightly forward; repeat

(see LECTURE)

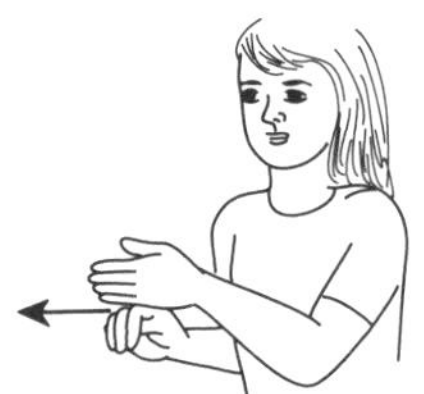

MINOR

M moves out along little finger side of left palm-right hand

(see STRAIGHT)

MINUS

Side of horizontal index finger hits on left palm-out hand

(See NEGATIVE)

MINUTE ♔

Side of palm-out index on left vertical palm twists to point forward

MIRROR

Flat hand in front of face; pivots back and forth slightly several times

MISCHIEF

Thumb of L on temple; wiggle index

(see DEVIL)

MISER

Palm-in claw hand on chin; pulls down and closes to S

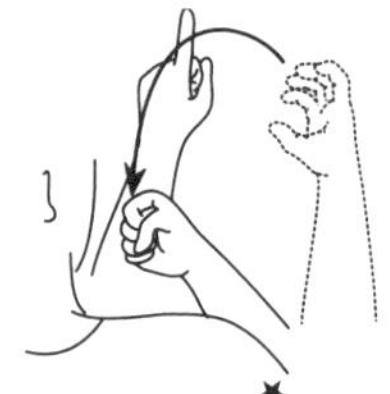

MISS ★

(verb)

Open right hand passes left vertical index finger and changes to S

MISS

(title)

Fingertips of M on cheek twist forward

(see GIRL)

MISSION

Left M at eye-level, right vertical index behind and slightly lower; index drops to point at M

(see AIM)

MISTAKE

Palm-in right Y taps on chin; repeat

(see WRONG)

MISTER
Fingertips of M on temple twist forward to palm-out R
(see HE)

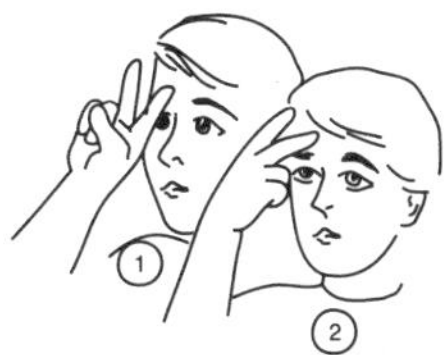

MISUNDERSTAND
Index of palm-out V on forehead, reverse to palm-in

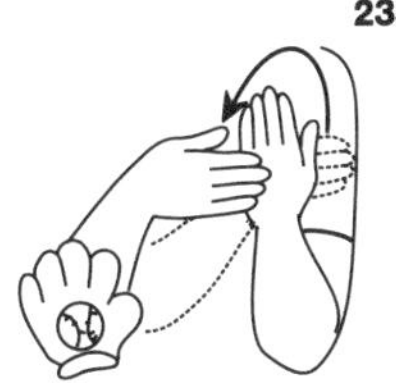

MITT
Flat right hand draws around edge of left hand from thumb to little finger

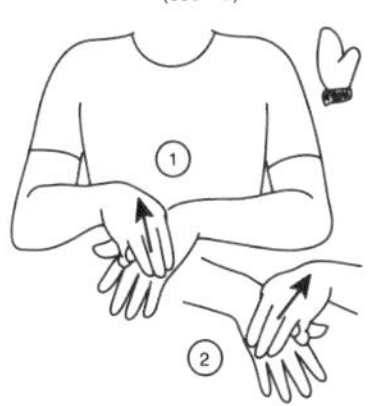

MITTEN
Fingertips of open palm-in M's draw on invisible mittens

MIX
Palms-facing claw hands, right above left, circle alternately

MIXTURE
Claw-hands, right above left, circle alternately; side of right U slides down vertical left palm *(mix + -ure)*
(see MARBLE)

MOAN
Side of M at throat shakes up and out under chin
(see GROAN)

MOBILE
Palm-down M wanders forward
(see WANDER)

MODEL
Tip of index on palm-up left, make horizontal circle together
(see DISPLAY)

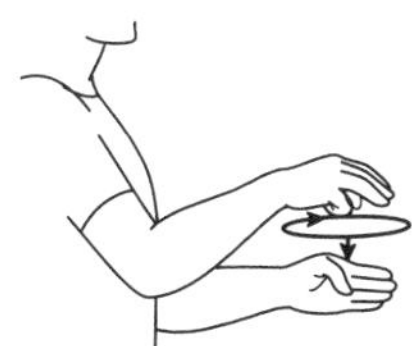

MODERATE
Left horizontal B points forward; right M circles once above and touches side of B
(see MIDDLE)

MODERN
Back of M brushes down, along left palm and up
(see NEW)

MODIFY
M-hands, palm-to-palm, reverse positions quickly, twice
(see CHANGE)

MOLASSES
Index finger brushes across chin and flicks forward, wiping

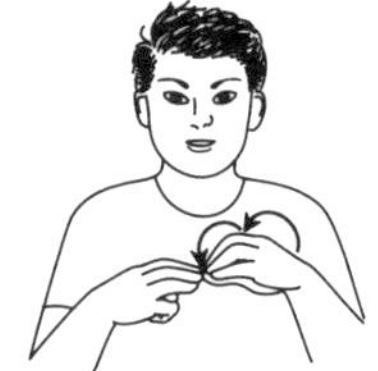

MOLD
M pointing left, makes series of small lumps down back of left flat-O

MOLE
Bent hands rest against cheeks and "dig," flapping

MOLECULE
Left extended-A, palm-down, right M circles near left thumb
(see ATOM)

MOM
M taps near chin
(see MOTHER)

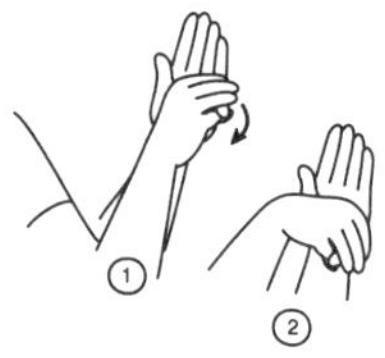

MOMENT
Side of M on vertical left palm, twists to point downward
(see MINUTE)

MOMENTUM
Wrist of right M pushes left horizontal index forward
(see CONTINUE)

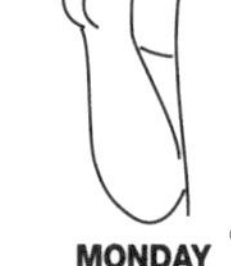

MONDAY
Palm-out M circles slightly

MONEY
Back of flat-O taps left palm twice

MONKEY
Scratch sides upwards twice with tips of claw hands

MONOTONE
M draws straight line to right
(see FLAT)

MONSTER
Palm-out claw hands rise to sides of head and claw

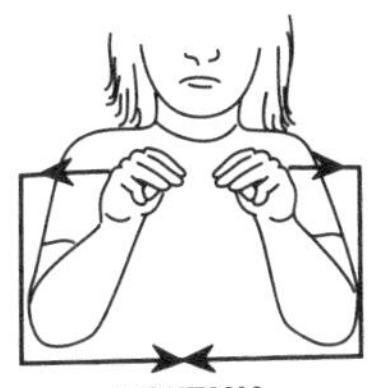

MONTANA
Palms-out, M's make a rectangle *(outlining the state)*

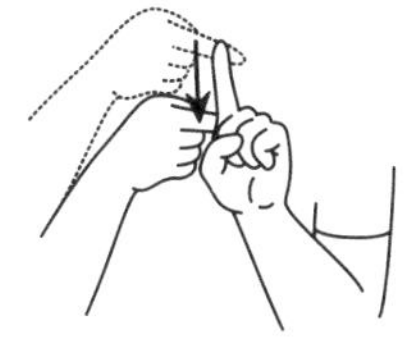

MONTH
Back of right index finger slides down back of left index finger

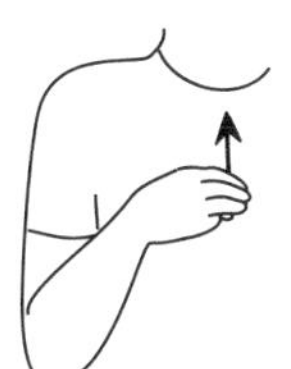

MOOD
M-fingers move up chest once
(see FEEL)

MOON
Side of small C near right eye

MOOSE
Thumbs of flat hands near temples; move hands out and up
(see DEER)

MORAL
Side of M on chest near heart, make circle and touch again
(see CHARACTER)

MORALE
Side of M circles on chest near heart, ending in E
(see CHARACTER)

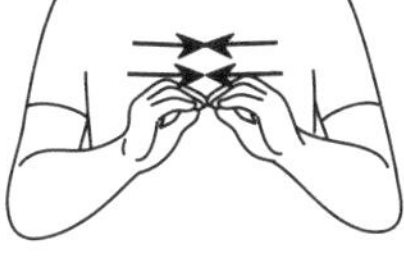

MORE
Flat-O's bounce tips together twice
(see EXTRA)

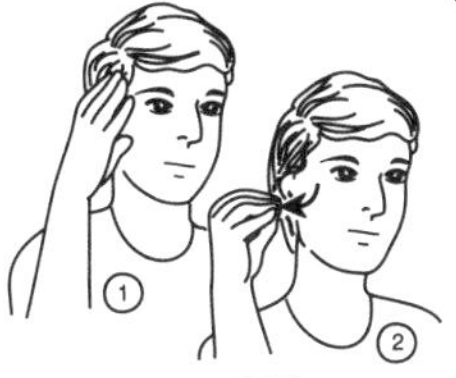

MORMON
Fingertips and thumb of right hand on cheekbone closes to flat-O; repeat

MORN
Left hand on right arm by elbow, right palm-up hand rises

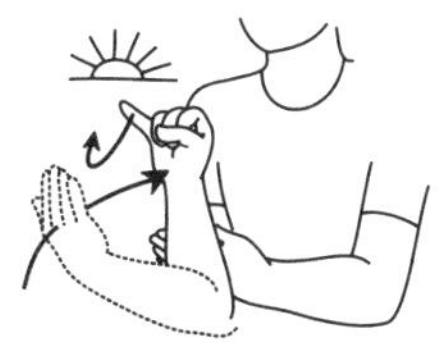

MORNING
Left hand rests in crook of right elbow, right palm-up hand rises; changes to an I-hand and twists to palm-out

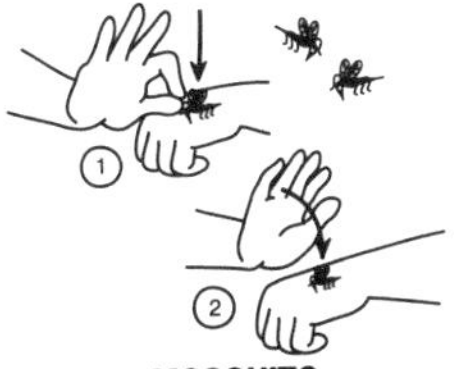

MOSQUITO
9 touches back of left hand; slap hand

MOSS
Fingertips of M circle on back of left palm-down S-hand

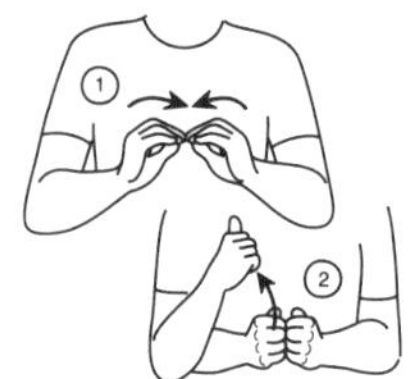

MOST
Flat-O's slightly arc, tips together; A-hands together, right A moves up *(more + -est)*

MOTEL
Right cheek rests on back of left hand; right M under palm
(see BED)

MOTH
Palms-in M's, crossed at wrists, fingers flutter while moving forward

MOTHER
Thumb of palm-left 5-hand taps jaw near chin
(see MOM)

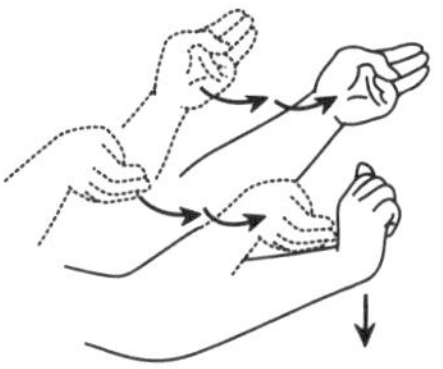

MOTIVATE
Palm-out M's push forward twice, drop palm-out A down *(motive + -ate)*

MOTIVE
Palm-out M's push forward; repeat
(see ENCOURAGE)

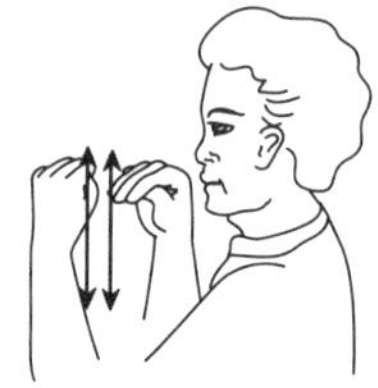

MOTOR
Right M behind left M, move up and down alternately, like pistons
(see ENGINE)

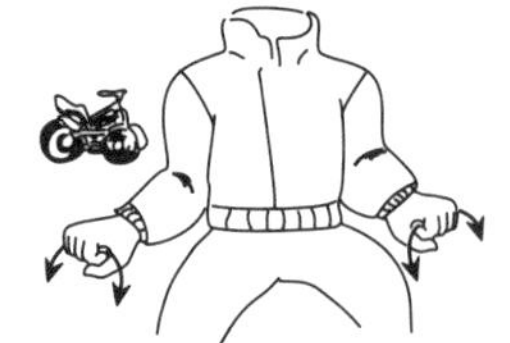

MOTORCYCLE
S-hands hold handlebars and twist inward *(rev up)*

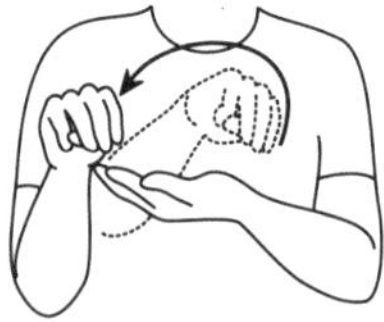

MOUND
Right M arcs through air from left heel to fingertips
(see AMOUNT)

MOUNT
Fingertips of M drop onto back of palm-down left hand
(see ON)

MOUNTAIN
(Alt. 1)
Right hand draws mountain tops; left stays still

MOUNTAIN
(Alt. 2)
Right fist raps on left wrist; then push flat hands upward to the right

MOUSE
Index finger flicks past tip of nose several times

MOUTH
Index circles mouth once
(see ORAL)

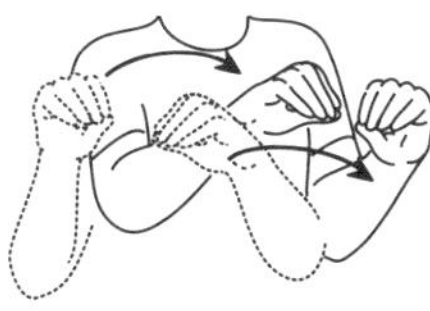

MOVE
Palm-down flat-O's arc to right

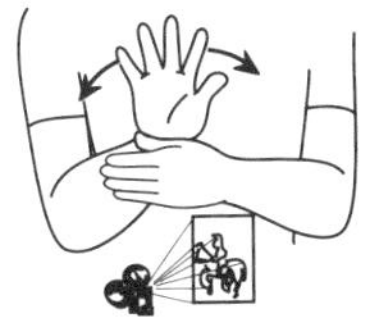

MOVIE
Heel of palm-out 5 rests on side of palm-in left hand; 5 waves slightly, side-to-side
(see FILM)

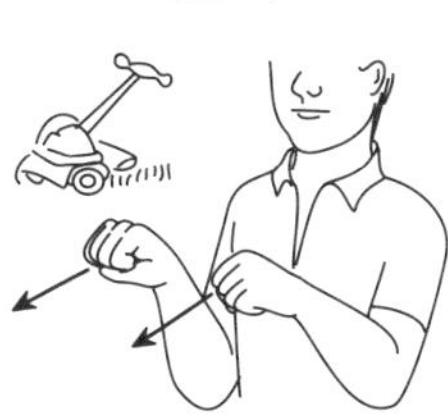

MOW
Push mower several times

MRS.
Palm-in M on cheek twists forward to palm-out S

MUCH
Cupped 5-hands face each other; arc hands apart

MUD
M flaps under chin
(see DIRT)

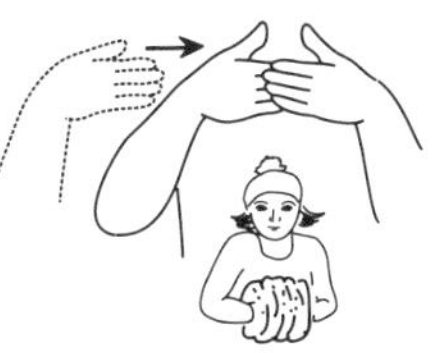

MUFF
Palms-in, right flat hand moves behind left as if into muff

MUFFIN
Fingertips of flat-O on left palm; open to claw hand

MUG
Side of X on left palm; rises off

MULE
Thumb of flat hand on temple, flap hand forward twice
(see HORSE)

MULTIPLE
Fingertips of M on left palm twist upwards to palm-in
(see ONCE)

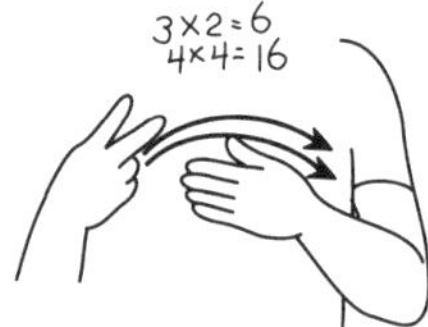

MULTIPLY
Back of palm-in V brushes sideways across left palm several times

MUMBLE
Side of M-hand near mouth shakes forward a short distance

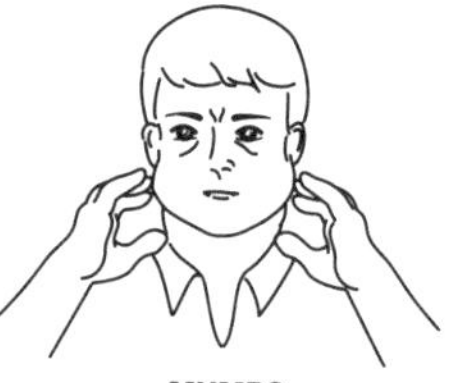

MUMPS
Claw hands on sides of neck

MUNCH
C-hand faces horizontal left index, changes to flat-O; repeat several times while moving left
(see NIBBLE)

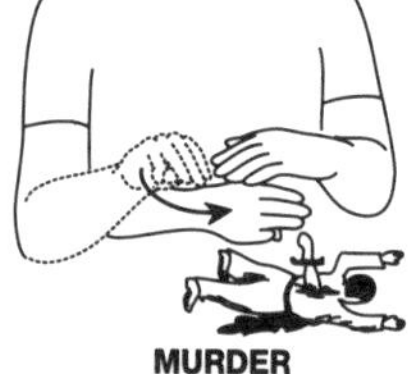

MURDER
Tips of open M-hand twist diagonally under left palm
(see KILL)

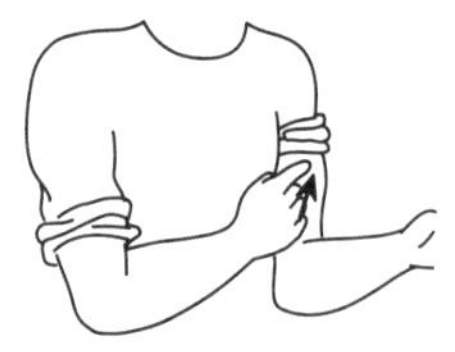

MUSCLE
Right index finger pokes left bicep muscle twice

MUSEUM
Palm-out M's draw house
(see HOUSE)

MUSHROOM
Bent right hand caps left flat-O

MUSIC
Fingertips of right flat hand pointing toward left palm, arcs side-to-side behind palm

MUST
Palm-down X-hand jerks sharply downward once
(see NECESSARY)

MUSTACHE
G-hands on upper lip move sideways to extended-A hands *(as if shaping the mustache)*

MUSTARD
Fingertips of M-hand circle several times on left palm

MUTTER
M near mouth vibrates slightly

MUTUAL
Palm-down Y-hands move together side-to-side

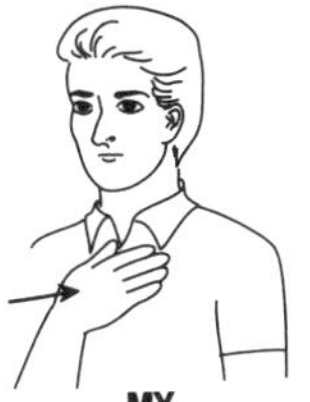

MY
Palm of flat hand on chest

MYSTERY
Right M-hand moves down from chin to under left hand
(see HIDE)

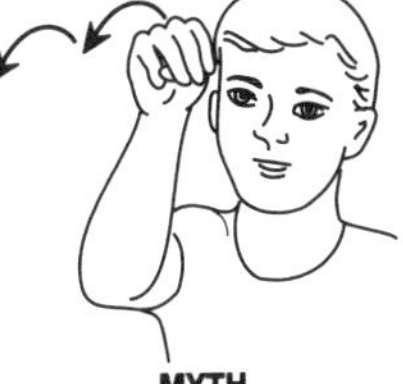

MYTH
Right M arcs twice off forehead
(see IDEA)

NOTES

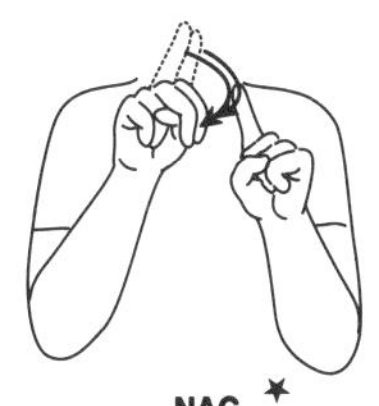

NAG ★

Right N fingertips peck vertical left index twice

(see PECK)

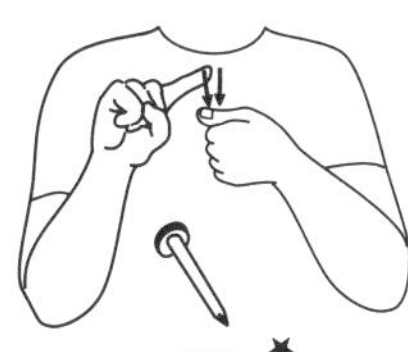

NAIL ★

Right index fingertip taps on thumbnail of left A-hand

NAIL POLISH

Fingertips of right open N-hand brush back and forth across nails of left hand *(can be nail + polish)*

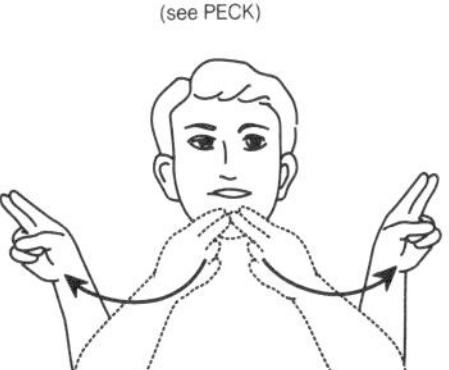

NAIVE

Palm-in H-fingers on chin, open outwards to palm-out

(see INNOCENT)

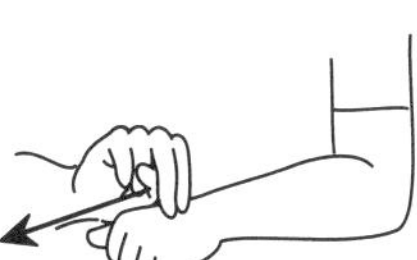

NAKED

Fingertips of right N brush off back of left A-hand

(see BARE)

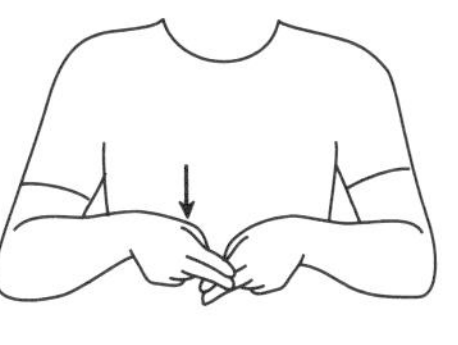

NAME 

Right H touches left H at right angles

NAP

Open N moves down in front of face, cheek resting on left hand

(see BED)

NAPKIN

Right palm-in A brushes off chin several times

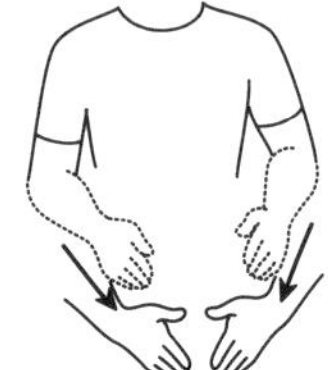

NARROW

Hands converge forward to fingertips almost touching

NASAL

Fingertips of N approach and touch bridge of nose; tap

NASTY

Back of N-fingers jerks out twice from under chin

NATION

Right N circles over, then drops on back of left S

(see REPUBLIC)

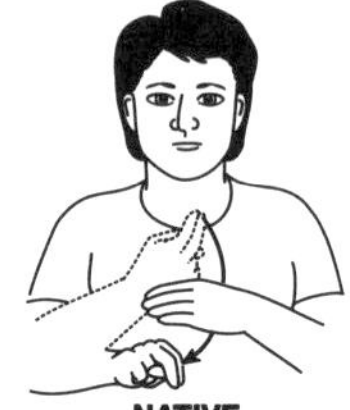

NATIVE

Palm-in right N behind flat hand, back of N brushes downwards under left palm and out to palm-down

(see NATURE)

NATURE

Back of right A against left palm; A twists down and out under hand to palm-down

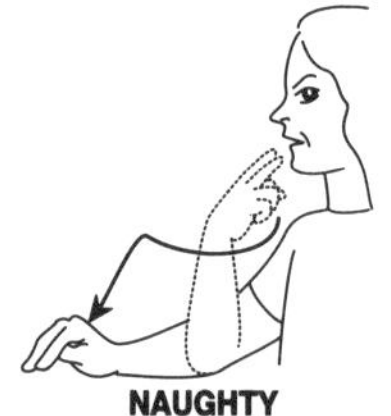

NAUGHTY

Open N on mouth swings outward and throws downward

(see BAD)

NAUSEA

Claw hand circles on stomach

(see DISGUST)

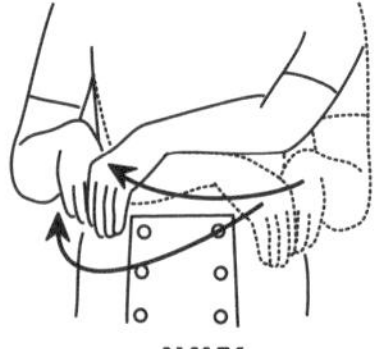

NAVY

B-hands move together from left to right side of waist *(buttoning pants)*

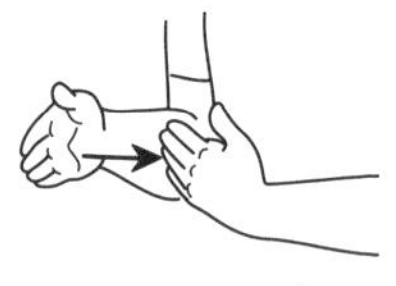

NEAR 

Palm of right hand moves nearer back of left hand

NEAT
Heel of N slides across left palm
(see CLEAN)

NECESSARY
Right palm-down N jerks down sharply; repeat
(see SHALL)

NECK
Fingertips touch neck

NECKLACE
G-hand outlines necklace on chest

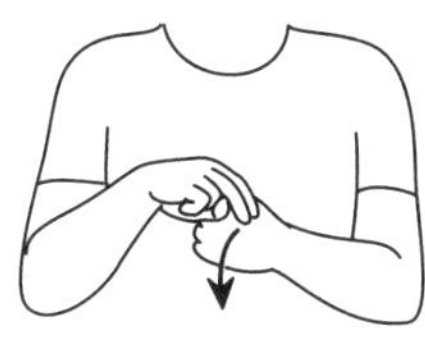

NECTAR
N slides down back of left palm-in S
(see JUICE)

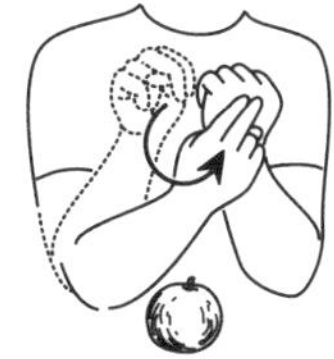

NECTARINE
N, palm-out to palm-in, circles left S
(see APRICOT)

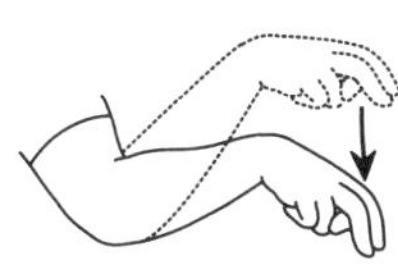

NEED
Palm-down N jerks slightly down
(see MUST)

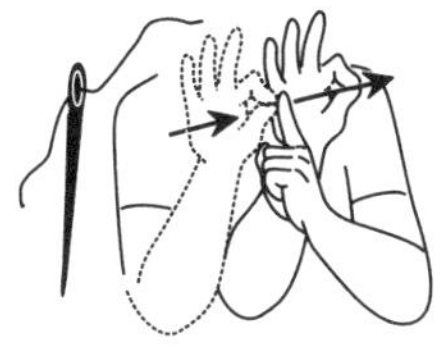

NEEDLE
9-hand threads left fingertip

NEGATIVE
Side of N strikes palm
(see MINUS)

NEGLECT
Right open N flips down and to side from nose
(see IGNORE)

NEGOTIATE
Index taps left palm each time both move forward and back

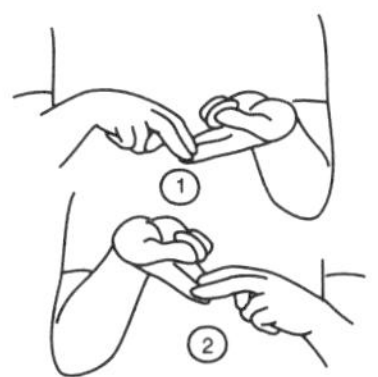

NEIGHBOR
Palms-facing, open N-hands rest, first right on left, then left on right
(see FRIEND)

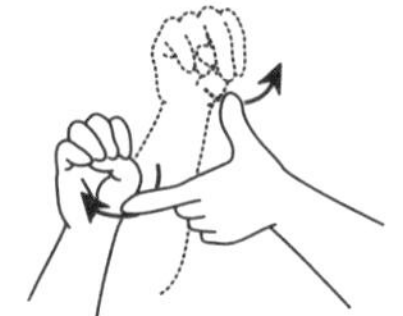

NEITHER
Right N swings back off left L-thumb, then E swings forward off fingertip
(see THEN)

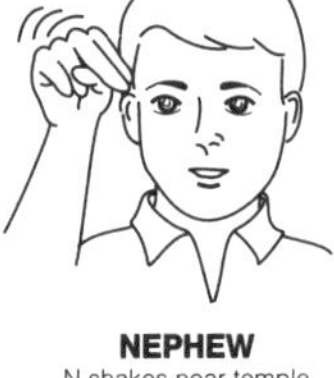

NEPHEW
N shakes near temple
(see AUNT)

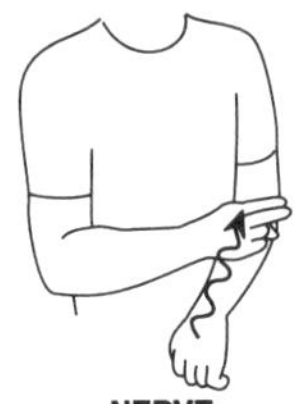

NERVE
N wiggles up left arm *(tracing nerve)*

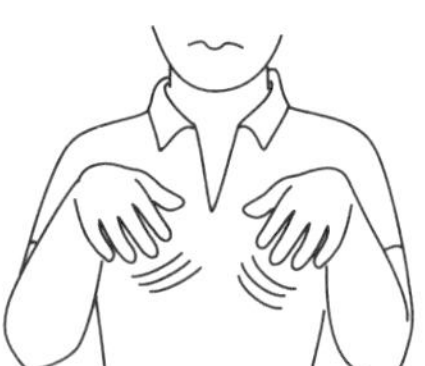

NERVOUS
Palm-down 5's shake

NEST
Open N's, touching, palms-up, swing upward to face each other
(see JAR)

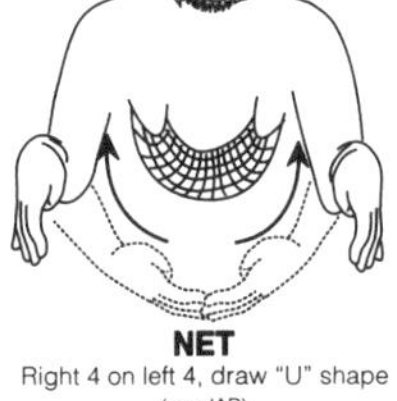

NET
Right 4 on left 4, draw "U" shape
(see JAR)

NEUTER
N fingertips touch temple then jaw
(see PARENT)

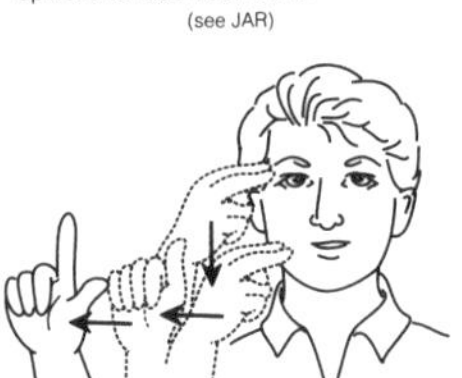

NEUTRAL
N touches temple then jaw; add right palm-out L *(neuter + -al)*

NEUTRON
Left extended-A, palm-down; right N circles near left thumb
(see ATOM)

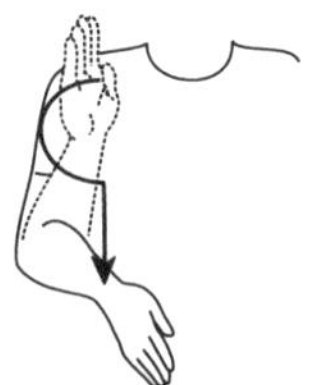

NEVER
Tip of open hand draws large question mark in front of body

NEW
Back of right palm-up flat hand arcs down, brushes across left palm and arcs up slightly

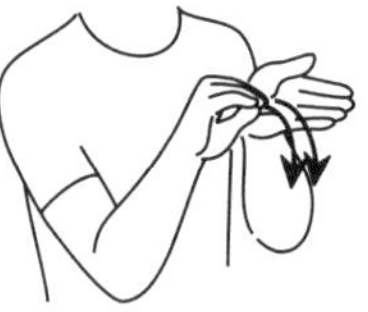

NEW ORLEANS
O brushes off left palm; repeat

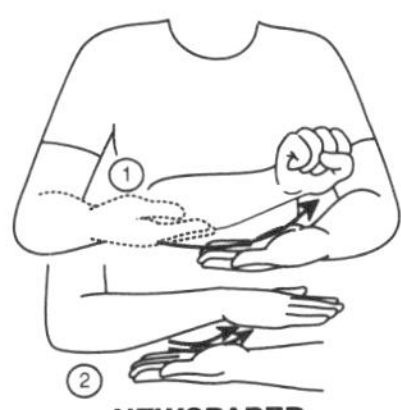

NEWSPAPER
Back of palm-up right hand brushes across left palm, changes to S; heel of right palm brushes heel of left twice

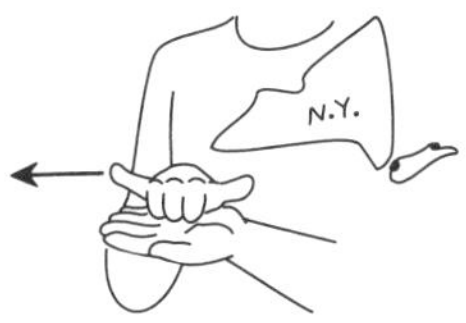

NEW YORK
Palm-down Y slides across left palm

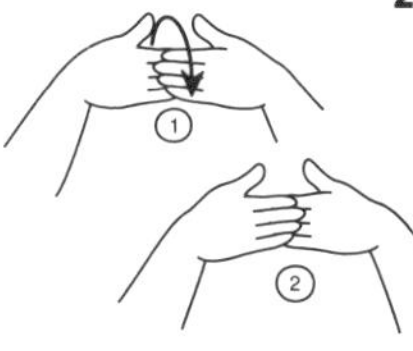

NEXT
Flat hands, palms-in; one in front of other, back hand lifts over to front

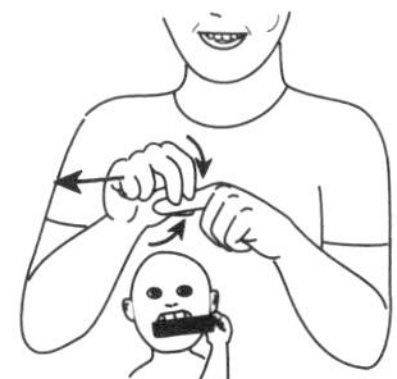

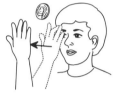

NIBBLE
Thumb, index and middle fingers nibble left index several times
(see MUNCH)

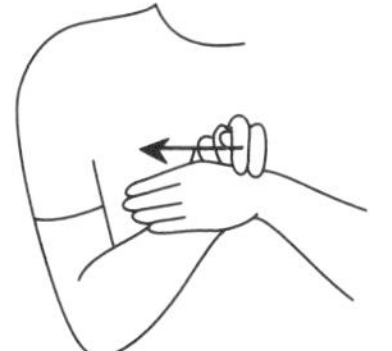

NICE
First 2 fingers of N slide along top side of palm-in left hand
(see DECENT)

NICKEL
Middle finger of 5 touch temple once, and pulls away
(see CENT)

NIECE
N shakes near jaw
(see AUNT)

NIGHT
Drop bent hand over edge of left

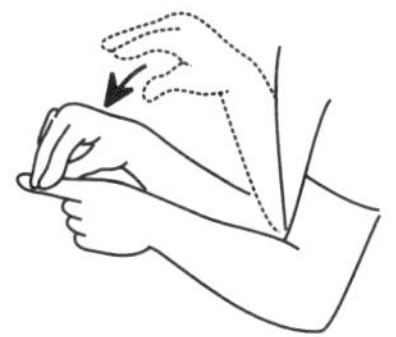

NIP
Thumb, index and middle fingers nip left index finger

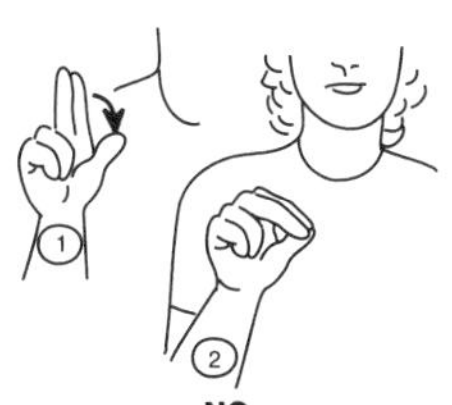

NO
First two fingers close onto thumb

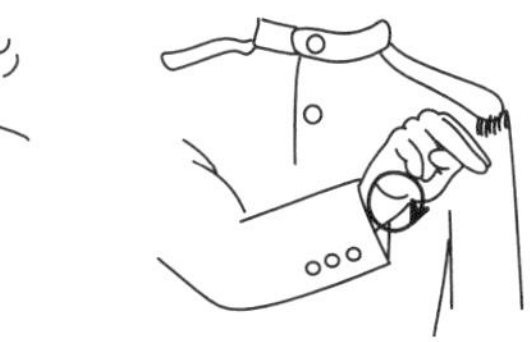

NOBLE
Palm-down extended-N circles near left shoulder, then touches
(see CHARACTER)

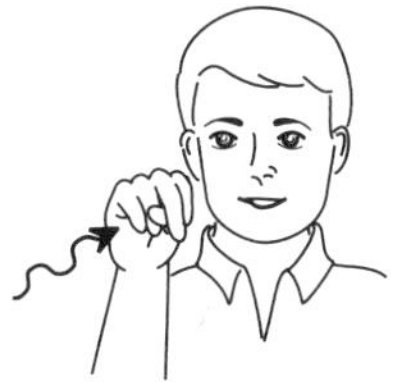

NOISE
Palm-out N shakes up to ear
(see SOUND)

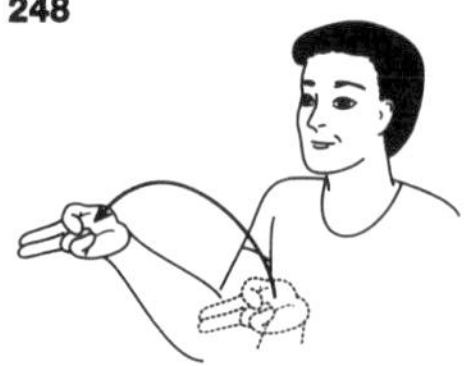

NOMINATE
Palm-up hand arcs up and forward
(see BID)

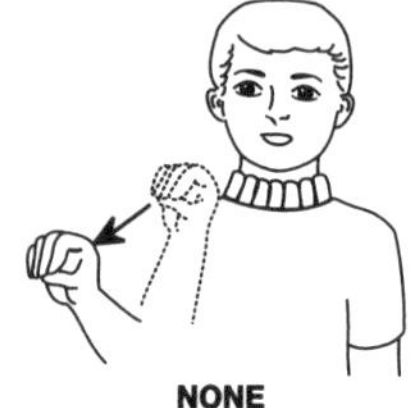

NONE
Palm-out O moves diagonally right
(see NOTHING)

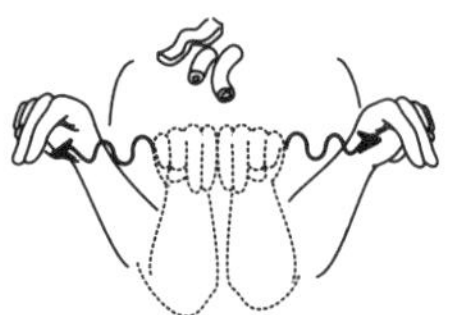

NOODLE
Palm-down N's touching, separate shaking to sides
(see SPAGHETTI)

NOON
Right vertical arm rests elbow on back of left hand

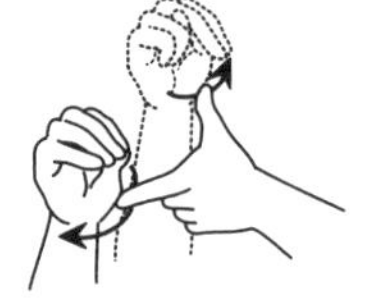

NOR
N back off left L-thumb; O forward off fingertip of index
(see THEN)

NORM
Palm-out N-hands tap together

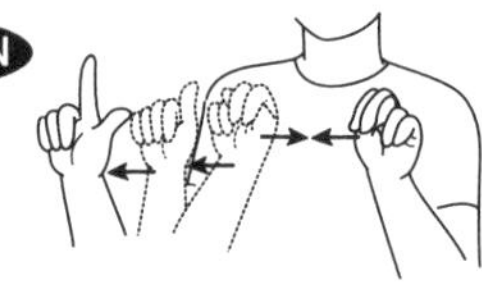

NORMAL
Palm-out N-hands tap together; right changes to L-hand *(norm + -al)*

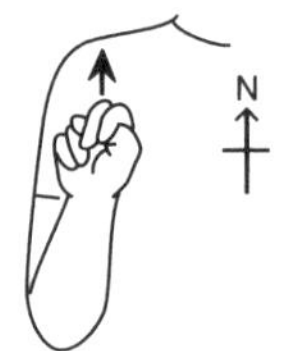

NORTH
Palm-out N moves up
(see UP)

NORWAY
(U.S. Sign)
N circles near forehead
(see DENMARK)

NORWAY
(Norwegian Sign)
Palm-out N draws mountains

NOSE
Right index points to nose

NOSTRIL
Right index fingertip circles nostril

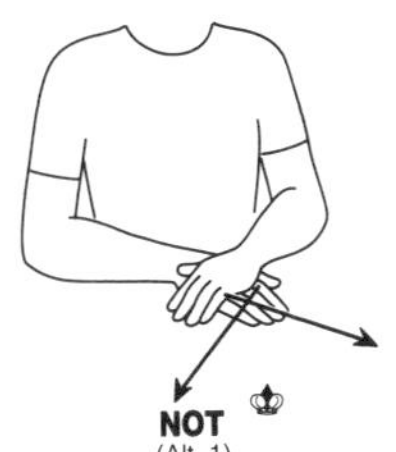

NOT
(Alt. 1)
Flat hands cross, separate sideways

NOT
(Alt. 2)
Thumb of right A-hand under chin brushes outward
(see AM)

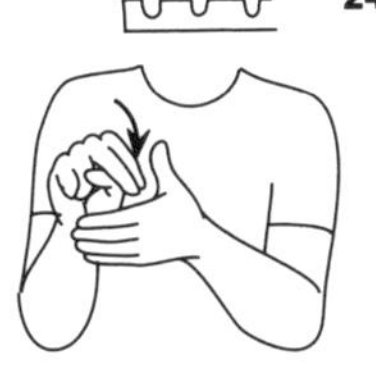

NOTCH
N jerks down toward palm-in left hand
(see MARK)

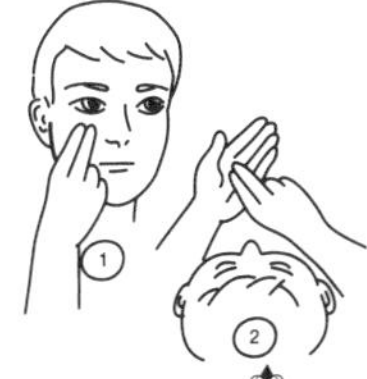

NOTE
Fingertips of palm-in H at eye twists out and down to touch left palm

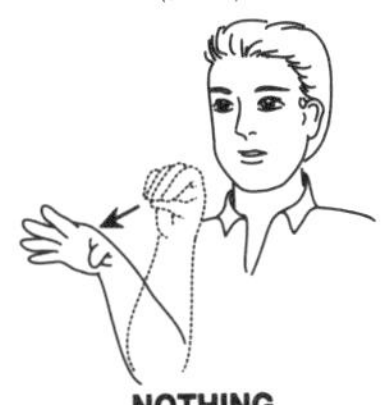

NOTHING
Palm-out O moves forward right, opening sharply
(see NONE)

NOTION
From side of forehead fingers of N-hand arcs up and out
(see IDEA)

NOUN
Fingertips of N tap side of left H index
(see WORD)

NOVEMBER
(Alt. 1)
N arcs over left vertical hand
(see CALENDAR)

NOVEMBER
(Alt. 2)
N shakes down from under chin in 3 steps *(3 syllables)*

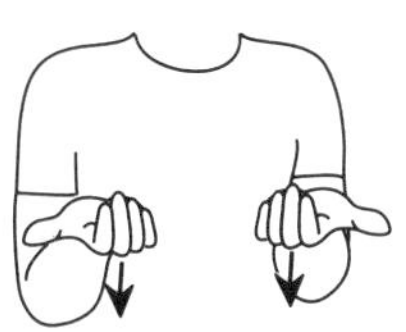

NOW
Palm-up bent hands drop slightly
(see IMMEDIATE)

NUCLEAR
N circles and drops on left palm, changes to palm-out R *(nucleus + -er)*
(see MIDDLE)

NUCLEUS
N circles and drops on left palm
(see MIDDLE)

NUDE
N brushes off back of left U
(see BARE)

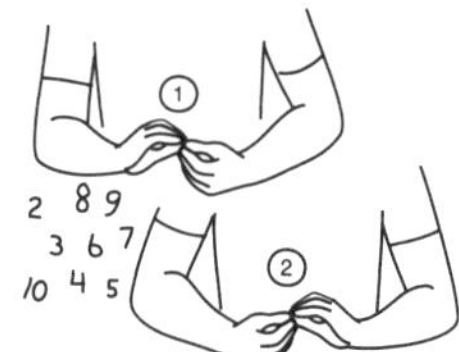

NUMBER
Flat-O tips touch, one palm-up, one palm-down, reverse; repeat
(see DIGIT)

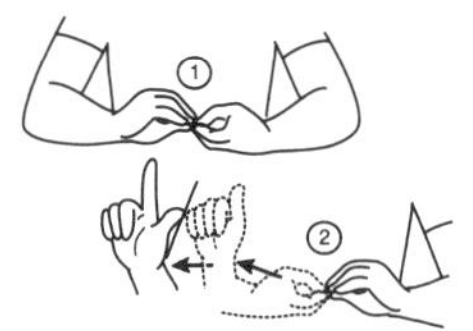

NUMERAL
Flat-O tips touch, one palm-up and one palm-down, reverse; right hand adds *(number + -al)*

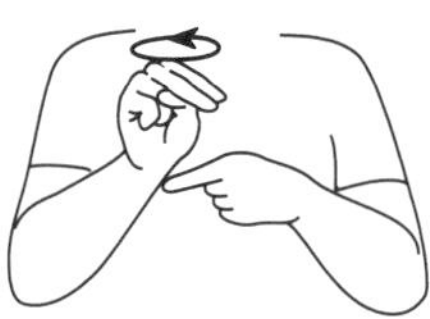

NUMERATOR
N circles above left index
(see FRACTION)

NUN
N arcs over face
(see VIRGIN)

NURSE
Fingertips of N tap left pulse twice
(see DOCTOR)

NUT ♔
Thumb flips out from under teeth

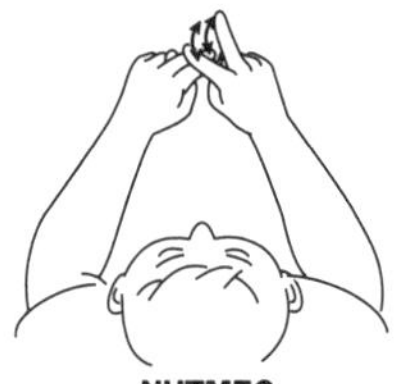

NUTMEG
Palm-down right V-fingers alternately tap back of left N-fingers
(see SALT)

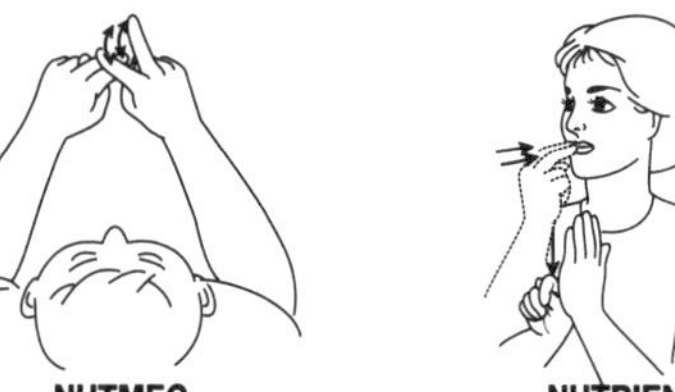

NUTRIENT
N-fingers tap just below lower lip, then side of palm-out T slides down vertical left palm *(nutrition + -ent)*

NUTRITION
N-fingers tap just below lower lip

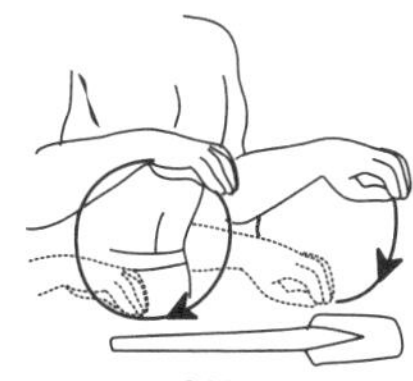

OAR
O-hands row

OAT
O brushes up through left C-hand
(see GRAIN)

OATH
Index at chin, to palm-out O against left horizontal hand
(see PROMISE)

OATMEAL
Palm-up O circles towards mouth from palm-up left hand
(see SOUP)

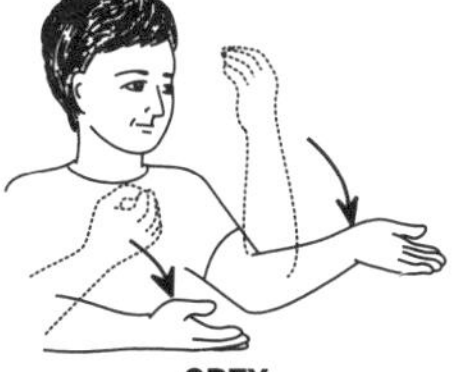

OBEY
Flat-O's, left near forehead, right near chin, both drop down and open

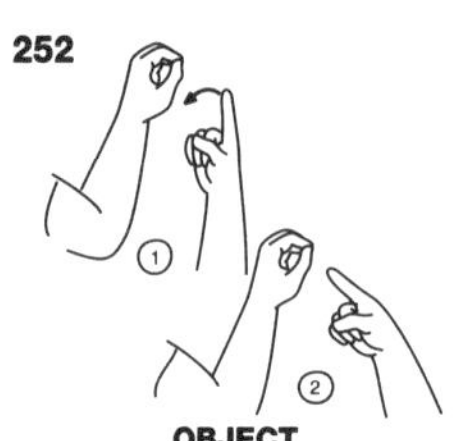

OBJECT
(noun)
Right index behind left O, index finger turns down to point at O
(see AIM)

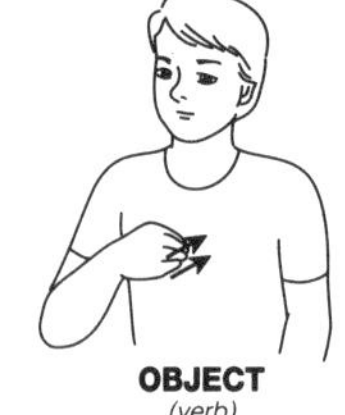

OBJECT
(verb)
Palm-in O hits chest; repeat
(see COMPLAIN)

OBJECTION
Palm-in O hits chest; right S slides down vertical hand *(object + -tion)*

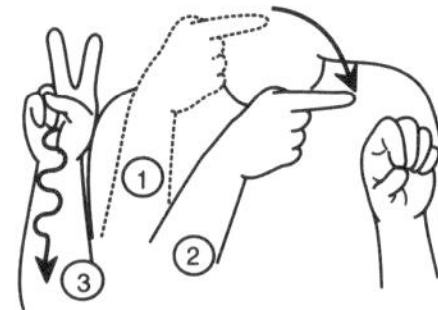

OBJECTIVE
Right index behind left O, index finger turns down to point at O; V-hand shakes downward *(object + -ive)*

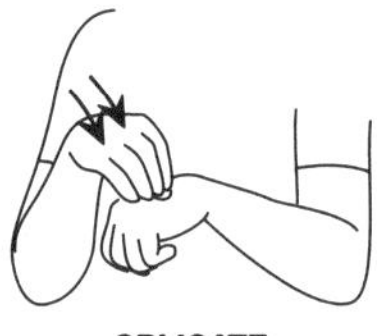

OBLIGATE
Right O taps back of left hand
(see WORK)

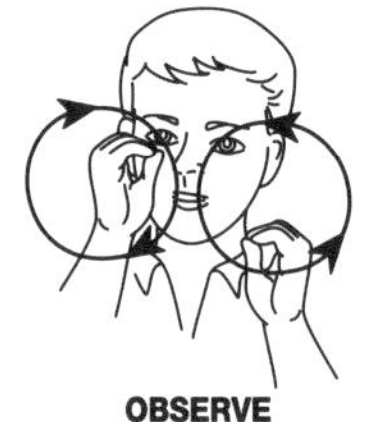

OBSERVE
Palms-facing, O's circle alternately before face

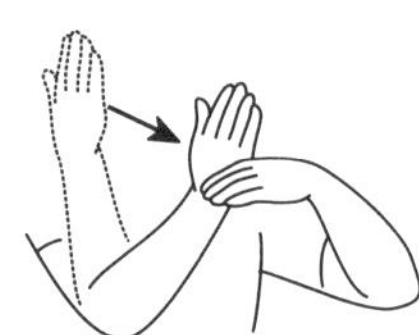

OBSTACLE
Side of right palm-in flat hand strikes thumbside of palm-down left hand
(see IMPAIR)

OBSTINATE
Thumbs of flat hands on temples, fingers close sharply to palms
(see STUBBORN)

OBTAIN
Heel of right O, palm-left, on top horizontal left S; both hands move backwards towards body
(see GET)

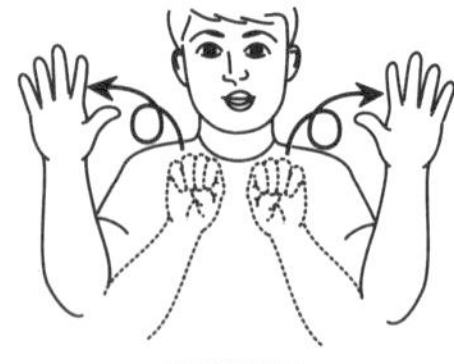

OBVIOUS
Palm-out O's arc sideways, up and out and open to 5's
(see CLEAR)

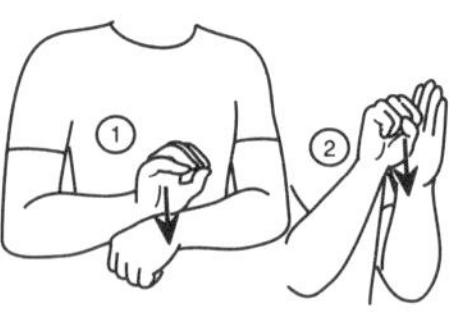

OCCUPATION
Palm-out O touches left wrist; S slides down vertical left palm *(occupy + -tion)*
(see OCCUPY)

OCCUPY
Palm-out O touches left wrist
(see SET)

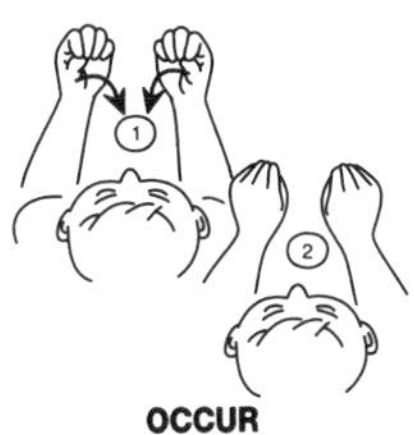

OCCUR

Palm-up O's twist to palm-down
(see HAPPEN)

OCEAN

Palm-down O's move wave like up and down forward, opening to 5's

OCTOBER
(Alt. 1)
O arcs over left vertical hand
(see CALENDAR)

OCTOBER
(Alt. 2)
O's before eyes, circle back to sides
(see MASK)

OCTOPUS

O sits on left palm-down 5-hand, 5 doing "push-ups" from flat-O's to 5's
(see SQUID)

ODD

Palm-left O arcs in front of nose to palm-down O
(see STRANGE)

ODOR
O-hand brushes upward at nose
(see SMELL)

OF
Open hands approach and link thumbs and index fingers

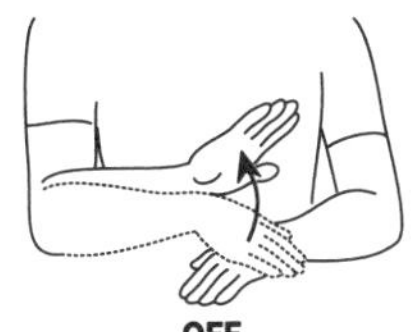

OFF
Right palm on back of left hand; lift off

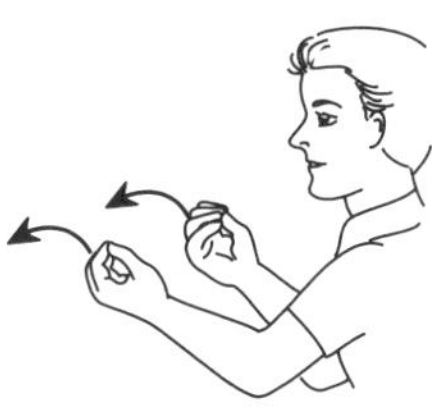

OFFER
Palm-up O's, side-by-side, arc forward
(see SUGGEST)

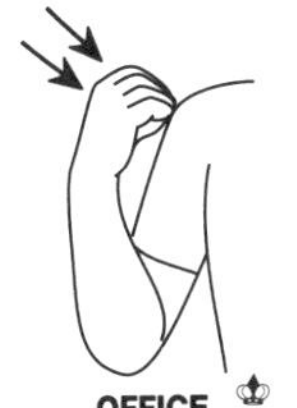

OFFICE
Tips of right O tap right shoulder

OFTEN
Right bent fingertips touch heel of left palm, then move to fingers
(see FREQUENT)

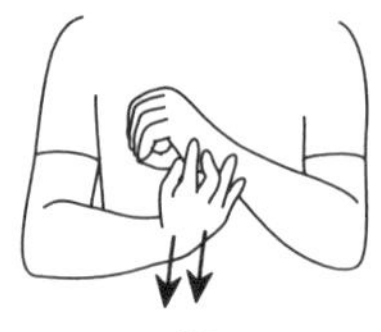

OIL
Thumb and middle finger grasp side of left O; slide down and shut; repeat
(see GRAVY)

OINTMENT
Thumbside of O circles counter clockwise over palm-up left hand

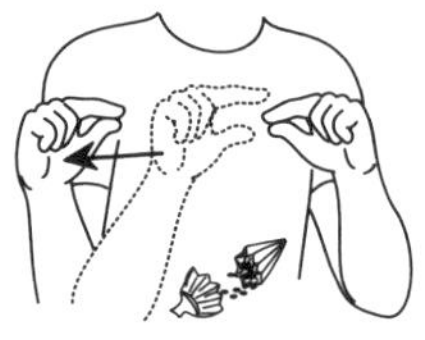

OKRA
Right G-fingers pull off closed left index and thumb; repeat

OLD
Right C-hand at chin, moves down, closing to S

OLIVE
Right O, palm-left, shakes slightly
(see BLUE)

OLYMPICS
9-fingers link alternately three times in the form of a triangle (olympic rings)

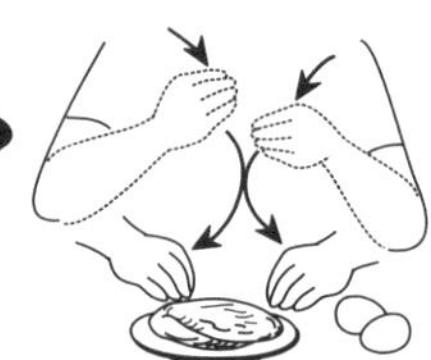

OMELET
O's strike fingertips and fall apart
(see EGG)

OMIT
O's throw down to side, opening palm-down 5's

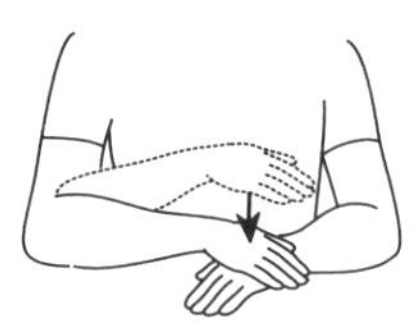

ON
Right palm touches back of left hand
(see MOUNT)

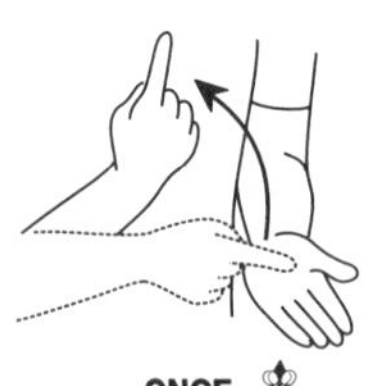

ONCE
Tip of palm-down right index finger on left palm-up; index twists to pointing upward

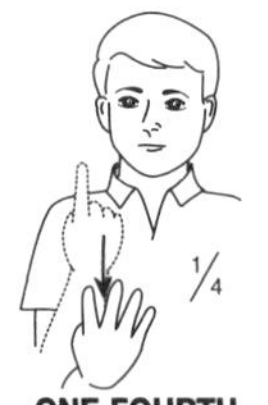

ONE FOURTH
Palm-in I-hand moves down to a palm-in 4-hand

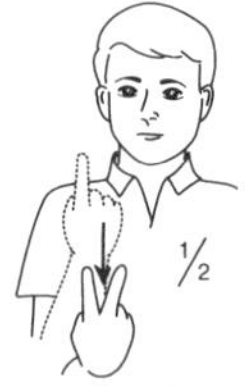

ONE HALF
Palm-in I-hand moves down to a palm-in 2-hand

ONION
Right X twists at corner of eye; repeat

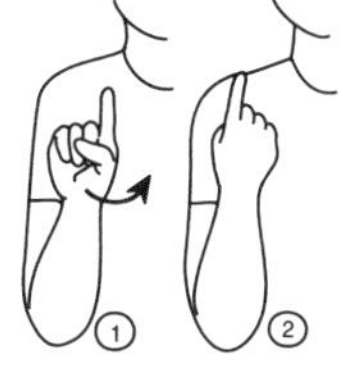

ONLY
Palm-out index twists to palm-in

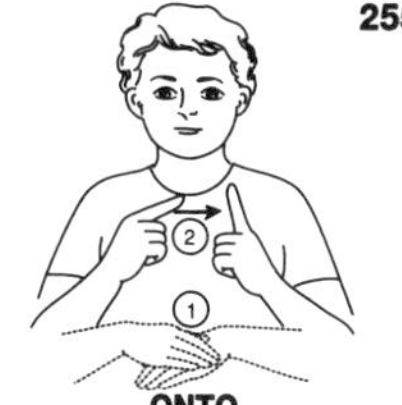

ONTO
Right palm touches back of left hand; right index approaches and touches left vertical index finger

ONWARD
Right palm touches back of left hand; palm-out W moves forward

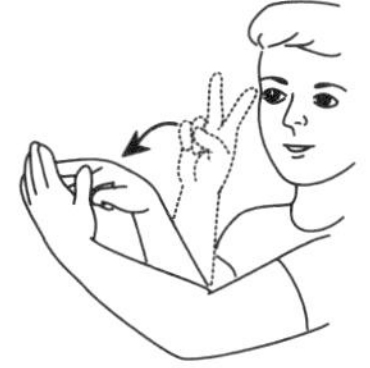

OPAQUE
V from eye moves forward, is stopped by left hand

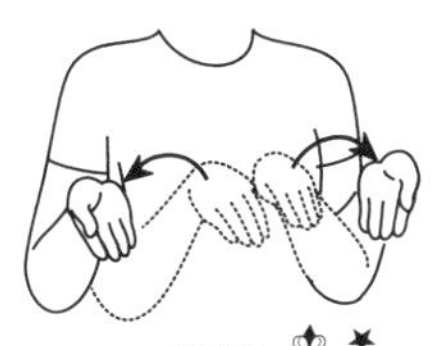

OPEN ♔ ★
B-hands, palms-down and sides touching, twist apart, palms facing up

OPERA

O arcs out twice from mouth
(see SING)

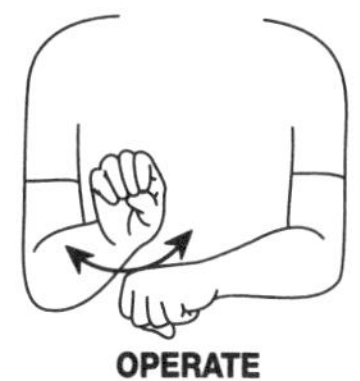

OPERATE

O arcs side-to-side, hitting back of left palm-down S
(see BUSY)

OPINION
(Alt. 1)
O arcs out near forehead
(see IDEA)

OPINION
(Alt. 2)
Side of O circles near temple

OPOSSUM/POSSUM

Little finger of right hand hangs from little finger of left hand

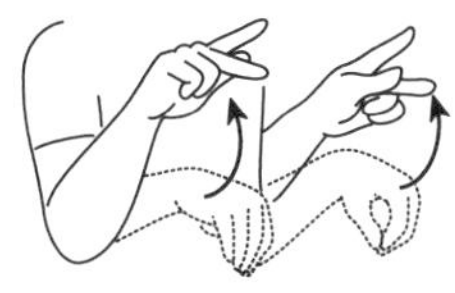

OPPORTUNE

Both palm-down O's change to P's arcing upward
(see ALLOW)

OPPOSE
Indexes point at each other; hands jerk apart

OPTION
Right O moves back from index of palm-in left V
(see CHOOSE)

OR
Palm-out O off left palm-in L-thumb, then forward off fingertip
(see THEN)

ORAL
O circles before mouth
(see MOUTH)

ORANGE
Right C-hand squeezes in front of chin; repeat

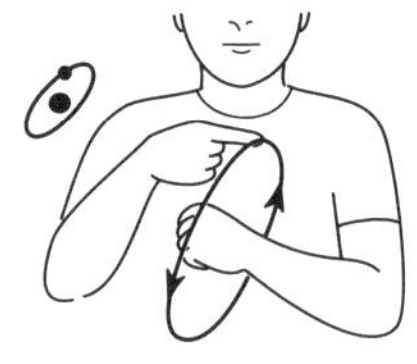

ORBIT
Index circles left palm-in S-hand
(see PLANET)

ORCHARD
Elbow of palm-out O on back of left hand; twist, moving slightly right
(see TREE)

ORCHESTRA
O's swing apart, then together; repeat (conducting the orchestra)
(see CONDUCT)

ORDER
Palm-in index on chin twists to palm-out; jerks to point forward
(see COMMAND)

ORDINANCE
Palm-out O on fingertips then on heel of vertical left palm
(see LAW)

ORDINARY
Palm-out parallel O's circle together slightly outward and back
(see STANDARD)

ORE
Back of right O, palm-up, taps back of palm-down left S

ORGANIZE
Palm-out O-hands separate and circle horizontally to palm-in
(see CLASS)

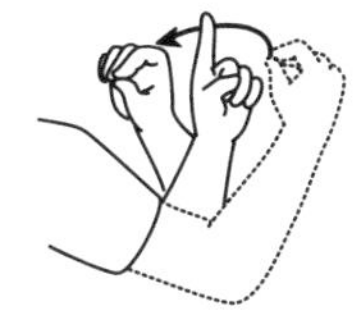

ORIENT
Right O circles left vertical index
(see ATMOSPHERE)

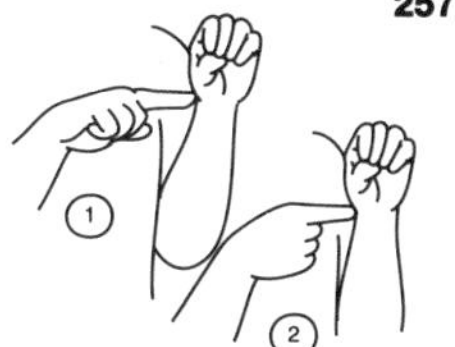

ORIGIN
Right index fingertip touches wrist of palm-out left O, then twists
(see START)

ORNAMENT
Fingertips of right O face left vertical palm and shake slightly as O moves down palm and arm
(see DECORATE)

ORPHAN
O touches temple, then jaw
(see PARENT)

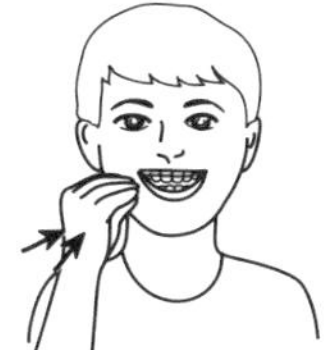

ORTHODONTIC
Fingertips of O tap at side of mouth
(see DENTIST)

OSTRICH
O-hand nods, resting elbow on back of left open hand
(see GULL)

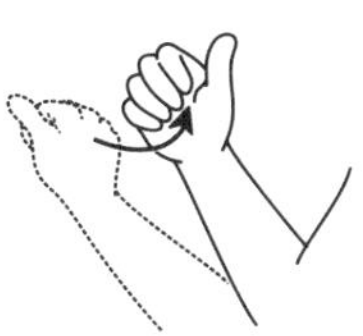

OTHER
Palm-down A-hand thumb extended; twist over to palm-up

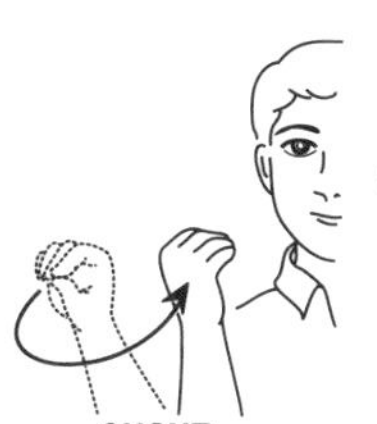

OUGHT
Palm-out O twists to palm-in
(see SEEM)

OUNCE
O rocks on index finger of H-hand
(see WEIGH)

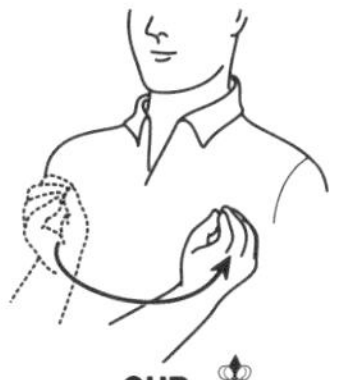

OUR ♔
(Alt. 1)
O-hand, on right side of chest, circles to left

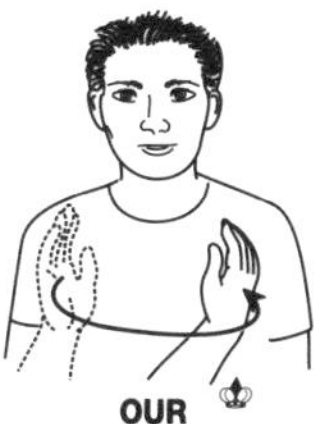

OUR ♔
(Alt. 2)
Cupped hand on right side of chest, circles to left

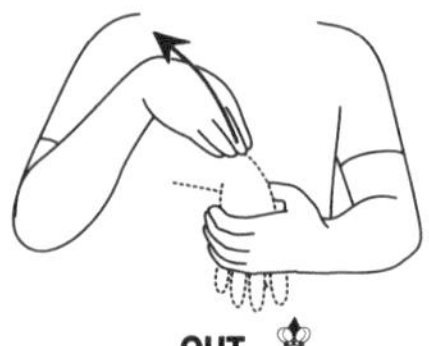

OUT

Right open hand pulls out from palm-left C and closes to O-hand

OUTFIT

Right flat-O pulls out form palm–left C; thumbtips of F–hands touch *(out + fit)*

OUTLINE

Right flat-O pulls out from palm-left C; L slides along left index *(out + line)*

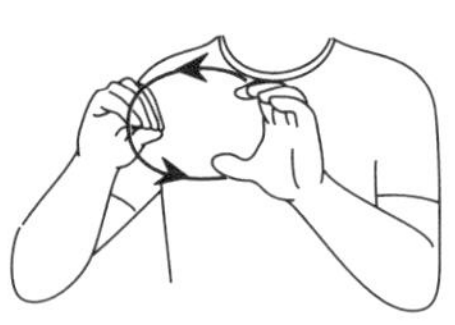

OVAL

Right O circles behind left C-hand

OVEN

Right O circles under left palm

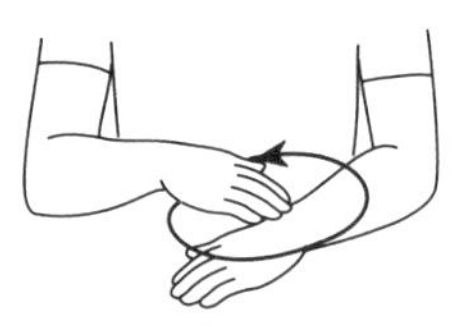

OVER

Palm-down right hand circles over back of left

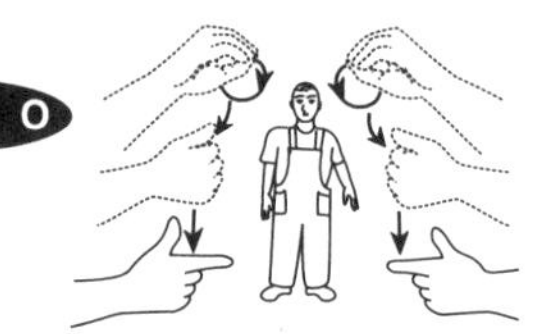

OVERALLS

O's circle on chest, change to palm-in A's, then to L's, dropping

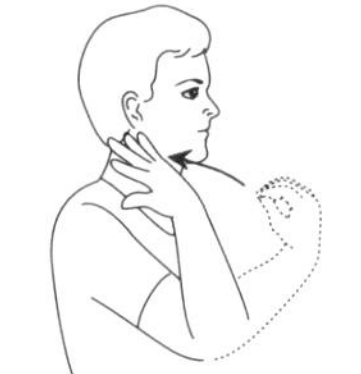

OVERHEAD PROJECTOR

Palm-in O moves inward and opens to relaxed 5 near shoulder

OVERWHELM

Palm-in right vertical 5 in front of palm-in left vertical index, 5 moves towards index and pushes it toward body

OWE

Index fingertip taps heel of palm-up left O; repeat

(see DEBT)

OWL

O's at eyes twist inward repeatedly

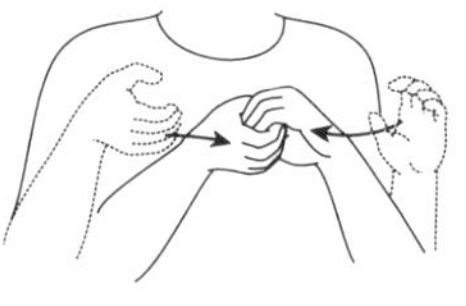

OWN

Right C approaches left horizontal C and link as O-hands

O

OXYGEN
Palm-out O's arc upwards to nostrils

OYSTER
Right hand cups over left palm-right O; flaps up and down

NOTES

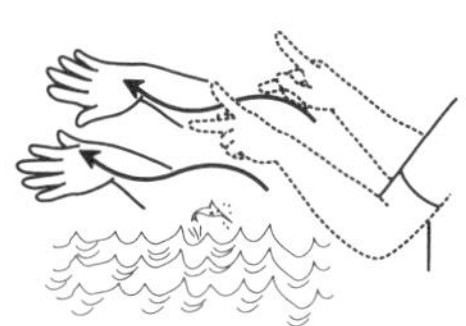

PACIFIC
P's arc slightly upwards, change to open hands and flow forward
(see OCEAN)

PACIFIER
Place side of small C on mouth

PACK ★
Flat-O's alternately "pack" circularly

PACKAGE
P-hands move up sides of box and together, tie a knot and separate

PAD ★
Middle finger of right P taps pad of left thumb

PADDLE ★
P-hands paddle at side

PAGE
P turns page on left palm
(see RECIPE)

PAGEANT
Palm-down P moves slightly sideways, down, and sidewise, changing to T
(see CARNIVAL)

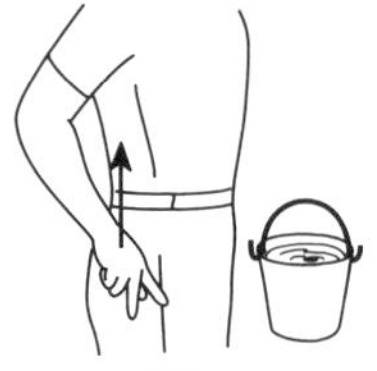

PAIL
P-hand, at side, rises
(see BUCKET)

PAIN ★
P-hands point at each other, twist toward each other; may repeat
(see HURT)

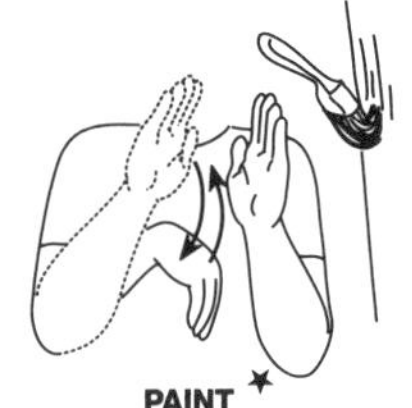

PAINT ★
Right flat hand fingertips brush up and down vertical left palm

PAIR
Thumb and finger of right hand close fingers of left 2-hand
(see COUPLE)

PAJAMA
Middle fingers of P's brush down chest; repeat
(see DRESS)

PAL
L-thumb slides from left side of chin to right side

PALACE
P's face each other, arc up several times, closer together each time
(see CASTLE)

PALE
Palm-in O near chin, moves up to 5-hand in front of face

PAMPHLET
Middle finger of P slides along bottom edge of flat left hand
(see MAGAZINE)

PAN
Middle finger of P-hand outlines pan rim and handle

PANCAKE

Flat hand moves out and inverts *(as if flipping pancake)*

(See FLAPJACK)

PANDA

Palm-in P circles eye

PANEL

Right palm-out P slides toward elbow from left wrist

(see BOARD)

PANIC

P's, palm-out, shake downward slightly toward body

(see AFRAID)

PANSY

Middle finger of right P touches each side of nose

(see FLOWER)

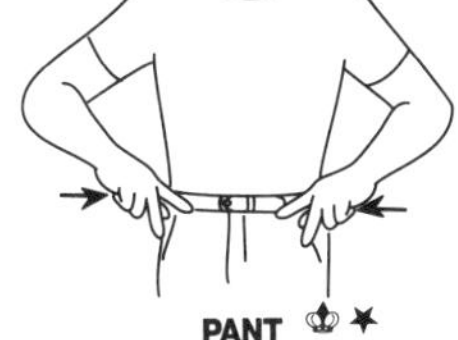

PANT

P's tap at waist twice

PANTHER

3-hands move from side of mouth outward; repeat

(see CAT)

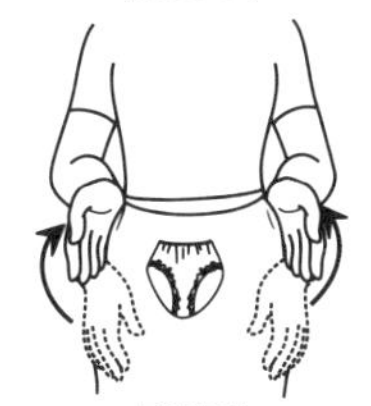

PANTY

Tips of cupped hands touch hips; hands arc up so heels touch waist

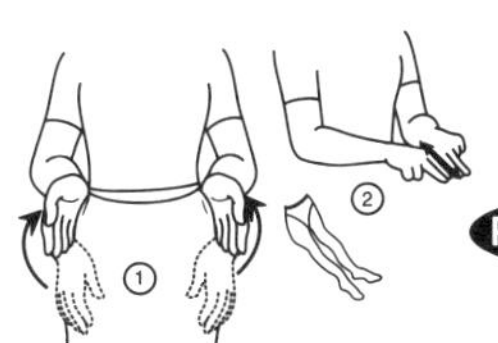

PANTY HOSE

Tips of cupped hands touch hips; moves so heels touch waist; H-hands alternately slide up and down against each other *(panty + hose)*

PAPER

Palm-down right heel brushes across palm-up left heel slightly to left; repeat

PARACHUTE

Palm-up O under open hand; both swing downwards together

PARADE

Palm-down P's, one behind the other, jerk away from body in upward jerks

(see MARCH)

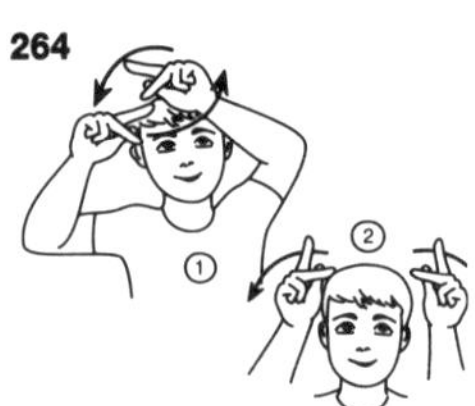

PARADISE
Right P passes under and over left P above head; P's separate
(see HEAVEN)

PARADOX
Parallel P's move to cross indexes
(see CONFLICT)

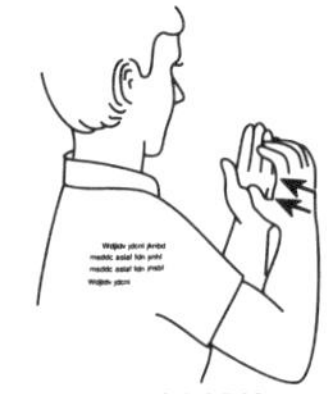

PARAGRAPH
Thumb and fingertips of C tap vertical left palm

PARAKEET
Tips of bent index and thumb tap at side of mouth
(see BIRD)

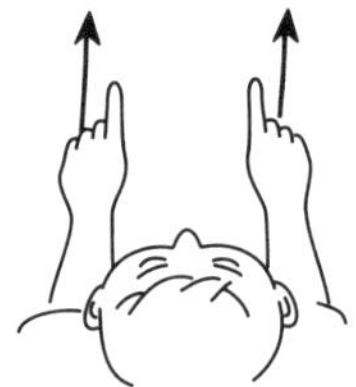

PARALLEL
Palm-down indexes move forward
(see HALL)

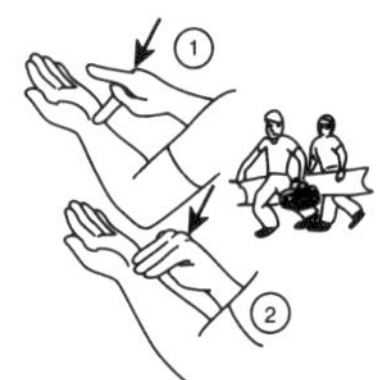

PARAMEDIC
Middle finger of P touches pulse, then fingers of M touch
(see DOCTOR)

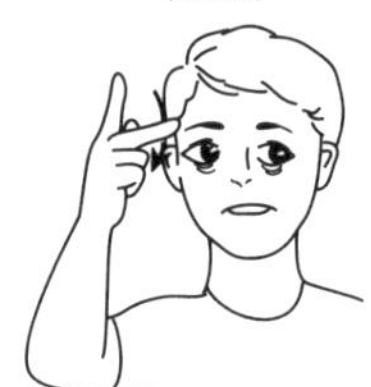

PARANOID
P-hand stationary, middle P finger flexes and scratches temple; repeat
(see SUSPECT)

PARAPROFESSIONAL
Middle finger of P taps on base of thumb of palm-right left hand, then slides forward on hand; add L-hand

PARASITE
Right P middle finger rests on left index; both drop slightly
(see DEPEND)

PARATROOPER
Left 5-hand on right index finger, both swing down

PARDON
Middle P-fingertip brushes off left fingertips; repeat
(see EXCUSE)

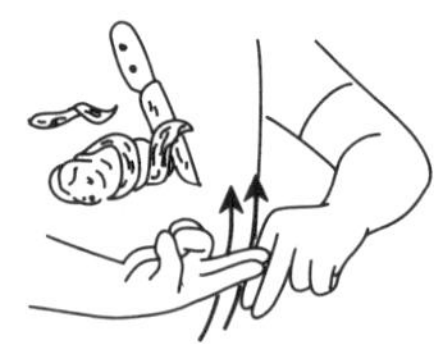

PARE
Back of H brushes inward off back of left H-hand as if paring

PARENT ♔
Middle fingertip of P-hand touches temple, then jaw

PARENTHESIS
P's draw parentheses

PARIS
V's face each other, arc up and together to meet fingertips

PARK ★
Set palm-left 3 on left palm

PARLIAMENT
Palm-in P, middle fingertip touches left side of chest, then right side
(see MEMBER)

PARROT
Hand in front of chin, bent index and thumb tap each other
(see BIRD)

PARSNIP
Index finger slices side of left P; repeat
(see TOMATO)

PART ★
Middle fingertip of P draws arc on palm-up left hand
(see SOME)

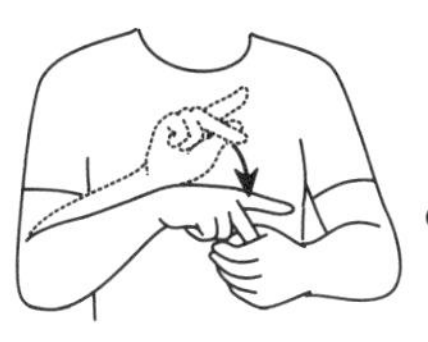

PARTICIPATE
Middle finger of P arcs into left O
(see JOIN)

PARTICLE
Palm-left horizontal P arcs downward, middle fingertip flicking little fingertip of horizontal left I
(see PIECE)

PARTICULAR
Pull up index of left palm-out P
(see EXCEPT)

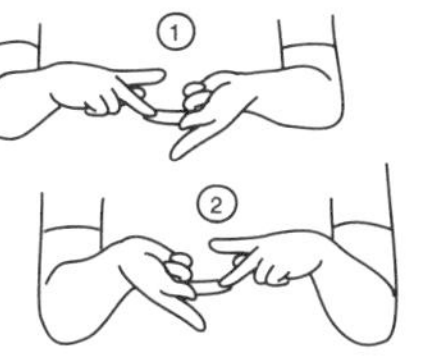

PARTNER
Middle fingers of P's, touch first right on left, then left on right
(see FRIEND)

P

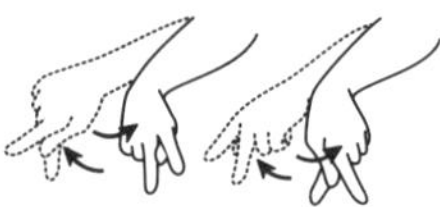

PARTY
P-hands swing at wrists from side-to-side rapidly
(see PLAY)

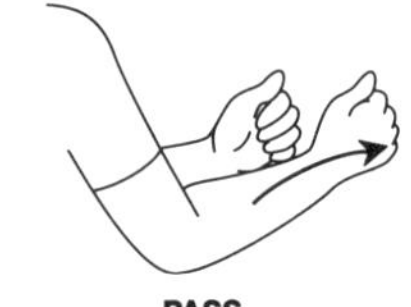

PASS
A-hands palms-facing, right slightly behind; right hand passes left hand brushing knuckles

PASSENGER
Middle finger of P-hand rides forward on thumb of left horizontal C-hand
(see RIDE)

PASSION
Palm-in C moves down middle of chest several times
(see HUNGER)

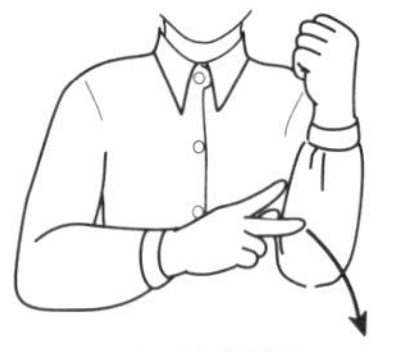

PASSOVER
(Alt.1)
Left forearm vertical, right P brushes down past elbow; may repeat

PASSOVER
(Alt. 2)
P-hand arcs forward across left palm-down flat hands

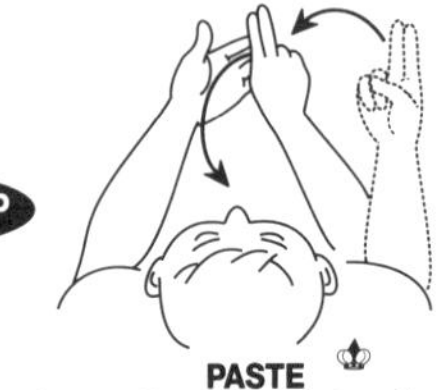

PASTE ♔
Palm-up H turns to palm-down; fingers sweep across left palm

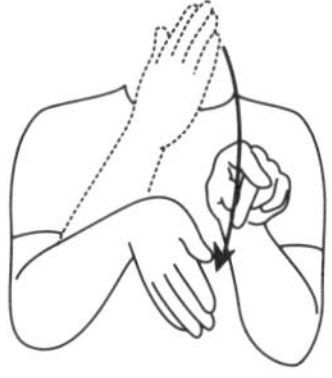

PASTRAMI
Right palm slices side of thumb of left P; repeat
(see SLICE)

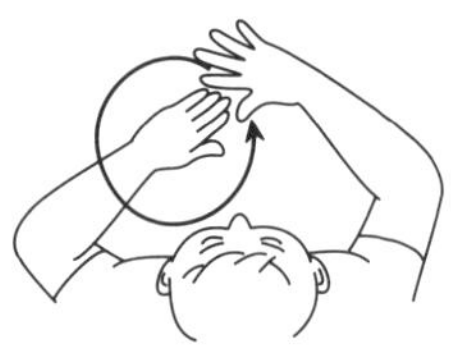

PASTURE
Palm-down flat hand over back of horizontal left hand, circles toward elbow and back along arm
(see GROUND)

PASTRY
Middle finger of P circles on the back of palm-in S-hand
(see DOUGH)

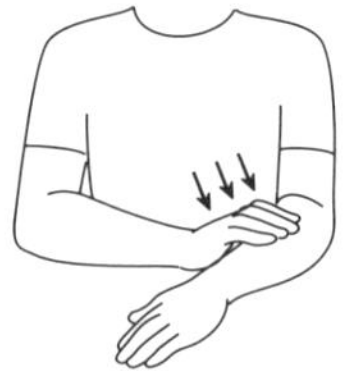

PAT
Pat left arm several times

PATCH
Left S, horizontal and palm-in; fingertips of right P arc up and across back of fist
(see COVER)

PATH
Palm-down P's move forward, weaving or winding slightly side-to-side
(see WAY)

PATIENT
Thumb of right A-hand moves down lips and chin
(see TOLERATE)

PATIO
Palm-down P arcs out from horizontal left arm, circling back to fingers *(outlining patio)*

PATRIOT
Place side of right P-hand on left upper chest

PATRIOTIC
Place side of right P-hand on left upper chest, right hand changes to C *(patriot + -ic)*

PATROL
Palm-in C outlines patrol belt

PATTERN
Side of P shakes towards and touches vertical left palm
(see COPY)

PAUSE
Right palm-down P behind palm-up left hand; flutter left fingers
(see WAIT)

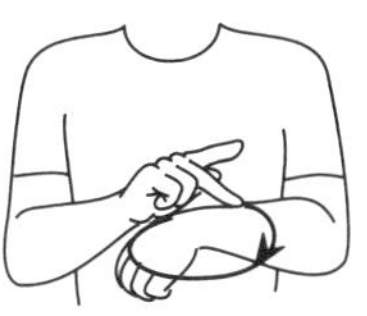

PAVE
Palm-down right P circles over back of horizontal left hand
(see TAR)

PAW
Middle finger of right P-hand cuts off left hand at wrist
(see FOOT)

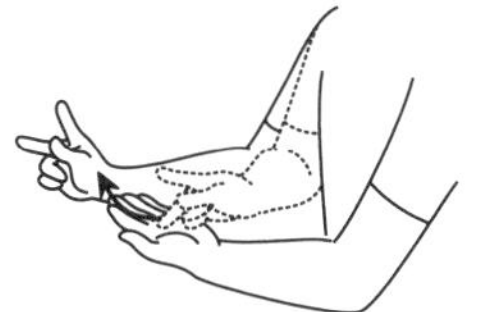

PAY
Middle finger of right P on left palm; flips up and out

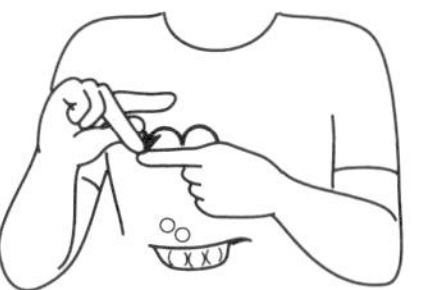

PEA
Middle finger of right P taps across left horizontal index
(see BEAN)

PEACE
P-hands, left in front of right at chin; separate downward
(see QUIET)

PEACH
Fingertips of right 5 draws down to flat-O on cheek, repeat *(feeling fuzz)*

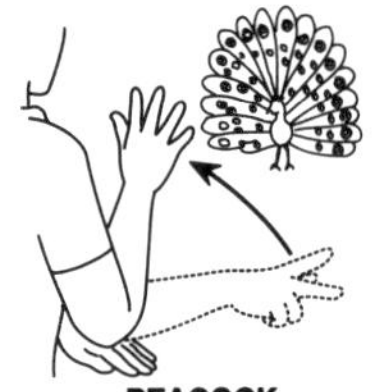

PEACOCK
Right elbow on back of left hand, palm-down P rises and opens to 5 *(like tail)*

PEAK
Index fingers rise to touch
(see CLIMAX)

PEANUT
P-index and then thumb of A-hand jerk from under teeth
(see NUT)

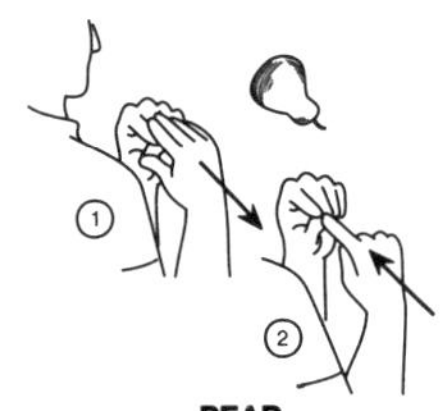

PEAR
Right hand grasps left flat-O and slides off into flat-O; changes to index which touches left fingers

PEBBLE
Back of palm-up P taps back of left palm-down S
(see STONE)

P

PECAN
Index of P flicks from under front teeth
(see NUT)

PECK
Index and thumb peck at back of left index finger
(see NAG)

PECULIAR
Palm-left P arcs left in front of eyes
(see STRANGE)

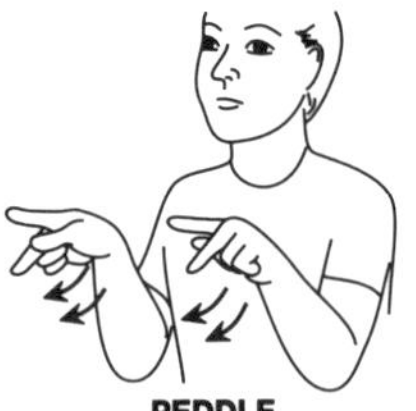

PEDDLE
Palm-down P's jerk out and up twice
(see SELL)

PEEK
Peek through P-fingers

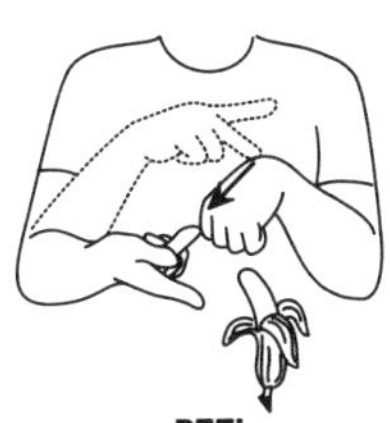

PEEL
(Alt. 1)
Middle finger or right P slides down back of left S-hand and fingers, twisting outward

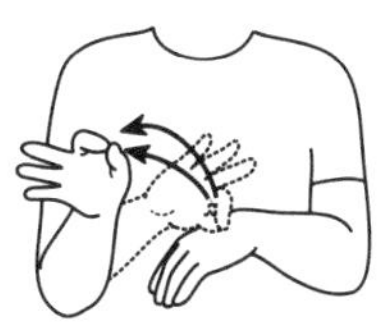

PEEL
(Alt. 2)
Right 9 peels from back of palm-down left hand

PEN
Middle fingertip of P writes on left palm
(see WRITE)

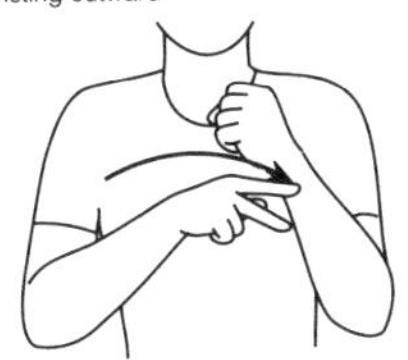

PENALTY
Right P makes a striking movement near wrist of left S-hand held upward

PENCIL
Thumb and index finger at mouth, then write on left palm
(see WRITE)

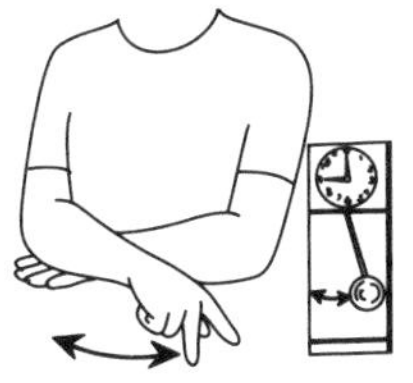

PENDULUM
P-arm down; swing it on the edge of left horizontal flat hand

PENETRATE
Index thrusts through middle and third fingers of left hand

PENGUIN
Inside of wrists on hips, hands bent back, tilt body from side-to-side

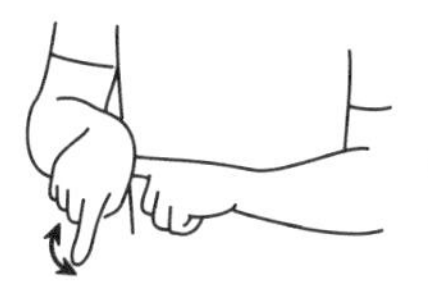

PENIS
Right index points down, wrist on horizontal left index; moves slightly up and down

PENNANT
P waves in breeze, left index on arm
(see FLAG)

PENNY
Middle finger of P taps temple, moves out, then shakes
(see CENT)

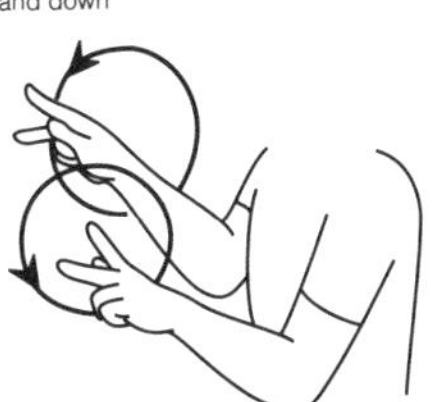

PEOPLE
Palm-out P's circle alternately forward up and down

P

PEPPER
Thumb-side of 9-hand shakes pepper

PEPPERMINT
Middle finger of P on chin; moves out to M-hand

PER
Middle fingertip of P strokes down thumb of vertical left A
(see EACH)

PERCEIVE
V at eye, circles forward to palm-down pointing at left vertical index
(see PERSPECTIVE)

PERCENT
O-hand moves diagonally up to right, then down tracing % symbol

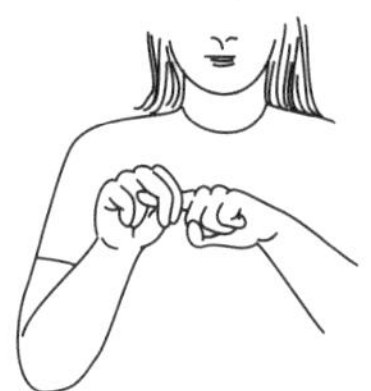

PERCH
Right bent fingers perch on left index
(see SIT)

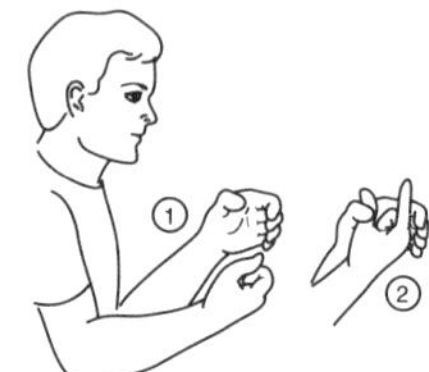

PERCOLATE
Left horizontal C, right palm-up S near C; right index flicks up repeatedly

PERFECT
Right P circles, facing left palm-in P, then middle fingertips touch
(see EXACT)

PERFORM
P's, palm-out; backs brush alternately down chest
(see ACT)

PERFUME
Right 9-hand at left side of neck tips bottle onto neck

PERHAPS
Palm-down P pivots several times side-to-side

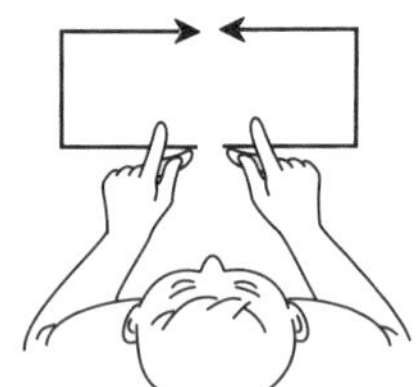

PERIMETER
Middle fingertips of P's touch, outline horizontal rectangle and touch again
(see SQUARE)

P

PERIOD
P circles forward once near left palm, then touches palm
(see HOUR)

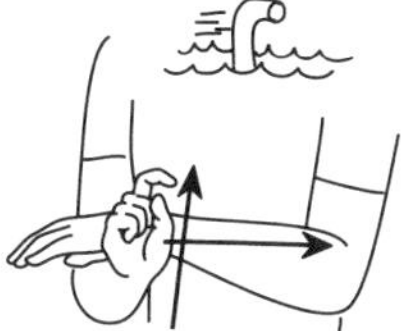

PERISCOPE
X rises outside left forearm and moves slowly toward elbow

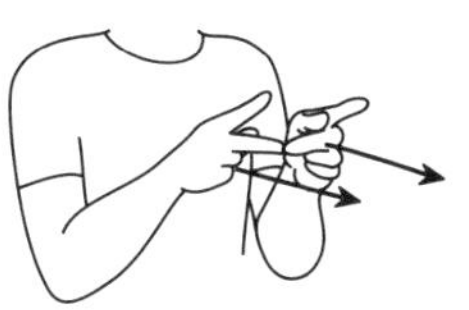

PERMANENT
Middle fingers of P's touch, and both move forward
(see CONTINUE)

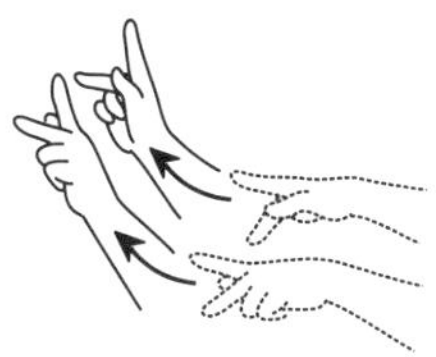

PERMIT
Palm-down P's twist to palm-out
(see ALLOW)

PERPENDICULAR
Inverted index rests on side of horizontal left index

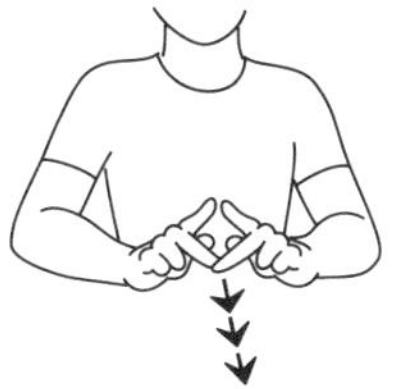

PERPETUAL
Middle fingers of P's touch and both move forward in three short movements
(see CONSISTENT)

PERSECUTE
Horizontal X's, right hits forward off top of left ; then left off right
(see TORTURE)

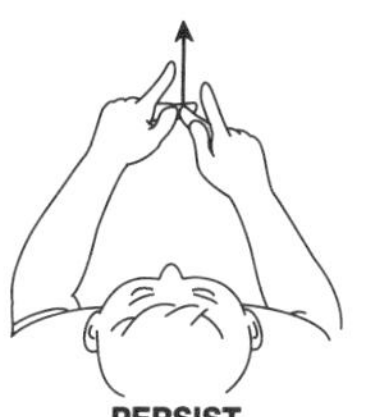

PERSIST
Middle fingertip of right P on middle fingertip of left P, both move forward
(see CONTINUE)

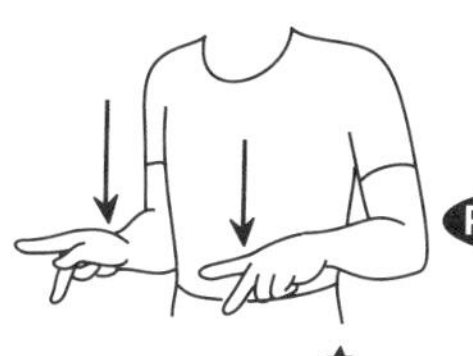

PERSON
Palm-down P's move straight down

PERSONALITY
Right P-hand circles clockwise then touches on left shoulder
(see CHARACTER)

PERSPECTIVE
P swings from eye in arc halfway to left palm-in P
(see PERCEIVE)

PERSPIRE
Wipe sweat from forehead with inverted index finger

P

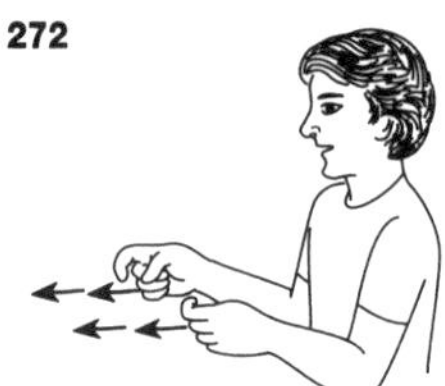

PERSUADE
Palms-facing, horizontal X-hands jerk forward twice
(see URGE)

PERVERT
P's touch forehead and stomach, twisting slightly
(see SICK)

PEST
Right P rides forward on back of wiggling left fingers
(see ANT)

PET ♔ ★
Pet back of left hand

PHILADELPHIA
P arcs sharply down to right
(see CHICAGO)

PHILOSOPHY
P nods down near center of forehead
(see WISE)

PHOBIA
Palm-out 5's, right behind left, right hand shakes
(see AFRAID)

PHONE ★
Right S-hand *(holding telephone)* rests on cheek

PHOTO
Side of P moves from eye to palm of vertical left hand
(see PICTURE)

PHOTOGRAPH
Right P arcs back against left palm-out flat hand

PHRASE
Middle fingertips of P-hands shake apart sideways
(see SENTENCE)

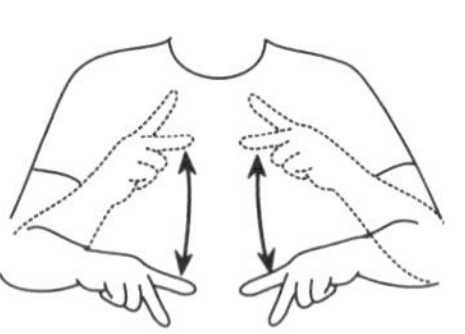

PHYSICAL
P-hands on chest and then on ribs
(see BODY)

P

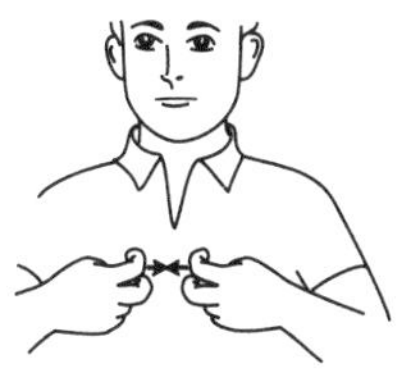

PHYSICS
Horizontal bent-V's bump several times
(see ELECTRIC)

PIANO
Wiggling fingers play piano up and down keyboard

PICCOLO
Palm-in fingers of right hand play back and forth on left index

PICK ★
(Alt.1)
Palm-down G-hand rises while fingers close *(picking up)*

PICK ★
(Alt. 2)
9-hand with thumb and index open; moves back closing index and thumb

PICKLE
Index of G-hand touches chin, then shakes outward

PICNIC
Palm-in P's circle up towards mouth alternately *(there are many different local signs for this word)*
(see BANQUET)

PICTURE ♛
C moves from side of eye to palm of left vertical hand

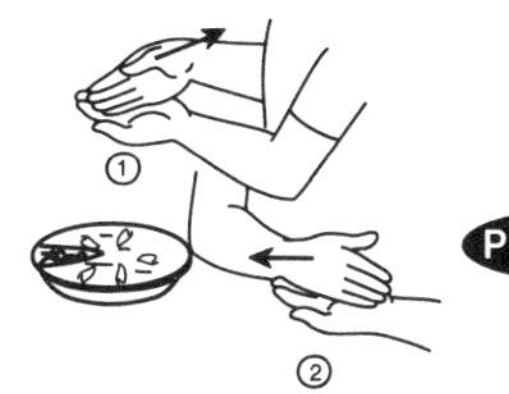

PIE
Side of right hand draws an X on left palm *(cutting pie)*

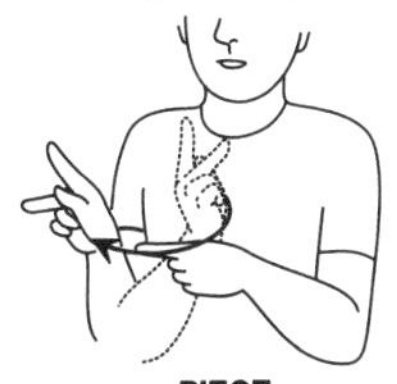

PIECE
Middle finger of P arcs down, hitting side of left index
(see CHIP)

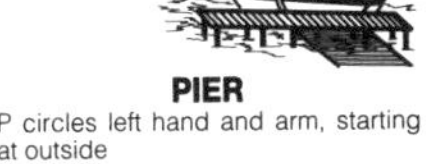

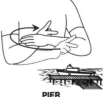

PIER
P circles left hand and arm, starting at outside
(see DOCK)

PIERCE ★
Right palm-left index thrusts through left palm-in V-hand

PIG
Palm-down flat hand flaps under chin
(see HOG)

PIGEON
At chin, close index finger of P to middle finger; repeat
(see BIRD)

PIGLET
Right hand palm-down under chin, flap fingers together, then drop slightly to stop above palm-up left hand

PILE
P outlines a pile in left palm
(see AMOUNT)

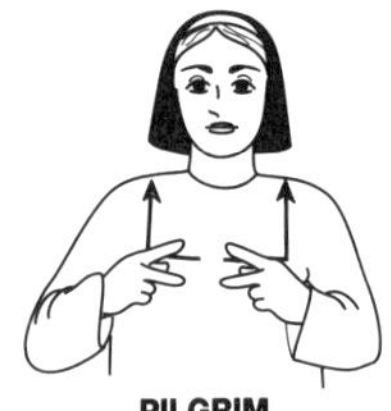

PILGRIM
Middle fingertips of P's on chest move to side, then up chest

PILL
Thumb and finger flick toward mouth *(popping pill in)*
(see VITAMIN)

PILLOW
Rest head on back of left hand; with right pat underside of invisible pillow
(see BED)

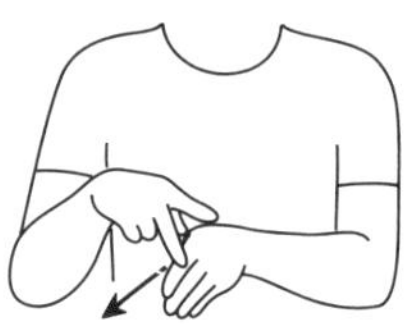

PILOT
Right P middle finger on index of left palm-right B-hand, both hands move diagonally forward
(see LEAD)

PIMPLE
Index finger flicks repeatedly off thumb as hand moves around face
(see MEASLES)

PIN
9-hand "sticks" two invisible pins in right shoulder

PINAFORE
Palm-facing 4's at sides of chest curve down body *(ruffles on pinafore)*

PINCH
Thumb of 9-hand slips past tip of index while resting on back of left hand *(takes a pinch)*

P

PINE ★

Right P fingertips slide down left palm-right vertical arm

PINEAPPLE

Middle finger of right P twists at corner of mouth

(see APPLE)

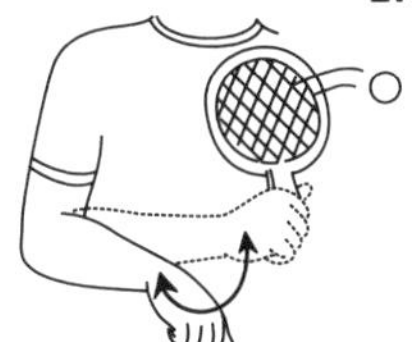

PING-PONG

Right wrist swings A-hand from side-to-side *(holding paddle)*

(see RACKET)

PINK

Middle finger of P brushes down chin

(see RED)

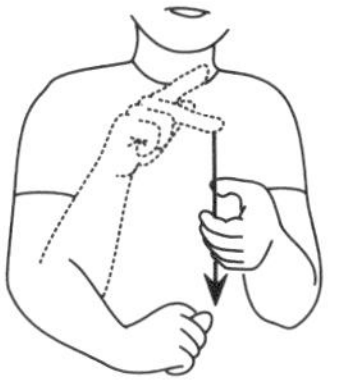

PINT

Right P passes down to T through left horizontal C-hand

(see GALLON)

PIONEER

Middle finger of P from eye arcs down along left palm and forward

(see INSPECT)

PIPE ★

Thumb of Y at mouth

PIRATE

Hand covers right eye from above

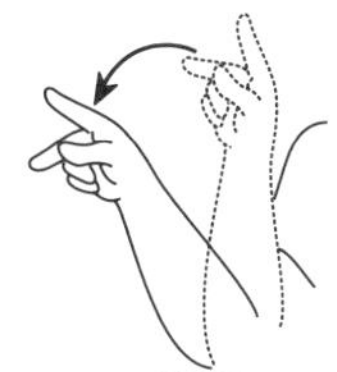

PITCH
(Alt. 1)

P throws forward from near shoulder

(see THROW)

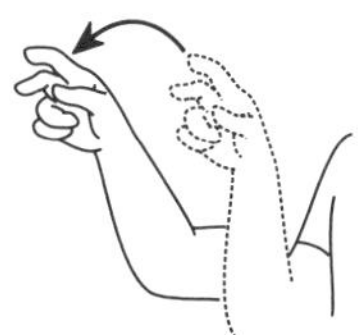

PITCH
(Alt. 2)

Right bent 3-hand throws forward from near shoulder

(see THROW)

PITCHER

Right S-hand pours

PITCHFORK

Tip of left index against wrist of right palm-up claw, both lift backwards

P

PITTSBURGH
9 index and thumb brush down left chest rapidly several times

PITY
Right middle finger strokes the air, hand arcing up and down
(see SYMPATHY)

PIXIE
P's swing off shoulders to sides
(see ANGEL)

PIZZA
(Alt. 1)
P draws a triangle above left palm

PIZZA
(Alt. 2)
Bent-V hand draws Z in air

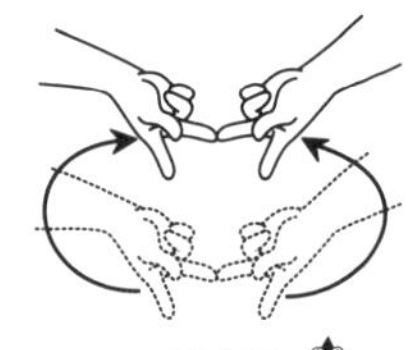

PLACE ♔
Middle fingers of P's touch ahead of you, circle, then touch nearer you

PLAGIARIZE
P at left elbow moves quickly along arm toward wrist
(see STEAL)

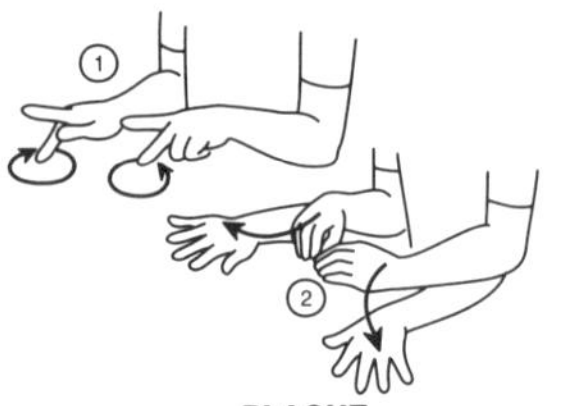

PLAGUE
P's circle, change to flat-O's, spread to 5's which move outward
(see EPIDEMIC)

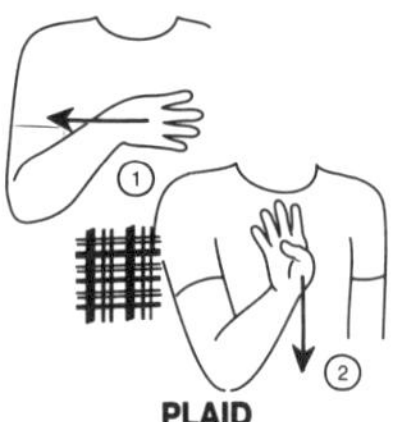

PLAID
With 4-hand, draw plaid on chest, palm-in across; palm-out down
(see SCOT)

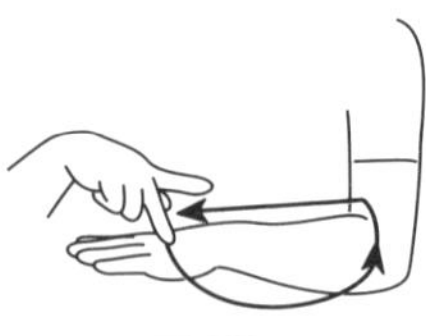

PLAIN
Middle finger of P on back of left hand circles out and back to arm, along arm to hand
(see GROUND)

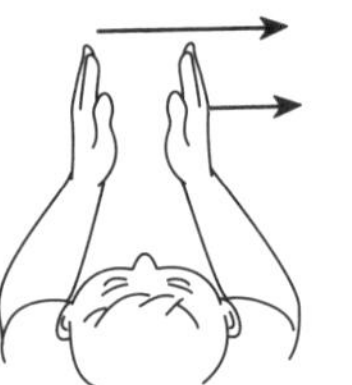

PLAN
Parallel flat hands, palms-facing, move to right

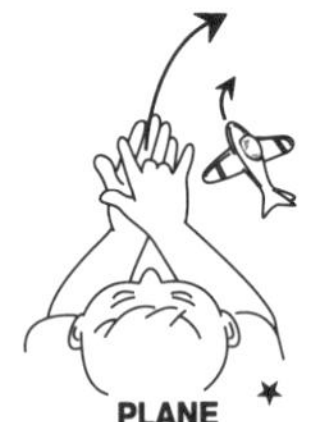

PLANE ★
Palm-down I-L hand on left palm, move right hand forward slightly

PLANET
P vertically circles around left S-hand
(see SATELLITE))

PLANT ★
Flat-O "grows" through horizontal C like a plant into palm-out P
(see GROW)

PLASTER
Left vertical hand, palm-up right P arcs up and in, brushing left palm in passing and ending palm-down
(see PASTE)

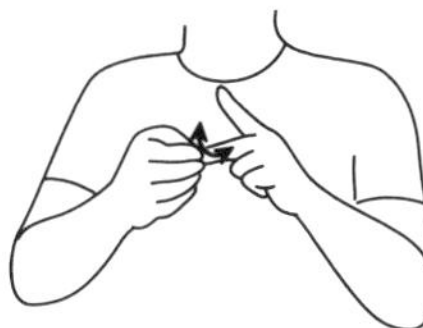

PLASTIC
Grip middle finger of left P and flex back and forth

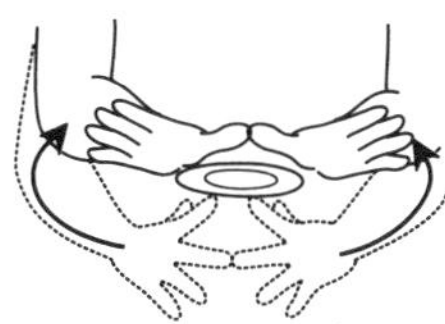

PLATE ★
Middle fingers touch; outline plate with palms, touch thumbs
(see DISH)

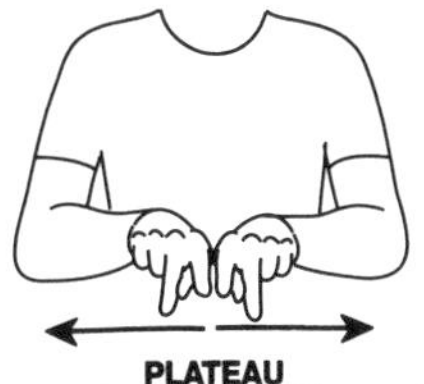

PLATEAU
Sides of palm-down P's touch, separate to sides
(see FLOOR)

PLATTER
Palm-down P makes oval circle around palm-up left hand

PLAY ♔ ★
Y-hands face each other; shake

PLEASE
Palm rubs on chest in circle
(see APPRECIATE)

PLEDGE
Palm-in index at chin to palm-out P on back of left hand
(see PROMISE)

PLENTY
Fingers of right palm-down 5 on top of left S, move off and forward, fingers fluttering

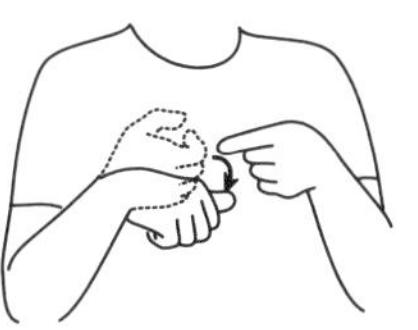

PLIERS
Invisible pliers "tighten" left index

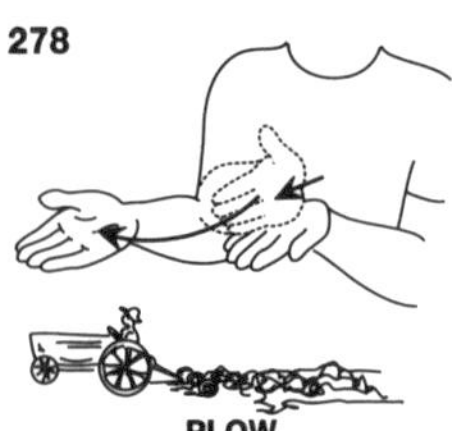

PLOW
Side of flat hand slides along left palm forward to palm-up

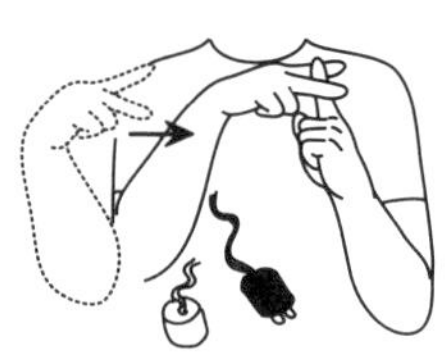

PLUG
Right index and middle finger plug onto vertical left index

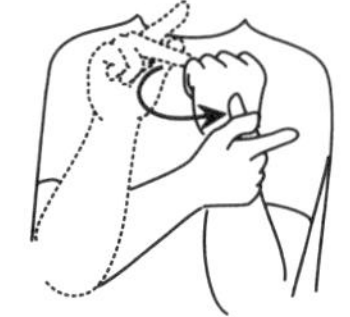

PLUM
Middle finger of right P slices around left palm-in S-hand
(see APRICOT)

PLURAL
P middle fingertip arcs right three times in succession

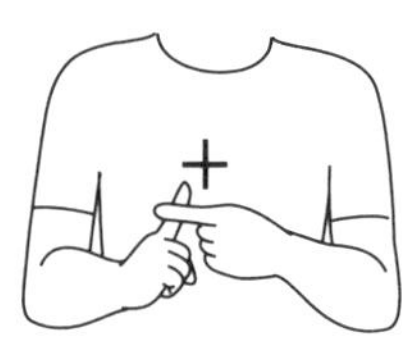

PLUS
Index fingers form plus sign
(see POSITIVE)

PNEUMONIA
Fingertips of bent hands rub up and down chest

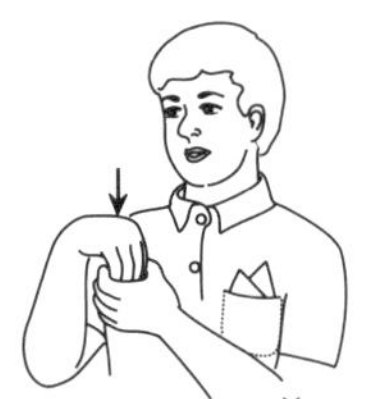

POCKET ★
Right flat-O hand slides into left horizontal C *(put wherever pocket is)*

POEM
Right P arcs behind left palm, ending in palm-out M
(see MUSIC)

POET
Right P arcs behind left palm, ending in palm-out T
(see MUSIC)

POETRY
Right P arcs behind left palm, ending in palm-out Y
(see MUSIC)

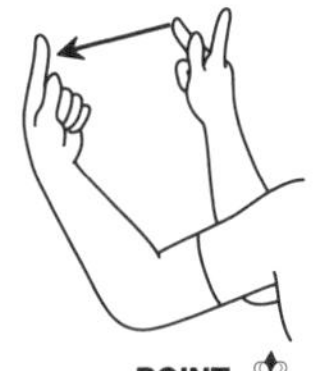

POINT ♔
Middle fingertip of P moves to left index fingertip

POISON
Right P middle finger rubs in circle on left flat palm
(see MEDICINE)

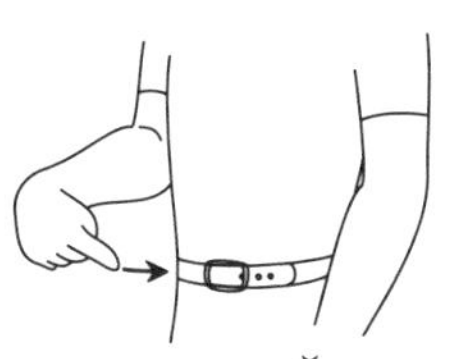

POKE ✶

Right index pokes self in side

POLAND

(Alt.1, *U. S. Sign*)

A-thumb flicks off nose tip; repeat

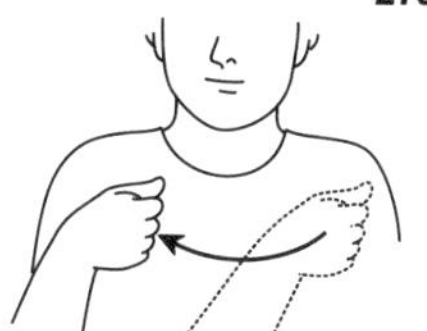

POLAND

(Alt. 2, *Poland Sign*)

Palm-in A-hand touches left side of chest, then right side of chest

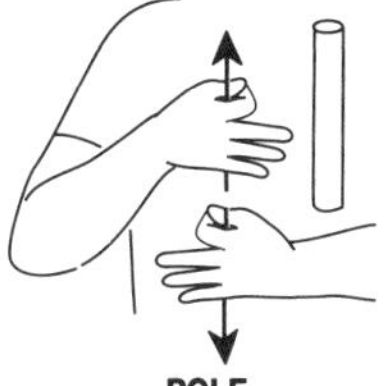

POLE

Palm-in 9's, right above left, separate vertically *(showing shape)*

(see TUBE)

POLICE

Small C shows badge on left shoulder

POLICY

Side of P on fingers of left flat vertical hand, changes to Y on heel

(see LAW)

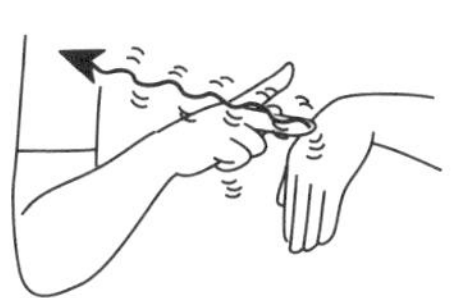

POLISH

(verb)

Middle finger of P-hand rises off back of left hand shaking

(see SHINE)

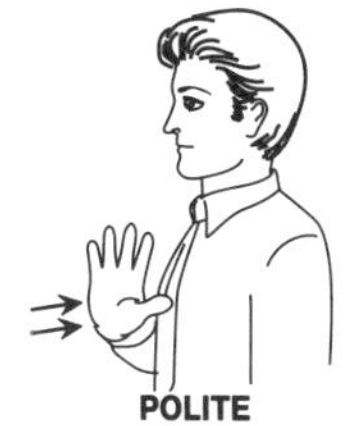

POLITE

Side of thumb of palm-left 5-hand taps chest

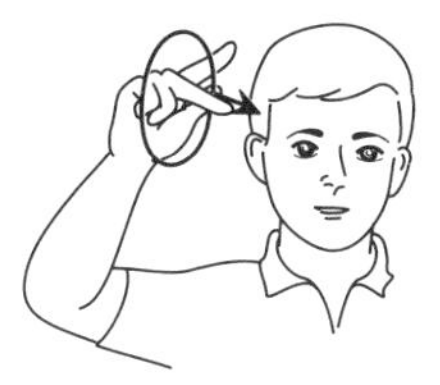

POLITIC

P circles once near temple, then touches temple

(see GOVERN)

POLLUTE

P wiggles under chin

(see DIRT)

PONCHO

Palm-in flat hands brush off shoulders and out

(see DRESS)

POND

Middle fingers of P's touch, separate shaking outward and forward in a circle, touch again

(see LAKE)

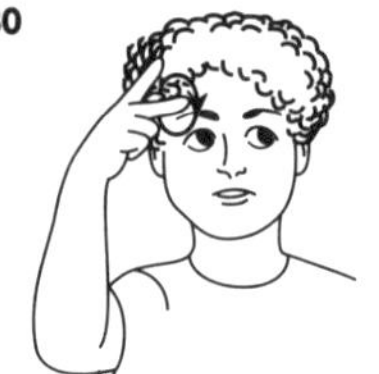

PONDER
Middle finger of P circles on forehead
(see REASON)

PONY
Side of P at temple nods from wrist
(see HORSE)

POOL ★
Back of P arcs down to right across left palm and up again

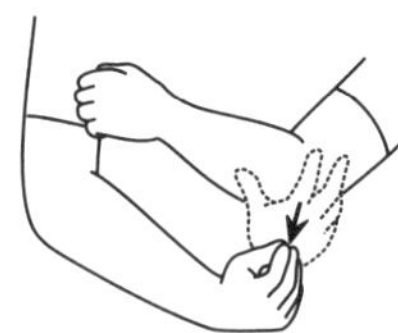

POOR
Right hand grasps left elbow, close to flat-O; may repeat

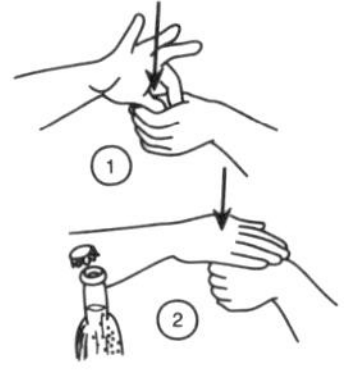

POP
Put 9 inside of left horizontal S, then slap top of S with flat hand

POPCORN
Palm-in S's, indexes flick up alternately

POPSICLE
V-fingertips twice stroke down chin
(see ICE CREAM)

POPULAR
Right claw hand moves to left vertical index finger and taps side of index

POPULATE
Middle fingertip of P brushes across 5 fingers of palm-in left hand

P

PORCH
P's outline form of porch
(see DECK)

PORCUPINE
Back of right 4-hand rests against left S; rotates upward like quills rising

PORK
Thumb and finger of 9 grasp side of left P and shake
(see MEAT)

PORPOISE

Right P moves up and down twice along left arm

(see DOLPHIN)

PORT

Fingertip of P on palm-up left hand arcs up and toward elbow

PORTABLE

Fingertip of P on left hand arcs toward elbow; palm-down A's drop slightly *(port + -able)*

POSITION

P's touch; separate and circle back to N's touching

(see PLACE)

POSITIVE

Index at chin drops to hit left index

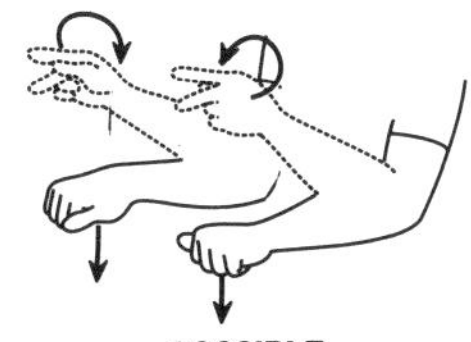

POSSIBLE

(Alt. 1)

P's face each other, twist to palm-down A's; drop slightly

(see ABLE)

POSSIBLE

(Alt. 2)

Palm-down S's move down at wrists; repeat several times

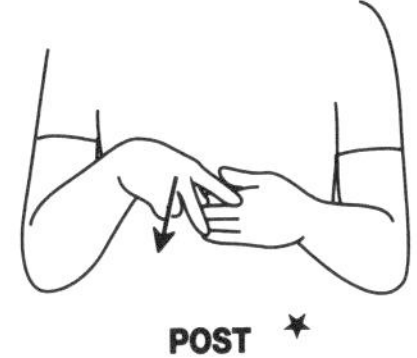

POST

P moves from back of left hand straight forward

(see AFTER)

POSTER

P's outline poster

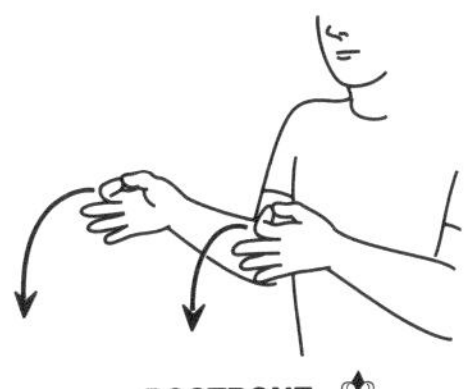

POSTPONE

Palms-facing, horizontal 9's arc forward

POSTURE

Side of palm-down P against vertical left palm, P rises

(see TALL)

POT

P's make shape of pot, palms-facing to palms-down

(see JAR)

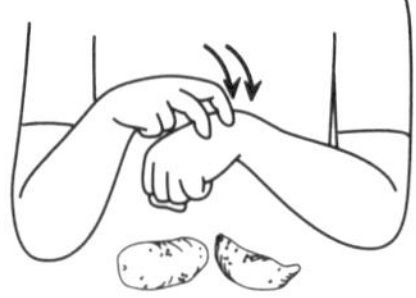

POTATO
Bent 2 fingers tap on back of left S
(see IRELAND)

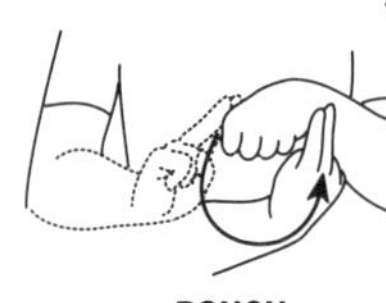

POUCH
Right H draws pouch under palm-down left S-hand
(see BAG)

POUND ✶
Rock middle finger of P on index of horizontal left H-hand
(see WEIGH)

POUR ✶
Extended-A lifts and "pours" into side of left horizontal C

POUT
P's beside mouth pull down
(see GRIM)

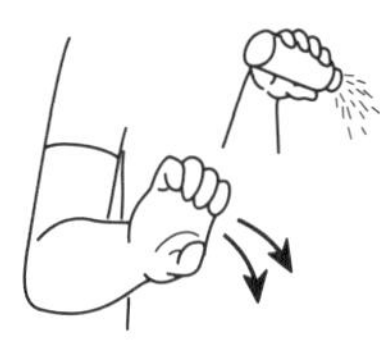

POWDER
C-hand shakes to sprinkle

POWER
Middle finger of right P draws muscle on left arm
(see STRONG)

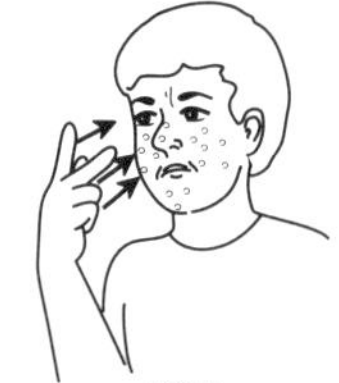

POX
Middle finger of right P-hand makes spots on face
(see MEASLES)

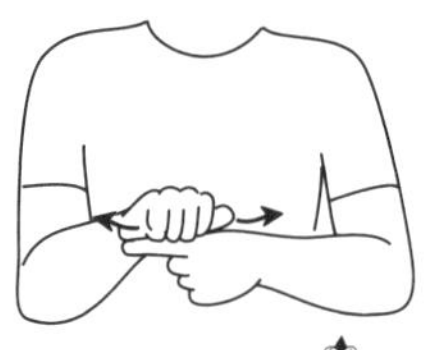

PRACTICE ♔
Palm-down A brushes back and forth on left index

PRAISE
Flat hand on chin, then clap hands
(see COMPLIMENT)

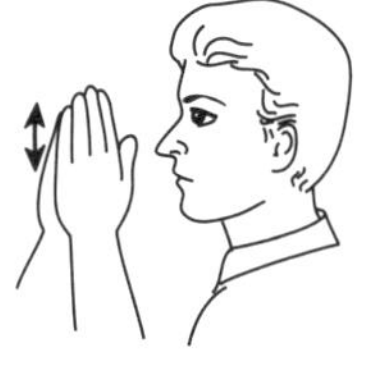

PRAY
Palms-together, hands move slightly up and down before face

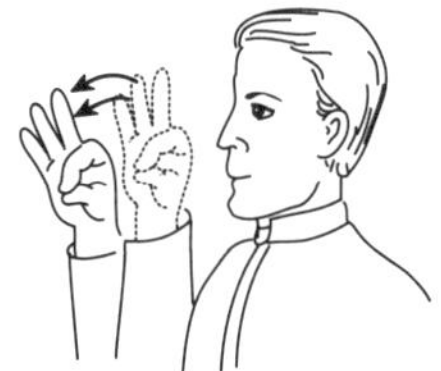

PREACH
Palm-out 9 near side of head jerks slightly forward; repeat
(see LECTURE)

P

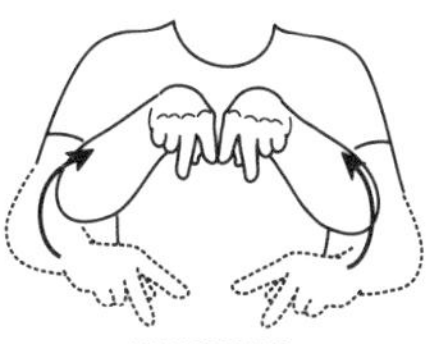

PRECIOUS
Palm-down P's arc up and touch
(see IMPORTANT)

PRECIPITATE
P's move down in small jerks
(see RAIN)

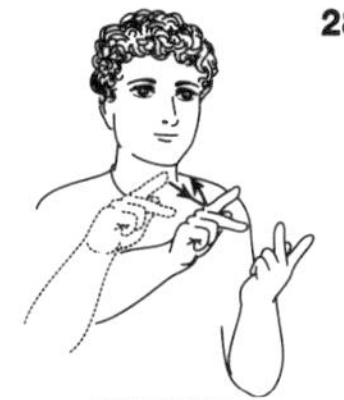

PRECISE
Palm-in left P, palm-out right P, right jerks slightly toward left and recoils
(see POINT)

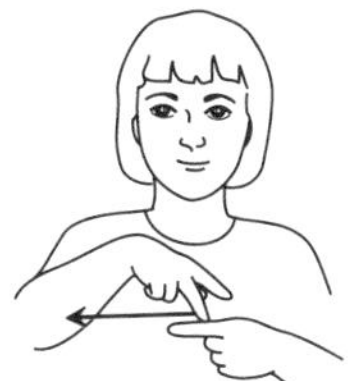

PREDICATE
Middle fiingertip of P on horizontal left index, slides off to right

PREDICT
Palm-in V, from eye, arcs under left hand and up
(see PROPHECY)

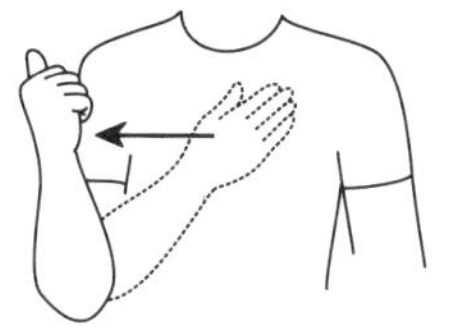

PREFER
Flat hand on chest closes sideways to a palm-in A-hand

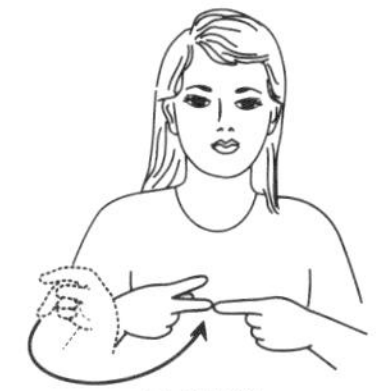

PREFIX
Left horizontal index points right; right P arcs left to touch tip of left index
(see AFFIX)

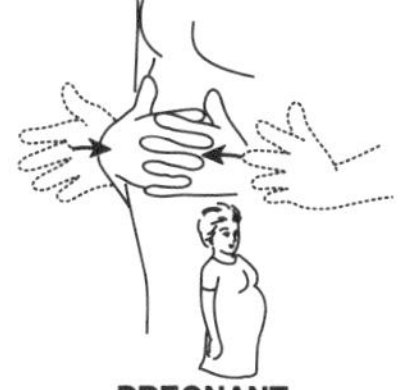

PREGNANT
Fingers of 5-hands mesh

PREJUDICE
Middle fingertip of P hits left palm
(see AGAINST)

PREMIER
Palm-down P at forehead moves out to palm-out R
(see FOR)

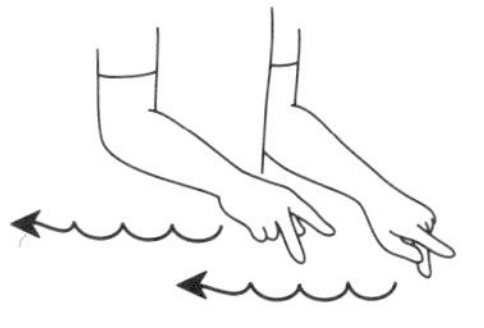

PREPARE
Parallel palm-down P's move to right in small downward arcs

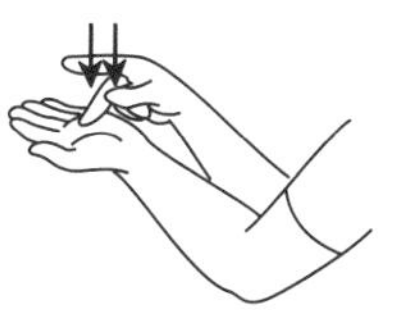

PRESBYTERIAN
Middle finger of right P taps on left palm-up hand
(see LUTHERAN)

PRESCRIBE
Middle fingertip of P at chin, swings outward to touch horizontal left palm

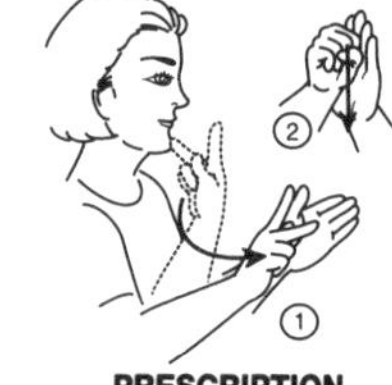

PRESCRIPTION
Middle finger of P at chin, swings outward to touch horizontal left palm; side of right S slides down vertical left palm *(prescribe + -tion)*

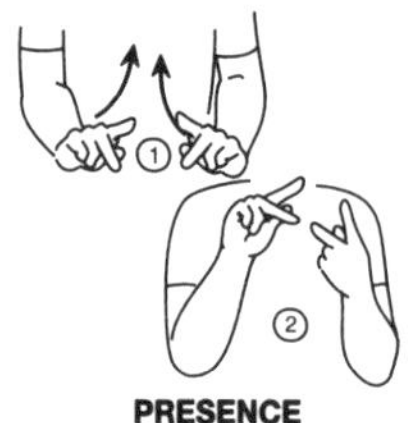

PRESENCE
P's swing up to face each other before chin, right slightly before left
(see CONFRONT)

PRESENT
P-hands, palms-facing but turned slightly upwards drop slightly

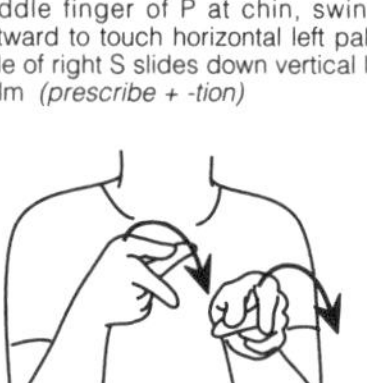

PRESENT
(verb)
P's left behind right, with indexes pointing forward, arc forward and up
(see SUGGEST)

PRESERVE
Fingers of V tap back of left P–hand
(see SAVE)

P

PRESIDENT
Palm-out C's at temples rise to sides, closing to S's
(see SUPERINTENDENT)

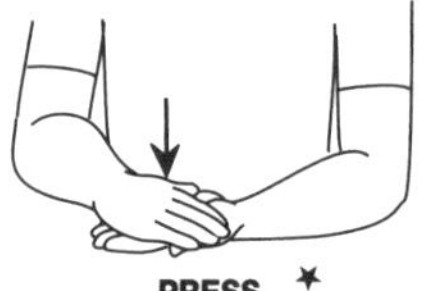

PRESS ★
Palms press together, right hand on top at right angles

PRETEND
Side of P brushes across chin; repeat
(see FALSE)

PRETTY
Middle fingertip of P circles face
(see FACE)

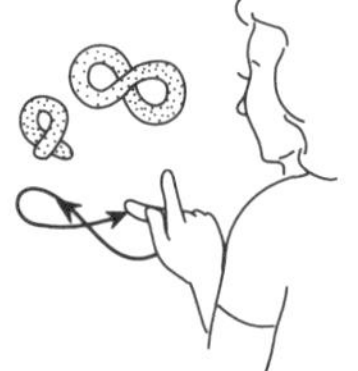

PRETZEL
Palm-down right P draws a figure 8

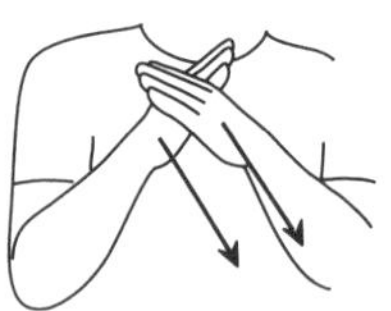

PREVENT
Crossed flat hands move forward
(see GUARD)

PRICE
Middle fingertip of P strikes downward on left palm
(see COST)

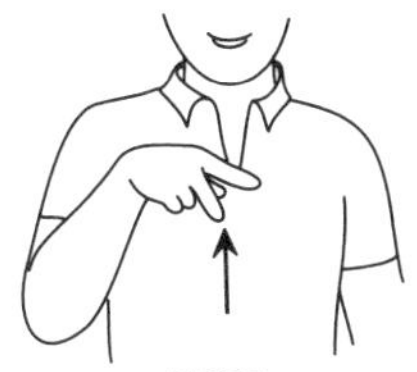

PRIDE
Middle finger of P draws up chest
(see FEEL)

PRIEST
Side of G-hand slides across neck

PRIMARY
P circles under left palm; add R then Y *(prime + -ar + -y)*

PRIME
P circles under left palm
(see BASE)

PRIME MINISTER
Palm-out P at forehead moves out to palm-down M
(see FOR)

PRINCE
P-hand touches left shoulder, then right side of body near waist
(see CHRIST)

PRINCESS
P-hand arcs from left to right shoulder, then drops down trunk

PRINCIPAL
Middle finger of right P circles over, drops on back of left palm-down S

PRINCIPLE
Side of right P on left fingers of vertical flat hand, then on heel
(see LAW)

PRINT ★
Right G-hand, slightly above left palm, drops and closes on left palm
(see IMPRINT)

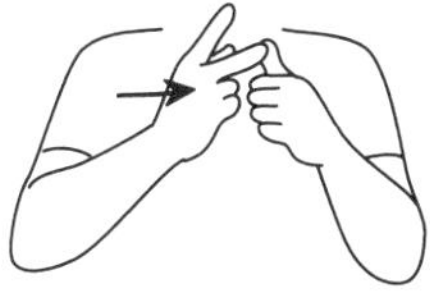

PRIOR
Middle fingertip of right P taps left extended-A thumb
(see FIRST)

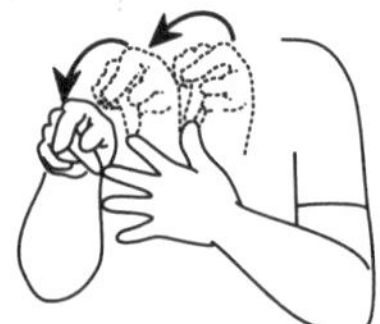

PRIORITY
Palm-in left 5, pointing right; middle finger of palm-out right P bounces off thumb, index, and middle fingers
(see CRITERIA)

PRISON
5-hands right behind left; right hits left
(see JAIL)

PRIVATE
Index of palm-out P taps lips
(see SECRET)

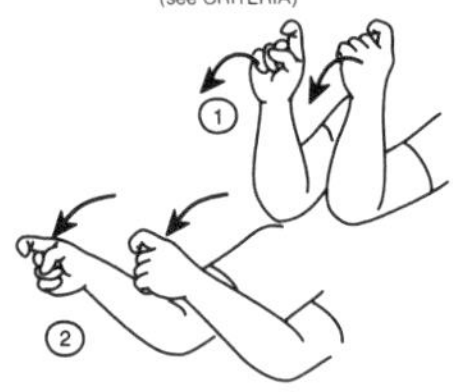

PRIZE
X-hands, palms-facing, right ahead of left, drop to the right
(see GIFT)

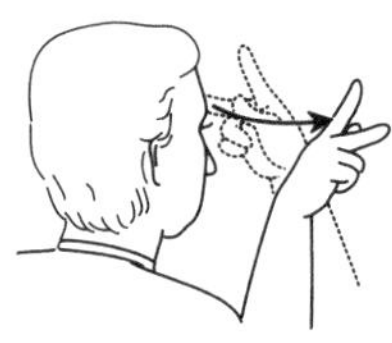

PRO
Middle fingertip of P on forehead twists to palm-out
(see FOR)

PROBABLE
Horizontal P-hands face each other; raise and lower alternately
(see BALANCE)

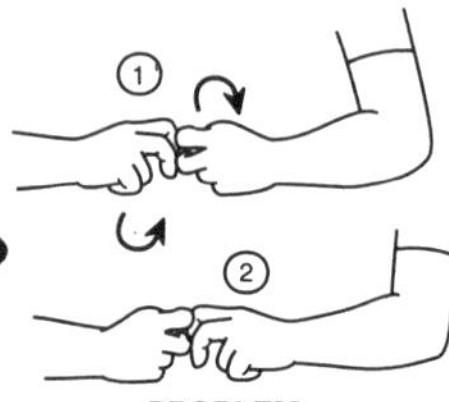

PROBLEM
Bent-V's, knuckles touching with right palm-up, left palm-down; twist to reverse position
(see HARD)

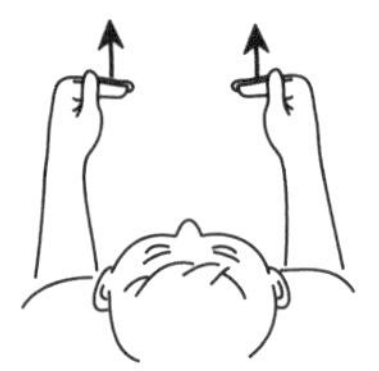
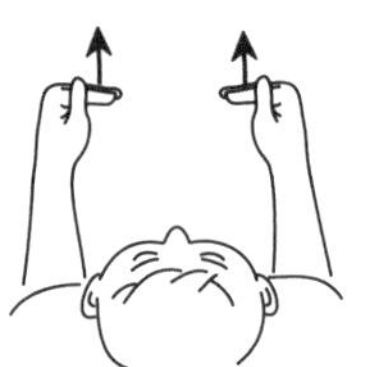

PROCEED
Palms-facing bent hands in front of body move forward

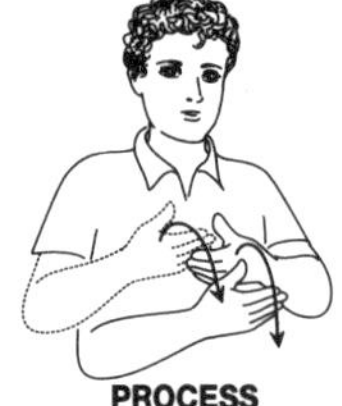

PROCESS
Horizontal bent hands, right behind left; right hops forward over left, then left hops forward over right

PROCLAIM
From corners of mouth, P's swing out
(see ANNOUNCE)

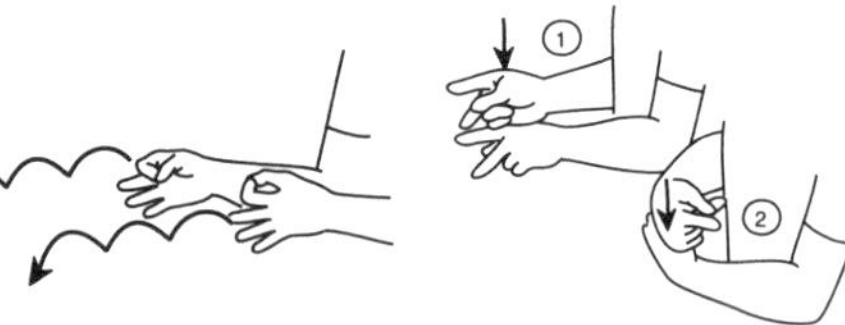

PROCRASTINATE
9's palms-facing, together both hands arc forward several times
(see POSTPONE)

PRODUCE
Touch right P on left, twist hands to palm-in and touch again
(see MAKE)

PROFANE
Middle finger of palm-in P touches lips, twists out and throws down
(see BAD)

PROFESS
Middle fingertip of P slides forward on side of left flat hand

PROFESSION
Middle finger of P slides forward on side of left hand; right S slides down vertical left hand *(profess + -tion)*

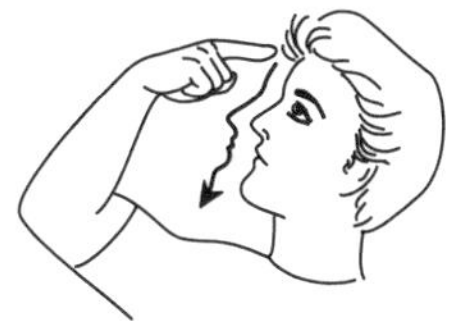

PROFILE
Index finger traces profile
(see HANDSOME)

PROFIT
Side of palm-down 9 on body near waist; slide down

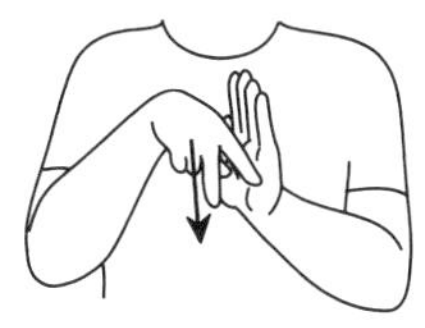

PROFOUND
Side of right P slides down left palm-right vertical hand
(see DEEP)

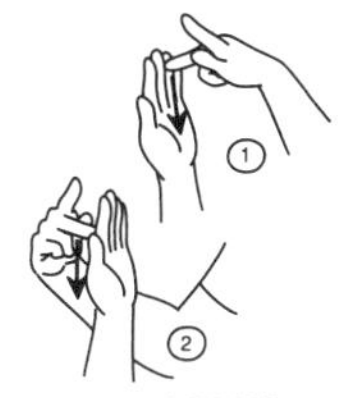

PROGRAM
Middle fingertip of P-hand moves down palm-in left hand, then down back of hand
(see PROJECT)

PROGRESS
Bent hands circle over each other several times while moving forward

PROHIBIT
Side of right P strikes sharply against vertical left palm
(see FORBID)

P

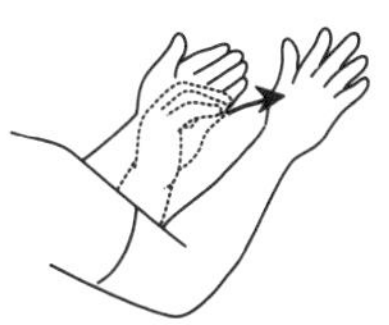

PROJECT
(verb)
Side of right flat-O against left palm, moves forward and opens

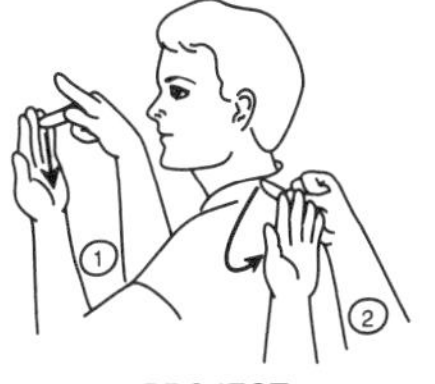

PROJECT
(noun)
P moves down left vertical palm, then makes J on back
(see PROGRAM)

PROLOGUE
Both P-hands swing inward to touch middle fingertips
(see INTRODUCE)

PROMISE

Index from chin, to rest flat hand against top of left hand

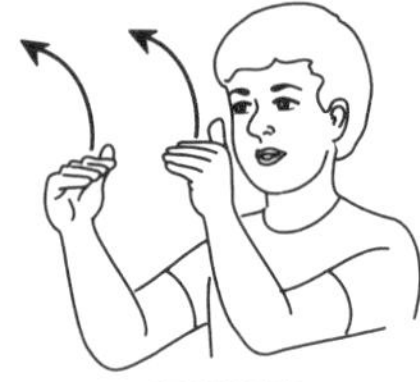

PROMOTE

Bent hands, face each other; arc in and up

(see ADVANCE)

PRONOUN
(Alt. 1)

Right palm-down P touches side of H, changes to N

(see WORD)

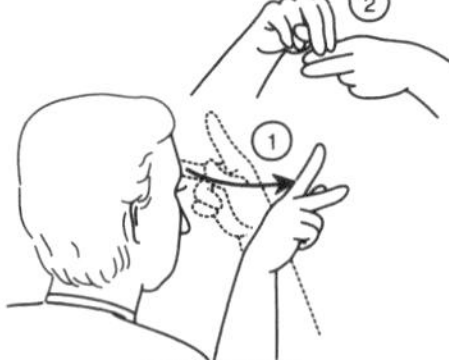

PRONOUN
(Alt. 2)

Middle fingertip of P on forehead twists to palm-out; fingertips of N tap index side of left H *(pro + noun)*

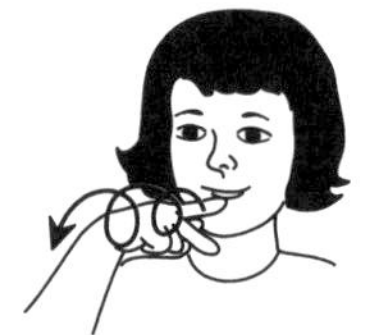

PRONOUNCE

Palm-down P, pointing left, circles out from mouth

PROOF

Back of F drops onto left palm

(see PROVE)

PROPAGANDA

Right P in front of left palm-right S; P shakes forward

(see EXAGGERATE)

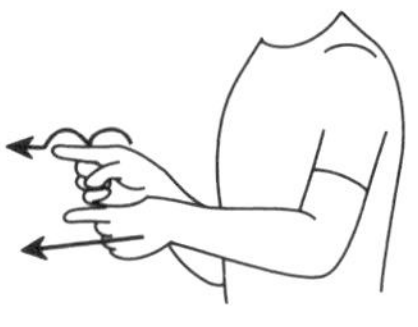

PROPER

Right 1-hand above left 1-hand, both pointing forward; right hand hits left several times; both move forward

PROPERTY

Palm-up flat hand circles outward to right, changes to palm-down and circles left and back

PROPHECY

P from eye arcs under left P and up

(see PREDICT)

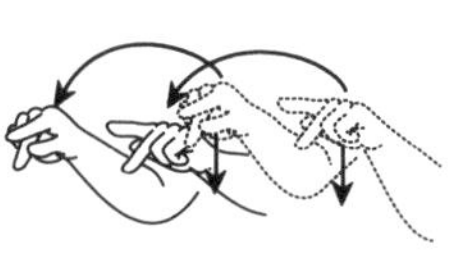

PROPORTION

Parallel P-hands move slightly down, back up and to the right, and slightly down again

PROSE

Middle finger of P moves in wavy motion down across left palm

(see READ)

PROSTITUTE
Palm-in bent hand, side of little finger against cheek, fingertips brush up cheek and forward; repeat

PROTECT
P's, left behind right, both move forward, not touching
(see GUARD)

PROTESTANT
Bent-V knuckles tap twice on palm-up left flat palm
(see LUTHERAN)

PROTON
Left extended-A, palm-down; right P circles near left thumb
(see ATOM)

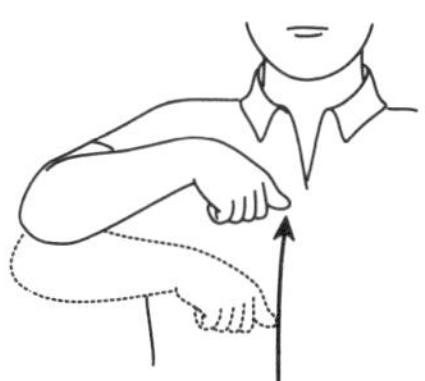

PROUD
Palm-down right extended-A thumb draws upward on chest
(see FEEL)

PROVE
Back of right V drops onto left palm

PROVERB
P's together; slide out and slightly up to bent-V's that twist inward
(see QUOTE)

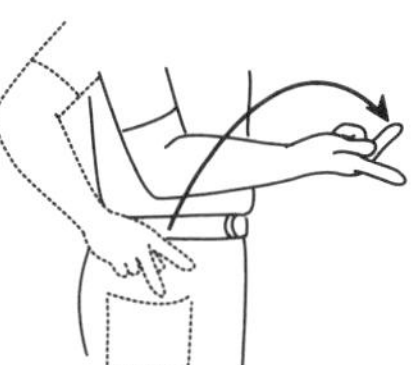

PROVIDE
P rises out of pocket and twists forward to palm-up
(see CONTRIBUTE)

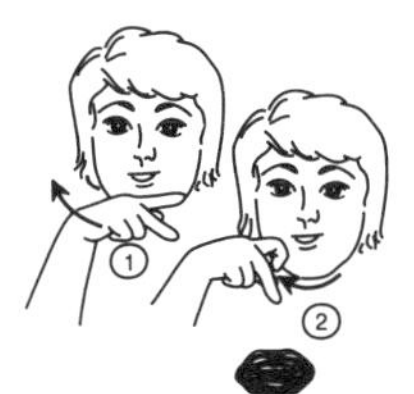

PRUNE
P draws across chin, index crooking
(see DRY)

PSYCHIATRY
Middle finger of right P taps left wrist
(see DOCTOR)

PSYCHOLOGY
Little finger of flat right hand taps left thumb joint from behind; repeat

PTERANODON
Both palm-out P hands fly

P

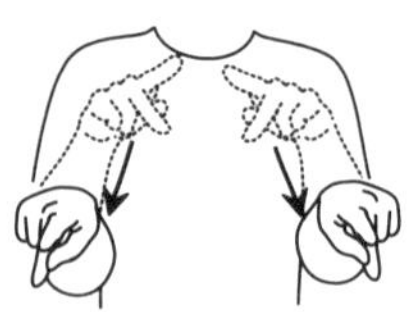

PUBLIC
P's move out and forward
(see BROAD)

PUBLICITY
Right P in front of left palm-right S; P pushes forward like a trombone; repeat rapidly
(see ADVERTISE)

PUDDING
Right palm-up P-hand ladles up to mouth twice from left palm
(see SOUP)

PUDDLE
P outlines puddle in wavy circle on back of left hand
(see LAKE)

PUFF ★
P at mouth moves out to F

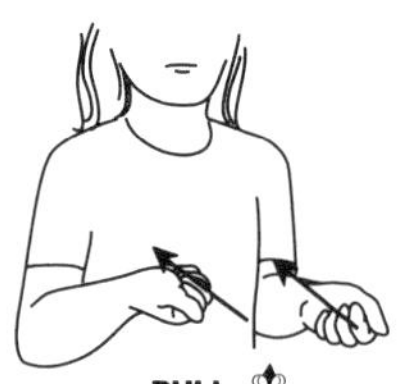

PULL ♔
Palm-up A-hands pull toward body

PULSE
Flat hand fingers grasp palm-up left wrist, thumb on bottom
(see DOCTOR)

PUMP
Right inverted A pumps up and down next to left palm-down S-hand

PUMPKIN
Middle finger of P taps on back of left palm-down S-hand
(see MELON)

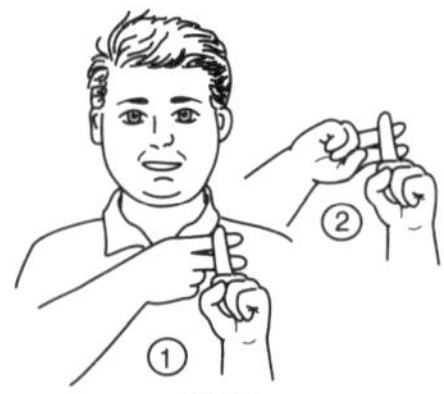

PUN
Right horizontal palm-in V fingers against vertical left index; right reverses to palm-out and touches left index again

PUNCH ★
Right P, slightly behind left palm-right index, moves forward to hit index with middle finger
(see BEAT)

PUNCTUATE
Fingertips of right P-hand jerks toward left palm
(see MARK)

PUNISH
Index finger strikes down on left elbow

PUPIL
Side of P brushes off left palm twice

PUPPET
Closed X-hands, palm-down, move alternately up and down *(pulling strings on puppet)*

PUPPY
Right P-thumb is rubbed by right middle finger several times
(see DOG)

PURCHASE
Back of right palm-up P moves forward off left palm
(see BUY)

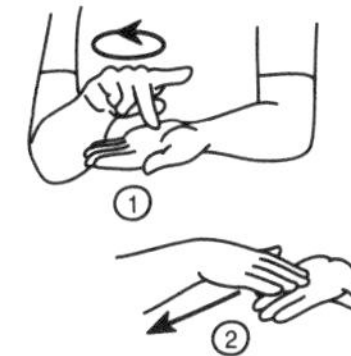

PURE
P circles over left palm, then flat hand wipes off left palm
(see HOLY)

PURPLE
Right P shakes from wrist
(see BLUE)

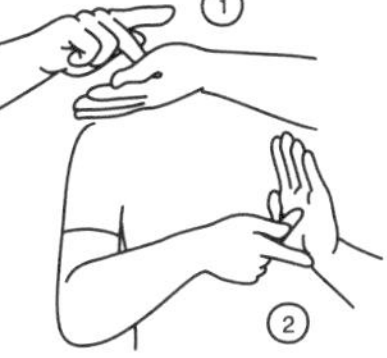

PURPOSE
Middle fingertip of P on left palm, both hands twist and touch again
(see MEAN)

PURR
Horizontal R vibrates near throat

P

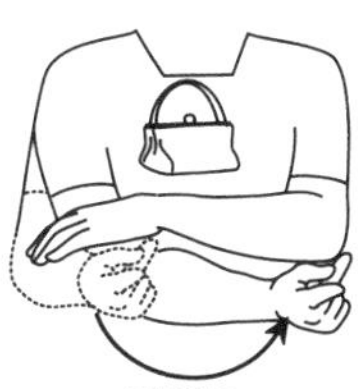

PURSE
Right P draws bag under left arm
(see BASKET)

PURSUE
Right P behind left A, both move forward left, P circling slightly
(see CHASE)

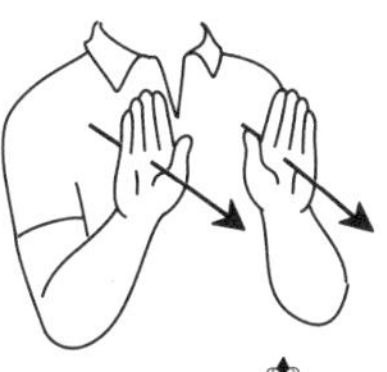

PUSH ♔
Palm-out flat hands push forward

PUT
Palm-out flat-O moves forward to put something down
(see INSTALL)

PUZZLE
Palm-out index finger jerks back to an X on forehead

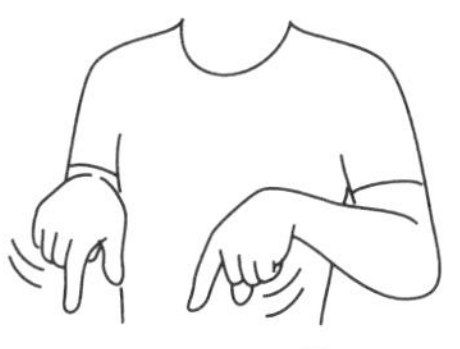

QUAKE ✶
Both Q-hands shake

QUAKER
Clasp hands and rotate thumbs

QUALIFICATION
Q circles slightly then touches near right side of chest; S slides down vertical left palm *(qualify + -tion)*

QUALIFY
Palm-down Q circles slightly near right side of chest, touches chest
(see CHARACTER)

QUALITY
Palm-down Q circles slightly, touches vertical left palm near side of chest
(see ROLE)

QUANTITY
Fingertips of palm-down Q touch heel of horizontal left palm, arc to touch back of Q on fingertips of left palm
(see AMOUNT)

QUARREL
Index fingers point to each other, move rapidly side-to-side
(see WAR)

QUART
Right Q passes to T down through left horizontal C
(see GALLON)

QUARTER
Index of palm-in L at temple moves out slightly, flutter last 3 fingers together of palm-in 25
(see CENT)

QUEEN
Right Q on left shoulder, then on right side of body
(see CHRIST)

QUEER
Right palm-left Q arcs in front of eyes to palm-down
(see STRANGE)

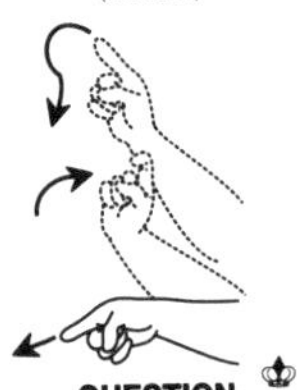

QUESTION
Flick a question-mark: 1 back to X, and forward to point with index finger

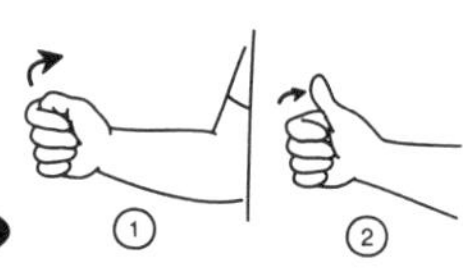

QUICK
Thumb inside right fist, snaps out

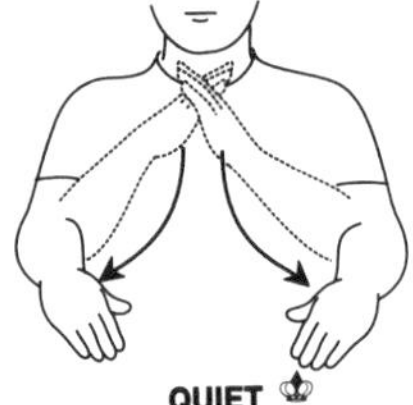

QUIET
Flat hands cross under chin and separate downwards

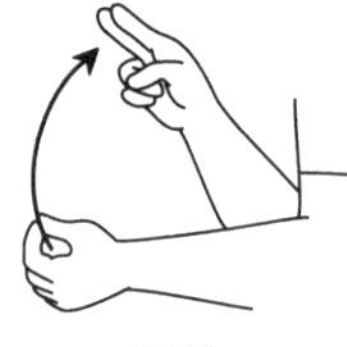

QUIT
H-fingertips in O; pull out and up
(see OUT)

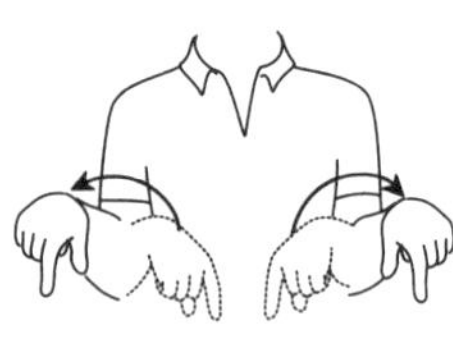

QUITE
Palm-down Q's separate and arc to the sides
(see MUCH)

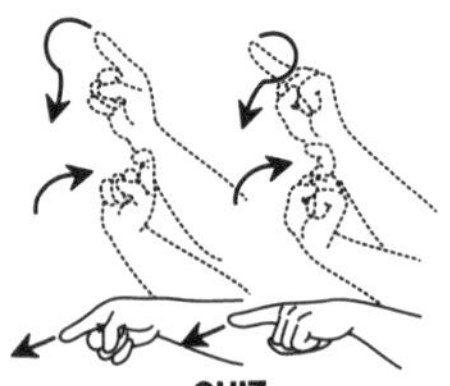

QUIZ
Flick "question" 1 back to X and forward to point with both hands
(see QUESTION)

QUOTE
Bent V's twist slightly, outlining quotation marks; may repeat

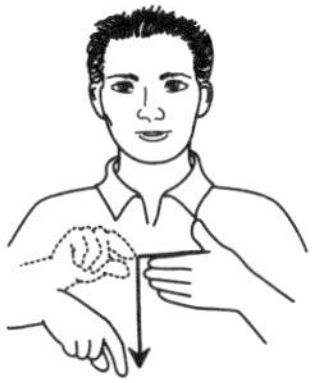

QUOTIENT

Q points forward, slides right on side of horizontal left palm-in hand and down end of hand, ending in palm-down Q

(see FINISH)

NOTES

RABBI

Palm-in R-hands outline prayer-shawl down chest

RABBIT

Palm-in U-fingers at temples wiggle backward together

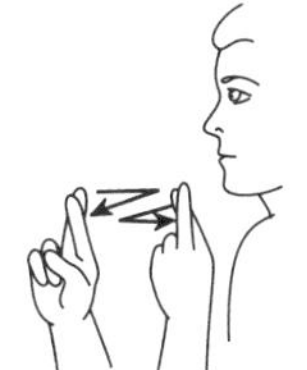

RACE

Vertical R's, palms-facing; move alternately forward and back

(see COMPETE)

RACCOON

R's outline bottom of mask

RACK

Palm-down R's at head level separate, drawing shelf

(see SHELF)

RACKET/RACQUET

R swings back and forth at wrist, hitting ball

(see PINGPONG)

RADAR
Right R points downward above horizontal left C and circles with wrist movement only

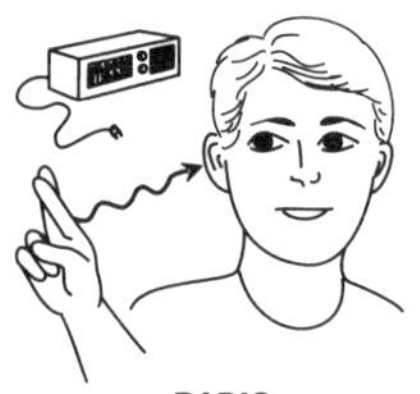

RADIO
Right R rises from side to ear, shaking slightly
(see SOUND)

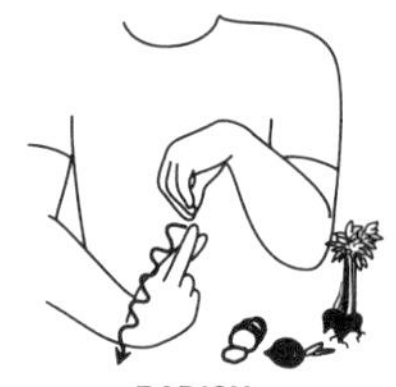

RADISH
R shakes down from fingertips of left palm-down flat-O

RADIUS
Palm-down R near palm-right left C, R moves slightly right
(see DIAMETER)

RAFT
Right flat hand on left floats forward with wavy motion
(see DRIFT)

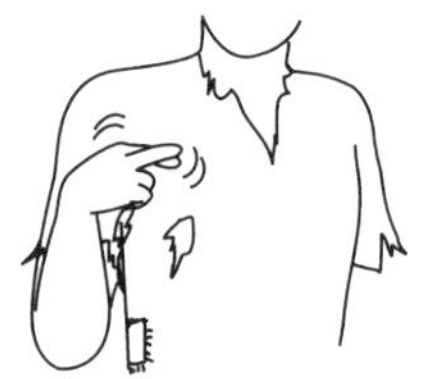

RAG
Right R-fingertips rub on chest near right shoulder

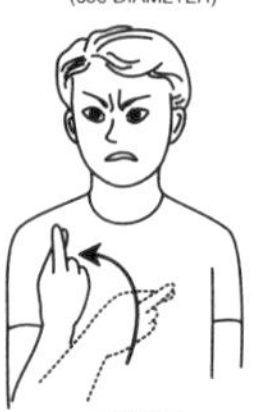

RAGE
Palm-in R near stomach jerks up to near shoulder
(see ANGER)

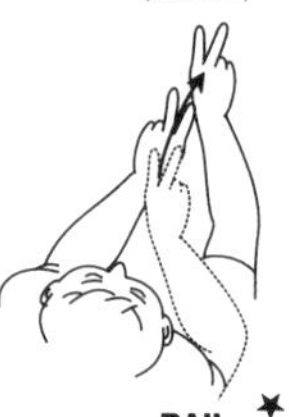

RAIL ★
Right palm-down V-hand slides forward off left palm-down V-hand
(see TRACK)

RAIN
Both palm-down claw-hands drop sharply; repeat
(see SNOW)

RAINBOW
(Alt.1)
Palm-in 4 at left arcs overhead to right
(see SKY)

RAINBOW
(Alt. 2)
Palm-down claw hands drop sharply; palm-in S-hands arc up to V-hands *(rain + bow)*

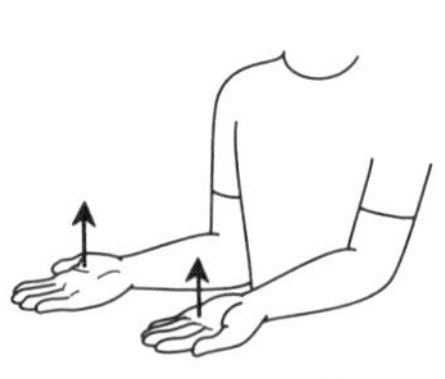

RAISE ★
Palm-up flat hands rise

R

RAISIN
R hops down back of S-hand
(see GRAPE)

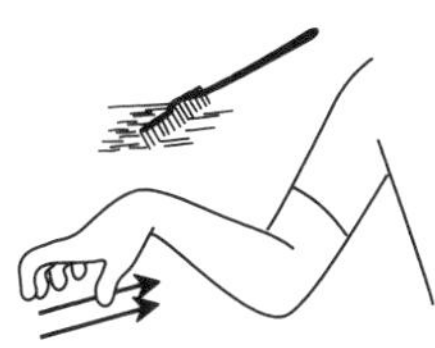

RAKE
Claw hand rakes several times

RAM ★
R's circle back like horns from temples

RAMP
Palm-down right R on top of palm-down flat left hand, slopes off to side

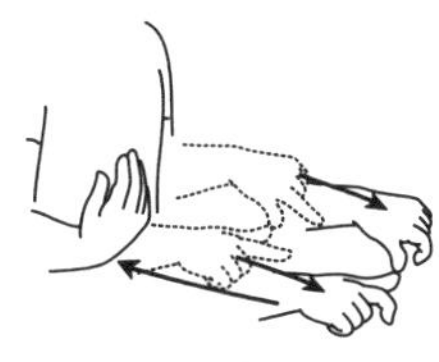

RAN
(Alt. 1)
Palm-down L-thumbtips touch; index fingers flick while hands move forward; right hand flips back *(run + p. t.)*

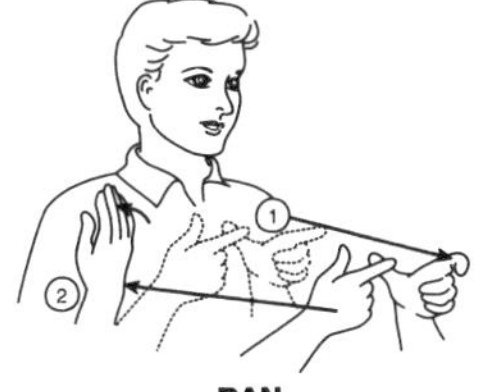

RAN
(Alt. 2)
Index of right L hooked around thumb of left L, move forward, left index wiggling; right hand flips back *(run + p. t.)*

RANCH
Extended thumb of R moves under chin, left to right
(see FARM)

RANGE
R circles over left arm
(see GROUND)

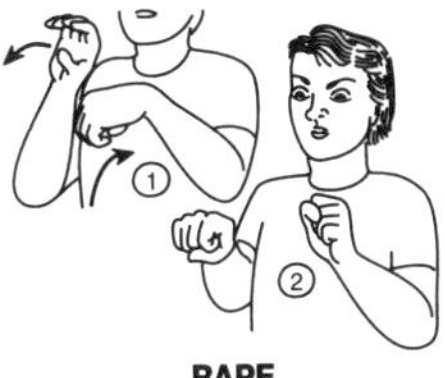

RAPE
Palm-out C's; right slides past left as both close to S's

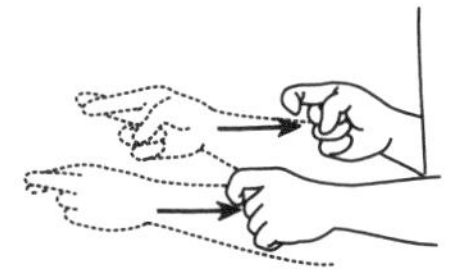

RAPID
Horizontal R's, left ahead of right, jerk back into X's
(see FAST)

RARE
Back of R slides off left palm toward the right

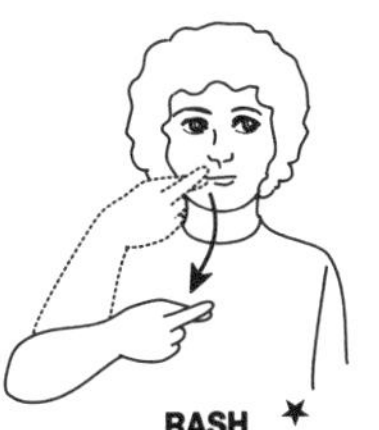

RASH ★
Horizontal palm-in R brushes down lips, slightly inward to touch chest

RAT
R brushes past nose; repeat
(see MOUSE)

RATE
Fingertips of right R-hand tap palm-up left hand

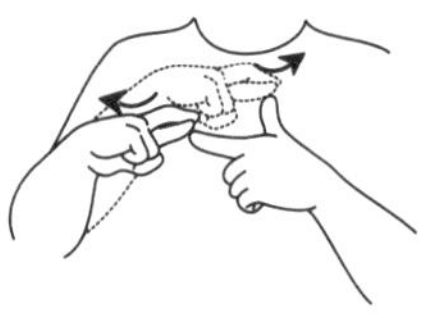

RATHER
Fingertips of palm-down R bounces off left L-thumb, then to fingertip
(see THEN)

RATTLE
Right R-hand shakes

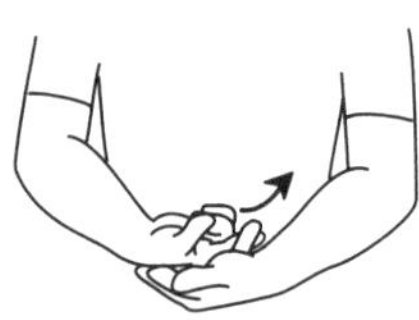

RAW
Palm-up R arcs left across palm
(see NEW)

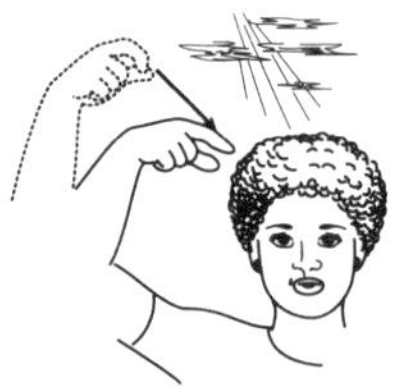

RAY
Thumb and index of closed G point at head from above right, move toward head and open

RAZOR
Side of slightly bent R-fingers brushes off cheek (in shaving motion); repeat
(see SHAVE)

REACH
Back of R approaches left palm
(see ARRIVE)

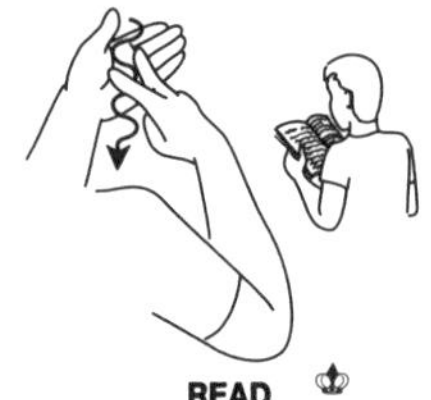

READ ♔
(present tense)
Right palm-down V-fingertips move down left palm-in palm in wavy motion

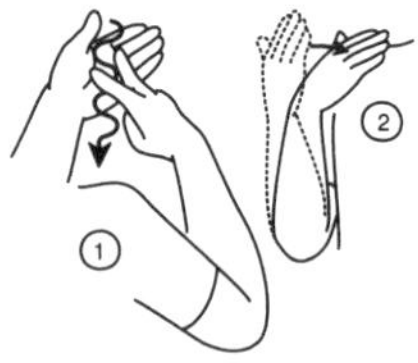

READ
(past tense)
Right palm-down V-fingertips move down left palm with wavy motion; then flat hand flips toward shoulder

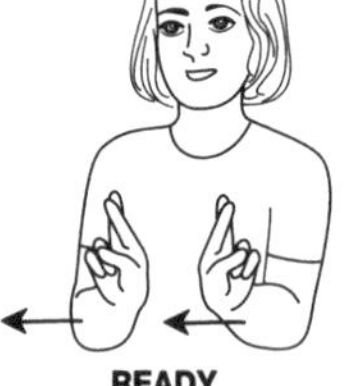

READY
Both R-hands move to the right

REAL
(Alt.1)
Fingertips of right R slide across palm-up left hand

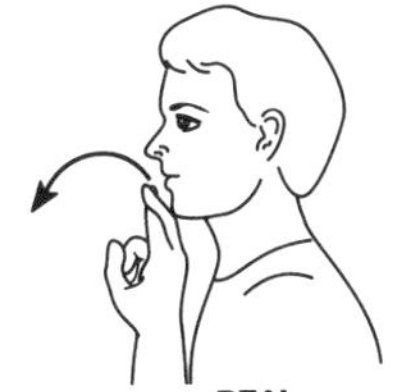

REAL
(Alt. 2)
R at lips arcs up and forward
(see CERTAIN)

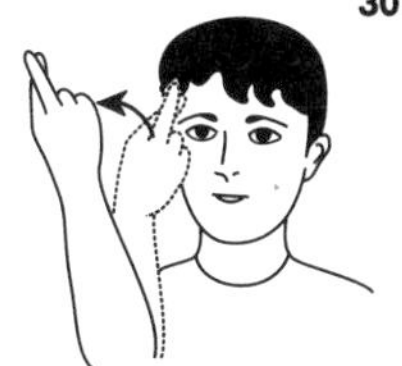

REALIZE
R on forehead twists up and forward from wrist ending palm-up
(see UNDERSTAND)

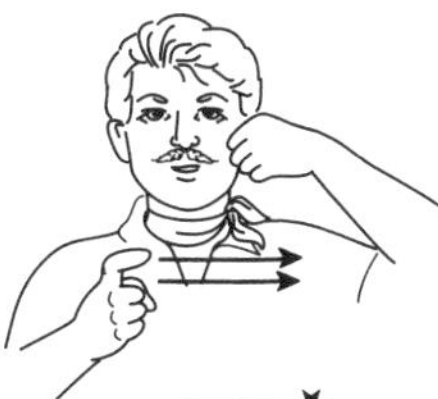

REAP ✶
Left palm-in horizontal S held at head level, right horizontal X sweeps under left hand

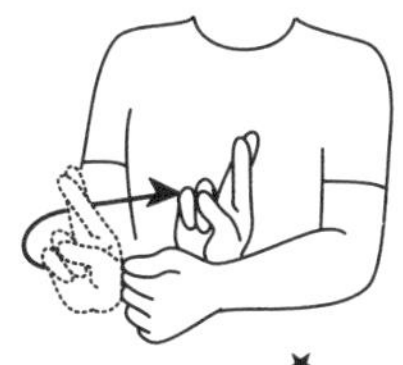

REAR ✶
Right palm-out R, next to left A, arcs outward and back to end behind A
(see HIND)

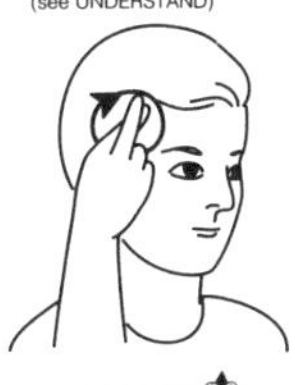

REASON ♔
R-fingertips circle near temple

REBEL ♔
(verb)
Palm-in S turns quickly to palm-out S

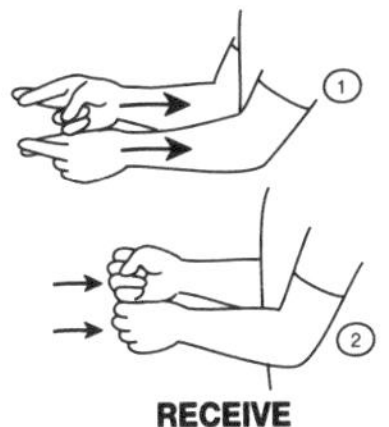

RECEIVE
Right R on left R, pull both toward body, closing to S's
(see GET)

RECENT
Side of X-hand on cheek, palm-in; wiggle finger

RECESS
R-hands face each other and swing back and forth, pivoting at wrists
(see PLAY)

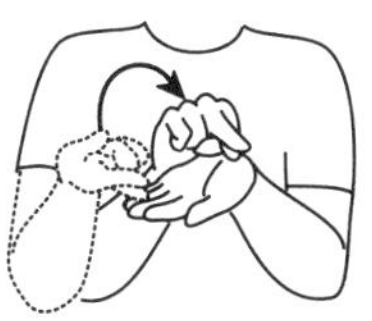

RECIPE
Right palm-up R on left palm, flips to palm-down
(see PAGE)

RECOGNIZE
R at eye drops to palm of left hand
(see NOTE)

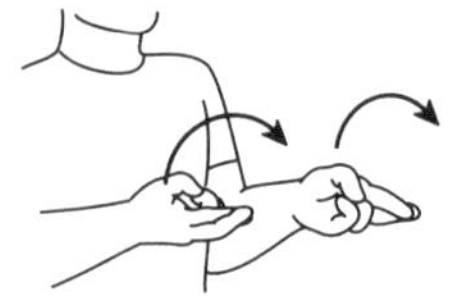

RECOMMEND
Both palm-up R-hands, move forward and slightly up
(see SUGGEST)

RECORD
(verb)
Right R-fingers write across left palm
(see WRITE)

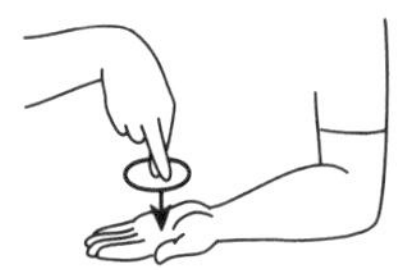

RECORD
(noun)
Tip of inverted right R circles above, drops on left palm

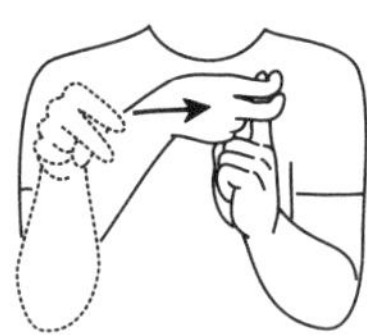

RECRUIT
Right bent V-fingers grab index

RECTANGLE
R's outline rectangle
(see SQUARE)

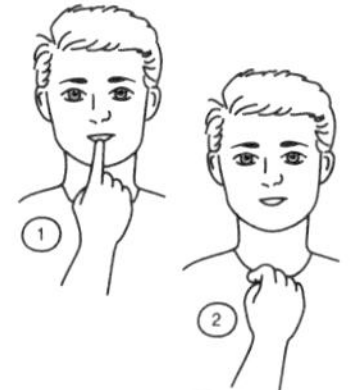

RED
Palm-in, index finger touches lip. brushes down and closes
(see PINK)

REDUCE
Right flat hand descends in stages above left flat hand

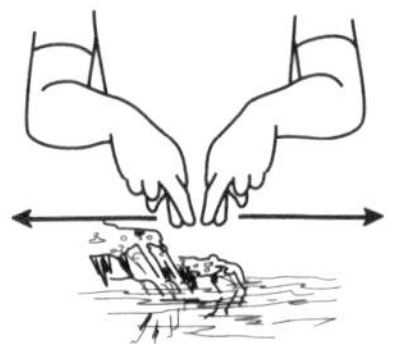

REEF
R's point downwards; fingers touch, then separate sideways
(see FLOOR)

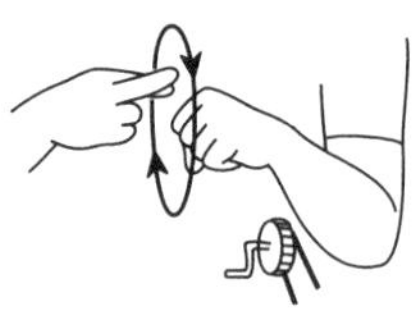

REEL ★
Right R circles around left S
(see SPOOL)

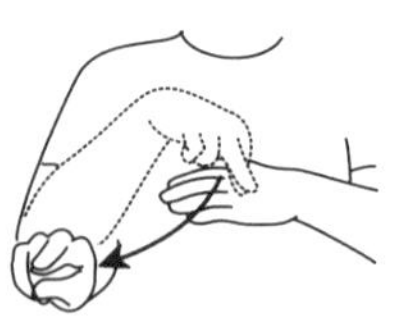

REFER
Right palm-down R on back of flat left hand swings outward
(see SEND)

REFEREE
Palm-out R-hands move alternately up and down
(see BALANCE)

REFLECT
Fingertips of right R hits left palm-in hand and reflects back, palm-in

R

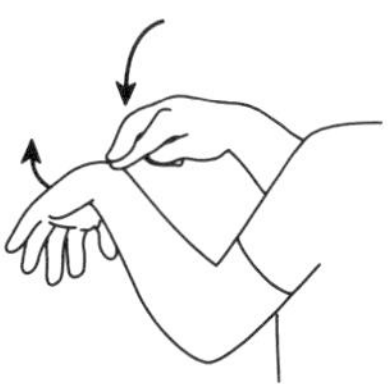

REFLEX
Right R taps on wrist of limp left hand causing a reflex up-flip

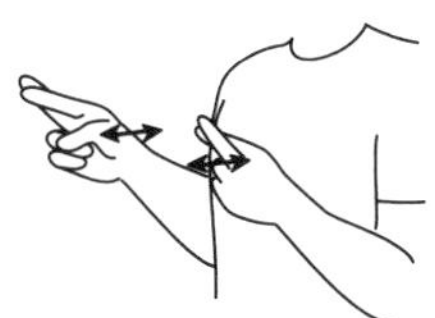

REFRIGERATE
R's move back and forth toward each other in shivering motion
(see COLD)

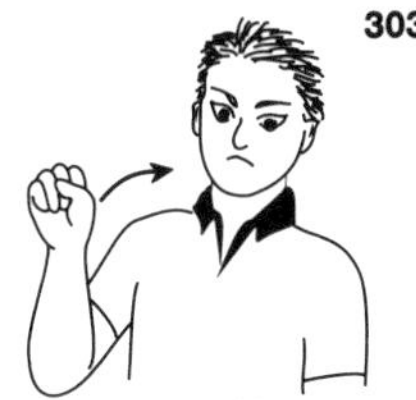

REFUSE
Right palm-left S-hand jerks back toward shoulder

REGION
(Alt. 1)
Fingertips of R's touch, then circle back to touch again
(see PLACE)

REGION
(Alt. 2)
R curves around vertical left index
(see ATMOSPHERE)

REGISTER
Right R-fingertips hop backwards once on left palm

REGRESS
Fingertips of right R move down in hopping motion on left arm
(see DETERIORATE)

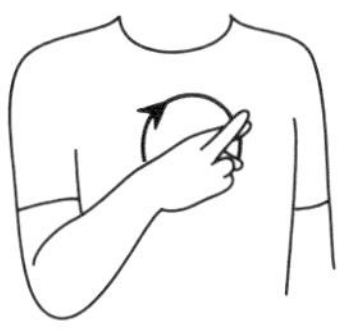

REGRET
Right palm-in R circles on chest
(see SORRY)

REGULAR
Right index above left, both pointing forward; right makes small clockwise circles, hitting left on each cycle

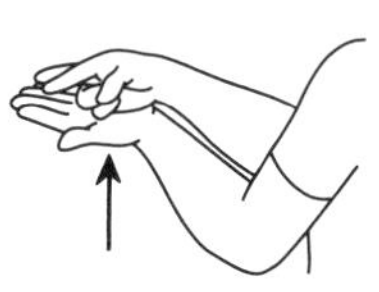

REHABILITATE
Side of R on left palm; both rise
(see HELP)

REHEARSE
Right heel of R brushes back and forth on left index
(see PRACTICE)

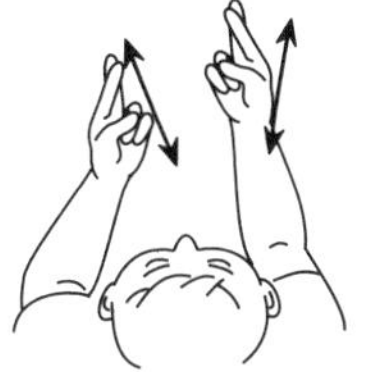

REIGN
Palm-up R's move alternately forward and back
(see MANAGE)

REINDEER
Thumbs of R-hands on temples, move out and up
(see DEER)

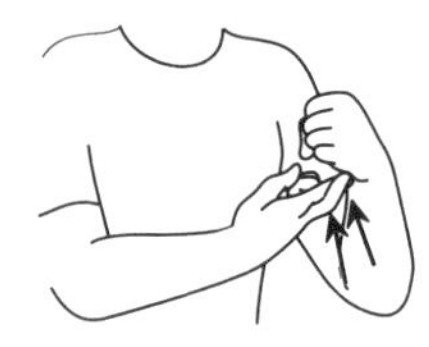

REINFORCE
Fingers of right R taps bottom of palm-in left S-hand
(see HELP)

REJECT
Side of flat right hand sweeps forward sharply off left palm

(see RID)

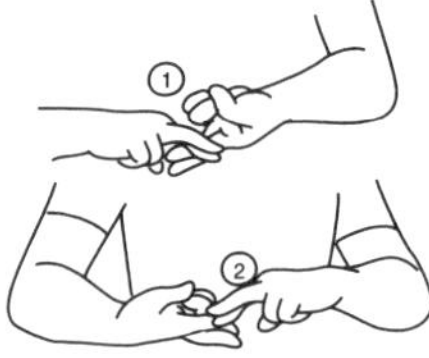

RELATE
R-fingers rest first right on left, then left on right

RELATIVE
R-fingers rest first right on left, then left on right; right V shakes downward *(relate + -ive)*

RELAX
Crossed palm-in R's rest on chest

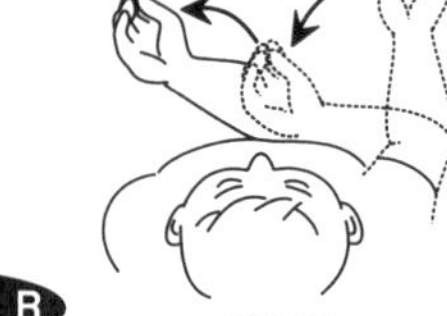

RELAY
Palm-up flat-O arcs in and over to body, then arcs out to palm-up on opposite side of body
(see TRANSFER)

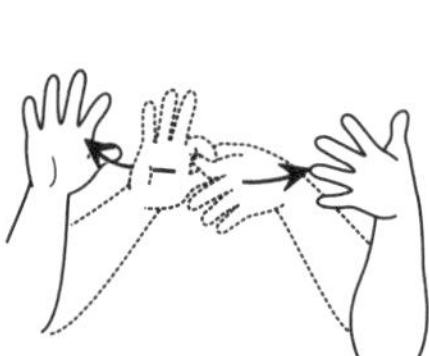

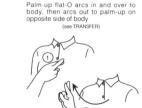

RELEASE
Linked thumbs and indexes of 9's open and separate sideways

RELIEVE
Palm-down R's, right above the left on chest, both move down
(see SATISFY)

RELIGION
Palm-in R on heart arcs down and forward to palm-out

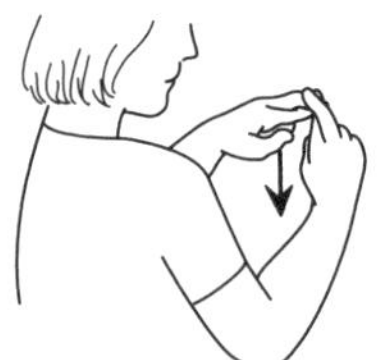

RELY
Palm-down R's cross at fingers and move slightly down
(see DEPEND)

REMAIN
Right R-fingertips on left R-fingertips, both move forward
(see CONTINUE)

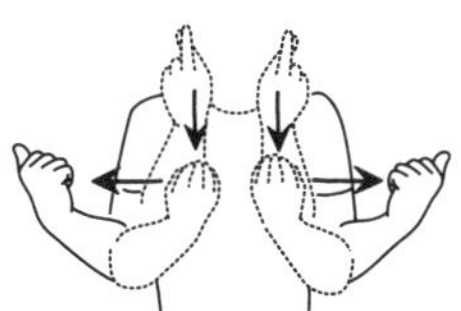

REMEDY
Palm-in R's close to palm-up flat-O's, which close to A's as they separate
(see MELT)

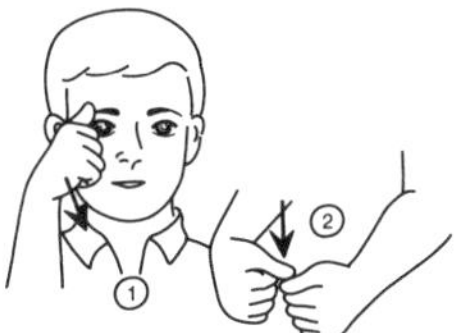

REMEMBER
Thumb of A on forehead; drops to touch left A-thumbnail

REMIND
Right R-fingertips tap forehead
(see THINK)

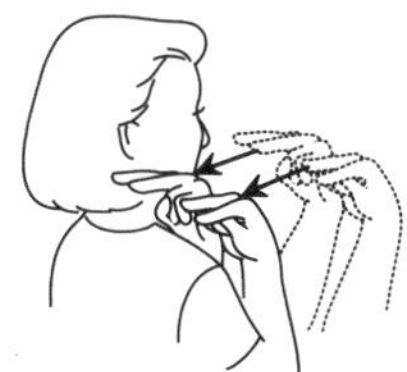

REMINISCE
Palm-in V's in front of face swing back over right shoulder

REMOTE
Vertical R-hands palm-to-palm, right arcs forward
(see FAR)

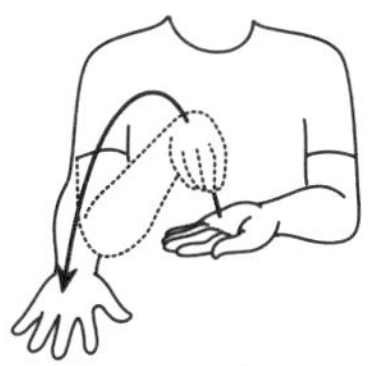

REMOVE
Fingertips of flat-O on left palm arc off to throw open hand down
(see DISPOSE)

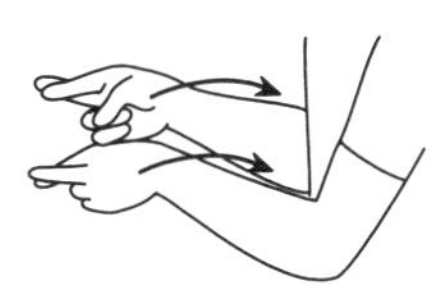

RENT
Horizontal R's, right on left, arc back toward body
(see BORROW)

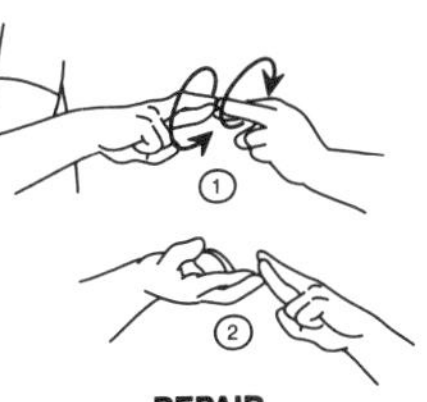

REPAIR
R-tips touch; twist in opposite directions and touch again
(see FIX)

REPEAT
Right palm-up R turns over and strikes left palm; can be repeated
(see AGAIN)

REPEL
Palm-out R hits palm-in left vertical hand and bounces back
(see REFLECT)

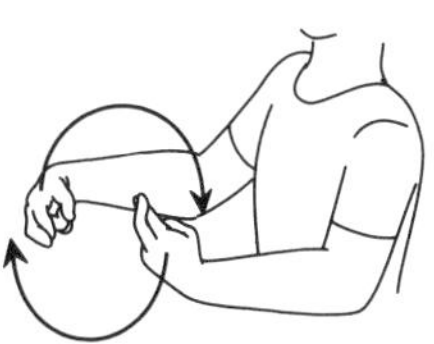

REPLACE
Horizontal R-hands facing each other, right in front of left, circle each other once
(see EXCHANGE)

REPLY
Palms-in, right R near lips, left R ahead to left; both hands turn palm-down, left one ahead
(see ANSWER)

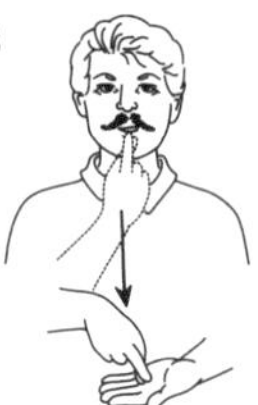

REPORT
Right palm-in R on lip twists to palm-down R on left palm
(see MENTION)

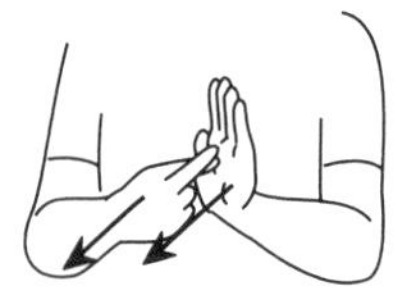

REPRESENT
Tip of right palm-in R on left palm, move both forward
(see SHOW)

REPTILE
R circles forward from under chin
(see SNAKE)

REPUBLIC
Palm-down right R circles over, then drops on back of left S-hand
(see NATION)

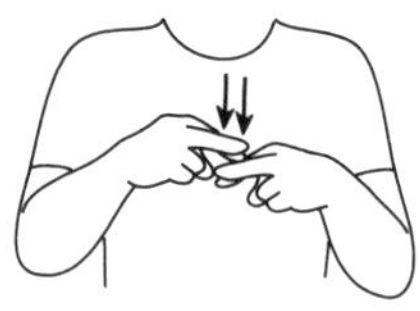

REPUTE
Horizontal R's, right R taps left R
(see NAME)

REQUEST
R hands, palms-facing, touch and arc toward self
(see ASK)

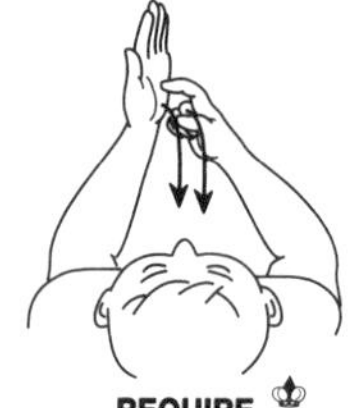

REQUIRE ♔
Tip of right X on left palm, both arc together toward body

RESCUE
Separate palm-in crossed R's to sides, twisting to palm-out
(see FREE)

RESEARCH
Fingertips of R at eye swings down to brush forward twice off left palm
(see INSPECT)

RESENT
Palm-in R on chest twists sharply out and throws palm-down
(see HOSTILE)

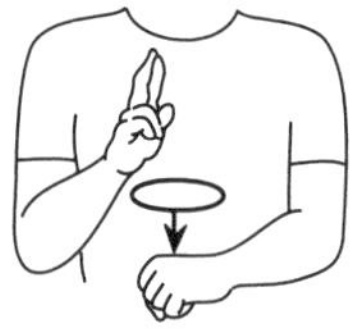

RESERVE
(Alt. 1)
R circles over back of left S and drops onto S-hand
(see APPOINT)

RESERVE
(Alt. 2)
R-fingertips tap back of left S-hand
(see SAVE)

R

RESIDE
Palm-in R's slide up body
(see ADDRESS)

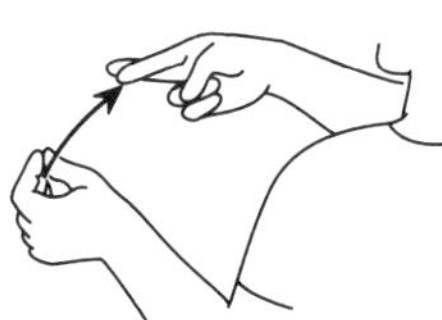

RESIGN
R-fingertips arc back out of left O
(see OUT)

RESIST
S-hand, palm-out and elbow out, jerks slightly forward and right from chest

RESOURCE
Palm-up R arcs slightly sideways
(see THING)

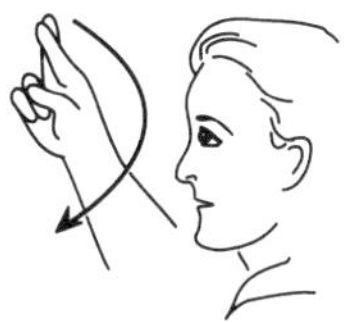

RESPECT
Palm-left R-hand arcs in and down near forehead
(see GOD)

RESPONSIBLE
Both R-hands on right shoulder
(see BURDEN)

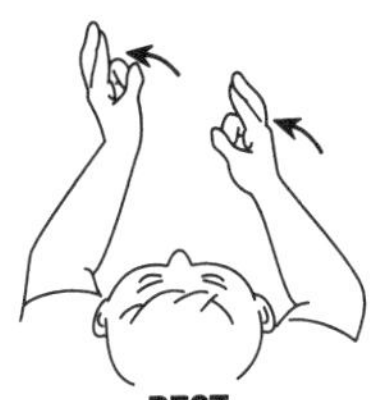

REST
Horizontal R's, right slightly behind left, both move slightly down

RESTAURANT
R touches on each side of mouth
(see CAFE)

RESTLESS
Palm-up V on left palm, V wiggles back and forth

RESTRAIN
Right palm-in claw at neck drops slightly down to S

RESTROOM
R-hand bounces once towards right

RESULT
(Alt.1)
R-fingers on side of palm-in flat left hand slides along hand and down
(see FINISH)

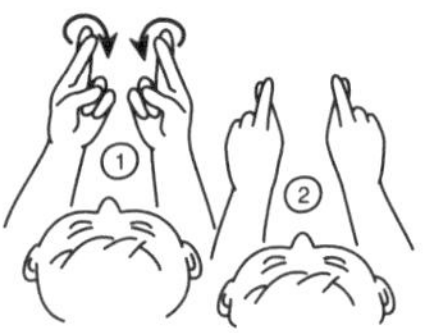

RESULT
(Alt. 2)
Palm-up R's twist to palm-down
(see HAPPEN)

RETARD
Right R-hand draws up back of left hand and wrist
(see SLOW)

RETIRE
Extended thumbs of R-hands tap front of shoulders
(see LEISURE)

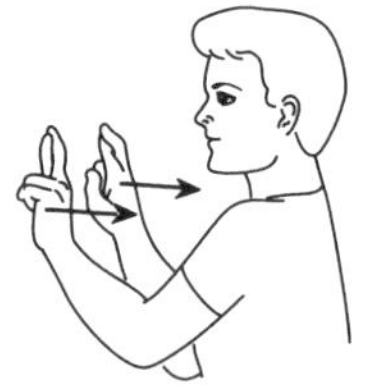

RETREAT
Palm-out vertical R's, right behind left, move back toward body

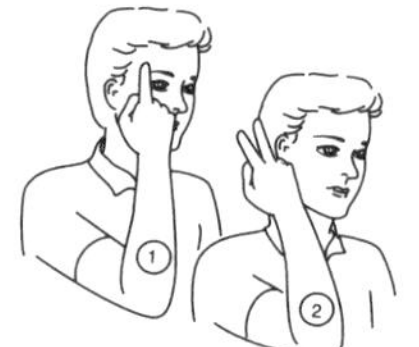

RETROSPECT
Palm-in index at forehead swings to V-hand over right shoulder

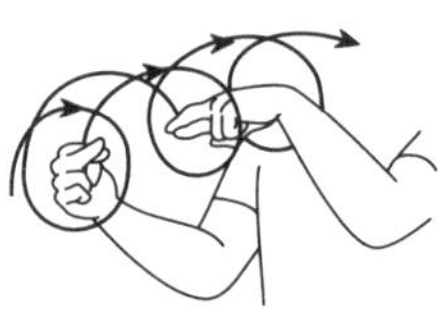

RETURN
R's point at each other, circle alternately toward body

REVEAL
Palm-down R's open outward
(see OPEN)

REVENGE
Modified A-hands hit each other sharply and separate

R

REVERSE
R-hands one on top of the other, palm-to-palm, reverse position
(see CHANGE)

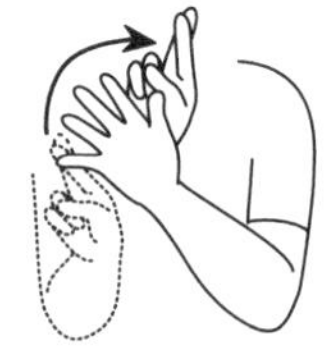

REVIEW
Right R sweeps up across fingers of left palm-in horizontal 5

REVISE
R-hands, palm-to-palm, reverse positions quickly twice
(see CHANGE)

REVOLT

Palm-in R twists back toward shoulder to palm-out

(see REBEL)

REVOLVE

Vertical R's point at each other; revolve around each other while moving right

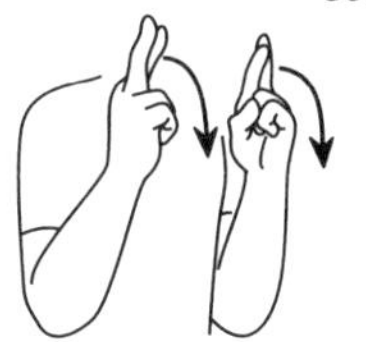

REWARD

Verical R's palms-facing, one slightly behind the other, both arc forward

(see GIFT)

RHINOCEROS

C-hand from nose arcs up to S

RHUBARB

Flat-O slides up through left C twisting to palm-out R

(see GROW)

RHYME

(Alt. 1)

Right R-fingertips touch left thumb and middle and little fingertips *(alternate rhyming lines)*

RHYME

(Alt. 2)

Palm-down R's tap sides

(see SAME)

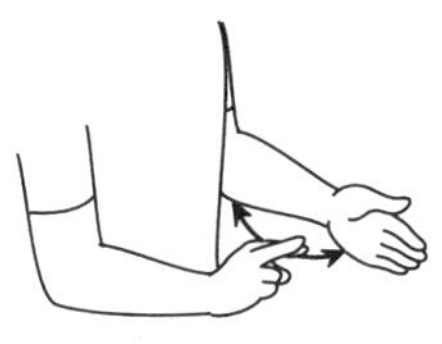

RHYTHM

Right palm-down R swings side-to-side behind left palm

(see MUSIC)

RIBBON

Right palm-in I wiggles away and slightly down from left palm-out R

(see CORD)

RICE

R-hand ladles up to mouth twice from left palm

(see SOUP)

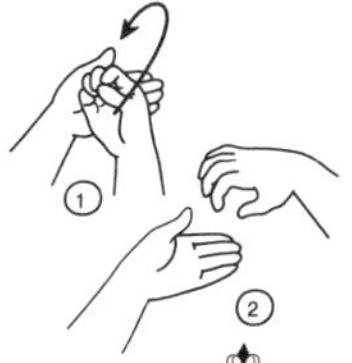

RICH

Back of right palm-up flat-O on left palm turns over and opens above palm to a claw hand

RID

Side of right R sweeps forward sharply off left palm

(see REJECT)

RIDDLE
Palm-out R draws question mark
(see QUESTION)

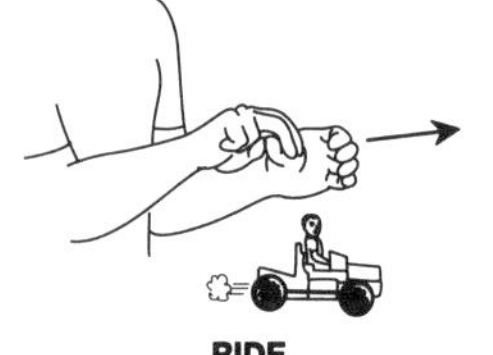

RIDE
First two fingers of right hand sit on thumb of horizontal palm-right C-hand; both move forward
(see PASSENGER)

RIDICULE
Index of right I-1 hand at corner of mouth, both palm-down I-1 hands, right behind left, jerk diagonally left; repeat

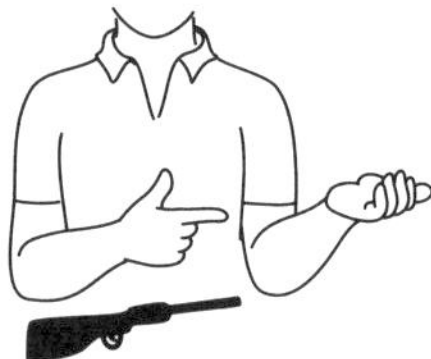

RIFLE
Right index, thumb extended, points left toward left palm-up bent hand *(as if holding rifle)*

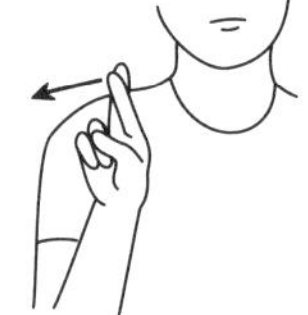

RIGHT ★
Palm-out R moves slightly right

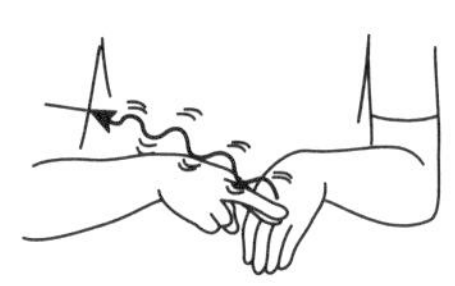

RING ★
R shakes away from left ring finger
(see DIAMOND)

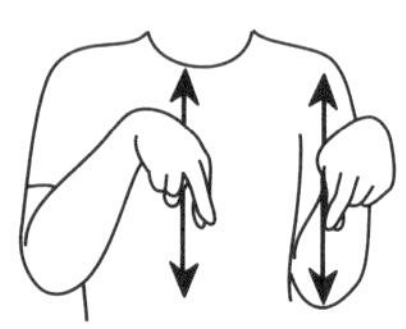

RINSE
Inverted R-hands rise and fall simultaneous twice
(see DIP)

RIOT
Inverted right R points at vertical left R; circle while moving up and right
(see STORM)

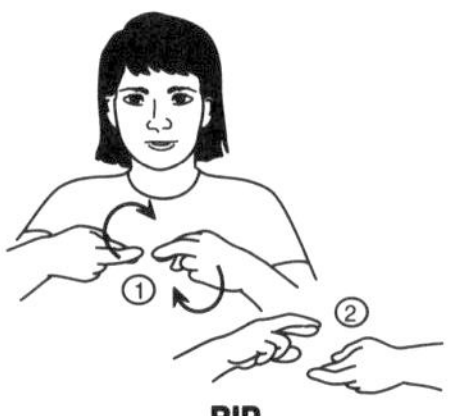

RIP
R's point at each other, touch tips; right twists inward and left outward
(see TEAR)

RIPE
Horizontal right R moves inward, brushing across left S-hand
(see FULL)

RISE ★
Palm-up R rises
(see UP)

RISK
Back of right R brushes up back of left horizontal palm-in S; repeat

RIVAL
Palm-in R fingertips point at each other, arc apart sideways
(see OPPOSE)

RIVER
Palm-down R's ripple forward to left up and down
(see BROOK)

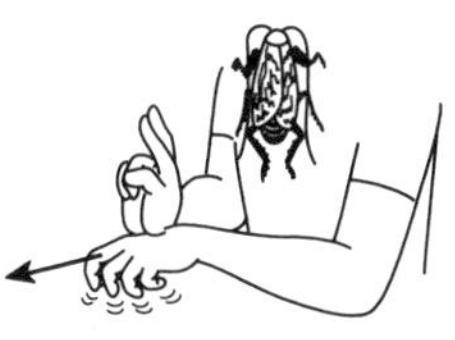

ROACH
R rides forward on back of wiggling fingers of left hand
(see ANT)

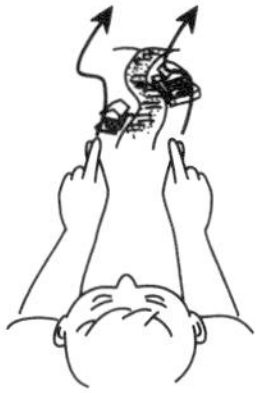

ROAD
Palm-down R's move forward, weaving slightly side-to-side
(see WAY)

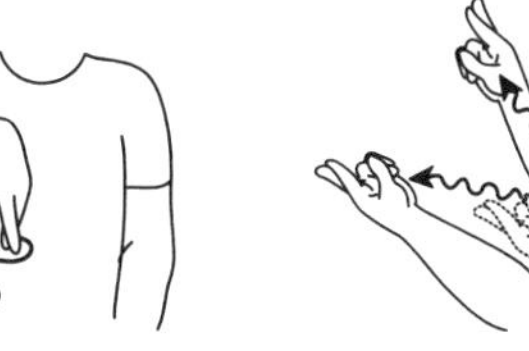

ROAM
Right R, pointing down, moves forward in a wavy path
(see WANDER)

ROAR
R's face each other, right above left at chin; move outward, separating vertically with wavy motion

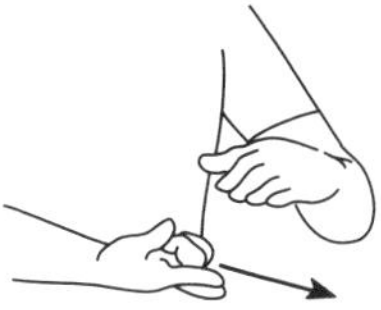

ROAST
Slide palm-up R forward under palm-down left hand
(see BAKE)

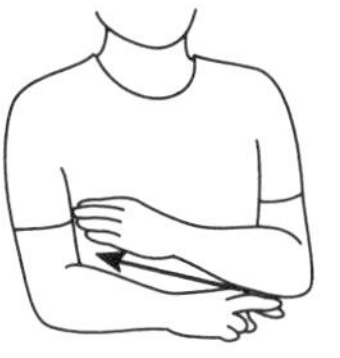

ROB
R slides along under horizontal left arm, from elbow to wrist
(see STEAL)

ROBE
Palm-in R-hands arc inward on chest
(see COAT)

ROBIN
Right R-fingers open and close on thumb by mouth
(see BIRD)

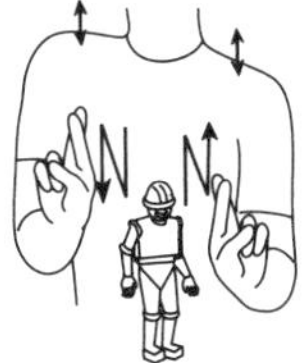

ROBOT
Palm-out R's; hands and shoulders move up and down alternately

ROCK ★
Back of R raps on back of left palm-down S; may repeat
(see STONE)

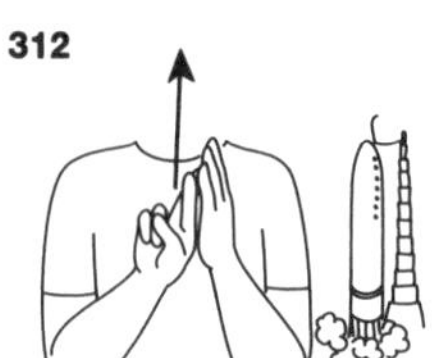

ROCKET
Side of R on left vertical palm, R moves upward
(see ASTRONAUT)

RODENT
Brush tip of nose alternately with R's
(see MICE)

RODEO
Right inverted V, palm-in, astride left flat hand, right arcs off forward, returns: repeat

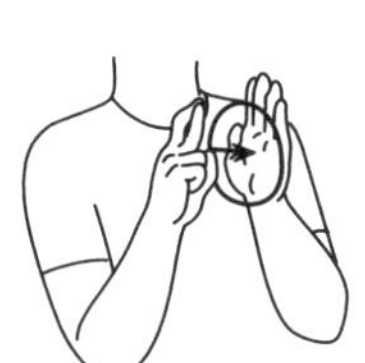

ROLE
R circles near and then touches vertical left palm
(see QUALITY)

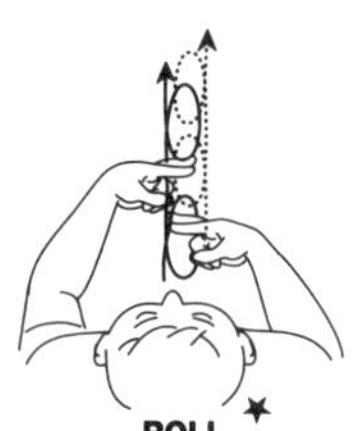

ROLL ★
Both R-hands, palms-facing body, roll forward around each other alternately from chest

ROMANCE
Palm-in R's cross at heart
(see LOVE)

ROMANTIC
Palm-in R's cross at heart, then right makes palm-out C *(romance + -ic)*

ROME
Fingertips of right R touch forehead, then nose
(see LATIN)

ROOF
R's outline roof

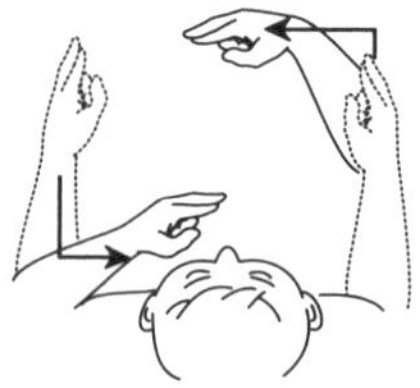

ROOM
R-hands box in a room
(see BOX)

ROOST
Fingertips of right R sits on left palm-down 2 fingers
(see SIT)

ROOSTER
Thumb of palm-left 3 taps on forehead

ROOT
Right flat-O "grows" down through left horizontal C to a 5

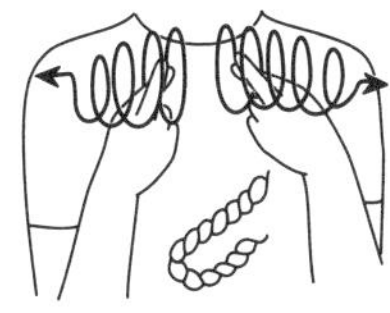

ROPE
Palm-in R-hands point at each other, separate in spiral movement

ROSE
R touches on each side of nose *(smelling rose)*
(see FLOWER)

ROT
Thumb of R flings off nose to the left
(see LOUSE)

ROTATE
R, pointing down, rotates
(see SPIN)

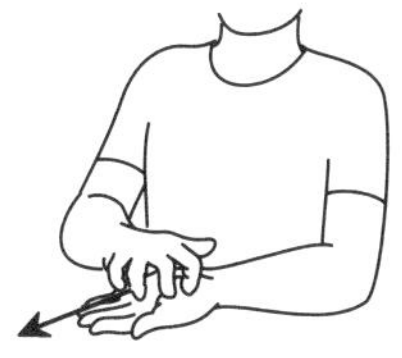

ROUGH
Fingertips of right claw on left palm; move claw sharply forward and off
(see COARSE)

ROUND ★
Palm-out R circles once
(see CIRCLE)

ROUTE
Left palm-down 5; right R brushes forward on back of left index and off

ROUTINE
Heel of right R on back of palm-down left S both hands drop slightly
(see HABIT)

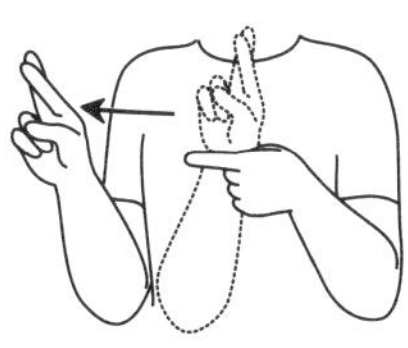

ROW
Heel of palm-out R slides along and off side of left index
(see BAR)

ROYAL
R at left shoulder then at right waist
(see CHRIST)

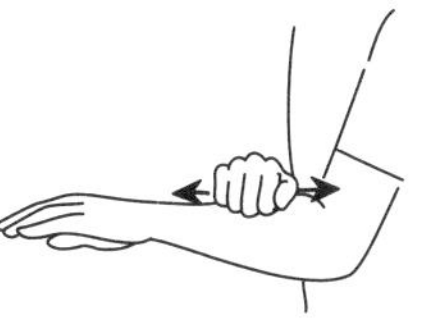

RUB
Palm-down A rubs on back of left arm

RUBBER
Side of right X-finger slides down cheek; repeat

RUBELLA
R-fingers spot face
(see MEASLES)

RUDE
Palm-in R on chin; twist to palm-out and throw down
(see BAD)

RUG
R drags across back of left hand
(see CARPET)

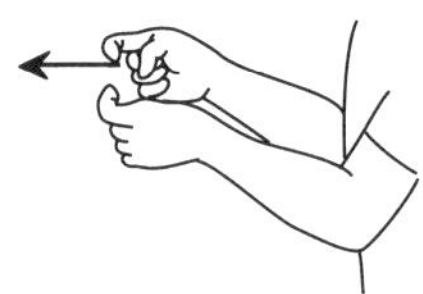

RUIN
Horizontal X's, right on left; right X *(only)* moves sharply forward
(see SPOIL)

RULE
R on the fingers of left vertical hand; then moves down to the heel
(see LAW)

RULER
Side of right R touches fingers of verical left palm, then heel; then palm out right R stands alone *(rule + -er)*

RUMMAGE
R's point downwards; rummage through pile

RUMOR
R-fingertips touch near chin, separate and circle horizontally out, shaking, to touch again
(see GOSSIP)

RUN
(Alt. 1)
Index of right L hooked around curved thumb of left L, both move forward, left index wiggling

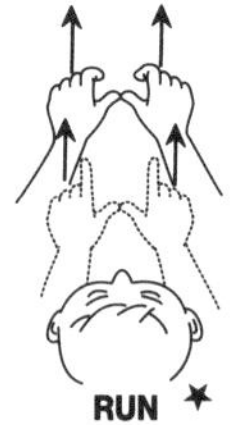

RUN ★
(Alt. 2)
Palm-down L-thumbtips touch; hands move forward, index fingers flicking in and out rapidly

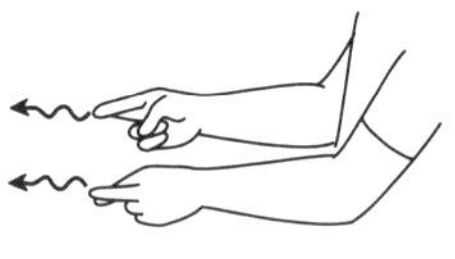

RUSH
Parallel R-hands shake forward
(see HURRY)

RUSSIA

Thumbs of palm-down 5-hands tap waist; repeat *(as in Russian dance)*

RUST

Fingertips of palm-in R at side of mouth drop to brush downwards across back of fingertips of palm-in horizontal left hand

(see BLEED)

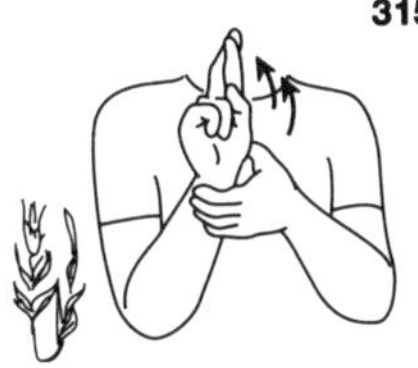

RYE

R brushes up through left horizontal C-hand; repeat

(see GRAIN)

NOTES

SABBATH
Right F-hand lowers past horizontal left arm *(as in sun setting)*

SACK
Right palm-left S draws bag under palm-down left S
(see BAG)

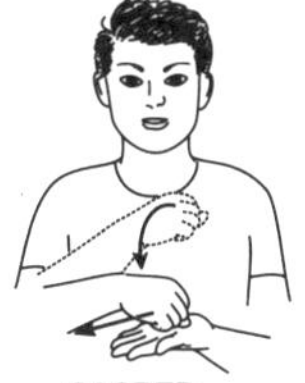

SACRED
Side of S on heart arcs to sweep forward across palm-up left hand

SAD
Open hands pull down in front of face

SADDLE
Fingers hook over flat palm-in left hand like a saddle

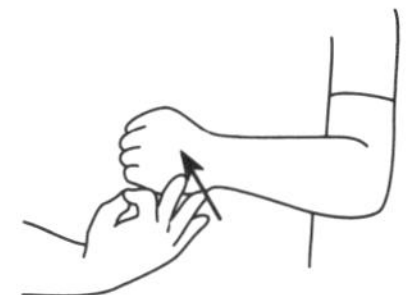

SAFE
Fingertips of F tap back of left S
(see SAVE)

SAID
Index circles up and outward near mouth; then right flat hand flips back toward shoulder *(say + p. t.)*

SAIL
Side of right 3-hand on flat palm; both hands move forward in slight up-and-down motion

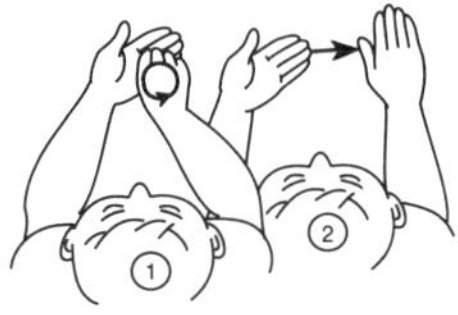

SAINT
Palm-down S circles above left palm, then flat hand slides off end of palm
(see HOLY)

SALAD
Palms-up V's toss salad
(see COLE SLAW)

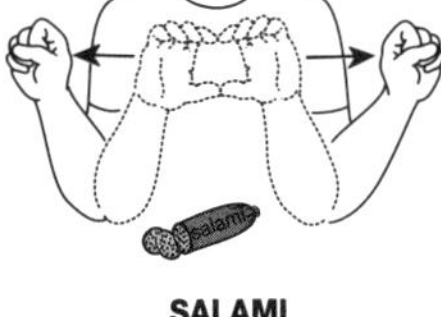

SALAMI
Palm-out C's separate to S's

SALE
Flat-O, palm-down above left palm, flips up at wrist several times
(see SELL)

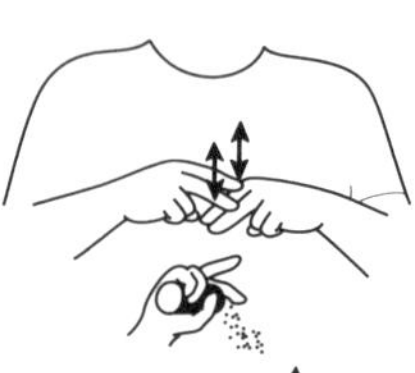

SALT ♔
Index and middle fingers tap alternately on left palm-down U-fingers

SALUTE
Right B at forehead, palm-out
(see SCOUT)

SAME ♔
Palm-down parallel index fingers touch sides together

S

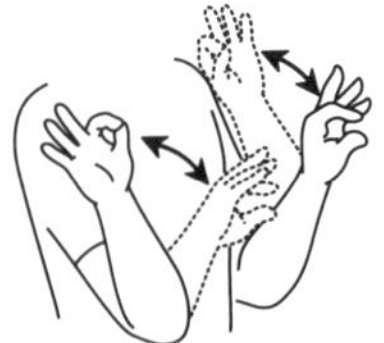

SAMPLE
Palm-out open 9-hands; alternately pull back to 9-hands, while moving slightly to the right

SAND ★
S-hands, palms-up; rub thumbs across fingernails

SANDAL
Index finger hooks between left index and middle fingers, then draws back across hand
(see THONG)

SANDWICH

Right hand, palm-up, inserts filling between thumb and fingers of left hand

SANG

Side of U from corner of mouth arcs forward and out, then palm of hand flips back toward shoulder *(sing + p. t.)*

SANITARY

Palm-down S on palm-up left hand, S changes to flat hand and wipes forward on left palm

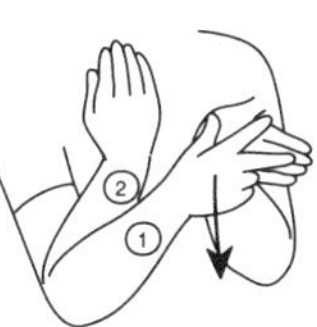

SANK

(Alt. 1)

Drop palm-left 3 down from palm-right left hand; palm of hand flips back toward shoulder *(sink + p. t.)*

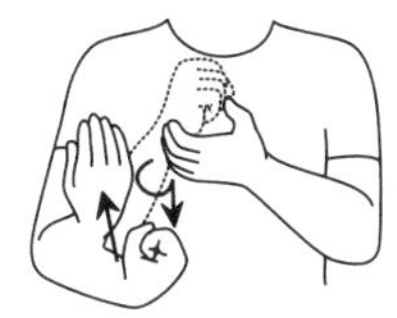

SANK

(Alt. 2)

Right S rotates down through horizontal left C-hand; palm of hand flips back toward shoulder *(sink + p. t.)*

SANTA CLAUS

Palm-in C at chin curves down to touch chest ending palm-up

SARCASM

Index of right 1-I hand at corner of mouth arcs out and left past bottom of palm-in 1-I hand

(see TRICK)

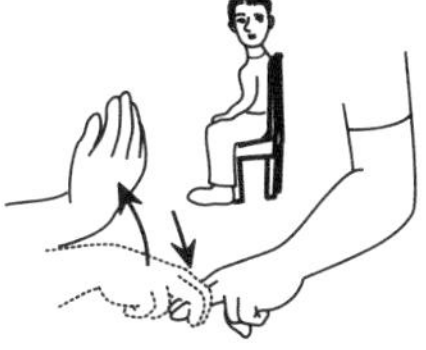

SAT

Right 2 fingers sit on left palm-down U; then palm of right hand flips back toward shoulder *(sit + p. t.)*

SATELLITE

Right S above palm-down left I-hand, right makes circle around left index

(see PLANET)

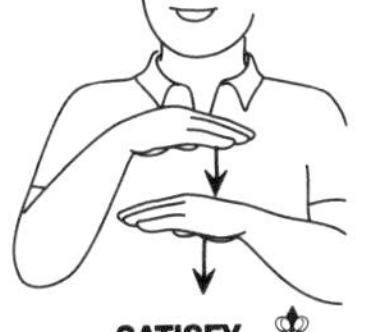

SATISFY ♔

Sides of palm-down B's resting on chest, right above left; both move downward

SATURDAY

Palm-out S-hand circles slightly

(see MONDAY)

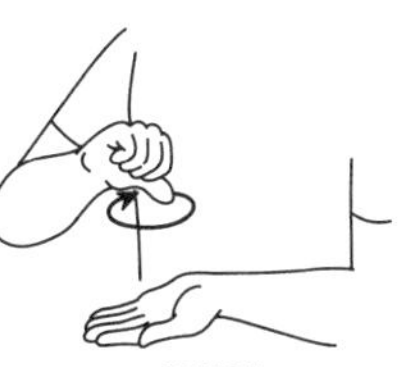

SAUCE

Palm-down extended-A hand circles above left palm as if pouring

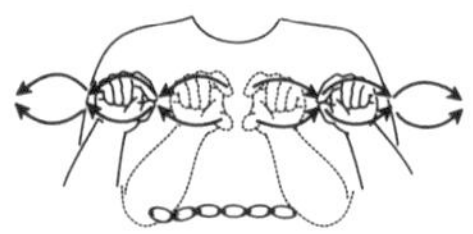

SAUSAGE
G's, moving sideways, open and close fingers to outline sausages
(see BALONEY)

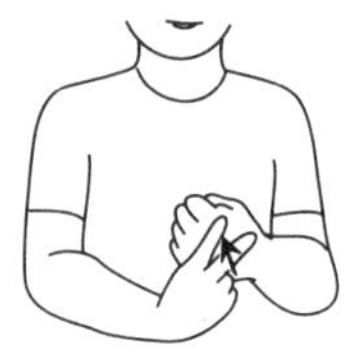

SAVE ♔
Fingers of right palm-in V tap back of palm-in left S

SAVIOUR
Palm-in S-hands, crossed at wrists, twist to sides ending palm-out; then parallel flat hands move down sides of body
(see FREE)

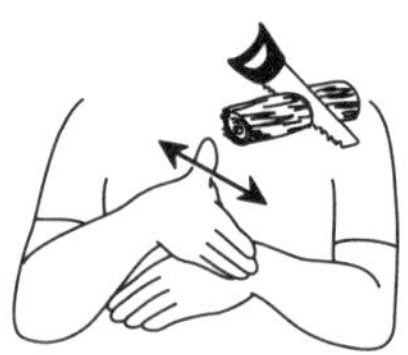

SAW
(Noun)
Edge of right hand saws on back of left *(may be done with right S-hand)*
(see LOG)

SAW
(Verb)
Palm-in V from eye moves outward; flat hand flips toward shoulder *(see + p.t.)*

SAY
Index of right hand circles up and outward near mouth
(see IMPLY)

SCALE ★
Side of right S slides across the back of palm-in flat left hand

SCARE
S-hands, palms-in, move toward each other, opening to palm-in 5's
(see FRIGHT)

SCARF ★
Both flat-O hands draw scarf around neck and tie at side
(see BONNET)

S

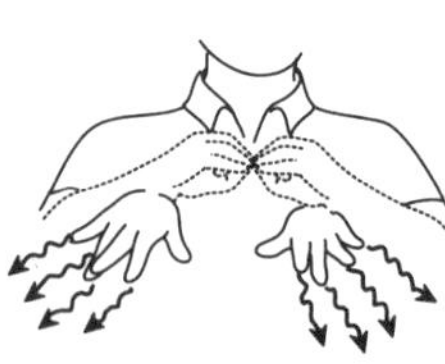

SCATTER
Flat-O tips together; open to palm-down 5-hands that separate while fluttering fingers

SCENE
Palm-out S on back of left hand, S circles slightly out and back

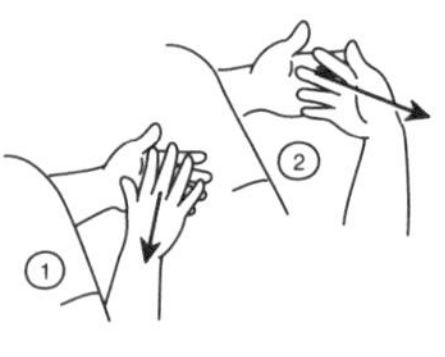

SCHEDULE
Fingertips of right palm-out 5 draws down left palm; then turns palm-in and draws across palm

SCHEME
Palm-in S at side of forehead rises up and away in shaking motion
(see DREAM)

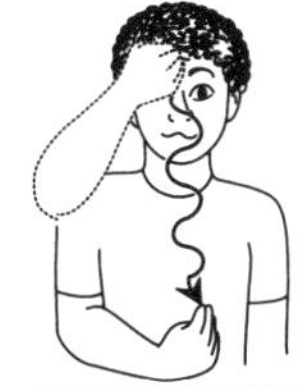

SCHIZOPHRENIC
Palm-in bent hand outlines crack down midline

SCHOOL
Both hands clap
(see ACADEMIC)

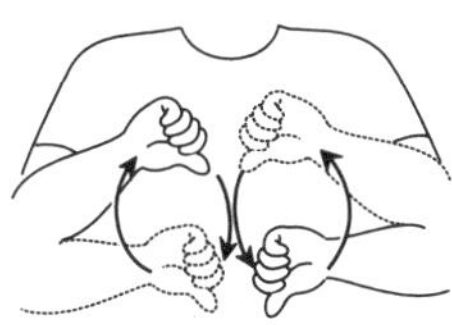

SCIENCE ♔
Extended-A hands alternately pour in circles

SCISSOR
Horizontal index and middle finger open and close forward
(see CUT)

SCOLD
Shake index finger at someone

SCOOP ★
Fingertips of palm-up C-hand, scoops across palm-up flat hand

SCOOT
S-hand, palm-down, flicks up sharply to palm-out S

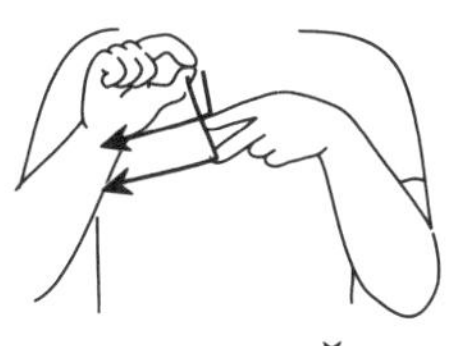

SCORE ★
Right closed thumb and index check off left 2-fingertips of V-hand

SCORPION
X rides on back of left hand while left hand moves forward fingers wiggling
(see ANT)

SCOT
4-fingers draw a cross on left upper arm; changing from palm-in to palm-up
(see PLAID)

SCOUT ★
Three fingers of palm-out hand salute
(see SALUTE)

SCRAMBLE
Palm-down S circles over left cupped hand like scrambling eggs

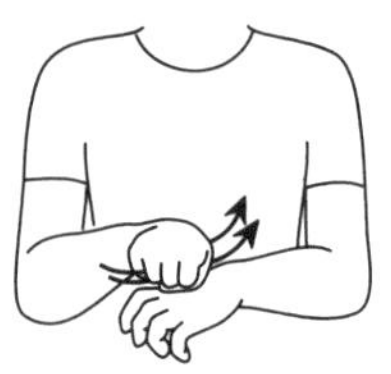

SCRAPE
Palm-down right S scrapes toward body off back of palm-down left claw hand several times

SCRATCH ★
Claw scratches left palm

SCREAM
Palm-in claw shakes up and diagonally forward from chin, rapidly
(see HOLLER)

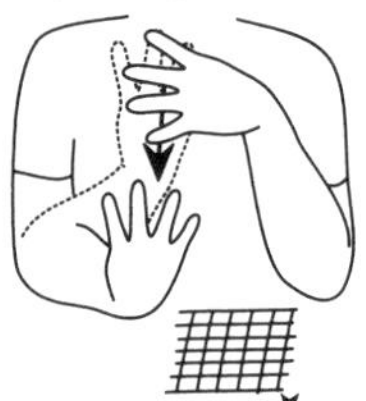

SCREEN ★
Palms-in, right vertical 4 falls inside left horizontal 4

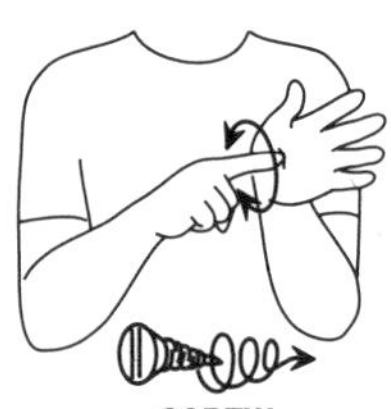

SCREW
Index finger twists in middle of left palm

SCREWDRIVER
H-fingers twist in palm of left hand

SCRIPT
Right palm-out S moves down vertical palm-in left hand

SCRUB
Knuckles of palm-down right A on palm-up left A, scrub with short back and forth movement

SCULPT
Extended thumb of A sculpts on palm; repeat several times

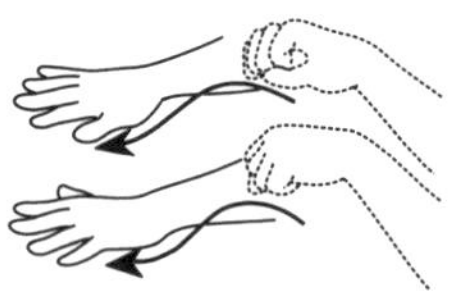

SEA
Palm-down S's sweep up and down forward, opening to 5's
(see OCEAN)

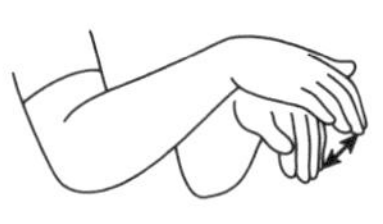

SEAL ★
Right on left bent hand, close right flat hand on left; repeat

SEAM
Left closed G points right; right 9 sews finger and thumb together

SEARCH
Palm-left C-hand makes several circles in front of eyes
(see SEEK)

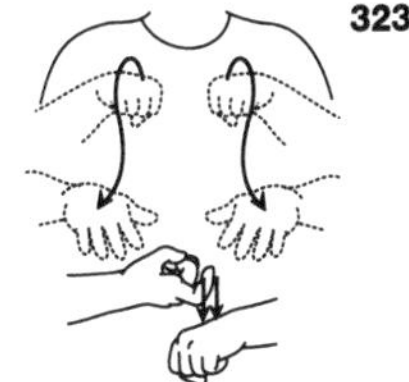

SEASHELL
S's sweep up and down forward, opening to palm-down 5's; back of right X taps back of left S *(sea + shell)*

SEASON ★
S moves downward with a wavy motion
(see WEATHER)

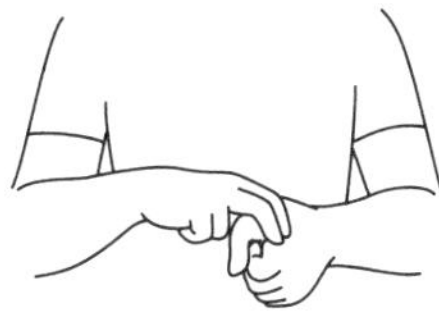

SEAT
2 fingers sit on side of left S-hand
(see SIT)

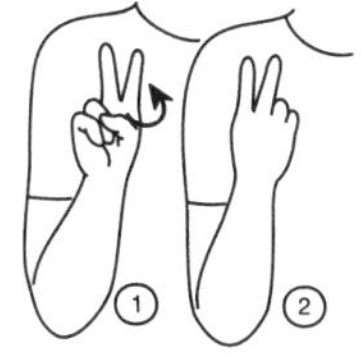

SECOND
Palm-out 2 twists to palm-in
(see THIRD)

SECRET
A-thumb taps chin; repeat
(see PRIVATE)

SECRETARY
(Alt. 1)
Closed index and thumb tip takes pencil from ear and writes across left palm
(see WRITE)

SECRETARY
(Alt. 2)
Fingers of H takes pencil from ear and writes across left palm
(see WRITE)

SECTION
Side of right S arcs toward body on palm-up left hand
(see SOME)

SECURE
S-hands, back-to-back touching, both jerk toward body

SEE
Palm-in V from eye moves outward

SEED
Palm-down thumb of flat-O rubs fingers, hand moving right *(sowing seeds)*

SEEK
Small C makes circles in front of eyes
(see SEARCH)

SEEM
Bent hand pivots at wrist to palm-in
(see OUGHT)

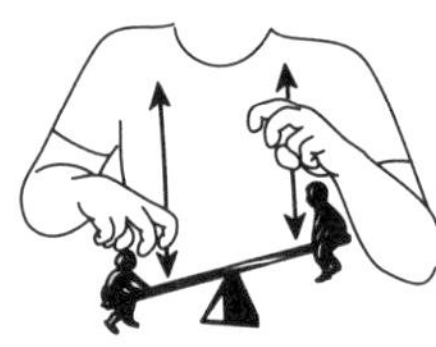

SEESAW
Palm-down bent-V hands face each other, alternately rise and drop

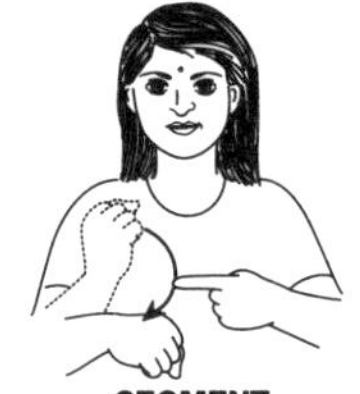

SEGMENT
Right palm-in S arcs down to clip tip of horizontal left index
(see CHIP)

SELDOM
Palm-left right index brushes up on left fingertips, then on left palm
(see SOMETIMES)

SELECT
Heel of right S-hand rests on index of left V, then pulls back toward chest; left hand is stationary
(see CHOOSE)

SELF
Thumb-up extended-A hand moves forward *(use for all -self's except myself, in which A turns to face in and touches own chest)*

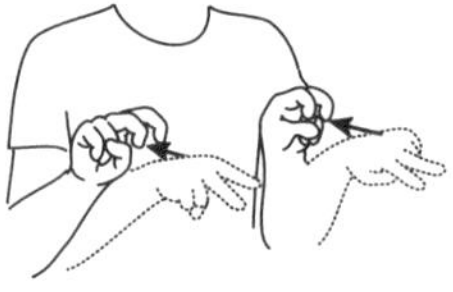

SELFISH
Palm-down V's pull back to bent-V's

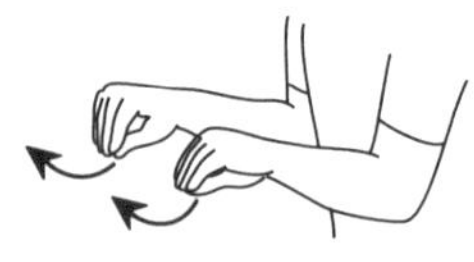

SELL
Both flat-O hands, palms-down, flip up at wrist; repeat

SEMESTER
Side of right S circles once then touches on left palm
(see HOUR)

SEMINARY
Palm-down S on palm-up left hand, S rises in circular movements
(see COLLEGE)

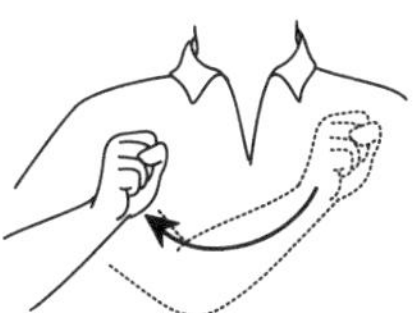

SENATE
S on left shoulder, then on right
(see MEMBER)

SEND
Right palm-in fingertips on back of palm-in left hand; right hand flips forward to palm-down

SENIOR
Right palm-down palm taps vertical thumb of left 5
(see FRESHMAN)

SENSE
Bent middle finger of right hand taps behind ear; repeat
(see CONSCIOUS)

SENSITIVE
Middle finger of palm-in 5-hand on heart flicks sharply outward

SENTENCE
9-hands touch at index and thumb-tips; separate, shaking slightly

SEPARATE
Palms-down, backs of bent hands together; separate hands
(see ISOLATE)

SEPTEMBER
(Alt. 1)
S arcs over vertical left hand
(see CALENDAR)

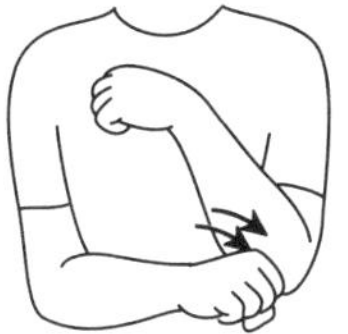

SEPTEMBER
(Alt. 2)
Palm-down right S brushes down left elbow twice
(see AUTUMN)

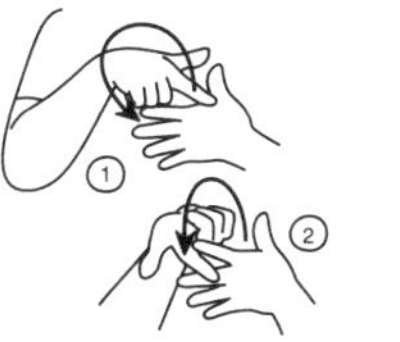

SEQUENCE
Index of palm-down L between left thumb and index; turn to palm-up between index and middle fingers

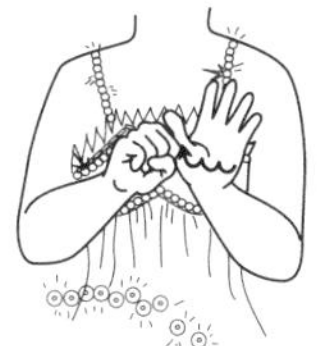

SEQUIN
Side of right S taps across left palm, *(like sequins)*
(see BEAD)

SERGEANT
3-hand index and middle fingers draw chevron on left shoulder

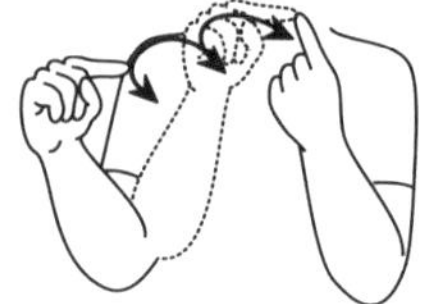

SERIES
Right index on left palm-in vertical index; right index dots off to right

SERIOUS
Palm-left right S-hand moves forward from chin
(see CERTAIN)

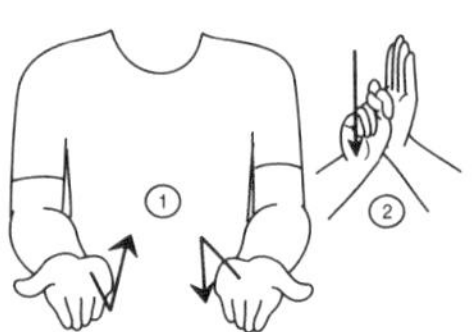

SERVANT
Palms-up, move hands alternately to and from body; side of T slides down left verical hand *(serve + -ant)*

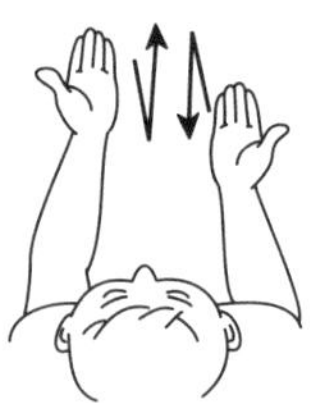

SERVE
Palms-up, move hands alternately to and from body

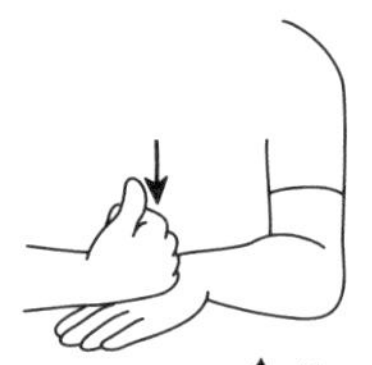

SET ♔ ★
Palm-in right extended-A is set on back of left hand

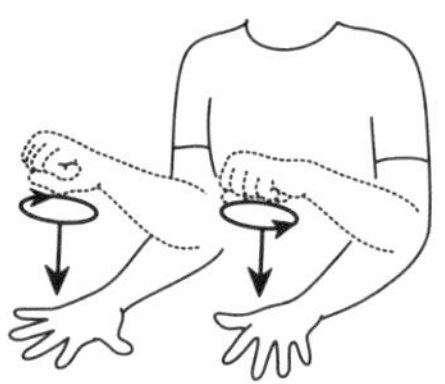

SETTLE
Palm-down S-hands circle and drop to palm-down 5's

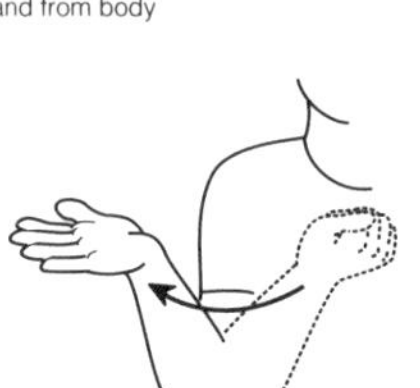

SEVERAL
Palm-up A moves sideways to open, one finger at a time

SEW
Right 9 sews left thumb and fingertip of 9-hand
(see TAILOR)

SEWER
S at chin drops to sink through horizontal left C, twisting to palm-in

SEX
Palm-out X at temple, then on jaw
(see PARENT)

SHADE
Both S-hands fall and cross at wrists
(see DARK)

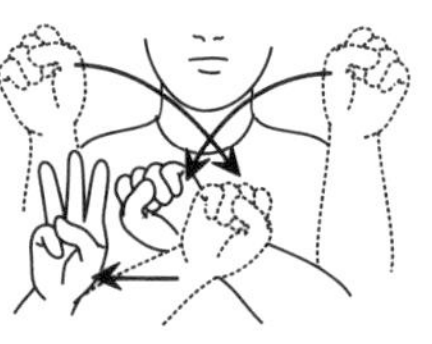

SHADOW ★
Both S-hands fall and cross at wrists; add palm-out W *(shade + -w)*

SHAKE

Shake palm-left S-hand

SHAKESPEARE

Right palm-left S-hand shakes and throws a spear *(shake + spear)*

SHALL
(Alt. 1)
Palm-down X nods several times

(see NECESSARY)

SHALL
(Alt. 2)
S-hand at side of face moves forward to palm-left L

(see SHOULD Alt. 2)

SHALLOW

Left vertical palm; side of right palm-down hand against heel of left, right rises a bit

SHAME ♔

Flat hand brushes up cheek, over and out, from palm-in to palm-up

SHAMPOO

Hands make washing motion on head

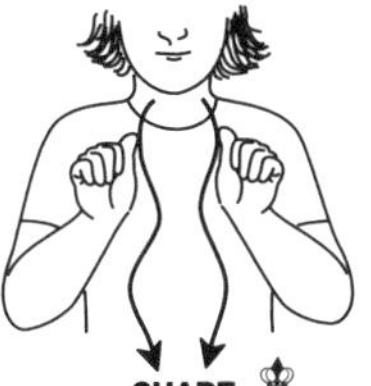

SHAPE ♔

Palm-out A-thumbs outline shape

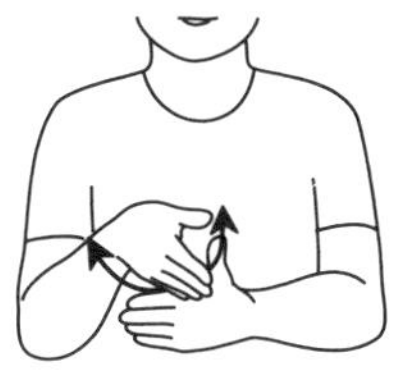

SHARE

Side of right hand arcs from side-to-side, on side of palm-in left hand between thumb and index fingers

SHARK

Right flat hand fingertips between left ring and middle fingers; swim forward

(see FISH)

SHARP ♔

Right middle finger flicks away from left index tip, turning palm-down

SHAVE

Thumb of Y draws along cheek, palm-left; repeat

(see RAZOR)

SHE
E slides along jawline and forward
(see GIRL)

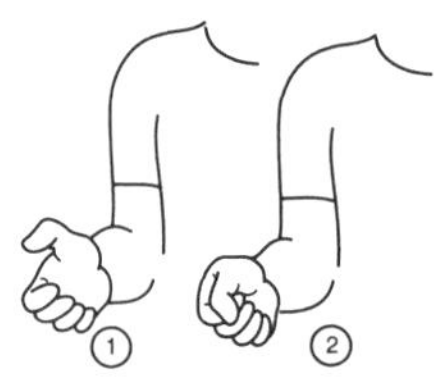

SHEARS
Mime holding a pair of shears; open and close hand

SHEEP ♔
Palm-up V clips wool off left arm

SHEET
Right arm swings up and in, over left hand near chest
(see BLANKET)

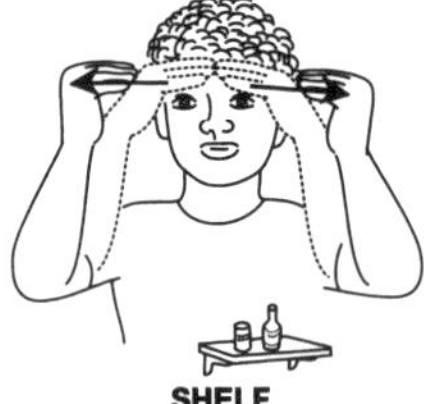

SHELF
Fingertips of bent hands touch at eye-level, then separate
(see RACK)

SHELL
Back of right X taps back of palm-down left S
(see STONE)

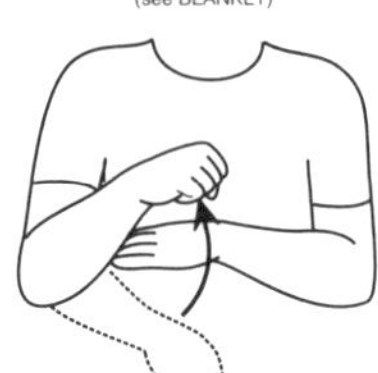

SHELTER
Right palm-in S arcs over left palm-down, flat hand
(see BLANKET)

SHH
Index finger shushes lips

SHEPHERD
Palm-up V clips wool off left arm; palm-out U-hands circle horizontally to palm-in *(sheep + -herd)*

SHIELD
Left arm across body, palm-out right S circles up and right in front of arm
(see ARMOR)

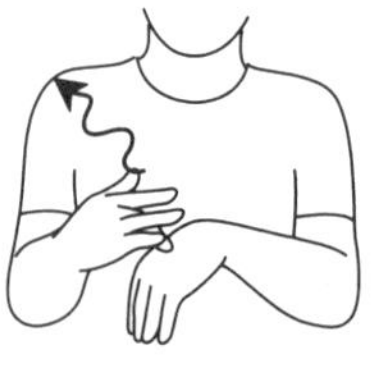

SHINE
Bent middle finger of right hand rises off back of left hand, shaking
(see POLISH)

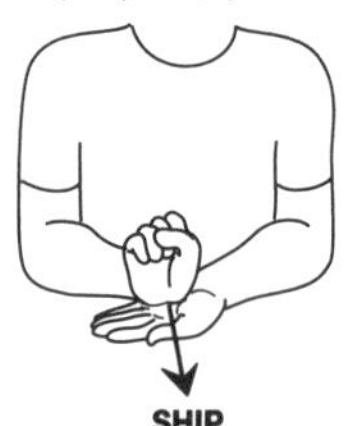

SHIP
S on left palm; both move forward

SHIRT
Both S-hands on chest, arc inward and downward
(see COAT)

SHIVER
Shoulders drawn slightly together, A's shake in front of body
(see COLD)

SHOCK
Index touches forehead, then drop hands into palm-down claws

SHOE
Palm-down S's bump together twice

SHOOT
Index jerks back to X *(pulling trigger)*
(see SHOT)

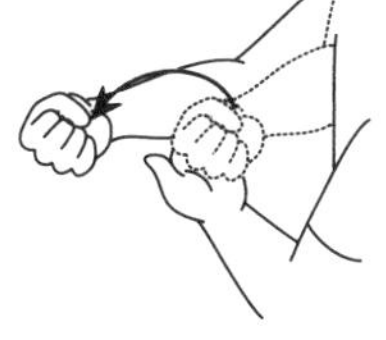

SHOP

Back of S on left palm; S arcs forward
(see BUY)

SHORE
Fluttering fingers of right palm-down 5 sweep, wave-like, onto and back from left palm-down hand
(see TIDE)

SHORT
Side of right H rubs back and forth on side of left H-hand

SHOT
Index points forward, pulls back to palm-out T-hand
(see SHOOT)

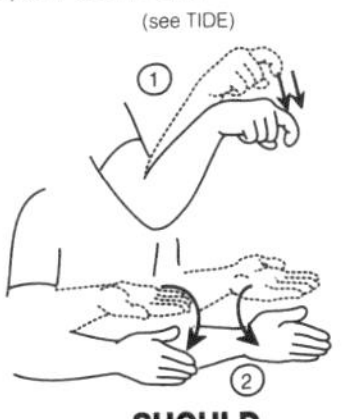

SHOULD
(Alt. 1)
Palm-down X nods; flat hands, palms-up, turn to palms-facing *(shall + p. p.)*

SHOULD
(Alt. 2)
Palm-out S-hand, at side of face, moves forward to D
(see SHALL, Alt. 2)

SHOULDER

Pat opposite shoulder

SHOUT
C before chin jerks up and forward
(see CALL)

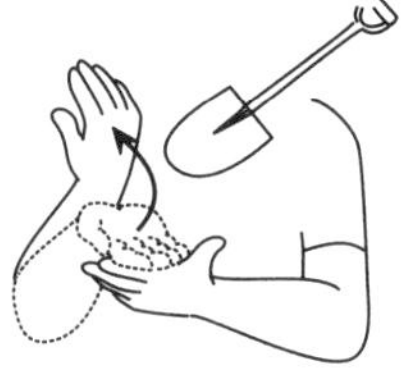

SHOVEL
Back of right hand slides forward in palm of left hand and flips up

SHOW
Index on left palm; both move forward

SHOWER
From above, closed hand opens to 5-hand in repeated motions

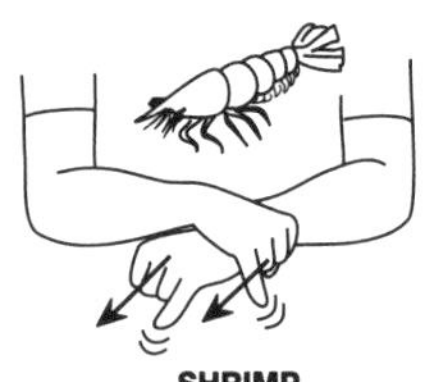

SHRIMP
Wrists of palm-down I's crossed, move to front and right, wiggling I-little fingers
(see CRAB)

SHRINK
(Alt. 1)
5-hands face each other, approach, changing to S's

SHRINK
(Alt. 2)
5-hands, palms-facing, one above the other, approach changing to S's

SHUT
Side of palm-in right hand drops on side of palm-in left B-hand

SHY
Bent hand, palm-in, moves up cheek
(see SHAME)

S

SICK
Bent middle fingers, touch right on forehead, and left on stomach

SIDE
Palm-in right hand brushes down past side of palm-down left hand

SIFT
Palm-up right 4 above palm-up left hand, 4 "sifts" above left, fingers fluttering slightly

SIGH

S-hands palms-facing near chest, right above left; move out and in again

(see BREATH)

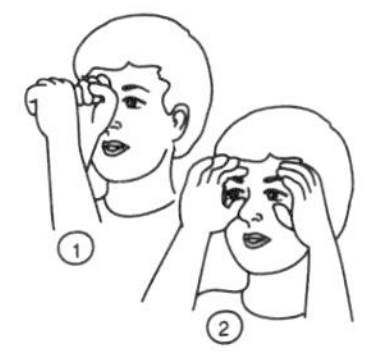

SIGHT

S-hands before eyes, left before right, separate sideways opening to C's

SIGN

(Sign Language)

Palm-out indexes circle alternately

SIGN ★

(noun, verb)

U-fingers touch palm, circle to side, touch palm again

SIGNAL

Palm-out flat-O opens to 5, quickly closes again; can repeat

(see FLASH)

SILENT

S's one behind the other at chin; separate downward

(see QUIET)

SILLY

Palm-left Y-hand shakes in front of eyes

SILVER

S at ear shakes down to the side

(see CALIFORNIA)

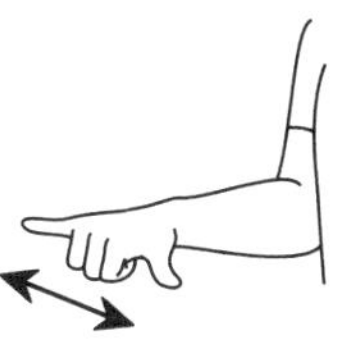

SIMILAR

Right palm-down Y moves slightly from side-to-side

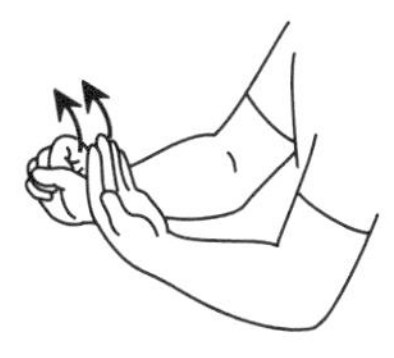

SIMPLE

Right S brushes up back of left bent fingers twice

(see EASE)

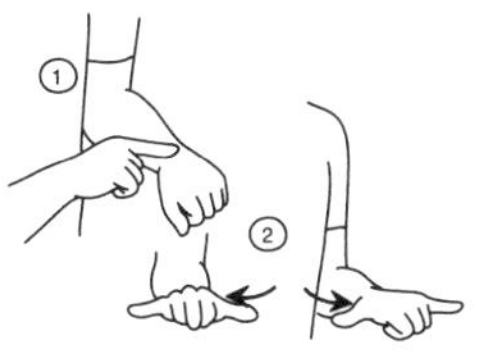

SIMULTANEOUS

Right index touches left wrist; then separates to palm-down Y's

SIN

Palm-in indexes point at each other, circle toward each other in front of body in opposite directions; repeat

SINCE
Palm-in indexes on right shoulder, arc up and out to point forward

SING
Palm-out U from corner of mouth arcs forward and out, slightly to the side

SINGLE
Vertical right index, palm-in, circles slightly horizontally
(see BACHELOR)

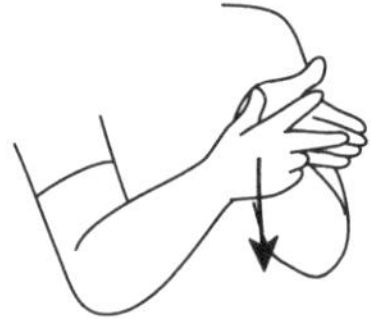

SINK
(Alt. 1)
Drop palm-left 3-hand down from palm-right left hand

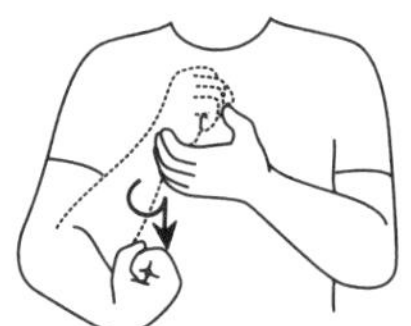

SINK
(Alt. 2)
Palm-out right S rotates down through horizontal left C-hand
(see DRAIN)

SIP
Tips of right G arc up to mouth
(see DRINK)

SIR
S at temple goes forward to palm-out R
(see HE)

SIREN
Flat-O repeatedly opens and closes as it revolves within left C-hand

SISTER
(Alt. 1)
Extended-A hand touches jawline; drops to both index fingers together
(see BROTHER)

SISTER
(Alt. 2)
Extended right A-hand touches jawline; drops to L-hand on left L-hand

SIT
Right index and middle fingers sit on left palm-down U-hand

SITE
Palm-down 5 slightly circles horizontally

SITUATE
S-hands touch, circle horizontally toward body, and touch again
(see PLACE)

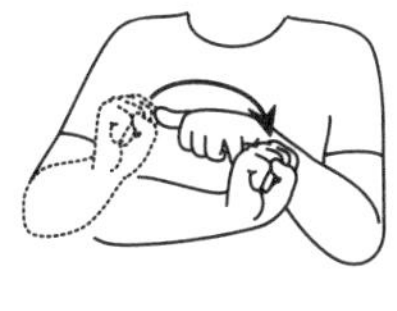

SIZE
S moves from little finger to thumb of palm-down left Y-hand

SKATE
Palm-up bent-V hands alternately move back and forth

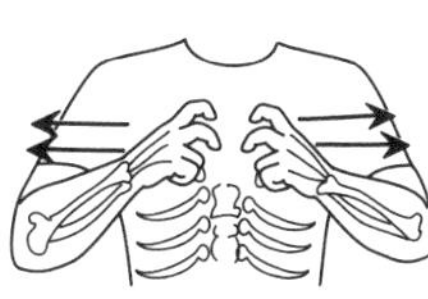

SKELETON
Palm-in horizontal bent-V's scratch outward on chest; repeat

SKEPTIC
Palm-in V, in front of face, bends fingers several times, shake head side-to-side at the same time

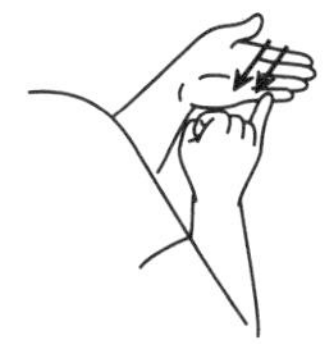

SKETCH
Right I-hand points little finger at left palm and moves quickly down, repeat several times
(see ART)

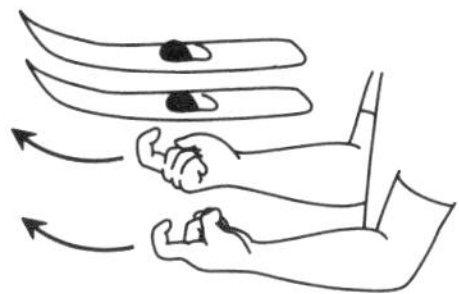

SKI
Palm-up X's arc forward

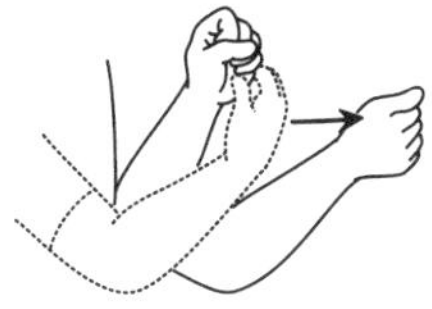

SKILL
Right hand grasps side of palm-left S; slides off forward into A
(see EXPERT)

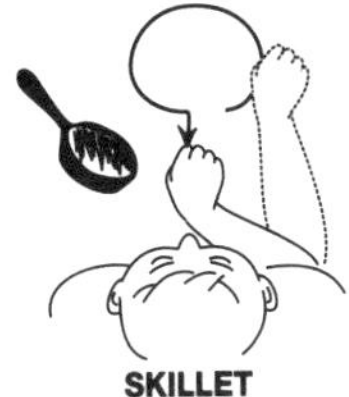

SKILLET
Palm-down S circles horizontally once, then pulls back toward body
(see PAN)

SKIN
Pinch skin on back of left hand

SKINNY
Palm-in I's, right above left, tips of little fingers touching; draw apart

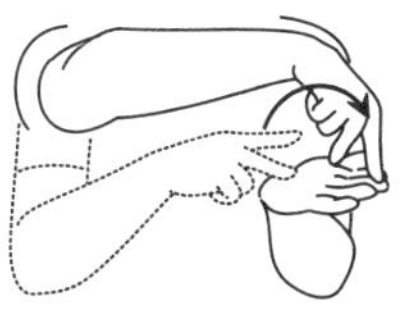

SKIP
Middle finger of right K skips upward to index finger on left flat palm
(See JUMP)

SKIRT
Thumbs of 5-hands brush down and out from waist

SKULL
Wrists of palm-in bent-V hands cross below neck

SKUNK
K moves back across middle of head

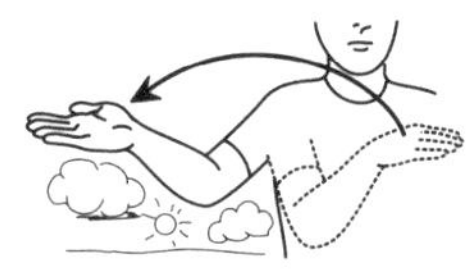

SKY
Palm-down flat hand at left arcs to palm-up hand at right
(see RAINBOW)

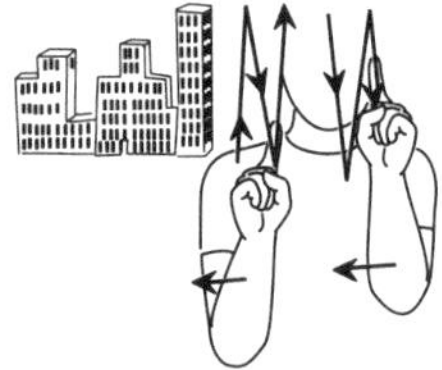

SKYSCRAPER
1-hands alternately move up and down, moving hands to right

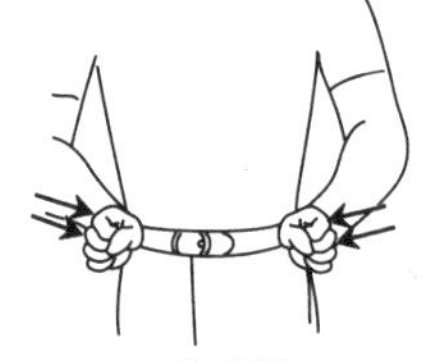

SLACK
Heels of S-hands tap waist
(see PANT)

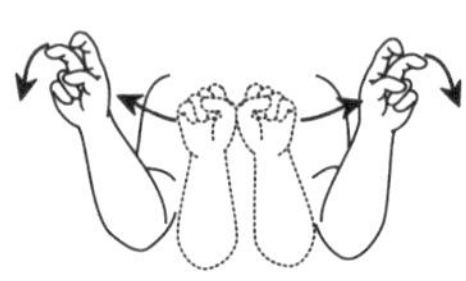

SLANG
S's together, separate to bent-V's that twist slightly down
(see QUOTE)

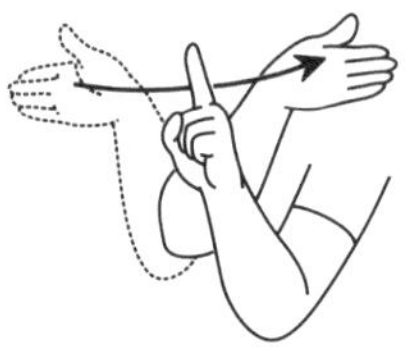

SLAP
Open right hand slaps left index
(see BEAT)

SLAVE
Palm-down S's, crossed at wrists, swing side-to-side

SLED
Back of right bent-V on left palm; both arc forward
(see TOBOGGAN)

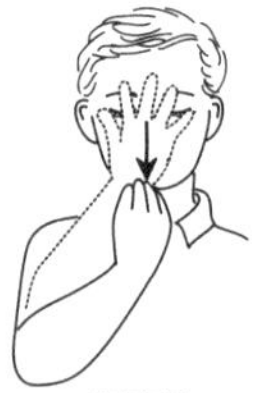

SLEEP
Right palm-in 5-hand in front of face, drops to flat-O

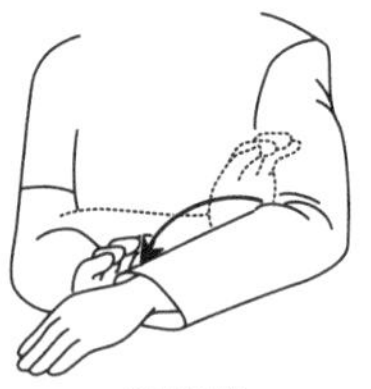

SLEEVE
C-hand moves from left elbow to wrist

SLEIGH
Palm-in 1-hands circle forward to palm- up X-hands that pull back

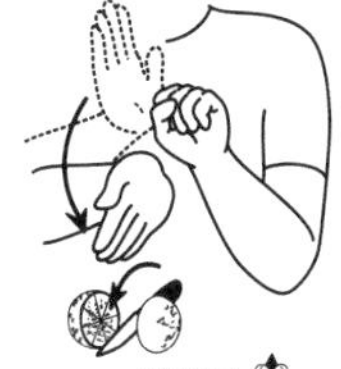

SLICE
Right palm slices side of left S; may repeat several times

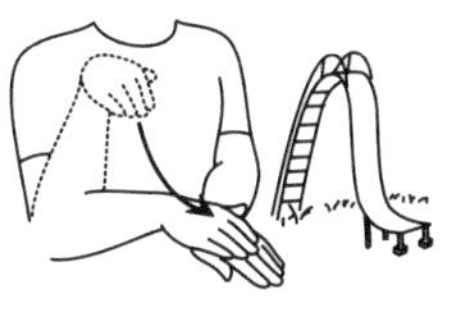

SLIDE ★
Right palm-down hand slides down and outward over back of left hand

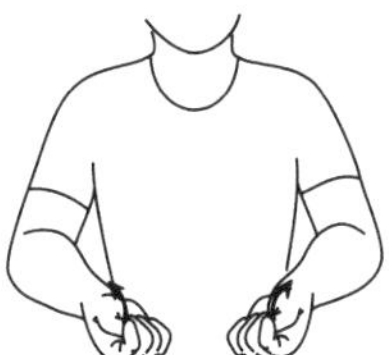

SLIGHT
Close palm-up hands with index over thumbnail; then flick thumbs out
(see BIT, Alt.1)

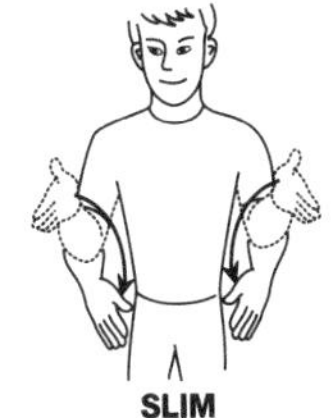

SLIM
Near body, palms-facing each other, hands curve in and down
(see DIET)

SLIP ★
Flat hand arcs out along left palm
(see LAP)

SLIPPER
Palm-down flat hand slides in and out of palm-up left C-hand

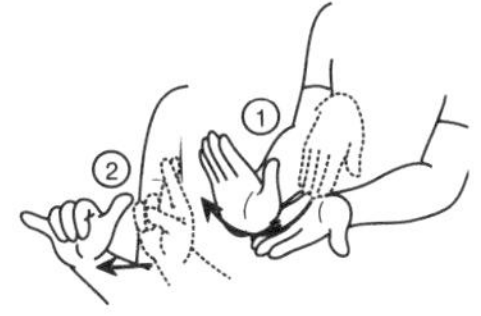

SLIPPERY
Palm-down hand slips down and out palm-up left hand; change to make palm-out R, then Y-hand *(slip + -er + -y)*

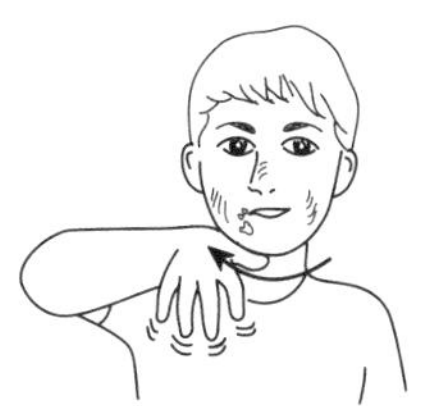

SLOP
Thumb under chin, 5-hand moves to right under chin, fingers fluttering

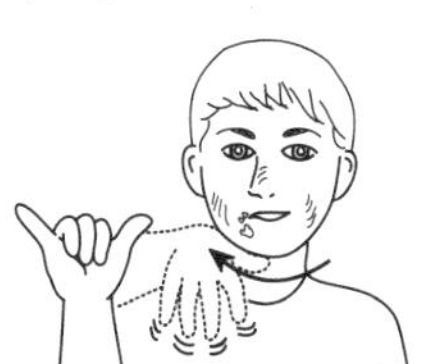

SLOPPY
Thumb under chin, 5-hand moves to right under chin, fingers fluttering; then add Y *(slop + -y)*

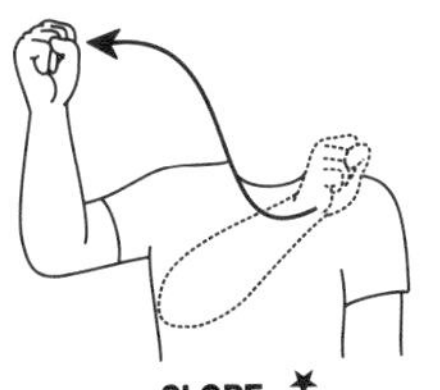

SLOPE ★
Right S-hand outlines slope up and out to the right

SLOW
Both palms-down, right hand moves up back of horizontal left hand

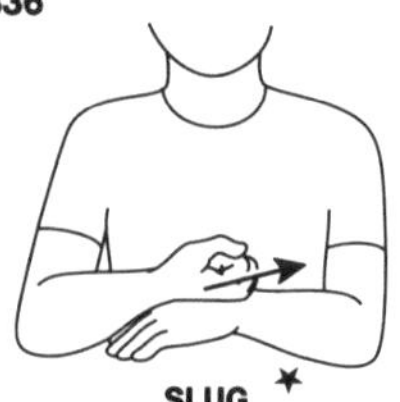

SLUG ★
Palm-up S moves along left arm
(see CATERPILLAR)

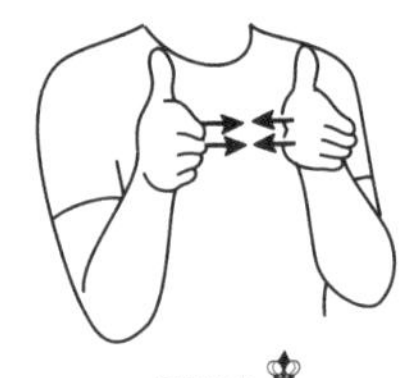

SMALL ♔
Flat hands, palms-facing, jerk slightly toward each other; repeat

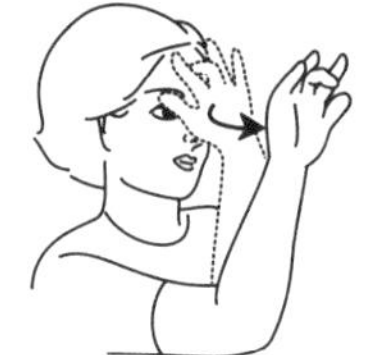

SMART
Bent middle finger on forehead snaps off and twists to palm-out
(see WIT)

SMELL ♔
Palm-up hand near nose brushes upward several times

SMILE ♔
Index finger sides of bent hands curve corners of mouth up

SMOG
Palm-in open hand and palm-out S-hand pass each other in front of face
(see DARK)

SMOKE ★
Right palm-in V at corner of mouth, slightly zig-zags upwards

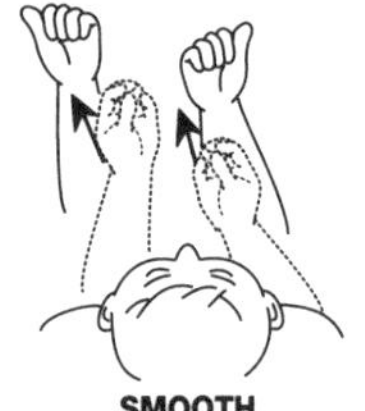

SMOOTH
Palm-up flat-O's both move slightly forward while thumbs move across fingertips to A-hands

SNACK
Middle finger snaps up to G at mouth

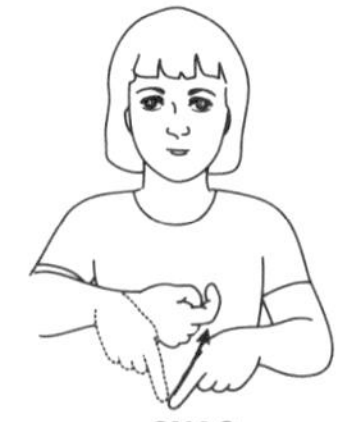

SNAG
Indexes pointing slightly downward, right index scrapes up left and ends in X

SNAIL
Heel of bent-V slides up left forearm
(see CATERPILLAR)

SNAKE
Back of bent-V hand under chin circles forward
(see REPTILE)

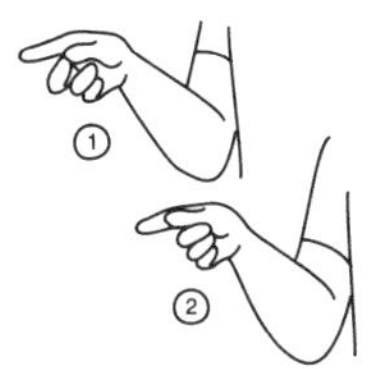

SNAP
Tips of middle finger and thumb together, index extended, snap to G

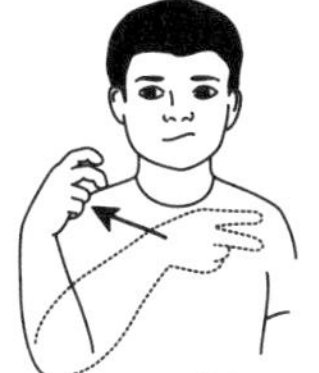

SNATCH
Horizontal V jerks right to bent-V
(see STEAL)

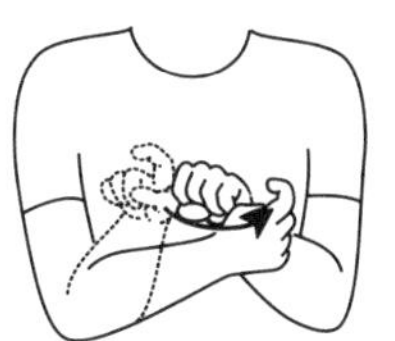

SNEAK
X-hand sneaks around left S to peek at little finger of left hand

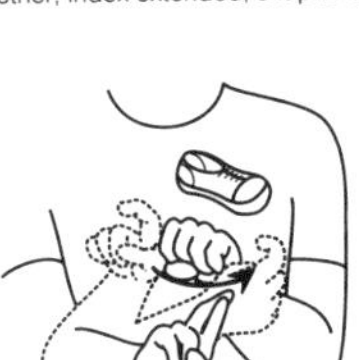

SNEAKER
X-hand sneaks around left S to peek at little finger of left hand; add R *(sneak +-er)*

SNEEZE
Index finger under nose, jerk head back and then forward slightly

SNIFF
X-hand against nose, sniff with head moving slightly up

SNIP
Fingers of V-hand snip corner of first knuckle of left S; may repeat
(see CUT)

SNOB
Index finger on nose tilts head back, little finger out
(see ARROGANT)

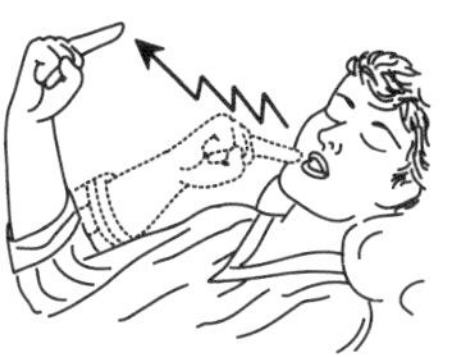

SNORE
Index zig-zags out from mouth

SNOW
Hands drop slowly, palm-down, fluttering fingers
(see RAIN)

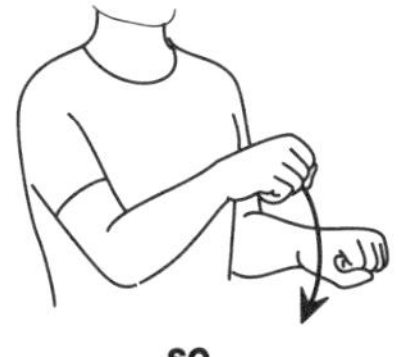

SO
Right S moves sharply down, striking side of left S in passing

SOAP
Flick fingers of bent right hand back, off left palm; repeat

SOCCER
Side of flat right hand kicks wrist of palm-down left S-hand several times
(see KICK)

SOCIAL
Right S curves around vertical left index finger
(see ATMOSPHERE)

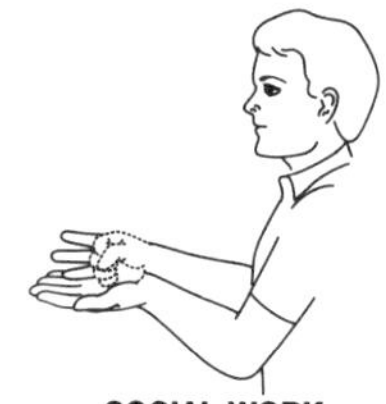

SOCIAL WORK
Side of horizontal S-hand on left palm, quickly changes to W-hand

SOCIETY
S curves around vertical left index; thumbtip of Y slides down vertical hand *(social + -ity)*

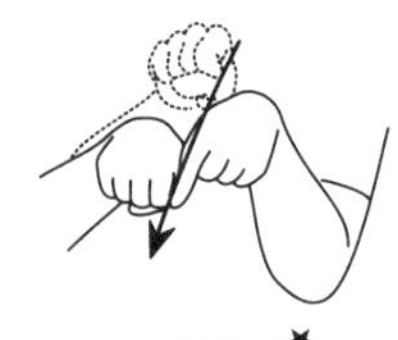

SOCK *
S hits forward along side of palm-down left index finger

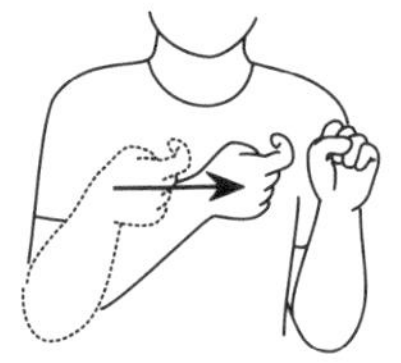

SOCKET
Palm-in horizontal right X-hand taps palm-out left S
(see ELECTRIC)

SODA
Fingers of palm-down right hand flutter up from palm-right left S-hand
(see YEAST)

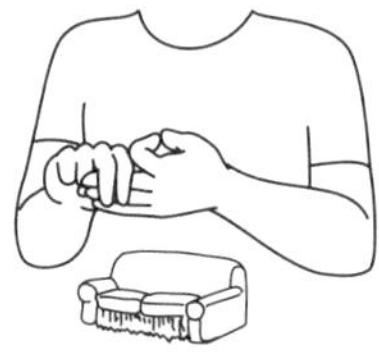

SOFA
First right two fingers sit on middle finger of palm-in left F-hand
(see SIT)

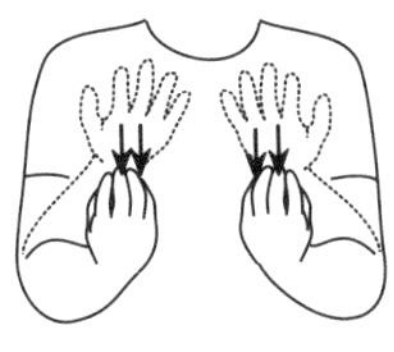

SOFT
Palm-up open hands drop slightly, closing to flat-O's; repeat

SOIL
Flat-O thumb rubs on balls of fingers

SOLAR
Right S behind left, palms-out; right circles around left to palm-in
(see EQUATOR)

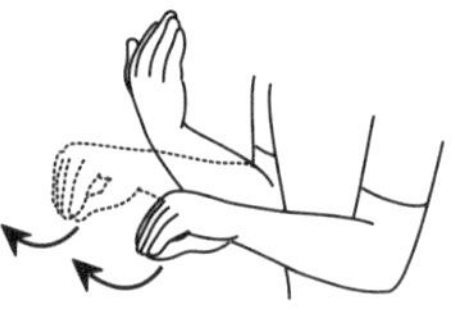

SOLD
Palms-down flat-O's flip up at wrist; right flat hand flips towards shoulder *(sell + p. t.)*

SOLDER
Index of palm-in L-hand circles near left S-hand
(see WELD)

SOLDIER
Palm-in A's tap at shoulder and side; repeat *(holding gun)*
(see MILITARY)

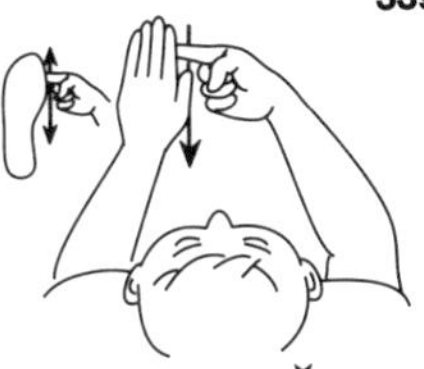

SOLE ★
Index finger slides backwards under horizontal left palm

SOLID
Right A knocks on left palm

SOLUTION
Thumb of palm-up flat-O slides past fingertips to A-hand as hand moves right; S slides down vertical flat hand *(solve + -tion)*

SOLVE
Thumb of palm-up flat-O slides past fingertips as hand moves right, becoming palm-up A-hand

SOME ♔
Side of right hand draws small arc across left palm

SOMERSAULT
Right S twists twice off left palm *(doing somersaults)*
(see TUMBLE)

SOMETIMES
Index touches left palm, moves toward body, circles back to palm; repeat
(see SELDOM)

S

SON
Right A-hand at temple drops in an arc to open palm-up on palm-up left arm

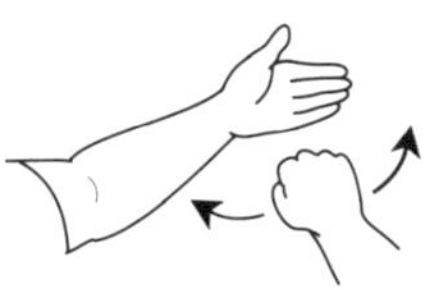

SONG
Right S arcs from side-to-side behind left flat palm
(see MUSIC)

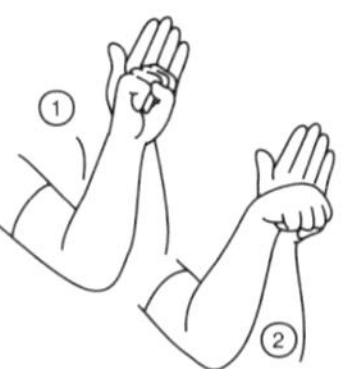

SOON
Side of palm-out S on left palm; twists to palm-down
(see MINUTE)

SOPHISTICATE
Thumb of 3 brushes off chin; repeat

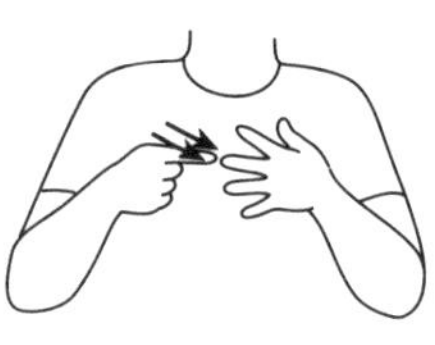

SOPHOMORE
Index taps middle finger of left 5
(see FRESHMAN)

SORE ✶
Right S-hand twists on chin; repeat
(see SOUR)

SORRY
Palm-in A-hand circles on chest
(see REGRET)

SORT
Right index tip of L-hand brushes inward on palm-up left heel, repeat on middle of palm, then fingertips

SOUL
Right 9-hand rises, shaking, from horizontal flat-O near heart

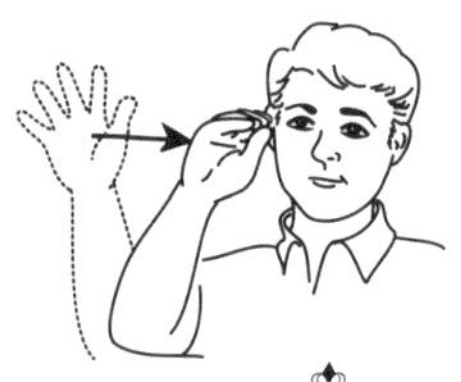

SOUND ♔
Right palm-out 5 moves to ear, closing to flat-O hand

SOUP ♔
Right H-hand ladles twice from left palm to mouth

SOUR ♔
Index finger on chin, twists to palm-in

S

SOURCE
Palm-out left S, right index touches left wrist and twists to palm-in
(see START)

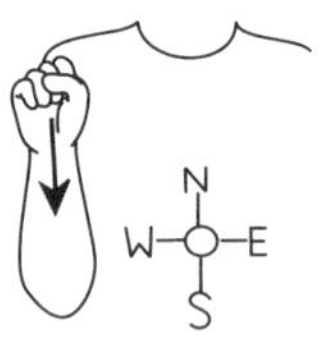

SOUTH
Palm-out S moves down
(see DOWN)

SPACE
S arcs up in front of face

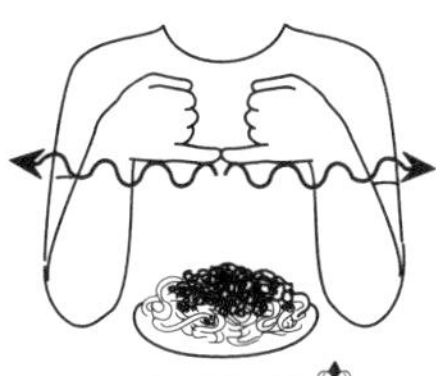

SPAGHETTI
Tips of palm-in I's touching, separate with a shaking movement

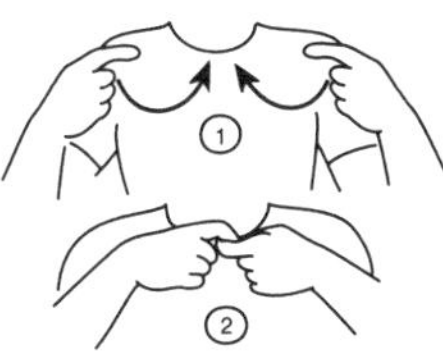

SPAIN
Index fingers on shoulders drop to interlocking X's *(fastening cape)*
(see HISPANIC)

SPANK
Right flat hand spanks heel of left vertical flat hand

SPARK
Right index flicks up alongside left vertical index; repeat

SPARKLE
Right flat-O at tip of vertical left index, right hand rises to side, fingers opening and fluttering

SPARROW
S-hand near mouth, changes to G-hand on chin, thumb and index repeatedly touch

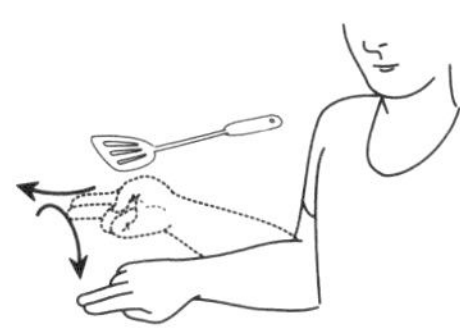

SPATULA
Palm-up U slides forward and flips over to palm-down
(see PANCAKE)

SPEAK
Palm-left 4 at chin moves forward and back; repeat

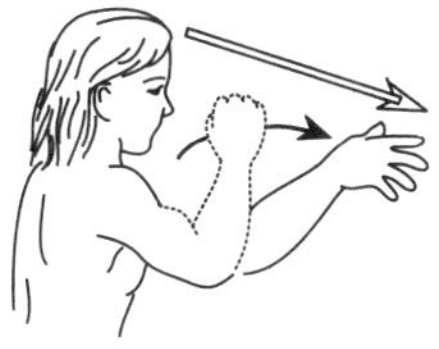

SPEAR
Mime throwing a spear

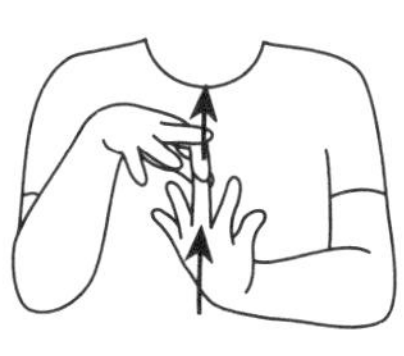

SPECIAL
Thumb and index of 9 pulls middle finger of palm-in 5 upward
(see EXCEPT)

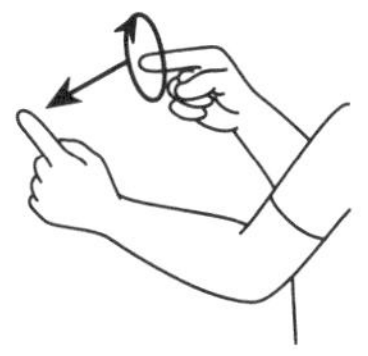

SPECIFIC
Tip of 1-hand makes small circle then jerks toward left vertical index
(see EXACT)

SPEECH
Bent-V circles in front of mouth
(see MOUTH)

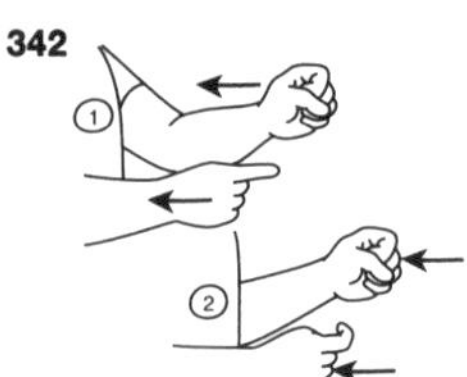

SPEED
Left horizontal S ahead of right horizontal index, jerk both toward body, closing index to X-hand
(see FAST)

SPELL ✶
Palm-down hand moves right, while fingers flutter

SPEND
Back of right flat-O on left palm slides off, closing to A-hand
(see BUY)

SPICE
Right index and middle finger of V-hand alternately tap left palm-out S
(see SALT)

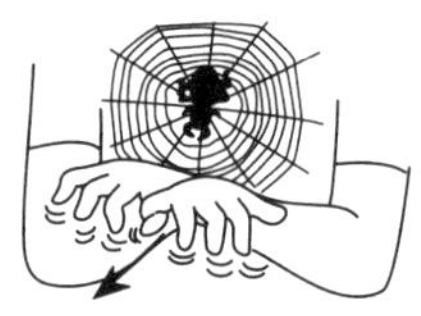

SPIDER
Little fingers interlock and fingers wiggle forward

SPILL
C-hand tips forward off left palm

SPIN ♔
Right index pointing down, left index pointing up, rotate fingers

SPINACH
Both S-hands palms-facing with heels together, hands open

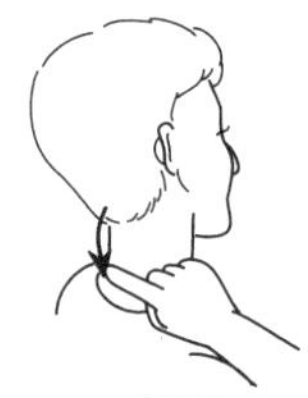

SPINE
Index of right hand on back of neck moves downward
(see MENINGITIS)

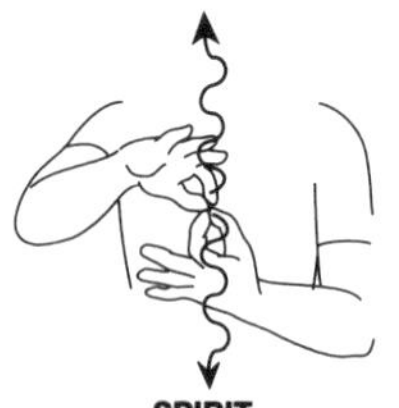

SPIRIT
9-hand's right over left, palms-facing, separate in wavy motion
(see GHOST)

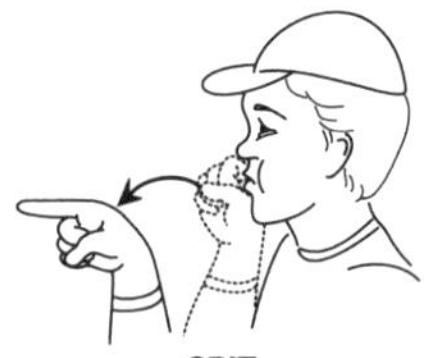

SPIT
Right S at mouth, index snaps out, pointing forward

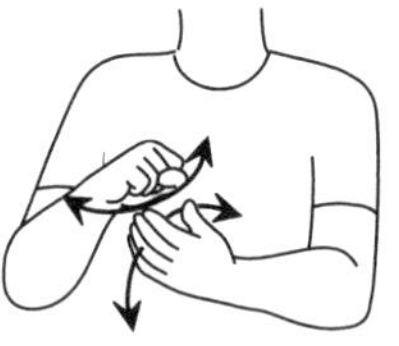

SPITE
Palm-in left hand and right S brush back and forth forward and back
(see THOUGH)

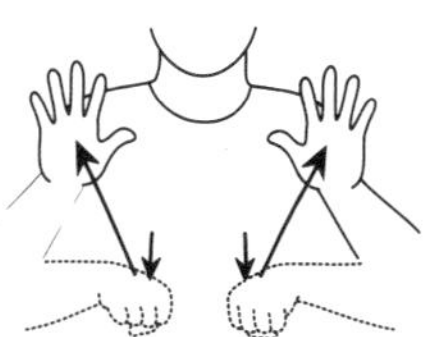

SPLASH
Palm-down S's drop; 5's splash up

SPLICE
N's move together with right fingertips resting on left fingernails

SPLINTER
Index is splinter that goes into left palm

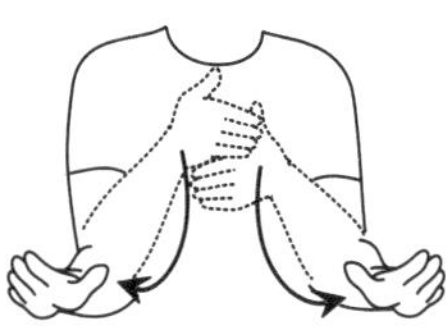

SPLIT
Flat hands, right on left at right angles; drop, separating to sides

SPOIL
Left S palm-down, right X points forward and strikes forward across S
(see RUIN)

SPOKE
Palm-left 4 hand at chin moves forward and back; repeat, then flat hand flips toward right shoulder *(speak + p. t.)*

SPONGE
Hold sponge between claw hands, fingertips touching and move fingers downward in squeezing motion

SPOOK
Palms-facing S's right over left, right rises above in wavy motion
(see GHOST)

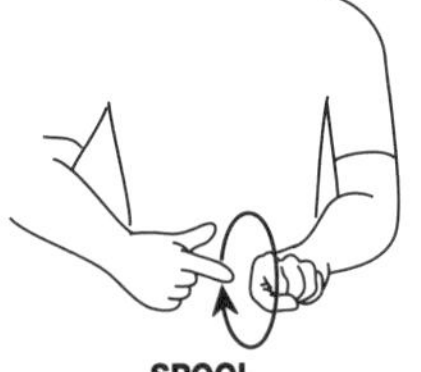

SPOOL
Fingertip of right L circles around side of left S-hand
(see REEL)

SPOON
Right H-hand circles up from left palm
(see SOUP)

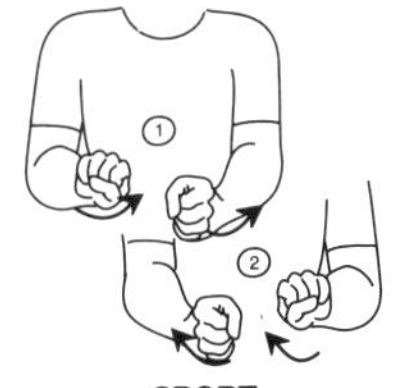

SPORT
S-hands swing side-to-side
(see PLAY)

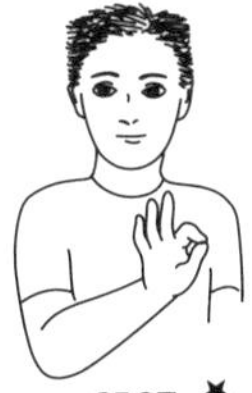

SPOT ★
Side of F placed wherever spot is

SPRAIN
Bent-V's palms-facing, near each other twist sharply in opposite directions
(see TWIST)

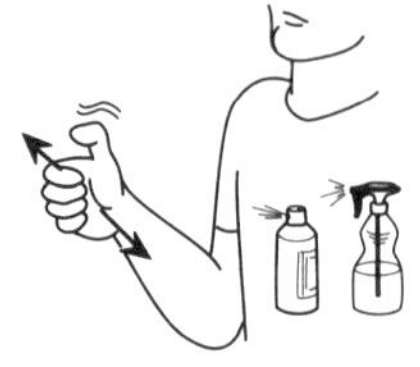

SPRAY
Thumb pushes aerosol spray knob, moving the "can" left and right

SPREAD
Flat-O hands, palms-down, spread to palm-down 5's

SPRING ★
Flat-O "jumps" upward through horizontal C to 5; repeat
(see GROW)

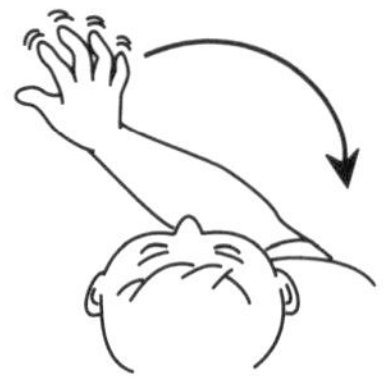

SPRINKLE
Palm-down 5 circles horizontally, fluttering fingers
(see DRIZZLE)

SPURT
Palm-out S-hands together; right index flicks forward

SPY
Side of palm-left B-hand at corner of eye, moves slightly to right, then back

SQUAD
Palm-out S's touch, circle outward and touch again as palm-in D's
(see BAND)

SQUARE ♔
Indexes draw a square
(see RECTANGLE)

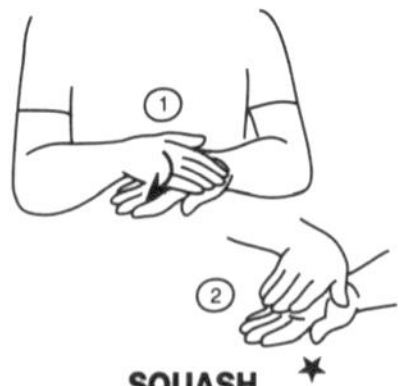

SQUASH ★
Right palm twists on left palm *(in squashing motion)*
(see CRUSH)

SQUEAL
S at throat shakes forward

SQUEEZE
Horizontal S's, right above left, open and close several times *(as if squeezing)*

SQUID
S sits on 5; 5-hand does push-ups
(see OCTOPUS)

SQUIRM
Palm-in S-hands holding arms to sides, body squirms

SQUIRREL
At chin, tap bent-V fingertips together, keeping heels together

STAB
Side of fist stabs left palm-in palm

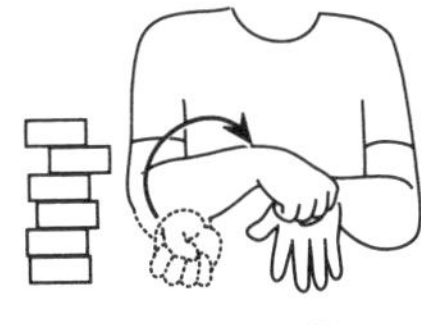

STACK ✶
Palm-up S arcs over to the left ending palm-down on back of left hand
(see CARGO)

STADIUM
Palm-down claw hands, fingers-facing, separate and arc upwards

STAFF
Right S-hand at right shoulder then F at left shoulder
(see MEMBER)

STAGE
Heel of S slides across left arm
(see BOARD)

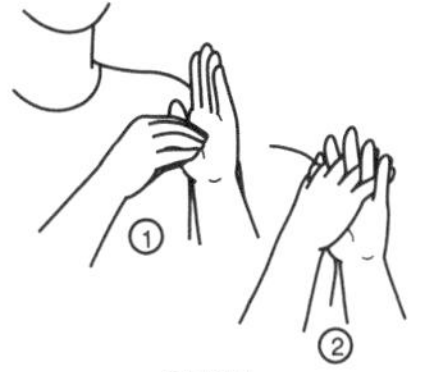

STAIN
Right flat-O fingertips on left vertical palm, changes to open fingers that penetrate fingers of left hand

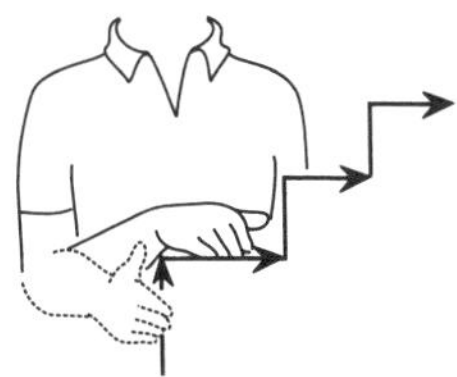

STAIR
Right palm traces stair steps

STALE
Right X-finger draws across left S
(see DULL)

STALL
Palm-in S's touch, separate, face each other, move towards body
(see DECK)

STAMP ★
Side of S-fist hits left palm-up palm
(see APPROVE)

STAND
V-fingertips stand on left palm

STANDARD ♔
Palm-down Y's move in circle horizontally together

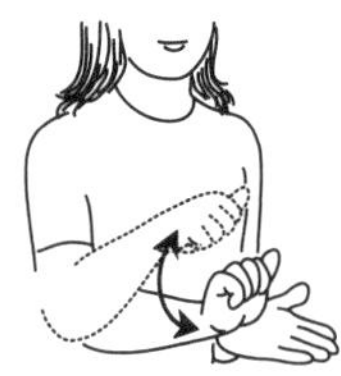

STAPLE
Heel of A-hand presses stapler on the heel of the left hand

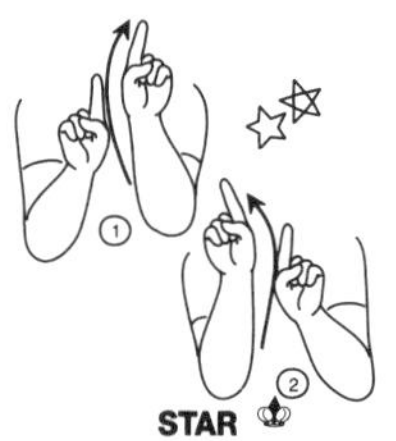

STAR ♔
Side of right index finger strikes upward against left index finger; left strikes upward against right

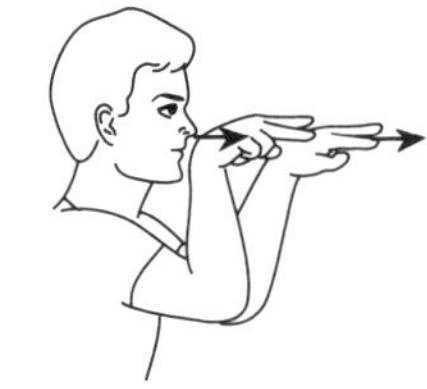

STARE
Both V-hands, palm-down near eyes, right behind left; move forward slightly
(see GAZE)

START ♔
Right index between left index and middle finger of 5-hand; twist right hand

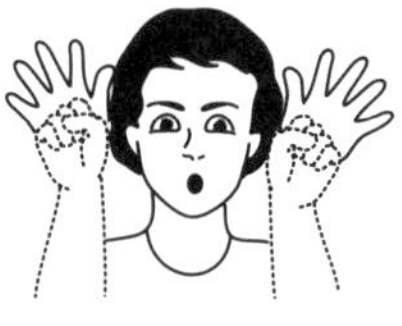

STARTLE
S's at sides of eyes spring open to 5's

STARVE
Palm-in C-hands, one above the other, move down middle of chest once
(see HUNGER)

STATE
Side of right S on fingertips of left vertical flat hand arcs down to heel
(see LAW)

STATION
Palm-out S's touch, then outline roof and sides
(see HOUSE)

STATIONARY
Thumbs of palm-down Y's touch, separate and drop slightly

STATIONERY
Heel of palm-down right S hits across heel of palm-up left hand; repeat
(see PAPER)

STATISTICS
Palm-out S's cross, right brushing back of left in passing; repeat
(see ARITHMETIC)

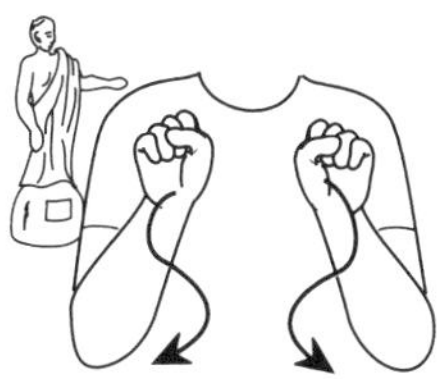

STATUE
Palm-out S's outline statue
(see SHAPE)

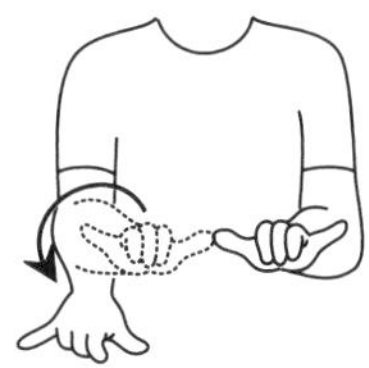

STAY
Palm-down Y thumbs together; right arcs slightly down to right
(see LODGE)

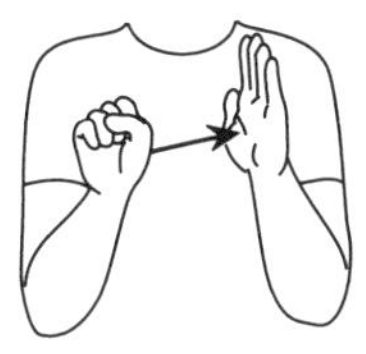

STEAD
Side of S hits heel of left vertical hand

STEAK
Right hand pinches thumb knuckle of left palm-up S; shake both hands
(see MEAT)

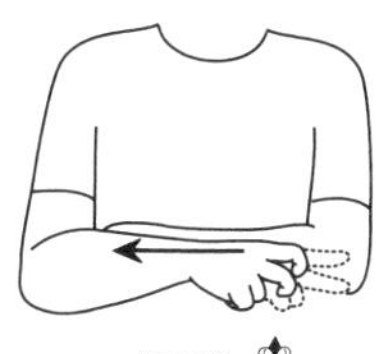

STEAL ♔
Right palm-down V-hand pulls to bent-V from left elbow

STEAM
W spirals upwards from chin

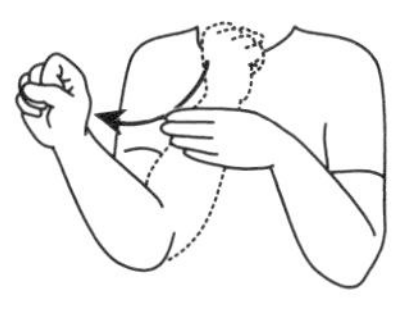

STEEL
Right palm-in S arcs right, hitting side of left index, ending palm-out
(see METAL)

STEEP
Right hand on back of left, hands point upward; right slides up left

STEGOSAURUS
Palm-down right S on back of left wrist, hop up forearm

STEM
Tips of finger and thumb of right G slides up left vertical index

STEP
Flat hands, palms-down, one hand steps forward

STEREO
5-hands swing from outward to facing toward ears

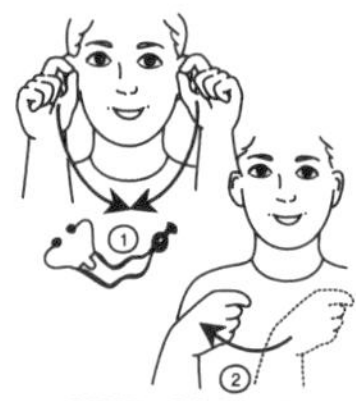

STETHOSCOPE
Indexes and thumbs grip at ears; drop hands to meet on chest; then right hand touches chest at left and right

STEW
Right S pointing down above left horizontal C opens to 5; repeat

STICK ✶
Fingers of G's close on each other

STILL ✶
Inverted Y-hand swings down and then up, forward

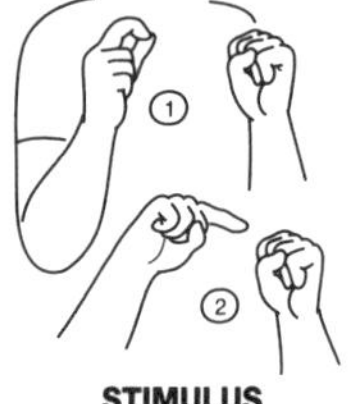

STIMULUS
Index of right S repeatedly flicks toward left S

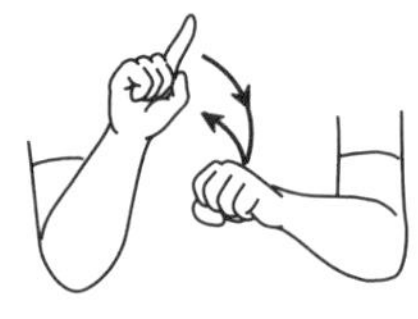

STING
Index finger hits back of S sharply

STINGY
Right claw on left palm scrapes to a closed S-hand

STINK
Pinch nose with thumb and index

STIR ✶
A-hand stirs, thumb pointing down

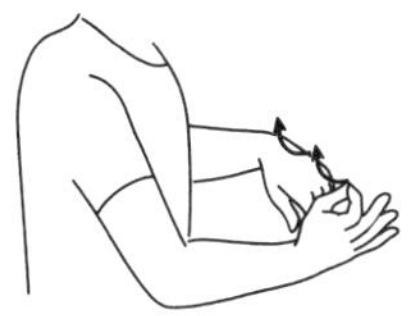

STITCH
Tip of 9-hand "stiches" up back of palm-down left hand

STOCK
Palm-out S behind palm right left C, S circles slightly, then pushes slightly towards C-hand
(see STORE)

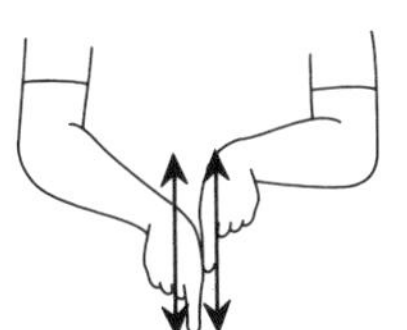

STOCKING
Pointing downward, index fingers slide back and forth against each other
(see HOSE)

STOLE
Right palm-down V pulls to bent-V from left elbow; then flips toward shoulder *(steal + p. t.)*

STOMACH
Fingertips of bent hand pat stomach

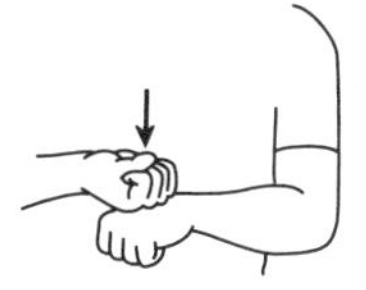

STONE ♔
Back of right palm-up S raps back of left palm-down S; repeat

STOOD
Right V-fingertips stand on left palm; then flips toward shoulder *(stand + p. t.)*

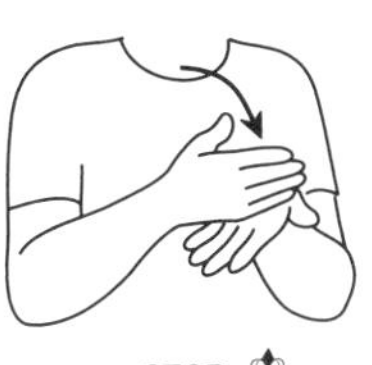

STOP ♔
Side of right palm-left flat hand strikes left flat palm

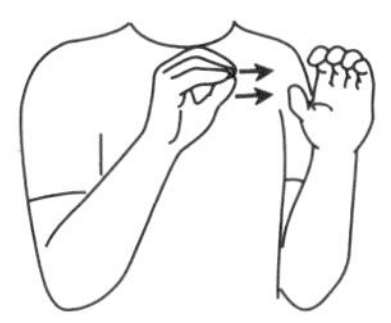

STORE ♔ ★
Right flat-O behind left C, nods rapidly toward and from side of C-hand

S

STORM ♔
Claw hands circle alternately, slightly upwards, over head

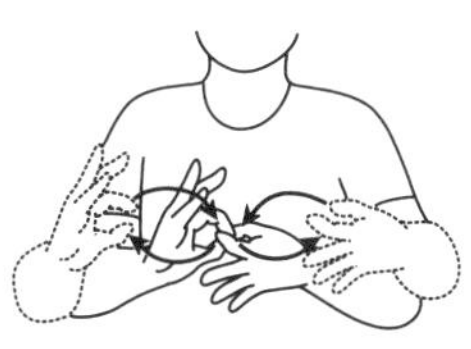

STORY
Open 9-hands approach, thumb and index fingers link, and separate still closed; repeat

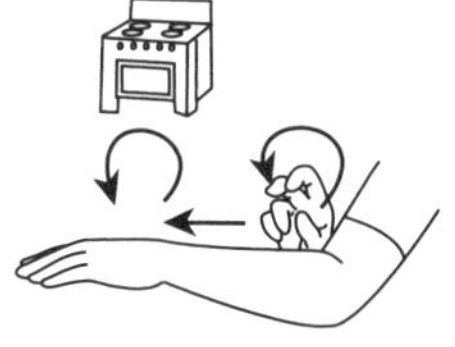

STOVE
Thumb and bent-V turn on 2 burners of the stove, along left arm

STRADDLE
Inverted V straddles side of flat left hand and rocks side-to-side

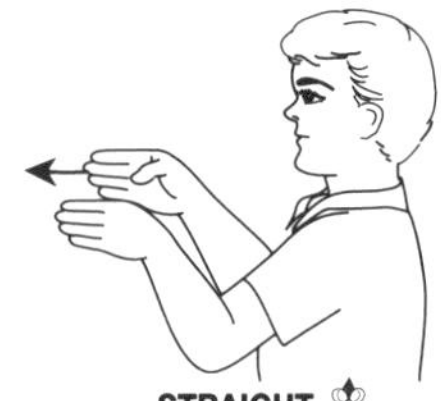

STRAIGHT
Side of right B slides forward on side of left B-hand

STRANGE
Right palm-left C arcs in front of nose to palm-down C-hand

STRAW
Palm-out S brushes up through horizontal C; repeat
(see GRAIN)

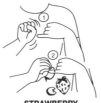

STRAWBERRY
(Alt. 1)
S shakes by little finger of palm-in horizontal left I; then add "berry"

STRAWBERRY
(Alt. 2)
Palm-in 9 at lips moves out

STRAY
Index fingers pointing downward, tips touching, right wanders off
(see DEVIATE)

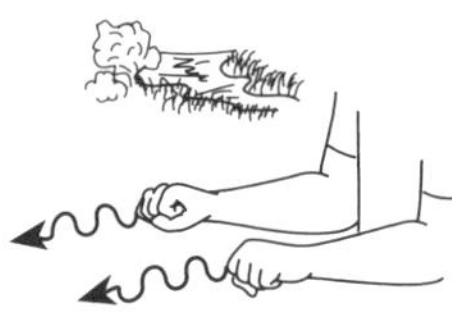

STREAM
Palm-down S's ripple forward to left, up and down
(see BROOK)

STREET
Flat hands pointing down with right slightly before left, hands sweep to the left

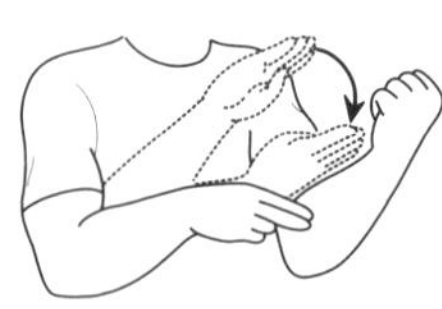

STRENGTH
Right B-hand draws muscle on left arm; add H-hand *(strong + -th)*

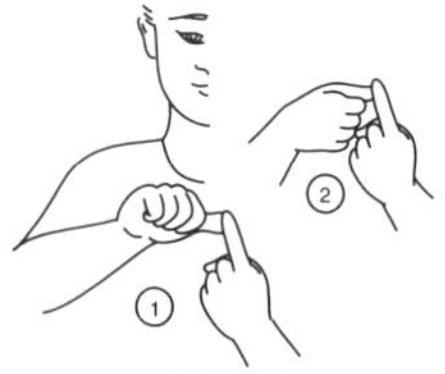

STRESS
Tip of right A on tip of vertical left index, right twists forward to palm in
(see EMPHASIS)

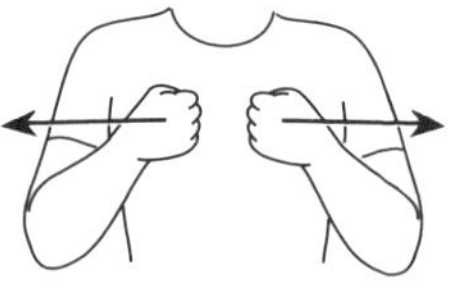

STRETCH
Palms-in S-hands pull apart

STRICT
Side of bent-V hits bridge of nose lightly

STRIKE
Right palm-in S-hand strikes palm-out vertical left index
(see BEAT)

STRING
Palm-in I-fingertip shakes from left S
(see CORD)

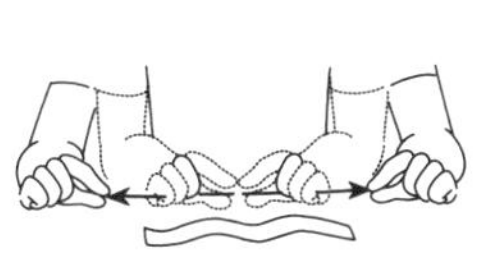

STRIP ★
G fingertips together, pull to sides and close thumb and finger

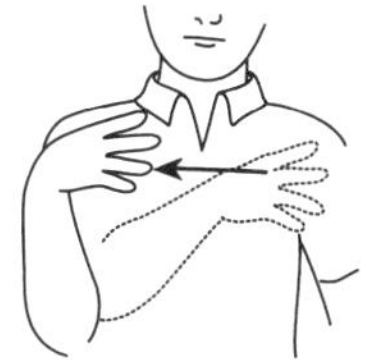

STRIPE
Palm-in 4-hand slides across chest to the right

STRIVE
S hands palms-facing arc slightly down and forward
(see ATTEMPT)

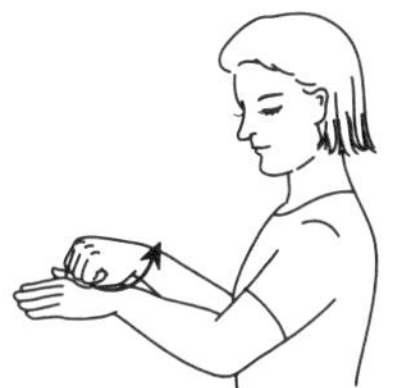

STROKE
Palm-down S strokes inward once on back of palm-down left hand
(see PET)

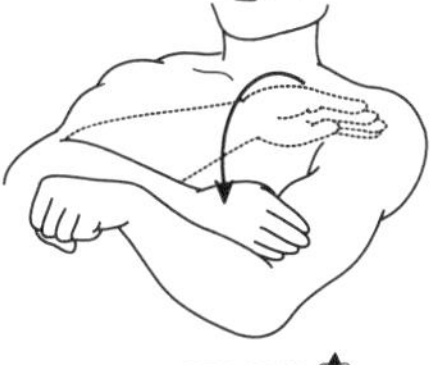

STRONG ♔
Right B-hand draws muscle on left arm

STRUCTURE
S-hands build alternately upward on each other
(see BUILD)

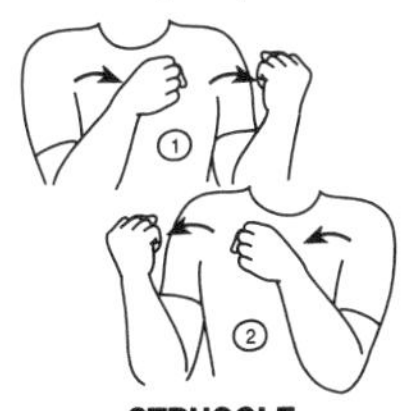

STRUGGLE
S's, palms-facing, rock side-to-side
(see WAR)

STUBBORN ♔
Thumb touching temple, fingers flap forward together

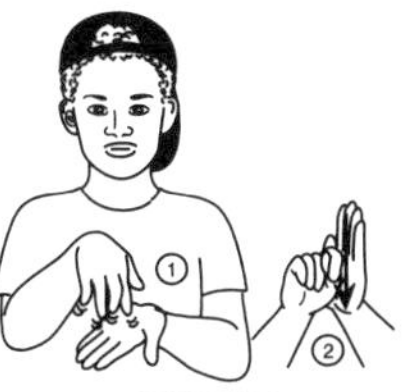

STUDENT
Right fingers wiggle above left palm; T-hand slides down left vertical hand *(study + -ent)*

STUDY
Right fingers wiggle above left palm

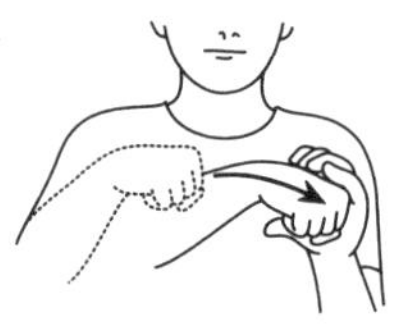

STUFF
Right palm-down S makes stuffing motions towards left C-hand
(see STORE)

STUMP
Left arm vertical, palm-down right S draws across arm near elbow

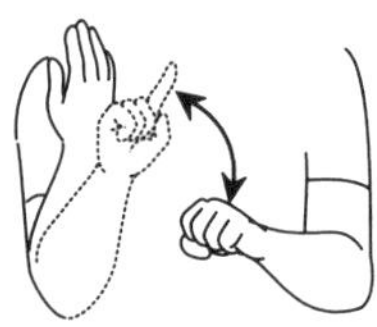

STUNG
Index finger of right hand hits back of S sharply, then flips toward right shoulder *(sting + p. t.)*

STUPID
Back of V hits forehead
(see DUMB)

STYLE
5 hand on torso, move upward on body fluttering fingers
(see FANCY)

SUBJECT
Side of right S on left fingers of palm-up flat hand, then on heel
(see LESSON)

SUBMARINE
Thumb-up horizontal palm-left 3-hand glides under left palm

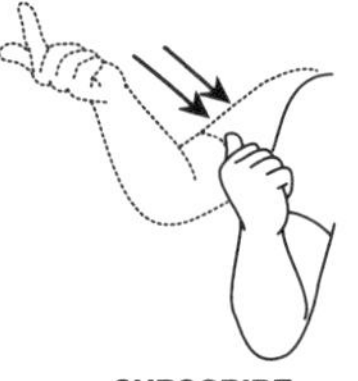

SUBSCRIBE
Palm-up L-hand moves back toward body, closing to A; repeat

SUBSTANCE
Back of palm-up S on heel of palm-up left hand, then on fingertips

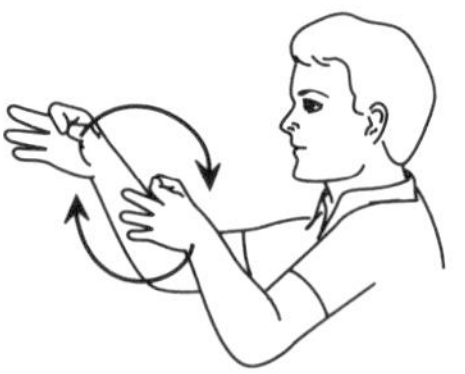

SUBSTITUTE
9-hands, right in front of left, circle each other vertically once
(see EXCHANGE)

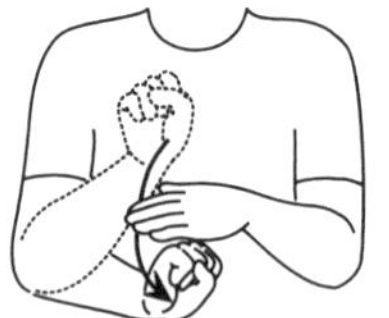

SUBTLE
Palm-out S moves from over palm-down left hand to under it
(see HUMBLE)

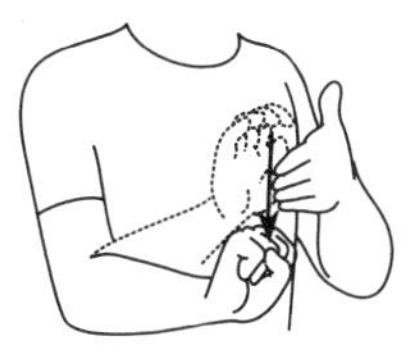

SUBTRACT

Fingertips of right C scratch left palm downwards to S

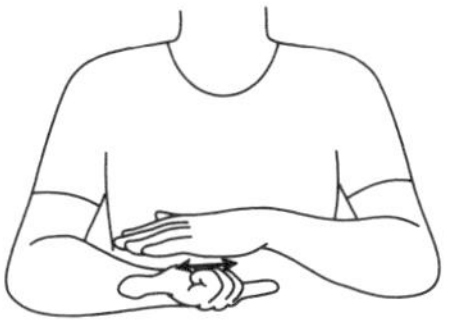

SUBWAY
(Alt. 1)

Right palm-up Y, moves side-to-side under left palm-down flat hand

(see XEROX Alt. 2)

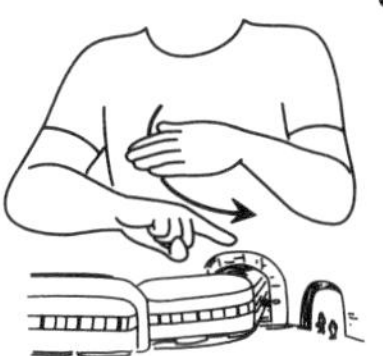

SUBWAY
(Alt. 2)

Right 1-hand dives down under flat palm-down left

(see ENTER)

SUCCEED

Palm-in index fingers at temples twist out to sides and up

(see SUCCESS)

SUCCESS ♔

Index fingers at temples twist out and up to sides, twisting twice

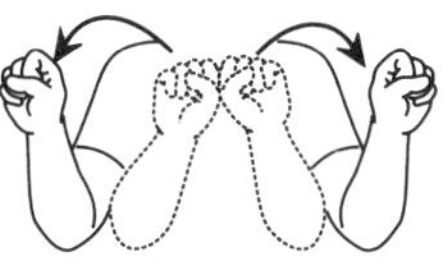

SUCH

S-hands together, arc up and apart

(see MUCH)

SUCK ★

Right palm-down 5-hand moves to flat-O near mouth

SUCKER

A-hand pulls an invisible sucker out of mouth several times

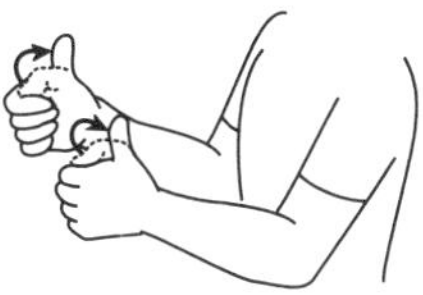

SUDDEN

Thumbs of both hands flip out from under index fingers

S

SUFFER

Thumb of A on chin, twists several times

SUFFIX

Left horizontal index points right, right S arcs left to touch tip of left index

(see AFFIX)

SUGAR

Fingertips of palm-in hand brush downward off chin; repeat

(see CUTE)

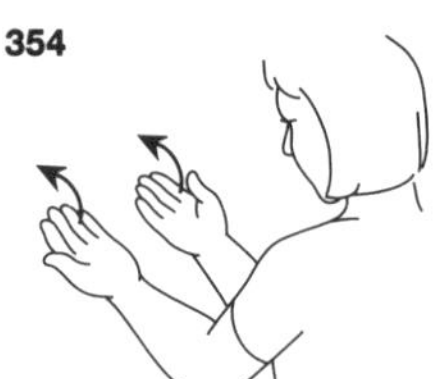

SUGGEST ♔
Palm-up hands arc up and forward

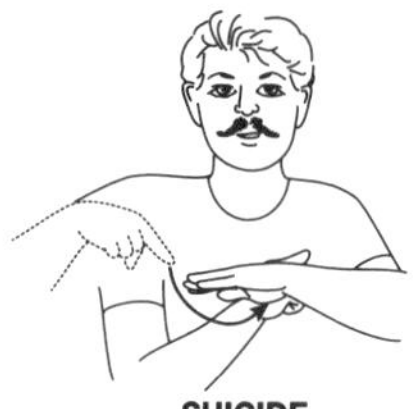

SUICIDE
Right index points inward, brushes in under left palm and touches chest
(see KILL)

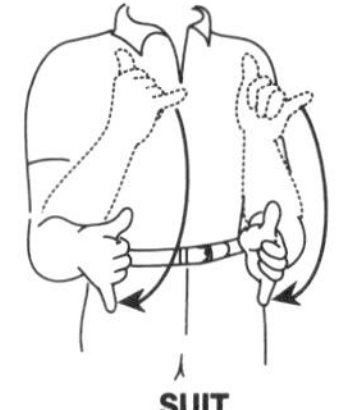

SUIT
Y-hands face each other, thumbs on chest, then arc down to little fingertips touching body

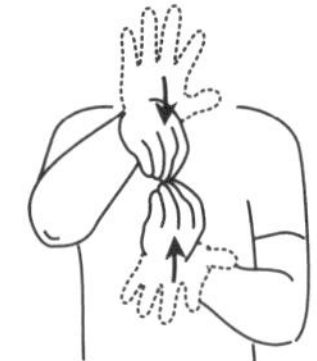

SUM ★
Right 5, palm-down, over left 5, palm-up; move toward each other and meet as flat-O's

SUMMARY
Horizontal 5-hands face each other, approach, close to right S on left S

SUMMER ♔
Palm-down X is dragged across forehead *(wiping sweat)*

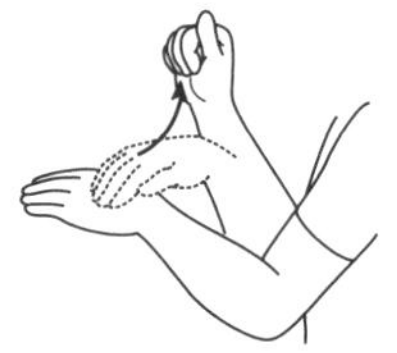

SUMMON
Fingers of right hand on back of left hand, arcs back to A-hand

SUN
Side of C by eye swings up to side

SUNDAE
Right extended-A thumb swirls up from left C-hand in a narrowing spiral

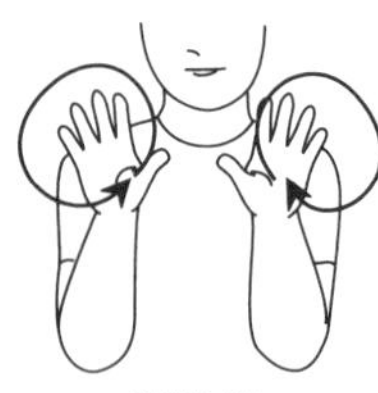

SUNDAY
Palm-out open 5's circle out to sides

SUNG
Side of U from corner of mouth arcs forward and out; palms-up twist to palms-facing *(sing + p. p.)*

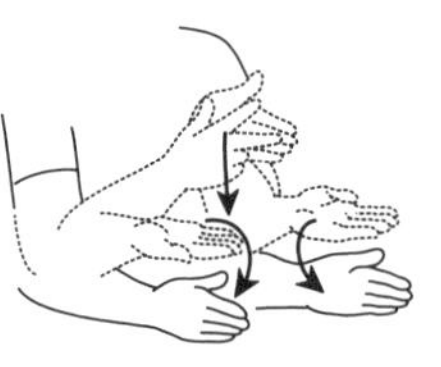

SUNK
Drop palm-left 3-hand down from palm-right left hand; both hands, palms-up, twist to palms-facing *(sink + p. p.)*

SUNRISE
Palm-down left hand points right; right O rises outside of left hand

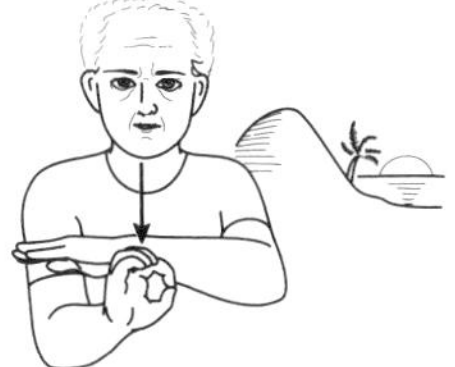

SUNSET
Palm-down left hand points right; right O sinks outside of left hand
(see DUSK)

SUPER
S circles over palm-down left hand
(see OVER)

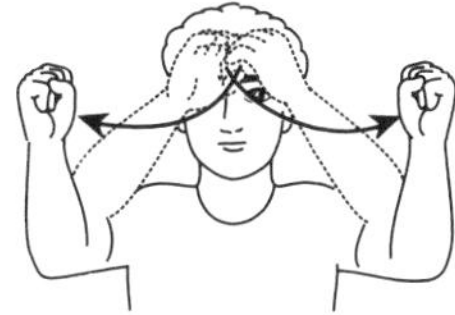

SUPERINTENDENT
C's at forehead, left in front of right, separate and close to S's
(see PRESIDENT)

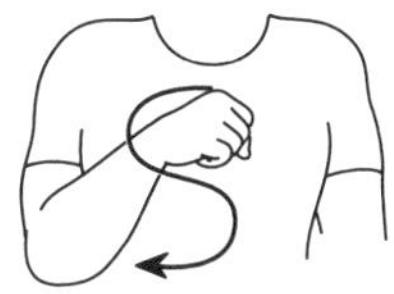

SUPERMAN
Right S-hand draws S on chest

SUPERSTITION
Right index touches temple, then both palm-out S's shake downwards from sides of head

SUPERVISE
Right S on side of left horizontal V; both circle horizontally
(see CARE)

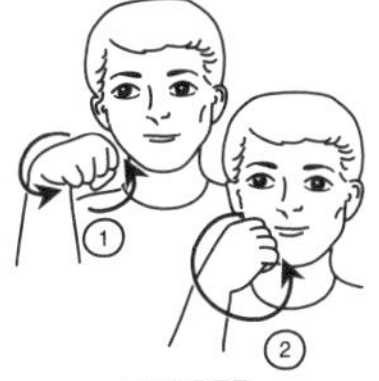

SUPPER
S circles forward near mouth
(see EAT)

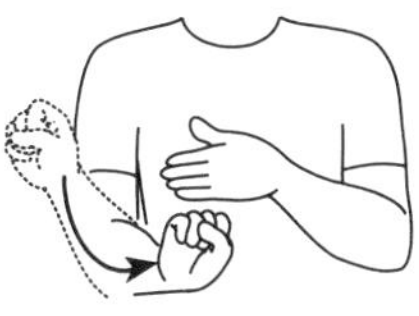

SUPPLEMENT
Right S arcs down to underside of palm-in horizontal left hand
(see ADD)

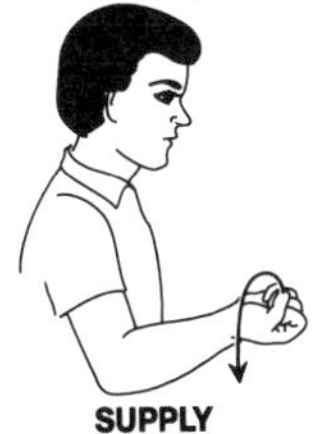

SUPPLY
Palm-up S arcs once to right
(see THING)

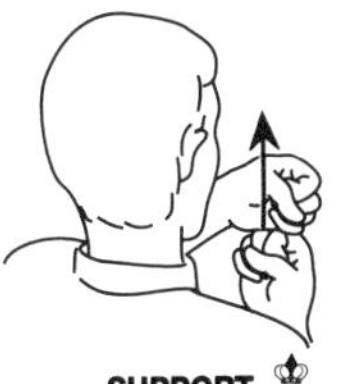

SUPPORT
Support side of left S with top of right palm-in S; push up

SUPPOSE
Palm-in I-hand at temple moves out in two arcs

SUPPRESS
Left horizontal S, palm-in, right flat hand pushes S downward

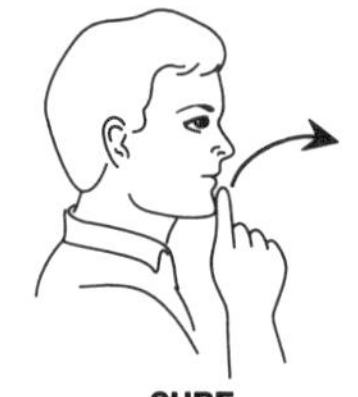

SURE
Palm-left index finger at chin arcs up and forward
(see CERTAIN)

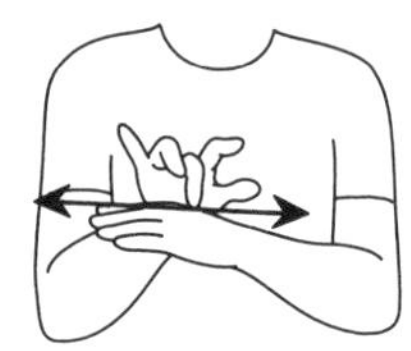

SURFACE
Right bent middle finger brushes back and forth on back of flat palm-down left hand

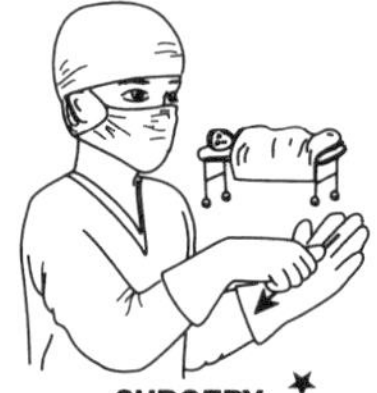

SURGERY ★
Thumb of extended-A cuts down open palm *(can be done on body where surgery is done)*

SURPRISE
Closed X-hands, facing each other near eyes, snap open to L-hands
(see AMAZE)

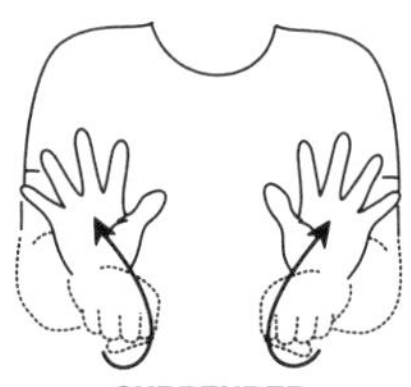

SURRENDER
Palm-down S-hands open and swing up to 5-hands

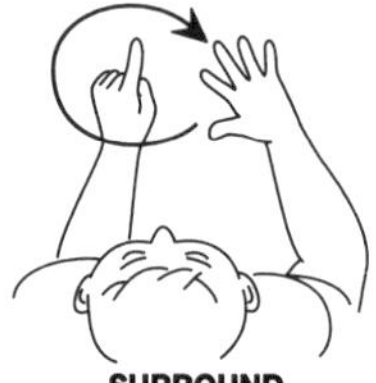

SURROUND
Horizontal right 5-hand circles vertical left index

SURVIVE
S-hands, palms-down, slide up chest
(see ADDRESS)

SUSPECT
Index scratches right temple
(see PARANOID)

S

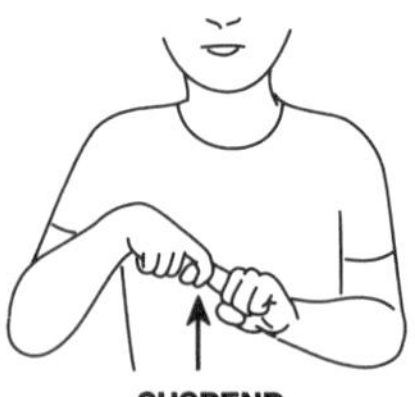

SUSPEND
Right X hooks on horizontal left index and both move upward

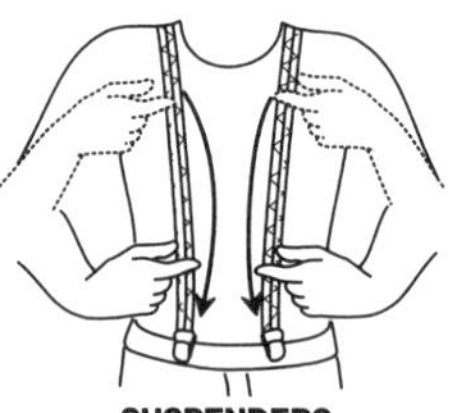

SUSPENDERS
Finger and thumbtips of G's draw suspenders down trunk

SWALLOW
Side of right index of palm-left hand arcs down throat

SWAM
Palms-down, breast stroke forward; right hand flips back *(swim + p. t.)*

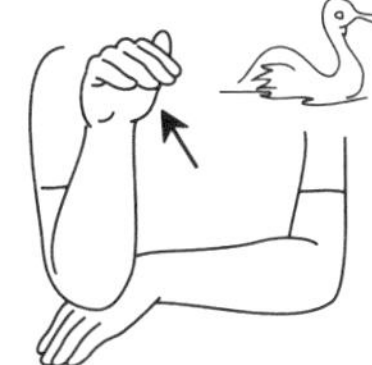

SWAN
Right elbow rests on back of left hand, arm and hand draws back to form S-shape

SWAY
Right vertical hand, palm-left, move back and forth at wrist

SWEAT
Palm-down 4 moves left over forehead, fluttering fingers

SWEATER
S-hands pull sweater down over head

SWEDE
(U.S. Sign)
S circles near forehead
(see DENMARK)

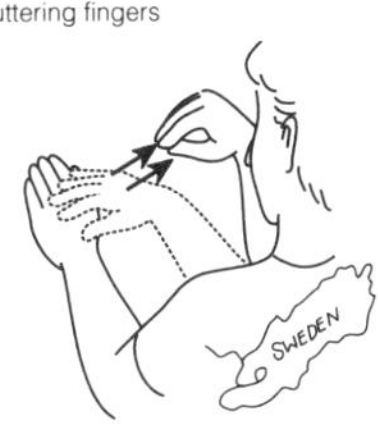

SWEDEN
(Swedish Sign)
5-hand draws up from back of left hand and closes to flat-O; repeat

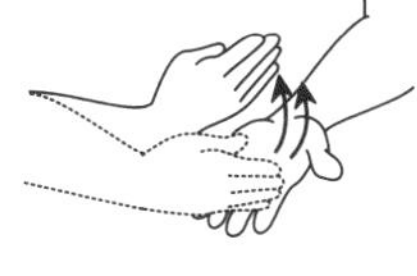

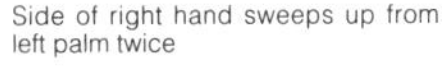

SWEEP
Side of right hand sweeps up from left palm twice

SWEET
Fingertips rub chin circularly
(see HONEY)

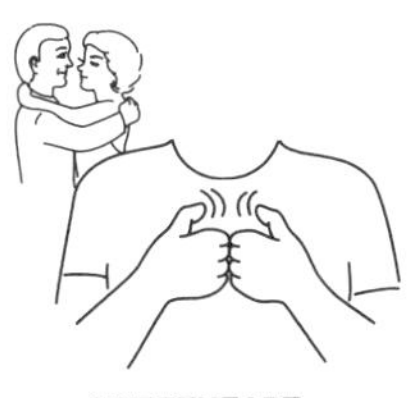

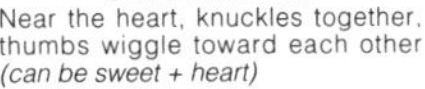

SWEETHEART
Near the heart, knuckles together, thumbs wiggle toward each other *(can be sweet + heart)*

SWELL ★
Claw hands near eyes move forward

SWIFT
Horizontal S's, palms-facing, slightly to the left with left ahead of right, arc quickly back towards body
(see FAST)

SWIM
Palms-down, breast stroke forward

SWING
Right bent-V sits on 2 fingers of left hand and swings forward and back
(see TRAPEZE)

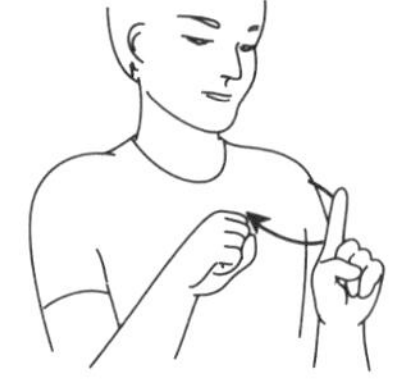

SWIPE
Left vertical index, right S touches tip, arcs sharply back toward body

SWITCH
Index fingers one over the other, almost touching, reverse positions vertically
(see CHANGE)

SWOLLEN
Claw hands near eyes move forward; add N-hand *(swell + p. p.)*

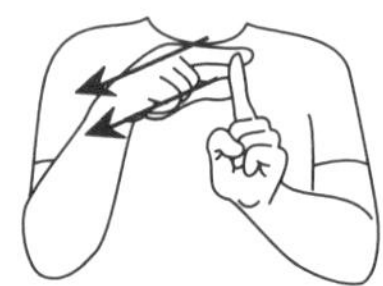

SWORD
Right A-hand draws sword out of left horizontal C at side

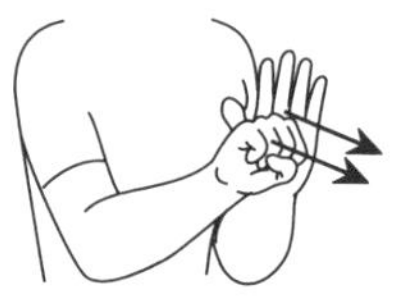

SYLLABLE
Right G-hand brushes tip of left index several times

SYMBOL
Right S on vertical left palm, both move forward together
(see SHOW)

SYMPATHY
Right bent middle finger touches heart, then bent middle fingers of both hands stroke outwards

S

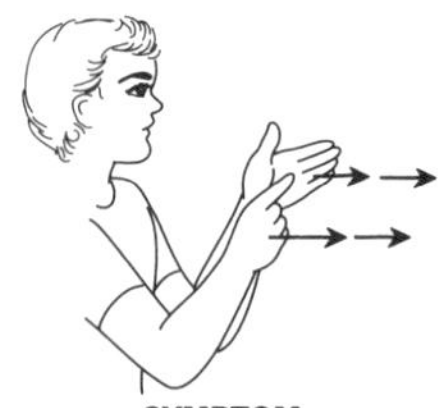

SYMPTOM
Tip of right index touches horizontal left palm; both hands move forward in two very short movements
(see SHOW)

SYNAGOGUE
Heel of S taps back of left hand; repeat
(see CHURCH)

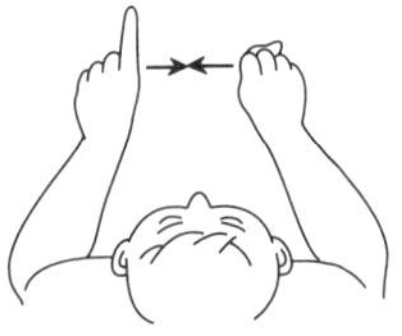

SYNONYM
Left index and right S-hand, palms-down, tap sides together
(see SAME)

SYNTAX
Palm-down S's touch, shake slightly separating sideways
(see SENTENCE)

SYRUP
Palm-in little finger of I-hand brushes side of mouth; repeat

SYSTEM
(Alt. 1)
S's together, separate sideways and down; repeat lower down
(see ANALYZE)

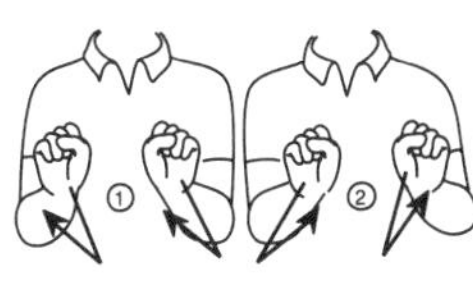

SYSTEM
(Alt. 2)
S-hands move forward left, back, then forward right
(see METHOD)

NOTES

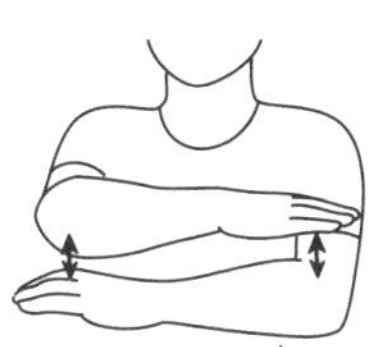

TABLE

Palm and elbow of bent right arm bounce on left bent arm

TACK

Right S "hammers" using wrist movement toward left thumbnail

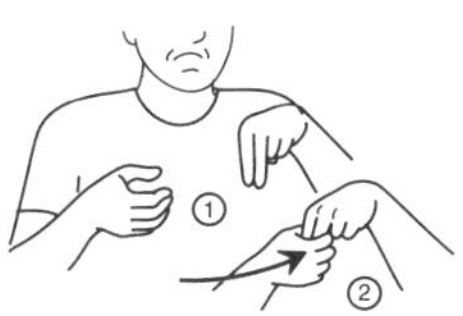

TACKLE

Right horizontal C forcefully grabs inverted left U

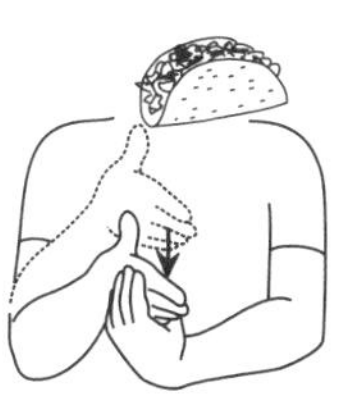

TACO

Right flat hand slips between thumb and fingers of "taco shell" shaped left, *(like filling a taco)*

TAG

Flat right hand slaps left shoulder once

TAIL

Right wrist rests on left index finger; wag hand with index extended

(see WAG)

TAILOR
Right 9-hand sews near left T-hand
(see SEW)

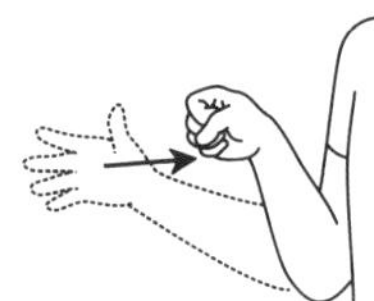

TAKE
5-hand draws back toward body closing to S-hand

TALE
Both T's together, palm-out, separate in a wiggling motion
(see DECODE)

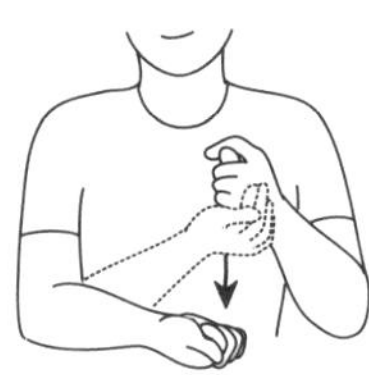

TALENT
Right hand clasps side of left T-hand and slides off to A-hand
(see EXPERT)

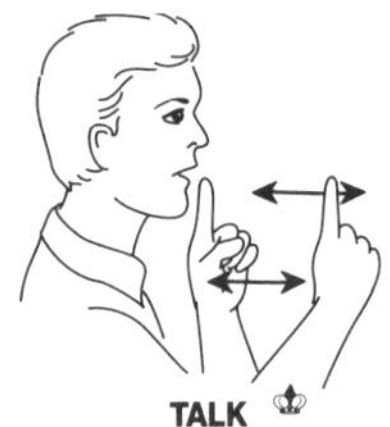

TALK
Index fingers of both hands move alternately to and from lips

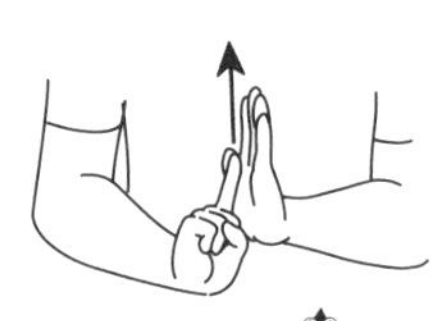

TALL
Right 1-index finger slides up vertical palm-right left hand

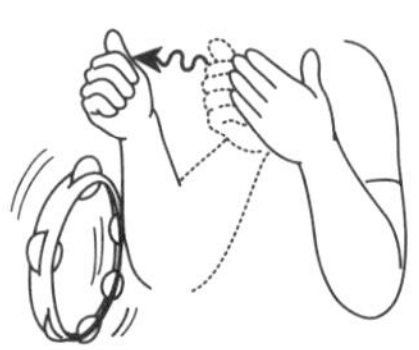

TAMBOURINE
A strikes on left flat verrtical palm and shakes away from it to the right

TAME
Right T-hand strokes back of palm-down left hand
(see PET)

TAN
Side of T moves down on cheek
(see BROWN)

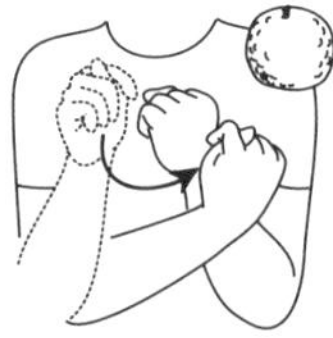

TANGERINE
Right T moves from in back of left S to the front ending palm-in
(see APRICOT)

TANK
Palms-facing T's, right behind left; right moves back, and both change to K's
(see CAR)

TANTRUM
(Alt. 1)
Palm-in T's near chest jerk up
(see ANGER)

TANTRUM
(Alt. 2)
Both palm-in T-hands alternately beat up and down

TAP ★
Right T taps left palm

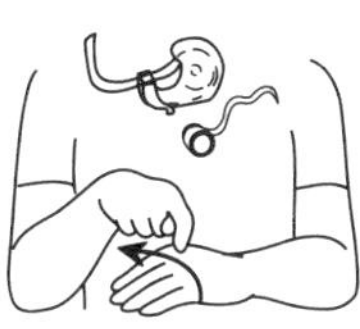

TAPE
Right palm-down T-hand pulls across back of left fingers

TAR
Right T circles on back of left palm down S-hand
(see Pave)

TARANTULA
Fingers of right 5, palm-down, slowly climb left forearm

TARDY
Side of right T on left vertical palm twists to palm-down
(see MINUTE)

TARGET
Right index behind left T; index jerks down to point at T
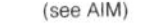
(see AIM)

TART
Right T twists on chin
(see SOUR)

TASK
Right palm-down T arcs to left, hitting back of left wrist
(see JOB)

TASTE
Right middle finger touches lower lip

TATTLE
Right S-hand at side of mouth, index flicks out several times

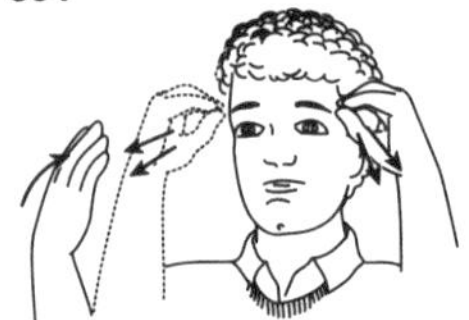

TAUGHT
Flat-O's pointing to temples move forward slightly; right hand flips toward shoulder *(teach + p. t.)*

TAX
Thumb of right T strikes straight down left palm
(see COST)

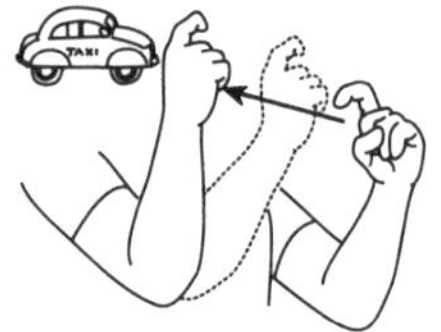

TAXI
Right X moves back from behind left X
(see CAR)

TEA
Circle 9 above left horizontal O as if swishing a tea bag

TEACH ♔
Flat-O's pointing to temples move forward slightly; repeat

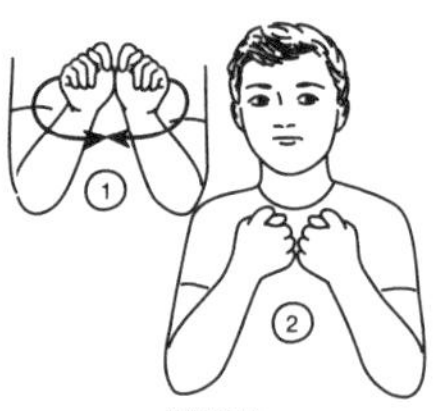

TEAM
Palm-out T's separate and circle horizontally out to palm-in
(see CLASS)

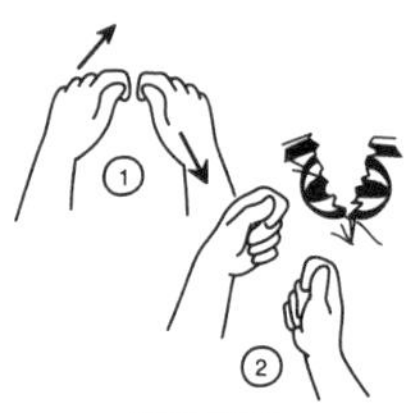

TEAR (rip)
Thumbs and indexes together; pull right back and left forward *(as if tearing something)*

TEAR (cry)
Both palm-in T-hands drag alternately down cheeks

TEASE
Horizontal X's, right on left, right brushes quickly forward on left; repeat

TECHNICAL
Right bent middle finger taps side of palm-in left hand

TECHNOLOGY
Fingertips of H twist near right temple several times

TEDDY BEAR
Palm-in T's, arms crossed near shoulders; change to palm-in claw hands and scratch chest slightly

TEEN
T touches first at temple, then at cheek
(see PARENT)

TEETER TOTTER
Both palm-down T's move up and down alternately

TEETH
Right X-hand crosses right to left in front of teeth
(see TOOTH)

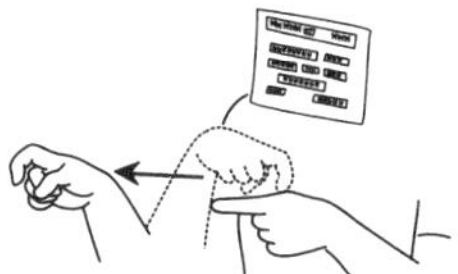

TELEGRAM
Palm-down X moves quickly along left index finger and off

TELEGRAPH
Right palm-down X taps along left index finger

TELEPHONE
Right Y-hand, thumb near ear, little finger near mouth

TELESCOPE
Right O behind left O at eye, twist to focus telescope

TELEVISION
Fingerspell T + V

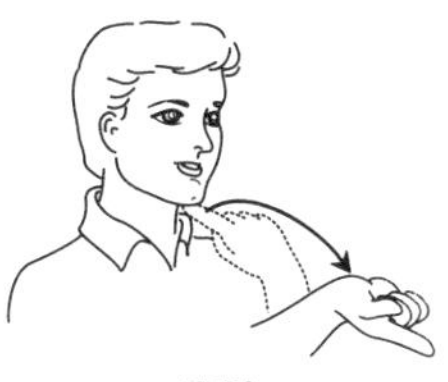

TELL
Palm-down index of right hand under chin flips out to palm-up

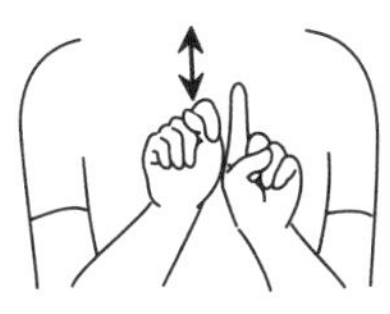

TEMPER
Right T slides up and down side of palm-out left index
(see THERMOMETER)

TEMPLE *
Heel of T taps on back of S; repeat
(see CHURCH)

TEMPORARY
Side of right T slides back and forth a bit on side of left H-hand
(see SHORT)

TEMPT
Right X-index taps elbow

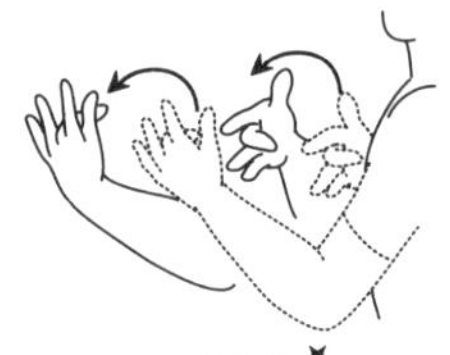

TEND ★
Bent middle fingers, right on chest and left ahead, both arc forward

TENNIS
Right A-hand swings racket

TENT
Palms-facing V-fingertips touch; separate while moving down and out
(see TEPEE)

TEPEE
T's together; separate while moving down and out
(see TENT)

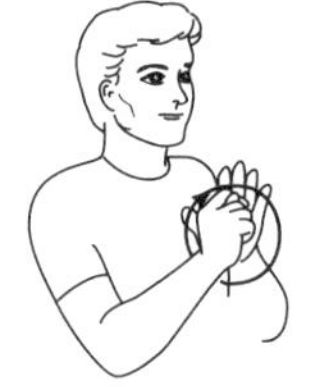

TERM
T on palm-right left hand; circles and touches palm again
(see HOUR)

TERMITE
Right T-hand rides forward on back of left wiggling fingers
(see ANT)

TERRIBLE
T-hands shake down and toward body; palm-down A's drop slightly *(terror + -ible)*

TERRIFIC
T's make small sideways circles; flat palm-out hands push forward slightly
(see FABULOUS)

T

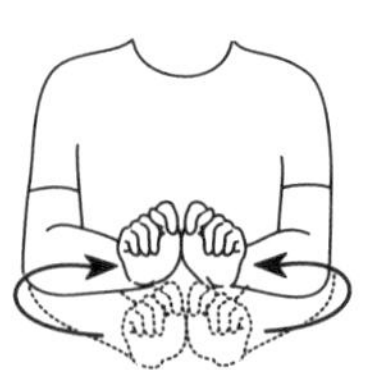

TERRITORY
Palm-out T's, circle back to body
(see PLACE)

TERROR
T's shake down and toward body
(see AFRAID)

TEST
Indexes change repeatedly from 1 to X, moving downward

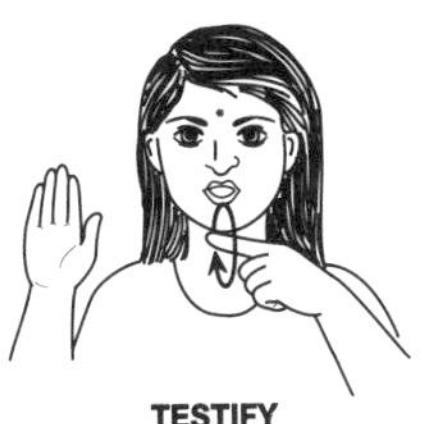

TESTIFY
Vertical right hand palm-out near shoulder; horizontal index of left hand circles near mouth

TEXAS
X moves down with a curve, palm-out

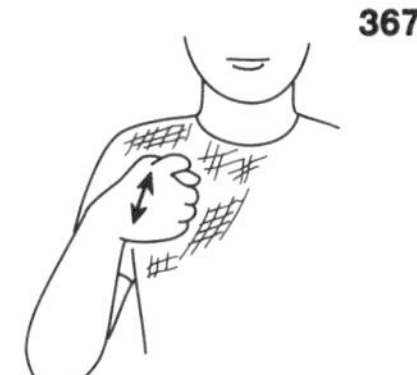

TEXTURE
Palm-in T rubs on chest near shoulder
(see CLOTH)

THAN
Fingertips of right flat hand slaps down across left fingertips

THANK
Fingertips of right palm-in open hand at chin drops to palm-up
(see GRATITUTDE)

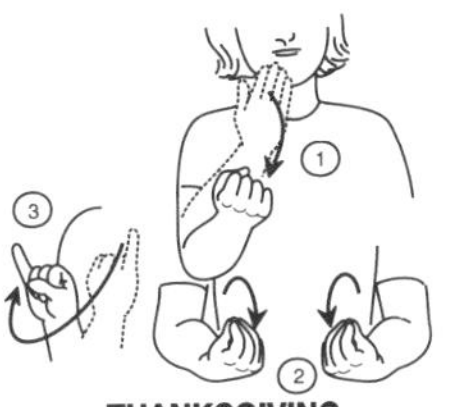

THANKSGIVING
Fingertips of open hand at chin drops to S; palm-up flat-O's arc forward, right I swings from palm-in to palm-out
(thank + -s + give + -ing)

THAT

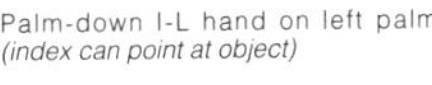

Palm-down I-L hand on left palm
(index can point at object)

THE
(Alt. 1)
Palm-in T; twist to palm-out

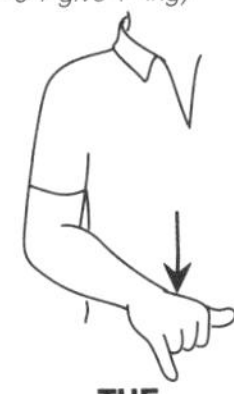

THE
(Alt. 2)
Palm-down Y drops slightly

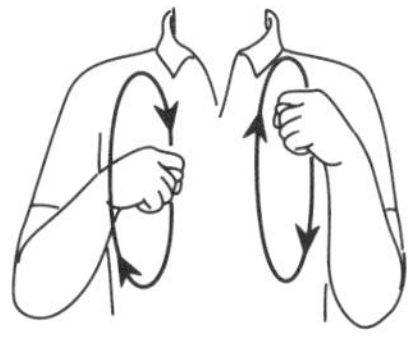

THEATER
T's brush alternatley down chest
(see ACT)

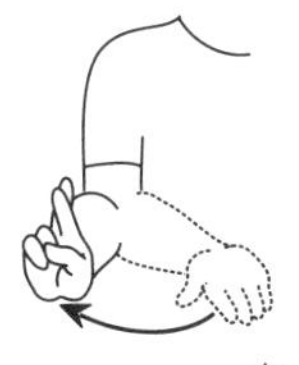

THEIR
Palm-up hand at left of body sweeps right to palm-out R-hand

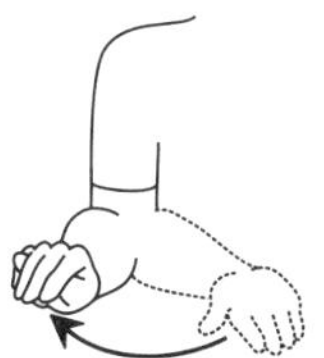

THEM
Palm-up hand at left of body sweeps right to palm-out M-hand
(see THEIR)

THEME
Right T circles beneath left hand
(see BASE)

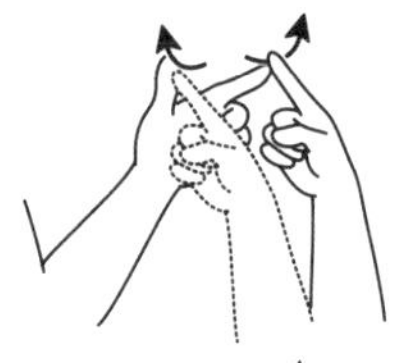

THEN
Right index moves off left thumb of L-hand, then off tip of left index

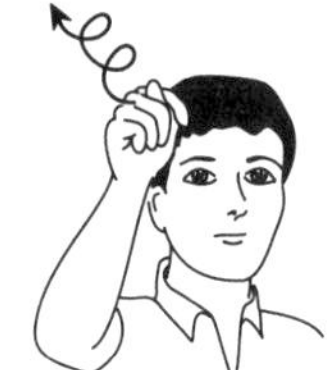

THEORY
Right T circles from forehead upward to the right
(see IDEA)

THERAPY
Left palm lifts right T-hand
(see HELP)

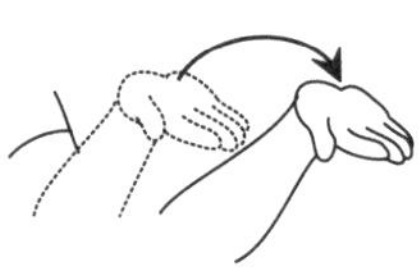

THERE
Right palm-up hand arcs forward

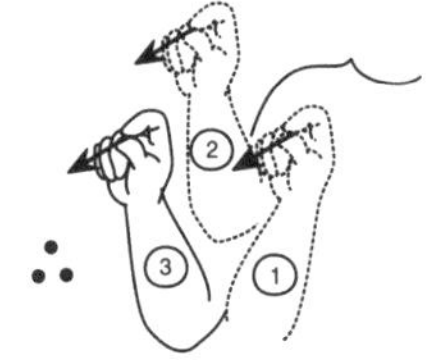

THEREFORE
Closed index and thumb make 3 dots in the air in a triangle shape

THERMOMETER
Right index finger slides rapidly up and down side of left index finger

THESE
Palm-down Y on palm of left hand; move Y across left fingers
(see THAT)

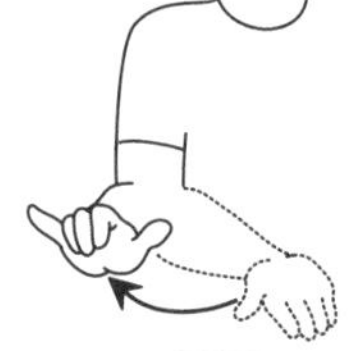

THEY
Palm-up hand at left of body; sweep right to palm-out Y
(see THEIR)

THICK
Heel of small C moves to the right along back of left hand

THIEF
Fingers of H slide from corner of nose to the right

THIGH
Right T-hand pats thigh

THIMBLE
Put thimble on left middle finger

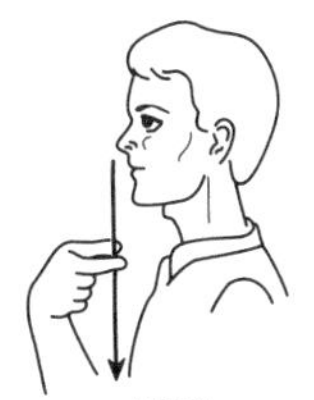

THIN
Fingertips of palm-in G-hand move down near face and body

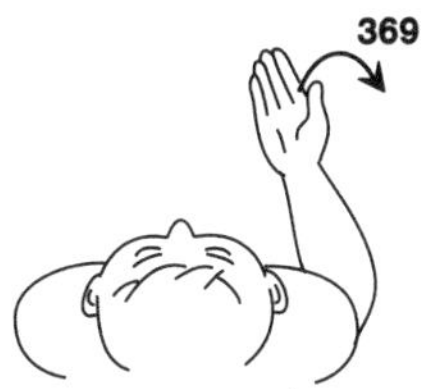

THING
Palm-up flat hand arcs slightly up and down to the right

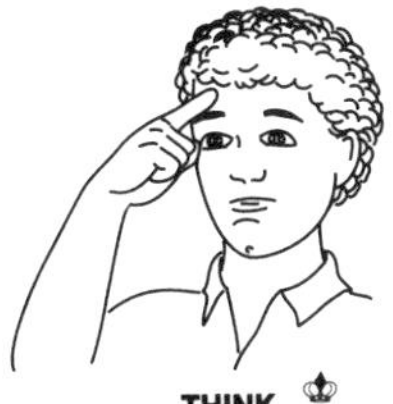

THINK
Index finger above brow on forehead *(may circle slightly)*

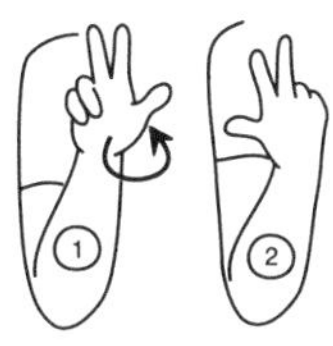

THIRD
Palm-out 3 twists to palm-in
(see SECOND)

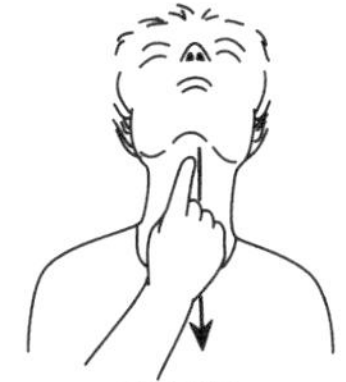

THIRST
Draw index finger down throat

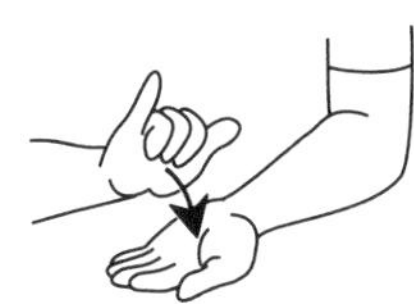

THIS
Right palm-down Y drops on palm of left hand
(see THAT)

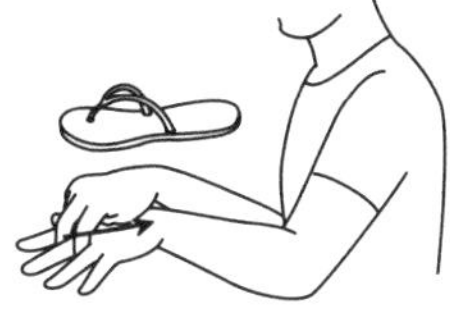

THONG
Left palm-down 5-hand, right bent-V draws back on left middle finger
(see SANDAL)

THORN
Right hand pulls "thorn" out of vertical left index finger

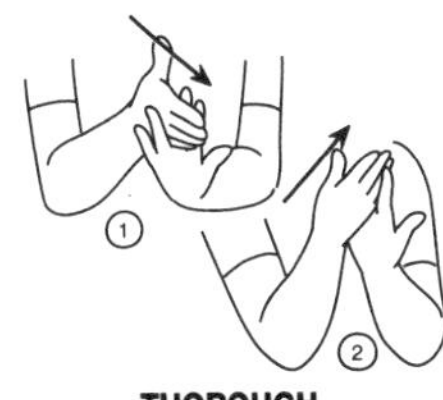

THOROUGH
Right hand slides through fingers of left; returns in the opposite direction
(see THROUGH)

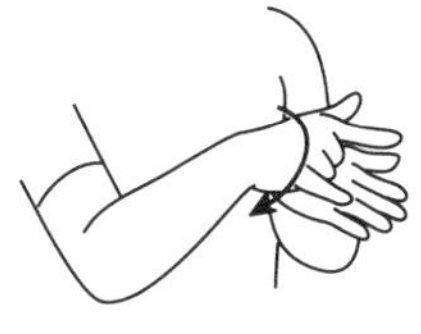

THOSE
Palm-down I-L hand on palm of left hand; moves across left fingers
(see THAT)

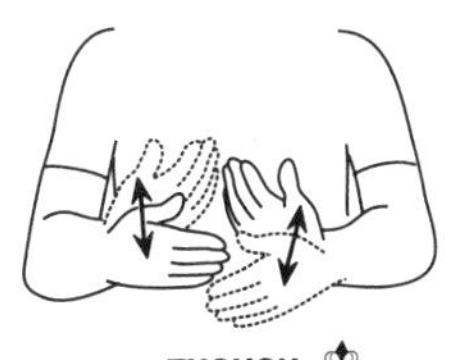

THOUGH
Slap fingertips forward and back against each other alternately

THOUGHT
(noun)
Palm-in T circles near temple
(see REASON)

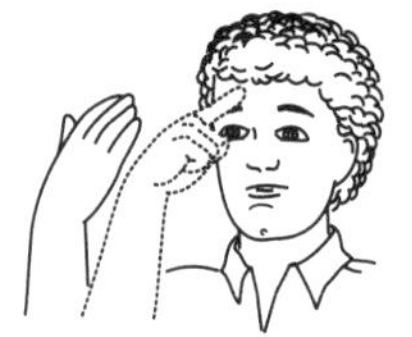

THOUGHT
(verb)
Index finger above brow on forehead; flat hand flips back toward shoulder *(think + p. t.)*

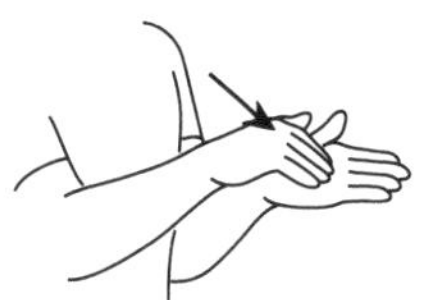

THOUSAND
Fingertips of bent hand strike left palm

THREAD
I-fingertip shakes down from left T
(see CORD)

THREAT
Back of right T arcs up, hitting back of left S; repeat
(see DANGER)

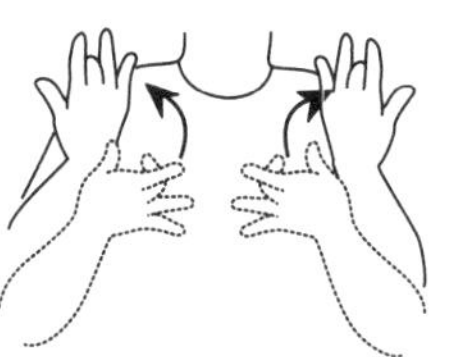

THRILL
Middle fingers on chest flick upward

THROAT
Slide fingertips of palm-in G-hand down throat
(see THIRST)

THROB
Palm-in A-hand bounces from heart to left horizontal palm

THRONE
Bent 3's hold arms of "throne"

T

THROUGH ♔
Open hand slides outward between fingers of left hand

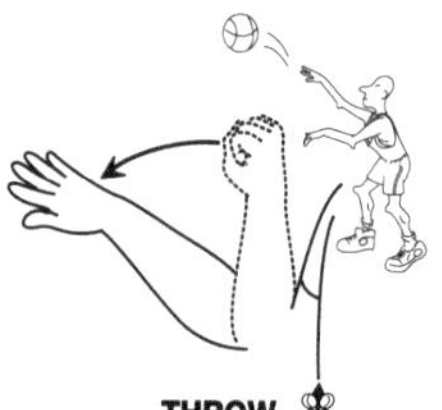

THROW ♔
S-hand throws forward into 5-hand

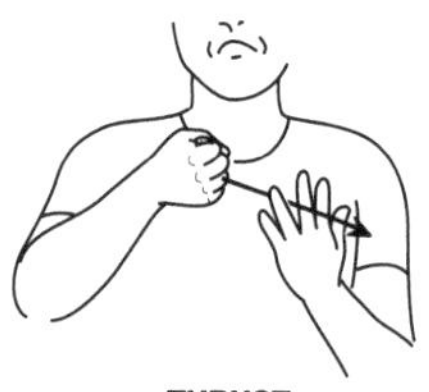

THRUST
Palm-in left vertical 5; horizontal right S thrusts forward through fingers
(see THROUGH)

THUMB
Right fingertip rubs left thumb

THUNDER
Right index finger at ear, then both S's jerk forward and back alternately
(see VIOLENT)

THURSDAY
T-hand to H-hand *(can be done with H alone circling slightly)*
(see MONDAY)

TICKET
Bent-V fingers slide onto side of palm-in left hand *(punch ticket)*

TICKLE ✶
Right index finger tickles near side

TIDE
Palm-down right T slides up onto back of left hand; slides back off
(see SHORE)

TIE ♔ ✶
Horizontal U-fingers circle around each other, then separate

TIGER
Both palm-in claw hands, near cheeks, move outwards *(drawing whiskers)*; repeat
(see CAT)

TIGHT
Right claw on left horizontal S; twist slightly right, as if to tighten cap

TILE
Palm-down T moves to the right on back of flat left hand
(see CARPET)

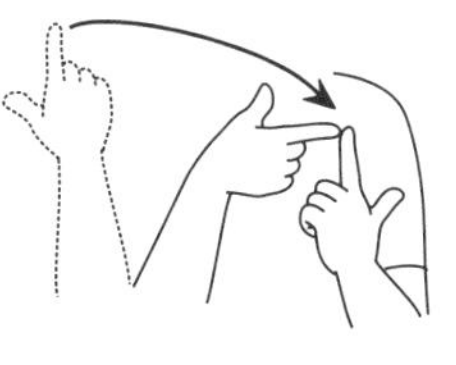

TILL ✶
Index of right palm-in L arcs over to touch index of palm-in left L
(see TO)

TIMBER
Arm of right T, elbow resting on back of left hand, shakes
(see TREE)

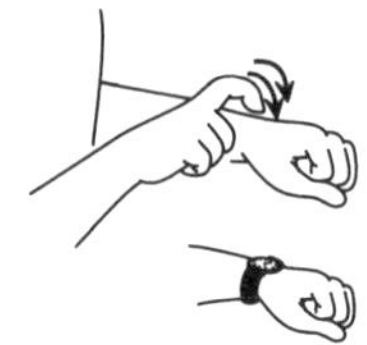

TIME
Right index X-finger taps left wrist

TIMID
Side of palm-in T on cheek twist slightly forward
(see SHY)

TIN
Palm-in T arcs right to palm-out, hitting side of left hand
(see METAL)

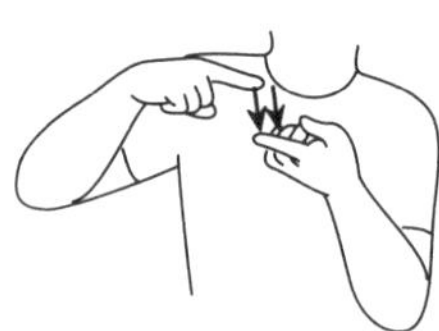

TINY
Palm-down right index bounces just above palm-up left index
(see MINIATURE)

TIP ★
Right index taps tip of left T-thumb
(see CAP)

TIPTOE
Tiptoe with indexes pointing downward
(see WADE)

TIRE ♔ ★
Both palm-down T's near chest arc down to palm-up

TIRED
Palm-down T's near chest arc down to palm-up; right flat hand flips toward shoulder *(tire + p. t.)*

TISSUE
Heel of right T-hand strikes across left heel; repeat
(see PAPER)

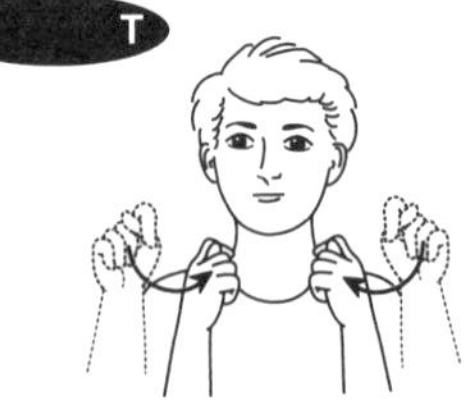

TITLE
Palm-out T's twist to face each other
(see QUOTE)

TO ♔
Horizontal index finger approaches and touches left vertical index finger

TOAD
S at left elbow flicks out to V when jumping; land with S; flick to V again, while moving down left arm

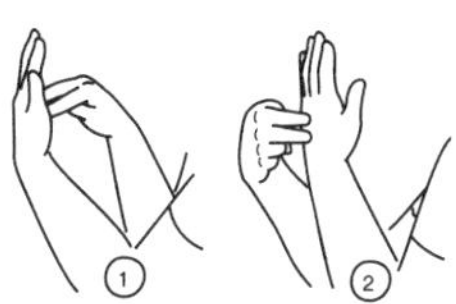

TOAST ✶
Right V stabs on left palm and then on back of hand

TOBACCO
Fingertips of flat M twist back and forth on cheek
(see GUM)

TOBOGGAN
Palm-up T rides forward on left palm
(see SLED)

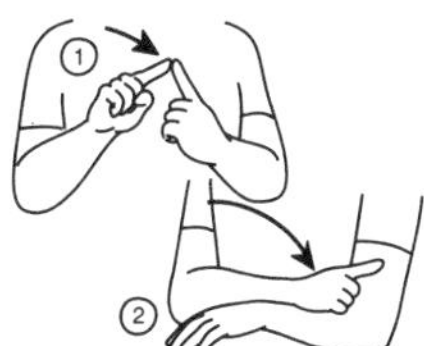

TODAY
Touch right index to left index, then arc to rest on bent left arm *(to + day)*

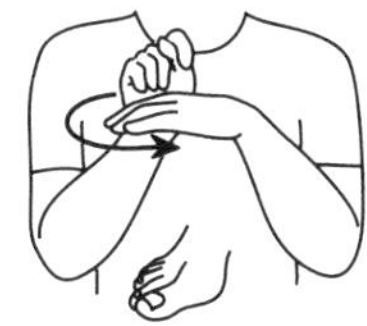

TOE
Right T-hand passes around fingertips of flat hand
(see EDGE)

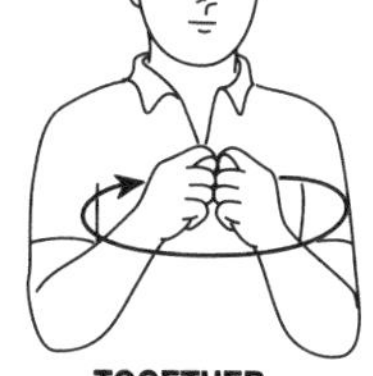

TOGETHER
Palms-facing T-hands touching, circle together once
(see STANDARD)

TOIL
T bounces back and forth on left S
(see BUSY)

TOILET
Palm-out T shakes

TOLD
Right palm-in index under chin, flips out to palm-up; flat hand flips toward shoulder *(tell + p. t.)*

TOLERATE
Side of T draws downward over chin
(see LONESOME)

TOMATO ♔
1-finger from chin strikes past fingertips of left horizontal flat-O

TOMB
Palms-down T's arc back toward body
(see BURY)

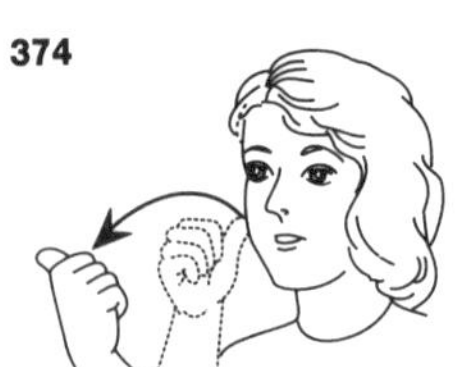

TOMORROW
Thumb of A-hand on cheek, moves forward and twists to point forward

TON
Side of T rocks on index of H-hand
(see WEIGH)

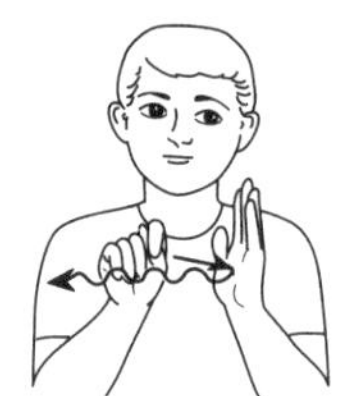

TONE
Side of right T hits vertical left palm, shakes to right

(see BELL)

TONGS
Palm-down right V clips onto vertical left index
(see CUT)

TONGUE
Index points to tongue

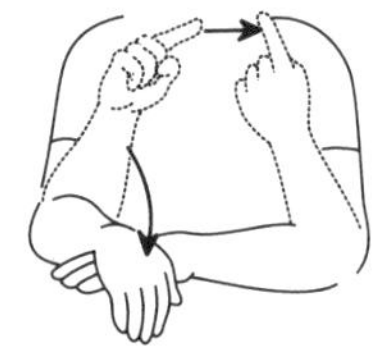

TONIGHT
Touch right index to left index, drop right bent hand over edge of left hand *(to + night)*

TONSIL
Index finger touches each side of neck

TONSILLECTOMY
Palm-in V at side of neck moves forward to bent-V; repeat at other side

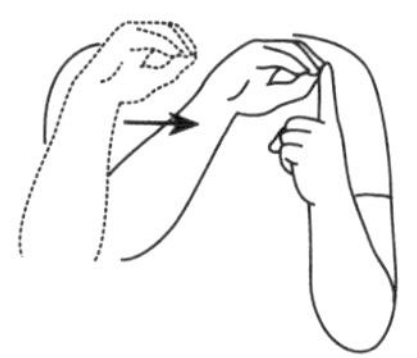

TOO
O approaches and touches left index
(see TO)

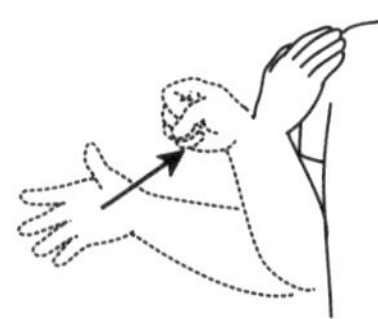

TOOK
5-hand draws back to body, closing to S-hand; flat hand flips back towards shoulder *(take + p. t.)*

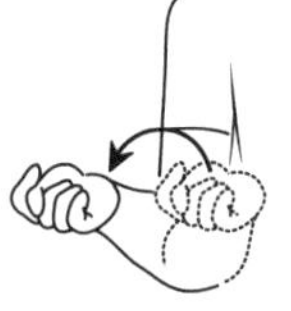

TOOL
Palm-up T-hand arcs right
(see THING)

TOOTH
Index points to a tooth

TOOTHBRUSH
Right index brushes back and forth in slight up and down wiggle at mouth

TOOTHPASTE
Right thumb and fist squeeze out toothpaste along horizontal left index

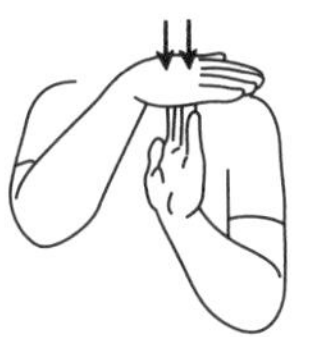

TOP ★
Right flat hand taps the tops of left palm-right fingers
(see CAP)

TOPIC
Side of T-hand touches left palm-up fingers then heel
(see LESSON)

TORCH
Right O above left horizontal S, opens to 5, rises with fingers fluttering
(see FLARE)

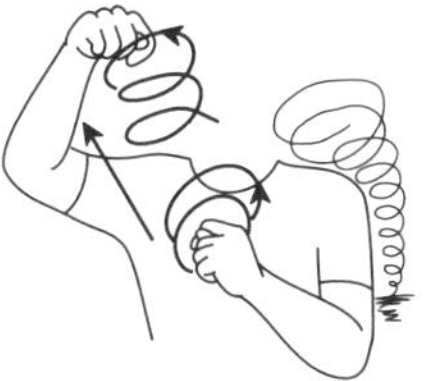

TORNADO
T's facing each other, rotate around each other, rising to the right
(see STORM)

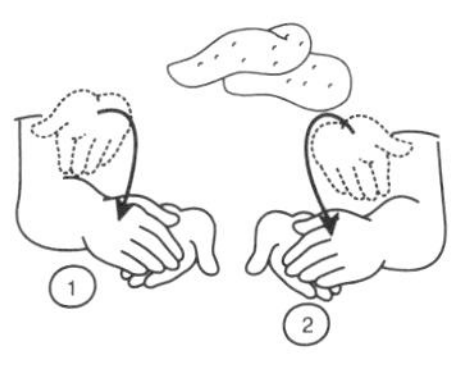

TORTILLA
Right hand on left, then left hand on right, *(press a tortilla)*

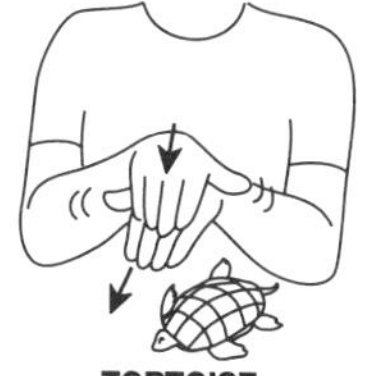

TORTOISE
Hands point forward, right on left, move forward, wiggling thumbs

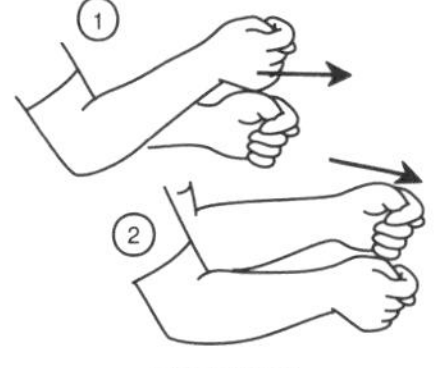

TORTURE
Horizontal T's, right hits forward and off left, then left off right
(see PERSECUTE)

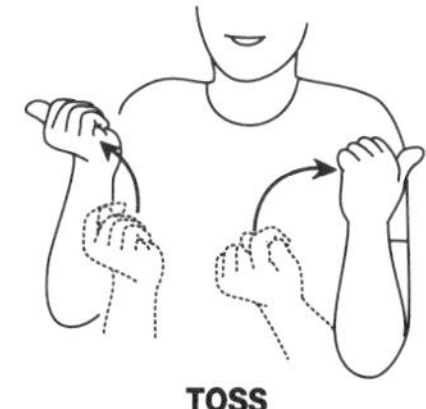

TOSS
Palm-up T-thumbs snap out while hands move to sides

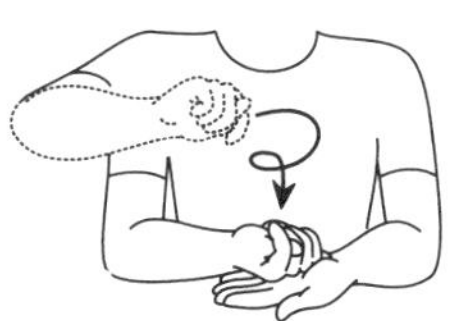

TOTAL
Palm-down T, over left palm, circles and inverts to palm-up T on palm
(see WHOLE)

TOTAL COMMUNICATION (TC)
Palms-facing, right T and left C move alternately forward and back
(see TALK)

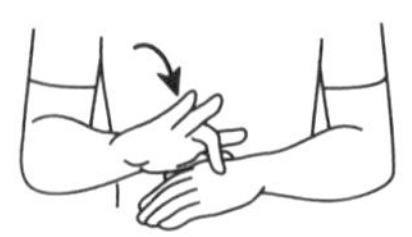

TOUCH
Middle finger of right hand touches back of left hand

TOUGH
Right bent-V hits back of left palm-down S in arc down to the right
(see HARD)

TOUR
Palm-down bent-V makes small circles while moving left

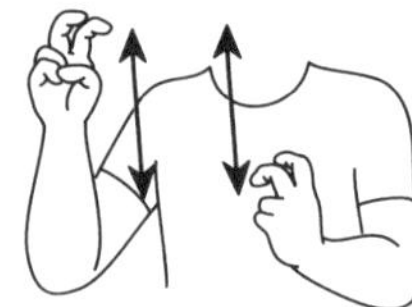

TOURNAMENT
Bent-V's palms-facing, move up and down alternately

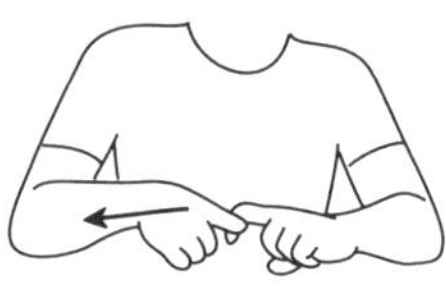

TOW
Right X pulls left X toward the right

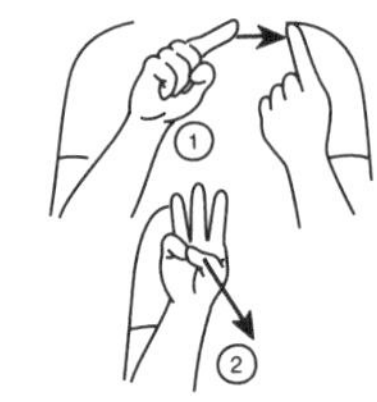

TOWARD
Touch right index to left index; palm-out W moves forward *(to + -ward)*

TOWEL
Open hands circle near cheeks; repeat

TOWER
Palm-out T's swing in and then up
(see CHIMNEY)

TOWN ♔
Fingertips tap several times while moving from left to right *(indicating roof tops)*

T

TOY
(Alt. 1)
T-hands, one palm-out, one palm-in, swing back and forth, pivoting at wrists
(see PLAY)

TOY
(Alt. 2)
Palm-in T-hands shake towards palm-out repeatedly

TRACE ★
Palm-down T draws wavy line on left palm, toward body
(see ART)

TRACK ✶
Palm-out T at side of palm-down left V; T moves forward

TRACTOR
Both T's steer large wheel
(see DRIVE)

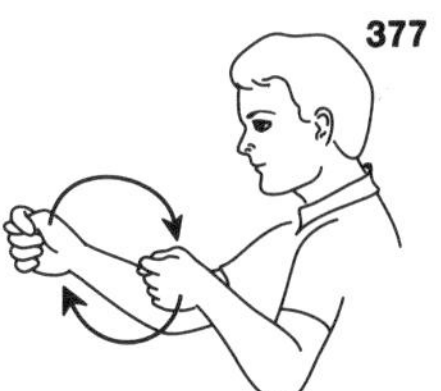

TRADE
T-hands, right in front of left, circle each other vertically once
(see EXCHANGE)

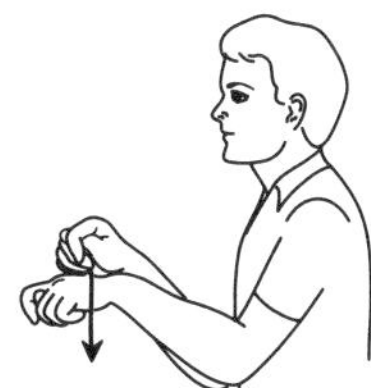

TRADITION
(Alt. 1)
Palm-down T's, right on left, both move downward
(see HABIT)

TRADITION
(Alt. 2)
Right T on left T near right shoulder. both move forward and down

TRAFFIC
Palms-facing 5's brush each other, moving rapidly forward and back
(see FREEWAY)

TRAGIC
T's arc down from corners of mouth, outlining a sad mouth
(see GRIM)

TRAIL
Palm-down T weaves towards body

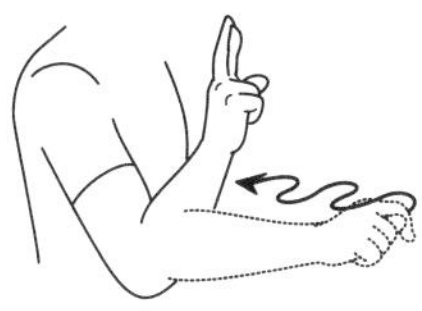

TRAILER
Palm-down T weaves towards body; add R-hand *(trail + -er)*

TRAIN ✶
Palms-down H-hands, right fingers rub on back of left fingers

TRAIT
Side of T circles near left shoulder, then touches it
(see CHARACTER)

TRAITOR
Left T, right index pointing forward, slides around T to point left
(See BETRAY)

TRAMPLE
Palm-down hands walk forward with squashing movements
(See WALK)

TRAMPOLINE
Right inverted-V stands on left palm, jumps up and down as left moves slightly up and down
(See JUMP)

TRANQUIL
Palms-facing T-hands near chin separate down and sideways
(see QUIET)

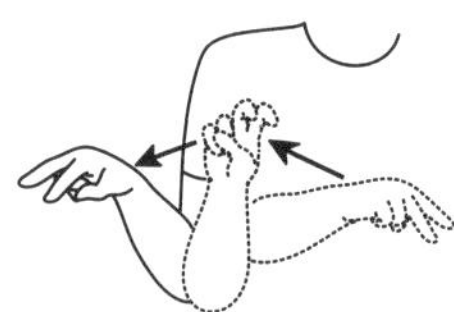

TRANSFER
Palm-down V lifts to bent-V and shoots to right to palm-down V again
(see RELAY)

TRANSFORM
T-hands face each other, right above left; reverse

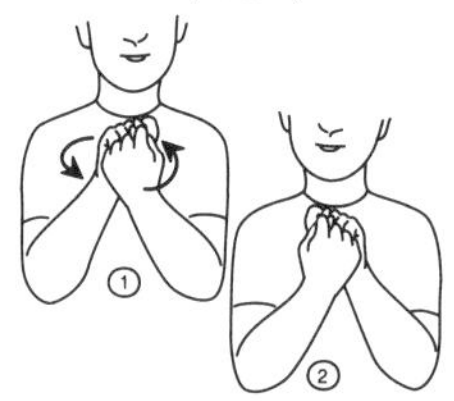

TRANSLATE
Palms of T-hands touch, twist to reverse position; may repeat
(see CHANGE)

TRANSPARENCY
Palm-out T's make vertical square
(See SQUARE)

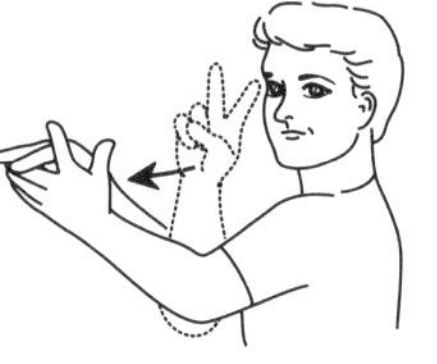

TRANSPARENT
Right V, from eye, points between first and second fingers of left hand

TRANSPORT
Palm-up T's at left arc toward right
(see BRING)

T

TRAP
Bent-V fingers drop to trap left index

TRAPEZE
Fingertips of inverted-V stand on left index; swing both hands
(see SWING)

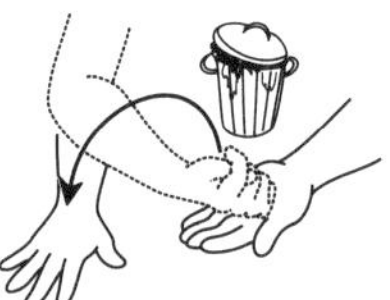

TRASH
Back of T on left palm, slide forward and throws off to palm-down 5-hand
(see DISPOSE)

TRAVEL

Index fingers circle each other; moving out, around, and slightly upward

(see VOYAGE)

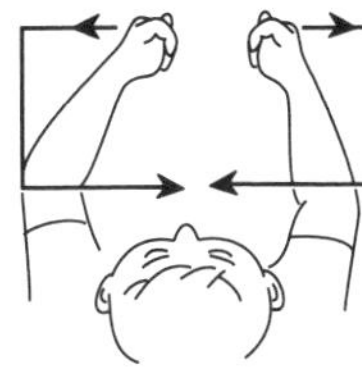

TRAY

T's draw shape of tray horizontally

TREASURE

Palm-up T on left palm rises to palm-down T over palm

(see RICH)

TREAT

Palms-up T's push forward; repeat

(see URGE)

TREE

Right 5-hand with elbow on back of left hand, shakes

TREMENDOUS

L-hands with bent indexes pull apart in exaggerated gesture

(see MUCH)

TRIANGLE

Indexes draw a triangle

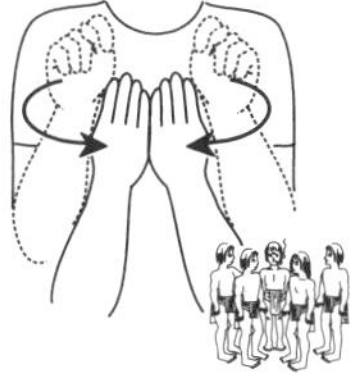

TRIBE

Palm-out T's separate, circle out to palm-in B's touching

(see BAND)

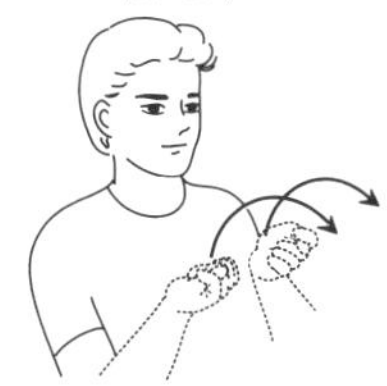

TRIBUTE

Palm-up T's arc up and forward

(See GIFT)

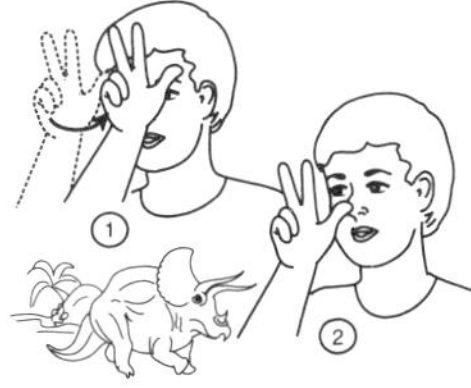

TRICERATOPS

Thumb of 3-hand on right side of forehead, moves to left side of forehead, then to nose

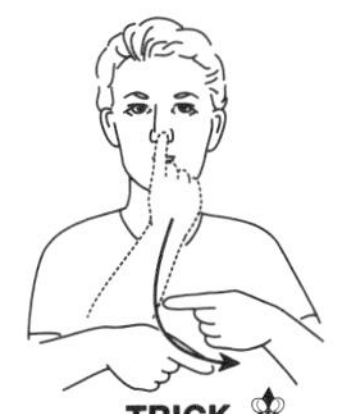

TRICK

Right index on nose quickly twists sideways under left 1-hand, both palms ending inward

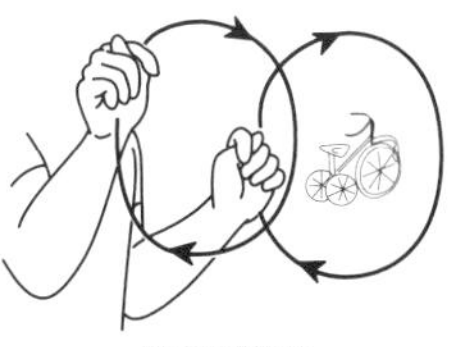

TRICYCLE

T-hands circle up and out alternately

(see BICYCLE)

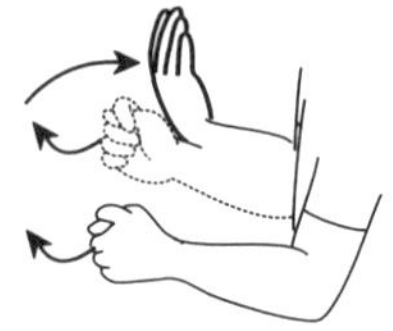

TRIED
T-hands, palms-facing, move forward; right flat-hand flips toward shoulder *(try + p. t.)*

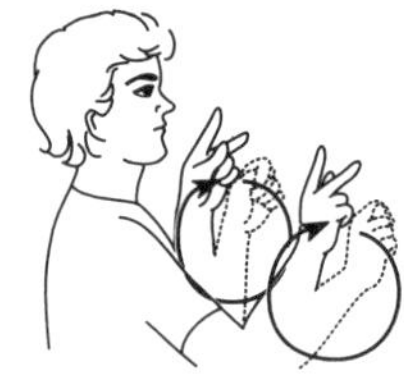

TRIKE
Palm-out T's circle alternately forward, ending in K's
(See BICYCLE)

TRILLION
Palm-down T arcs forward from left heel to hit fingertips
(see BILLION)

TRIM ✶
V-fingers scissor across tip of left T
(see CUT)

TRIP ✶
Middle fingertip trips over left index

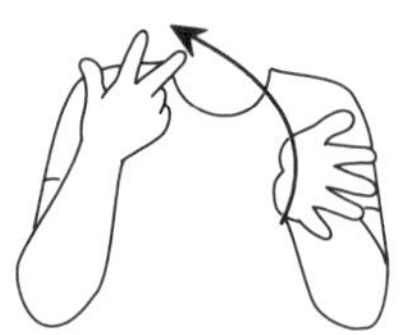

TRIPLE
Middle finger of 3 brushes up left palm
(see ONCE)

TRIUMPH
Right T spirals up off left S-hand
(see WIN)

TROMBONE
Thumbs of both A-hands, palms-facing, at lips; right moves out and back several times

TROOP
Palm-out T's, right slightly behind left, move forward in small downward arcs

T

TROPHY
Tips of palm-in Y-hands touch
(see SHAPE)

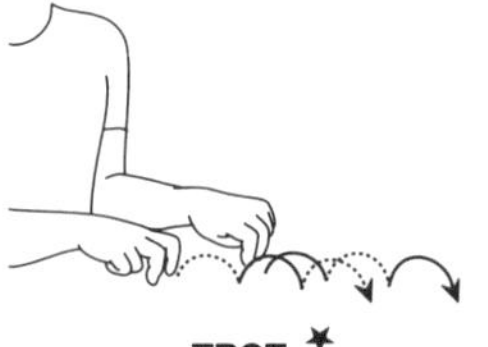

TROT ✶
Palm-down bent-V hands alternately arc forward
(see WALK)

TROUBLE
Palms-facing, flat hands circle alternately in front of face
(see WORRY)

TROUSER
T-hands tap sides at waist
(see PANT)

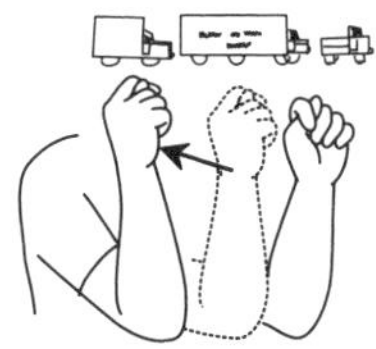

TRUCK
Palms-facing T's, right behind left; move right hand back
(see CAR)

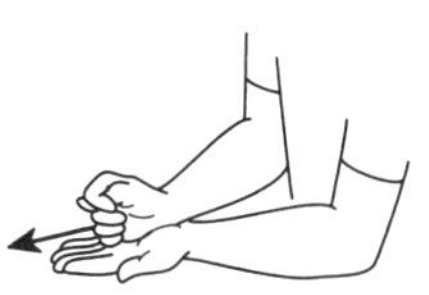

TRUE
Side of T on left palm; slide forward across palm and fingers
(see HONEST)

TRUMPET
Right fingers play outside left T at lips

TRUNK ★
T's, palms-facing, draw down on chest

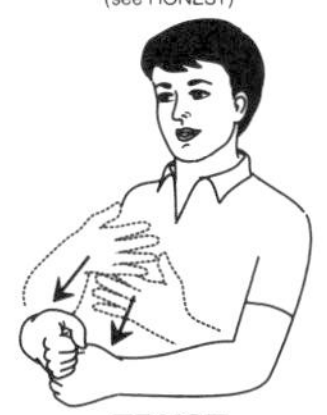

TRUST
5-hands near shoulder, one above the other, pull out and close to S's

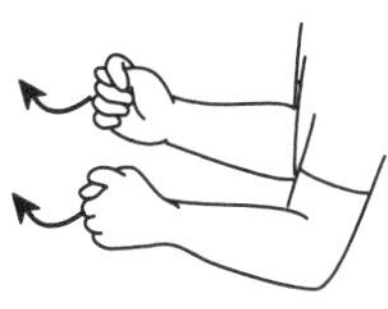

TRY
T-hands, palms-facing, move forward
(see ATTEMPT)

TUB
Palms-up T's swing upward to palms-facing *(outlining tub bottom)*
(see JAR)

TUBA
Right T against left T at lips; right moves out and rises to 5-hand

TUBE
Right G-fingers on left G-fingers; right hand moves up
(see POLE)

TUESDAY
Palm-out T circles slightly
(see MONDAY)

TUG ★
T's tug diagonally inward; repeat
(see PULL)

TULIP
T touches each side of nose
(see FLOWER)

TUMBLE
Inverted V-fingertips on left palm roll forward off palm
(see SOMERSAULT)

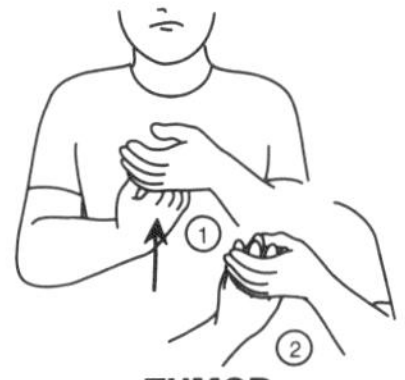

TUMOR
Right palm-up flat-O rises into left horizontal C and opens slightly *(place near site of tumor)*
(see GROW)

TUNA
Palm-left T-hand swims forward
(see FISH)

TUNE
Right T-hand arcs from side-to-side behind left palm
(see MUSIC)

TUNNEL
Right index spirals through left palm-down C-hand

TURKEY
Right G-hand, pointing down at chin, shakes down

TURN
Horizontal right hand curves around left vertical index

TURNIP
Index finger slices side of T; repeat
(see TOMATO)

TURQUOISE
Right palm-left T, pointing forward, shakes slightly
(see BLUE)

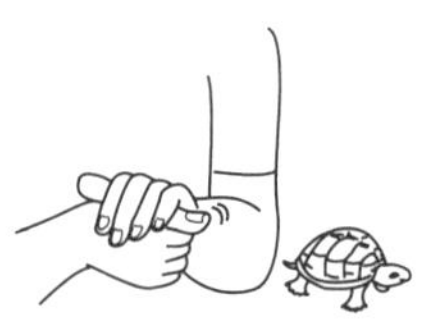

TURTLE
Left hand covers right palm-left A; wiggle right thumb

TUTOR
T-hands at temples move slightly forward; repeat
(see TEACH)

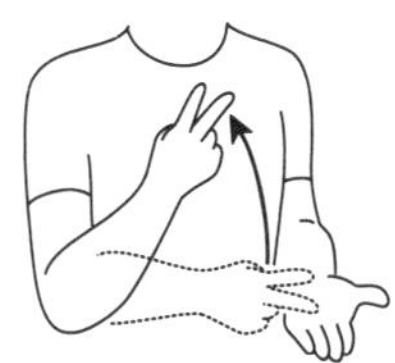

TWICE
Middle finger of 2 touches left palm, twist up to palm-in
(see ONCE)

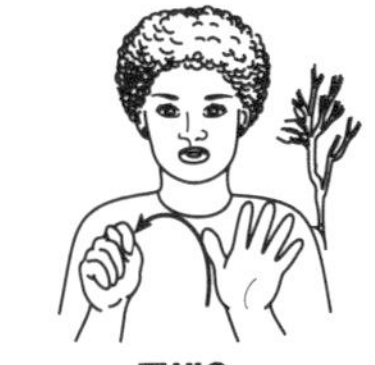

TWIG
Left palm-out 5; palm-out right T touches thumbtip and arcs off to right
(See BRANCH)

TWIN
Side of palm-left T touches left, then right corner of mouth
(see BACHELOR)

TWINE
Right T-hand touches side of left palm-out T, shakes off to right
(see CORD)

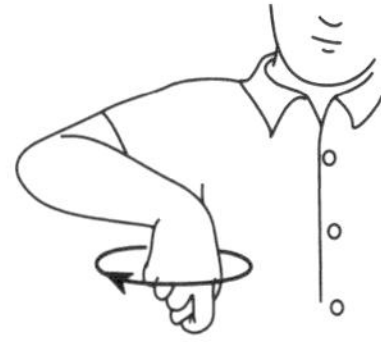

TWIRL
Upside down T twirls
(see SPIN)

TWIST
Right palm-down V above left palm-up V; reverse positions
(see SPRAIN)

TYLENOL
Right T circles on edge of left palm-up flat hand

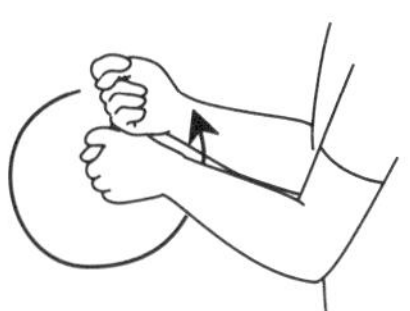

TYPE
Right T on left T; then circle vertically around each other
(see KIND)

TYPEWRITER
Relaxed palm-down 5's, fingers wiggle *(in typing motion)*

TYRANNOSAURUS REX
T on left shoulder, then R on right side of waist

NOTES

UGLY
Palm-down index fingers cross near nose; pull to X's at sides of face

UMBRELLA
Horizontal S's, right above left, right moves up once from left S

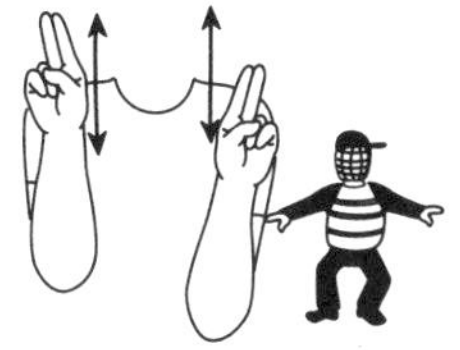

UMPIRE
U-hands move up and down alternately
(see BALANCE)

UNCLE
U shakes near temple
(see AUNT)

UNDER
(Alt. 1)
Horizontal A slides under left palm
(see BRIBE)

UNDER
(Alt. 2)
Right extended-A thumb circles under left flat hand

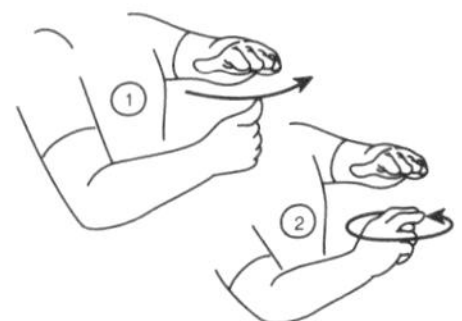

UNDERNEATH
Horizontal A-hand slides under left palm; then N-hand circles under palm *(under + -neath)*

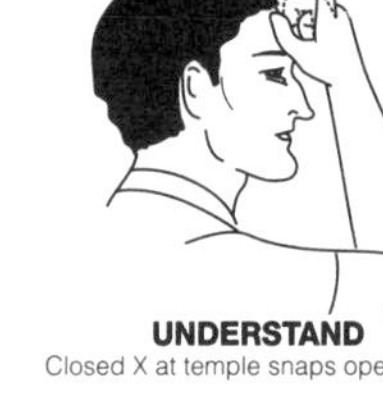

UNDERSTAND
Closed X at temple snaps open to 1

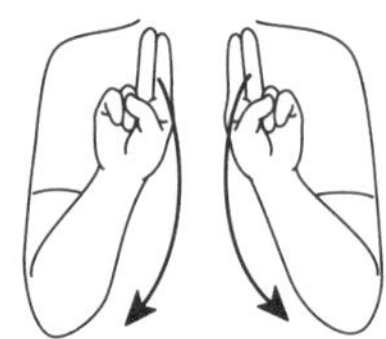

UNIFORM
Palm-out U's move down body
(see COAT)

UNION
Side of U-hands touching; circle horizontally together
(see STANDARD)

UNIT
Horizontal right H touches fingertips, then palm, of palm-up left hand
(see LESSON)

UNITE
U's at sides of body, arc down and towards each other, then touch

UNITED STATES
U-hand circles, S-hand circles

UNIVERSE
Right H on left H; circle right H forward around left hand and rest on top
(see WORLD)

UNIVERSITY
Horizontal palm-down U circles up from left palm
(see COLLEGE)

U

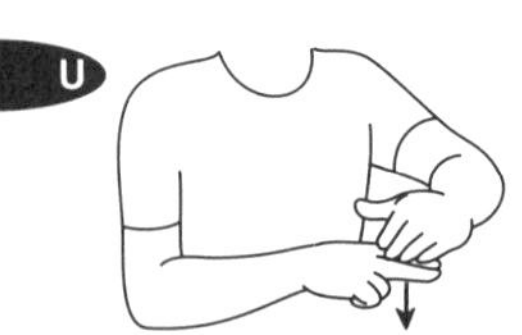

UNLESS
Right U, palm-down under left flat palm, drops slightly
(see LESS)

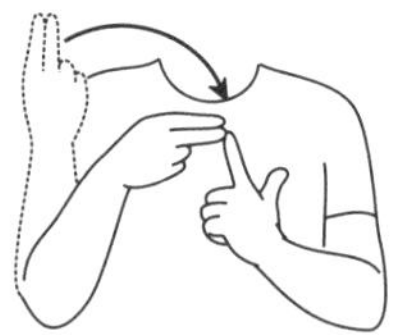

UNTIL
Right palm-in U arcs over to touch tip of palm-in left L
(see TO)

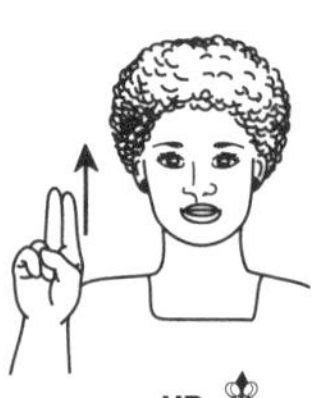

UP
Palm-out U moves up

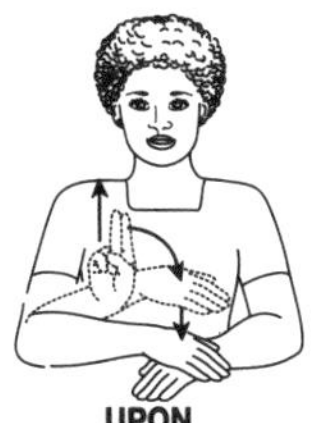

UPON
U moves up, right palm touches back of left hand *(up + on)*

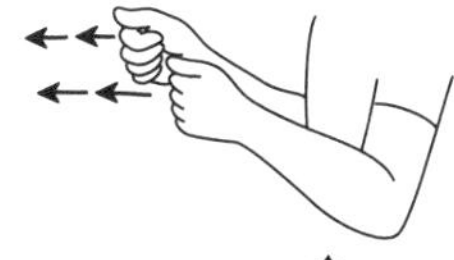

URGE ♔
Horizontal A's, slightly to the side, jerk forward twice

URINE
Middle fingertip of P taps nose

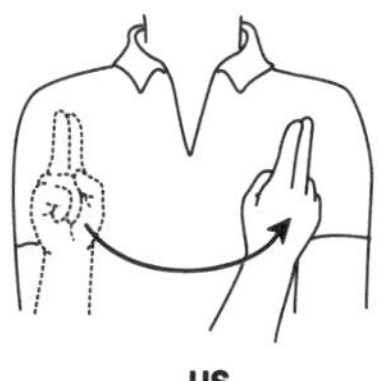

US
Right U-hand at right side of chest circles to left side
(see OUR)

USE
(Alt. 1)
Heel of U-hand bounces on back of left palm-down S-hand
(see BUSY)

USE
(Alt. 2)
U-hand circles, clockwise slightly

USUAL
Heel of U bounces on back of left hand; add L-hand *(use + -al)*

NOTES

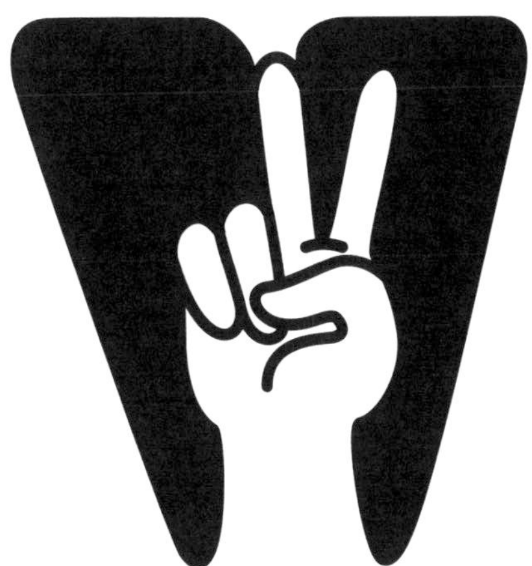

VACANT
Heel of V slides along back of left hand
(see BARE)

VACATION
Palm-in horizontal V's tap on sides of chest; repeat
(see LEISURE)

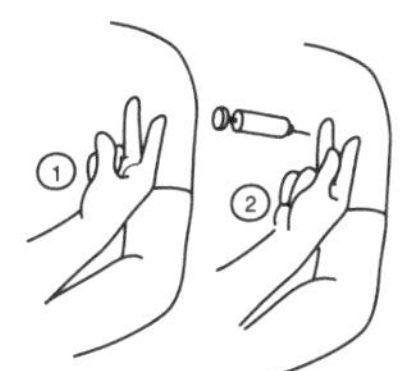

VACCINE
Back of V fingers on upper left arm; thumb of V drops to index

VACUUM
Palm-down V pulls back to the right

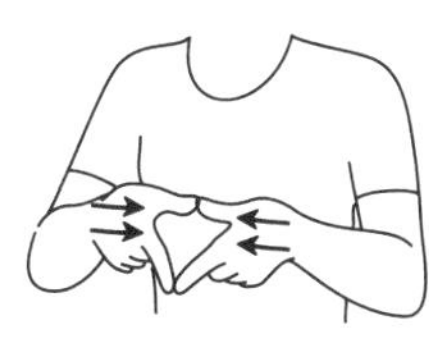

VAGINA
Thumbtips and index tips touch, indexes pointing downward

VAGUE
Left palm-in 5-hand in front of right palm-out 5-hand; circle alternately

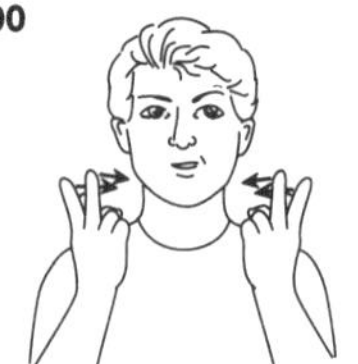

VAIN
Palm-in V's near sides of head, drop fingers toward shoulders, hands remain stationary; repeat

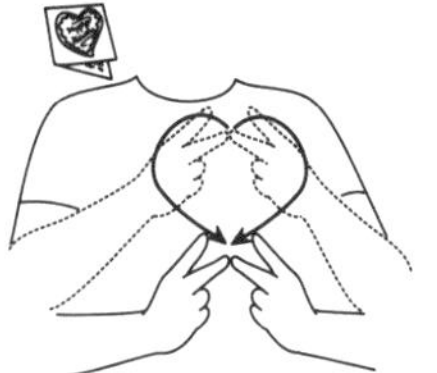

VALENTINE
Palm-in V's draw heart over heart
(see HEART)

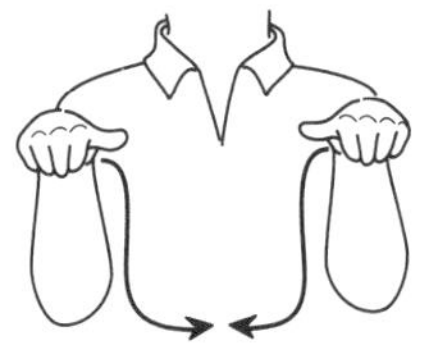

VALLEY
Beginning at sides, palms-down, flat hands draw valley
(see CANYON)

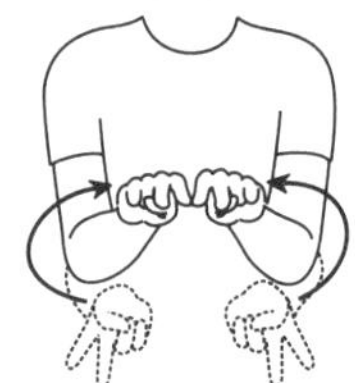

VALUE
Palm-up V's circle up to touch palm-down
(see IMPORTANT)

VAMPIRE
Bent-V arcs to hit neck with fingertips

VAN
Right V-hand behind left V-hand; right moves backward
(see CAR)

VANE
Back of right V-hand rests on left index; rock back and forth like a vane

VANILLA
V circles on back of left flat hand
(see CHOCOLATE)

VANISH
Right open hand, palm-in, moves down through palm-in left horizontal C and closes to flat-O hand

VAPOR
V wiggles up through left horizontal C
(see EVAPORATE)

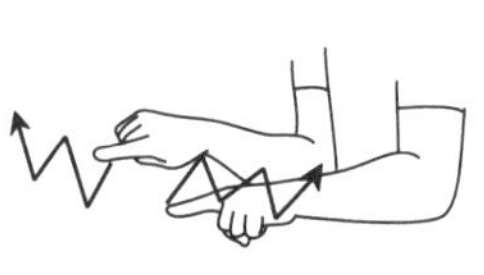

VARY
1's , palms-down, move alternately up and down to each side

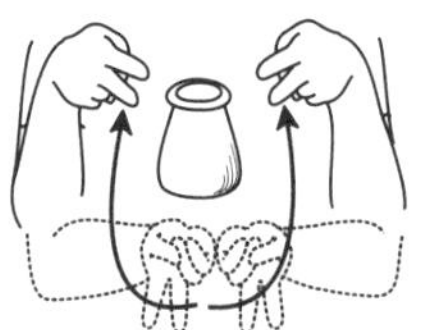

VASE
Palm-up V's outline vase
(see JAR)

VASELINE
Heel of V-hand circles on left palm
(see MEDICINE)

VAST
Heels of horizontal V's touch, then hands separate sideways
(see BROAD)

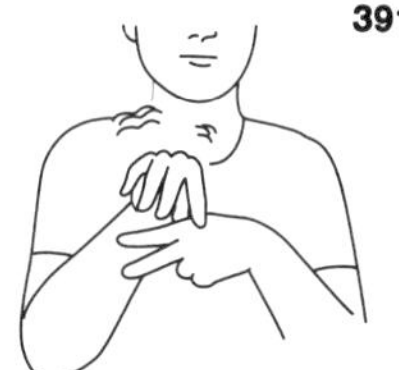

VEAL
Right hand pinches side of left horizontal V and both shake
(see MEAT)

VEGETABLE
Index fingertip of V on cheek; twist
(see APPLE)

VEHICLE
Palm-left V behind palm-right V, separate and change to L's
(see CAR)

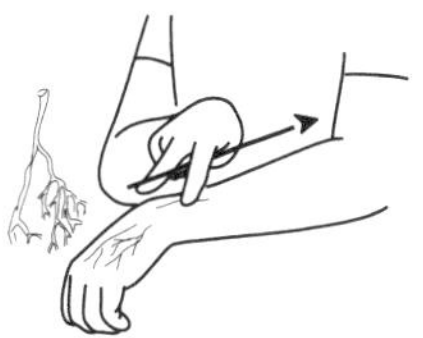

VEIN
Fingertips of palm-down V draw up back of wrist

VENT
Right palm-out V rises from thumb side of left horizontal C
(see EVAPORATE)

VENTURE
Inverted V wanders forward
(see WANDER)

VERB
Index finger of palm-in V slides across chin below mouth

VERSE
Side of G finger and thumb slide across vertical left palm

VERTICAL
Palm-out V pulls downward
(see DOWN)

VERY
Fingertips of palms-facing V-hands touch and then arc apart

VESSEL
Palm up-V's arc twice to side
(see CARRY)

VEST
Palm-in V-hands arc inward on chest
(see COAT)

VETERAN
Index of palm-out V brushes down side of head; repeat
(see EXPERIENCE)

VETERINARIAN
Heel of right V taps on left pulse
(see DOCTOR)

VIBRATE
Palm-down 5-hands jerk forward and back alternately, quickly

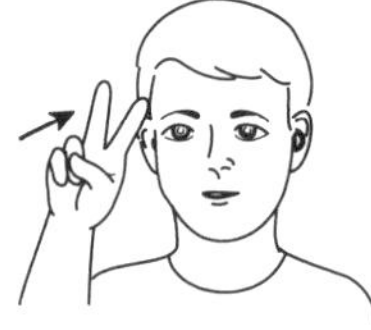

VICE
Palm-out V index taps temple
(see WIT)

VICTIM
Knuckles of palm-in A hit side of palm-out left V-hand
(see BUMP)

VICTOR
Right V on left horizontal S; V spirals quickly upward
(see WIN)

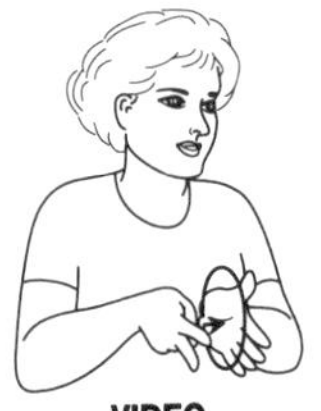

VIDEO
Right V circles once near horizontal left palm, then touches
(see H0UR)

V

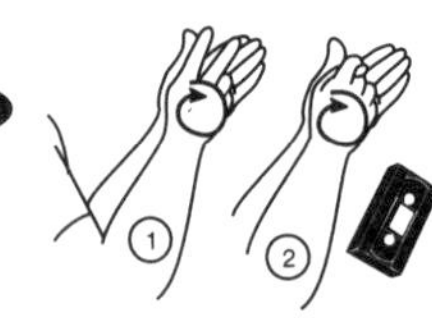

VIDEOTAPE
Right V and then T circle vertically against left palm

VIEW
Palm-down V sweeps left above left arm, *"scanning"*

VIGOR
Palm-in V's on sides of chest pull out to palm-in R's
(see BRAVE)

VILLAGE
Index of V taps fingertips of left hand; both hands circling
(see TOWN)

VINE
V grows and wiggles out and down from left horizontal C
(see GROW)

VINEGAR
Index finger of palm-left V on chin; twist to palm-in
(see SOUR)

VIOLENT
Palm-out V's move sharply side-to-side
(see THUNDER)

VIOLET
Right V touches first one side of nose, then the other
(see FLOWER)

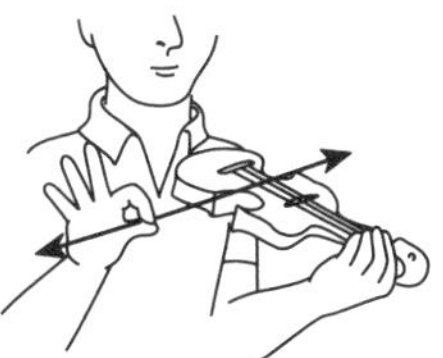

VIOLIN
9-hand plays violin

VIRGIN
V outlines face from left temple, over head, to chin
(see NUN)

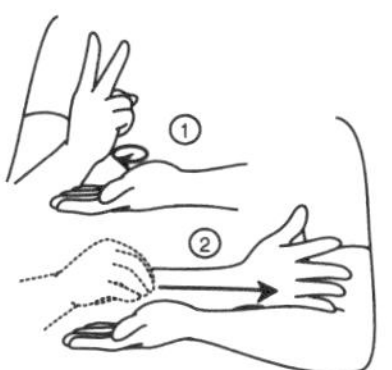

VIRUS
V circles over left palm, then flat-O opens and spreads up left arm
(see CANCER)

VISIBLE
Palm-out V's at sides of eyes drop to palm-down A's which drop slightly
(see ABLE)

VISION
Tip of index of V at corner of eye twists to palm-down V at right; sweeps left

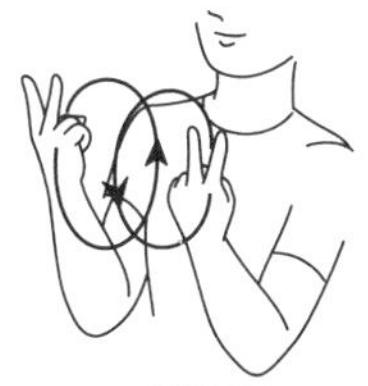

VISIT
Palm-in V's circle vertically *(may go in and out or out and in)*
(see PEOPLE)

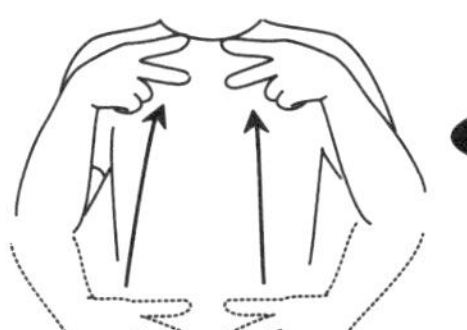

VITAL
Palm-in V's slide up body
(see ADDRESS)

VITAMIN
Side of V throws toward mouth
(see PILL)

VOCABULARY
Fingertips of palm-down V tap on side of left index; repeat
(see WORD)

VOCATION
Palm-out V arcs side-to-side, hitting back of palm-down left S
(see BUSY)

VOICE
Fingertips of palm-in V move up throat and out under chin

VOLCANO
From flat-O to 5, right arm repeatedly rises out of left horizontal C

VOLLEYBALL
Hands push up ball several times

VOLUME
Index finger of right V on heel of left palm, arcs to touch middle fingertip
(see AMOUNT)

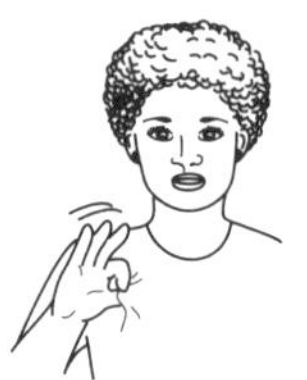

VOLUNTEER
At side of chest, right index and thumb of 9 tug material forward

VOMIT
5-hands one behind the other, arc out from throat *(can be done with one hand)*

V

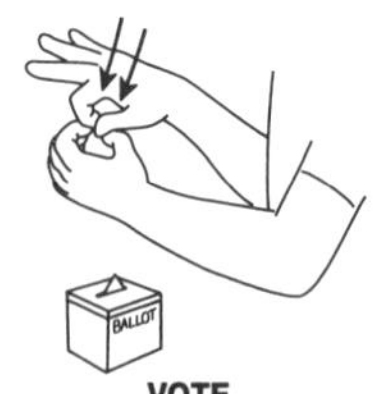

VOTE
Thumb and finger of right 9-hand go into left O; repeat

VOW
Palm-in index on chin, changes to V with heel on back of left hand
(see PROMISE)

VOWEL
Palm-out V brushes across fingers of palm-in left 5
(see ALPHABET)

VOYAGE
Right V pointing down, above left V pointing up; rotate alternately forward
(see TRAVEL)

VULTURE
Draw palm-down V under nose, while bending V fingers

NOTES

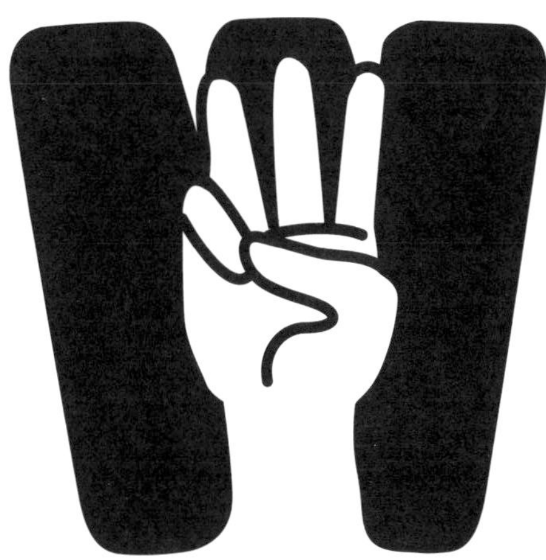

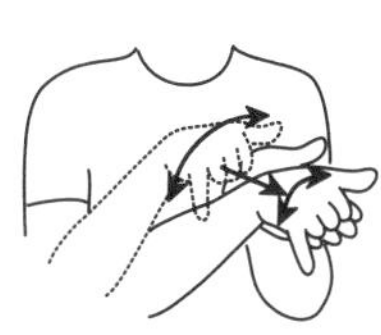

WADDLE
Inverted right Y rocks *(waddles)* forward on left horizontal palm

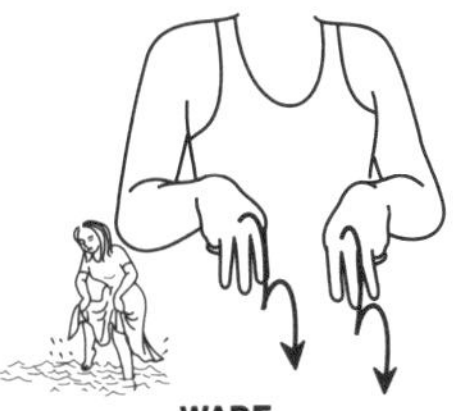

WADE
Inverted W's alternately arc up and forward several times
(see TIPTOE)

WAFFLE ★
Right W palm-down on left flat palm; lift again

WAG
Inverted right W, hanging over left horizontal index, wags
(see TAIL)

WAGON
W's, palms-facing, right behind left; right moves back
(see CAR)

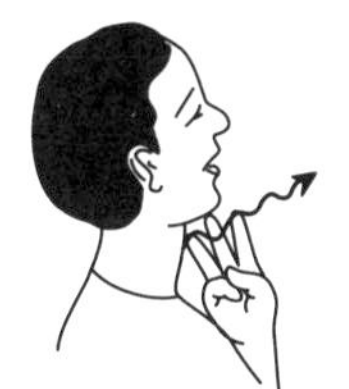

WAIL
Right palm-in W-hand shakes up and out from throat
(see GROAN)

WAIST
W-hand drags across waistline

WAIT ♔
Palm-up right hand behind palm-up left, all fingers fluttering

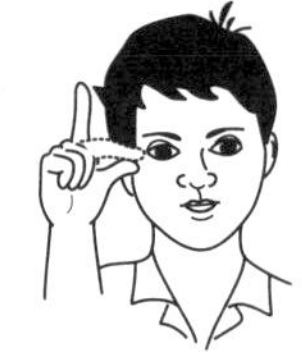

WAKE
Closed right G-hand at corner of eye opens to L-hand

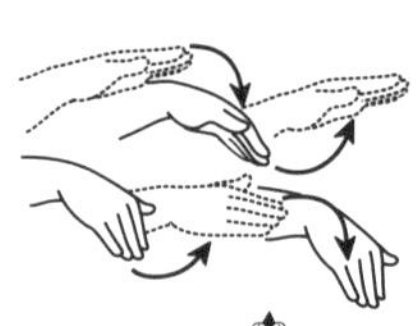

WALK ♔
Palm-in flat hands alternately flip up while moving forward

WALL
Palm-in W's together, separate, turn palms-facing and move toward body

(see DECK)

WALLET ★
Inverted W slides down hip *(as if putting wallet into pocket)*

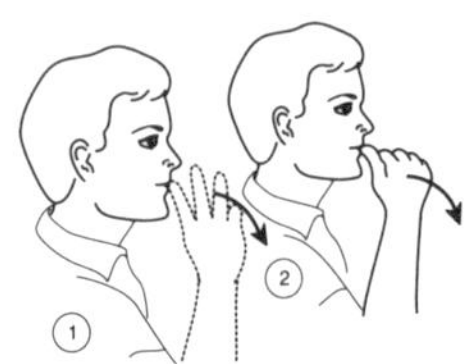

WALNUT
Index of palm-left W and then thumb of A jerk from near teeth

(see NUT)

WALRUS
From mouth, both C's curve out and down to S's *(forming tusks)*

WANDER ♔
Right index pointing down moves forward on wavy path

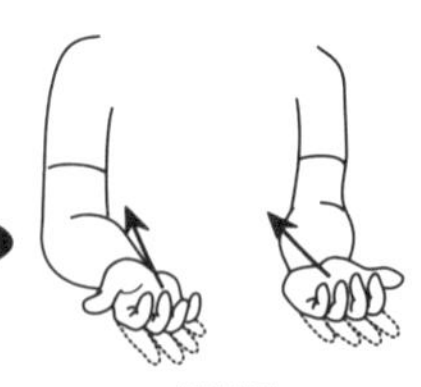

WANT
Palms-up 5's pull back to claws toward body

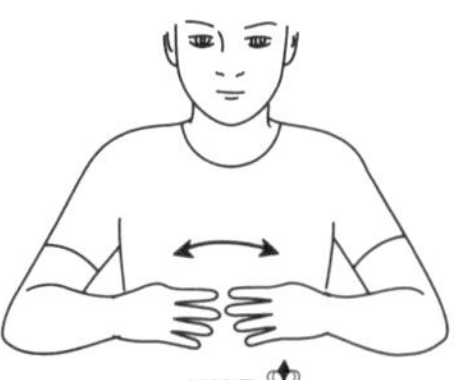

WAR ♔
Palm-in 4's move side-to-side

WARD ★
Palm-out W moves forward

WARE
Palm-up W arcs slightly up to right
(see THING)

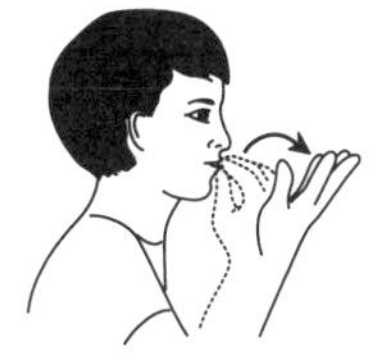

WARM

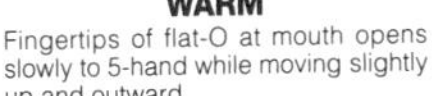
Fingertips of flat-O at mouth opens slowly to 5-hand while moving slightly up and outward

WARN
Hand slaps back of left S-hand sharply
(see CAUTION)

WART
Fingertips of right flat-O on cheek *(or wherever wart is)*, hand then flicks open to W-hand

WAS
(Alt. 1)
Palm-in W-hand moves back toward right shoulder
(see WERE)

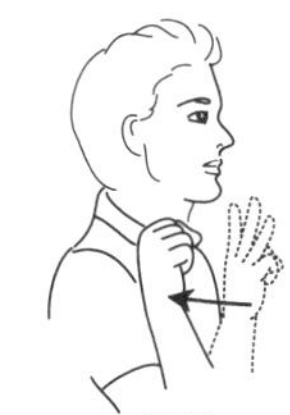

WAS
(Alt. 2)
W changes to S while moving toward right shoulder
(see WERE)

WASH ♔
Palm-down A-hand scrubs circularly in flat left palm

WASHINGTON
Palm-in W from shoulder circles forward and to the right

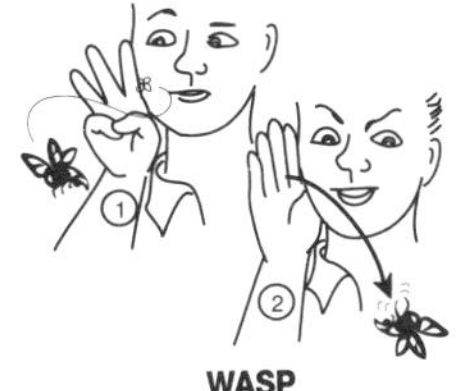

WASP
Side of W at cheek, then brush off wasp with open hand
(see BEE)

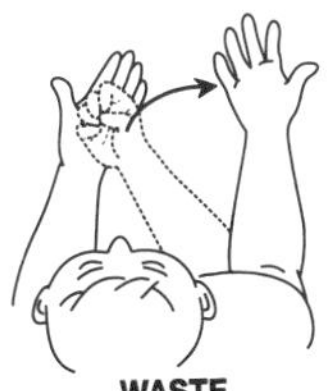

WASTE
Flat-O, palm-up on left palm, slides off and opens to 5-hand

WATCH ★
Palm-out V-index at eye; twist down to back of left wrist

WATER
Index finger of palm-left W taps chin

WAVE
Right hand waves

WAVER
Horizontal B-hands, right hand rocks side-to-side on left hand

WAX
Fingers of W circle on back of left hand
(see DUST)

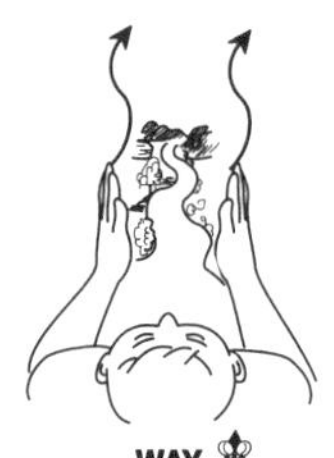

WAY
Parallel flat hands move forward, weaving slightly side-to-side *(may be done with W's)*

WE
Palm-left W on right side of chest circles to left side ending palm-right
(see OUR)

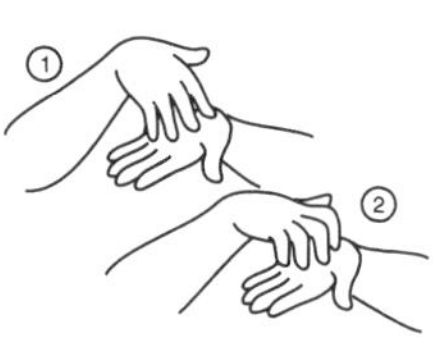

WEAK
At right angle, fingertips on left palm; bend fingers; repeat

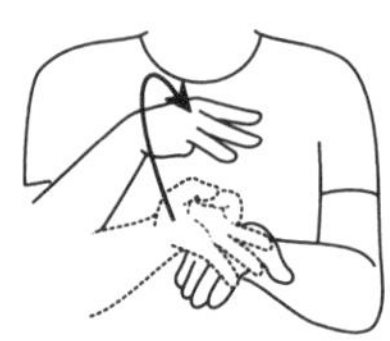

WEALTH
Back of W on palm-up left hand, arc up and over to palm-down
(see RICH)

WEAPON
W points down at side, pulls up to point forward and thrusts
(see SWORD)

WEAR
Palm-out W arcs side-to-side hitting back of left palm-down S
(see BUSY)

WEARY
Fingertips of W's touch chest and drop downward to palm-up
(see TIRE)

WEATHER
Palm-out W shakes downward

WEAVE
Right palm-down 5-hand makes weaving motion in and out of fingertips of palm-down 5-hand

WEB
Palms-down, right W fingertips lie on back of left W-fingertips

WED
Flat hands swing together and left clasps right

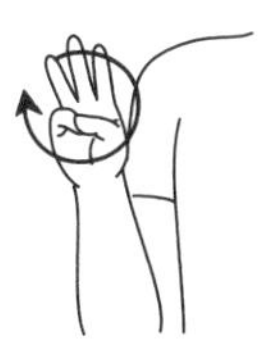

WEDNESDAY
Palm-out W circles slightly
(see MONDAY)

WEE
Horizontal W's, palms-facing close together, move slightly toward and away from each other
(see SMALL)

WEED
Flat-O grows rapidly through C, twisting to palm-out W
(see GROW)

WEEK
Right 1-hand brushes horizontally across left palm

WEEP
Both palm-in, W-hands drag alternately down cheeks
(see CRY)

WEIGH ♔
Middle finger side of right H rocks on side of left H index

WEIRD
Right W-hand arcs past eyes while fingers flutter
(see STRANGE)

WELCOME
Right palm-up W curves horizontally toward body
(see INVITE)

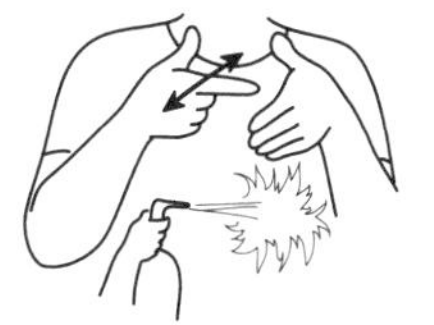

WELD
Index of right L points at palm-in left hand; move back and forth
(see SOLDER)

WELL ★
Horizontal W-hands face each other; drop straight down

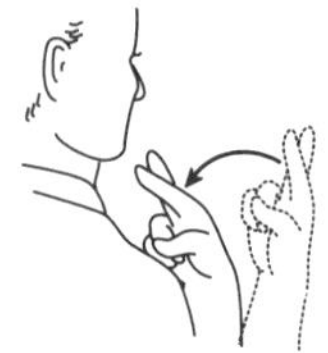

WERE
(Alt. 1)
Palm-in right R-hand moves back toward shoulder
(see WAS)

WERE
(Alt. 2)
Pass palm-out W to R back toward right shoulder
(see WAS)

WEST
Right palm-out W moves left

WET ♔
Drop right palm-in flat hand off chin, then open and close both flat-O's

WHALE
W makes 2 curves to the left, outside bent left arm
(see DOLPHIN)

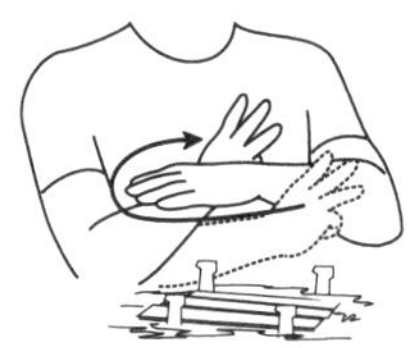

WHARF
Right W outlines left palm-down arm starting on outside
(see DOCK)

WHAT
Index fingertip of right hand brushes down across left fingers

WHEAT
Palm-out W brushes up through left horizontal C-hand
(see GRAIN)

WHEEL
Palm-left W rotates vertically forward

WHEELBARROW
Grasp handles of wheelbarrow and arc forward

WHEN
Indexes touch, make a circle with right index fingertip; return tip-to-tip

WHERE
Palm-out index shakes sideways

WHETHER
Palm-out W bounces off thumb, then off fingertip of left L
(see THEN)

WHEW
Shake limp right palm-down hand side-to-side

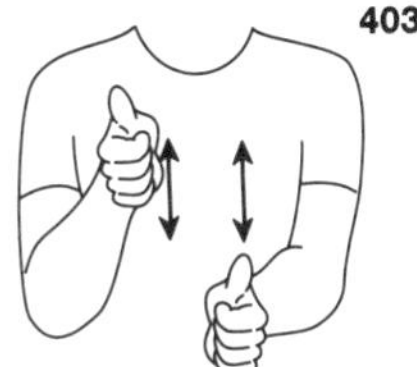

WHICH
Extended-A hands, palms-facing, alternately move up and down
(see BALANCE)

WHILE
W-hands face each other near right shoulder, arc down and forward
(see DURING)

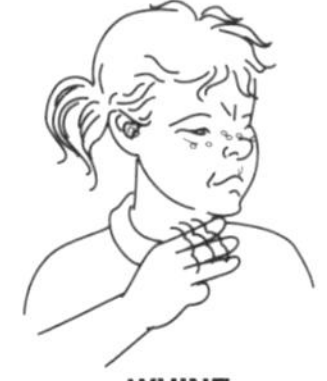

WHINE
Palm-down W vibrates at throat

WHIP
Fingers of horizontal W whip past left index; may repeat
(see BEAT)

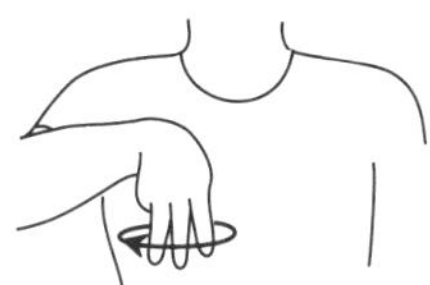

WHIRL
Upside down W circles rapidly
(see SPIN)

WHISKEY ♔
Side of right W taps on side of left I-1 hand; repeat

WHISPER
Whisper behind hand; fingers wiggle

WHISTLE
Palm-in bent-V fingers near mouth

WHITE
5-hand on chest moves outward, closing to a flat-O hand

WHO
Thumb of L on chin; wiggle index finger

WHOLE
Palm-down flat hand circles and turns over, resting palm-up on left hand

WHOM
Thumb of L on chin, wiggle index finger; add M-hand *(who + -m)*

WHOSE
Thumb of L on chin, wiggle index finger; add S-hand *(who + -s)*

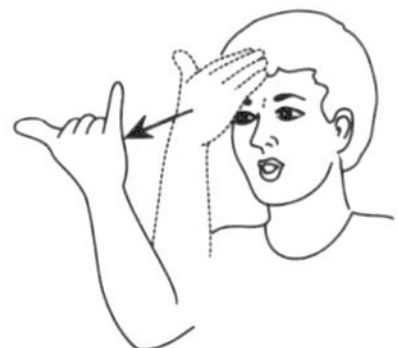

WHY
Palm-in fingers of open hand on forehead, move out to palm-in Y

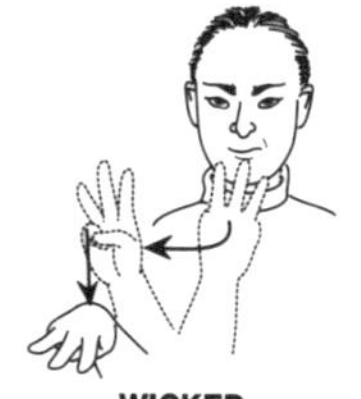

WICKED
Fingertips of palm-in W on chin; twist to palm-out and throw down

(see BAD)

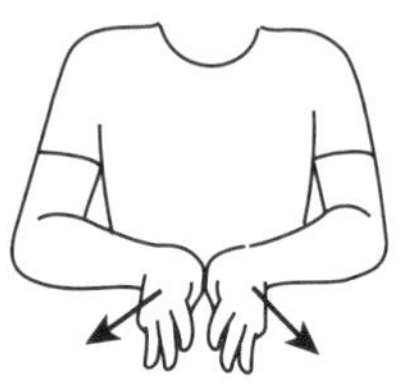

WIDE
W-hands, palms-facing and thumbs touching, separate, moving slightly out and forward

(see BROAD)

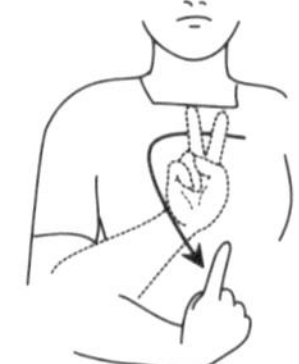

WIDOW
Palm-out 2-hand twists to palm-in, becomes 1 and moves forward

(see ALONE)

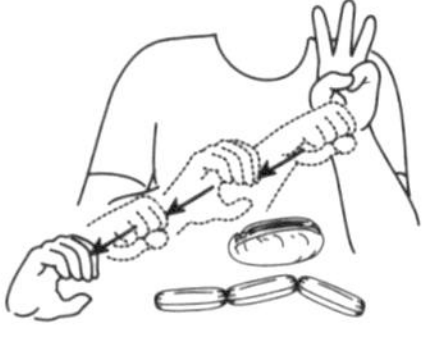

WIENER
Right S's and C's pull out of left W alternately

(see BALONEY)

WIFE
Thumb of A at jaw to clasped C's

(see HUSBAND)

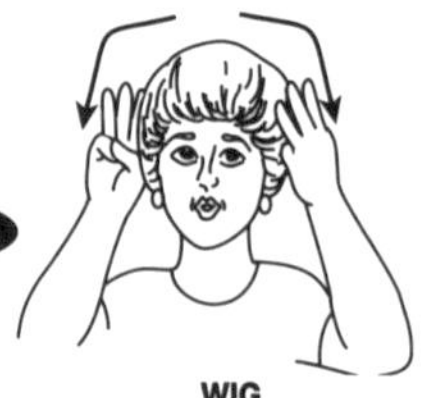

WIG
W-hands pull on wig

WIGGLE
Horizontal palm-left W wiggles forward

(see FISH)

WILD
W-hand twirls off temple

(see IDEA)

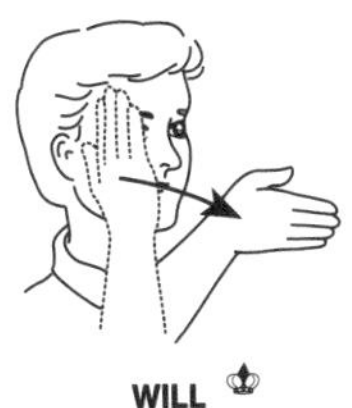

WILL ♔

Right flat hand palm facing side of head; arcs forward

WIN ♔

Close right S on left S; spiral right S quickly upward

WIND
(verb)

Fingertips of palm-down W on wrist; circle W horizontally forward

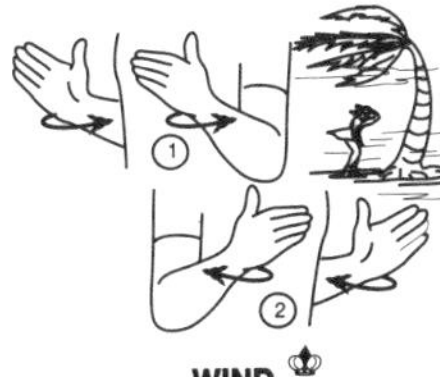

WIND ♔

Horizontal hands swing back and forth, twisting at wrists, as wind "blows" them

WINDMILL

Right palm-left W circles vertically near left index

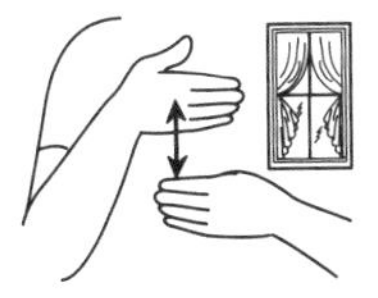

WINDOW

Sides of palm-in flat hands hit to open and close

WINE

Palm-in W circles on cheek
(see BEER)

WING

Left hand on right shoulder; flap right hand at the side

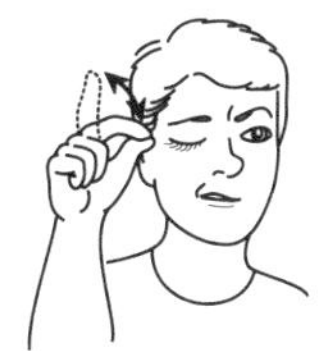

WINK

Thumb of L at eye, shut and open index finger

WINTER

Both W's face each other; shake slightly *(shivering)*
(see COLD)

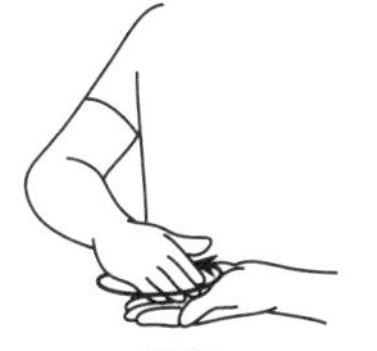

WIPE

Right palm wipes circularly on left palm
(see WASH)

WIRE

I-fingertip shakes outward from left W
(see CORD)

WISE

Palm-down X-hand nods near center of forehead

(see PHILOSOPHY)

WISH

Palm-in W slides down chest

(see HUNGER)

WIT

(Alt. 1)

Index of W on temple; W swings outward from wrist

(see SMART)

WIT

(Alt. 2)

Index finger of W touches near end of eyebrow

(see VICE)

WITCH

Right X moves from nose to rest on left palm-up X near chin

WITH

A-hands together, palm-to-palm

WITHDRAW

Palm-out W moves back toward body, changing to D-hand

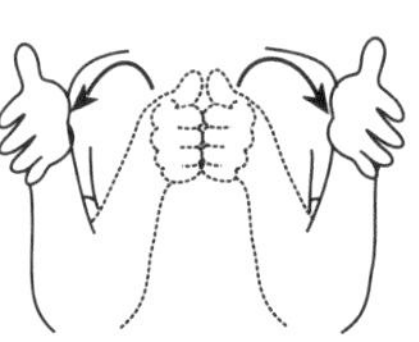

WITHOUT

Knuckles together, horizontal A-hands move apart to 5-hands

WITNESS

Index finger of W touches near end of eyebrow; palm-out N slides down side of vertical left palm *(wit + -ness)*

WIVES

Thumb of A at jaw to clasped C's; right hand changes to S *(wife + -s)*

WOLF

Hand at nose, pull out to flat-O

(see BEAK)

WOMAN

Thumb of A-hand at jaw moves up to show height with bent hand

WOMEN
Thumb of A-hand at jaw; measure several heights with bent hand

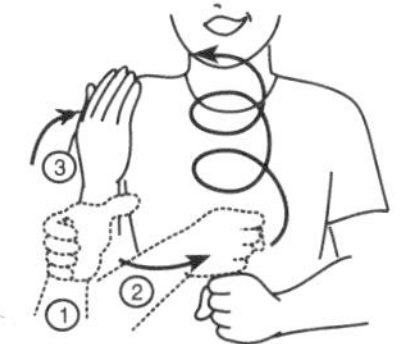

WON
Close right S on left S; spiral right S quickly upward, then flips back towards shoulder *(win + p. t.)*

WONDER
Palm-in W circles near temple
(see REASON)

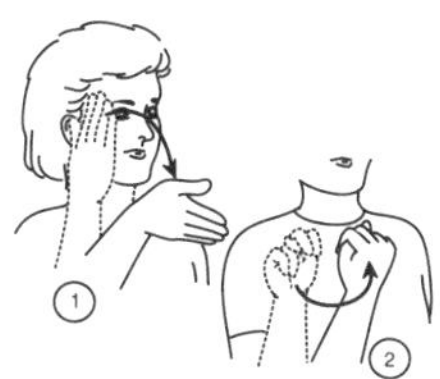

WON'T
Flat hand palm facing side of head, arcs forward; then palm-out N twists inward *(will + -n't)*

WOOD
Elbow of W on back of left hand; twist W slightly side-to-side
(see TREE)

WOOL
Back of right W-hand slides up horizontal left arm
(see SHEEP)

WORD
Fingertips of right G touch left index

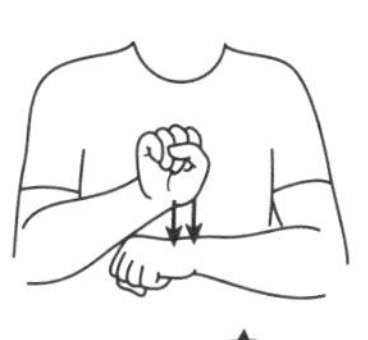

WORK
Right palm-out S taps back of left palm-down S; repeat

WORKSHOP
Palm-out W's together; circle out and meet as palm-in S's
(see BAND)

WORLD
Horizontal W's, right W on top of left W; circle right around left vertically

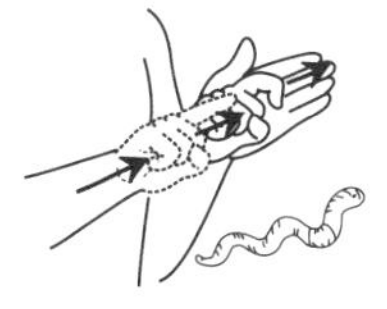

WORM
Side of right index crawls along left palm, alternating 1 and X

WORRY
Palms-facing W-hands alternately circle before face
(see TROUBLE)

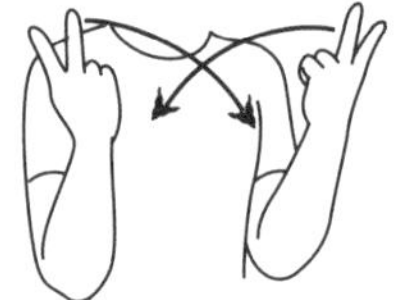

WORSE

Palms-in V's arc from sides to cross wrists ending palms-in

WORSHIP

Left hand closed over right, move toward body in slight vertical circle

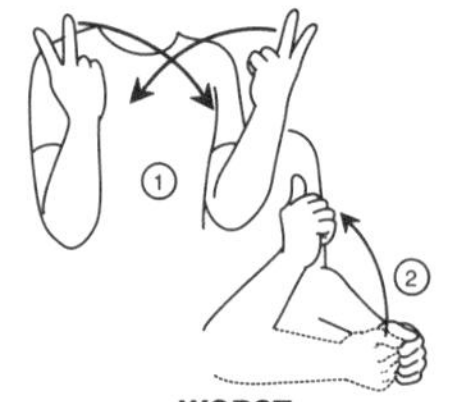

WORST

Palms-in V's arc from sides to cross wrists; A's together, right moves up *(worse + -est)*

WORTH

Palm-up W's rise in vertical circle to meet, palm-down

(see IMPORTANT)

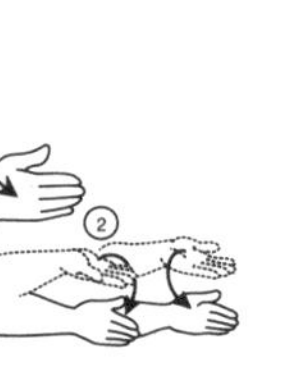

WOULD

(Alt. 1)

Palm facing side of head, arcs forward; then flat hands change to palms-facing *(will + p. p.)*

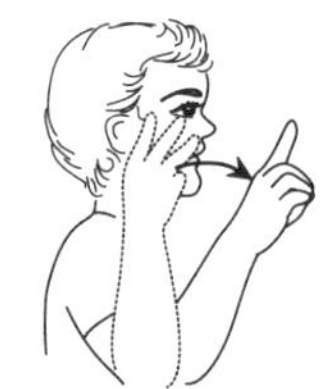

WOULD

(Alt. 2)

Palm-out W-hand, at side of face, moves forward to D-hand

WOUND

Palm-in W's point at each other, approach, twisting slightly

(see Hurt)

WOW

W's on each side of O-mouth; push slightly forward

WRAP

Palm-in horizontal W's circle each other, separate

(see TIE)

WREATH

Palm-out W's touch, circle vertically, and touch again

(see BULB)

WRECK

Right S-fist hits side of left W-hand

(see BUMP)

WRENCH

Index and middle finger of W-hand "tighten" left index once

(see MECHANIC)

W

WRESTLE
Keeping fingers straight, 5-hands mesh, shake forward and back slightly

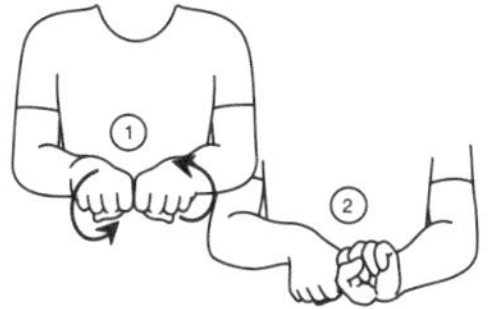

WRING
Palm-down S's together, right S twists downward to palm-in

WRINKLE
Right W draws wavy wrinkles wherever they belong

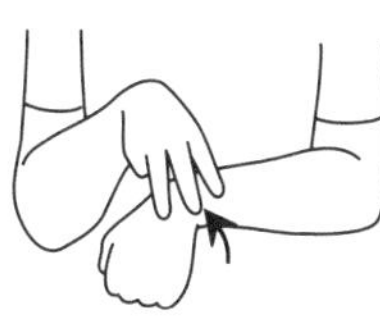

WRIST
Palm-down W draws across left wrist

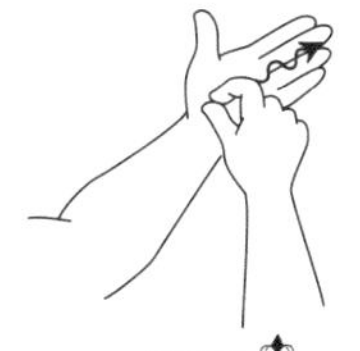

WRITE
Thumb and finger of closed X write on left flat palm

WRONG
Palm-in Y on chin
(see MISTAKE)

NOTES

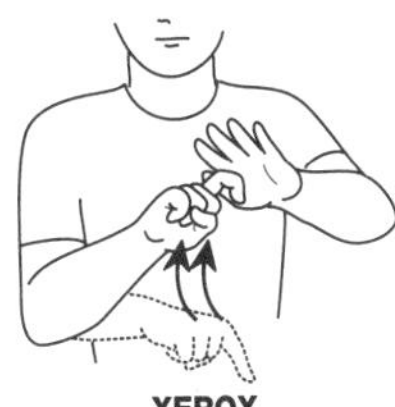

XEROX
(Alt. 1)
Palm-down index rises to X under left palm *(may repeat several times)*
(see COPY)

XEROX
(Alt. 2)
Right X-hand moves side-to-side under left palm-down flat hand
(see SUBWAY Alt. 1)

X-RAY
X-hand; then palm-in flat-O opens, moving toward chest

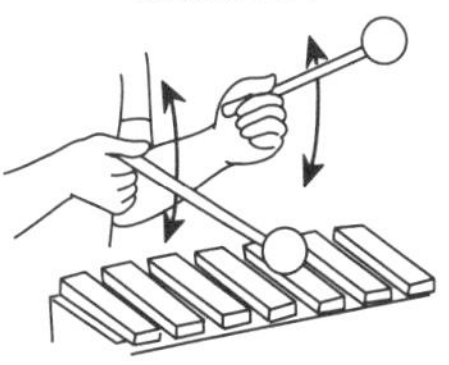

XYLOPHONE
Horizontal A's alternately play from side- to-side on xylophone

NOTES

YARD
Palm-down Y on back of left flat hand moves up to inside of elbow
(see MILE)

YARN
Palm-in I-hand wiggles from left Y
(see CORD)

YAWN
Palm-out S-hand at side of mouth, opens to bent-3 hand *(mouth opens at same time)*

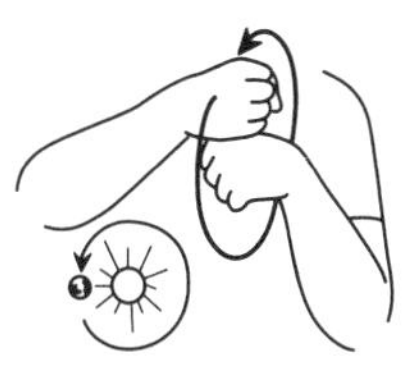

YEAR
Right horizontal S rests on left S; right circles vertically around left
(see WORLD)

YEAST
Right palm-down relaxed 5-hand above cupped left palm, right rises, fingers fluttering
(see SODA)

YELL
Palm-in Y moves up and out from chin
(see CALL)

YELLOW
Palm-left Y shakes
(see BLUE)

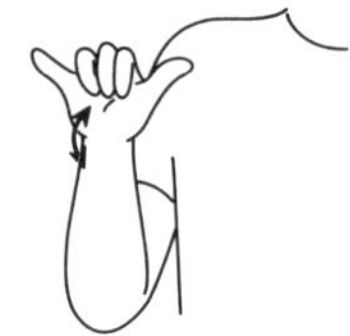

YES
Right Y-hand nods *(can be done with S-hand)*

YESTERDAY
Thumbtip of right Y touches near chin, then near ear

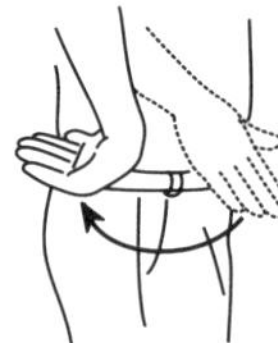

YET
Palm slaps gently backwards near side; may repeat

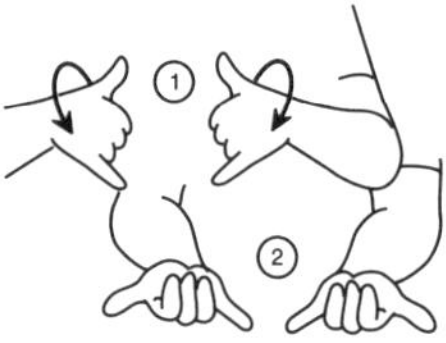

YIELD
Palm-in Y's, fingertips-facing, arc forward to palm-up
(see GIVE)

YOGURT
Right palm-up Y circles from left palm to mouth
(see SOUP)

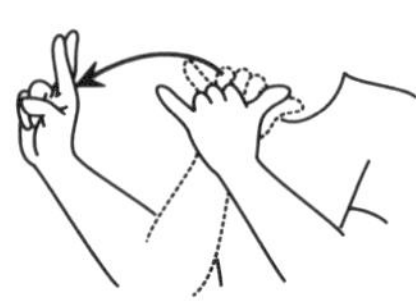

YONDER
Y's, palms-facing and touching, right hand slightly arcs forward and changes to palm-out R
(see FAR)

YOU
Index points at person addressed

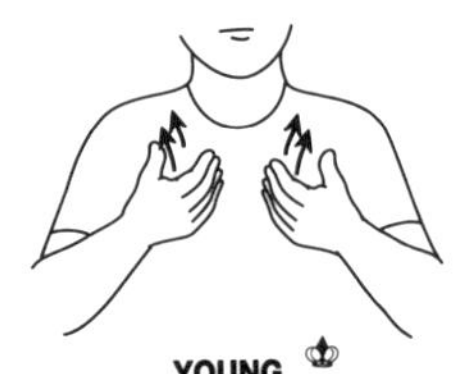

YOUNG
Tips of both bent hands brush upward twice off chest

YOUR
Vertical flat palm moves toward person addressed

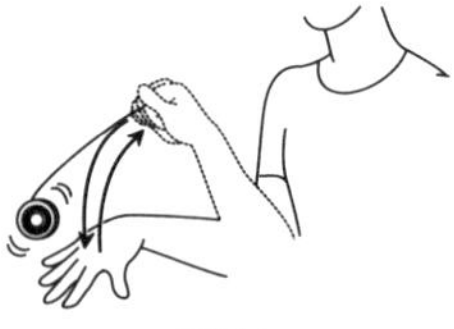

YOYO
Palm-out A drops to palm-down 5; repeat several times

ZEBRA
Horizontal 4-hands mark stripes on body

ZERO
Palm-out O circles once vertically

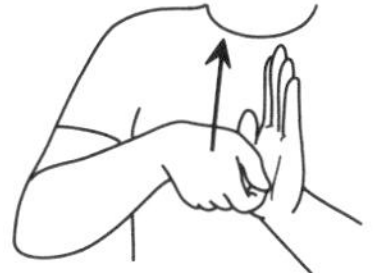

ZIP
Thumb touches knuckle of index finger (*as if holding tab of zipper)*; zip up palm

ZIPPER
Thumb touches knuckle of index finger *(as if holding tab of zipper)*; zip up palm; add R-hand *(zip + -er)*

ZONE
Right index draws Z on thumb side of palm-in horizontal left S

ZOO
Right index finger draws Z on palm of left 5-hand

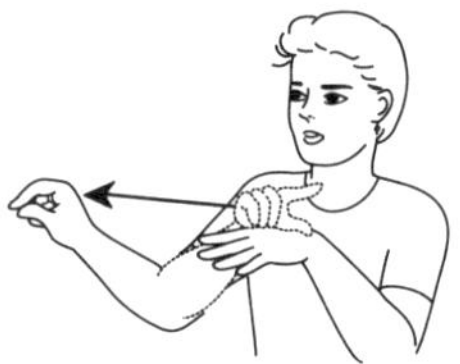

ZOOM

Thumb of right G rests on back of left palm-down flat hand; move G rapidly forward across hand and off, closing finger and thumb

SIGNS GROUPED BY FAMILIES

The following groups of signs are those which are similar in movement and belong together conceptually. We have found doing this has helped people to remember signs with greater ease. If a group of words originated from a traditional sign, we used that sign as the head of the family. If all the words are new, we merely alphabetize the list.

—The head of the family is shown with a ♔ after the word in the text.

—An asterisk (*) means look for a slight variation.

—Where we say, "(see ____)," the ____ will be the head of the family. When there are only 2 words in a family, we cross-referenced them.

ABSENT
lack
delinquent

ACT
drama
perform
theater

ADD
amend (alt 2)
supplement

ADDRESS
biography
dwell
exist
inhabit
life
live
reside
survive
vital

ADMIT
confess
commit

ADVERTISE
commercial
publicity
exaggerate*
propaganda*

ADVICE
advise*
affect
counsel
effect

AFFIX
prefix
suffix

AFRAID
anxious
coward
fear
horror
panic
phobia
terror

AGAINST
con
prejudice

AIM
goal
mission
object
target

ALGAE
bacteria
cell
fungus
gene

ALLOW
grant
let
opportune*
permit

ALPHABET
consonant
vowel

AM
are
be
is
not*

AMOUNT
batch
heap
mound
pile
quantity
volume

ANGEL
elf
fairy
gremlin
leprechaun
pixie

ANGER
fierce*
fury
irritate
rage
tantrum

ANNOUNCE
declare
proclaim

ANT
beetle
cricket
insect
pest
roach
scorpion
termit

APPLE
fruit
grapefruit
pineapple
vegetable

APPOINT
engage
reserve (alt 2)

APRICOT
fig
nectarine
plum
tangerine

ARITHMETIC
algebra
calculus
deduce
figure
geometry
math
statistic

ART
architect
craft
diagram*
draw
etch
sketch*
trace

ASTRONAUT
eject
rocket

ATMOSPHERE
culture
environment
local
orient
region
social

ATOM
electron
molecule
neutron
proton

ATTEMPT
effort
strive
try

AUNT
cousin
niece
nephew
uncle

AVOID
dodge
evade

AXE
chop
hatchet

BACHELOR
single
twin

BAG
pouch
sack

BAD
evil
naughty
profane
rude
wicked

BAKE
casserole
roast

BALANCE
assess
clumsy
court
doubt
evaluate
judge
may
probable
referee
umpire
which

BALONEY
frankfurter*
sausage
wiener

BAND
club
commission
council
crew
squad
tribe
workshop

BANQUET
dine
feast
picnic

BAR
line
row

BARE
empty
naked*
nude*
vacant

BASE
cellar
denominator*
element
fundamental
inferior
kindergarten
-neath
prime
sub-
theme

BASKET
April(alt 2)
hamper
purse

BAY
cove
gulf
harbor

BEAT
abuse*
curse*
hit
lash
punch
slap*
strike
whip

BED
hotel
motel
nap*
pillow

BELL
chime
chord*
echo
jingle
tone

BIG
enormous*
grand*
great
huge
immense
large
tremendous

BICYCLE
bike
cycle
tricycle
trike

BILLION
million
trillion

BIRD
chicken*
crow
duck
parakeet
parrot
robin

BLACK
coal
gray

BLANKET
sheet
shelter

BLEED
blood*
rust

BLOOM
blossom*
bud

BLUE
green
olive
purple
turquoise
yellow

BOARD
panel
stage

BODY
anatomy
flesh
health
physical

BONNET
kerchief
scarf

BOOK
album
Bible*
bibliography
booklet

BORROW
credit
rent

BOTHER
annoy
disturb
interfere

BOX
apartment
case
condo (alt 2)
den
garden
kitchen
room

BRANCH
limb
twig

BRAVE
hero
vigor

BRING
import
transport

BROAD
general
public
wide
vast

BROOK
creek
river
stream

BULB
globe
wreath

BUMP
bang
crash
damage*
victim
wreck

BURY
grave (alt 1)
tomb

BUSY
chore
commerce
employ
function
industry
labor
operate
toil
use
vocation
wear

BUTTER
jam
lard
margarine
mayonnaise

BUY
cash
invest
purchase
shop
spend

CABBAGE
cauliflower
lettuce

CALENDAR
April (alt 1)
August (alt 1)
February (alt 1)
December(alt 1)
January (alt 1)
July (alt 1)
June (alt 1)
March (alt 1)
May (alt 1)
November (alt 1)
October (alt 1)
September (alt1)

CALIFORNIA
gold
silver

CALL
shout
yell

CANCER
diabetes
germ
infect
virus

CAP
lid*
tip*
top

CAR
auto
automobile*
bus
jeep*
tank*
taxi
truck
vehicle*
wagon
van

CARE
custody
supervise

CARGO
load
freight
stack

CARNIVAL
festival
pageant

CARPET
linoleum
mat
rug
tile

CASTLE
mansion
palace

CAT
kitten
leopard*
panther*
tiger*

CATERPILLAR
creep
slug*
snail*

CELEBRATE
anniversary*
ceremony*

CENT
dime
nickel
penny
quarter

CENTIMETER
centigram
high school
millimeter

CERTAIN
fact
serious
sure

CHANGE
adapt
adjust
alter
amend
convert
distort
evolve
modify*
reverse
revise*
switch*
translate

CHARACTER
attitude
feature
moral
morale
noble
personality
qualify
trait

CHICAGO
Detroit
Philadelphia

CHILD
dwarf
midget

CHINA
Asia
Japan
Korea

CHIP
flake
fragment
particle*
piece
segment*

CHOCOLATE
caramel
cocoa
fudge
vanilla

CHOOSE
choice
elect
option
select

CHRIST
duke
emperor
king
lord
majesty
prince
queen
royal

CHURCH
auditorium
synagogue
temple

CIRCLE
ever
hoop
round

CLASS
bunch
department
family
group
herd
league
organize
team

CLEAR
bright*
obvious

CLOTH
fabric
flannel*
rag
texture

COAT
blouse
jacket
robe
shirt
uniform
vest

COLD
chill
refrigerate
shiver*
winter

COLLEGE
graduate
seminary
university

COMPLAIN
fuss
gripe
object

CONDUCT
harmony
orchestra

CONFUSE
aphasic
bewilder

CONTINUE
constant
maintain
momentum*
permanent
persist
remain

COPY
duplicate
imitate
pattern*
xerox*

CORD
cable*
fiber
ribbon
string
thread
twine
wire
yarn

COST
charge
fee
price
tax

COUNT
accounting*
calorie

COUNTRY
county
foreign

COVER
frost
glaze
laminate
patch

CRAB
lobster
shrimp

CRACKER
crackerjack*
matzo

CRUSH
crunch*
demolish
squash

CRY
tear
weep

CUT
scissors*
snip
trim
tongs*

DANGER
harm
risk
threat

DARK
dim
eclipse
fog
haze
shade
smog

DECK
porch
stall
wall

DECODE
fable
tale

DEER
antelope*
antler
elk*
moose*
reindeer*

DENMARK
Finland
Norway
Swede

DEVIL
demon
mischief

DIAMOND
gem
jewel
ring

DIP
dye
rinse

DIRT
mud
pollute

DISPLAY
exhibit
model

DISPOSE
abort
garbage
junk
remove
trash
waste

DO
behave
manner

DOCK
pier
wharf

DOCTOR
chiropractor
medic
nurse
paramedic*
psychiatry
veterinarian

DOLL
cartoon
fun

DOLPHIN
porpoise
whale

DOUGH
flour
graham
pastry

DOWN
low
south
vertical

DRESS
attire
costume
gown
pajama
poncho*

DRIFT
float
glide
raft

DUMB
goof
idiot
stupid

EASE
convenient
simple

EAT
breakfast
dinner
gobble
lunch
meal
supper

EDGE
border
crust
hoof
lawn
toe

ELECTRIC
battery
physics
socket

ENJOY
amuse
entertain

ENTER
invade
infiltrate*
subway

EQUAL
equate
equivalent*
even*

EQUATOR
latitude
solar

ESCAPE
elope
evacuate
flee

EVAPORATE
gas
vapor
vent*

EXACT
perfect
specific

EXCEPT
especially
particular
special

EXCHANGE
replace
substitute
trade

EXCUSE
apologize*
dismiss*`
pardon

EXPERT
competent
excel
skill
talent

FABULOUS
elaborate
marvel
terrific

FACE
beauty
Hawaii
lovely
pretty

FALSE
fake
pretend

FANCY
elegant
luxury
style*

FAR
distant
extreme
remote
yonder

FARM
agriculture
Arizona
ranch

FAST
rapid
speed

FEEL
emotion
mood
pride
proud

FIND
discover
locate

FINE
courtesy
polite

FINISH
complete
end
expire
quotient
result

FIRE
blaze
bonfire*

FIRST
January
prior

FISH
mermaid
shark*
tuna
wiggle

FIX
mend
repair

FLAG
banner
pennant

FLAT
level
monotone

FLOOR
diploma
plateau
reef

FLOWER
daffodil
pansy
rose
tulip
violet

FOR
premier
prime minister
pro

FORBID
ban
crime
flunk
prohibit

FRACTION
denominator
numerator

FREE
liberty
rescue

FRESHMAN
junior
sophomore
senior*

FRIEND
acquaint
colleague
mate
neighbor
partner
relate

FULL
mature
fertile

GALLON
liter
pint
quart

GENERATE
heredity
inherit
legend

GET
receive
obtain

GHOST
goblin
haunt
spirit
spook

GIFT
award
dedicate
prize
reward
tribute

GIRL
female
her
Miss
Mrs*
she

GOD
admire
esteem
honor
respect

GOVERN
capitol
federal
mayor
politic

GRAIN
alfalfa
barley
crop
hay
oat
rye
straw
wheat

GRAVY
grease
oil

GROAN
growl*
howl*
moan
wail

GROUND
continent
-dom
ecology*
empire
field
land
meadow
pasture
plain
range

GROW
asparagus
broccoli
celery
furnace*
herb
ivy*
plant
rhubarb
spring*
tumor
vine*
weed

GUARD
barrier
defend
protect
prevent

HABIT
custom
routine

HALL
gallery
lane
mall
parallel

HAPPEN
chance
event
fate
incident
luck
occur
result

HAPPY
cheer
enjoy
glad
joy
merry

HARD
difficult
firm
harsh
problem
tough

HAVE
had
has

HE
fellow
guy
him
his
mister*
sir

HEART
February
valentine

HELP
aid
assist
facilitate
hint
rehabilitate
reinforce
therapy

HIDE
conceal
intrigue
mystery

HIND
behind
rear

HOLD
clutch
grasp
grip

HOLY
divine
pure
saint

HONEST
earnest
frank
genuine
real
true

HORSE
colt
mule
pony

HOSPITAL
ambulance
clinic
infirmary

HOUR
age
century
decade
era
period
semester
term
video

HOUSE
barn
cabin
condo (alt 1)
factory
garage
hut
museum
station

HUNGER
appetite
depress
desire
passion*
starve
wish

HURT
ache
injure
pain
wound

ICE CREAM
lollipop
popsicle

IDEA
abstract
concept
fantasy
fiction
hypothesis
myth
opinion
theory
wild

IGNORE
apathy
neglect

IMPAIR
dam
obstacle

IMPORTANT
essence
main
precious
value
worth

INFLUENCE
contagious
infest

INSPECT
clue
explore
investigate
pioneer
research

INVITE
guest
hire
welcome

JAIL
cage
prison

JAR
bowl*
nest
net*
pot
tub
vase

JUICE
cider
lime
nectar

JUMP
ballet
hop
leap
skip
trampoline*

KILL
assassin
murder
suicide*

KIND
breed
generous
type

LAW
constitute
curriculum*
doctrine
formula
ordinance
policy*
principle
rule
state

LECTURE
minister
preach

LEISURE
holiday
idle*
retire
vacation

LESSON
agenda
course
subject
topic
unit

LIE
exhausted
lounge

LIST
detail
ingredient

LONESOME
patient
tolerate

LOVE
dear
fond
hug
romance

LUTHERAN
Presbyterian
Protestant

MAGAZINE
brochure
catalogue
journal
ledger
pamphlet

MAKE
create
devise
manufacture
produce

MANAGE
control
dominate
handle
reign

MARK
decimal*
notch
punctuate

MASK
Halloween
October

MEAN
define
intend*
purpose

MEASLES
freckle
pimple*
pox
rubella

MEAT
beef
ham
liver
steak
veal
pork

MEDICINE
alcohol
aspirin*
drug
vaseline

MELON
cantaloupe
jack-o-lantern*
pumpkin

MELT
cure
dissolve
heal
remedy

MEMBER
committee
congress
delegate
faculty
legislate
parliament
senate
staff*

METAL
aluminum
brass
copper
iron
lead
steel
tin

MIDDLE
center
intermediate
nuclear*
nucleus

MINUTE
instant
late
moment
soon
tardy

MONDAY
Friday
Saturday
Thursday*
Tuesday
Wednesday

MONEY
economy
finance

MONKEY
ape
gorilla

MOUSE
gerbil
hamster
rat
mice*

MOUTH
oral
speech

MUCH
big
great
huge
immense
large
quite
such
tremendous

MUSIC
carol*
chorus
hymn
lyric
melody
poem*
poetry*
rhythm
song
tune

NAME
anonymous
cite
identify
repute

NATURE
instinct
litter
native

NEAR
close
intimate

NEW
fresh
gospel
modern
raw

NOT
dis-
il-
im-
in-
ir-
mis-
non-
un-

NOTE
detect
memo
recognize

NUT
peanut*
pecan
walnut*

OCEAN
Atlantic
Pacific
sea

OFFICE
boss
capital
captain

OLD
ancient*
elder

ONCE
double
multiple
triple
twice

OPEN
expose
hatch
reveal

OPPOSE
allergy
contrast
disagree*
enemy
foe
rival

ORDER
command*
claim*
exclaim

OUR
us
we

OUT
extract
quit
resign

OVEN
broil
grill

PANCAKE
flapjack
spatula

PANT
slack
trouser

PAPER
kleenex
tissue
stationery

PARENT
adult
foster
gender
neuter
orphan
sex
teen

PASTE
glue
plaster

PEOPLE
folk
visit

PERSON
human
-ist

PET
stroke
tame

PICTURE
illustrate
photo

PLACE
acre*
area
district
island
lot
position*
region
situate
territory

PLAY
game
party
recess
sport
toy

POINT
designate
precise

POSITIVE
affirm
assure
confirm
plus

POSTPONE
delay*
extend*
procrastinate

PRACTICE
coach
drill
intern
rehearse

PROMISE
guarantee
oath
pledge
vow

PROVE
evident
proof

PULL
haul
tug

PUSH
aggress
buggy*
cart*

QUESTION
quiz*
riddle

QUIET
calm
gentle
peace
silent

QUOTE
idiom*
proverb*
slang*
title

REBEL
defy
revolt

READ
essay
prose

REASON
logic
meditate
ponder
thought
wonder

REQUIRE
condition
demand
impress
insist

RICH
fortune
treasure
wealth

SALT
allspice
basil
cinnamon
nutmeg
spice

SAME
rhyme
synonym

SATISFY
content
relieve

SAVE
conserve
preserve
reserve(alt1)
safe

SCIENCE
biology
chemistry
experiment

SELL
auction
peddle
sale*

SEND
deliver
export
refer

SENTENCE
grammar
language
linguistic
syntax

SET
lay
occupy

SHAME
ashamed
bashful*
shy

SHAPE
contour
form
image
statue

SHARP
acute
blade

SHEEP
lamb
wool

SHOE
boot
galoshes

SHORT
abbreviate
brief
temporary

SHOW
code
demonstrate
example
indicate
represent
symbol
symptom*

SICK
disease
pervert
ill (alt 2)
flu

SING
chant
opera

SIT
bench
chair
couch*
perch
roost
seat
sofa

SLICE
carve
pastrami

SLOW
gradual
retard

SMALL
compact
little
wee

SMELL
fragrant
odor

SMILE
chuckle
comic
giggle*
grin
laugh*

SOME
factor
part
section

SOUND
hear
listen
noise*
radio*

SOUP
broth
cereal
dessert
granola
oatmeal
pudding
rice
yogurt

SOUR
bitter
sore
vinegar

SPAGHETTI
bacon
macaroni
noodle

SPIN
twirl
whirl

SQUARE
perimeter
rectangle
transparency

STANDARD
circumstance*
common
company*
ordinary
together
union

STAR
constellation
galaxy

START
begin
commence
initial
initiate
origin
source

STEAL
plagiarize
rob
snatch *

STONE
brick
concrete
fossil
gravel
mineral
ore
pebble
rock
shell

STOP
cease
halt
interrupt

STORE
bank
grocer
market
stuff

STORM
cyclone
hurricane
riot
tornado

STRAIGHT
career
crooked*
direct
major
minor*
profess

STRANGE
fool
odd
peculiar
queer
freak
weird*

STRONG
authority
energy
intense
might
power

STUBBORN
donkey
obstinate

SUCCESS
accomplish
achieve*
succeed*

SUGGEST
offer
present (v)
recommend

SUMMER
desert
humid
July

SUPPORT
allegiance
crutch

SWORD
holster
weapon

SYMPATHY
compassion*
pity*
mercy

TABLE
counter
desk

TALK
communicate
converse
dialogue
interview
total communication

TALL
develop
erect
posture

TEACH
educate
instruct
tutor

THAT
these
this
those

THEIR
them
they

THEN
alternate
either
neither*
nor*
or
rather
whether

THERMOMETER
barometer
centigrade
degree
Fahrenheit
meter
temper

THING
component
device
equip
french fries*
furnish
item
material
resource
supply
tool
ware

THINK
familiar
know
mind
remind

THOUGH
gray
matter
spite

THROUGH
thorough*
thrust

THROW
dart
pitch

TIE
bind
wrap

TIRE
fatigue
weary

TO
till
too
until

TOMATO
beet
cucumber
parsnip
turnip

TOWN
city
village

TREE
forest
grove
jungle
lumber
orchard
timber
wood

TRICK
irony
sarcasm

UNDERSTAND
comprehend
realize

UP
elevate
high
north
rise

URGE
persuade
treat

WAIT
hesitate
pause

WALK
hike
trample
trot

WANDER
journey
mobile
roam
venture

WAR
battle
crusade
quarrel
struggle

WASH
launder
wipe

WAY
canal
glacier
path
road

WEAK
delicate
fragile

WEATHER
climate
season

WEIGH
ounce
pound
ton

WET
damp
dew

WHISKEY
liqueur
liquor

WHOLE
certify
entire
include
total

WILL
destine
future

WIN
triumph
victor

WIND
air
breeze

WITH
accompany*
escort*

WORD
noun
pronoun
vocabulary

WORK
duty
obligate

WORLD
civil
geography*
international
universe
year

WRITE
author
chalk
literate
manuscript
pen
pencil
record (v)
secretary*

YOUNG
adolescent
juvenile

PRODUCTS from MODERN SIGNS PRESS, INC.

Basic Tools and Techniques

- **Signing Exact English** The Dictionary, the heart of the SEE system
- **Signing Exact English Interactive CD ROM** with all Dictionary information and ability to print illustrations and descriptions
- **Teaching and Learning Signing Exact English**
- **Student Workbook**
- **Vocabulary Development Flash Cards**
  - **Kit A**
  - **Kit B**
  - **Kit C**

Video Tapes

- **Curriculum Tapes**
  - **Beginning level** – 14 lessons
  - **Rather Strange Stories** (Intermediate level)
- **SIGN WITH ME** Produced at Boys Town National Research Hospital
  - **Building Conversation**
  - **Building Concepts**
- **See Me Sing** Songs and stories
- **Visual Tales** (available in Signed English or ASL)
  - **The Father, The Son and The Donkey**
  - **Village Stew**
  - **The Greedy Cat**
  - **The Magic Pot**
  - **The House That Jack Built**
- **Signed Cartoons** (available in Signed English or ASL)

Three Pigs	**Three Bears**	**Casper**	**Animal Antics**
Raggedy Ann	**Jingle Bells**	**Pup's Christmas**	**Shipshape Shapes**
Rudolph	**Cinderella**	**Numbers**	**Red Riding Hood**

- **Show and Tell Stories**
  - Series 1 – Brown Bear, Brown Bear and This Is Me
- **Informational Tapes**
  - **Deafness the Hidden Handicap**
  - **Growing Up with SEE**
- **Video Tapes in Spanish/English**
- **Sign for Friends** David Parker

Children's Collection

- **Coloring Books**
  - **ABC's of Fingerspelling**
  - **Sign Numbers**

Storybooks

Talking Finger Series - Popsicles are Cold, At Grandma's House, Little Green Monsters, I Was So Mad

In Our House

Be Happy Not Sad (two books including coloring workbook)

Grandfather Moose (finger rhymes)

Cosmo Gets An Ear A story about a hard of hearing boy and his hearing aid

Greeting Cards

Color Your Own Cards (in both signs and words)

All Occasion

Birthday

Christmas

Special Products

Music In Motion

Pledge of Allegiance Poster

Signing Exact English in Spanish

Signs Everywhere

Sign with Kids A curriculum for teaching kids sign language

Signing Bear "Honey"

More Yet To Come

FOR MORE INFORMATION ON OTHER PRODUCTS
MAIL – PHONE – FAX
TO REQUEST A FREE CATALOG

Modern Signs Press, Inc.
P.O. Box 1181
Los Alamitos, CA 90720

562/596-8548 V
562/493-4168 V/TDD
562/795-6614 FAX
email modsigns@aol.com
www.modsigns.com

NOTES

NOTES

NOTES

NOTES

NOTES

NOTES

NOTES

NOTES

NOTES

NOTES

NOTES

NOTES

NOTES